A Trip Through the 12 Steps
with a doctor and therapist

Also by this author:

The Alcoholic / Addict Within:
Our Brain, Genetics, Psychology, and the Twelve Steps as Psychotherapy

available from amazon.com

A Trip Through the 12 Steps

---

with a doctor and therapist

Andrew P. MD

Contact the author at alcoholism.addiction@gmail.com
or
visit the author's website at
www.alcoholism-addiction-psychology.com

Contents

Introduction

I couldn't wait to do the Steps.

I was languishing in a drug and alcohol detox center, a sick, broken, defeated man. My obsessive use of drugs and alcohol had taken nearly everything from me, but I just couldn't stop. I had been practicing medicine and psychotherapy for more than a decade, yet I couldn't figure out what was wrong with *me*, how to get the drugs and alcohol to release their dark hooks from my soul. I was convinced I must be some species of lunatic. *Why couldn't I stop the insanity that had taken over my life?* It seemed simple: *all I had to do was stop the drugs and alcohol, right?* But why couldn't I do that?

I knew I was vanquished. I no longer carried any pretenses whatsoever that I could control or stop my drinking and drug use. I had accepted that my life was no longer under any kind of control of my own. Drinking and drug use had long ago stopped being fun, and I had crossed that line where I knew I couldn't live without my drink and drugs, yet I couldn't bear to go on living in such misery. So, I was planning my own death. Just before I went over that cliff, some friends picked me up off the floor (literally) and dropped me off at the detox center. So, here I was, a walking dead-man who had already accepted his own death.

Here before me at the detox center sat some guys from Alcoholics Anonymous – some were from Narcotics Anonymous, and a few from Cocaine Anonymous – who were there to tell us besotted wretches about their program of recovery. They were all like me – some were worse – except for one glaring difference: they were sober and living productive and happy lives. I had no idea how they managed to get their lives back, but I definitely wanted what they had. They told me the way to go about it was to do the 12 Steps. I could see with my own eyes that these guys had found a way out of the same misery that I was living, and I wanted it too – *right now!* So, I was hungry to do the Steps. I wanted to get better.

*

1

EVERYBODY's life has the capacity to be beautiful. EVERYBODY's. As a doctor and therapist, and as someone who has experienced the remarkable positive personal transformation that comes from doing the Steps, I'm so happy you're here. I've seen many, many people whose lives had become empty miserable shells become miraculously transformed by doing the 12 Steps. And it's not because they suddenly became wealthy, but because they were released from the obsession with drugs and alcohol and all the mental carnage that comes with it. Even the simplest of life is sweet after being released from the cruel grip of active addiction.

It's painful to watch a person drive his or her own life off a cliff with drugs or alcohol, especially when there exists a simple solution. Obsessive fixation to alcohol or drugs is an activity fit only for beasts yet practiced by no kind of beast but man. And it can beat the best of us. However, the great news is this: anyone – I repeat, *anyone* – is capable of a full recovery from any kind of addiction. Many among us feel recovery is impossible. They're too overwhelmed – they believe they are too addicted, too far gone, have burned too many bridges, and they are too filled with fear to get sober. If that's you, you're in the right place; the 12 Step program is for people like you. I know this first-hand, because I was one of them.

Addiction to drugs or alcohol doesn't just affect people who are vulnerable or down on their luck. Addiction and alcoholism know no discrimination: they consume anybody, regardless of ethnicity, gender, age, income, culture, religion, and background. There are well-defined risk factors, but no one is immune; many victims of addiction have few risk factors or none. It happens to one out of seven of us, whether we are rich or poor, healthy or sick, successful or destitute. It's not Samuel Colt who made all men equal, alcoholism-addiction did.

One thing's for sure: no matter how high our starting point, if we stay on that road of compulsive drug or alcohol use long enough we all end up in the same place. Addiction-alcoholism is serious business; it may be the greatest threat to your health, happiness, and life that you will ever face. And it has a strong hold on us that doesn't just go away once we stop drinking or using. We're stuck with the brain changes that will cause us to end up right back where we were, even decades after our last drink or drug – if we fail to see to our ongoing recovery. This is a serious affliction, and it requires some serious attention. That's why we're here, beginning a trip through a program of recovery that includes all the tools we need for life-long recovery and a return to health, happiness, and good function.

*

There's no such thing as an "expert" in the 12 Steps. The 12 Step program isn't like that. There's no hierarchy, no formal leadership, no person of greater value than others, and no one who can claim to be any more of an expert than anyone else. So – full disclosure – I am no expert in the 12 Steps. However, I have written this book because I can offer a perspective and some insight into the 12 Step process based on my experience as a physician and psychological therapist, and as an addictions researcher. I will bring together the breadth of the 12 Step literature with the most up-to-date information available from the psychological, medical, behavioral, and social sciences. I will also blend into the narrative the principles and techniques used by psychotherapists and counselors, along with principles and writings on spirituality. The 12 Step program provides the "how" of recovery, I use the science to provide the "why." This is useful for people who want to know more about their condition and the program, and it allows us to get a better result from our own trip through the Steps. It also gives us some extra insight to help us to be more effective sponsors as we help others through the Steps. My role here is to provide a framework to help you optimize the benefits and find more insight on your trip through the Steps.

Part of the genius of the 12 Step program is that we don't have to understand addiction-alcoholism to get sober and heal. Good thing, too, because I certainly didn't understand it when I sat in the detox center. However, in this book I have intertwined information about how the addicted mind works and how people come to be addicted. The information helps us to understand ourselves and to understand how the Steps work to address the underlying causes of our substance addiction.

My readers may be people who are new to the 12 Step program and going through the Steps for the very first time, people who are taking another trip through the Steps after years in recovery – as many of us do, people who wish to learn more about the Steps in order to better sponsor and guide newcomers through the Steps, and people who just wish to know more about addiction-alcoholism and our remarkable program of recovery. Even medical professionals and addictions counselors may find the information enlightening, to learn more about our program and how it works. There's something here for everyone, regardless of your purpose.

I can't emphasize enough the importance of having a sponsor when we are in recovery. I consider trying to work through the Steps and maintain sobriety without a sponsor as being akin to trying to give yourself CPR while you are in cardiac arrest – not a good idea. The explanations and perspectives I give in this book are based on my expertise in the science of addictions and in my own personal experience in recovery. Yet, there is so much more to learn from an experienced sponsor, and a sponsor can personalize the experience for you and help you through your sticking points. Importantly, a good sponsor will call you out on our bull-crap if you're not being entirely honest with yourself – which will happen – and will challenge you in those moments your addict-alcoholic brain bee-lines for the easier, softer way – which it will. This book should be regarded as just one of many tools for recovery, and definitely not a replacement for a sponsor.

Although the concept of a sponsor is not specifically named in the basic text of the Big Book – and some purists argue that it's therefore not really a part of the 12 Step program, taking a deeper look at where that term came from sheds light on why sponsorship holds such an important piece of the puzzle for recovery in the 12 Step program. In the very early days of A.A., as the very first A.A. groups developed a reputation for success, local hospitals would refuse to accept admissions for hard-core drunks unless someone from one of these A.A. groups would "sponsor" the patient. This involved the designated "sponsor" visiting the patient in hospital and introducing him or her to the 12 Step program, and taking the patient under their wing after discharge. This "sponsorship" proved so effective that the practice became a custom in the 12 Step program, a custom that remains rightfully firmly in place today.

Just as this book is not a replacement for a sponsor, it's also not a replacement for the 12 Step literature – that is, books that are official publications of Alcoholics Anonymous World Services. Rather, this book should be viewed as a study guide to help you get more from the 12 Step literature. In fact, the 12 Step literature is tightly woven into this book, and readers will find that they gain a familiarity with the important books from the 12 Step program as we progress through the Steps together. Throughout the book, I've indicated references to scientific sources by a floating number (like this[1]) so that you can look up the reference I used – if you wish – in the back of the book. However, for the 12 Step literature I have included the name of the book and the page number right there in the text so that readers can follow along in their own books as we go along. The most important 12 Step books that appear are *Alcoholics Anonymous*, which I refer to by its nick-name, the "Big Book," and the book *Twelve Steps and Twelve Traditions*, as these contain the meat and potatoes of the information we need. However, I have also included the 12 Step books *Came to Believe, Living Sober, Pass it On, As Bill Sees It,* and various *A.A. Grapevine* publications, including its monthly magazine.

Even though the Big Book and much of the other primary 12 Step literature was written about alcohol, it applies directly to any addictive substance or behavior. When I quote the Big Book and other 12 Step literature throughout this book, I ask readers to remember that even though the quotations use the term "alcoholism" we should simply substitute the term "alcoholism-addiction." Those readers who have other addictions should just mentally insert the name of their poison or vice.

While we're on the subject, let's clarify some necessary terminology. The word "addiction" isn't a proper medical term. Until 2013, the accepted medical terminology for addiction was "[insert name of substance] dependence" and "[insert name of substance] abuse." Since 2013 it has been "substance use disorder." However, I prefer to use the term "addiction." It's unequivocal, to the point, and understood by everybody. The medical community keeps changing their terminology, but we always understand the word "addiction." Different types of drugs have differing characteristics, but they all have the same end effect when it comes to addiction. This includes alcohol, which is just another type of addictive drug. However, out of respect for the way people commonly use the term "alcoholism" as separate from "addiction," I have decided to use the term "alcoholism-addiction" or "addiction-alcoholism" throughout this book. Occasionally, I just use the word "addiction." I don't want to offend anyone's sensitivities, but I believe everyone can get behind the term "alcoholism-addiction."

It's appropriate to note that substance use is not the only type of addiction that entraps people as their negative psychology propels them to seek a dysfunctional coping mechanism. Behavioral addictions – sometimes referred to as *process addictions* – have a very similar mechanism of action on the brain as do drugs of addiction, and many people who come to the 12 Step program do so to overcome such addictions. These include such addictive behaviors as gambling, compulsive eating, compulsive shopping, pornography, and co-dependency. Anybody who's using this book to work through the Steps to overcome such addictions is in the right place; just substitute "drugs or alcohol" with whatever your addiction happens to be. There are 12 Step fellowships for all of the process addictions, such as Gamblers Anonymous, and Over-eaters Anonymous, and the Steps help any and all of us, regardless of our particular poison.

In this book I refer to alcoholism-addiction as a disease. I know that many people recoil at that concept, just as I did as a physician before I became involved in addiction research and came to understand the basis for calling it a disease. For anyone who is interested, I have included as Appendix 1 at the end of this book an explanation of why alcoholism-addiction is a disease.

I've been asked a number of times what is meant by the term (from the Big Book) that we have an "allergy" to alcohol (or drugs). Well, that term is medically appropriate. People tend to think of having an allergy as being when someone begins sneezing, or swelling up, or getting itchy, or breaking out in red spots when they ingest or are exposed to something they are allergic too. Sure, that's a common form of allergy. However, an allergy is, in the broad sense, a chronic condition involving an abnormal response to a foreign substance. In our case, alcohol or drugs do not cause the immune response that we think of as an allergy; rather, they produce structural and functional brain changes that result in abnormal thought processes and behaviors. That's our allergy to drugs or alcohol: a chronic condition involving an adverse reaction to a foreign substance. The point is that we must learn to regard alcohol as a poison for us rather than a beverage; likewise with drugs of addiction.

Speaking of terminology used in the Big Book, I ask readers to excuse the use of early 20th century masculine pronouns and other misogynistic language in the passages that are cited from the original 12 Step literature. The language in the Big Book can be somewhat off-putting because of its misogynistic use of pronouns, and the chapter "To Wives," which give the impression that the information is applicable to men. However, women in recovery were a part of the 12 Step program from its very beginnings, and are well represented in the Big Book; many of the stories are written by our sisters in recovery.

Although the style of language used in the Big Book appears objectionable to the modern eye, we must remember that the Big Book was written in the 1930s, a time when male pronouns were used by default. Even when I was growing up in the 1970s and 80s this practice was still in use. So, why hasn't the Big Book text been updated to reflect the more gender-neutral style of writing that's in use today? The introduction to *Twelve Steps and Twelve Traditions* explains:

> In recent years some members and friends of A.A. have asked if it would be wise to update the language, idioms, and historical references in the book to present a more contemporary image for the Fellowship. However, because the book has helped so many alcoholics find recovery, there exists strong sentiment within the Fellowship against any change to it (p. 14).

If readers can get past and accept the style of writing for what it is – a reflection of the times in which the Big Book was written – then the healing power of that remarkable book will open up to them. It's about not throwing out the baby with the bathwater.

By the by, you may note that, unlike in the Big Book and other A.A. literature, I do not capitalize the term "higher power." I do this for a reason: capitalizing the term implies a divinity and for many people their understanding of a higher power does not involve a divinity. So, at the risk of offending A.A. purists, I chose to vary from this A.A. practice in the interest of inclusiveness to all of our brothers and sisters in recovery. If I offend anyone by this decision, I ask for understanding and I apologize in advance.

The Big Book has taken a lot of heat because of its use of the word "God," while the program is emphatically open to people of any and all beliefs, including atheists. Because of this, some outsiders have labeled and rejected the 12 Step program as "religious." However, the program is explicitly open to people of all or any beliefs. Personally, I am not religious and I have never once felt any pressure to be religious during my time in the 12 Step program. In writing this book I took extra care in making sure that people of all beliefs or non-beliefs are given opportunity to find the message within each Step consistent with each individual's own context and sensitivities. When approached with an open mind, the 12 Step program invites all, constrains none.

*

If we can get past the somewhat dated language and terminology of the Big Book we can avail ourselves of one of the most fascinating and amazing books in print.

The Big Book is one of the best-selling books of all time, having sold more than 30 million copies. Time magazine has recognized its considerable influence by including it on its list of the top 100 best and most influential books in the last 100 years. The U.S. Library of Congress has recognized it on its list of 88 "Books that Shaped America." However, all its accolades aside, the Big Book has impressed me immeasurably for other reasons.

As a scientist it amazes me that the principles and suggestions contained in the Big Book – even though it was written in the 1930s – are entirely consistent with the most up-to-date science that we have available to us today. In fact, most of the core principles and techniques used by present-day addiction therapists are derived from this 80+ year-old program. The 12 Steps are an especially effective form of cognitive-behavioral therapy (CBT), yet they were developed half a century before CBT was invented. Extraordinary.

As a therapist, I was stunned as I first went through the Steps and I realized that the process is actually a form of psychotherapy, and an incredibly effective one at that. What amazed me most, though, was that this extraordinary form of psychotherapy is delivered by laypersons with no medical training; one alcoholic-addict in recovery helping another. The Big Book is the manual for how to do that.

I credit the turning point in my disease and my life with reading the Big Book. When I was in the detox facility they gave me a copy of the Big Book. I was only about 20 pages in when a light switched on in my brain; I realized that I was not a write-off as a human being, that I was simply an addict-alcoholic displaying the typical symptoms of alcoholism-addiction, and that there was a way out. I could see that there were millions of people just like me who had fallen, and then followed this pathway to recovery and life. I could see that there was redemption, forgiveness, self-forgiveness, and a return to good health and function – all within my reach. This realization was like a lightning bolt of hope in my brain, and I went from dead man walking to hope, determination, and resolution in an instant. And this all occurred from reading the Big Book. What a feeling!

Now, years later, as I grow in my recovery and my life, I find that the Big Book grows with me. The Big Book is my constant friend, not only as a tremendous tool for my recovery, but also a great guide for effective living. It's my go-to stress-reliever, over-riding my natural tendency to seek comfort in the bottle or needle. I have read my Big Book through many times, and every time I read it I see new things in the pages and between the lines that I hadn't previously noted. The message I take from the sage words depends on where I am in my recovery and what's happening in my life at that time. It's almost like it's a different book every time I read it through. I hope you allow this amazing book into your life as well.

The Big Book is organized so that the first 164 pages contain the meat and potatoes of the 12 Step program, and the rest of the book is comprised of short stories from people like us who are in recovery, sharing with us their experience, strength, and hope. Even people who are not into reading find the Big Book an easy read because we learn all about ourselves. Please do get a copy and make sure it never collects dust.

*

The 12 Steps are about healing. They're about ending the pain. They're about healing destroyed relationships. They're about living life on life's terms. They're not about nagging or guilting us into saying "no" to drugs or drink. Rather, they're about ridding us of our emotional, mental, and spiritual burdens so that the need to run and hide in drink or drug falls away. They're about new life skills so that we don't get back to the same train-wreck mentality that brought us down in the past. I treasure the new life skills that I have obtained from doing the 12 Steps; if only I would have had these wonderful life talents much earlier in life.

Through the lens of psychology, the 12 Steps convert us from the absolute worst example of negative psychology – the sewer-pit psychological mess of active drug or alcohol addiction – to a level of positive psychology that has been proven to be well above that of average, happy, functioning people, as we will see. And it's not based on material wealth or success. There are many people of great material success who are not happy people, ridden with conflict, self-doubt, pessimism, and negative feelings. Meanwhile, there are many without two nickels to rub together who are happy, at peace, and well adjusted. The difference between happiness and misery is not material wealth; rather it's positive psychology. Even t. "positive psychology" sounds awesome. The first time I heard it - before I came to be addicted to drugs and alcohol – I thought *Cool! I ι ,ι t know what that is, but I want it!* So, what is this "positive psychology?"

"Positive Psychology" is a relatively new and very hot term in psychology, and with good reason, because it's an awesome thing to have. Positive psychology is the scientific study of what makes life most worth living.[1] By understanding positive psychology, we can apply it to our lives to optimize our well-being and happiness. Positive psychology focuses on the thoughts, feelings, and behaviors that make people happy and fulfilled, rather than the traditional approach of psychology to study what makes people unwell and how to fix it. It focuses on positive experiences, positive emotions and feelings, and positive institutions. People with positive psychology are optimistic, grateful, happy, and have a positive outlook on life, in adversity as well as in triumph. Positive psychology has been associated by an overwhelming body of research evidence to be associated with multiple measures of mental and physical health, including recovery from addiction-alcoholism. We'll learn all about positive psychology and how to use the Steps to optimize our own positive psychology as we progress through the Steps together.

Negative psychology is a painful state of mind to be in. It impairs our ability to deal with life. We see the worst in everything, we project the outcome of all our stressors into a worst-case scenario, and we regret and obsess on past events, creating significant fear and anxiety. When our mind is filled with such negativity, we have very little capacity to handle new stresses, and we are quick to anger; we get stressed and anxious over little things, and we are robbed of a modicum of peace and happiness. We have no resilience or hardiness, and are vulnerable to the smallest of stresses. Negative psychology creates such uncomfortable thoughts and feelings that we turn to anything to get a break from the pain. That's when we are ripe for addiction, as we turn to substance use – usually without any intention of becoming addicted – as a quick and easy way to numb the pain.

People with active addictions to alcohol or drugs are an extreme case of negative psychology. Their self-esteem and feelings of self-worth are in their boots. They are wracked with guilt, shame, and remorse. They are angry at everyone and everything, and resent and blame everyone. They have lost meaningful connections.

So, we get a vicious cycle of downward-spiraling negative psychology and substance abuse, both of which feed off each other. The genius of the 12 Steps is that they are singularly effective at putting an end to this negative psychology that is both cause and effect of addiction, thereby removing the need to drink or use. This breaks that self-perpetuating vicious cycle of substance use and negative psychology. In my professional and personal opinion, the 12 Step program is – by far – the most effective way to impart a positive psychology, and it does so quickly, and without monetary cost.

Many of the people who suffer through addiction-alcoholism are lacking in the usual risk factors for substance use, such as an uncaring upbringing, past trauma, low income, and a family history of addictions. Many had beautiful, loving families, a good upbringing, good jobs, an education, nice homes, and enjoyed good health. So, it isn't always obvious what makes someone one of the one in seven people who become addicted when they drink alcohol or use drugs. Equally as weird, is that many of us were previously able to go through life with the ability to drink alcohol or even do drugs without any problem. Then, suddenly, a switch got flipped and we became obsessive drinkers or users.

When we look at the stories of a large number of people who have become addicted, the watershed moments that seemed to engage them in increasing substance use were surprisingly consistent. In some, especially adolescents, substance use was the only way they felt comfortable in social situations. Many reported using the substances to self-medicate mental health symptoms that they may or may not have been aware of; depression and anxiety were especially common. Still others reached a watershed moment where their life stressors became overwhelming, and they turned to substance use to cope. Many turned to substance use to cope with traumatic events in their past, either recent or distant. Some just liked how the drugs or alcohol made them feel, but then couldn't stop. You will see as we progress through the Steps together that the 12 Steps are remarkably effective at helping people address whatever it was that made them drink or use obsessively.

*

From a medical perspective, the 12 Step process takes advantage of an ability of the brain to adapt and change according to what we are doing and what we need it to do, a physiological property known as *neuroplasticity*.[2] The term "plasticity" refers to the ability of our body tissues to adapt to our needs. For example, muscles have plasticity: if we lay around and don't use them they shrink and lose tone. They become weak and diminished. After all, our body sees no point in maintaining big muscles if we never use them. However, if we exercise and stay active, our muscles respond by growing in size and strength to meet our needs. Likewise, laying around and watching TV requires little brain effort, so our brain will respond accordingly. However, if we use our brain and challenge it, it will grow in capacity and ability. It really does work like that. This is neuroplasticity – brain plasticity.

We come to recovery in a state of negative brain plasticity. If we've been in active drug or alcohol use long enough, our life has degenerated to

10

the point where we are not using our brain very much, and certainly not challenging it. Even worse, as we will discuss later on, addictive substances change the structure and function of our brain in a negative way, leaving lasting dysfunctional adverse physical changes. As such, we can really use some positive brain plasticity. Enter the 12 Steps!

As we progress through the Steps we are constantly challenging our brain and setting new demands on it, learning and adopting new habits, new ideas, and new ways of thinking. The learning curve is steep and it pushes our brain plasticity to new, healthy levels that we may not have previously known. Step Eleven is particularly potent at inducing positive growth and development of brain function.

Just to give an example of the impressive power of the brain to adapt to positive change – i.e. neuroplasticity – I'll illustrate using the scenario of a typical stroke victim. A stroke occurs when the blood supply to a part of the brain gets cut off by a blockage of the artery that supplies that part of the brain. The affected brain tissue dies, rots away, and never grows back, actually leaving a vacant hole. If the affected part of the brain is the part that controls the individual's left arm, then she will be unable to move her left arm after the stroke. However, over the next eight months or so, with the proper therapy, the stroke victim can gain back function of her left arm, often just as well as before the stroke. *But how is that?* The part of her brain that controls her left arm is dead and rotted away. The answer is neuroplasticity. Her brain – with the proper therapy – was able to adapt and form alternative pathways around the dead brain tissue to control the left arm. However, if she had just sat around and not participated in therapy to help her develop new brain pathways, her arm would've ended up permanently paralyzed. This is the same neuroplasticity that helps us to heal and overcome the anatomical, physiological, and functional ravages done to our brain by our substance use. The 12 Steps provide us with the therapy to form new brain pathways – positive neuroplasticity.

Achieving positive brain plasticity is difficult to do. Therapists try to do it with their patients, but they only have their patient in front of them an hour or two a week. Many people don't have the regimented neuroplasticity regimen in place required to achieve positive brain plasticity. However, the 12 Step program is an extremely effective, regimented, guided system of brain plasticity, and we are most fortunate to have the opportunity to benefit from it. But, we must complete the 12 Steps in order to see these healing benefits.

*

So, why should anyone do the 12 Steps? Some people who go to 12 Step meetings are sober despite never having made it past the first one or three Steps. Well, there's a good answer for that. Recovery from alcohol or drug addiction is not simply the absence of drinking or using drugs. By the time we come to recovery we are socially, financially, physically, mentally, and spiritually unwell. Our self-esteem is in our boots, and we are angry, blameful, and resentful. We are wracked with guilt, remorse, and self-loathing. Although we might begin healing physically once the drug and alcohol use stops, the rest must be healed if we are to find happiness, peace of mind, and health and good function again. If we don't take care of the things that made us obsessively use drugs or alcohol, we won't find happiness and wellness, and we are at considerable risk of relapse.

In my time in the 12 Step fellowship and in my research work I have met many people who participate in the 12 Step fellowship, but who haven't done the Steps. Most are chronic relapsers. However, I have met some people who have a lot of sobriety but have never done the Steps. That's fine, that's their choice, but I will say two things about that: 1) they weren't as sick as me, because I couldn't have gotten and stayed sober without the Steps, and 2) they are short-changing themselves by missing out on the full healing power and life-enhancing properties of the program afforded by the Steps.

As one brother in recovery said at a recent A.A. meeting I attended: "I avoided doing the Steps when I came to the fellowship. I was sober two years but nothing had changed. I was still obsessed with alcohol. I wanted to hang myself." Another speaker I recently heard: "when I came to the fellowship I had been two and a half years without a drink or drug. However, my way of thinking was still totally screwed up, and I was incapable of making a rational decision. Alcoholics and addicts who still suffer are not always the ones who are still drinking or using." Another member said after coming back from a relapse: "I didn't do the Steps and I didn't know how to feel better, so I did what I knew to feel better – I went drinking and using." Incidentally, all three of these individuals have since done the Steps and were emphatic that they wished they had done so in the very beginning of their time in the fellowship.

*

Do **you** need to do the 12 Steps to get sober? Well, only you can answer that, although it may be wise to get an opinion from a loved. However, I remind you, the 12 Steps are not so much about not drinking or using as they are about healing. If you're living under the dark cloud of a negative psychology, if you're living with anger, resentment, guilt, shame, self-doubt, elevated pride but low self-esteem, a negative outlook on life, and troubled interpersonal relationships, then you may wish to consider taking the time to benefit from the 12 Steps. Most people find the process to be a turning point in their lives; I certainly did.

We must exercise some caution when deciding whether or not we need help to stop the miserable cycle of compulsive drinking or using. After all, one of the core symptoms of alcoholism-addiction is a persistent over-confidence in our ability to control or stop our drinking or using on our own, even after multiple failed efforts to do so. As we will discuss in our trip through the Steps together, there are other powerful psychological forces that induce us to lack insight into the extent of our disease, and to refuse help. The pull of drink or drug is very powerful, and the consequences of relapse are devastating, even fatal.

So, the odds are stacked against us having an objective opinion about whether or not we need some help in getting and staying sober. That's why it's wise to consult a loved one, or someone who is in recovery before you reject committing to doing the Steps.

The Big Book suggests on pages 31 and 32 a way to see if you can control your drinking or using, in case you are not sure. Basically, it suggests trying to control it, and seeing how you fare. Too, I have a few suggestions that may indicate whether you are someone who may benefit from a program of recovery. If you find that alcohol or drugs are affecting your behavior, if you can't control or stop it despite a sincere desire to stop, if you keep drinking or using despite that fact that it is having negative affects on your health, relationships, finances, job, and important responsibilities, then you are probably in need of some help. Alcoholic-addicts display a remarkably uniform set of behaviors that are not seen in "normal" people. If we are lying to cover our drinking or using, hiding our alcohol or drug use, leaving work early to drink or use, becoming angry when people confront us, and blaming our substance use on others (*you'd drink too if you had my wife!*), then we are behaving like an alcoholic-addict. If we hit the bottle or needle after arguments or other stressors, all the more so. There are other indicators that we have a problem, such as: driving while impaired, experiencing blackouts, feeling guilt over our substance use, or needing a drink or drug to start our day.

*

I use my "transmission" analogy to explain why giving the 12 Step program a try makes good sense. I'm not a car-guy, but let's say I decided to restore an old car in my garage. As a rookie, it would be a tough project, to say the least. I've heard that rebuilding a transmission is really tough, even for experienced gear-heads. So when I got to the point in the project where it was time to rebuild the transmission, I would be likely to fail if I tried doing it on my own without any help. *Right?*

Well, let's say that my next-door neighbor is a mechanic who has worked in a transmission shop for 20 years. He rebuilds transmissions for a living. I would be an idiot to not ask my neighbor to help me rebuild my transmission, *right?* After all, I will pretty much definitely fail if I try it on my own. But, being hardheaded, I try rebuilding the transmission on my own, but I fail and make a mess of it. There are parts everywhere. Now, do I ask my transmission-expert friend for help? *Nope.* I'm too hardheaded. So, I try it a couple of dozen more times, failing every time. So – finally – I swallow my pride and ask for my neighbor's help. An hour later, I have a working, finished transmission. So, why didn't I just get my neighbor's help in the first place, right? Well, repeatedly trying to stop our drinking or drug use on our own when there is help at hand is just as insane as repeatedly trying to rebuild a transmission on our own when we have a transmission expert living next door.

Alcoholism-addiction is – as we will see on our trip through the Steps together – characterized by a pathological proud stubbornness to seek or accept help. We typically try multiple times to stop our drinking or using on our own, sometimes with some success, but we end up failing. After all, one of the core defining symptoms of alcoholism-addiction is an inability to control our drinking or using. Yet we try, sincerely believing each time that THIS time we will stop. As the Big Book tells us: "the idea that somehow, someday he will control and enjoy his drinking is the great obsession of every abnormal drinker. The persistence of this illusion is astonishing. Many pursue it into the gates of insanity or death" (p. 30). When someone from the 12 Step program who has been in successful long-term recovery offers us a way out, it seems insane to say no, much like me refusing the help from my transmission expert neighbor. However, when we finally reach the point where we are willing to do whatever it takes – *anything* – to finally get better, then we will finally accept the help we need. In the 12 Step program we refer to this point as "reaching our bottom." However, beware; when we do the 12 Steps we must commit ourselves and put our best effort forward, as we will discuss in Step One. For our disease is so powerful, that it is said that every "bottom" has a basement. Some of us are fortunate in that we reach our bottom and seek and accept help before we have lost too much. Others reach the grave before they reach their bottom. We reach our bottom when we decide to stop digging; it's up to us. The help and the solution are there, and they don't cost a cent. The 12 Step program lays the tools we need at our feet... we just need to pick them up.

*

I'm sure you're as anxious as I am to get going on the Steps, so I'll keep the introduction short. There are, however, a few key concepts we need to

14

nail down before we get to it. The first of these involves setting the scene for self-forgiveness.

One of the most valuable gifts we derive from doing the Steps is self-forgiveness. Among other things, the first nine Steps are about self-forgiveness, but much of our ability to forgive and like ourselves again comes from learning about our disease. Of course, this comes from doing the Steps, but it also comes from interacting with other people in recovery, listening at meetings, reading our Big Book, and doing our best to learn about the science of addiction. One key aspect that we get from these efforts is that it begins to dawn on us that all those horrible things that we did were not manifestations of being a bad person; rather they were simply the symptoms of the disease of addiction-alcoholism. We lied and deceived during our active drug or alcohol use like few other people ever do – but we are not liars and deceivers. Rather, we are alcoholic-addicts with active disease displaying the typical symptoms. Lying, deceiving, and all those other horrible things we did all fall under the umbrella of our disease's typical brain effects. As we'll discuss on our trip through the Steps, we don't use this fact to excuse our behavior – we must take full responsibility for our past actions. Rather, this fact puts our past wrong-doings into context and demonstrates that we were not bad people who needed to become good, but sick people who needed to become well. Our alcoholism-addiction is part of who we are, but it doesn't define us. Thus, we use our alcohol or drug use to put our past behaviors into context, not as an excuse to hide behind.

Another important point that we must discuss before we get started is that ours is a serious, uniformly fatal, complex disease. The aspects of alcoholism-addiction that make it complex are its chronicity, the depth of its grasp on its victims, the self-perpetuating nature of its effects, the high incidence of co-occurrence with other mental health disorders, its deep social stigma, and the lack of any kind of cure. Although people may achieve remission, they remain susceptible to relapse for the rest of their lives. As such, we must be all-in, fully committed to doing what we need to do to achieve and maintain long-term sobriety and a return to happiness, good health, and good function. The Big Book is clear about this: "rarely have we seen a person fail who has thoroughly followed our path…. Remember that we deal with alcohol – cunning, baffling, powerful…! Half measures availed us nothing" (p. 58-59).

We can't expect to sit in a chair and have our recovery fall into our lap; we must make our recovery happen, and we must have both feet in our program of recovery, or this serious, life-long, powerful disease will win out. In 15 years of medical practice, never once have I seen people with cancer only go for half of their treatments, or pick and choose which ones they go for. They go to them all, because they know that they need to be all-in if they want to beat their deadly disease and keep it from coming back. So it is with us.

There's a phrase in *Twelve Steps and Twelve Traditions* that sticks with me because it defines beautifully the bottom line of what we get from committing fully to recovery; we become: "men and women spared from alcohol's final capacity" (p. 31). When we consider the staggering number of beautiful lives wasted and lost because of addiction-alcoholism, the impact of that phrase really hits home. Our disease is a powerful one. We must commit to recovery, all-in. If we don't our disease will certainly win.

*

Besides a full commitment to recovery, there are two other requisites for sobriety that we must take on as we enter the Steps. These are absolute requirements of the 12 Step program that solidify our commitment to recovery, yet these concepts are foreign to the mind-set of people in active addiction-alcoholism. They may therefore be something that many among us may not be accustomed to at present: being open-minded to new ideas, and being rigorously honest. Let's discuss these quickly before we get into the Steps.

The negative mind-set of the active alcoholic-addict is not conducive to open-mindedness. As we'll discuss as we progress through the Steps together, the negative psychology of addiction-alcoholism is characterized by anger, resentment, suspicion, a need to be "right" to compensate for a low self-esteem, and a need for control. Being open to considering new ideas doesn't come easily to us. However, if we've hit our bottom and are truly desperate to do whatever it takes to get better, being open-minded is possible. As the Big Book tells us:

> We often found ourselves handicapped by obstinacy, sensitiveness, and unreasoning prejudice. Many of us have been so touchy that even casual reference to spiritual things made us bristle with antagonism. This sort of thinking had to be abandoned. Though some of us resisted, we found no great difficulty in casting aside such feelings. Faced with alcoholic destruction, we soon became as open minded on spiritual matters as we had tried to be on other questions. In this respect alcohol was the great persuader. It finally beat us into a state of reasonableness. Sometimes this was a tedious process; we hope that no one else will be prejudiced for as long as some of us were (p. 48).

Being open-minded doesn't necessarily mean accepting something as fact; it just means being willing to consider another viewpoint. Sometimes

16

we can benefit from something that we don't accept simply by being open-minded to it. Prying open our angry, judgmental minds and keeping an open mind allows us to consider and perhaps adopt some new ideas and some new ways of doing things. When you think about it, that's not a bad idea because in the past our best thinking and our way of doing things only got us to our rock bottom. Being open-minded to new ideas and new ways of doing things is our way out of the old, dysfunctional ways that our alcoholic-addict minds stubbornly cling to.

Spirituality is a perfect example. Many of us come to the program with a belief that spirituality means religion, and many of us can list religion and God among our resentments. However, if you keep an open mind, we will explore how spirituality and religion are not at all the same thing, and many deeply spiritual individuals are committed atheists. Those who are open-minded enough to consider the facts may find that they have much to gain, without having to make any changes whatsoever to their belief system.

*

Along with open-mindedness, another important skill that we need to heal and get the most out of the Steps is what the Big Book refers to as "rigorous honesty." Like open-mindedness, the alcoholic-addict mind-set makes rigorous honesty an uphill battle for us. One of the core features of our disease in all its glory is deceit. We lie to cover up our drinking or drug use. Then, as we spiral downwards we lie to hide why we didn't show up for work, why we didn't come home last night, where all our money went, and why we need to borrow money. Then we lie to cover our lies, and so on. So, by the time we come to recovery rigorous honesty is far from the forefront of our minds. As the Big Book explains: "more than most people, the alcoholic leads a double life. He is very much the actor. To the outer world he presents his stage character. This is the one he likes his fellows to see" (p. 73).

It's difficult to be honest about our past. It was – for most of us – the lowest point of our lives, and our behaviors were embarrassing, shameful, and contemptible. Too, being addicted to alcohol or drugs carries a heavy burden of social stigma and shame. In fact, many of our behaviors may best be left unrevealed to people who don't understand addiction-alcoholism. However, the 12 Step fellowship is the easiest place in the world to finally stop the lies. When we're surrounded by people who understand our behavior – because they've been there themselves – and they are being rigorously honest with us, it breaks down our need to lie. We know that there is no judgment, no stigma, no jaw-dropping, and no secrets with these people. If we try to lie they see right through us, and they'll call us on it because they know it's for our own good. The 12 Step fellowship is a safe place for us to tell our stories. We want to be part of the group, to be honest like them. Being honest becomes a normal part of our participation.

We not only lie to everyone else when we are in active alcoholism-addiction, but we also lie to ourselves, which is known as denial. Self-deceit and lying to ourselves is based on an important psychological phenomenon known as *cognitive dissonance*.[3] I'm not here to turn you into a professional psychologist, but the concept of cognitive dissonance will come up many times in our trip through the Steps, so we need to understand what it is. Our mind likes to think of us as good people. When our behavior doesn't line up with our mind's beliefs about how a good person should behave – like when we are drinking or using drugs and doing all the associated behaviors – it creates a psychological discomfort known as *cognitive dissonance*. This psychological discomfort can be relieved by stopping the "bad" behavior, thereby eliminating the cognitive dissonance. However, we find that we can't stop our drug or alcohol use, so the "bad" behavior continues and keeps getting worse. Because we can't change the behavior that's causing the cognitive dissonance, our mind seeks other ways to reduce the psychological discomfort. The mind does this by making excuses for our behavior, and trying to ignore it or minimize it by lying to ourselves. We deny that our drinking or drug use is a problem, or we make excuses for it. After a while, our mind starts believing its own lies. The truth hurts too much, so our mind changes the truth to protect itself from pain and guilt. That's cognitive dissonance.

When we hear other people being honest it allows us to start being honest with ourselves. As the Big Book tells us: "if our [the 12 Step fellowship] testimony helps sweep away prejudice, enables you to think honestly, encourages you to search diligently within yourself, then, if you wish, you can join us on the Broad Highway. With this attitude you cannot fail" (p. 55).

We can't heal from something that we deny or refuse to talk about. In the 12 Step program we say that we are only as sick as our secrets. Rigorous honesty is how we keep from being sick. The lies and deceit and secret-keeping only got us into trouble; we can only begin to heal if we let go of old behaviors, starting with the lies and deceit. Once we get over that hump and let go of our need to conceal, the truth is truly liberating. It feels great to stop the lies and to get things off our chest. The more we let go of our secrets and tell our story – our true story – the better we feel. It's the beginning of healing; with every secret we let go of we heal a little more. Later in recovery – when our disease tries to re-assert itself – rigorous honesty will keep us from those little lies that add up to lead us to relapse. So let's make that decision to be rigorously honest and get better. It feels good, and it's a prerequisite to self-forgiveness and healing.

*

The elephant in the room when it comes to addiction-alcoholism is mental health. Data from the U.S. National Institutes of Health tell us that more than half of people with addiction got there by self-medicating their mental health symptoms with drugs and/or alcohol.[4] As well, addiction and other mental health disorders share considerable overlap in their genetics and environmental causes (i.e. their risk factors), the brain chemistry involved, and symptomatology.

As we'll discuss in our trip through the Steps together, mental health disorders - especially depression and anxiety - are very closely linked with substance addiction in a reciprocal fashion. Many people with mental health disorders aren't even aware that they have a diagnosable and treatable problem; many have been living with the symptoms for so long that they just think it's normal for them. However, substance use and mental health disorders can each cause each other, and they worsen each other when they occur together. Many people become addicted to substances in order to "self-medicate" their mental health symptoms; conversely, many people develop mental health symptoms from their substance use. The two are so intricately woven together that it's very difficult to treat one without treating the other at the same time.

Drugs and alcohol oppose the actions of medications that treat mental health disorders, so that even people who seek treatment are unlikely to get better as long as they continue drinking or using when treatment is initiated. The two must both be treated if there is to be any success.

The point here is that anyone who is coming into recovery would be wise to consider the issue of a mental health disorder – particularly anxiety and depression – in his or herself, and be open to seeking outside help from a doctor. By definition, mental health disorders cannot be diagnosed in someone who is actively using drugs or alcohol, because the symptoms can be produced or mimicked by substance use. However, symptoms that preceded the drug or alcohol use or that persist while in recovery should be a cause for concern.

This subject is very near and dear to me, because chronic depression is a part of my own story, and attempts to self-medicate with alcohol and drugs were part of my addiction. Even though I knew very well that I was depressed and that there is effective treatment available, my alcoholic-addict focus on the here and now overcame my better judgment. Too, when I did start on the appropriate medication to treat my depression it did very little for me because the drugs and alcohol were negating the medication's effects. When I came to recovery the medication finally had a chance to work, and it wasn't long before the medication had me feeling much better –

once I was in recovery. My story is far from unusual. So, let's keep our antenna up for mental health symptoms in ourselves and others. If there's any concern or doubt, it's probably better to be safe than sorry, and seek a professional opinion. We'll talk more about this as we progress through the Steps together. *OK?*

*

Finally, before delving into the Steps, it's important that we have a word about a certain word: "suggestion." The word "suggestion" pervades the 12 Step literature, reminding us that the 12 Steps are mere "suggestions." From the Big Book: "here are the steps we took, which are suggested as a program of recovery" (p. 59), "we believe we can make some definite valuable suggestions" (p. 86), "when the man is presented with this volume it is best that no one tell him he must abide by its suggestions" (p. 144), "our hope is that when this chip of a book is launched on the world tide of alcoholism, defeated drinkers will seize upon it, to follow its suggestions" (p. 153), and "to return to the subject matter of this book: it contains full suggestions" (p. 143). From *Twelve Steps and Twelve Traditions*: "A.A. does not demand belief; Twelve Steps are only suggestions" (p. 5), "our Twelve Steps to recovery are suggestions" (p. 129), and "all of its Twelve Steps are but suggestions" (p.26). So why are the 12 Steps presented as suggestions rather than instructions?

Alcoholic-addicts invented stubborn. Especially when actively using or drinking or in early recovery our alcoholic-addict pride is likely to make us buck at orders or must-do's: "long ago, trustees and staff members alike found they could do no more than make suggestions, and very mild ones at that" (*Twelve Steps and Twelve Traditions*, p. 173), "this doesn't mean an A.A. won't take advice or suggestions from more experienced members, and but he certainly won't take orders" (*Twelve Steps and Twelve Traditions*, p. 173).

However, as we take on a mind-set of open-mindedness and willingness and shed our alcohol- or drug-induced stubbornness, we should begin to view these suggestions as more than mere suggestions: "we know these suggestions are sometimes difficult to follow, but you will save many a heartbreak if you can succeed in following them" (Big Book, p. 111).

Because of these truths, the 12 Step program never advocates strong-arming anyone into recovery, and therefore does not deal in imperatives. However, if we're here of our own will, and we have reached our bottom and truly want to be healthy and well again, we should view the "suggestions" of A.A. as imperatives: "unless each A.A. member follows to the best of his ability our suggested Twelve Steps to recovery, he almost certainly signs his own death warrant" (*Twelve Steps and Twelve Traditions*, p. 174).

One thing that I learned very early on in my own recovery in the 12 Step program is that the "suggestions" in the 12 Steps are must-do's if we want to get better. When our sponsor or a long-timer makes a suggestion to us, we are wise to take it as a must-do. Doing so has never failed me. I have received many very subtle "suggestions" from long-timers who I thought barely knew me and which seemed like odd suggestions at the time, but these always proved to be very wise once I acted on them. If you get your hackles up when someone dares make a "suggestion" to you, I suggest you take some time before you reject it. I "suggest" that you wait and consider it when the raw emotion of indignity has passed.

I have seen people do the Steps out of order, or only do certain Steps because *some don't apply to me*. However, they are cheating themselves of the magnificent healing power of the 12 Step program. If we are serious about recovery, the time for doing things our own way is over. We can ask ourselves: *how has doing things my own way worked out for me so far?* Doing things our way has nearly killed us, so let's commit to treating the "suggestions" that are made of us as imperatives. As we will learn in Step Three, our self-will is not our friend. We have to relinquish that alcoholic-addict need for control; we need to be teachable and open to suggestions.

*

Ready to change your life for the better? Let's just quickly re-iterate the points I just made, because optimal success depends upon committing to a few attitude changes that go against the grain for we alcoholic-addicts. Those are: willingness, keeping an open mind, and a commitment to be all-in. We must be willing to at least consider new ideas and to give our utmost effort to do the things that are suggested of us. And we must commit to taking the program as a whole, not picking and choosing the parts that suit us or that are most convenient for us. The time for the easier, softer way is over. That means taking suggestions as instructions for actions, not as optional requirements. That means doing the Steps in order – all of them – not jumping around or doing certain ones. That means getting a sponsor and using him or her, reading the Big Book, having contact with someone else in recovery every day, going to meetings, getting a home group, and becoming involved. Recovery is serious undertaking that seeks to overcome a deadly, all-consuming disease. We must be ready to do whatever it takes, and to face facts with courage. You have nothing to lose but your chains. Ready? Let's get to it.

Step One

We admitted we were powerless over alcohol – that our lives had become unmanageable.

I'll never forget my first exposure to powerlessness over alcohol. I was an intern, fresh out of medical school, still years away from my own experiences with drug and alcohol addiction. I was working on an internal medicine ward in a large hospital and one of my mentors was a Hepatologist (a liver specialist) who told me about a clinical study that he was running. He was looking at how many alcoholics with end-stage alcoholic cirrhosis of the liver would quit drinking if their life depended upon it.

The liver is a very forgiving organ, and it can bounce back from pretty serious adversity if we give it a chance. The people that my professor recruited for his study all had a very good chance of surviving and becoming well again **if** they stopped drinking. However, if they continued drinking their average life expectancy was about four months. Four hellish months. When you die of cirrhosis you are really, really wretchedly sick and miserable. It's a hard way to die.

I thought this Hepatologist was crazy, and I politely told him so. I reasoned that given the choice between being wretchedly sick and dying in a few months, and a return to good health, the choice was a no-brainer. I thought he was wasting his time, because 100% of those alcoholics would quit drinking as soon as they were given the choice. Right?

Well, at this point in my life I was still uninitiated to the power of addiction-alcoholism over the mind and the will, still years away from my own experience with powerlessness. So, it was obvious to me that *anybody* – alcoholic-addict or not – would quit drinking if given the choice between life and health, and horrible death. I had learned about addiction-alcoholism in medical school, but there was one thing about it that wasn't in any textbook or lecture and I had no way of really understanding... powerlessness.

As it turned out, my professor's clinical study showed that 82% of the alcoholics continued drinking right up to their slow, painful death. Eighty-two percent?!? How could that be? That stuck with me for years because I couldn't figure it out. It defied logic, it defied psychology, and it defied understanding. It didn't make sense to me as a doctor, and it definitely didn't make sense to me as a person. *Why didn't they just stop?* Even if those people wanted to kill themselves, why didn't they commit suicide quickly, rather than by suffering a slow, lingering, and miserable decline? I didn't understand any of it until I went through the experience of alcoholism-addiction myself, years later.

It turns out that addiction-alcoholism does something to our mind; it warps our normal psychology, and changes how we think and behave. It defeats the power of our will and renders even the strongest among us unable to help ourselves, and it does it through what the 12 Step program refers to as *powerlessness.*

In our Step One discussion we'll review why some people become powerless over drug or alcohol use, and why so many of us refuse to admit, accept, and concede that powerlessness, even when it's painfully obvious. We'll discuss what happens to our brain and mind and why our thought processes become so badly disrupted. We'll discuss why alcoholism-addiction is so completely illogical, why it's known as the disease of paradoxes. We'll also lay out exactly how to counter these effects of drugs and alcohol on our will. And we'll tie all that information into doing a really awesome Step One.

*

Consider this story from Cheryl B. from Illinois:

> How can I, a tough girl raised on the south side of Chicago, survivor of an active alcoholic upbringing, single mother of two, bringing home the bacon, frying it up in a pan, be powerless? It did not make sense and it kept me out there long after alcohol stopped working and was the cause of two painful relapses after entering Alcoholics Anonymous.
>
> My alcoholism had progressed to the point that at 31 years old, I did not want to live anymore even though I had everything to live for: two beautiful, healthy children, good physical health, plenty of family, I owned my home and had lots of stuff. Growing up poor, I thought money was the answer, but I was absolutely miserable and could not figure it out. I found myself crying out some nights, while completely sober, 'What is wrong with me?'

My bottom began with another night of just going out for a "few." Driving home drunk around 4 a.m., I smashed my new car into a light post after exiting an off-ramp from the expressway. By chance I did not hurt anyone or myself, but the car took a beating. I was in a fairly desolate area about three miles from my home. I managed to get my car over to the side of the road after trying to drive it with the front end jacked up like an accordion, and began to walk home. There I was, walking down a dimly-lit road surrounded by forest preserves and thought to myself, 'And you are the mother of two kids.'

I had had numerous drunken episodes and nightmarish things happen during my 15 years of drinking, particularly the last half, but this time I was given grace. The next morning as my eyes opened, and last night's memories came rushing in, I knew I couldn't live that way anymore and needed to ask for help. This was solidified moments later when I hazily stumbled out of my bedroom, and my 11-year-old daughter looked up at me with her big brown eyes and in all her innocence asked, 'Mommy, where's our car?'

I went to my brother, who had already started recovery, and told him I thought I had a drinking problem and would like a list of meetings. He wanted me to go with him, but in my usual fashion I thought I could handle it all by myself. Surprisingly, it didn't take long for me to realize I was getting nowhere that way and I took him up on his offer.

He took me to his meetings and introduced me to some women. Thanks to an awesome home group and sponsor, I started to learn about the disease of alcoholism. I was so fortunate to be around solid AA and strong teachers. I did not know during my drinking career that I was in the grips of a disease that I was powerless over. I could look back and see my drinking was never normal, but that was all I could understand. I also knew that even though I made several promises to myself to stop, I could never stay stopped. I had no idea, in other words, what I was dealing with.

I was taking a lot of actions in the group but I was still picking and choosing what I would and would not do. I know now that I had not completely surrendered. The time came when my disease started talking to me and told me 'You weren't that bad, you can handle it now. Things would be different this time. You have learned so much.'

I listened to that insane thinking and started to believe that self-knowledge and will power was the key to managing and controlling my drinking. At 11 months sober, I went back out determined to beat this thing. Within 2 months, I was right back where I left off. Doing the things I swore I wouldn't do again even with all my newfound knowledge. I had lost control over my drinking once again and began withdrawing from my family, and driving drunk, and that hole in my soul was back in full force.

I decided that 'maybe those AAs were right.'

Thank God I had built a support group during the 11 months that I was in AA. I called my friend to complain about my dilemma and she simply told me to meet her at the meeting. It was divine intervention that I said yes as I had no intention of coming back just yet; after all it still wasn't 'that bad.' Coming back was a bit of a struggle, but after a while, I felt triumphant. 'I will never drink again. I get it now,' I told friends. 'I love AA!'

Turns out you can hit a bottom and then keep on digging. Four months later, I drank again.

I was finally beginning to understand that this disease had me and I was powerless with no defense against it. No matter how strong I was, no matter how much I knew, no matter how much I loved AA, it didn't matter. This time coming back into AA was extremely difficult. There was no honeymoon and I thought I was losing my mind. Two and a half months into this sobriety, I contemplated killing myself. I started to believe that maybe AA wouldn't work for me. I knew it worked in others because I saw it, but maybe I was one of those people who were "incapable of being honest with themselves."

I felt like I was hanging by a thread through my early sobriety but with the help of my sponsor who kept reminding me to pray and stay in some kind of service, other newcomers and people sharing at meetings, I kept coming back. Today I believe my entire journey was necessary for me to accept in my heart and soul that I was truly powerless over alcohol. I now have respect for the disease of alcoholism. It beat me up and brought me to my knees. Turns out it is OK to be powerless, because if I don't have the power or the answers then I have to seek out one who does and that one is my god, whom I found in Alcoholics Anonymous. My god almost always uses my fellow "trudgers" in the rooms to pass along the message he wants me to receive.

I have also learned that I am also powerless over people, places and things. I still wander into the god zone from time to time trying to take over. When I do, I become frustrated, emotional, and obsessive. There is still a fighter in me, although she does tire much sooner than before.

I don't know why I was chosen but I show my gratitude by putting my hand out to the suffering alcoholic the best I can. Today, I take care of my family and I am there for them. I continue to go to meetings to hear the message and to remember that alone, I am powerless. I still believe that the insanity of that first drink will return if I'm not giving this gift away and staying plugged into Alcoholics Anonymous and a god of my understanding. My sponsor assures me this is a healthy fear and I agree.

I often say to the newbie, 'Watch that First Step, it's a doozy!' Most of the time they look at me like I am off my rocker, but that's OK because I know exactly what it means. Step One is the only step I have to do completely and because of that I have not had to pick up a drink since July 6, 1997. (Copyright © The A.A. Grapevine, Inc. (June 2011). Reprinted with permission.)

Cheryl's story illustrates perfectly the reason that accepting our powerlessness is the first Step to recovery. We can do all the right things but as long as we maintain that stubborn belief that somehow, someday we will be able to control our drinking or using we will almost certainly fail. Cheryl did all the right things: hitting her bottom, seeking help from her brother in recovery, attending meetings, and even racking up some good sobriety time. However, as long as she maintained her belief that she could assert control over her drinking, more bottoms awaited her.

But Cheryl is not an odd or unusual case. Even though a non-alcoholic-addict would call her insane because of her refusal to just give in and accept once and for all that she is not able to control her drinking, this is typical, characteristic thinking and behavior of the addicted mind. As the Big Book tells us: "the idea that somehow, someday he will control and enjoy his drinking is the great obsession of every abnormal drinker. The persistence of this illusion is astonishing. Many pursue it into the gates of insanity or death" (p. 30). In order to move forward in recovery and shed the insanity we must completely lay this illusion to rest: "the delusion that we are like other people, or presently may be, has to be smashed" (Big Book, p. 30).

Cheryl's story sets the scene for our study of Step One. We are going to mesh together the vast experience from the 80+ years of success of the 12 Step program with the findings of the latest research in neuroscience and behavioral sciences to explain: 1) who is powerless over alcohol and drugs, 2) why people become powerless, 3) why people who are completely powerless have such difficulty in accepting and admitting it, 4) how to eliminate these barriers to Step One, and 5) how to bring all this information together to complete a Step One that will lay a solid foundation for a lasting recovery.

*

I was dumbstruck when I came to the 12 Step program and no one ever said to me: *dude! You gotta stop drinking or using, or you're going to lose everything and die.* No one ever said anything like that. I was expecting some premium weapons-grade nagging and ass-kicking and for them to ride me about my drinking or using until I stopped. (It wouldn't have worked, mind you, because I had already heard all that a thousand times.) But it turned out that – contrary to my pre-existing beliefs about the 12 Step program – it wasn't about that at all. Rather, the 12 Step program is about learning to live life in a way where the need for drugs or alcohol falls away. The 12 Steps impart a new set of life skills that enable a transition in our ability to cope with life to a new way of living where we can handle whatever life throws at us, without having to drink or use to handle it. Although I was surprised by this approach to addiction-alcoholism, it turns out that it's brilliant, because – as we will see as we progress through the Steps together – science has since demonstrated that this is exactly how substance addiction is best addressed. As a psychotherapist I realized as I worked my way through the Steps that the process was actually a simple but incredibly effective form of psychotherapy that's designed to move us from an extreme of negative psychology to an extreme of positive psychology. And I was singularly impressed by its ingenuity and sheer potency, despite its compelling simplicity! As we progress through the Steps together we will discuss what this transformation from negative to positive psychology means and why it works, and how to best use the Steps to achieve this life-affirming gift.

My personal and professional opinion is that the virtuous life skills and psychological health that the 12 Steps impart would benefit anybody and everybody, addict-alcoholic or not. After all, as you will see as we pass through the Steps together, most people suffer from the same kinds of stress intolerance, character defects, and interpersonal liabilities that we did, but they are fortunate enough not to have the genetics or life situation that made them turn to drink or drug to cope as many among us did. Any person would benefit from the life skills and spiritual well-being that comes from embracing the 12 Steps. They should teach the 12 Steps in high school! In fact, there are several hundred organizations that teach the 12 Steps to people who have no substance addiction problems at all. Rather, they use the 12 Steps for life skills training for business, life coaching, and leadership training. If you are – like me – gob-smacked when you first hear people in the fellowship refer to themselves as "grateful alcoholic-addicts," rest assured that the reason they say that is because they would otherwise never have known the salutary and invigorating effects of the 12 Steps in their lives.

Here, we are focused not on those who use the 12 Step program to further their skills for business, but for those who are pursuing their drug or alcohol use into the gates of insanity or death; people like Cheryl in our story from Grapevine. The 12 Step program is fundamentally for people who can't control or stop their drinking or drug use. There are people who are problem drinkers or drug users but once they realize their substance use is wrecking their health and their lives they can stop and walk away from the drinking or drug use. That certainly wasn't me. If people can quit on their own, then all the better for them. However, for those of us who can't, the 12 Steps are there to help us overcome our powerlessness.

As for me, when I was a medical intern – before I personally experienced alcoholism or addiction – powerlessness didn't make sense. Not at all. I was one of the *why don't they just quit* crowd. *Twelve Steps and Twelve Traditions* describes what happens to us: "when men and women pour so much alcohol into themselves that they destroy their lives, they commit a most unnatural act. Defying their instinctive desire for self-preservation, they seem bent upon self-destruction. They work against their own deepest instinct" (p.64).

The transition that we undergo when we move from being "normal" drinkers or users to alcoholic-addicts is described in the Big Book:

> For most normal folks, drinking means conviviality, companionship and colorful imagination. It means release from care, boredom and worry. It is joyous intimacy with friends and a feeling that life is good. But not so with us in those last days of heavy drinking. The old pleasures were gone. They were but memories. Never could we recapture the great moments of the past. There was an insistent yearning to enjoy life as we once did and a heartbreaking obsession that some new miracle of control would enable us to do it. There was always one more attempt – and one more failure (p. 151).

That sums it up pretty well. We crossed that line where drinking or using wasn't fun anymore. Instead of doing it for festive social occasions, we drank or used to escape reality, cope with bad feelings, cope with mental health symptoms, to avoid withdrawal symptoms, to get out of bed, to tolerate life. And soon we did it because we had to, we couldn't stop. We had become powerless over our substance use.

When our alcohol or drug use crosses that line and is no longer a choice, we become increasingly detached from life as our substance use takes more and more of our time, attention, and resources. Our lives become increasingly unmanageable. The 12 Step program uses the term "unmanageable," but for many of us this is the same unmanageability that a train conductor experiences when the train leaps off the tracks at high speed. This unmanageability of life perpetuates our substance use as the stress, frustration, hopelessness, and fear of our unmanageable, downward spiraling life becomes unbearable. Our powerlessness to control our drinking or using and our unmanageable lives are closely tied together. The only way to make life manageable again is to arrest the substance use. As with any problem, we can't address our quandary with substance use unless we first acknowledge that the problem exists. This is what Step One asks of us.

We are powerless over many things in life that affect us: the weather, traffic, other people's behavior – and we have no trouble realizing that. Why, then, is it that so many people can't do the same when they see that their reaction to alcohol or drugs is beyond their control, even though it's obvious? Well, it's because of the way psychoactive substances interact with our brain and mind functions. We'll discuss exactly how substances do this and how to use the Steps to put an end to it.

*

Dr. Bob Smith, co-founder of Alcoholic Anonymous, wasn't going to admit his powerlessness: "he would do anything, he said, but that" (Big Book, p. 155). Dr. Bob had just met Bill Wilson, who recounts:

> A certain resident of the town [i.e. Dr. Bob], who, though formerly able and respected, was then nearing the nadir of alcoholic despair. It was the usual situation: home in jeopardy, wife ill, children distracted, bills in arrears and standing damaged. He had a desperate desire to stop, but saw no way out, for he had earnestly tried many avenues of escape. Painfully aware of being somehow abnormal, the man did not fully realize what it meant to be alcoholic (Big Book, p. 155).

Dr. Bob, a practicing physician, was like many of the rest of us: aware that he was defeated and unable to escape the cold grasp of his drinking or using, yet not fully aware or accepting of his powerlessness. He was aware he was "abnormal;" abnormal, yes, but normal compared to the rest of us alcoholic-addicts. He was, in fact, just a normal, garden-variety alcoholic-addict. But being powerless isn't about being abnormal; it's about being a normal addict/alcoholic. *Twelve Steps and Twelve Traditions* gives a good description of the level of our powerlessness and the impact of our admission of powerlessness:

> We have warped our minds into such an obsession for destructive drinking that only an act of Providence can remove it from us. No other kind of bankruptcy is like this one. Alcohol has become the rapacious creditor, bleeds us of all self-sufficiency and all will to

resist its demands. Once this stark fact is accepted, our bankruptcy as going human concerns is complete (p. 21).

Step One asks a lot of alcoholic-addicts. It's difficult for us to throw our hands up in the air and admit defeat, to make our "bankruptcy complete." However, Step One is front-loaded with the benefit of knowing that admitting defeat comes with the promise of a victory that soon follows. It's an admission of defeat required only as a prelude to victory. There's a power that comes from accepting our powerlessness, because it's the key to taking back our lives again. Admitting powerlessness is all carrot and no stick.

*

Is powerlessness just an invention of the 12 Step program? Nope. The medical profession has long been familiar with powerlessness, which they refer to as "physical and psychological substance dependence." In fact, one of the core symptoms of addiction-alcoholism that the DSM-5 (the diagnostic manual that defines substance use disorders) specifies is the inability to control or stop the substance use despite obvious negative consequences – in other words: powerlessness over the substance.[1,2]

Why is anyone powerless over drugs or alcohol? Why can't we use willpower to stop? Addiction-alcoholism is a chronic physical disease of the brain, not a weakness of willpower, or a failing of morality.[3] Addiction-alcoholism is accompanied by a number of physical, physiological, and functional changes in the brain, and these changes are largely permanent (for a detailed account of these brain changes, see my book *The Alcoholic/Addict Within*). These brain changes cause the unusual set of thoughts and behaviors that preside over the lives of people in active substance addiction, as we will discuss as we walk through the Steps together. But the physical changes in our brain also debilitate our brain's ability to choose – our ability to engage willpower.

Researchers in neuroscience have found that addictive substances disrupt our brain's natural decision-making mechanisms, particularly the system that suppresses urges for impulsive behaviors, which is the system that forms the basis of what we call willpower.[4] These functional changes in the brain can actually be seen on a type of brain imaging scan known as functional magnetic resonance imaging (fMRI).[5]

Other research into the neuroscience of addictions has shown that substance use induces the development of anatomical and physiological errors in brain function that impair our ability to learn from experience and to change our behaviors and make decisions based on an otherwise obvious realization that our behavior will result in harm.[6] Further, similar substance

30

use-related brain changes also appear to impair the brain's ability to inhibit unwise or harmful behaviors.[7] Since these functional mechanisms form the very basis of what we call willpower, this suggests that addictive substances seriously impair our ability to engage willpower. This provides a neuroscience basis for powerlessness over alcohol or drugs: our brain's ability to exert power over substance use is incapacitated by the physical effects of the substance. As Dr. Alan Leshner, former director of the U.S. National Institutes of Health puts it: "once addicted, the individual has moved into a different state of being."[8] As such, the science supports the premise of Step One: the addict-alcoholic is beyond his or her own help; the addict-alcoholic is powerless.

Such research bolsters my respect for the 12 Step program and its founders because it provides a scientific validation of the principles of the program as, in this case, it provides compelling evidence confirming the concept of powerlessness.

If we are skeptical about the 12 Step program's suggestion that we are powerless over drugs or alcohol, then perhaps we can accept it when hard science tells us the same. Although the initial use of drugs or alcohol is voluntary, a matter of choice, when addiction develops the brain changes in substantial ways that take over the brain's inherent mechanisms for motivation so that the drug or alcohol use becomes the dominant motivational priority.[9] As one addictions researcher puts it: "addiction is like the Trojan horse, welcomed under false pretenses only to usurp the power that first received it."[10]

*

Not everyone becomes powerless over drug or drink when they partake. In fact, most people can go through life without ever becoming addicted when they drink or use drugs. We know from well-established statistics that almost everybody tries or uses alcohol and over half the population tries or uses drugs, but only 10-26% of people become addicted in their lifetime (statistics vary, depending on the population surveyed).[11,12] Just because alcohol and drugs are addictive substances doesn't mean that everyone becomes addicted and powerless. Most people can walk away from drugs or alcohol once it becomes a problem for them. Good for, them, I wish I were one of them. But for the rest of us – the ones who need the 12 Step program – we have no power to do that.

By the time someone walks through the door of a 12 Step meeting, he or she has likely tried earnestly many times and many ways to quit drinking or using. Strong-arming ourselves into recovery with willpower hasn't worked. No matter how much willpower we have, how intelligent we are, and how disciplined and hard-working we are, we haven't been able to beat it. We are powerless.

The Big Book is straightforward about willpower and addiction-alcoholism:

> the fact is that most alcoholics, for reasons yet obscure, have lost the power of choice in drink. Our so-called willpower becomes practically non-existent. We are unable, at certain times, to bring into our consciousness with sufficient force the memory of the suffering and humiliation of even a week or a month ago. We are without defense against the first drink (p. 24).

When Bill Wilson wrote this passage in the late 1930s, he and his fellow recovering alcoholics knew that willpower was useless for their disease, but they didn't know why; "for reasons yet obscure," he said. However, more than 80 years later, we now know exactly why this is, as we will discuss over the next few pages.

I'm a person with *a lot* of willpower, bordering on abject stubbornness. Raw willpower allowed me to quit smoking, survive brutal training in the army, earn two black belts, and have some success as a boxer. Sheer power of will got me into medical school and through the butt-kicking of my medical training. With my willpower I can bust through fatigue, hunger, pain, just about anything. In fact, before I was addicted to alcohol I was always able to take it or leave it. I had tried drugs before too, and didn't get caught up in them. But all of a sudden my willpower was a big fat zero when it came to drug or drink. *So why was I now powerless?* The failure of my usually considerable willpower was the greatest mystery to me in my struggle to escape active addiction-alcoholism. Time and again I tried to engage my willpower to stop the self-destructive madness of my substance use, always confident in my ability to take back control of my life, but time and again I failed. *Why?* When I came to the 12 Step program they told me it was because I was powerless over alcohol and drugs. I didn't understand it, but it was enough for me; I readily accepted my powerlessness, even though I didn't understand it. I didn't need to understand; I just wanted to get sober and get better. Later, though, I needed to know why.

Willpower is the ability to resist short-term temptations in order to meet long-term goals; the capacity to override an unwanted thought, feeling or impulse.[13] We often use other words for willpower, such as self-discipline, determination, drive, resolve, or self-control. Willpower is a great thing to have in life, but even at the best of times it is unreliable. Willpower is a daily – sometimes hourly or minute-by-minute – battle of the wills, and a difficult one when it comes to something with such a powerful hold on us, such as our substance of addiction. This can be an excruciating battle, which is why trying to recover by willpower alone is often referred to as "white-knuckling it." A single moment where that willpower fails, and we are back at it again. This is widely the experience of powerless people who try quitting on their own.

Studies have shown that willpower for addiction-alcoholism not only doesn't work, but is actually harmful.[14] That's right: harmful. Even among people who are high in willpower, the state of the will has no effect on recovery.[15] Interestingly, the 12 Step program identified the futility of willpower for recovery from addiction based on experience more than half a century before it was identified by clinical research.

So, how can willpower be harmful to recovery? Willpower is an effort to suppress and push down the pain and other reasons behind our addiction, rather than confronting them.[16] This is never a successful approach, and it is the reason why addiction recovery programs use counseling techniques to help people address the underlying causes of addiction, rather than trying to teach them ways to make their willpower stronger.

Trying to rely on willpower diverts us from making connections with people who could help us. As one addict in recovery says: "the opposite of addiction is connection."[17] Willpower is an *internal* process, where we keep the problem within ourselves, relying on a person who is physically, mentally, and spiritually sick and unreliable – ourselves. It's a cardinal feature of the psychology of addiction-alcoholism that people overestimate their ability to control their substance use on their own, are neurotically secretive about their substance use, and have an uncanny ability to rationalize just about any bad decision, particularly if it relates to substance use. As we will see in Steps Two and Three, spirituality is about making connections with people outside ourselves, and it's the antidote to the secretive, selfish behavior of addiction-alcoholism. Trying to rely on willpower prevents us from letting other people in.

Another problem with willpower is that it requires constant thinking, and we forget things. The psychology of addiction has a peculiarity whereby we have a pervasive belief that, especially after a period of abstinence, we can try drinking or using again, that we have learned our lesson, so that THIS time things will be different. This dysfunctional thinking – the insanity of alcoholism-addiction – takes over and we gladly drop all the effort it takes to maintain willpower. After all, we don't need to put in the pain and effort to sweat out willpower when we can control our drinking or using, *right?* This is what happens when powerless people try to rely on willpower rather than addressing the dysfunctional thought processes underlying their addiction.

Even if we are able to stop drinking or using for a period of time using willpower, the underlying causes of the addiction, and the mental carnage from the substance use and related behaviors remain. Life would not be any better, our muddled and dysfunctional thought processes would continue their sinister workings, and the inability to handle life's stressors would not be any different. Past traumas would remain unaddressed. With willpower we are dry, but not healed. It's a tenuous recovery, at best.

*

There are other reasons that willpower doesn't work for those of us who are powerless. Willpower is about effortful regulation of the self by the self, making the right choice despite temptations otherwise. However, we have long ago reached the point where our substance use is no longer a choice.[18] Addiction-alcoholism occurs when people cross the line where their drug use is no longer a choice. If addiction-alcoholism was a choice and therefore subject to willpower, we would have quit drinking or using way back when it was no longer fun and it began wrecking our lives.

The psychology of addiction-alcoholism is characterized by a focus on the here and now, the self, and instant gratification. It's about escape from the present reality. There's a big disconnect between willpower and this prevailing drive for the here and now that presides over the addicted mind. Willpower is about determination to put off gratification now in favor of benefits in the future. By its very nature, addiction-alcoholism is defined by continued obsessive use of alcohol or drugs now despite obvious negative consequences in the future. The here and now is all that matters. The addicted mind doesn't care about consequences, so putting off gratification of the obsession for drug or drink now to avoid problems later isn't even a consideration. Willpower is rendered defunct by the very nature of the effects of psychoactive substances on our mind.

When we try to apply our best willpower to our drinking or drugging, we burn it out. Willpower is not available to the human mind in infinite quantities; rather, it's a limited resource that becomes depleted.[19] An convincing body of research evidence has demonstrated that repeated efforts to use willpower burns it out, making willpower progressively less effective.[20] Resisting the urge to drink or use diminishes our strength for resisting the next temptation. This is why some people may find they are able to withstand the temptation to drink or use in the early stages of their addiction, but soon find that they can no longer prevail when they try to apply their willpower. Powerlessness develops as willpower burns itself out.

*

In Step One we are taking a big mental leap by giving up on our faith in willpower, which, as we have seen, is actually not an effective way to stop drinking or using anyway. One of the barriers to people's ability to do their Step One is that they cling to the belief that they can use willpower to stop their drug use or drinking. Their willpower has worked for them in every crucial life situation in the past, so why not now, they wonder. Many try over and over again and still cling to that belief. It's not until we accept that our willpower is useless against addiction-alcoholism – that we are powerless over drugs or alcohol – that we can let go of that insanity and get on with our recovery.

Our willpower has failed us miserably and Step One instead asks us to take on a willingness to take responsibility for our situation, to concede and own our powerlessness, and to commit to a program of recovery that is specifically designed for people who are powerless over drugs and alcohol. However, we can still use our willpower to help our recovery. Our willpower has failed against drugs or alcohol, but we can use willpower as our mind clears from its chemical cloud and begins working properly again. Powerlessness over alcohol and drugs is for life, so we never will be able to use willpower to control our drinking or using, even decades into recovery. However, we can use our willpower to get to meetings, work the Steps, adopt an attitude of open-mindedness and willingness, and work with a sponsor. Our willpower is not an effective defense against drinking or using for us, but we can apply it to make sure that we do the recovery activities that will allow us to finally break free of the insanity of our addiction.

The futility of willpower in escaping addiction-alcoholism shines through in the stories in the Big Book. By reading these stories we can be comforted by seeing that we are not alone in our powerlessness, that it doesn't make us weak or unworthy. Too, we can see in these stories that finally admitting their powerlessness and letting go of their belief in willpower was the turning point for these people in finding life in sobriety again. These stories are of great comfort to me anytime I am troubled or down, or my recovery needs a boost. Every one of them reminds me that I am powerless over alcohol and drugs, something I must remember for as long as I wish to remain healthy and happy in recovery.

*

Many people come to the 12 Step program already well aware of their powerlessness and are readily willing to admit it. They have long ago come to terms with the fact that stopping the insanity is beyond their power. That was my case. Here I was, a practicing doctor and psychotherapist, yet I was completely unable to fix myself, to halt this obsessive alcohol and drug use that was consuming my life and my soul. I had tried "everything" to stop: my usually considerable self-discipline and willpower, going for counseling, seeing my doctor, everything I could think of. My repeated failures to halt my substance use for anything more than a few days despite all my best efforts and my sincere promises to myself and my loved ones had convinced me that there was nothing inside of me that could help me. I was resigned to my alcoholism-addiction. I was past the point of arguing about whether or not I was powerless.

I couldn't keep living this empty and miserable life, yet I couldn't live without using and drinking. I was beat down, a tortured soul; physically sick, mentally and psychologically tormented, and spiritually sick. Every time I woke up I was disappointed to see that I was still alive. That's a pretty sad state to be in. As we'll discuss shortly, I was a living, breathing embodiment of extreme negative psychology. I couldn't keep living that way, but I was absolutely powerless to do anything about it. So, I resigned myself to the only way out: death. I had long ago swallowed my fate and accepted that I was completely powerless over drugs and alcohol; I needed no convincing. However, many among us really struggle with that realization of utter defeat.

To the outside observer, a reluctance to admit powerlessness appears as full-on lunacy. Everyone is entitled to be a little batty, but alcoholic-addicts abuse the privilege. However, it's not lunacy or stupidity. Not at all. Rather, it's simply the textbook effects of our psychoactive substances on our brain's function, which produces a set of symptoms that are so illogical and bizarre as to appear to the outside observer as some species of madness. Small wonder that they say that only an alcoholic-addict can understand another. These thought processes and behaviors are too counter-intuitive and incomprehensible for those who haven't been through the experience themselves.

Why are people so resistant to recognizing or admitting their powerlessness over drugs and alcohol when it's so blatantly obvious to everyone else? Well, there are a lot of reasons, and they all involve the way that drugs and alcohol manipulate our natural thought processes and behaviors when we become subjugated by addiction. Let's talk about why this happens, what these substances do to our brain functions, and how we can stop these effects so that we can rock our Step One and get on with recovery and living. The first of these factors is the bizarre pride of alcoholism-addiction.

*

The most pathetic thing about this guy was that he didn't even know how pathetic he was, but everyone else did. Ryan was in the detox center for, the staff told me, the 19th time. He had our disease through and through,

36

but it wasn't his fault. It was his wife's fault, it was his boss's fault, and it was the world's fault. If only the world wasn't stacked against him, he could live a good and sober life. And he was angry about it. Angry? He was the kind of guy who could get in a fight playing solitaire, or start a brawl at a bake sale. To hear this guy talk you'd think he was crazy, triple-dipped in psycho. But he wasn't. Ryan was just a prideful alcoholic-addict.

This guy Ryan wanted to be done with the drugs and alcohol, so he told us every time. Every time he was in the detox center he told the same story: THIS time he was done with it. He was an older guy, but he married a younger girl back when he was working and living a normal life. Of course, he had long ago burned his bridges with his wife, and then his friends, and he now lived outdoors in the summer and in any homeless shelter where he could find a bed in the winter. Sometimes he spent the night in Tim Horton's when the shelters were full. Every cent he could get went straight to drugs and alcohol, and I'm sure he was resorting to unsavory tactics to get money, because he had been long ago fired from his job. Ryan and his wife had two kids together – both under five years old – and he cried about how much he wanted to be with his wife and kids again. But, rightfully, she would have nothing to do with him until he got himself sobered up. She didn't want him around the kids because of his erratic, angry behavior. This guy wanted so bad to be done with the drugs and alcohol, because he had so much to live for... if only he could live again. But there was a single thing keeping him from getting what he wanted.

This guy couldn't accept that he was powerless over drugs and alcohol. Every time he was in detox he begged to get healthy again, to have his wife and family and job and life back. Life was once so good. We told him that all that was possible, but he had to give in and admit that he was powerless over drugs and alcohol before he could move forward. No one could doubt that this frequent flyer at the detox center was powerless over substances of abuse. But he did.

Time after crummy time, he maintained that he was a **man**, that his parents had raised him to look after himself, that there is no way that he is going to admit defeat over drugs and alcohol. It was just a matter of getting his head screwed on right. *I have to do this on my own*, he said, *I got this. I'll do it for my kids*. Was it craziness? Nope, it was the bizarre pride of alcoholism-addiction.

By the way, Ryan died of an overdose just hours after checking himself out of his 19th trip to detox. I went to his little funeral. Hardly anyone was there. His wife was there, and when I offered my condolences I sensed that she was relieved that her ordeal with Ryan was finally over. A sad, but all-too-common ending to the effects of substance use on the human mind.

Why was Ryan such a tortured soul? What force in the dark recesses of his addicted mind kept him in such a fatal denial? Why did he have to pursue his stubborn illusion that he could control his drinking and using all the way into the gates of insanity and death? Why did he not accept the help that was offered to him time and again? Because of pride. His pride was the agent of his demise. But it wasn't just ordinary pride, it was the extraordinary pathological pride of alcoholism-addiction that killed him. But how can a guy who was so thoroughly sick, dispossessed, and living on the street have such a huge pride?

*

The pathological psychology of alcoholism and addiction includes a peculiar form of pride that asserts itself into a position of control over thought processes and behaviors, presiding over the lives of active alcoholic-addicts and forming a major barrier to recovery. Alcoholism-addiction is often referred to as the disease of paradoxes, and the strange pride of alcoholism-addiction is one such paradox because it involves a pride that is exceptionally elevated in the presence of an exceptionally diminished self-esteem. This pride makes it very difficult for many among us to take that first Step and admit powerlessness.

The psychological basis of this elevated pride is, ironically, paradoxically rooted in a pathologically depleted self-esteem. The lower the self-esteem, the higher the pride. It's a false pride, created by the addicted mind to compensate for a shattered self-esteem, yet only we are fooled by our own masquerade. The further life tumbles downward and the more pathetic we become, the more our mind is driven by cognitive dissonance to present a false front, to convince others – and ourselves – of how awesome we are. For most people, pride is a by-product of accomplishment, possessions, their feelings of self-worth. In other words, they have something to at least partly back up their pride, over-inflated as it may be. In the practicing alcoholic-addict, pride becomes over-inflated, and defensive in nature... usually with nothing to back it up. Yet, it's powerful enough to prevent us from accepting our powerlessness over alcohol, and is a major factor in the reluctance of people like us to seek or accept help. It's an extreme example of what early 20th century Swiss psychiatrist and all-around smart guy Dr. Carl Jung was referring to when he said about addict-alcoholics that "people will do anything no matter how absurd, to avoid facing reality."[21]

This substance-induced pride is an instinctive mechanism that our mind generates to compensate for our ruined self-esteem, to reduce the psychological pain that comes from knowing how low we have become. In order to compensate for our own sorry behavior and increasingly pathetic situation, we will project a fabricated positive view of ourselves to others by inflated demonstrations of pride, and conversely by criticizing and nit-

38

picking others in efforts to cut them down beneath us. We are not only trying to convince others of our awesomeness, we are trying to convince ourselves. It's why people who are drunk or high will respond with aggression to the slightest affront or discourtesy. We become consumed by being "right" and can't admit when we are wrong, and we can't acknowledge our defects. Small wonder others find us obnoxious and can't stand to be around us.

This façade of pride takes a lot of effort as we become constantly consumed by our need to project a false image; the effort required can be exhausting. Many of our character defects come into play in our efforts to maintain this fake pride and try to sell it to others (and to ourselves). In order to do this we are secretive, we lie, we cheat, we are jealous of others, we are judgmental and look for fault in others, we try to cut others down to elevate ourselves, and we are defensive and aggressive when anything or anyone challenges our pride. This pride brings out the ugly in us. People see this behavior, and we don't fool anybody for long; the pride of alcoholism-addiction is dysfunctional, ineffective, illogical, and a tremendous waste of brain-power.

It's largely this bizarre pride that keeps many people from admitting powerlessness, even when they know very well deep down inside that they and nothing else on earth can arrest their obsessive use of drugs or alcohol. The psychological need is not only to fool others with this projection of pride, but to fool ourselves to reduce our psychological discomfort at our pathetic situation. The addicted mind deflects any challenge to its flimsy belief in this pride, including the suggestion of our powerlessness over drugs or alcohol. What Step One asks of us is offensive to our substance-soaked mind's need to maintain this façade of pride.

It is said that everyone must hit their bottom before they can admit their powerlessness. Hitting our bottom is the point where our mind finally turns the corner and becomes willing to drop the need for the façade of pride. Some are fortunate enough to hit their bottom before too much has been sacrificed, some are not. Many hit a bottom and think it can get no worse, but quickly find out that every bottom has a basement. For some, like our friend Ryan, their bottom is six feet underground.

*

However, even this otherwise unyielding pride can be convinced to admit powerlessness. Even though Step One asks us to admit defeat (to the objective observer it merely asks us to acknowledge the obvious), it does so with promise of a solution, a victory. It involves letting go of the fake pride in order to open the path to a healthy self-esteem based in reality, one of the rewards of advancing through the 12 Steps. The 12 Step program offers a well-travelled solution to addiction-alcoholism, but no one can solve a problem that they won't admit they have. Therefore, Step One sets the solution in motion. It's like that match we strike to light a bonfire. It's so much easier for the psyche – even the delicate ego of the alcoholic-addict – to admit defeat when it is coupled with the promise of a worthy reward:

> Upon entering A.A. we soon take quite another view of this absolute humiliation. We perceive that only through utter defeat are we able to take our first steps toward liberation and strength. Our admissions of personal powerlessness finally turn out to be firm bedrock upon which happy and purposeful lives may be built (*Twelve Steps and Twelve Traditions*, p. 21).

Once accomplished, this admission of powerlessness is a huge relief. It feels wonderful to stop the running, hiding, sneaking around, and lying. It represents an end to being dead-tired of dancing like some kind of hideous puppet on the end of the strings held by drugs and alcohol. Confessing powerlessness to other people is a liberating experience. You will commonly hear people in the fellowship talk about how great it felt the first time they finally let go and said "I'm ___, and I'm an alcoholic/addict." It takes way too much effort to lead a fake life. As *Twelve Steps and Twelve Traditions* tells us: "when we have finally admitted without reservation that we are powerless over alcohol, we are apt to breathe a great sigh of relief, saying, 'Well, thank God that's over!'" (p. 73).

Admitting powerlessness did something else for me as well. All my messed up thought processes and behaviors were, in fact, typical of the psychology of addictions, but I didn't know that. I thought there was something seriously wrong with ME. I had learned about addiction and alcoholism in medical school and seen a lot of it in medical practice, but I had no idea about what the life of these people was actually like. When I lived it myself I thought I was a special case; that only I had been messed up so badly. It was an immense relief when Step One said that this complete and utter powerlessness is a normal part of addiction, that it's OK to admit it, and that we must admit it to get better. I felt a rush of warmth come over me, intense relief that the running and hiding was finally over. I could finally come out of the proverbial drug and alcohol closet and get my dirty secrets in the open. Like me, other people find relief in discovering that they are not unprecedented messed up humanoids, that their behaviors were just like millions of others who came before us, and that there is a way out that begins with admitting our problem.

Newcomers to the 12 Step program hear people in the fellowship with significant recovery time say with ease that they, too, were and are powerless over drugs and alcohol, yet these newcomers can see that the others are living sober and productive lives. Newcomers can see through the example of the others that being powerless isn't the end; rather, it's the beginning to reclaiming life. We feel relief at knowing that powerlessness is not unique to us, but is a **normal part** of the addiction-alcoholism experience. We see that everything is going to be OK, as long as we are willing to admit powerlessness.

So it is that admission of powerlessness is not about breaking us down before building us up, as if we were at Marine Corps boot camp or something. Rather, we can understand that admitting powerlessness is the beginning of the solution; that it is a therapeutic and uplifting thing to do. When we grasp that perspective, even our alcoholic-addict pride will allow us to embrace Step One with due conviction.

*

Denial – even partial denial – of our powerlessness to drugs or alcohol is a major barrier to recovery. Most people would rather deny a hard truth than face it; for alcoholic-addicts this psychological tendency is magnified. However, for people in active addiction-alcoholism denial can kill us, as our friend Ryan found out. Substance addiction has a powerful hold on us; so powerful that we were driven to keep using or drinking as our life deteriorated in front of our eyes and we got sicker and sicker. To break such a crushing grip requires an all-in commitment to recovery. In fact, it requires an all-or-nothing commitment. If we harbor even a sliver of doubt of our powerlessness, our alcoholic-addict mind will talk us into believing that we can handle our booze or drugs; if not now, then a little later on. This is a peculiarity of our disease's effects on our mind, so prevalent and pervasive that it is referred to in the 12 Step program as the "insanity of alcoholism-addiction." Step One suggests (requires) that we make sure that any lingering doubt is snuffed out once and for all. To proceed in recovery without a total acceptance of powerlessness is to invite failure:

> We know that little good can come to any alcoholic who joins A.A. unless he has first accepted his devastating weakness and all its consequences. Until he so humbles himself, his sobriety – if any – will be precarious.... The principle that we shall find no enduring strength until we first admit complete defeat is the main taproot from which our whole Society has sprung and flowered (*Twelve Steps and Twelve Traditions*, p. 21-22).

But what's this thing about being "humble?" We have to humble ourselves to do our Step One? Why do we have to humble ourselves? Everybody knows that humility is bad, right? Well, hold on a minute. There is a mistaken belief that is widely held in Western society that humility is the opposite of confidence, the antithesis of self-esteem. People widely believe that to take on humility means to degrade oneself; after all, the word "humility" sounds a lot like "humiliation." However, they couldn't be more wrong.

Rather, humility is a realistic appreciation of one's limitations as well as one's strengths. Humility is having a healthy self-esteem that comes from an unshakeable understanding of our own self-worth without having to maintain a false front of pride that we show the world. Humility is not about needing to prop up our feelings of self-worth by impressing others through our material worth or demonstrations of grandeur. Humility is not only about dropping the false front; it's also about not needing a false front. As part rock-star, part Trappist monk Thomas Merton said: "pride makes us artificial and humility makes us real."

Studies in the behavioral sciences have shown that humility is a highly desirable virtue, that it's a character trait that can advance one's fortunes in the world.[22,23,24,25,26,27,28] Humility is associated with a number of improved outcomes in life, including pro-social behavior, academic excellence, better job performance, and receiving respect from others.[29] However, most importantly, humility is a tool that allows us to crush the negative psychology that is both cause and effect of our obsessive substance use.[30] Humility has been shown to be a powerful tool in helping us to handle life's inevitable hardships; in psychological terms, humility gives us life resilience.[31] That's precisely what the 12 Step program does to get people sober: teaching them to live life on life's terms without having to use drugs or alcohol to escape from bumps in the road.

It may surprise you that I consider humility to be the most valued character virtue that I have been gifted from living the Steps. It's key to my spirituality and recovery, but it has also gotten me through some tough experiences that I would otherwise never have had the strength to bear. Humility plays a central role in my happiness, my effectiveness in life, and my ability to connect with other people. I have found that – far from degrading me – my humility has become the basis of my newfound and deeply valued unvarnished self-esteem. As one researcher in the social sciences points out: "humility and modesty do not require self-disparagement, negativity, or a contemptuous attitude toward the self."[32]

We will discuss humility in much more detail as we wind our way through the Steps, particularly in Step Seven. In the meantime, I ask that readers open their minds to the idea that humility is a positive virtue that is key to our recovery, our conversion to a positive psychology, and our spirituality. When we see the word "humility" in the 12 Step literature we should not recoil from it.

With this perspective of humility, it shouldn't come as a surprise that humility is the bedrock principle of all twelve of the Steps: "indeed, the attainment of greater humility is the foundation principle of each of A.A.'s Twelve Steps. For without some degree of humility, no alcoholic can stay sober at all" (*Twelve Steps and Twelve Traditions*, p. 70). In fact, research in the social sciences has shown that without humility, motivation for learning how to stay sober and to make sober lifestyle changes is likely to be low.[33] Step Seven is the where the rubber meets the road for humility and we really learn to embrace and live this key virtue, but Step One lays the footing. Humility doesn't come naturally to most people, and certainly not to alcoholic-addicts, so Step One sets the tone for this unnatural but salubrious process: "every newcomer in Alcoholics Anonymous is told, and soon learns for himself, that his humble admission of powerlessness over alcohol is his first step toward liberation from its paralyzing grip" (*Twelve Steps and Twelve Traditions*, pp. 72-3).

*

From a psychological viewpoint, Step One provides the basis for the commitment to what I refer to as "closing the mental door." The "mental door" is the psychological phenomenon where individuals who are seeking recovery keep a pathway, a doorway, to their drug or alcohol open in their mind. They leave that door that leads to their substance use open just a crack, "just in case." Just in case we have a really bad day, or just in case recovery ends up being too hard, our addict-alcoholic mind likes to know that there is a pathway – an open possibility – to picking up again. The problem is that any time we leave that door open, even just a crack, we will always end up going through it eventually, usually before very long. The 12 Step program – as with any program of recovery – only works if we are all-in. That means closing this mental door that leads back to our drinking or using. Not jut closing that mental door, but slamming it shut. This is when we are mentally fully committed to recovery.

What kinds of things do we do to keep that door open a crack? We leave our dealer's number on our phone. We leave that bottle hidden in our garage. We don't tell our loved ones that we are in recovery. We don't get a sponsor. We plead some indisposition to the 12 Step program. We find some excuse for holding back. Our excuses that allow us to keep that mental door open a crack are the result of muddled thinking: excuses clothed as unfounded concerns.

Only when an alcoholic-addict is ready to close this mental door completely will recovery be possible. Our substance has such a powerful hold on our brain that we can only recover if we have both feet in the program; one foot in and one foot out just doesn't work. As the Big Book tells us: "rarely have we seen a person fail who has thoroughly followed our path" (p. 58). If we truly want sobriety and a return to good health and function we need to be all-in and thoroughly follow the path to recovery. We know what that path is, and we know when we are deviating from it. Thoroughly following that path includes closing that mental door that leads back to our drink or drug. The willingness to do so comes when we have finally reached our bottom, when we are so thoroughly finished with the insanity that we are willing to surrender and do whatever it takes to get better.

In my research work in addiction-alcoholism, I've observed three stages of mental readiness for recovery. First of all, we are content with our substance use, usually in denial about addiction to it, and we don't want to quit – even if we could. In stage two, we become aware of the negative effects our drug or alcohol use is having on our lives, we begin to feel physically, mentally, and spiritually sick, and we realize we need to stop our substance use. In this phase, we cling to the belief that we can quit by ourselves, despite multiple failures at it. We "cherry-pick" bits and pieces of help, but we still need to be in control. Repeated failures follow every earnest effort to quit. In the third stage, we become so desperate to quit that we are finally ready to admit that we are unable to do it ourselves and are willing to commit ourselves to the help we need. We have reached our bottom. Until we reach our bottom, including an admission that we are powerless, we don't stand much of a chance at recovery. Only then will we slam shut that mental door and commit ourselves to a program of recovery... all-in.

*

I do some volunteer work at a drug and alcohol detox center, and I'm always amazed by the resistance that many of the people in there show to accepting that they are powerless over their substance use. Our friend Ryan was certainly not an isolated case. These are people who are completely mentally, physically, socially, financially, psychologically, and spiritually defeated, and yet they cling to the belief that they can beat their addiction and get sober on their own. They have tried many times to do it their way – one guy had been in the detox center 29 times – yet still can't admit that they are powerless and that for them there is "... no such thing as the personal conquest of this compulsion by the unaided will" (*Twelve Steps and Twelve Traditions*, p. 22). My last drink or drug was years ago, and the cravings, thoughts, and obsession with drug and drink have long since left me, so I am struck by the paradoxical outlandishness of this persistent belief. I can't judge, however, because I was once exactly the same, and I could easily end up the same again if I ever stop accepting my

44

powerlessness. So why do we cling to this insanity? Well, as we've already discussed, the weird pride of alcoholism-addiction exerts a powerful deterrent to admitting and accepting help. Now let's look at another major impediment to admitting powerlessness: fear.

Consider Kate's story:

> Many fears kept me on the fence with sobriety for a long time. Fear of accepting I had a problem, fear of the label of alcoholic and the fear of a new way of life I heard about in recovery. When I drank, I felt free of my overwhelming emotions and problems. Drinking was my solution to dealing with fear and how could I handle life without it? What would life look like without alcohol? How would I manage to handle things? I was afraid.[34]

It's incredible how overwhelmed we can be by fear when finally faced with the decision to commit to quitting alcohol or drugs, and how much it's a barrier to getting sober. For reasons that will become clear shortly, the addict-alcoholic mind is especially geared to breed worry, anxiety, and fear. As the Big Book explains: "this short word [fear] somehow touches about every aspect of our lives. It was an evil and corroding thread; the fabric of our existence was shot through with it" (p. 67). The alcoholic-addict facing recovery experiences fear on a number of levels:

- Fear of living without our substance as our escape,
- Fear of facing all of life's problems that have piled up and worsened,
- Fear of confronting the guilt, shame, fear, self-loathing, and anger and other negative feelings without our substance,
- Fear of failure in recovery,
- Fear of the future, especially what will happen with our finances, work, and relationships,
- Fear of the unknown, and
- Fear that other people will find out about our addiction-alcoholism.

The power of addiction to alcohol or drugs has such an anxiety-inducing power on the brain that sometimes we're just plain afraid: "we're not always sure *what* we're afraid of; sometimes it is just a vague, generalized, nameless fear" (*Living Sober,* p. 38).

Fear in general – but especially the fear associated with the addicted mind – is a dysfunctional human reaction to our environment, because it is largely a self-destructive product of our imagination. *Instinctual fear* is a natural self-preservation mechanism: for example, we fear a wild bear, or walking too close to the edge of a cliff. Those are understandable, life-preserving functional fears. However, there are few fears in our world that are functional and self-preserving. Most of the fears that dominate our thoughts and govern our actions are unhealthy, neurotic, counter-productive, and destructive. This is especially so when these fears keep us from accepting help to escape active substance addiction.

Dysfunctional, neurotic fears are seldom based in reality. Rather, they are a by-product of our past experiences, our social conditioning, and most especially the effects of psychoactive substances on our brain. This fear is based on our emotional insecurities and the precarious fragility of our ego. These fears have an operatic self-destructive effect on our mind; swirling around and provoking pessimism, dread, and obsessive rumination about a future event that likely will never be. It makes us self-focused and mistrustful of others, a major barrier to healthy, loving relationships. This fear is a major source of anger and defensiveness. This neurotic fear is a cornerstone of the extreme negative psychology of addiction-alcoholism; it simply poisons the soul.

The most tragic thing about this dysfunctional, non-instinctual fear is that it's entirely self-manufactured, not based in reality, and completely unnecessary. The truth is that there are very few realistic possibilities that warrant the fears that we hold for them. This is what Mark Twain was referring to when he said: "I have been through some terrible things in my life, some of which actually happened." Fear is both a liar and a bully. Fears manipulate us into doing things – or, more commonly, *not* doing things.

Much of our fear is from "projecting," which is the unfortunate human tendency to project into the future and imagine how our problems will further develop. This generates fear and anxiety because we have a tendency to blow things out of proportion, to think the worst, to be pessimistic. This is especially true when we have a negative psychology. We worry, dread, and fear what hasn't happened and what probably never will, thereby putting ourselves through torture for naught. Alcoholic-addicts are expert ruminators; we lay awake at night and allow ourselves to be consumed by our anxieties of the future. In the dark of night, our mind can dream up terrible, monstrous outcomes that await us, anticipating the cruellest of evils. We suffer intense fear and anxiety, completely generated by our imagination. The problem is that for people like us, our go-to solution to this self-generated fear and anxiety is to seek refuge in the bottle or needle.

Let's look at some of the specific fears that keep us from accepting our powerlessness and committing to Step One. And then we'll look at how to use the tools from the 12 Step program to overcome these neurotic fears; I'll also throw in some suggestions from psychology.

*

It's easy to feel alone, isolated, and picked on when life spirals downwards from addiction-alcoholism. It's hard to understand our own behavior and continued use of the drug or drink, because it doesn't make sense. Life's problems become so huge and overwhelming that it feels like there's no way out. We are terrified by what the future holds and we are afraid of facing the horrible future without our drug or drink to "get us through." Our mind screams to keep the door to our drug or drink open, just in case the fear is too much and the future is too much to bear.

Part of the abnormal psychology of alcoholism-addiction is a terrible tendency to blow things up in our mind and scare ourselves – the "making a mountain out of a molehill" thing. Many among us end up laying awake at night ruminating, thinking up worst-case scenarios, and making things look worse than they are. We create dreadful monsters in our minds, terrifying ourselves. Our self-inflicted, imaginary fears create despair and rob us of all power of reason. Our go-to refuge is our drug or drink. When we think of living without drugs or alcohol, we project it as being too much for us. Recovery seems overwhelming.

The mind in active addiction is pathologically pessimistic as part of the deep negative psychology that accompanies substance use, and this is the basis of the deep fear that accompanies substance use. We are pessimistic about the future, so the future scares us. This is yet another way that addiction propagates itself. As life crumbles, we become increasingly withdrawn from reality by our substance use and we become increasingly pessimistic. As our psychology becomes progressively darker and more negative, the mounting fear causes us to withdraw further into our drink or drug use. Addictive substances produce chemical changes in the brain that cause anxiety – an excessive fear reaction – by disrupting the neurotransmitters involved in creating anxiety. This anxiety is temporarily relieved by using or drinking, but this further worsens the anxiety afterward. The addiction propagates itself by creating fear and driving us to cope with that fear by drinking or using in a vicious downward cycle.

Another specific fear that presents a barrier to recovery is the fear of withdrawal. When people who are regular users of alcohol or drugs stop they usually develop uncomfortable and (sometimes) dangerous withdrawal symptoms. The process by which the body rids itself of the substances and its metabolites is referred to as detoxification (detox). If people are using more than one kind of drug they may get more than one kind of withdrawal syndrome, increasing the fear level. Withdrawal is dreaded and fear of it keeps many people from even trying.

Although withdrawal from opioid drugs (such as heroin, methadone, or oxycodone) has the scariest reputation, it's withdrawal from alcohol that's most dangerous. People seldom die from opioid withdrawal, no matter how horrible they feel. When people die from opioid withdrawal it's usually from dehydration from vomiting and diarrhea when they had no one there to care for them. In practice, this usually occurs when they are thrown into a jail cell and left to detox alone without any supervision or help. But this seldom happens. Alcohol withdrawal, on the other hand, can be fatal, particularly if seizures or delirium tremens ("the DTs") develop (anyone who wishes to learn more about withdrawal can do so on my website: www.alcoholism-addiction-psychology.com). However, withdrawal and detox can be done safely and comfortably with proper medical supervision, **if** we let go of our obsessive need for secrecy and control, and let down our guard enough to seek and accept help. This is what Step One is asking of us; to let go and allow others inside our bubble.

*

When it comes to our fears, we have to take a leap of faith. We have to allow ourselves to understand that there is help out there – a solution – for all of our fears. The solution is contained within the 12 Step program, and it has been working for millions of people like us for more than eighty years. And it doesn't take much of a leap of faith to see that it works. We meet within the fellowship people who are like us but got better and now live happy and productive lives, no longer ruled by fear. We see people who have been addicted to multiple drugs, who have overdosed and were resuscitated, who were driven from successful lives to homelessness, who were hospitalized, who were addicted to behaviors like gambling or shopping, who were sexually or physically abused as children, who have been incarcerated or institutionalized, and so on. There is always someone in the fellowship we can identify with, who has shared our experience, no matter how horrible it may have been. They had fears like us, maybe even worse. And they all got better and found sobriety, good health, happiness, and good function again. We see them now and they are no longer dominated by fears. Why is that? Because they did their Step One – admitting their powerlessness – and continued on to do the Steps. The Steps are a powerfully life-changing pathway to learning to end the fears and negative thought processes that generate them. We can see that in the people around us in the fellowship. And we read the stories of people like us in the Big Book, or A.A. Grapevine, or hear their stories at meetings. When we see these people and hear their stories it doesn't take much of a leap of faith at all to forego our fears and give ourselves completely over to the program of recovery. We just need to realize and accept that by admitting our powerlessness we, too, can draw a line in the sand, and begin the healing process that will end the power of fear over our mind. We must remember that these are not fears that protect us from danger – like a fear of bears. Rather, these are dysfunctional, neurotic fears that are a product of our substance use.

Taking a leap of faith and accepting powerlessness is a lot easier when we can see with our own eyes that it has worked for many others who are just like us:

> There is a solution. Almost none of us liked the self-searching, the leveling of our pride, the confession of shortcomings which the process requires for its successful consummation. But we saw that it really worked in others, and we had come to believe in the hopelessness and futility of life as we had been living it (Big Book, p. 25).

I was duly impressed at my first 12 Step meetings, as I met many people who were as bad or worse than me but were now living healthy, happy, productive lives, something I never would have thought possible. I wanted what they had and I was willing to do whatever it took to get it. And they told me exactly how to get it. However, in order to have what they had I had to start by letting go of my fear of life without drugs or alcohol.

*

One of the things that Step One does for us is that it is our entry point to an abundance of help; not just any help, but help from people who have been through exactly what we have been through. You will note that the first word in Step One is "we;" this is significant because the 12 Step program is a "we" program. No one does it alone; in fact, "Never Alone" is one of the slogans of the program. We are unlikely to accept that help if we believe we don't need it because we still cling to the belief that we can do it on our own. If I am driving my car and I believe that I know where I am going I am not going to stop for directions. Once I realize and admit that I am lost, only then will I stop and ask for help to find my destination. Until then I drive around aimlessly, like a fool. Likewise, until we admit powerlessness we lack the will to seek and accept help to overcome the powerful draw of our poison.

There is little that dispels fear quite like having support, other people doing life with us, backing us up. A call to our sponsor or another friend in recovery does a lot to sooth our fears when they creep up in our mind. Even opening the Big Book and reading one of the stories of recovery in the back assuages our anxieties. And we can seek help from outside the program once we admit powerlessness. That could be seeking help for mental health issues – as we will discuss shortly – or getting medical assistance from a doctor or a detox center to help us detox safely and comfortably from our substance use. It could be seeking help from a counselor or a therapist for issues that we struggle with. Getting help from people inside or outside of the fellowship is best done as soon as fears or problems arise, rather than waiting for a crisis. I have learned that when my car starts making weird noises it's much easier and cheaper to get it looked at right away rather than waiting until it breaks down at the side of the road. So it is with my recovery. Step One is where we give ourselves permission to accept help; it is the antidote to the fatal words "I got this." Admitting powerlessness is the beginning of the end to our fears.

*

The 12 Step program is specially geared to provide us with tools to manage fear, because it acknowledges the central role that fear plays in addiction-alcoholism. Life is always going to have trials and tribulations whether we are sober or not, and it can be scary sometimes. That's just life. However, our natural tendency to create fear out of nothing will prevail unless we have some way of putting an end to it. Everything we want is on the other side of fear. Fear keeps us from having the courage to face recovery, and if we don't have tools that allow us to handle fear then we are sure to relapse. What's nice is that some of these tools are so simple we can pick them up on day one in the program, and therefore use them to help us overcome the fears that are keeping us out of recovery.

One surprisingly simple yet potent fear-crushing tool is the slogan "One Day at a Time." This five-word idiom may sound unassuming, but it is psychologically powerful. I will illustrate with my own experience.

One of my great fears that kept me drinking and using was a fear of life. I was overwhelmed by how many problems I had in my life, and of course they all got much worse during my active substance addiction. I was terrified about what tomorrow would bring, and I always projected my problems in my mind, blowing them way out of proportion. Because of this, my biggest trigger to drink or use was ordinary life stressors and the fears they provoked. My stress was stressing me out to the point where I was too stressed to deal with my stress. Every time something bad happened – no matter how small – in my mind it spelled certain doom. I drank and used to escape that fear. My fear kept me from even trying to stop my substance use.

Taking life one day at a time has been a powerful tool for me, and it has lifted that fear of life and fear of living life without alcohol and drugs. It worked for me from the beginning, while I was still in the detox center. It's about taking life one day at a time, guided by the Serenity Prayer. Here's how it works: every day when I wake up I do my best to do what I can *that day* to make my problems better. I seek the courage to do what I can to address my problems today. The problems that I can do nothing about, I accept. I forget about yesterday, because ruminating on the past is pointless

50

and a waste of brain-power. I accept what has happened in the past because I can't change it. As for tomorrow, I let it take care of itself. If I find myself ruminating about what tomorrow may hold, or projecting my problems into the future I stop myself by repeating to myself: *one day at a time*. Projecting my problems and worries into the future is counter-productive, wasted brain-power, self-manufactured artificial stress. It was my obsessive worrying and ruminating about the past and the future that were the most powerful trigger for my drinking and using. I had to let go of those things, and taking life one day at a time has allowed me to do that. A major cause of my obsessive drug and alcohol use simply fell away when I applied that simple slogan to my way of thinking.

The same approach can be applied to our fear of living without our drug or drink. When I was in detox and I would hear someone say that he had 30 days clean and sober, I would think *there is no way that I can go thirty days without drinking or using!* It would fill me with fear and self-doubt about my ability to succeed in recovery. I felt overwhelmed. When we are in active addiction or alcoholism, going a day or two without drinking or using can be really hard to get our head around. Sometimes we can put together a few days or more without drug or drink, but that's it. The thought of not drinking or using for a lifetime is totally overwhelming. Even the thought of thirty days seems impossible. We are fearful: *how will I face life without drinking or using?*

However, the trick is to stop thinking about staying clean and sober for a lifetime, or even for 30 days. We must just concern ourselves with today. Anybody can stay clean and sober for one day, right? Well, we just concern ourselves with staying clean and sober today. We do the things we need to do to be in recovery today – go to a meeting, seek help, connect with someone who's in recovery, delete our dealer's number from our phone, read from our Big Book – and let tomorrow take care of itself. Worrying about staying sober tomorrow is just wasted brain-power. We need to learn to just concern ourselves with today: do the things we need to do to stay sober today, and let tomorrow look after itself. Focusing on today is easy enough, focusing on a lifetime is not.

When we take our sobriety one day at a time, we just focus on staying sober today, and forget about tomorrow. As simplistic as that sounds, it works. For me, I was less overwhelmed by the thought of just staying sober today. Soon, that "one day at a time" adds up to a lot of days. And it becomes easier as time goes by.

Taking life one day at a time doesn't mean that we can't plan for the future. We still set goals and make plans, but we don't plan the outcome. We don't allow whether or not we are happy or having a good day rest on how our plans turn out. However, we must eliminate projecting our problems into the future; that's not planning for the future, that's just useless anxiety-generating speculation. That kind of thinking will kill us.

*

Getting ourselves into recovery is a difficult task. When it comes to any kind of difficult task, this "one day at a time" approach is a potent tool. It is supported by considerable research and is even used by the U.S. Navy SEALs for mental toughness when facing the most daunting tasks. In psychological terms, "one day at a time" is known as *chunking*. Chunking is a widely recognized technique for self-motivation. The U.S. Navy SEALs – famous for their mental toughness and ability to endure any kind of hardship – employ it as a mental technique to help them get through physically or mentally demanding situations. Rather than focus on the entire task ahead and getting overwhelmed, they break the task down into bite-sized chunks that they can focus on, one piece at a time. For example, during their BUD/S training (considered to be the most grueling military training in the world), Navy SEALs trainees don't focus on completing the 24 weeks of hell that they must face, or they would feel overwhelmed and fearful. Rather, they focus on getting through the particular task that they are confronted with *right now*. If they are facing their notoriously punishing obstacle course, they focus on getting through that and giving their very best effort. They forget about everything else, they just focus on that particular task, one task at a time. If even that seems overwhelming, they break it into further chunks, such as each individual obstacle, one obstacle at a time.

The 12 Step program employs chunking very effectively with its focus on staying sober "one day at a time." Rather than becoming overwhelmed by the thought of having to stay clean and sober for months or years, we break down sobriety into bite-sized chunks – one day at a time. If the day is tough, we can break it down into one hour at a time. The program also uses the same concept for helping us cope with life when we are overwhelmed. Rather than focus on dealing with all our problems, we break it down to what we can do to help our problems *today*, one problem at a time if necessary, and forget about the rest. Like the U.S. Navy SEALs, we use chunking to get through sobriety's difficulties and life's challenges.

*

We will speak about the concept of a higher power in Steps Two and Three, including directly addressing the issue for atheists and agnostics. In the meantime, suffice it to say that the higher power concept is a powerful antidote to fear. Many people whose higher power is not named "God" or who don't have a concept of what a higher power is to them have found that even going through the motions of using the higher power concept has a powerful and soothing effect on their fears and anxieties. As we will discuss in the upcoming Steps, compelling research has supported the higher power concept as an effective tool for coping with fear and life's stressors.

It breaks my heart every time I see someone sick and suffering under the lash of substance addiction, yet who rejects what the 12 Step program has to offer because *I can't do the Steps because I don't believe in God*. The mistaken belief that the 12 Step program is religious or requires belief in God seems to provide a convenient excuse for people who have not yet hit their bottom. When we hit our bottom we are willing to do anything to get better, even if it means being open-minded about the higher power concept. I know that if I ever walked down the halls of the cancer ward of any hospital and announced that there is a way for these sick and suffering people to get a daily reprieve from cancer every day for the rest of their lives based on a higher power, I doubt I would have refusals. Unfortunately, it's not always the same on a drug and alcohol detox ward. Our disease is, indeed, cunning and baffling.

One woman who isn't even an addict-alcoholic explains how she has found great value in the higher power: "chemical addiction has never been an issue for me, yet I've used the 12-Step program to address other troubles, such as negative thinking, eating disorders, and chronic fear... even the first few steps can be transformative, providing new perspectives on persistent problems."[35] She's an atheist, by the way. She goes on to explain the value that she gets from the higher power, despite being an atheist:

> This higher-power concept can apply to any crisis in which we feel helpless. Sorrow, sickness, loss, rejection, fear: sometimes these feel like "hitting bottom," and we cannot crawl out on our own. For those of us who cannot pray, that higher power in those moments might be music. Running. Foreign-language flash cards. Working well. Footage of whales, Mars, Paris. The fact that forests exist.
>
> A hobby. A relationship. A practice. A promise. A memory— even just one, which shines brightly enough to make us believe its ilk will happen again.
>
> If we believe in nothing—as depression, trauma and self-loathing tend to make us do—our higher power might be whatever we love. If even that sounds too expansive, then: whatever we like slightly better than ourselves.
>
> Whatever intrigues, inspires or distracts us.
>
> That tiny difference between us and whatever-else becomes a form of faith.

Even this atheist finds great comfort in a higher power. A higher power provides an alternative comfort, to give us strength in facing and challenging fears as a replacement to avoidance through drinking or using. As the Big Book explains: "as we felt new power flow in, as we enjoyed peace of mind, as we discovered we could face life successfully, as we became conscious of [our higher power's] presence, we began to lose our fear of today, tomorrow or the hereafter" (p. 63).

For those readers who are skeptical about the higher power thing, bear with me. We will discuss this further, from a very clinical and scientific perspective for those who are so inclined, and from a philosophical perspective for those who prefer.

We have been in a negative psychology and fatally pessimistic for a long time; our heads have been filled with negative thoughts that have no bearing in reality, even if we convince ourselves that they do. Our minds have been out of control. It may take us a while to get used letting go of unfounded fear and worry. It will come. In Step Eleven we will develop some useful meditation skills that will help repair the undisciplined, wandering, worry-filled mind left over from our substance use. In the meantime, let's take life and sobriety one day at a time, and let's be open-minded to the idea of a higher power as a potent antidote to fear.

*

We've discussed how fears and anxieties are creations of our mind in all its dysfunctional glory. Indeed, experience has shown that our fears tend to be remarkably unfounded. It is the common experience of millions of addict-alcoholics that once they got sober, things started to get better. It always turns out that we have blown our problems way out of proportion in our minds, as alcoholic-addicts do, and taking our problems one day at a time and applying the Serenity Prayer stops us from driving ourselves crazy. This removes one of the main triggers to drink or use: fear. As the fear and anxiety subsides, we are able to face life and its challenges with a clear head.

I encourage those who find themselves suddenly possessed with fear to read the stories from the back of the Big Book. These stories show the fears that people like us faced and how these fears passed in recovery. The stories are very comforting, and a powerful way to relieve fear. Whenever I find myself dealing with fear or a problem that I feel overwhelming I take out my Big Book and read one of the stories in the back. It's ten minutes well spent, because I am invariably of a different mind-set when I put my book back on the shelf. Likewise, listening to speakers at 12 Step meetings is as soothing as it is therapeutic for the fearful.

I was amazed at how unfounded my fears about life were when I found recovery. My life was a train-wreck, I had lost pretty much everything that was important to me, and I had burned many bridges. I didn't see much point to even trying to get sober, because I thought that life in recovery would suck, *so what was the point of getting sober?* However, I was amazed at how people and things started coming back to me once I was in recovery and healing by working through the Steps. Addiction consumes all of our time, resources, and brain-power; when the substance use stops we finally have the time and energy to take care of life again. When we stop running and hiding from life, we can turn around and face our fears, deriving courage from our support system. The 12 Step fellowship provides a tremendous support system for helping newcomers to transition back to life. As we confront our fears with a sober mind, it surprises us how they melt away. They are exposed for what they were: inventions and exaggerations of our substance-soaked mind. Not everything will be easy, but we learn the courage and confidence to face life.

It has been the broad – if not universal – experience within the fellowship that life comes together again, usually better than ever before, as long as we take care of *one thing*: our recovery. First things first. When we read the stories in the Big Book we can see that the same has been the experience of people in the fellowship for the past 80+ years. According to the Big Book, by the time we are doing Step Nine: "our whole attitude and outlook upon life will change. Fear of people and of economic insecurity will leave us. We will intuitively know how to handle situations that used to baffle us. We will suddenly realize that God is doing for us what we could not do for ourselves" (p. 84). Those promises come true. But, in order to get to Step Nine we must first conquer Step One and accept our powerlessness over addictive substances.

*

One virtue that is imparted by the 12 Step program is especially fatal to fear and anxiety: acceptance. Many of our fears are based on preoccupations with things going wrong in life, problems arising, and things not turning out well for us. We fear losing what we have and not getting what we want. But those fears are based in unreasonable expectations that everything has to go right for us and we must get what we want for life to be good. Life is never going to go just right and problem-free for anybody, no matter who they are. We have to accept that not everything in life is going to go our way. Yes, it's disappointing when things don't go well, but we can either drive ourselves crazy pining over it, or we can decide to be happy. The point is that we will be OK no matter how things go in life. The 12 Steps are about living life on life's terms, come what may. As we learn to live life on life's terms, we learn to accept that things are not always going to go just right for us all the time in life, but we know that we will be OK regardless of how things turn out. The human animal has the capacity for great resilience when armed with a positive mind-set, even in the face of great adversity. Even the most psychologically broken individual is capable of great things with the proper frame of mind. This is precisely the process by which the 12 Step program works: by guiding broken people into the frame of mind that allows them to fulfill their full potential for resilience.

It's completely unreasonable to expect life to go smoothly without any hiccups. We're setting ourselves up for failure and disappointment when we entertain such an expectation. Unfortunately, such unrealistic expectations come naturally to many of us, and those inevitable failures and disappointments make people like us turn to drugs or alcohol. So, we learn as we pass through the 12 Steps that life isn't always going to go our way. That's just life. Even the richest, healthiest, best looking person on the planet can't expect to never run into set-backs, disappointments, tragedy, and sadness from time to time. When we accept that life will not always go our way, we knock the legs out from underneath that beast called fear.

Rather than expecting that everything will always go just fine, we adopt a different mind-set. Life is not about never *facing* hardship; rather, it's about how we *endure* hardship. When times are tough, it helps to remember a few simple mantras: *this, too, shall pass*, and *the sun sets on every day*. We will talk later about finding meaning in life. One way that people find meaning in life is by how they endure the inevitable hardships of life. Meaning comes from handling hardships by acceptance, fortitude, using our strength to help others through the ordeal, and maintaining our integrity. Contrast that to enduring hardship by complaining, feeling sorry for ourselves, taking from others to make ourselves feel better, and drinking or using drugs and you will understand the point. More about that later.

Acceptance is not something that comes naturally to humans. We like to feel and act like victims, we like other people's pity, we like to complain and get angry, and we hate accepting things that aren't how we want them to be. Acceptance is definitely an acquired trait, and one that becomes second nature to us as we progress through the Steps. The Serenity Prayer says it all. We should accept the things we can't change. The choice is to burn with rage over our perception of unfair treatment from the world, or to be happy and grateful for what we do have. Most people go through their entire lives with very poor levels of acceptance, but we alcoholic-addicts don't have that luxury. For us the peace of mind that comes with acceptance is a matter of life and death; our survival and ability to lead a sober and productive life depends upon it.

When I was practicing medicine I was always impressed by people's capacity for extraordinary levels of acceptance. I knew people who had been blind since birth, people who had been confined to a wheelchair at a young age, people with catastrophic diseases, and people who had suffered great loss. What stood out for me is how many of these people had long ago stopped feeling sorry for themselves and instead got on with life on life's terms. Many challenged themselves to fulfill and even exceed their abilities in order to make the utmost of life. They had long ago accepted their tragic circumstances and got on with living. The choice was to feel sorry for themselves and drive themselves crazy with the *why me???* mind-set, or to find happiness and fulfillment in life. My problems always suddenly seemed small and petty whenever I interacted with such people and saw their attitude toward life. I always felt guilty for feeling sorry for myself over my own pithy issues. We, too, have the capacity for such salubrious and life-affirming levels of acceptance, and there's no better way to learn that healthy mentality than by a trip through the 12 Steps.

Whenever I have a sponsee who is stuck on the "poor-me" mentality I take him to volunteer at our local homeless shelter for an evening or two. The message gets across pretty swiftly. Likewise, a colleague of mine – a physician who is not an alcoholic-addict – had become stuck on her problems in life and was really letting it get her down. I took her to volunteer at our local soup kitchen and she definitely got the message. She needed to get outside herself (we will talk about what this means in Step Two) and get her focus off herself and her problems. It did the trick; she found the experience so refreshing that she goes back to volunteer there regularly on her own. Acceptance and gratitude are purely a matter of perspective, and sometimes a good "perspective adjustment" is just what we need.

Acceptance of our life situation frees us from constant dissatisfaction with what we have and an obsessive focus on what we don't have. Such a mentality is toxic. With such a mind-set, even when we get something we find it strangely unsatisfying because we immediately start pining for the next thing we want. It's a terrible thing to go through life never being satisfied with what we have. It's a major cause of a negative psychology because other noxious emotions follow: we become angry, resentful, self-pitying, and envious because we are not getting what we think we deserve to have. Negative behaviors – such as lying, stealing, and a toxic pride usually follow as well. The antidote to this toxic mentality is gratitude, something we will discuss and develop as we progress through the Steps together. Gratitude and acceptance are powerful fear-crushing tools for happiness and peace of mind, essential parts of our recovery.

*

How about that other fear that undermines our willingness to accept our powerlessness, the fear that other people will find out about our addiction? It's a valid fear, because our disease carries a significant social stigma. Even I, a practicing doctor, always believed (prior to my personal operatic initiation to addiction-alcoholism) that people with substance addictions are bad people who wake up every day and make bad decisions. They annoyed me. I was very judgmental about it. Scary, but it's true.

My ego and fear of being "discovered" were keeping me from recovery. I had opened up to the idea of trying out 12 Step meetings, but I refused to go because I didn't want to be seen at a meeting. After all, *I'm a practicing doctor in this community, what if someone sees me, right?* In the end, I didn't go to 12 Step meetings out of my fear of being discovered. All that changed when I finally hit my rock bottom. I was exposed to 12 Step meetings as I languished near death in a detox center, and what I heard really made sense to me. At that point, I was so sick and tired of being sick and tired that I didn't care anymore. It felt good to say *I'm Andrew and I'm and alcoholic and addict* at meetings; all the lies, deceit, fear, and misery could finally end. And the fear of discovery began to melt away very quickly. Being an alcoholic-addict in recovery is now part of my identity. My addiction-alcoholism doesn't define me, but it is part of who I am. Far from being labeled as a bad doctor or a bad person because of my past, I have found that I have received nothing but respect and kudos from patients and the public because I have come forward and admitted my problem and got the help that I needed. In hindsight, my fears about being discovered were because I didn't want anybody or anything to interfere with my drug and alcohol use. My fears about being ridiculed or rejected once I came forward for help were unfounded. Besides, as I progressed through the Steps and my ego and hubristic pride became replaced by healthy self-esteem and humility, I lost any concern about what anyone would think. I no longer needed to project a fake image to prop up my pride, and there was no way I was going to allow delusions about what others *might* think interfere with my precious, hard-won sobriety.

The truth is that we delude ourselves anyway, when we think that our drug or alcohol use is a secret. Our odd and insane behavior is evident to people around us, one way or another, long before we think it is. Alcoholics Anonymous co-founder Dr. Bob Smith was the same way as I was: "he lived in constant worry about those who might find out about his alcoholism" (Big Book, p. 155). And, of course, Dr. Bob was just as blockheaded as I was, lacking the insight and imagination to see that everybody already knew anyway: "he had, of course, the familiar alcoholic obsession that few knew of his drinking" (Big Book, p. 155). We are only fooling ourselves if we think that our addiction is a secret to those around us. So, as long as we bumble along thinking that it's a big secret to everyone, we are just making ourselves look the fool. That's why people are impressed when they see us come clean (i.e. admit our powerlessness) and take action. Denial and *I got this* serve only to make us so much more the fool in other people's eyes, as does refusing to acknowledge the obvious: our powerlessness.

In the end, the fear of being discovered by others proves to be unfounded. It would be a much more valid fear to be concerned about what people will think of us if we continue on our path of active addiction-alcoholism and continuing our denial, failing at our pathetic efforts to act as if all is well. People respect honesty, and they respect recovery.

*

There's a gorilla in the room that pertains to fear that must be considered as we transition to recovery, and that is anxiety disorders. As we have already discussed, more than half of people with substance addiction have a co-occurring mental health disorder.[36] Mental health disorders and addiction share many of the same genetic and environmental causes, share similar symptoms, and have a closely related abnormal brain chemistry. One of the most common mental health problems that co-occurs with addiction is the anxiety disorders.

Anxiety disorders cause addiction-alcoholism because people attempt to self-medicate their anxiety with alcohol or drugs. Many aren't even aware of having a treatable anxiety disorder; they have been living with their anxiety symptoms for so long that they just believe it's normal for them. Unfortunately, while they may feel temporary relief from their anxiety symptoms when they use drugs or alcohol to numb their overactive minds, after the drink or drug wears off the rebound effect worsens the abnormal brain chemistry that caused the anxiety. So it is that a vicious cycle develops: anxiety symptoms leading to substance use for relief leading to worsened anxiety symptoms leading to more substance use and on and on in a downward spiraling vortex of addiction-alcoholism and worsening anxiety. Before long tolerance to the drug or alcohol develops and the amount and frequency of substance use increases. Then withdrawal occurs when the individual doesn't use or drink and addiction-alcoholism is in place.

Conversely, alcohol or drug use can cause an anxiety disorder. Of course, this usually (but not always) resolves when people are in recovery. That's why recovery in itself is curative of excessive fears in many individuals. Anxiety disorders are primarily caused by abnormal levels of certain brain chemicals known as *neurotransmitters*. Psychoactive substances disrupt these same neurotransmitters, thereby causing the anxiety symptoms.

So, substance use and anxiety disorders can cause and worsen each other. They can also greatly lower our chances of recovery unless both are treated at the same time. As such, it's very important that people who think they may have an anxiety disorder discuss it with their healthcare provider very early on in recovery.

As we have discussed, addiction-alcoholism is characterized by heightened fears and anxieties, so how can we tell if we have an anxiety disorder or if we are simply experiencing the effects of our substance use? Well, that can be tough. One crucial factor is to look back to see if there were any anxiety symptoms that pre-dated the substance use. In general, anxiety that is pathological involves panic attacks, physical symptoms (such as rapid heart rate, chest pain, or dizziness), fear of being around people, unreasonable fears, or anxiety that occurs for no apparent reason.

Because substance use causes anxiety that is difficult to distinguish from a true anxiety disorder, the DSM-5 (the American Psychiatric Association Diagnostic and Statistical Manual, 5th edition, the standard diagnostic manual for mental health disorders) cautions against diagnosing anxiety (or any other mental health disorder) in anyone who is actively using drugs or alcohol. It's important that we disclose our substance use to our doctor.

I suggest that anyone who has any doubts or concerns that they may have an anxiety disorder should discuss it with their healthcare provider as soon as possible. Most anxiety disorders are easily treated. This is one of those cases where seeking outside help is a must, for the sake of our recovery and our return to health, happiness, and good function. Bill Wilson himself suffered from an often debilitating chronic mental health disorder – depression – that certainly played a role in his addiction to alcohol (as did I). Says the Big Book:

> We [do not] disregard human health measures. God has abundantly supplied us with fine doctors, psychologists, and practitioners of various kinds. Do not hesitate to take your health problems to such persons. Most of them give freely of themselves, that their fellows may enjoy sound minds and bodies. Try to remember that though God has wrought miracles among us, we should never belittle a good doctor or psychiatrist. Their services are often indispensible in treating a newcomer and in following his case afterwards (p. 133).

This sage advice definitely applies to seeking outside help for a mental health disorder.

*

So that's fear. It's effects on causing and propagating our substance use are profound and it also represents a significant barrier to recovery in general and Step One in particular. Small wonder that Shakespeare

60

respected the power of fear: "of all base passions, fear is the most accursed."[37] Fear is a liar and a bully, but fortunately we have tools to stop it from ruling our mind and wrecking our happiness, peace of mind, and health. Like the strange pride of alcoholism-addiction, fear is a barrier to recovery that can be addressed simply by picking up the tools that the program lays at our feet as we progress through the Steps.

So, where does this leave us with Step One? We must recognize that we have fears that are holding us back from accepting and admitting our powerlessness, and that these fears are human nature, but unfounded. They are a fatal flaw of human psychology that is magnified by psychoactive substance use. We have some tools already available to us to allay these fears, and we will gain many more as we grow through the Steps. In the meantime, we use our tools and take that leap of faith that it's OK to let go of our need for control and admit powerlessness so that our healing can begin.

When we get to Step Four we will directly confront our specific fears and learn to end their unkind connection to our drug and alcohol use. We will put the nail in the coffin of the fears that have been doing their very best to drive the nail into *our* coffin. In the meantime, we can use the tools we have discussed to help us to arrest the fears that keep us from completing our Step One.

*

For many of us, recovery is the hardest thing we will ever have to do. It takes effort and commitment on an ongoing basis. Sitting back and waiting for recovery to magically fall into our lap never works. And we are never cured; what we get is: "a daily reprieve contingent on the maintenance of our spiritual condition" (Big Book, p. 85). We will discuss in the upcoming Steps what this means and how we go about getting it. For now, the point is that our recovery requires a lifelong commitment, lest we fall back to where we were before. Not one of us is going to put in such effort and commitment unless we are absolutely convinced that we are now and will always be powerless over addictive substances. No way will we put forward the time and energy required to achieve and maintain recovery if we don't think it's necessary, if we believe that at some point now or later, we can control our substance use. As such, our admission of powerlessness must be on an ongoing basis: we are just as powerless over drugs and alcohol at thirty years of recovery as we are at one week. This is firmly supported by the neuroscience of addiction-alcoholism, as we will see in the pages that follow. This is why I sometimes refer to Step One as Step Twelve-and-a-half; it's the first Step, but our commitment to its principles must be on an ongoing basis.

I was fortunate in that when I came to the 12 Step program I was already fully aware of and willing to admit my powerlessness over drugs and alcohol. I had tried everything, and I was thoroughly beaten. But what of those who aren't? They say that we must hit our bottom before we are ready for Step One, but that bottom doesn't necessarily have to be rock bottom. I know many people whose bottom was the grave, too late for us to help, like our friend Ryan. When I hit my bottom I was about to go over that cliff myself. I wanted to die, because I believed that death was the only way out of the miserable and cruel existence that my life had become. But, I also know many people who realized and conceded their powerlessness early on, before their bottom became too deep and they lost everything. Alcoholism-addiction is a progressive and uniformly fatal disease; if we stay on that road long enough we all end up in the same place, regardless of how high our station in life when we started. So, the sooner we get off that road, the better. Accepting powerlessness – as Step One suggests that we do – is precisely how we get off that road to nowhere. Ideally, we want to help people while their bottom still isn't too low:

> It was obviously necessary to raise the bottom that the rest of us had hit to the point where it would hit them. By going back in our own drinking histories, we could show that years before we realized it we were out of control, that our drinking even then was no mere habit, that it was indeed the beginning of a fatal progression (*Twelve Steps and Twelve Traditions*, p. 23).

People who doubt their powerlessness – their inability to control their drinking or using – can try some simple tests. The validated questionnaires that doctors use are available online, and you can take them yourself in private (see my website for some of these tests: www.alcoholism-addiction-psychology.com "Am I an Alcoholic-addict?"). The 12 Step literature suggests a simple but effective test: "step over to the nearest barroom and try some controlled drinking. Try to drink and stop abruptly. Try it more than once" (Big Book, p. 31-32).

The Big Book describes this ruinous but common dilemma, when our lives are spiraling downward and our drinking or drug use is out of control, but we are not yet ready to accept or admit our powerlessness:

> Most of us have been unwilling to admit we were real alcoholics. No person likes to think he is bodily and mentally different from his fellows. Therefore, it is not surprising that our drinking careers have been characterized by countless vain attempts to prove we could drink like other people. The idea that somehow, someday he will control and enjoy his drinking is the great obsession of every abnormal drinker. The persistence of this illusion is astonishing. Many pursue it into the gates of insanity or death (p. 30).

62

Denial of powerlessness – even when our powerlessness is screamingly obvious to all around us – is common: "many who are real alcoholics are not going to believe they are in that class. By every form of self-deception and experimentation, they will try to prove themselves exceptions to the rule, therefore non-alcoholic" (Big Book, p. 31). Overcoming this self-deception and denial is crucial to our Step One and to our recovery. One way to do that is to look at the science that demonstrates the validity of the concept of being powerless over addictive substances. Let's do that now.

*

We have already discussed pride and fear as powerful forces that keep us from accepting and affirming our powerlessness. But, fear and pride are only part of our resistance to conceding the obvious: that we have "pass[ed] into a state where the most powerful desire to stop drinking is of absolutely no avail" (Big Book, p. 24). How can so many among us in active addiction-alcoholism really believe that they are not powerless over their drink or drug when it's so obvious? Are they crazy? Well, in the 12 Step program we often refer to that mind-set as "insanity," but these people are not crazy. Rather, they are merely exhibiting the typical, run-of-the-mill, garden-variety psychological symptoms of addiction-alcoholism. We may feel insane, but we are simply typical alcoholic-addicts.

Addiction is caused by the effects of drugs or alcohol on our brain and mind, so it's not surprising that they affect how our brain and mind function; that's why they are known as psychoactive substances. Part of what makes addiction a disease is that psychoactive substances manipulate the brain's natural flaws and quirks in order to increase and propagate the substance use. As we progress through the Steps we will discuss the specifics of how alcohol and drugs do this, and we will see how to maximize the power of each Step to undo these powerful psychological holds that our drug or drink has over us; in other words, we will learn how to untangle this disease from our brain and psyche. In the meantime, let's have a look at the powerful hold that these hijacked psychological processes hold over us, and see exactly how they render us powerless, removing the power of our will from the ability to control our drug or alcohol use.

Many people wonder why alcoholism-addiction is referred to as a disease. I wondered that myself, even as a practicing doctor. To be honest, I didn't buy into the so-called disease model of addiction one bit. However, since focusing my medical practice on addictions and becoming involved in research I now see very clearly that alcoholism-addiction is indeed a disease. If you're not sure about it and would like to know why, I provide an explanation in Appendix 1 at the back of this book.

Substance addiction – like other diseases – involves a foreign substance entering our body and manipulating our natural body processes to propagate itself. Substance addiction does so by altering the brain chemistry, resulting in changes to the structure of the brain and interfering with proper function. The human brain has some peculiarities and weaknesses that addiction-alcoholism is able to take advantage of, and this produces the pathological psychology – the bizarre thought processes and behaviors – that are so characteristic and consistent among people with addiction-alcoholism. The result is a syndrome of thought processes and behaviors that are so illogical and odd that it makes us difficult to understand by other people. These very bizarre psychological processes are exactly why many powerless people can't see their powerlessness. Let's talk about these brain glitches now.

*

The human mind has an odd set of eccentricities in the *cognitive functions* that affect our ability to get our head around Step One. Cognitive functions are the brain's "higher functions," such as thinking, planning, memory, anticipating, and decision-making. Our cognitive functions are what allow us to understand and relate to the world around us, and they determine our actions and behaviors. Being imperfect creatures, we humans have glitches in our cognitive functions; these glitches are known as *cognitive biases*.[38,39] These are patterns of thinking that are innate to the human psyche that deviate from rationality. These cognitive biases cause people to create their own reality; they may be thought of as systematic errors of inductive reasoning. Usually they are relatively benign processes and don't affect us much because logic and reason generally prevail, but in alcoholism-addiction they are driven to extremes by the psychoactive substances that we imbibe. They cause us to maintain the irrational belief that we can control our drinking or using, despite all evidence to the contrary, and they cause people who are obviously powerless over alcohol or drugs to reject the idea.

As we go through these various types of cognitive bias you will probably recognize many if not all of them in your own thoughts and behaviors from your drinking and using days. These processes occur subconsciously, but when we are aware of them we can recognize their effects and protect ourselves. There are dozens of different cognitive biases embedded in our minds, but some are particularly relevant to our inability to accept powerlessness. Let's have a quick look at these so we can get some insight into our dysfunctional thinking. This kind of awareness of our

64

mental flaws allows us to challenge these irrational thought processes when they occur – and they will.

Probably the most powerful cognitive bias that makes us cling to the belief that we can control our drinking or using is known as the *confirmation bias*. This is where we ignore facts that aren't in line with what we want to believe, and over-emphasize facts that support what we want to be true. We want so badly to believe that we are not addicted – because it is such a terrible, socially unacceptable thing – that we subconsciously ignore facts that tell us that we are addicted. The idea that we are powerless goes totally against what we want to believe, so our confirmation bias causes us to reject the idea of powerlessness when it is suggested to us.

This confirmation bias, by which we cling to the false belief that we can control our drinking or using, provides a convenient excuse for us to keep using our substance despite the negative consequences, and it tells us that we don't need any help to stop. After all, why bother getting help for something that you are perfectly capable of accomplishing on your own? I'm always amazed by the power of the confirmation bias in propagating addiction–alcoholism. The effect of addictive substances on our mind is so strong that otherwise rational, logical, intelligent people cling to the belief that THIS time they will be able to control their drinking and using on their own, despite overwhelming evidence to the contrary. The 12 Step founders referred to this effect – long before the confirmation bias had been identified by science – as the "insanity of alcoholism-addiction." This flaw in our higher brain functions is so powerful that it drives many among us to financial, social, physical, mental, and spiritual ruin, and even to the grave. In recovery, the confirmation bias asserts itself in people who drift away from an ongoing program of recovery, which is why we see so many people relapse when they no longer do the things they need to do to maintain their recovery. They say that our disease is always waiting for us out in the parking lot doing push-ups. Well, the confirmation bias – which convinces us that we have been in recovery long enough so that NOW we will be able to our control drinking or using – is the muscle that allows our disease to do those push-ups.

The effect of the confirmation bias is worsened by what's known as the *Semmelweis reflex*. This is our tendency to reject new evidence that contradicts our established beliefs. The confirmation bias makes us ignore the facts that go against what we want to be true, and the Semmelweis reflex causes us to reject anything that contradicts our beliefs. It's easier for our minds to reject the facts than it is to change our beliefs. This is especially true when we utterly want our beliefs to be true; such as our desire to believe that we could stop our drinking or using if we really put our mind to it. The Semmelweis effect is what makes us close-minded, something we must overcome if we are to make any progress in overcoming our addicted mind-set.

Another cognitive bias, the *subjective validation bias*, ties in with the Semmelweis effect. This is our mind's tendency to believe that something is true if it supports what we believe or what we want to believe. The subjective validation bias is what makes us reject the opinions of our loved ones who tell us that we have a serious substance use problem and need help, and accept the opinion of our fellow drinkers and users who tell us that everything is OK.

Our ability to think logically about our substance use is further worsened by the *irrational escalation bias*. I refer to this as the "in for a penny, in for a pound" bias, because it's where we become more and more stubbornly attached to our beliefs because of all the effort that we have already put into defending them. This is pure stubbornness, where we stick to our guns even though there is convincing evidence that we were wrong, because we have already invested so much time and energy into defending our belief. We are doggedly doubling down and sticking to our guns because we don't want to lose face by giving in to those who say we need help.

You can really see the irrational escalation bias when you work with sick, miserable people in the detox center who will not admit powerlessness over their drug or drink even though they have been struggling unsuccessfully to beat it for years. I have seen people who have hit rock bottom and ended up in detox multiple times still unable to admit defeat to their drug or drink. People just hate admitting they were wrong all along. This is the irrational escalation bias bolstered by the toxic effects of psychoactive substances.

Another similar cognitive bias that affects our Step One is the so-called *ostrich effect*. This is our tendency to ignore obvious negative information. This cognitive bias is named after the (false) belief that ostriches try to avoid danger by burying their heads in the sand; likewise, we have a natural tendency to try to avoid a negative situation by ignoring information that is negative. We bury our heads in the sand hoping it will just go away. For "normal" rational people, overcoming the ostrich effect isn't very difficult, as they would rather face their problems and deal with them than pretend the problem doesn't exist and hope that it just goes away. However, substance addiction is in its very nature an extreme avoidance behavior, where we use our drug or drink to escape life's problems. As such, for the active alcoholic-addict, the ostrich effect comes naturally to us as yet another way to avoid facing reality, and it makes us especially resistant to the requirements of Step One.

Another oddity of human psychology that keeps us from being able to concede our powerlessness is known as the *illusory truth effect*. This peculiarity of our minds is the tendency to believe that a statement is true if it's easier to process or if it has been stated multiple times, regardless of its actual veracity. In other words, the more we tell ourselves and others that we can stop if we want to, the more we believe it ourselves. If you think about it, you've probably told yourself a million times that: *I've had enough! Monday, I'm going to quit*, and we've probably all told others a billion times: *I got this! I'm just going through a rough patch right now. Once this [insert stressful experience] is over I'm going to stop drinking/using.* The illusory truth effect makes us start believing our own lies once we've lied enough. And we lie **a lot** to cover our drinking and using.

Restraint bias is yet another flaw of human reasoning that constitutes a barrier to Step One. The restraint bias is the tendency to overestimate one's ability to show restraint in the face of temptation. The restraint bias is greatly magnified by substance addiction's disruptive effect on the brain, because a core characteristic of addiction is an over-inflated belief in one's power of self-control. When we over-estimate our power over drugs or alcohol we are not going to admit powerlessness.

The cognitive bias known as *naïve realism* prevents us from allowing other people to reason with us to make us see that we need help, that we can't stop our substance use on our own. The naïve realism bias is the stubborn belief that we see reality as it really is, and that those who don't agree with us are uninformed, stupid, irrational, or biased. It makes us stubbornly stick to our guns as we maintain our belief that: *I got this!* This is tied in with the cognitive bias known as the *illusion of validity bias*. This is our stubborn belief that our understanding of the facts is accurate and that our judgments and decisions are correct, even in the face of contradictory evidence. Our interpretation of the facts is correct, everyone else's is wrong. We believe we are right and no one can convince us otherwise. Our mind is closed and nobody is going to open it.

Even if someone were to succeed in convincing us that we need help and that we are unable to get sober on our own, the cognitive bias known as *belief revision conservatism* makes us further unable to relent. This is our tendency, when we do accept facts that go against our beliefs, to only change our beliefs a little bit rather than to completely concede defeat. As such, we may admit that we need help, but only *some* help. We can still get sober on our own, but we will pick and choose little bits of help here and there when we think we need it. We accept help, but with one foot in and one foot out.

Have you noticed how people with addictions get defensive when they are confronted about their substance use? If you are like me you can identify with this. This is partly due to the *hostile attribution bias*. The hostile attribution bias is the tendency to interpret others' attempts to help us as having hostile intent, even when it's really done out of love or truly good intentions.

As we have discussed, our alcoholic-addict's pride is an effort to compensate for our rock bottom self-esteem by over-inflating our own merits and cutting down other people's value. The *illusory superiority bias* is an error of reasoning that makes this pride effect even worse. This is also known as the "Lake Wobegon effect" (fans of author Garrison Keillor will understand this reference), the "better-than-average effect", or the "superiority bias". This is where we overestimate our own abilities and underestimate the abilities of others. The illusory superiority effect causes us to recognize that other people may be powerless over drugs or alcohol, but we ourselves are not, because we are, after all, awesome compared to them. Too, when the addictions counselor or our sponsor tells us things that rub our pride the wrong way, we reject the advice because "the counselor is just stupid."

Reinforcing the overconfidence in our ability to quit our drink or drug use on our own caused by the lake Wobegon effect, our reasoning is further impaired by the *optimism bias*. This is also known as the "wishful thinking bias," the "valence effect," and the "positive outcome bias." This is our tendency to be unreasonably optimistic about our own abilities, such as our ability to quit drinking or using. The really weird thing about the optimism bias is that it occurs even in the most pessimistic of people, such as people in active addiction-alcoholism.

One final cognitive bias that is especially relevant to our recovery is the *backfire bias.* This dysfunctional reactive thought process causes us to strengthen our support for our existing belief (or what we want to believe) when we hear convincing information that we are wrong in our belief. This is yet another brain flaw that causes us to hunker down and stick to our belief that we can get sober on our own when people present us with compelling facts to try to convince us otherwise.

My point here is not to attempt to make all my readers experts in psychology, but rather to demonstrate that there is plenty of reason that we may be wrong when we refuse to accept and admit that we are powerless over alcohol or drugs. For those who struggle with Step One, an awareness of these flaws of reasoning that affect the human mind may help us to re-evaluate our belief in our power over our substance use. This self-awareness may be key to finding the open-mindedness we need when we advance through the Steps, beginning with Step One.

Do we have to lay back and just accept these dysfunctions of the mind? No! We can overcome them, and we must. Doing so is one of the challenges of Step One, because we have to challenge our dysfunctional thinking in order to develop the open-mindedness and willingness to accept what Step One asks of us and to progress through the rest of the Steps. Researchers in behavioral sciences have spent considerable time working out how we can mitigate these biases, because they affect everyone to some degree. Even for non-addict-alcoholics, they affect how people interact with others, make decisions, and form opinions. Marketing experts understand these cognitive biases and prey on them to get us to buy things we don't need and to influence how we vote. Since these biases represent a deviation from reality, they can be harmful and cause us to make bad decisions and form erroneous opinions. Unfortunately, they are outright destructive for people with substance addictions, because they become pushed to the extreme; as we have discussed, they are a major barrier to Step One. Thankfully, behavioral scientists have found some ways to attenuate or even halt their effects on us. They call these *debiasing* techniques.[40,41] Let's look at them now so that we can apply them to our recovery.

The first debiasing technique is simply to be aware of these cognitive biases, and to recognize their influence on our thoughts and beliefs. Psychologists refer to this as *metacognition*, but I prefer to call it just being mindful that our thought processes are subject to a great deal of flaws. The 12 Step program is very clear that we should be open-minded, and that's an effective way to defeat these cognitive biases. We are more likely to be open-minded and open to new ideas if we are mindful that our thoughts, beliefs, and opinions are subject to significant bias. Thus, we give ourselves permission to challenge our existing beliefs and to see if they line up with the facts, and to be open to new information. This is important, because the human mind is stubborn and resistant to new ideas, and the addicted mind is doubly so. Our old ideas and ways of doing things brought us disaster, so challenging ourselves to consider new ideas is one of the best decisions we could ever make.

The next debiasing technique is to pause and try to visualize the situation from the other person's perspective before jumping to conclusions. Imagine if we were sober, "normal" individuals and we saw ourselves behaving as we do. Would we think everything was fine, or would we think there was something seriously wrong? If the other person has been through addiction or alcoholism and is in healthy and happy recovery and has helped other people get sober, could he or she be right and could I be wrong? Could I be biased in my viewpoint? This technique of putting ourselves in another person's shoes and trying to see things from his or her perspective is known as empathy, and it's a skill that will become second nature to us as we grow in spirituality on our trip through the 12 Steps.

Another way to prevent cognitive bias from wrecking our Step One is to slow down our thought process. Cognitive bias works on a reflexive basis, where we make snap conclusions and react immediately and with emotion to information we hear. If we step back and carefully consider the new information before we jump to conclusions we can avoid the emotional reaction that hardens us to the facts and makes us reject information out of hand, regardless of its merits.

Eliciting feedback from other people also helps us to defeat cognitive bias. So, if someone is trying to explain to us that we are powerless and we get our back up and become indignant, we should go and talk it over with people we love and trust, to see what they think about the matter. We can either ask them how they feel about the other person's opinion, or ask for their feedback on our reasoning process. And we must be open to considering what they tell us.

Developing an attitude of open-mindedness is a powerful tool for defeating the cognitive biases that do their best to impair our ability to think clearly and logically. This means resisting our knee-jerk emotional reaction to new information and ideas, and instead taking the time to consider the new information carefully. That way we engage our higher brain functions rather than allowing cognitive bias to make our decisions for us. The 12 Step program emphasizes this virtue from the very beginning because it is a life skill that will serve us well beyond helping us get through Step One. Open-mindedness is a significant advantage in business, relationships, education, and general function in life.

As we progress through the 12 Steps and grow in humility and healthy self-esteem, our vulnerability to cognitive bias will shrink away. Many of our flawed thought processes are emotionally charged, based on our need to nurse an inflated pride based on a low self-esteem. It's that bizarre pride of alcoholism-addiction working against us once again. As this fake pride and flawed thinking fall away, our beaten-down self-esteem finally has a chance to flourish.

These debiasing techniques will help people who are stuck on Step One to take a more objective look at themselves and perhaps realize and admit that they are in fact powerless, if in fact they are. But it does more than that. As we will see in Steps Two and Three, the 12 Step program requires us to keep an open mind, and these cognitive biases are exactly what keeps us from having an open mind. So, being mindful of the many types of bias that our addict-alcohol's mind uses to control our thoughts and behaviors will prove to be a helpful tool as we progress through the Steps on our way to good health and function.

*

The psychology of addiction-alcoholism is characterized by a sense of victimization, the so-called "poor-me" syndrome. For many people drinking or drugging is a coping mechanism for the stressors of life. Then, as addiction develops and we become more detached from normal life the problems worsen and life and addiction both spiral downwards.

It's only natural that people who feel wronged in life wonder *why me?* They begin to feel victimized and fall prey to a peculiarity of human psychology called *learned helplessness*.[42,43] This describes what happens when we face life stressors and problems that accumulate and overwhelm us to the point that we don't even know where to start to deal with them, so we just give up. Learned helplessness is a psychological consequence of repeated exposure to negative, uncontrollable situations, and affected individuals end up just shutting down and stop trying to change their circumstances. Learned helplessness is a toxic mind-set, a sad and hopeless feeling, and a great contributor to a negative psychology. Unsurprisingly, it is highly associated with depression and anxiety.[44] Active addiction-alcoholism and the resulting decline in life circumstances is an extremely negative, uncontrollable situation, so learned helplessness is highly prevalent in people with our disease. Step One is a powerful first step in changing this toxic mind-set, because it requires us to admit that our awful situation is, in fact, beyond our control, but there is a way we can finally change our circumstances, starting with admitting our problem. Although we may be in a state of learned helplessness, we finally see that there is help, hope, and a realistic expectation for a brighter future, and Step One tells us exactly how to begin the process. Too, we see that we are not facing life alone anymore; we have the fellowship, a higher power, and a sponsor behind us.

Self-pity, known to psychologists as *self-victimization*, is also a horrible mental trap. It's an expression of learned helplessness, and is another symptom of a deeply negative psychology. Self-victimization is a causative factor in many of the serious complications of a negative psychology, such as depression, emotional loneliness, anxiety, substance use, and suicide.[45] Self-pity is also heavily associated with anger and rumination, both dangerous causes of addiction-alcoholism.[46] Like learned helplessness, self-pity is a toxic mind-set.

Being convinced that we are passive victims makes us feel helpless and hopeless. It's poison to the mind and spirit and lies behind many of the character defects that play a central role in the spiritual sickness that pervades our addiction-related behaviors. Self-pity makes us angry, because it's natural for victims to be angry. But that anger is based in blame, and we blame everybody but ourselves for our problems. The anger and resentments that come out of this are a profound burden that weighs down our soul. But, what of people who truly are victims, those who have been abused or subjected to some other undeserved outrage? Well, we will discuss this at length in Step Four. I believe that the 12 Step program is – by far – the most effective intervention for people with a traumatic and tragic past. This is important, because it is so much better to stop such things from the past from haunting us and remaining a reliable daily source of unhappiness. We are re-victimized every day when this happens. More on that in Step Four.

This self-victimization – this pervasive view that the world is out to get us – is the basis of a negative psychology that has lethal effects on our thinking, our view of ourselves, our view of the world, and our hope and reason for living. This is known as an *external locus of control*.[47] That means that we come to believe that things that happen to us – our very future – depend on things outside of our own control. This is a pretty ugly feeling. It means that we come to believe that any effort we would put forward to make our lives better doesn't matter, because control of what happens in our lives lies outside ourselves. It's just a waste of time to even try to make life better, there is no point. As this mentality worsens, people naturally just give up trying, and just lay back and wait for things to happen to them. This awful feeling propels people to drink or use, to escape form the terrible hopelessness that it entails. It's escapism. We stop trying to work on our problems and instead focus on blaming others. We have learned to be helpless. When that happens, our mind instinctually looks for coping mechanisms to smother the anxiety and pain that comes with our feelings of abandoned hopelessness; our mind doesn't care if they are healthy or dysfunctional, it just wants quick relief.

This external locus of control makes us believe that we drank or used because our spouse is such a tyrant, or because our finances had gone so badly, or because we didn't get that great job we interviewed for. Those stressors surely contributed to the stress that brought us to seek our chemical coping mechanism, but we see them as an excuse for our substance use, when in reality they are just part of life.

These toxic, negative mind-sets – learned helplessness, self-pity, and an external locus of control – are a big part of the reason that simply not using or drinking is not treatment for addiction. If this negative psychology is not corrected, our sobriety will be fine... until our spouse annoys us again, or we suffer financial set-back, or we blow another interview, or someone upsets us, or we're just having a bad day. These poisonous mind-sets can be a significant barrier to recovery. *Why bother doing the Steps if I'm still a helpless victim of the world, and nothing I do matters?*

You will note that all three of these pernicious twists of psychology involve a belief that we are powerless over our lives and the world; we see ourselves as helpless victims who shouldn't even bother to try to make good in life. A truly odd twist of the psychology of addiction-alcoholism is that many of these people – who feel completely powerless over life – have such a resistance to admitting powerlessness over drugs or alcohol. This is one of the reasons that alcoholism-addiction is often referred to as the disease of paradoxes.

As a trained therapist with more than 15 years of clinical experience, it is my opinion that the 12 Step program is the most effective approach to relieving people from the negative psychology of alcoholism-addiction, including the devastating effects of the poisonous mind-set of learned helplessness, an external locus of control, and self-pity. My own opinion is supported by the medical and behavioral sciences research literature.[48,49] I hope that you, too, will experience this remarkable psychological transformation as we grow through the Steps together. It all begins with overcoming that strangest of paradoxes of alcoholism-addiction – our resistance to admitting powerlessness over drugs and alcohol.

*

All these causes of muddled and dysfunctional thinking are driven by two of the core symptoms of alcoholism-addiction: 1) an obsessive need for control, and 2) a pronounced lack of insight. These symptoms represent a major barrier to recovery in general, and to Step One in particular. Let's look at these symptoms quickly, so that we can recognize them in ourselves and put a stop to their power over us.

Part of the abnormal psychology of addiction-alcoholism is a pathological need for control. This is yet another paradox of addiction, because it doesn't make much sense that someone with an external locus of control – a belief that life is totally beyond our control – would need to try to control everything. However, this need for control is based solely on the addicted brain's need to protect its access to drug or drink. This need for control is why people will pick and choose the help they get, taking a bit of help here and a bit there, but always staying in control and never fully giving themselves over to a program of recovery. The addicted mind needs this control to protect its pathway back to the drink or drug, *just in case.* This is the "open door" concept that we've already discussed.

Another core symptom of addiction-alcoholism psychology is a conspicuous *lack of insight.* This is a medical term used to describe when someone has a disease but is unaware of it, often to the point of believing they are being lied to about it. People in active addiction are largely unaware of or unable to understand their dysfunctional thoughts and behaviors, and therefore recoil when it is suggested to them that they may be powerless over their substance use. Much of the lack of insight in addict-alcoholics is denial, as we don't want to believe that we are as bad off as we are. It's a natural reflex to protect our mind from the pain of cognitive dissonance and to try to maintain our false front of pride in our own mind. However, a lot of lack of insight is not due to denial at all, but to a genuine lack of awareness of how disrupted and corrupted our mental processes really are. Many people in recovery look back at how they thought and what they believed to be true when they were in active addiction and can't believe they actually thought the way they did. In hindsight, the behaviors that we saw as normal or justified back then horrify us when we are in recovery and have some insight. The psychological technique of metacognition – giving people insight into their psychological state and thought processes – is a highly effective way of helping people to correct dysfunctional behaviors, and is a mainstay of all addiction therapy programs, including the 12 Steps.

We can use our knowledge of our dysfunctional psychological processes to help break down our need for control and our lack of insight. This alone will not fix or cure our addiction-alcoholism, but it will help bring out the willingness and open-mindedness that we need to do our Steps and heal, beginning right here with Step One. If you are powerless over addictive substances, recognize the substance-induced dysfunctions of your mind that keep you from acknowledging your powerlessness, and let's get on with recovery.

*

We have discussed the psychological barriers to Step One so that we can recognize these processes in ourselves (and in others when we become sponsors). Although it's unfortunate that our brain functions have flaws and quirks that our disease can use to trap us, one of the wonderful things about the human mind is that once we are aware of these dysfunctional thought processes we can recognize them and consciously overcome them. As we discussed previously, psychologists refer to this process of learning about our mind's dysfunctions and consciously overcoming them as metacognition, which I refer to simply as mindfulness.

Unfortunately, mindfulness/metacognition does **not** apply to our disease as a whole. Knowledge alone will not get us sober. The Big Book is clear on this point: "but the actual or potential alcoholic, with hardly an exception, will be *absolutely unable to stop drinking on the basis of self-knowledge.* This is a point we wish to emphasize and re-emphasize, to smash home upon our alcoholic readers as it has been revealed to us out of bitter experience" (p. 39). Bill Wilson himself tried to get sober based on self-knowledge, after his insane behavior was explained to him by a physician: "surely this was the answer – self-knowledge. But it was not, for the frightful day came when I drank once more" (Big Book, p. 7). For our disease, self-knowledge is an excellent tool for recovery, but it's not the solution. It doesn't heal us; for that we need to complete the Steps, armed with our self-knowledge.

Part of the genius of the 12 Step program is that we don't have to understand alcoholism-addiction to get sober. Good thing for me, because when I was languishing in the detox center ready to give myself over to the Steps I had no idea whatsoever what had happened to me. I hadn't a clue why I behaved the way I did, and why I couldn't use my usually considerable

74

willpower too quit my drinking and using when my life and health were crashing down around me. Thanks to immersing myself in the Steps and the fellowship, I was able to get sober and start healing, and when my mind and body were becoming clear again I was able to answer my curiosity about why and how addiction-alcoholism occurs. The 12 Step program allows us to get healthy and sober now, and figure everything out later – if we wish to.

The Big Book explains that our recovery doesn't depend on self-knowledge, but on having a spiritual awakening, finding spiritual health and well-being, and applying spiritual principles to our lives. We will discuss in our Step Two study what exactly this "spirituality" means, but suffice it to say in the meantime that it's not about religion. Chapter 2 of the Big Book tells the story of a "certain American business man" (p. 26) who sought out help from world-famous psychiatrist Dr. Carl Jung, before Alcoholics Anonymous was in existence. The A.A. publication *Pass It On* tells us that this certain American businessman was named Rowland H. This man spent a year under the care of Dr. Jung, and felt that the insight he had gained from the famed psychiatrist would be his key to sobriety. The Big Book explains:

> Above all, he [Rowland H.] believed he had acquired such a profound knowledge of the inner workings of his mind and its hidden springs that relapse was unthinkable. Nevertheless, he was drunk in a short time. More baffling still, he could give himself no satisfactory explanation for his fall.
>
> So he returned to this doctor [Dr. Jung], whom he admired, and asked him point-blank why he could not recover. He wished above all things to regain self-control. He seemed quite rational and well-balanced with respect to other problems. Yet he had no control whatsoever over alcohol. Why was that?
>
> [Dr. Jung explained]: 'here and there, once in a while, alcoholics have had what are called vital spiritual experiences. To me these occurrences are phenomena. They appear to be in the nature of huge emotional displacements and rearrangements. Ideas, emotions, and attitudes which were once the guiding forces of the lives of these men are suddenly cast to one side, and a completely new set of conceptions and motives begin to dominate them' (p. 26-27).

Rowland did, in the end, experience a spiritual awakening and got sober, and we read about him in the early history of A.A. This "vital spiritual experience" referred to by Dr. Jung is what the 12 Step program refers to as a spiritual awakening. It's this spiritual awakening that gets us sober and healthy and again, and keeps us there as long as we continue to grow and thrive in spiritual wellness. More about this in Step Two.

So what does all this information we are discussing about the inner workings of our mind do for us? Well, the self-insight we gain helps break down the barriers to doing the Steps, starting right here in Step One. An understanding of our mental barriers to recovery helps us to stop the dysfunctional thinking that keeps us close-minded and unwilling to give ourselves over to a program of recovery. As well, a knowledge of the dysfunctional thought processes at work in our disease helps us to understand why we must do the Steps to correct our negative psychology, and why we must maintain our recovery by continuing to do the things we need to do to remain in recovery for the long-term.

I have found, too, that people in recovery are hungry to understand what happened to them, why they became trapped as they did by their substance use, and why they behaved as they did. I was certainly that way when I got sober. Although it's not necessary for our recovery, this knowledge can be a useful tool for our recovery, and it helps us when we sponsor others and they have questions about their disease.

So, let's take our knowledge and insight of our pathological alcoholic-addict mental processes and use them in the right context. This knowledge on its own will never be enough to make a true alcoholic-addict sober and stable in recovery. Rather, it's yet another tool that we can use to strengthen our experience and understanding as we pass through the Steps to attain the mental and spiritual wellness that will form the basis of our new life in recovery. Let's use this self-knowledge to break down the mental barriers to what keeps us from having the willingness and open-mindedness to do our Steps, starting with Step One.

*

Just about anybody can admit powerlessness when they are languishing at their bottom – physically, mentally, and spiritually sick, and with their life a smoking train-wreck. However, Step One is not just asking us to admit that we are powerless *right now, at this moment*. It also requires ("suggests") that we make a lifelong commitment to owning our powerlessness, so that ten years from now, when life is good and we haven't had a drink or drug in a decade, our disease doesn't succeed in talking us into having "just one." To stop believing in our powerlessness is to invite relapse. If not now, eventually. Our powerlessness is with us for life.

Forgetting or abandoning belief in our powerlessness is a dangerous step toward relapse. Ours is a disease with no cure. Rather, we are gifted with a daily reprieve from its effects, as long as we take care of the things we need to do to stay in recovery. Foremost among these things is maintaining our affirmation of our powerlessness. Step One is not only the first Step in *achieving* recovery, it's also the first Step in *remaining in* recovery. One of the things that happens as we lose sight of our powerlessness is that we lose touch with our program of recovery. After all, why waste time with meetings and all that recovery stuff if we don't need it? With the diabolical victory of separating us from our sense of powerlessness, our disease then pushes our mind to rationalize our way to a drink or drug. Once we allow that to happen by losing sight of our commitment to Step One, that's it for us; we put ourselves at grave risk of relapse. We may not see it at the time, but this has been the experience of myriad people in recovery, as documented in the 12 Step literature and within the fellowship. Better to learn from their grievous experiences than to have to find out for ourselves. We have seen their burned hands after they touched the red-hot stove, so we shouldn't have to touch the stove ourselves to find out if we, too, will get burned.

I like to go to 12 Step meetings in the detox center where I got sober, because it keeps me in touch with my powerlessness. There are always people in there just off the street following a relapse after years of recovery, and it's always the same story, time after time: *I stopped going to meetings and lost touch with the program, then I tried drinking/using again and here I am. Next time I'm going to stay with the program.*

If you are not convinced by the experience of millions of others like us, you should know that the danger of relapse from letting go of our respect for our powerlessness is firmly supported by science. Repeated use of drugs or alcohol causes a low-grade inflammation in the brain that disrupts the pathways formed by connected brain cells. New pathways are formed in their place that include pathways that produce the compulsive cravings for addictive substances and the other aspects of the pathological psychology of our disease.[50,51,52,53] Addiction truly is a brain disease, and these brain changes affect multiple brain circuits and pathways, including those involved in reward and motivation, learning and memory, and inhibitory control over behavior. These new "addiction" pathways remain in place for life, and can be re-activated even decades into recovery, most often with even a single drink or drug.[54,55] As such, addiction-alcoholism is not only a brain disease, but is a *chronic* brain disease.[56] These recently discovered effects of addictive substances on the brain provide an explanation for the observed effect of relapse following even a single exposure to drug or drink even many years into recovery. Once rendered powerless by our disease, we truly are powerless for life.

Although the analogy is admittedly overdone, it's appropriate to compare addiction-alcoholism to type 1 diabetes. Both are chronic diseases that can't be cured but can be successfully managed by taking proper daily care. Both can be lethal as soon as affected individuals become complacent and stop doing the things they need to do to keep their disease in check. Acknowledging the chronicity of our disease – that our powerlessness is something that will be with us for life – is required by Step One and supported by neuroscience. We will speak much about fear and its sinister effects on our psychology and our addiction-alcoholism as we walk the Steps together, and we will discover how to release the grip of fear from our minds. However, there is one type of fear that is good for our recovery: a healthy fear of our disease re-asserting itself at any time, should we become complacent and forget our powerlessness.

I often refer to Step One as Step 12.5, because it is very much a maintenance and growth Step, like Steps Ten, Eleven, and Twelve. We must keep renewing our commitment to Step One on a daily basis for the rest of our lives, or we surely will fall. All we have to do is to read the stories in the Big Book, or talk to people in the fellowship to see what happens when people – even with tons of sobriety – lose sight of their powerlessness and drift away from their program of recovery. Thanks to modern neuroscience, we know that this observation from the beginnings of the 12 Step program is firmly rooted in scientific fact.[57]

I will tell you my point of view; see if it makes sense for you. I am privileged to have a second chance at life, even though I don't deserve it. I caused so much harm and wronged so many during my drinking and using days that I didn't deserve another shot at life. But, I have been given one. Thanks to the 12 Step program, I approach life in a much more healthy and functional way, and I am privileged to live and work among "normal" people. However, I am different from them in one major way: I am powerless over alcohol and drugs. The one thing that lies between me and relapse is my spiritual program of recovery, which will only work if I continue to acknowledge my powerlessness. If I let go of that, I give in to my powerlessness, and I will certainly lose my second shot at life. I can't bear the thought of going back to that same misery and dysfunction that I suffered through in my drinking and using days; therein lies my healthy fear that keeps me bonded to my cherished commitment to my powerlessness.

So, there are certain things we must do to hold on to our treasured second chance at life. First among those things we must do is to take care of our recovery by acknowledging our powerlessness and holding onto our program of recovery with all our might. That begins with a daily affirmation of our powerlessness on an ongoing basis. Step One is for life.

*

Thus far, we haven't talked much about the other part of Step One, the part where we admit that our lives had become unmanageable. I've left that for the end of our Step One discussion because very few people seem to have much difficulty recognizing that their life had become total unmanageable chaos. However, there are some important points about this "unmanageability" that we must acknowledge to properly complete our Step One.

We must recognize and acknowledge that the psychology of addiction-alcoholism causes us to blame everybody and everything else but ourselves and our drinking or using for the chaos that presides over our lives. Our cognitive dissonance and alcoholic-addict pride propel us to see ourselves as blameless or nearly blameless victims of the world, and to minimize our own role in the vicious tailspin that life has taken. Step One is where we must become willing let go of our blame-thrower and acknowledge that our life situation had everything to do with us and our drinking or using. Even when terrible things have happened to us that were beyond our control, it was our inability to cope with adversity and hardship that caused us to seek refuge in bottle or needle, greatly worsening our situation and completely defeating our ability to face life's challenges and do something about them. Regardless of the cause of our problems, when we added drugs or alcohol to the mix life became unmanageable.

We will learn exactly how to let go of the anger, resentments, self-pity, and blame-throwing as we progress through the Steps, but here in Step One we are acknowledging that the chaos that reigns over us had much to do with our powerlessness over alcohol and drugs. Affixing blame, escaping through drugs or drink, and harboring resentment and self-pity have been destroying us. Step One asks us to be willing to take ownership of our lives and problems as the first Step toward managing our lives in a sane and functional way. Our lives become manageable again if we accept responsibility and stop looking outside ourselves to lay fault. As the Serenity Prayer suggests, we must accept the things we cannot change, but find the courage to take action to do what we can to help ourselves by addressing the things that we can change. The biggest and most helpful thing that we can change: our outlook and attitude. That's why we are doing the Steps.

We have discussed how people in active alcoholism-addiction lack insight, meaning that they have great difficulty in recognizing how insane their behavior is. However, when we get sober and look back at our thoughts and behaviors we are stunned by how blind we were. Yet, at the time all the insanity seemed normal to us. Juggling creditors, lying, stealing, hiding booze or drugs around the house, lashing out at people who tried to help us, spending our grocery and rent money at the liquor store or dealer, trying to pretend that we were fine when we were really sick, blowing off our kids, friends, and family, and refusing help that was offered to us all felt like normal, rational behavior to us. We lacked insight and we were focused only on the here and now; the senseless behavior made sense to us. To anyone who asked us how things were going, we would say *fine!* and do our best to make it look that way.

Unmanageability of our life can be both cause and effect of our addiction-alcoholism. The point where I crossed that line from a guy who could take it or leave it when it came to drugs or alcohol to a guy who drank and used obsessively, occurred when my life began to tumble out of control after a divorce where the stress and conflict and related chaos made my life no longer manageable for me. I couldn't handle things, and I turned increasingly to drug or drink to numb the anxiety and negative feelings, and to escape from reality. As my drug and alcohol use increased, my increasingly erratic and dysfunctional behavior pushed my life further into chaotic disaster. For me unmanageability of life was both a cause *and* effect of my addiction-alcoholism.

Simply stopping our drug or alcohol use won't suddenly make our life manageable. We are still mentally and spiritually sick, still lacking in coping skills for handling life, and still an inch away from going back to our familiar escape with the first set-back. We will still resort to lying, stealing, and evading to try to succeed. We will still cower from adversity. We will still be angry, resentful, self-pitying, and blameful. The 12 Step program is designed to heal our scars, to guide us to take ownership of our lives, to develop in us a strongly positive psychology, and to teach us healthy coping skills for living life on life's terms. Step One readies us for that process by asking us to recognize and acknowledge the dysfunction that has wrecked our lives.

There is another purpose to the part of Step One where we acknowledge that our lives had become unmanageable, and that is that we make the association between our alcohol or drug use and the unmanageability of life. Saying that "our lives had become unmanageable" is another way of saying that our lives had become messed up and out of control. As we enter into sobriety with a commitment to owning our powerlessness, we must always make the association between our alcohol or drug use and an unmanageable life, a life that is messed up and out of control. When our disease begins to tell us that enough time has passed in sobriety, so that NOW we can take a drink or a drug and manage it, we need to immediately associate that drink or drug with an unmanageable life, because that is exactly what will happen if we allow our disease to lead us back down that perilous path. When we see or think of alcohol or drugs we should immediately associate the image with an unmanageable life. That will help us to remember our powerlessness in the face of our disease's efforts to get us to forget. In our study of Step Eleven we will see how this aspect of Step One ties in with the slogan "Remember When" as a powerful tool for life-long relapse prevention. For now, Step One suggests that we make the association between alcohol and drug use and an unmanageable life, and that we allow that association to sink deep into our brain.

*

So, we have discussed the flawed psychological processes that occur in substance addiction that make us powerless over drug or drink, and those that create a significant barrier to our ability to recognize and acknowledge that powerlessness. We have seen how we can counter these powerful effects on our thinking, so that we can take a step back and look at our situation with the open-mindedness and willingness that we need to concede our powerlessness.

Step One allows us to bust down these psychological processes that the addicted mind uses to substantiate continued drinking and using and to keep us from seeking and accepting help. By admitting that we are powerless, we destroy those negative, dysfunctional, harmful psychological processes and allow ourselves to look outside ourselves for the help we need. But, we must do more than simply say the words; we must accept it as fact and believe it.

The long and the short of what the science is telling us is that for people who are addicted to drugs or alcohol, the pervasive desire to quit on their own, their own way, using willpower is very unlikely to succeed, unlikely to be sustainable, and does nothing to heal the causes and effects of the addiction-alcoholism. In order to move forward to recover from substance addiction, individuals must first surrender their need for control and accept help. This requires an admission that they themselves are powerless over their substance use; exactly what Step One is suggesting that we do.

Many people have already accepted that reality by the time they come to the program, and have no problem acknowledging that they are powerless over their substance. Others are hardened to the idea of powerlessness, but when we understand the psychological processes that are causing this resistance to accept help, we can break them down.

Step One is deeply therapeutic. It tells us that it's OK to be powerless over a substance, that the realization of powerlessness is actually part of – indeed, the First Step toward – the solution. It's a relief to know that our powerlessness is just part of the normal course of addiction-alcoholism, that all the people we see in good health and sobriety in the fellowship were – and are – also powerless over their substance use. We are in good company.

*

If, after all this, anyone still harbors doubts about powerlessness, then I suggest turning to a sponsor and the fellowship. When we hear other people who have lots of recovery explain their powerlessness, and when we meet people who have relapsed after long periods of sobriety, then powerlessness becomes very real for us. Better to learn from others' mistakes than to repeat them ourselves.

There's a certain logic to being open-minded when someone who has successfully found recovery tells us that admitting powerlessness is the first step back to health and good function. Let me illustrate by reminding you of my transmission analogy – it's feeble, but indulge me; I like it. If I decided that I wanted to restore an old car and I set out to rebuild the transmission on my own I would undoubtedly fail multiple times. Transmissions are complicated to rebuild. Stubborn me would probably try a number of times to do it on my own, and I'm sure I would fall flat on my face every time. However, if I had a neighbor who rebuilds transmissions for a living, I would be a fool not to ask him for advice, and follow his instructions to the letter. Right? Well, so it is with alcoholism and addiction. If we have failed in all our attempts to stop our drinking and using and someone who has recovered from alcoholism-addiction and has helped many other people successfully do the same, we would be foolish not to heed his or her advice to the letter. Right?

Well, his or her advice is this: *admit you are powerless over alcohol/drugs, and that your life had become unmanageable.* Follow that advice, or keep failing to rebuild that transmission.

*

So why is admitting that we are powerless so important for recovery? Why can't we just say: *well, **maybe** I'm powerless over drugs or drink* and then proceed with the Steps? Admitting powerlessness allows us to drop the pretenses that have dominated our lives, to stop the flimsy lies and deceit, and to finally tell our story. It lifts from our shoulders the impossible burden of trying to maintain a fake exterior façade while we are dying inside. It allows us to stop holding back, to put both feet into our program of recovery. As the Big Book tells us: "many are doomed who never realize their predicament" (p. 92).

If you have understood, accepted, and conceded your powerlessness over drugs and alcohol, and that this powerlessness is a permanent feature of your makeup that will be with you for life, and that substance use has and always will make your life unmanageable, then you have gotten Step One. If your sponsor agrees, let's move on to Step Two.

First, one final – albeit tongue-in-cheek – comment about Step One. If Karl Marx had been an alcoholic he probably would have said:

Alcoholic/addicts of the world admit your powerlessness; you have nothing to lose but your chains!

Step Two

Came to believe that a Power greater than ourselves could restore us to sanity.

To begin the process of recovery we had to, in Step One, admit that we are powerless over alcohol and drugs. Step One lays the foundation for the life-affirming transformation from the deeply negative psychology of active addiction to the positive psychology necessary for a lasting recovery characterized by peace of mind, happiness, and resilience to life's ups and downs.

To complete our Step Two and move on to Step Three, we are asked to believe that a power greater than ourselves can restore us to sanity. Wait, what? Are we insane? Our defensive alcoholic-addict pride inflames at the very suggestion. But what is meant by Step Two when it suggests that we are insane? *Twelve Steps and Twelve Traditions* explains:

> Few indeed are the practicing alcoholics who have any idea how irrational they are, or seeing their irrationality, can bear to face it. Some will be willing to term themselves 'problem drinkers,' but cannot endure the suggestion that they are in fact mentally ill. They are abetted in this blindness by a world which does not understand the difference between sane drinking and alcoholism. 'Sanity' is defined as 'soundness of mind.' Yet no alcoholic, soberly analyzing his destructive behavior... can claim 'soundness of mind' for himself (p. 32-33).

In our study of Step One we discussed how psychoactive substances hijack the flaws and quirks of the human brain and push them to extremes. The resulting pathological and illusory thought processes and behaviors result in the classic symptoms of addiction-alcoholism. Although these thoughts and behaviors seem normal to us when we are in active addiction, they are harmful and dysfunctional; small wonder that they are referred to as "insanity." While "insanity" is not a medical term *per se*, it is a very accurate term for the complex pathological psychology that typifies alcoholism-addiction. This insanity results in a pattern of behavior and thought processes that result in a progressive detachment from normal life and a downward spiral as the normal functions of the mind deteriorate and remove us from reality, society, and normal life.

Step One was about realizing, admitting, and accepting that we are caught in this insanity, and that it's making life unmanageable. Step Two is where we begin the process of freeing ourselves from this all-devouring insanity.

At the risk of offending readers' sensitivities, I must point out that, from the medical perspective, alcoholism-addiction is a mental health disorder. People hate that idea, because the term "mental health disorder" is such a socially loaded term. We have visions of crazy people with a loss of touch with reality who have to be locked up to keep from hurting themselves or others. But – remember that ours is a program of rigorous honesty – that's kind of what we are like when we're actively drinking or using, *right?* That's certainly pretty much what I was like in my drinking and using days.

If anyone is really stuck on the insanity piece, they can think of "restore us to sanity" as "restore us to sane behavior." However, we must remember that seeing our addicted behavior as insanity doesn't label us and condemn us to a life of mental illness. Rather, our insane behavior is when we are intoxicated or seeking our drug or drink. Just about anybody can act insane when intoxicated. However, as the interval between our binges shrunk to the point of being continuous or at least daily and lasted months and years, all we had was insane behavior. As the Big Book explains: "whatever the precise definition of the word may be, we call this plain insanity. How can such a lack of proportion, of the ability to think straight, be called anything else?" (p. 37). By calling our behavior "insane," Step Two isn't calling us stupid; far from it. That's the whole point about addiction to drugs or alcohol: it turns anybody, regardless of how intelligent or accomplished they are, into purveyors of insane behavior. Again from the Big Book: "however intelligent we may have been in other respects, where alcohol has been involved, we have been strangely insane. It's strong language – but isn't it true?" (p. 38).

Those who still don't believe that they need to be restored to sane behavior (i.e. sanity) should ask a friend or loved one who has observed their behavior what they think about the issue. In our addiction, alcohol or drugs have exerted such power over us that we were willing to sacrifice all else in life, including sanity itself, to support our substance use. Intoxication removed our inhibition, memory, power of reason, and civility. When seeking our drug or drink we were willing to trample anyone or anything underfoot to fulfill our obsession. Our infantile excuses and attempts to cover up our addiction, the intoxicated driving, and the continued obsessive use of toxic substances even though they were making us sick and dispossessing us… it's all insanity. Even our way of thinking when in active addiction is insanity. Whether you call that insanity or not, we have come here to find an end to it and to be restored to normal behavior and function. If we could do that on our own, we would have done so long ago, but here we are. We didn't have the power to do so ourselves, so we are seeking some power greater than ourselves that can help us behave and live normally again. Step Two is suggesting to us that such help is there for us, and suggests that we accept the help.

Although addiction-alcoholism is a disease of that affects us mentally and physically, there is no mental or physical cure. No doctor will prescribe you a pill that makes you no longer addicted. You will never walk out of a psychiatrist's office cured of addiction. Rather, the 12 Step program addresses the fact that we came to addiction because we were spiritually sick, and we got increasingly more spiritually sick as our drinking or using progressed. The 12 Step program's success lies in the fact that it heals people spiritually. Step Two is where we dip our toes into that spirituality that promises to heal us as it has millions of others just like us over the past 80+ years. As we discuss Step Two we will look at what, exactly, spirituality is, why it is therapeutic for us, what science says about the issue, and how to optimize it to heal and enjoy lifelong recovery.

Step Two is asking us to accept that there is a power outside ourselves that can help us heal and restore us to sanity (i.e. sane behavior) again. We have only to look around ourselves in the fellowship or read the stories in the back of the Big Book to see abundant true-life proof that some kind of a power can restore people to sanity:

> Here are thousands of men and women, worldly indeed. They flatly declare that since they have come to believe in a Power greater than themselves, to take a certain attitude toward that Power, and to do certain simple things [the 12 Steps], there has been a revolutionary change in their way of living and thinking. In the face of collapse and despair, in the face of the total failure of their human resources, they found that a new power, peace, happiness, and sense of direction flowed into them (p. 50).

Who wouldn't want that?

*

With Step Two we are introduced to two concepts that are central to the 12 Step program of recovery, and these may be new and unfamiliar to many among us. These concepts are spirituality, and the idea of a higher power. Let's now look at exactly what those things are. I ask that all keep an open mind, because both concepts truly are inclusive and compatible with all people, regardless of race, creed, belief system, or frame of mind. As the Third Tradition tells us, the only requirement for membership is a desire to stop drinking or using; membership does not depend upon conformity, adopting beliefs, and certainly not on adopting a religion.

Step Two plays an undeserved role in turning away many people who desperately need help with substance addiction. This is especially tragic, because it really is unnecessary. Step Two leaves the uninitiated with the mistaken impression that the 12 Step program is religious, and this reputation has unfortunately been perpetuated in press and media.

Being a person who is decidedly not religious, I find this regrettable, because Step Two has changed my life in ways that go well beyond my sobriety and I wish the same for others, regardless of their beliefs. I know many people in the 12 Step fellowship who are agnostic, atheistic, or who just don't know about or care about religion, yet who – like me – treasure what Step Two has added to their lives. We will discuss the higher power concept and I ask anyone who struggles with it to hear me out on the matter with an open mind. Being open-minded is about hearing out an idea and giving it a chance by considering its merits and giving it a trial run, rather than rejecting it out of hand. That's all that is suggested of us.

As a physician and a therapist, I recognize the 12 Steps as a program of psychotherapy that is entirely consistent with the principles of addiction treatment in use today by professional addictions counselors at rehab centers. In fact, the majority of treatment programs are 12 Step-based, for reasons that will become apparent as we bring the science together with the Steps in our trip through the Steps. I also believe that the 12 Step process of instilling spirituality and a positive psychology is therapeutic for a number of other physical and mental disorders, including post-traumatic stress disorder, which modern medicine is woefully poor at treating. Wait, what? Did I also just say that the 12 Steps are useful for treating physical illness?

Until the early 1980s, treatment of illness – anything from colds to cancer to addictions – was based on the "biomedical" model of care, where the focus was on treating the disease, and health was considered to be the absence of disease. However, since the 1980s, healthcare has adopted a different approach to treating the sick, known as the "biopsychosocial" model of healthcare.

The biopsychosocial model of care is based on treating the whole person, which includes the biological, psychological, social, cultural, and spiritual (that's right, spiritual) aspects of sickness and disease. These elements of each person's makeup are all affected by illness and all need to be addressed to return people to good health and function. What that means for addiction-alcoholism is that simply the absence of using drugs or alcohol is not an effective treatment; otherwise we could just lock people in a room without any drugs or alcohol for six months to cure them of substance addiction. Rather, the biopsychosocial model of care recognizes that addiction-alcoholism is a disease that affects us socially, psychologically, culturally, biologically, as well as spiritually (that's right, spiritually), and all these aspects of the disease need to be addressed to bring people back to good health. Considerable research evidence supports this approach to healthcare in general and *especially* in treating addiction-alcoholism.[1,2,3]

Some illnesses are more physical than social, cultural, spiritual or mental; for example, a bladder infection is usually a simple matter of using an antibiotic medication, and then all is well. Other illnesses are more mental than physical, such as depression. Substance addiction covers all aspects of the biopsychosocial way of looking at disease: it's physical/biological – we get very ill physically, and most systems in our body are affected – it's mental – in fact it's classified as a mental health disorder – it's cultural and social – alcoholism-addiction deeply affects social relationships, crosses cultural and social values, and is heavily tainted with social stigma – and it's spiritual, as we will discuss shortly. However, there's no physical/biological cure for addiction; you will never walk out of the doctor's office with a medication that takes away your addiction. There's no mental cure for it; many of us have found out (me included!) that a psychiatrist isn't able to fix us. There's no social or cultural cure; our family's nagging and a desire to honor our cultural norms haven't fixed us. However, there is a spiritual treatment for our disease, which is the basis of the 12 Step program's long-standing ability to help millions of people find sobriety and a return to good health and function over the past 80+ years.

The 12 Step program is fundamentally a spiritual program of recovery, and you can't argue with success. A PhD psychologist who researches addiction-alcoholism treatment provides a good explanation of why the spiritual approach works so well: "when people find connection to a larger frame of meaning that allows self-transcendence and meaningful engagement in recovery practices and social re-engagement, they are more likely to change from addictive preoccupation to increased behavioral self-control, mindfulness and reconnection with others in ways that are meaningful for the person."[4] I have pointed out already that spirituality is not the same as religion, and shortly we will discuss what, exactly, spirituality is.

Many people may find it surprising that medical science uses the term "spirituality," but it does. Spirituality was once the domain of clergy and new-agers, but it is now firmly embraced by mainstream medical science.

Since the mid-1990s medical researchers have espoused spirituality because its obvious effects on health and illness could no longer be ignored. No longer a hoofy-doofy non-palpable thing, spirituality is now a measurable subject of significant medical research. The research into the effects of spirituality on health and well-being has progressed to the point where investigators are now documenting its effects on specific diseases. And it's a powerful thing, indeed!

It was about time that medical science took an interest in the health benefits of spiritual wellness. When I was in medical school in the 1990s it quickly became obvious to me that people who were "in good spirits" did much better when they were sick. From my first days on the medical wards, I could see that it was undeniable that people who had meaningful connections with others, with the world at large, and – for some – with some kind of a higher power did much better when they were sick than those who lacked these connections. As we will see shortly, these connections are what define spirituality. At the time, I had some religious beliefs, but I didn't understand what spirituality was. Nevertheless, the effects of these connections on people's resilience, happiness, and ability to beat illness were glaringly self-evident. I remember thinking that we could really help people overcome illness if we could help them to have these connections. Well, it turns out that these same effects had been observed since recorded history, and I was noticing the same thing that my predecessors had noticed going back centuries. Although I didn't know it at the time, science had already begun looking into the effects of these connections on illness, and how we can apply these benefits to our patients.

Medical science stubbornly refused to acknowledge the effects of these non-physical aspects of health for nearly two and a half millennia. At the time of Hippocrates (450 BCE), disease was considered to be a manifestation of sin, and medical care was based on supernatural beliefs, magical incantations, and religious ceremonies. Hippocrates's big contribution to medicine was that he was the first to reject this dubious approach to medicine in favor of the study of anatomy, physiology, and empirical observation. Hippocrates is considered the father of modern medicine because he spearheaded the end to the view that disease was best treated by appeasing the wrath of deities, and instead introduced the concept of using nutrition, exercise, and medications as the basis of health care. From that point on, medical science fanatically rejected anything that wasn't physical in its zeal to reject the old practices of magic and the supernatural in health care. That's why it took so long for modern medicine to acknowledge and embrace the very real impact of spirituality on health and disease.

By the 1990s, science could no longer ignore the obvious health effects of spiritual connections, and finally let go of its outdated rejection of anything that won't fit into a pill. Science had to admit defeat on rejecting the power of spiritual connections for two main reasons: 1) the effects of spirituality on health, well-being, and recovery from illness were being well supported by high-quality clinical studies, and 2) the advent of the biopsychosocial model of healthcare, where the entire patient is treated rather than simply the disease, which had a significant impact on the effectiveness of Western medicine.

This recognition of the health-affirming qualities of these connections on three levels – with other people, with the world in general, and with a higher power – coincided perfectly with the transition of medical care from the old biomedical model (where health is defined as the absence of disease) to the biopsychosocial model (where health is defined as the composite of good biological health, psychological health, social and cultural well-being, and spiritual health).

The effects of spiritual connections will be discussed in this book, as well as how we can harness and optimize these effects for ourselves. Just as a bit of a spoiler, there is a large body of compelling scientific research demonstrating that spirituality is associated with: psychological well-being, thriving, life satisfaction, psychological resiliency, mental health, protection against depression and depressive symptoms, reduced risk of alcoholism or drug addiction, ability to cope with stressors, happiness, improved immune function, physical well-being, physiologic resilience (ability to avoid illness), recovery from illness, disease, and injury, and improvement in a long list of chronic health conditions. Spirituality has well-documented associations in the science and medical literature with all those things. And, I would like to add from my own experience: awesomeness. Spirituality has improved the quality of my life immeasurably, mostly due to the peace of mind and resilient happiness that it has imparted on me. And above all, it has freed me from that cruelest of prisons: the obsessive need for drink and drug.

So, let's answer some questions here. What, exactly, is spirituality? How can spirituality stop me from using drugs and alcohol? How can spirituality overpower my powerlessness?

*

To begin our exploration of spirituality I will start by re-iterating once and for all that spirituality is not the same thing as religion. The common misconception that spirituality = religion is one of the main detractors from the 12 Step program for many people. I am not a religious person at all, but I am spiritual. Spirituality is the basis of my recovery from drug and alcohol addiction, and is a major factor in my ability to function in life at a level of effectiveness that I have never previously known. But I'm not religious. So if spirituality is not religion, what is it? What does it mean when the Big Book says: "what we really have is a daily reprieve [from our disease] contingent on the maintenance of our spiritual condition" (p. 85)? How can an intangible concept like spirituality possibly overcome the powerful draw of drugs and alcohol? What does a higher power have to do with spirituality? Do I have to have an understanding of a higher power to have a spiritual reprieve from alcoholism-addiction? Let's answer all those questions.

We can start defining spirituality by addressing the fallacy that spirituality is the same thing as religion. While it is true that religion professes to pursue spirituality, many people are religious but not at all spiritual, while many others are spiritual but not at all religious. It's not necessary to be part of a religious group to be spiritual, as some of the most hard-core spiritualists do their best "spiritualizing" in solitude and silence. Spirituality is, by its nature, a deeply personal and personalized phenomenon. Besides "religion" there are a couple of other words I think should not be coupled with spirituality: supernatural, New Age, otherworldly, and any word ending in –ism.

Before I offend anyone's sensibilities – or get struck by lightning – I want to say that I am not disparaging religion; rather, I am simply pointing out that spirituality and religion are not the same thing. As a spiritual person I am open-minded and accepting of all people's beliefs and value systems, regardless if they are similar to mine or not, as long as they are not harmful to anyone. In fact religion has a long history of playing a crucial function in societal cohesiveness, and provides a moral compass for society. Religion is very important for many people, and for some it is their primary contact with spirituality.

I am envious of anyone who has found a comfortable home in the arms of religion. For many, it provides a ready-made understanding of a higher power and a highly supportive community, as well as a direction for living. Such people may have a head start on spirituality. However, for those who have not found religion to be so welcoming, a paradigm of spirituality without the dogma and doctrine of religion offers a way for them to come to understand their transcendental selves on their own terms, in a way that makes sense to them. Psychiatrist Carl Jung practiced at a time and place (Switzerland, early 20th century) where religion was a defining part of the lives of most people, and participation in religion was a required part of community inclusion. He found in his practice that people who felt rejected by the religious community or who themselves rejected organized religion were left feeling dejected and alone. He also found that guiding them in finding their own personal spiritual perspective had a remarkable healing effect. So it is with spirituality even now, one hundred years later, for those who are disillusioned or uncomfortable with religion, or who find that religion's canon of beliefs doesn't fit well with what they observe in the world around them.

So, let's get the "spirituality equals religion" misconception out of the way right off the bat. There are a few fundamental differences between spirituality and religion. First of all, there are no rules to spirituality. There is no defined ideology or set beliefs that you must subscribe to; you as an individual seek your own understanding of the world as part of your own spirituality. While it may take some time to define your spirituality, I can say from experience that the search in and of itself is stimulating and fulfilling. People say that the search is never really over, and I agree with that.

Religion involves an organization, an institution, with certain rituals, values, practices, and beliefs about God or a higher power.[5] Religions have boundaries and guidelines, which might not coincide with each individual's personal beliefs or might not make sense for each individual. The restrictions of a religion may limit some people's search for meaning.[6,7] Crucially, some people may find that religion may not allow them to optimize their connections outside themselves. As I will demonstrate shortly, a search for spirituality is an innate characteristic that is genetically programmed into humans, and many people will seek out religion to fulfill this need for spiritual expression or understanding. However, spirituality is a much broader, personalized, and inclusive concept than is religion, simply because it allows for more leeway and does not exclude anyone.

Spirituality is refreshingly free of politics. Religion has taken on a global political significance.[8,9] Even wars have been based on opposing religious beliefs. I have yet to hear of anyone suffering discrimination or hate because they are spiritual, or of wars being fought over spirituality. Religion has been abused to lead many people to do things that are supported by their religion, but are decidedly not spiritual. For example, wars over religious principles, or rejection of other people based on their religion or sexual orientation in the name of religion, are not consistent with spiritual healthiness.

There are many people who are spiritual but not religious, but religious beliefs may form a part of their spirituality. They may believe in God as described by a certain religion, but do not belong to a particular religious denomination, or participate in organized religion. Religion can be a very important part of some people's spirituality.

*

It's really hard to define "spirituality." Try it. Most dictionaries shirk the effort, using circular definitions like "that which pertains to things spiritual." It's not something tangible that we can put in a box. Much of spirituality is tied to emotion: spirituality gives us passion, warmth, happiness, and a sense of peace. I found it interesting to note that the word spirituality is derived from the Latin word *spiritus*, which means "breath of life." I find that word association to be most appropriate because it describes precisely the effect that spirituality had on me when I was down and out, and had given up on life. It certainly breathed life back into me. It's about letting go, in a way, of dogmatic prescribed beliefs that don't make sense when held up to what we observe in the world, about letting go of our diffidence to asking questions and looking for the answers ourselves, untarnished by what others dictate to us as answers. Spirituality is a way of freeing our curiosity, contemplating things beyond the day-to-day melodrama of our lives, a mindfulness of things that otherwise go unnoticed. Yes, defining spirituality is like trying to define the smell of vinegar, or the taste of sweet. But alas, we're going to define it.

The indefinability of spirituality is part of its essence, because spirituality must necessarily be up to individual people to define what it means for them. Besides, it's not something tangible that we can hold in our hands, so putting words on it is kind of like nailing Jell-O to the wall. However, there are some characteristics of spirituality that allow us to come up with a definition that sticks. Whenever a person takes a moment to consider what life is about, where life and the universe come from, why things are as they are, and whether there is some driving force or direction to life and the universe... that person is being spiritual. That use of conscious thought to consider those intangible things is spirituality. Whenever someone looks for a connection with another person, or feels joined with the world, that person is being spiritual.

When I found myself in the situation where I had a "spiritual illness" and the way out was a "spiritual cure" I didn't understand at all what that meant. As a doctor I understood physical illness and mental illness, but I had no idea what these people were referring to when they spoke of a spiritual illness. Like many other people, I believed that spirituality and religion were the same thing, but there was nothing religious about what these people were talking about. However, even though I didn't understand it, it worked for me. After everything else had failed, I was no longer drinking or using drugs, and I was finding peace of mind and happiness for the first time in my adult life. Whatever this "spiritual cure" was, it was working for me when all else had failed. It opened my mind to the idea of spirituality, and it made me want to know more about it.

Once my head cleared from all my chemical misadventures, the scientist in me needed to find out what this "spiritual cure" was all about, and how it could be so powerful. So began my typically obsessive search through the scientific literature, the psychology journals, the popular media, and anything else I could find about what, exactly, spirituality is. I dug through religious writings and talked with people of religion. I even signed up for yoga. I read through essays from philosophers from history – Aristotle, Aquinas, Kant, Nietzsche – as well as some 20th century

92

philosophers. In the end, I came up with a definition of spirituality that made sense to me, and was consistent with what I had seen in my search and my own experience (and I learned to hold a pretty good downward-facing dog). I have run it by a couple of hundred people who are experienced with spirituality, and every one of them was supportive of my definition. Here it is:

> Spirituality is the connections that we make outside of ourselves. These connections can occur on three levels: 1) connections with other people, 2) connections with the world around us, and 3) for some people, connection with a higher power.

In order to illustrate this definition, let's take a look at my addiction and how I was able to overcome it. I was addicted to alcohol and drugs. It progressed to the point where I had pushed away all my friends, family, and colleagues. I just wanted to be left alone to my drinking and using. I stopped going to work. I isolated myself at home with the blinds shut, not answering the door, and ignoring my phone. For me a good day was being alone, shut out from the world, and entirely focused on drinking and using. Accomplishing nothing and talking to no one. Passing out and coming to on no particular schedule. I just drank and used drugs until I passed out. When I came to I repeated the process. I had no idea what time of day it was, and I didn't care. If it was 5 o'clock, I wouldn't know if it was 5 a.m. or 5 p.m., and I really didn't care. I wanted to be left alone, and I had no interest whatsoever in what was happening in the world outside of my house. If that sounds far-fetched, believe me, that's how people with substance addictions usually end up. I was sick on the first two levels of spirituality: I had no connections with other people, and I had no connections with the outside world. I pushed those things away, and I was glad to see them go. I just wanted to be left alone to my drink and drugs, at home with the blinds closed, in my own world.

I was also sick on the third level of spirituality: connection with a higher power. I was raised Christian, and I always believed in God and had a meaningful connection with God. I had not practiced formal religion for many years, but I nevertheless prayed and considered myself close with God. However, I was so angry about the disaster that my life had become that I blamed God: *I'm a decent person, I help others, so why is this happening to me? Why is my life such a disaster? What did I do to deserve this???* I was angry at God for my situation, and I blamed God for picking on me. I was no longer praying, and I rejected God for making me so miserable. My spirituality on the third level – connection with a higher power – was now zero. I was definitely spiritually sick on all three levels.

Addiction makes people sick physically, mentally, socially, and – as I have just explained – spiritually. However, there is no physical cure, and there is no mental cure. The cure for addiction must be spiritual, and that was how I found my way out of addiction. As I worked my way through the 12 Steps, my spiritual connections came back. My connections with other people healed and were healthier and more fulfilling than they had ever been, even before the drugs and alcohol. My connection with the world around me came back, as I took a renewed interest in my work and my hobbies, I began taking morning walks and enjoying nature and the fresh air, and I took an interest in the news and what was going on around me. I once again cared whether it was 5 a.m. or 5 p.m. And I developed a new understanding and connection with a higher power that made sense to me. This effect was so powerful that the obsession and physiological need to drink and use drugs simply fell away. Becoming spiritual did much more for me than just helping me to leave the drugs and alcohol behind; it gave me a peace of mind, serenity, and happiness that I had never previously known. My freedom from substance addiction and its miserable shadow came from spiritual health.

*

So, according to the above definition, spirituality is about transcendence – a connection with things outside of ourselves. Finding meaning and purpose in life, connectedness, inner strength, and self-transcendence are important components of spirituality. Small wonder that spirituality is the ideal antidote to addiction-alcoholism, a condition characterized by selfishness, turning inside ourselves, isolation, loneliness, and self-focus. The quality of these transcendent connections is what determines our spiritual health and, as we will see as we progress through the Steps, determine the powerful effects of our spirituality on our health, happiness, and release from the obsession with drugs and drink. Spiritual health has been shown by medical and psychological studies to be a substantial component of overall health and well-being.[10,11,12,13]

When we form connections with other people, these connections are not necessarily spiritually healthy. For example, people with antisocial personality disorder are very personable, interactive, and tend to know a lot of people. They are social schmoozers (contrary to popular belief, people with anti-social personality disorder do not avoid social contact – quite the opposite). However, they have a pathological fixation on cultivating interpersonal relationships for the sole reason of personal gain. If they can't manipulate or use someone to their own gain, then they have no interest in any connections. While they are socially interactive and make many connections outside themselves, the quality of their interpersonal

94

relationships is based on selfishness, greed, and covetousness. They are pathologically lacking in empathy or love. The spiritual quality of these connections outside themselves is less than zero; they are negative. That is people with antisocial personality disorder; funny how it sounds a lot like the connections we make with other people while we are in active addiction-alcoholism, isn't it? One of the salubrious effects of the Steps is that they help us to become people who make quality spiritual connections with others, a refreshing change to our antisocial behaviors while in active addiction. As you change with each Step, people around you will be blown away by the new you. Stay the course – it's worth it.

*

As we will see as we advance through the Steps together, spirituality is the antithesis of negative psychology. As we unload ourselves of the mental carnage that led to our substance addiction and also resulted from it, the dark emotions and feelings will begin to melt away. As we develop our spiritual health we purge ourselves of those dark aspects of human nature that make our psychology negative. Many of us have lived with such pain for so long that we've become used to it, but what a relief it is to finally break through the clouds.

It's a shared notion among experts and laypersons alike that spirituality moves us toward self-affirmation, positive character strengths, connectedness, hope, confidence, love, and a sense of wholeness. Life no longer seems to be a struggle against a seemingly cruel world, but just life; we stop swimming upstream against the current and instead go with the flow of life. We stop seeing life's difficulties as sources of mental distress and anxiety but rather as the challenges of everyday life. They are just the stuff of life, not evidence that deities and the world are out to get us. Spirituality, happiness, recovery, and positive psychology are strongly connected.

The secret to happiness – the quest of all the ages – is not a life that's devoid of problems. No, because no such life exists. Rather, the secret to happiness is a spiritual approach to life that endows us with resilience and hardiness to life's ups and downs, and a peace of mind that we are so grateful for that we are unwilling to yield it to any person or thing. We move from *I can't drink or use* to *I won't drink or use*, because we are unwilling to sacrifice our peace of mind and happiness to the gods of our addiction.

The nature of the 12 Step spiritual approach to recovery works – and has been widely adopted by addictions treatment professionals – because it emphasizes achieving positive experiences and changes rather than focusing on bad, dysfunctional, and psychologically painful behaviors.[14] Therefore, recovery is not about focusing on stopping compulsive behaviors

– a challenge that requires raw willpower that few can sustain – but instead focuses on moving to a positive adaptation to life.[15] It's all about perspective and attitude – i.e. positive psychology – and learning and adopting the behaviors and thought processes that we need to achieve that invigorating mind-set.

The very nature of positive psychology makes it a snug fit with spirituality. The field of positive psychology arose from a feeling among psychologists that perhaps psychology should shift its focus from what makes people unwell, to a focus on learning what makes people thrive and flourish.[16] Positive psychology is, therefore, the science of happiness, of well-being. Like the medical field in its shift away from defining health as the absence of disease, psychologists recognized that there's more to mental well-being than simply the absence of mental illness.

The resulting shift in research became what we now know of as positive psychology, and it quickly became the focus of psychotherapy. Likewise, spirituality is a shift from an inner focus and a feeling of being on the defensive against everything outside of ourselves and a disproportionate focus on our problems, to an attitude of acceptance, gratitude, and a realistic view of life and the world as something that will not always be favorable to us, but that life and everything in it is to be relished and enjoyed. Positive psychology and spirituality involve a life-changing shift in perspective. The very same person in the very same situation can have a complete change in quality of life and well-being simply by the shift in perspective that's brought on by positive psychology based in spiritual health.

Science has put this purported association between spirituality and positive psychology to the test. A huge study that looked at the relationship between spirituality and positive psychology found such a close connection between the two that the study authors concluded that spirituality may be considered to be foundational to positive psychology traits.[17] Similarly, numerous studies have provided ample evidence that people who are high in spirituality are also high in measures of positive psychology.[18] Another large study with almost 4,000 participants further examined the relationship between spirituality and positive psychology, and concluded that: "personal spirituality and positive psychology traits continue to go hand in hand."[19,20] The overwhelming evidence is that positive psychology is the end result of spiritual health.

The field of psychotherapy rapidly embraced positive psychology, as an obvious optimal goal for therapy was to move a patient from a negative, pathological frame of mind to a positive frame of mind. After all, people without addiction seek psychotherapy because they want to be happier, deal with problems better, find greater life satisfaction, improve their self-esteem, and reduce the stress that they feel from the outside world.

96

Addictions therapists quickly seized on the same process.[21] Of course, the 12 Step program has been taking precisely this approach since long before the advent of the discipline of positive psychology, so we are now seeing addictions treatment – even that which is not 12 Step-based – coming increasingly in line with the 12 Step process. Of course, in the presence of mental illness, proper medical care is also vitally important in the process of becoming well.

Spirituality can best be characterized by psychological growth, mindful consciousness, and emotional maturation. Spirituality entails the capacity to see life as it is – including the good and the bad – and to love life nonetheless. Happiness no longer depends on whether or not things are going our way; rather we learn the happiness of a soul that is lifted above every circumstance. We accept and embrace life on life's terms.

This spirituality, these connections outside ourselves, are an essential psychological need; this has been established by foundational psychologists like Carl Jung, Otto Rand, Abraham Maslow, and Rollo May, among others. Spirituality fulfills this primal human need, and the pursuit of spirituality pushes us outside of ourselves to optimize these fulfilling connections. Wondering how to do that? Stay tuned, because that spiritual growth is the result of these Steps.

As you will see as we progress through the Steps, spirituality accomplishes what positive psychology interventions endeavor to do: increasing positive feelings, positive behaviors, and a positive approach to life.

*

There have been substantial studies into A.A. members' scores of positive psychology that have confirmed the effect of the 12 Step program on their mental well-being.[22] These studies have provided objective evidence that spirituality and its associated improvements in quality of life are strong predictors of successful and sustained recovery from addiction-alcoholism.[23,24] The data from these studies demonstrate that A.A. affiliation is substantively associated with optimism, gratitude, a feeling of purpose in life, and spirituality. In fact, the positive psychology scores of the A.A. members were *significantly higher* than those found in comparison groups of healthy, successful people. This is especially significant when you take into account the fact that the starting point for these A.A. members, when they first came to A.A. as drunks and addicts, was dismal. In other words, the 12 Step program transformed them from about the most negative psychology that can be found anywhere – that of the miserable alcoholic-addict in active substance use – and transformed them to a state of positive psychology well above that seen in healthy, high-functioning, non-addict-alcoholic controls. It must be noted though, that these were not people who simply occupied a chair at meetings with one foot in the program and one foot out. Rather, all the study subjects fully embraced the program – both feet in – and had worked the Steps, and actively practiced the principles of the program in their daily lives. We will learn these principles as we conquer each Step.

Further research from the behavioral sciences has demonstrated that being too self-focused is harmful to our emotional and physical health.[25] In psychological terms, this inward focus is referred to as *self-focused attention*, the same selfishness and self-focus that we seek to eliminate with our efforts at spiritual health. As we become more self-focused, personality and behavioral pathologies (sicknesses) begin to emerge. Most notably, these pathologies that are brought on by excessive self-focus include depression, anxiety, substance use, suicide, and social isolation.[26] As such, the research confirms what the 12 Step program established decades prior as a major cause of alcoholism-addiction: a selfish inward focus, which is the exact opposite of spirituality.

Further, other clinical investigations have demonstrated that by taking steps to reduce self-focus – exactly what we are doing by taking care of our spiritual health – these adverse conditions are reduced and our overall well-being is improved.[27] This validates the entire process of the 12 Steps, which are focused on getting us outside ourselves, stopping our self-destructive excessive inner-focus, and developing spiritual health and a positive psychology. Let's look at the three levels of connections outside ourselves that constitute spirituality, starting with our connections with other people.

Quality connections outside ourselves require quality interpersonal skills, and these will only come through selfless motivations. As long as we remain self-focused, our interpersonal skills will be dreadful and spiritually worthless. As we will see in Steps Four through Nine, people in active addiction-addiction are ruled by character defects that bring out the worst self-centered behaviors, destroying any chance of truly meaningful connections with others. That's why codependent relationships are so exceedingly common among people in addictions. We become so focused on our drinking or using that we fail to see that to others we have a forbidding disposition. As we journey through the Steps and grow in positive psychology and spirituality, we see that the more that our motivations for our interpersonal connections move from visceral self-serving to connection-based outside ourselves, the greater the quality of our connections with other people and therefore the greater the spiritual value of these connections. As such, empathy, compassion, and communion with others produce greater spiritual value and form an important part of our recovery. Our connections outside ourselves move from selfish to

98

meaningful. The resulting quality connections with others become a priceless source of strength and fulfillment.

In order to achieve spiritually quality connections with others, we must recognize and strive to eliminate some of the character defects that are part of human nature: selfishness, jealousy, impatience, being judgmental, anger, resentment, and so on. It's not hard to imagine how these unlovely character traits can interfere with our ability to make quality connections with others. If we promote and nurture some of our positive character traits (such as love, understanding, selflessness, patience, tolerance, and generosity), we will have spiritually positive connections with others. These are precisely the interpersonal virtues that become instilled in us as we wind our way through the Steps and grow in spiritual well-being.

The Big Book cautions us that our pursuit of spiritual maturity is not a form of superiority, or a catch-all excuse that puts us above our more earthly responsibilities. Rather, the Big Book is emphatic that those of us with spirituality must not talk down to those still spiritually sick as if: "from any moral or spiritual hilltop" (p. 95). Similarly, alcoholic-addicts who are new to the ways of spiritual connectedness are warned against "spiritual intoxication" (p. 128). "Many alcoholics are enthusiasts. They run to extremes" (page 125). We are so enthralled by our new life and our – perhaps first ever – meaningful spiritual connections that it's easy to be so overwhelmed by the experience as to wrongfully shut out people and things that deserve our attention and understanding after all we have put them through. These are described as "vagaries of... spiritual infancy," and a "phase of development" (p. 129). The individual may use "spiritual justification" for retreating further inside him or herself, or by ignoring family obligations. The 12 Step program treats spirituality like a loaded gun, which must be used properly when first picked up by the uninitiated. For someone to go from the depths of spiritual sickness to sudden spiritual awareness can be heady stuff. We are warned to "...keep our heads in the clouds with Him [our higher power], but that our feet ought to be firmly planted on earth" (Big Book, p. 130). We must beware of flying off on a "spiritual tangent."

*

When it comes to the second level of spiritual connection, we may wonder: *how can we connect with the world?* Well, when I walk outside – sober – in the beautiful weather and I look around at nature I feel overwhelmed by a connection to it. I'm amazed by its beauty, I find the fresh air to be as good for the mind and spirit as it is for the body. I appreciate it, and it makes me feel good. When I gaze up at the stars on a beautiful night,

I'm amazed at the hugeness of the universe, the beauty and majesty of it, the comforting consistency of the march of the planets. I somehow feel right in my place. These are things that I never noticed or enjoyed while I was drinking and using, and they are examples of connecting with the world around us. I only feel these connections because I have the presence of mind to be mindful of these things as part of my spiritual growth.

Perhaps more to the point, connecting with the world also involves taking an interest in what's going on around us. Taking an active interest in our job, current events, what's going on at the kids' school, and generally being an engaged part of what's going on around us. These are things that we became detached from while we were actively drinking or using; many of us got to the point where we were completely divorced from the world around us. Our drug or alcohol use was our way of hiding from the world as we self-isolated, and we ended up physically hiding from the world as well. We felt the world was unkind to us, and we wanted no part of it.

Part of our spiritual connection with the world around us means understanding it, so that it makes some kind of sense to us. That means looking at the stars and the universe, looking at the world and all the things that occur in it, and making sense of it within the context of our spiritual understanding. Our spirituality must be consistent with what we observe or it will not be meaningful to us. That's part of the journey of spirituality: finding some way to make sense of the universe, the cosmos, and our world, as chaotic and nonsensical as it all may seem.

An important thing about spirituality is that our own spirituality must fit with and make sense of the world as we know it. Rather than being told the meaning of life and the truths of the world, spirituality allows us to discover it for ourselves. Some people reject religion because they find that it doesn't explain their world, or is inconsistent with what they see. For example, some people may ask: *if God is loving, beneficent, and all-powerful, then why is there so much evil and suffering in the world?* Some people may find an answer for such questions that makes sense for them, while others struggle with it. As well, religions may prescribe beliefs or practices that oppose some people's convictions, no matter how hard they try to change their convictions to match their religion. For example, some people may be convinced "pro-choice" advocates, but may belong to a religion that is staunchly "pro-life," and experience considerable inner conflict over the dissonance between their religion and their personal beliefs. Our spiritual journey involves finding meaning that is consistent with what we see and believe.

Religion tends to prescribe specific beliefs and practices that are meant as a spiritual connection, but the spirituality we seek is open-ended, up to each individual to search out and find, and is focused more on personal experiences, personal values, and connectedness for determining its parameters. As an academic and an individual who is very spiritual, I find any doctrinal approach to spirituality to be most unfortunate. While I respect anyone's beliefs as long as they are not harmful to others, I have found a personal discovery of spirituality and meaning to be most fulfilling. I find the prescriptive approach, where we are told how and what to believe and how to go about it, to stymie my own discovery. It may be that an open-ended self-discovery approach to spirituality is more therapeutic for addiction-alcoholism than is a prescriptive approach; while spirituality has been shown to be protective against alcohol and drug use, and to promote recovery from addiction-alcoholism, religion itself has not.[28]

Religion evokes adjectives such as institutional, formal, doctrinal, and even authoritarian. Spirituality has broader parameters, involving a very personal and emotional search for a sense of meaning and purpose, concepts and images of a higher power, and an understanding of why the world is the way it is and how things work. Spirituality has less to do with the worship of God and more to do with our perceived relationship and understanding of those forces considered higher than ourselves. However, we must be careful to not place too much emphasis on the separation of religion and spiritualty; to dismiss religion as inflexible and dogmatic while spirituality is considered freeing and enlightening does a disservice to both ideals. Religion and spirituality contain overarching frameworks that intertwine them. Both are considered means by which human beings strive to understand the universe and to transcend their daily lives.[29] People who find spirituality that makes sense to them within the community of religion should continue to do so, and be grateful for it.

If our spiritual understandings of the world don't match what we observe in the world, then our spirituality will not make sense to us and should be further explored. Psychologists – and common sense – tell us that our spirituality won't make sense to us if there is incongruity between what we see and what we believe.[30] For example, let's use a deck of playing cards to illustrate. Our understanding and belief about a deck of cards is that there are 52 cards, 4 suits, 2 colors, and aces, numbers 2 through 10, and jack, queen and king cards. If we pulled a card out of the deck that was a red 17 of spades it would be incongruent with our belief system about cards, so our belief system wouldn't be able to explain the card and it would turn our belief system on end. So it is with our spiritual beliefs. If our spiritual understanding of the world and a higher power aren't congruent with what we see in the world, then neither what we see nor our belief system will make sense to us. Anyone who is in that situation needs some spiritual discovery.

Not all people have a connection with a higher power as part of their spirituality, but this kind of transcendental connection is a very powerful and rewarding one, so I encourage all to be open-minded about it. We will discuss the science and spirituality of the higher power concept in our Step Three discussion, so I will only say a few things about it here. A higher power that is part of spirituality is not necessarily God, or if it is it's not necessarily God as defined by a specific religion. Many people accept that there is some kind of power in the universe that is behind the immutable laws of the universe, but don't know exactly what that power is, and don't try to define it. Science, too, is quickly coming to realize and accept that there is some kind of a higher power, but doesn't define that power. The discussion around the scientific community's rapidly increasing acceptance of the existence of some kind of a "higher power" is fascinating, but I will defer that discussion to our Step Three study. For those who don't have a ready-made understanding of a higher power, the higher power connection is less about figuring out what a higher power is than it is about acknowledging that *I am not the most powerful thing in the universe.* For those who do believe in God, their spiritual journey may include some changing or evolving of their understanding of and relationship with God.

*

One thing that vexes me is when I hear people reject spirituality because they "believe in science." Let's make one thing clear: spirituality is completely and totally compatible with science. I have three university science degrees, including at the doctoral level, and I take great offense when people poo-poo on spirituality because they "believe in science." I live, eat, and breathe science, and I make my living at it. If I wasn't such a spiritual person, I'd get really, really pissed every time I heard that. As one research scientist puts it: "science and spirituality have an evolving relationship, symmetry, and harmony."[31]

Let's see what some scientists of repute have to say about the matter. Carl Sagan (astrophysicist): "science is not only compatible with spirituality; it is a profound source of spirituality."[32] Neil DeGrasse Tyson (astrophysicist): "we are all connected; to each other, biologically. To the earth, chemically. To the rest of the universe atomically."[33] He feels a connection to the world and universe that is very profound. I like that. (Mind you, Neil DeGrasse Tyson is the same dude who made the profound observation that the Hubble Space telescope looks exactly like the NHL's Stanley Cup, which it kind of does.) Albert Einstein: "science without religion is lame. Religion without science is blind,"[34] "every one who is seriously involved in the pursuit of science becomes convinced that a spirit is manifest in the laws of the Universe – a spirit vastly superior to that of man, and one in the face of which we with our modest powers must feel humble,"[35] and "my religion consists of a humble admiration of the illimitable superior spirit who reveals himself in the slight details we are

102

able to perceive with our frail and feeble mind."[36] Theoretical physicist Stephen Hawking shows us that science and spirituality are not so different: "ever since the dawn of civilization, people have not been content to see events as unconnected and inexplicable. They have craved an understanding of the underlying order in the world. Today we still yearn to know why we are here and where we came from. Humanity's deepest desire for knowledge is justification enough for our continuing quest."[37] In fact, science and spirituality share a common focus: both endeavor to make sense of the world around us, including the universe.

The nature of science's derision for anything spiritual dates back to the days of Hippocrates in ancient Greece, as we have already discussed, where magic and religion first became replaced by empirical knowledge (i.e. facts based on observation and experimentation rather than by legend or mythology) as the primary driver of knowledge of how things work. "Science" became very protective of its territory and very defensive, endeavoring to separate itself jealously from "non-science" and, for centuries, spirituality was considered to be part of that obsolete pre-modern non-science. As one historian puts it: "figuratively speaking, the adolescent science, an heir to the Enlightenment, had to cut the umbilical cord to theology (and religion and spirituality) in order to become adult."[38] This is especially because of the prevalent belief that spirituality and religion are the same thing, a belief that remains widely held today. However, time has proven that this is not so. Science has admitted spirituality into the fold, and numerous studies are being conducted measuring the effects of spirituality on physical and mental health and disease. These studies are of similar design to studies of new medications and surgical procedures. As we have discussed, the current science-based approach to healthcare (the biopsychosocial model) includes treating the spiritual causes and effects of disease.

Science is simply a method of inquiry based on empirical observation, and the considerable effects of spirituality on disease and health are being observed and measured in proper clinical studies. So it is that these empirical observations of the effects of spirituality definitely have brought spirituality well into the realm of science.

*

Science cannot explain spirituality. We know that our brain is a collection of interconnected nerve cells (*neurons*), not unlike computer circuitry, but the brain is somehow much more than a sum of its parts and their connections. Somewhere in there a consciousness, emotion, creativity, and sentience are produced, and science has no idea where or how that seeming miracle occurs. Likewise, spirituality, which is based in emotion,

103

thought, consciousness, and a need for connection is not yet understood by science. Perhaps it will, one day, but as yet there is no understanding of how a collection of brain cells can have life, and think, and be capable of the abstract. However, because science cannot explain our consciousness and ability to think, plan, feel, and understand does not mean that those things don't exist, obviously. So it is with spirituality and its effects on our health.

Science cannot explain what exactly makes something alive. We can't take something that is dead and make it live. Likewise, we can't replicate biological tissue and then give it life. There is something – some essence – that gives life, and we humans have no idea what that is, and we definitely have no power over it. Likewise, science cannot replicate consciousness and cognition (the ability to think, plan, be creative, and feel). Even artificial intelligence, for all the hype, isn't even close to creating artificial circuits that are alive, or capable of creativity, anticipation, emotion, or compassion. There is something innate to the living brain, that most extraordinary of machines, that cannot be captured by computer circuits and algorithmic programming; the human mind is truly a phenomenon, in the true definition of the term: something unique and non-reproducible. Spirituality lies in the human mind, wherein it finds its power over the body, well out of the reach of present-day science.

The fact that we can't see spirituality and hold it in our hands doesn't mean that spirituality can't be studied by science. I have a degree in chemistry, and my entire four years of study in chemistry was based on the atomic theory of chemistry, which is the theory that all things are made of atoms that bond together and that we can change matter by changing the bonds between atoms. However, I (or anybody else) have never seen an atom. But no one would argue that chemistry is not a science because we cannot visually verify the existence of the atom, the very basis of the science of chemistry. However, science accepts atomic theory because we can measure the effects of the unseen atom in scientific experiments. Likewise, we cannot see spirituality, but we can – and do – measure its effects in scientific study.

So, why does the human brain need connections with others? Why do we need to connect with the world? Why do we wonder about a higher power or where we fit into the universe? Why do we need connections with a higher power, something greater than ourselves? And why are these things so important for our health and well-being? Well, fortunately we don't need an explanation from science to be able to enjoy and benefit from those things.

I can illustrate the point by recounting the experience of a physicist, who: "always held a purely scientific view of the world. By that, I mean that the Universe is made of material and nothing more, that the Universe is governed exclusively by a small number of fundamental forces and laws, and that all composite things in the material world, including humans and stars, eventually disintegrate and return to their component parts."[39] This scientist's views on science and the world changed one night after he inadvertently connected with his own spirituality. Our physicist was out on his boat one moonless but starry night, and, on a whim, he turned out all the lights on his boat and lay down and looked up. He was surprised by his first spiritual experience, or, as he called it, transcendental experience:

> After a few minutes, my world had dissolved into that star littered sky. The boat disappeared. My body disappeared. And I found myself falling into infinity. A feeling came over me. I felt an overwhelming connection to the stars, as if I were part of them. And the vast expanse of time – extending from the far distant past long before I was born and then into the far distant future long after I would die – seemed compressed to a dot. I felt connected not only to the stars but also to all of nature, and to the entire cosmos. I felt a merging with something far larger than myself, a grand and eternal unity.[40]

Ever since his experience, he "understood the powerful allure of the spiritual world, the nonmaterial and the ethereal, things that are all-encompassing, unchangeable, eternal, sacred."[41] However, he remained committed to the physical world, and to his life and career as a PhD physicist. He did not see the two worlds – his hard science world and his newfound spiritual awareness – as in any way incompatible. And, he notes, science cannot refute or disprove his spirituality:

> It was an extremely personal experience, and no one could refute the authority and validity of that experience. Furthermore, that experience is not easily analyzable by science. You could hook up all hundred billion of my neurons to a giant computer and read out all the electrical and chemical data during that experience, and you would not have come close to understanding the experience in the way that you can understand the reason why the sky is blue or the orbits of planets. It is the sum of such experiences that constitutes my spiritual universe.[42]

Our newly spiritual scientist offers an insightful take on reconciling science and spirituality:

> I would suggest that the contrast between the materiality of the physical world and the immateriality of the spiritual world goes deeper than religion and science, into the dualism and complexity of human existence. We are idealists and we are realists. We are

105

dreamers and we are builders. We are experiencers and we are experimenters. We long for certainties, yet we ourselves are full of the ambiguities of the *Mona Lisa* and the *I Ching*. Our yearning for the unprovable ethereals of the spiritual world and, at the same time, our commitment to the physical world reflects a necessary tension in how we relate to the cosmos and relate to ourselves. I have gone on that fraught journey myself. It is a winding and difficult path, with boundaries sometimes in clear view and sometimes dissolving into the mist. It is a journey sometimes of contradictions. It is part of being human.[43]

Fellow physicist Carl Sagan agrees: "When we recognize our place in an immensity of light-years and in the passage of ages, when we grasp the intricacy, beauty, and subtlety of life, then that soaring feeling, that sense of elation and humility combined, is surely spiritual. So are our emotions in the presence of great art or music or literature, or acts of exemplary selfless courage such as those of Mahatma Gandhi or Martin Luther King, Jr. The notion that science and spirituality are somehow mutually exclusive does a disservice to both."[44]

I dare anyone to try to tell these accomplished scientists that spirituality should be rejected by anyone who "believes in science."

*

We alcoholic-addicts are ripe for spirituality. A peculiar aspect of spirituality is that spirituality and spiritual awareness seem to follow significant life experiences, especially traumatic life experiences.[45] In fact, some researchers posit that the degree of spirituality that people may attain is limited by the amount of traumatic experiences that they have had in their life.[46] In other words, the more traumatic our recent life experiences the greater our capacity for accepting and understanding spirituality, and the greater the healing power these things will have for us. If your experience with addiction-alcoholism was anything like mine, it was deeply traumatic. This observation has not been limited to empirical science. Genius novelist Daphne du Maurier, known for her literary examinations of mood and emotion, observed "I believe there is a theory that men and women emerge finer and stronger after suffering, and that to advance in this or any world we must endure ordeal by fire."[47] We alcoholic-addicts have certainly endured an "ordeal by fire," and we are therefore ripe to benefit from it by "emerging stronger and finer" with a greater capacity for spirituality.

Trauma and facing death force us to examine – often for the very first time – our mortality, our views about meaning and purpose in life, and our

106

connections outside ourselves. For many people, such experiences propel them to think about or re-examine their understanding of a higher power.[48] Most trauma survivors and people who have faced death embark on a quest for spiritual understanding and connection, and the search can be a potent tool for dealing with the experience.[49] Thus, trauma may directly serve as a stimulus for spiritual growth that may not otherwise occur. This is why you may hear people in the fellowship describe themselves as a "grateful alcoholic or addict;" they are grateful because without the traumatic experience of active addiction-alcoholism they may never have found the peace and serenity of spiritual health.

The 12 Step program also acknowledges the value of serious trauma in making people suddenly open to spiritual awareness. The Big Book says that if we weren't so broken we might never have been open to spirituality: "faced with alcoholic destruction, we soon became as open minded on spiritual matters as we had tried to be on other questions. In this respect alcohol was a great persuader. It finally beat us into a state of reasonableness" (p. 48). The great persuader, indeed!

When people try to recover from a traumatic event or face death, they have a sudden need to understand the experience. We often go through life taking our life and safety for granted... terrible things happen to other people, not to us. Then an awful experience – such as enduring addiction-alcoholism – forces us to confront uncertainty and instability that threaten our existence. Our complacent sense of security in the world is challenged, even shattered. Our pre-existing beliefs in concepts such as identity, responsibility, justice, guilt, suffering, and forgiveness may be overturned. It makes us re-examine our sense of self, our relationships with others, and our concept of spirituality. Things that were once taken for granted in our hurried lives now come to the forefront of our thoughts. Ideas of spirituality comfort us, return our sense of security and order.

In a world of on-demand television, portable devices, a 24-hour news cycle, and social media there's little emphasis on things spiritual. For many of us life passes by without us casting a thought to spirituality, which is why most people don't understand it. Our world is filled with things designed to help us switch off our brains: Netflix, YouTube, social media, Internet surfing; I call it low-effort or no-effort thinking. However, when we do take the time to explore and understand spirituality it takes us beyond ordinary daily experience and affects our lives and relationships. It causes us to see things from a different perspective and changes our thoughts and behaviors. We end up – for some of us for the very first time – adopting higher values, inner freedom, and things that give life meaning that trump our previous values of material success, ego-boosting achievement, and accumulation of material wealth. It adds a priceless level of quality to life with a very low price tag. It seems that tragedy, trauma, or coming face to face with death hasten a person's thoughts toward things transcendental. Suddenly things that previously went by the wayside have now become important.

In my own case, my spirituality definitely followed a deeply traumatic experience: my addiction, which wrecked my life for four years, and nearly took my life. I became deeply spiritual in order to escape the addiction, and – liking what I saw – further explored it afterwards, as I grew in my sobriety. Prior to that, I was somewhat religious, although not participating in organized religion, but I had no awareness of spirituality. I valued relationships with others but I was still inner-focused. I am deeply spiritual now, thanks to the awareness of spirituality following my traumatic experience. For me spirituality was and is a life and death necessity. I am sure that if I ever let go of my spiritual way of living that my cascade of character defects, my poor ability to handle life's highs and lows and the other reasons behind my addiction will resurface before too long. As they say, my addiction is waiting for me out in the parking lot doing push-ups. The one thing that lies between me and my next drink or drug is my spiritual health.

So, trauma is a catalyst for spirituality. It's the silver lining to our suffering, and it would be an opportunity squandered to fail to embrace the gift of spiritual wellness by a heartfelt trip through the 12 Steps. Step Two is the introduction of spirituality into our recovery.

*

Spirituality is not an unnatural thing for us, not at all. Humans are spiritual beings.[50,51] Spirituality is a part of us; it's literally in our genes, our DNA. Humankind's search for spiritual meaning is ancient, with evidence of its importance being present in the anthropological record as far back as humankind itself.[52,53] It wasn't a cultural thing, because different cultures in different parts of the ancient world have left evidence of their search for meaning and spiritual connections without ever having had any contact with each other.[54] This curiosity, this need to find meaningful connections beyond ourselves is therefore in our very genetic make-up, and is part of our very nature. People are searching for peace, meaningful lives, and connections. French philosopher Pierre de Chardin said that: "we are not human beings having a spiritual experience; we are spiritual beings having a human experience."[55]

Humans are spiritual beings, and cues for spirituality are built right into our genes. To wit, we actually need spirituality to develop and thrive. Humans rely on interaction with others, and we cannot properly develop without it. Interpersonal interaction is critical for the survival and development of babies.[56] Infants are born to learn, but their developing brain circuits rely entirely on input from social interactions.[57] Humans are

108

born with the ability to recognize and understand facial expressions, and this forms the first basis of their understanding of human interaction. In fact, lacking the ability to recognize faces at birth may be behind the poor social function of autistic individuals. Our brain's higher functions (cognition) will not develop properly or even at all without this interaction. Interactions with people and things outside ourselves are a primal human need, not just a nicety.

Our ancient ancestors were only able to survive by banding together. They needed each other for protection, food gathering, hunting, and for propagating (i.e. breeding). Those who formed close connections with others were more likely to survive, especially when faced with adversity or danger. Nowadays, that need for connection continues in our present day selves, deeply embedded in our DNA and our most basic instincts. Connection with others makes us feel empowered and less anxious. Connection, especially transcendent connection (i.e. to something larger than ourselves), is an antidote to stress and hardship.[58] If you ever observe people who are have just experienced a traumatic event, they are hugging each other and (those who have a higher power connection) praying or seeking transcendent spiritual connection; they sense that they need connection to feel better and to not feel anxious or out of control. It's part of our survival instinct to seek connection and to want to attach when we feel stress or danger.

Humans have always been tribal creatures, surviving by hunting and protecting each other from danger, and we were never meant to be alone. This instinct remains, so that when we feel isolated our anxiety goes up and we feel more vulnerable to danger.[59] The alarms start going off in our brain when we feel isolated.[60] Certainly, we don't feel comfortable, at ease, or well. Humans were especially not meant to be alone under hardship.[61] Stress and adversity are much easier to cope with when we are not isolated.[62] Addiction-alcoholism is ultimately a problem of dysfunctional coping, trying to cope with an increasingly out of control, unmanageable life. Unfortunately, self-isolation and social dysfunction are distinct symptoms of addiction-alcoholism, further cutting our ties with people and things outside ourselves. This runs counter to our natural primal need for connections and provides an additional layer of psychological stress. We need to re-establish meaningful connections outside ourselves to break the cycle of addiction and to heal.

The effect that interconnections with others gives us is strengthened by connection with a power greater than ourselves.[63] The higher power attachment stays with us, and we can draw on that association anytime, anywhere, even if we are alone. An awareness of this connection helps us to stay focused as we face stressful situations.[64] This helps stave off the alarms that go off in our mind when we face danger or adversity alone.[65] Feeling a bond to something larger than ourselves overrides our immediate panicky, emotional, and selfish reactions.[66] This helps us to switch from the "toddler" brain (our primitive emotional, reflexive reactions) to the "adult" brain (our advanced cognitive functions in the pre-frontal cortex), and we think and act better.[67] Connection with a higher power enhances this powerful effect that comes with connections outside ourselves. Thus, a need for spiritual ties is a deep-rooted human need, and restoring and improving these connections is of great therapeutic value when we have lost these bonds. This is what we accomplish as we progress through the Steps.

The absence of spiritual connection is a cruel thing. Social isolation is used as a form of punishment, and even torture for prisoners of war. Social isolation drives people crazy, literally. The effects of spirituality on mental and physical health are very well documented, and people who are socially connected are healthier and live longer than those who are not.[68] In fact, it was proven in the 1980s and confirmed by numerous clinical studies since, that social isolation is as bad a risk factor for physical illness and premature death as are the very worst physical risk factors: smoking, obesity, sedentary lifestyle, and high blood pressure.[69] Given that these are the things that kill the vast majority of people in the world, that makes social connectedness a pretty crucial aspect of good health and function, not just a simple nice-to-have. For people who need to escape the powerful grasp of substance addiction it's an absolute must-have.

Social isolation, loneliness, or a lack of quality, supportive, and meaningful inter-personal relationships have well known effects on brain function and mental health. For example, social isolation is associated with declining higher brain (cognitive) functions, such as planning, problem-solving, memory, learning, etc., and is associated with an increased risk of Alzheimer's disease.[70] It's also associated with depression and other mental illness.[71] Promoting social connectedness has been shown to be an effective treatment for many serious mental illnesses, such as schizophrenia.[72,73,74]

Surprisingly, social isolation affects much more than our mental health. We know that a lack of social connectedness adversely affects our hormonal and nervous systems (it creates increased sympathetic tone and hypothalamic-pituitary-adrenal activation – for you physiology nerds), and negatively impacts the immune system (decreased inflammatory control, reduced lymphocyte proliferation, higher basal cortisol, increased oxidative stress, glucocorticoid resistance, and altered glucocorticoid gene expression – again, to keep the science nerds happy).[75] As such, insufficient connectedness outside ourselves can have serious physical health consequences.

However, if you are not the type of social butterfly who can juggle hundreds of close friends, fear not! Studies have shown that the health benefits of social connectedness depend on your *perceived* social connectedness. So, if you are fulfilled with a few good friends and have quality and supportive and meaningful contact with them, your health is just as safe as it is for the social butterflies.[76] The risk for mental, cognitive, and physical problems lies with those who feel isolated and lack quality interpersonal attachments.

It has been demonstrated in experimental studies that our body is driven by physical and mental cues to seek social connection when we are isolated; again this demonstrates that we are, by our very nature, social and spiritual animals.[77] Studies have also shown that quality social connections induce the same reward system in our brain (the ventral striatum of the mesolimbic dopamine system) as do drugs of addiction, albeit to a lesser degree.[78] Of course, some people with mental illness shun social contact as part of their symptomatology (this is also a prominent symptom of addiction-alcoholism), and social inclusion has been demonstrated by a large body of experimental evidence to be a very effective therapeutic measure for all types of mental health disorders, including addiction-alcoholism.[79,80,81,82,83] Other studies have consistently shown that spirituality restored a feeling of well-being and promoted recovery from substance use and other traumas, such as homelessness, sexual abuse, and other psychological pain.[84,85,86,87] All told, there is an overwhelming body of research studies that provide ample evidence that spiritual connections with others are therapeutic for our recovery. This is especially so when we belong to a 12 Step fellowship, because it provides us with a group of people who understand and seek quality bonds and also provides a culture of recovery and spirituality that we can model and emulate.

Research from the psychological and behavioral sciences tells us that spirituality gives us four things: (1) a source of values, meaning, and purpose beyond the self, (2) a way of understanding the world around us and our place in it, (3) inner awareness, and (4) personal integration (finding an inner unity and connectedness to others, the world around us, and a higher power).[88,89,90,91,92] Spirituality is not a separate characteristic but an inseparable part of all we are and do.[93] It's there within us all the time, but our modern world with its distractions and priorities prevents many people from ever contemplating or even developing an awareness of its inestimable value or how to get in touch with it.

Spirituality is about working to improve and develop our connections outside of ourselves so that we can experience the rich benefits of these bonds and explore their meaningfulness for us. But this takes some commitment to personal change, and some ongoing work and self-reflection to accomplish. That's because the things inside of us that enhance spiritual contacts are often distracted and derailed by our unlovely tendencies, such as our instincts for anger, greed, and ego. As we will see in the upcoming Steps, the addicted mind is burdened with anger, resentments, and fears that bring about self-serving character defects that are absolutely toxic to any chance of quality connections on any level. If we have taken on the thought processes and behaviors that are typical of addiction-alcoholism, then we have much work to do to become spiritually healthy. Fortunately, the 12 Steps provide us with a superb process for doing exactly that.

Meaningful spiritual connections on any of the three levels bring a passionate joy that – like spirituality itself – defies words. I can say from my research-based interviews with hundreds of people who have found meaningful spirituality (as well as from my own personal experience) that finding spirituality is a life-changing event. I can honestly say that since I have had a spiritual awakening (we will discuss spiritual awakenings in Step Twelve) I have known a peace and happiness such I had never previously known in my life. What's more, it has imbued me with a resilience and hardiness to all of life's stressors. My peace and serenity is so hard-won and so valuable to me that I cherish it and refuse to allow people or things to take it from me. It's been a potent tool in coping with life without running to hide behind drug or drink, as is my natural inclination.

So, when Step Two asks us to cast our faith in spirituality – and specifically a power greater than ourselves as part of that spirituality – to return us to sanity we should seriously consider it. Science strongly supports the therapeutic value of what Step Two suggests of us. Let's now look at the higher power concept, with a special focus on people who don't have a pre-existing understanding of a higher power, those who are not comfortable with the idea, and those who have an understanding of a higher power that doesn't quite fit with what they see in the world. For those who are comfortably in touch with a higher power, let's see if we can add to the quality of that attachment. We can all benefit from Step Two.

*

Now we turn our attention to the third level of spirituality – a connection with a higher power. This is the power that Step Two speaks of: "came to believe that a Power greater than ourselves could restore us to sanity." For some, this is a thorny issue and a barrier to participation in the 12 Step program. After all, the word "God" appears in the Steps, and some people don't like that. We will consider what that means for people who don't subscribe to the word "God" in our study of Step Three – the first Step that uses the word "God." However, for right now we will consider what Step Two asks of us: to consider a power greater than ourselves. What is a higher power? And what does it have to do with quitting drinking or using?

Whether a higher power concept nestles neatly with your belief system, or whether you are repulsed by the idea, including a higher power in your spirituality will make a difference in your life... if you allow it to.

112

Science has convincingly demonstrated the therapeutic effects of incorporating an acknowledgement that there is something greater than ourselves that we can connect with, and we have limitless testimonials to that effect. We will look at both – the science and the stories.

The term "higher power" was apparently coined by A.A., being first used from A.A.'s founding in the mid-1930s. While the term may be new, the concept isn't. It's also referred to by A.A. as a "power greater than ourselves." Other terms that could be used: the creative intelligence, the intelligent designer, the power of the universe, God, the supreme being, supreme intelligence, nature, life force, universal mind, spirit of nature, source of all, spirit of life. There are many more names, and the name doesn't matter. I'm sure the force behind the laws of the universe doesn't care what we call it. What matters is that it is something that we are personally comfortable with. Many people never view a higher power as some kind of an entity; rather they simply acknowledge that they are not the most powerful thing that exists. Really, through the lens of psychology, the higher power is about getting outside ourselves. One friend of mine in recovery who struggled with a debilitating addiction to alcohol and crystal meth for many years has effectively used the higher power concept as the foundation of his recovery, despite being a hardcore atheist. He has been sober for several years now, and still has no idea what a higher power is to him. He completed his Step Two by accepting that there is some kind of power outside himself that will enable him to end the insanity that ruled his life, and it worked perfectly for him. He even prays. He says a prayer and then just throws it up in the air. Even though he doesn't know where the prayer goes, he says that it really helps him. He's the perfect example of why being an atheist or not being comfortable with the higher power concept should not keep us from accomplishing Step Two. Get sober and healthy now; figure the higher power thing out later, if ever.

Psychological research has found the traditional imagery of a higher power to be detrimental for people who seek coming to an understanding of a higher power.[94] Specifically, the ego-centric and ethno-centric image of a higher power as an old Caucasian man with a long white beard flowing over his blindingly white robes as he sits on a golden throne on the clouds may not be helpful. There is no reason to believe that a universal force, a power greater than we could know, would make itself look like an elderly human. It would make sense that such an intelligence would exist in a form that is not conceivable to us, beyond our imagination, imperceptible to our limited sensory perception. Putting this unhelpful and unlikely image out of our mind may help some among us to come to terms with the concept. However, if that imagery works for you, then go for it!

I recommend to anyone who wishes to become more spiritually connected to have an open mind to a higher power. As we discussed, spirituality occurs on three levels: 1) connections with others, 2) connections with the world around us, and 3) connection with something greater than ourselves. Limiting ourselves to only two of three aspects of spirituality by closing our mind to the idea of a higher power would limit the healing power and strength of our spirituality from the outset. All that's required is to keep an open mind; there's no reason to try to figure it all out up front. As people explore their spirituality, they almost invariably come to an understanding of a higher power that fits with their world viewpoint and their belief system. This understanding may come after years of recovery; get sober now, figure out the higher power thing later.

Psychological research has demonstrated very convincingly that the involvement of a higher power concept and connection has a highly positive impact in our lives.[95] Specifically, it leads to an improved sense of well-being, better coping skills, greater acceptance of the difficulties in life, and improved mental and physical health (yes, physical health!).[96] It has even been suggested that spirituality might be THE fundamental, defining aspect of people's overall health.[97] It also leads to improved self-control, and less drug and alcohol use. One surprising finding in the research has been that surrendering our will to a higher power actually leads to a higher sense of control in our lives.[98] While this sounds paradoxical, this will not surprise a Twelve Stepper, because this effect is well known among those who are well practiced in spirituality. More on that in Step Three.

*

People may assume that a higher power means God or is only accessed through religion, and many are uncomfortable with that. After all, the word God appears not infrequently in the 12 Step literature, and we will discuss this in our Step Three study. Anyone losing out on finding sobriety in the 12 Step program based on this erroneous belief is deceived. Upon closer inspection, the Big Book is crystal clear that although the word God is often used, the higher power concept is all-inclusive and open to anybody's interpretation: a "God of our understanding." There is no right answer and no wrong answer for what a higher power is. The fact is that it doesn't matter; just going through the motions of accessing a higher power works. You can use the telephone pole outside the window as your higher power. Fortunately, there are plenty of non-God higher power concepts that make good sense, better sense than the telephone pole. We'll look at some of these shortly.

The higher power concept required for the 12 Steps is open to any interpretation of any individual. Bill Wilson, co-founder of A.A., said: "our concepts of a Higher Power and God – as we understand Him – afford everyone a nearly unlimited choice of spiritual belief and action" (A.A.

Grapevine, 1961). It certainly does not require religion, although those who practice a religious faith are fortunate in that they already have a ready-made higher power. There have been lawsuits against A.A. alleging discrimination against those who do not believe in God. There are also spin-off groups of A.A. for atheists. All this is totally unnecessary because, although the Big Book uses the word God often, it also makes it very clear that the higher power can be anything to anyone. In fact, one of the chapters in the Big Book is entitled "We Agnostics." I have seen many various – even weird and wonderful – interpretations of a higher power in my time in the 12 Step fellowship and in my research interviews, but I have never once even heard of anyone suffering ridicule or discrimination or challenge over their beliefs.

One alcoholic-addict in recovery found his higher power in his conscience: "God talked to me through my conscience." He realized that he had never listened before: "then one day I did try listening to God, and found that He had been talking to me for some time. About those checks I had cashed, knowing that they would bounce. About those rotten lies I had told. About some relationships I would not have wanted made into a movie. About the selfishness of my ways and the grievous hurt I had inflicted on my friends and relatives" (*Came to Believe,* p. 81). This seems to resonate with another recovering alcoholic, who felt that: "God – or good – emanates from within each of us" (*Came to Believe*, p. 83).

*

We alcoholic-addicts are predisposed to have a problem with the concept of a higher power. Anger and resentment are at the top of the list of what makes us drink or use, and the easiest target for this anger and resentment is God or whatever other higher power may be out there pulling our strings. *If there is a higher power, why would it do this to me?* I felt this way myself when I was drinking and drugging. I had previously always been a man of faith, but during my active addiction I became the opposite: I was resentful of God, angry at God for picking on me and making my life so miserable. How much more so, then, would someone who was not a person of faith be closed to the concept of a higher power while seething under the spell of addiction-alcoholism?

One alcoholic tells of how alcohol addiction disconnected him from his spirituality: "... with increasing dependence on the bottle and the anguish, heartache, and loneliness that went with it, there seemed to be a sharp and total decline in all spiritual beliefs and feelings" (*Came to Believe*, p. 88). One sister in recovery, raised in a family of faith, is typical of the mind-set that our disease brings out: "when I came to A.A., I was a self-ordained theist, a part-time agnostic, and a full-time antagonist – antagonistic toward everyone, everything in general, and God in particular" (*Came to Believe*, p. 24).

So, we alcoholic-addicts come hard-wired with a closed, resentful mind toward the concept of a higher power. We come to a 12 Step meeting and we're immediately turned off by the emphasis on spirituality, and repelled by the talk of "God." We are sick, hurting, angry, and afraid, and we definitely don't feel very "spiritual." Fortunately, the 12 Step program asks only for open-mindedness. Being open to the *possibility* of a higher power is all that is asked. Get sober and healthy now; figure out the higher power thing later.

Alcoholics Anonymous co-founder Bill Wilson found for himself that we don't need to have this higher power thing all figured out to move forward: "*It was only a matter of being willing to believe in a Power greater than myself. Nothing more was required of me to make my beginning.* I saw that growth could start from that point" (Big Book, p. 12). Such openness to a new idea is a great opportunity for us: "we were having trouble with personal relationships, we couldn't control our emotional natures, we were prey to misery and depression, we couldn't make a living, we had a feeling of uselessness, we were unhappy... was not a basic solution of these bedevilments more important [than our refusal to believe]?" (Big Book, p. 52). The example of people in the fellowship who have a successful recovery helps us understand: "when we saw others solve their problems by a simple reliance upon the Spirit of the Universe, we had to stop doubting the power of God. Our ideas did not work. But the God idea did" (Big Book, p. 52). Open-mindedness to the idea of a higher power is a small price to pay to partake of an effective treatment for alcoholism-addiction that has worked for so many millions of people like us.

I do some service work at a detox center, and I have seen many people come to the fellowship for help, but they are convinced that they have to figure out this whole "higher power" thing right then and there in order to take what the program offers. They sit there in full withdrawal from substance use – with minds clouded and sick – trying to figure out for themselves for the very first time what a higher power might mean to them. It would be comical if it weren't so tragic. I see them decline our help because they think they need to figure out the higher power thing first, right then and there. We need people sober now; there is time to figure out all the other stuff later. Some people in the fellowship take years to come to terms with the higher power thing, but at least they are living healthy and sober lives in the meantime. Get sober now; figure out the higher power thing later.

The Big Book says that: "God [of our understanding] could and would [help us] if He were sought" (p. 60). This search for our higher power is a long process for many of us. None of us should force the issue on our mind,

116

if our mind is not ready for it. Experience has shown that alcoholic-addicts in recovery often find their concept of a higher power in an unexpected way. Often they fall into it suddenly when they are not looking. For some, that search never ends: "I cannot say that I have found God as I understand Him, but rather that I have faith in Something which remains a mystery to me and which I continue to seek" (*Came to Believe*, p. 59). This alcoholic got sober now, and is concerning herself with figuring out the higher power thing later.

When, at some point, we stumble upon our higher power, the impact can be stirring. The woman just quoted, when she found her "faith in Something which remains a mystery to me" had a typical reaction:

> Strange things began to happen. I had thought I was happy in that first eighteen months of sobriety, but now everything began to look brighter; people seemed nicer; and I had moments of tremendous insight. It was as if words and sentences I had heard all my life had a deeper meaning and were reaching my feelings, rather than my intellect. It was as if my head and my heart finally had gotten glued together. I no longer seemed like two people in one, engaging in a tug of war. I experienced... a feeling of being totally forgiven, and never since have I felt the guilt that I had throughout my life prior to that time. More than once, I had a sense of Presence which I can only describe as being marvelously warm, uplifting, and comforting (*Came to Believe*, p. 58).

As spectacular as it sounds, this is a typical experience among 12 Steppers who find their higher power, and there are few joys in life as complete. We will look into this more in Step Twelve when we look at spiritual awakenings.

*

There's a compelling logic to keeping an open mind to new ideas that were closed to us of old. Our old ideas weren't working for us – look where they got us, time and again. As it says in *Living Sober*: "if you get on a bus bound for a town a thousand miles away, that's where you'll wind up, unless you get off and move in another direction" (p. 8). When new ideas come gift-wrapped in the assurance that they will get us where we need to be, then perhaps these new ideas deserve some consideration. Step Two requires only that we commit to keeping an open mind that there is some power out there that can get us sober. We certainly didn't have the power to do that ourselves; we are powerless over drugs and drink. Step Two asks us to take a leap of faith that there is some kind of power greater than ourselves that can end the insanity for us. It's not much of a leap of faith, either, because we can see people in the fellowship who have found a power greater than themselves that helped them overcome their powerlessness.

A connection to a higher power is a brilliant thing to have: a private companion, a reassuring presence, a focus of meditation, and a way out of our drinking or using. After suffering under the dark rule of our addiction, letting go and allowing some kind of exogenous strength to fill that emptiness is a soothing release, even if we aren't quite sure what that source of strength is. It's part of our newfound spirituality, the key to our recovery. The alcohol and drugs didn't work for us, so we have nothing to lose by trying a higher power.

One of the greatest gifts we get from engaging in the 12 Steps is self-forgiveness, something that could otherwise be very difficult to come by. We are people whose past actions have left us with a deep sense of guilt and shame, remorse, and self-loathing. Medical science knows that alcoholism-addiction is an issue of biology and not of morality, and that all those bygone actions that roil our crowded conscience fall under the umbrella of our disease's symptomatology. This is something that we, too, realize as we read the Big Book and see that our experience is far from unique or severe. However, we tend to apply society's stigma and judgmental attitudes about substance use on ourselves, and it's in our nature to be self-critical, especially in moments of reflection, and we are the person we are least likely to forgive. Self-forgiveness is hard to come by, but we can't move forward in sobriety and life without it.

Among the kindest virtues of the 12 Step program is that the fellowship sees past our disease-induced actions and sees the good person inside of us. We don't have anything to prove, we are forgiven the moment we come through the door the very first time. How could they judge us or blame us for how we have lived; they have been there themselves. By what right does the lion judge the wolf? It's well established in psychology that self-forgiveness is often only possible when we feel forgiven by others. We may not be able to find that forgiveness anywhere else than in the 12 Step circle when we first stagger out of our clouded and sullied life of addiction. This forgiveness is given freely and unconditionally. It is the milk of human kindness.

Connecting with a higher power also shows us that we are deserving of forgiveness and love. Psychological studies have shown that a feeling of forgiveness from a higher power is an especially potent predictor of our self-forgiveness.[99,100,101,102] We again feel deserving of love and forgiveness, allowing us to forgive and love ourselves again. The 12 Step program teaches us how to find that forgiveness. The first nine of the Steps are all about self-forgiveness, and to be freed from the indelicate effects of our guilt and shame and self-loathing is liberating indeed. Taking on a higher power

118

as part of our spirituality is a key part of the process of self-forgiveness; it's something worth being open-minded about.

Our loved ones will forgive us, but they don't understand us like fellow alcoholics and addicts do. They've heard us say we were getting sober so many times before that our words have become meaningless to them, and they may hurt us with their justified skepticism. However, this time we are *showing* them with our actions rather than *telling* them with words. The proof is in the pudding. When they see us going to meetings and becoming part of a fellowship of recovery, we get their attention. Actions mean something when words no longer cut it. Seeing our connection to our higher power goes a long way to helping that process along.

*

With good reason, ours is known as the lonely disease. The more our substance tightened its chains around us the more isolated we became. We used up more and more of our family and friends, and we were no longer tolerable in the workplace or social gatherings. We were just as happy to see people go from our lives; we wanted to be left alone and unharassed to our drink or drug. As depression creeped in, the tendency to avoid social contact deepened our loneliness. In recovery, we must watch for those tendencies if they try to weasel their way back into our behavior: our disease wants them to. And it can be devastating to our recovery: "thoughts of a drink seem to sneak into our minds much more smoothly and slyly when we are alone. And when we feel lonesome, and an urge for a drink strikes, it seems to have a special need and strength" (*Living Sober*, p. 36). A higher power in our life somehow gives us a warm feeling of not being alone no matter where we are. The ability to communicate with our higher power through prayer or meditation – as we will discuss in Step Eleven – further reassures us. This is a great tool to help us to keep our disease from sneaking its own diabolical tools – such as loneliness – back into our lives: "when you have used up all resources of family, friends, doctors, and ministers, there is still one source of help. It is one that never fails and never gives up, and is always available and willing" (*Came to Believe*, p. 35-36).

A certain recovering alcoholic found great comfort in the concept of a higher power:

> I have recently made a friend of Someone I wish everyone could know. This friend is never too busy to listen to me, my problems, my joys, and my sorrows. He gives me the courage to face life squarely and helps me conquer my fears. The counsel I get is always good, for this Friend is wise, patient, and tolerant. Sometimes, I do not heed

His advice, and then I must ask for and be willing to accept additional advice very humbly and sincerely.

Regardless of the mistakes I make, my Friend is always there, available to me at any time, day or night. I can talk, and He does not interrupt, no matter how I ramble on. Sometimes, while talking to Him, I receive a solution to my problem. Other times, just by putting my problems into words, I see how petty and unimportant it is. I feel as if my Friend is holding my hand and gently guiding me if I will listen. I feel that when I do not listen, my Friend is hurt, but never angry.

My friend is with me at work or at home, my constant companion wherever I go. He is my Higher Power as I understand it. He is the God I know (*Came to Believe*, p. 80).

*

There are many who came before us who have lived the same struggles with substance addiction and the higher power concept. It's a comforting thing to see that we are not alone, that we are like millions of others who came before us, including millions who recovered from our disease and lived happy and productive lives. It makes the leap of faith and open-mindedness that Step Two asks of us much easier, because we can see with our own eyes that there is indeed a power greater than these people that restored them to sanity. As one alcoholic in recovery tells us: "most emphatically we wish to say that any alcoholic capable of honestly facing his problems in the light of our experience can recover, provided he does not close his mind to all spiritual concepts. He can only be defeated by an attitude of intolerance or belligerent denial. We find that no one need have difficulty with the spirituality of the program. *Willingness, honesty and open mindedness are the essentials of recovery. But these are indispensable*" (Big Book, p. 568). Like those millions of alcoholic-addicts who came before us, we are invariably pleasantly surprised when we adopt an attitude of open-mindedness: "with few exceptions our members find that they have tapped an unsuspected inner resource which they presently identify with their own conception of a Power greater than themselves" (Big Book, p. 567-568).

For us hopeless alcoholic-addicts there are two choices: "one was to go on to the bitter end, blotting out the consciousness of our intolerable situation as best we could; and the other, to accept spiritual help" (Big Book, p. 25). But we can see with our own eyes in the fellowship and in the stories in the 12 Step literature what awaits us if we accept spiritual help, beginning with Step Two: "we saw that it really worked in others, and we had come to believe in the hopelessness and futility of life as we had been living it. When, therefore, we were approached by those in whom the

120

problem had been solved, there was nothing left for us but to pick up the simple kit of spiritual tools laid at our feet" (Big Book, p. 25).

A certain disconsolate drunk picked up those tools. He was brought to an A.A. meeting by a friend. He didn't think it was for him, but he went along anyway. He tells us what happened: "it was the second meeting that clinched my sobriety.... the chairperson called upon me to share.... As I spoke, I looked around the room. More importantly, I looked at the faces of the people in the room and I saw it. I saw the understanding, the empathy, the love. Today I believe I saw my Higher Power for the first time in those faces. While still up at the podium, it hit me – this is what I had been looking for all of my life. This was the answer, right here in front of me. Indescribable relief came over me; I knew the fight was over" (Big Book, p. 326). This "hopeless" alcoholic felt relief because he suddenly realized what Step Two tells us: that there is a power greater than ourselves that can restore us to sanity. What a relief, to finally realize that the fight, the inner battles, the dysfunction is over. Step Two is there for us, waiting for us to pick it up.

*

We should not be in any kind of a rush to figure out the higher power thing. Step Two does not ask us to identify, name, or draw a picture of what a power greater than ourselves is to us. It only asks for that leap of faith, the willingness to be open-minded to the idea that there is something greater than ourselves out there that can restore us to sanity. That's all we have to do to get through Step Two: come to believe that there is something out there that can get us sober and healthy, when we ourselves have been unable to do so on our own. We have only to look at others in the fellowship to see that Step Two is absolutely correct and true. We have only to reach down and pick up Step Two in order to start ourselves on the same journey as those who have what we want. We can get sober and healthy now, and figure out the higher power thing later (I keep repeating that for good reason; it's key to getting through Step Two and progressing without getting hung up on abstract concepts).

It's perfectly fine to leave the "what is" aspect of the higher power blank. I know many people with years of successful recovery who have done extremely well in their newfound spiritual and sober lives, but who still have a blank as a higher power. They don't know what their higher power is, they just know that something greater than themselves has helped them recover their sanity, their health, and their lives, freeing them from the daily obsession with drugs and alcohol. And that's good enough for them. They are in no particular rush to define their higher power, and rightfully so. They are comfortable and doing well with a blank for a higher power.

However, most people in the fellowship at some time or another develop some kind of an understanding of what their higher power is to them, and it often changes or evolves over time.

When someone does not believe in God and is not open to the concept of God, there are many other ways of finding that higher power. Commonly, the 12 Step group as a whole is used. After all, this is a collective of people recovering from addiction-alcoholism together, some with many years of sobriety and sage experiential advice to give. This group and their amazing support and wisdom is certainly a more powerful entity than the individual struggling to recover, so it makes sense when people use the group as their higher power.

Some people use music as their higher power. Music has a mollifying, comforting power. Music soothes and centers, and can form the basis of meditation. It also has an energizing and motivational power. It can inspire us, especially songs that are meaningful to us. It's not so strange that some have turned to music as their higher power.

For some, the concept of a higher power and God blur together. This isn't surprising, because God is but a name for a higher power, and there are many different definitions and understandings of God. One alcoholic-addict in recovery stumbled across this idea:

> While I was making some progress, I still didn't have a concept of God. So I went back to the Big Book, as I had done so many times before with other problems. The answer was on page 12, in Ebby's words to Bill: 'why don't you choose your own conception of God?'
>
> ...I sat down at my desk, got a pad of paper and a pencil, and asked myself, 'If you could pick the kind of God that you could believe in, what would He be like?'... Here was my chance. For the first time in my life, I could create something perfect. All right!
>
> I wrote across the page, 'God is the perfection I've been searching for all my life. He is too perfect to have human characteristics and faults.' That was the start.
>
> Then I wrote, 'God is the ultimate perfection. He is the perfect love, the perfect truth, the perfect goodness, the perfect understanding, tolerance, mercy, forgiveness. God is so perfect that no matter how evil, how unclean we may be, He'll forgive us if we ask, and grant us strength to overcome our shortcomings.'
>
> I sat back and told myself, 'You're a brain! You've come up with something brand-new here.' And then I realized that I was no brain – just a dunce. This was the God that Jesus was talking about two thousand years ago, when He stood on the hillside and said He had a Father in heaven who loved all human beings (*Came to Believe*, p. 63-64).

Many atheists and agnostics have found a way to approach the 12 Steps – and Step Two in particular – in a way that's comfortable for them and consistent with their beliefs. Let's look at how they did it. One such story is chronicled in the A.A. publication *Came to Believe*. Four men from A.A. were visiting a "hopeless" drunk who once again found himself wretched and retching in a hospital bed. He was interested in the 12 Step program, but said that it wasn't for him because the idea of God was part of the program. One of the men from A.A.: "...pointed out the plight of the patient, his helplessness, his illness.... He pointed out that he and the other three were sober and had managed to stay that way. They were working; they were happy. Surely, this made them stronger than the patient. The patient couldn't argue that point. Well then, couldn't they be considered a higher power of a sort, who possibly could help restore his sanity?" (p. 80). Happily, this approach worked for him, because he adopted the four men as his higher power, and found sobriety that lasted the rest of his life.

Another A.A. member unfamiliar with the idea of a higher power, came to an understanding after finding sobriety in AA. His approach is interesting:

> Long before nagging and pressures from others concerning my excessive use of alcohol made any impression on me, the nagging voice of conscience – my own inner voice of truth and right – apprised me of the irrevocable fact that I had lost control of alcohol, that I was powerless. I know now that inner voice was God, as I understand Him, speaking. For, as I had been taught from earliest memory and as A.A. has emphasized, God – or good – emanates from within each of us (*Came to Believe*, p. 83).

To this person the higher power is the voice, the conscience, and the inner good that's in all of us.

I know one A.A. member who uses his eight year-old daughter as his higher power. It works for him, because he's been sober for four years. I have daughters, and I can attest that a child has a power over a parent. That power could be called love. Intense love. And like any other interpretation of a higher power, it has the power to keep us sober. I like that. After all, who, being loved, is without power?

Some have chosen Love as their higher power. Some view humanity or humankind as that power. Others have chosen nature, or the universe. Or the mind. One friend who has been sober from drug and alcohol addiction for more than a decade tells me that when he was languishing in the detox

123

center for the ninth (and final) time, he finally gave in and accepted Step Two, using, for lack of any other understanding, Iron Maiden (the heavy metal band) as his higher power. He has since developed a new understanding of a higher power, but that worked for him when his chemical-soaked brain was fried as he withdrew from substance use and his anger and resentments prevented him from accepting any other higher power. Yup, Iron Maiden.

Some see a higher power in the 12 Step program itself: "I believe that the A.A. program is simply the will of God being put into practical, everyday use. And I think that the spiritual awakening [which we discuss in Step Twelve] is the realization that God will help the individual – if the individual is completely honest in his efforts." (*Came to Believe*, p. 85). Another feels the same: "God is a living part of A.A. I feel His presence each time I look into the concerned eyes around me. His greatest commandment is 'Love thy neighbor as thyself.' This seems to me the entire purpose of A.A." (*Came to Believe*, p. 89). *Twelve Steps and Twelve Traditions* also suggests using the fellowship as a higher power:

> You can, if you wish, make A.A. itself your 'higher power.' Here's a very large group of people who have solved their alcohol problem. In this respect they are certainly a power greater than you, who have not even come close to a solution. Surely you can have faith in them. Even this minimum of faith will be enough. You will find many members who have crossed the threshold just this way (p. 27).

Even the most resentful of skeptics can be animated by a power greater than themselves welling from the fellowship: "...I do believe in the power of collective thought, whether for good or evil. Thus, I believe that the collective thought of the body of Alcoholics Anonymous throughout the world must have some effect on alcoholics, whether they are aware of it or not" (*Came to Believe*, p. 87). One "unreachable" alcoholic felt vitalized by this same power:

> In Step Two, the 'Power greater than ourselves' meant A.A., but not just the members I knew. It meant all of us, everywhere, sharing a concern for each other and thereby creating a spiritual resource greater than any one of us could provide. Another woman in my group believed that the souls of dead alcoholics, including those of times before A.A., contributed to this fountainhead of goodwill. The thought was so beautiful that I wished I could believe it, too (*Came to Believe*, p. 84).

124

Ten years on she mused about what propelled her over her crippling pride and made her "reachable" and open: "the best answer is what my father used to call "the life force".... It is in all of us, I believe; it animates all living things; it keeps the galaxies wheeling.... I am cut down to size; I feel serenely that I am a small part of something vast and unknowable" (*Came to Believe*, p. 84-5). As a doctor and a scientist, I find her tidy explanation clear and unifying. After all, science acknowledges a "life force" that is as yet unexplained but much explored; something that makes otherwise inanimate organic compounds alive. Science cannot explain nor can it reproduce what this life force is. For those of a religious faith, that life force is named God. What that life force is called is up to each one of us.

It can be such a hurdle for proud, defiant, denying alcoholic-addicts to admit they are not the most powerful thing in the universe. We have only to surmount that small but most imposing of barriers and we have a chance at life again. Once the toxic clutter – the intoxication and sickness, the anger, resentments, the false pride, the guilt, and self-focus – begin to clear, the higher power concept can be properly considered. Later, through the clarity of hindsight, it's as if our higher power was there all the time, we just couldn't see it through the mental chaos. Most people, including non-alcoholic-addicts, never take the time to notice or to contemplate the other side of their instincts. It's like being a fish swimming along through life, and suddenly having the presence of mind to notice the water. The water surrounded the fish his whole life, he just never took the time to notice. So it is with our higher power.

That the thought processes that predispose us to rejecting a higher power are unique to our disease can be illustrated by analogy. An announcement in any hospital ward that acceptance of help from a higher power would avail remission from illness would be met with animated cheers. Yet so many who suffer from the sickness of addiction and alcoholism balk at the chance. Anyone suffering from any other infirmity would describe this stubborn refusal to accept help as some species of insanity.

*

Get sober now; figure out the rest later. That doesn't mean we have to change our beliefs at all, now or later: "what do I believe as a result? I can say that doubting God's existence was no barrier at all to a spiritual experience. Also, I can say that having such an experience didn't lead me to any certainty about God. Alcoholics Anonymous gives me the freedom to believe and to doubt as much as I need to" (Big Book, p. 374).

There were many people uncomfortable with the higher power concept who crawled this earth long before us, but who also found it to be no barrier to a spiritual solution for their addictions:

> My sponsor was a living damper on my intolerance. But even more, he told me that it would be all right for me to doubt God, that A.A. was not a religious program and, to belong, I did not have to adhere to any set of beliefs.
>
> He suggested that for me a good starting point would simply be recognition of the fact that I had failed in running the world – in short, acceptance of the fact that I was not God. He also suggested that I might try occasionally to act as if I believed. Somewhere I had heard that it is easier to act yourself into a new way of thinking than to think yourself into a new way of acting, and this made sense in the context of 'acting as if' (Big Book, p. 366).

This souse did find a spiritual higher power on his own terms: "I was able to accept the idea of a force that moved in the rooms and animated A.A. members with a sense of unconditional love. That satisfied my spiritual needs for a long time" (Big Book, p. 367). He was able to get sober and did not find A.A. to be a challenge to his beliefs, nor was it proselytizing any beliefs in God.

*

Seeking a higher power connection to overcome the strong arm of addiction has proven brilliant in the practical laboratory of 12 Step meetings over the past 80+ years, but it has also proven to be scientifically solid. Earlier we discussed how spirituality is consistent with science, that rejecting spirituality because "I believe in science" is utter nonsense. Now, for the sake of those of you whose higher power is a greater being, a creator, an intelligent designer, or God, allow me to dispel any misplaced beliefs that a higher power concept is not consistent with science.

Bill Wilson, the co-founder of A.A., was himself initially a non-believer in God. He was, however, convinced of the existence of a higher power, and his argument has an appeal to those who place emphasis on science:

> I had always believed in a Power greater than myself. I had often pondered these things. I was not an atheist. Few people really are, for that means blind faith in the strange proposition that this universe originated in a cipher and aimlessly rushes nowhere. My intellectual heroes, the chemists, the astronomers, even the evolutionists, suggested vast laws and forces at work. Despite

contrary indications, I had little doubt that a mighty purpose and rhythm underlay all. How could there be so much of precise and immutable law, and no intelligence? I simply had to believe in a Spirit of the Universe, who knew neither time nor limitation (Big Book, p. 10).

I love the logic of Bill's take on this. Personally, I have always been most taken by the simple but elegant argument, such as what I heard from a friend at an A.A. meeting just today: "today I went for a walk by the river. It was such a beautiful scene: blue sky, bright sun, birds flying, beautiful green trees, flowers in blossom, and the powerful river winding by. I know man didn't make this. Something or someone else did." That something or someone is what we may refer to as a higher power. While I find this the most convincing of evidence for a higher power, many among us prefer a more "scientific" explanation. After all, we were all brought up seeing science as fact, so we want to see the science. Well, the science definitely validates the existence of a higher power.

It is pure arrogance, it seems, to believe that there is nothing beyond the realm of human understanding – that nothing exists beyond that which science can readily explain or demonstrate. The second that we come to believe that there is nothing that exists that is beyond our current capacity to understand is the moment that science lays down and dies. Why pursue discovery if there is nothing out there to discover? So, using science to refute the existence of a higher power because science cannot explain it is contradictory to the very nature of science.

When it comes to our universe, science seems to be just playing around. A long-time amateur astronomer myself, I have come to the point where I roll my eyes at many of the new "discoveries" of science as it contemplates the infinite universe. A "cold patch" in deep interstellar space that defies explanation; a wobble in a star that can't be explained, the existence of a star that shouldn't be there, dark matter and dark energy that we can neither observe nor measure, parallel universes, anti-matter, ripples in the cosmic web, a rapidly expanding universe – to where? All these things have, to me, left science and soared into the existential. So a scientist contemplating the universe is no different than any one of us who contemplates the meaning of a higher power. It's not possible for any of us or for science to transcend all earthly knowledge. That's why we have imagination. It's imagination that led to the discovery of the atom, that led to the evolution of society, that leads us to ask questions and explore the deep reaches of the universe. So it is that our imagination allows us to conceive of the great power at work behind it all.

What is power? Among the very smallest of things is the atom. Yet the atom contains enough power to awe us. Splitting an atom, which we have achieved with some types of uranium and plutonium atoms, releases tremendous power. About 4½ pounds of plutonium is enough for a thermonuclear explosion that would dwarf Hiroshima. Each tiny atom contains massive power, and we have no concept of a number high enough to count the number of atoms in a human body, let alone the universe. But atoms can collect to have a power that is greater than the sum of their parts. Our brain is a collection of atoms that somehow produce a consciousness that can sense and interact with the environment, feel, think, understand, learn, ask questions, wonder, love, and feel. That power is not contained in the atom, so where does that power come from? I'm purposely trying to mind-boggle you here because this is mind-boggling stuff. Our mind reaches to understand things that are beyond reach. Things exist that we can't understand. But they exist. To deny the existence of anything because it is beyond our comprehension or not visible within our eyesight is arrogance of the highest order. And our arrogance can have nasty teeth: how many people in history were put to death for suggesting that the earth was round, or that the planets circled the sun? So I find it to be a very arrogant endeavor to try to demonstrate something as far beyond our understanding as the power that holds the universe together by our diminutive understanding of science.

When it comes down to nuts and bolts, we don't need to prove the existence of a higher power to benefit from it. When I came to the 12 Step program, I was desperate to get sober. Before me were hundreds of thriving, happy people who had achieved what I wanted. They had my attention. They were like me, many even worse, and they got sober and stayed that way. And they were loving life. So, I decided to surrender myself and do what they said I had to do to be sober and happy like them. They told me that I couldn't do it myself, that I needed a higher power. So, I did just that. I asked a higher power for help, even though I wasn't quite sure what that higher power was. As I got sober and my mind cleared, I worked my way through the Steps and found much more than successful sobriety. I found a new way to look at life, and a new way to live it. I found peace of mind and freedom of soul for the first time in my life. I'm not giving up what I've found for anybody or anything. And it involves having a higher power in my life, so I refuse to give that up, direct scientific proof or not. But, we people are a stubborn lot, so let's break out the science and look at what it says about a higher power.

*

Besides empty space, the entire universe is made up of matter and energy. No one would refute the existence of these two things that make up our entire existence. Yet science can't explain where matter and energy came from, where or how it was created. Even the late uber-astrophysicist Stephen Hawking, a card-carrying atheist, admitted that there was some power greater than the laws of physics that must have made matter, energy, and the physical laws of the universe before the "big bang." He couldn't, of course, explain what that power was, just that it was a higher power.

Physics tells us that energy cannot be created – this is known as the First Law of Thermodynamics. It can change from one form to another, but it can't be created. Because of this, at some point some power greater than these Laws of Physics must have created all the energy and matter that makes up the universe; otherwise, where did it all come from? The laws of the universe also tell us that entropy always increases. This means that all things naturally deteriorate to a more disorganized state. To see this, put a brand new Cadillac in a farmer's field and come back in twenty years to see what your Cadillac looks like. It will be a rotting heap of rusted metal. That's entropy. Science holds that life started as random chemicals – atoms of carbon, hydrogen, nitrogen, and oxygen – coming together and attaining progressively higher states of organization, ultimately progressing to the level of incredible complexity that life is today. This completely defies the law of entropy, so some power greater than these unalterable laws must have caused this to happen.

Famous American astrophysicist and NASA scientist Carl Sagan felt that: "the notion that science and spirituality are somehow mutually exclusive does a disservice to both." He united science and spirituality nicely: "science is not only compatible with spirituality; it is a profound source of spirituality. When we recognize our place in an immensity of light years and in the passage of ages, when we grasp the intricacy, beauty and subtlety of life, then that soaring feeling, that sense of elation and humility combined, is surely spiritual."[103] About the existence of a higher power Sagan had this to say: "an atheist has to know a lot more than I know. An atheist is someone who knows there is no God."[104] He believed that science would one day find compelling evidence of a higher power. I disagree... I believe it already has.

Science is not at all based on whether we can see something with our own eyes. No human eye or camera has ever seen a hydrogen atom, or dark-matter, or gravity, or X-ray radiation, or a radio wave, or.... There are many things we know about but we can't and probably never will be able to see. So, how does science know these things exist? We know something exists when someone comes up with a hypothesis – an explanation for something – and the explanation is supported by the laws of science and mathematics. Scientists then try to prove the hypothesis false. When no proof is found of it being false, it starts to become more believed. Then scientists look for things that can be explained by the hypothesis and when lots of these are found and it gets promoted to "theory" status. A theory is considered more or less fact. The first atomic bomb was built entirely based on "theories" and it sure worked, unfortunately. After a while, a theory is given law status. As we will see shortly, the laws of science support the existence of a higher power. No scientist has ever proven the existence of a higher power false. And there is no limit to the number of observations we can make to support a higher power: the existence of matter, energy, time and space, which had to come from some beginning; as Bill Wilson points out in the earlier quoted passage, the very laws of science, which are consistent in every way in every corner of the universe from the center of the atom to the vast reaches of space must have come from somewhere. The infinitely complex design of the human body, from the molecules to the cell to the organs to the body is "smoking gun" evidence of architecture of the highest order. The existence of a higher power passes the same empirical tests as do hypotheses, theories, and laws in science.

Science has no explanation for the essence of life, and certainly no power over it. We cannot give a dead body life again. We can combine biological compounds in a test tube but we can't give them life. Whatever this thing called life comes from is far outside the laws of the universe, and is therefore of a nature not yet understood or explained by science. Something more powerful than the laws of the universe and the understanding of our best science gives life.

It's scientifically antithetical that something as complex as a human eye could ever have arisen by natural forces acting on inanimate matter in an entirely random fashion. It's much less probable still that a human eye, kidney, brain, digestive system, immune system, respiratory system, reproductive system, all could have arisen randomly together, and gelled together so perfectly, even over the millions of years that this is said to have happened. It's easy to demonstrate that the mathematical probability of this happening randomly by chance is infinitesimal... in other words mathematically impossible. There has to have been a guiding intelligence at work. How could the greatest feat of engineering not have an engineer?

Many scientists share my convictions. Says John D. Morris, an accomplished and well-known research scientist with a doctorate in engineering: "any living thing gives such strong evidence for design by an intelligent designer that only a willful ignorance of the data could lead one to assign such intricacy to chance."[105]

There are, of course, many people of science who also put forward evidence and arguments for the existence of a creator. Many in the science community choose to call their theories and conclusions "creation science" and "intelligent design", which alludes to a higher power, a creator, an intelligent designer, perhaps what some might call "God." One example is the accomplished molecular biologist James Shapiro, who observed that the extremely complex process by which cells use DNA to change with their

130

environment and exclude adverse changes and the consistency of DNA across all living species amounts to what he calls "natural genetic engineering." Naturally, his research and conclusions have been seen as strongly supporting the intelligent design argument, as the processes he identifies in his publications are referred to as engineering. In other words, he finds the complexity of life to be evidence of an intelligent designer, an engineer, a higher power behind what and who we are, even though he can't explain who or what that engineer is. I share his convictions.

I was forewarned that medical school would shake my belief in a creator, and I was reluctant to follow any such path. In the end, I decided to hold my spiritual convictions up to the flame of science, to see if they would survive the test. To my surprise and delight, medical school confirmed and deepened my beliefs, and opened my eyes to spiritual vistas I hadn't previously known. As with Dr. Shapiro, whom we discussed in the previous paragraph, as I learned more about the indescribable complexity of life I became increasingly convinced that such a design could not possibly have been by random chance, and that there was a highly intelligent force behind it all. My concept of a higher power moved from faith to fact.

Faith is belief in anything we cannot see, and science relies very heavily on faith. Science cannot see the atom, yet its existence is accepted as fact because the laws of the universe support it. That is faith. As I mentioned, I did a university degree in chemistry, and all of my studies were founded on the faith that science requires, because my whole degree was based on the existence of the atom, something that neither I nor anybody else has ever seen. Imagine life without faith, believing only in that which we can see. Although we can't directly see a universal higher power, the science points to its existence because we can see its effects in all of creation itself, just like science points to the existence of the unseen atom. Our faith in the existence of the atom has led to countless scientific developments that have benefitted humankind immeasurably. Faith in a higher power has also enriched many lives. Medical science has demonstrated abundantly that those gifted with spiritual connectedness with a higher power have a far better chance at overcoming illness, and a more peaceful way of it if not. This is faith that advances our cause.

My three science degrees are long behind me, and in my years of practicing medicine I have repeatedly seen a higher power at work. Those of us who have contemplated where life, energy, and matter come from do not need science to bolster our spirituality. But, I cherish my spirituality, and I love the sciences. And I am at peace that the two get along so well.

*

Science holds no monopoly on figuring out the universe. This has been the focus of philosophy since humankind first found time to spare from day-to-day survival to turn thought and attention to bigger things. Even that (to me) confusing, convoluted discipline known as philosophy has the simplest of arguments for a higher power of the universe, a creator. Philosophers can't stomach the concept that the universe created itself because something cannot exist before it existed. It all goes back to "an uncaused cause", the philosophical argument that nothing comes from nothing. Somewhere, sometime, somehow, the universe had to have been caused by something; and that something may be thought of as a higher power. To propose that science can prove otherwise or even challenge this assertion is absurd. Even hardcore atheist Stephen Hawking conceded on this point.

Since the earliest recorded history those who engaged in deep thought have expended much effort into the question of the existence of a higher power. Philosophy can be a very hard read; during my one and only philosophy course in university I spent more time lost in space than I did lost in thought. I did, however, find much of the philosophical reasoning for the existence of a higher power to be quite neat, if it's boiled down to comprehensible nuggets. Interestingly, some of the logic used in the ancient philosophical arguments mirrors the logic used in science. For example, when I spoke above of how the fact that a human body is an incredibly complex machine, which implies a designer, a creator, a similar logic was used to argue for the existence of a higher power by philosopher William Paley early in the 19th century, in his "Watchmaker Analogy" argument. He mused that if he was walking along a path in the forest and happened upon a watch sitting on the ground, even though he didn't see it being created he knew that an intelligence had made it... it didn't just assemble itself there in the forest by random chance. Likewise, he pointed out, that the same complexity and purposeful utility as he sees in the watch can also be discerned in the natural world around him. Biological organisms show complexity and utility, and it's therefore natural and correct to conclude that these things were also designed and constructed by a higher power. Voltaire, an earlier philosopher of some fame, also saw logic in this argument, and phrased it with beautiful simplicity: "the Universe troubles me, and much less can I think that this clock exists and should have no clockmaker."[106]

St. Thomas Aquinas, a well-known philosopher who lived about a thousand years ago, argued that if the universe once didn't exist, then it must have had a cause to come into existence. If it has always existed, it also owes its existence to a cause. He said that this cause of the universe is what we understand to be God (a higher power). He also argued, and this may remind you of my above scientific arguments, that: "wherever complex design exists, there must have been a designer; nature is complex; therefore nature must have had an intelligent designer."[107] It's hard to argue with that.

The 18th century philosopher David Hume argued that the fact that there is a design to the world shows that there must have been a designer:

> Look round the world: contemplate the whole and every part of it: you will find it to be nothing but one great machine, subdivided into an infinite number of lesser machines, which again admit of subdivisions to a degree beyond what human senses and faculties can trace and explain. All these various machines, and even their most minute parts, are adjusted to each other with an accuracy, which ravishes into admiration all men who have ever contemplated them. [This machine] throughout all nature, resembles exactly, though it much exceeds, the productions of human contrivance; of human design, thought, wisdom, and intelligence. Since therefore the effects resemble each other, we are led to infer, by all the rules of analogy, that the causes also resemble; and that the Author of Nature is somewhat similar to the mind of man; though possessed of much larger faculties, proportioned to the grandeur of the work which he has executed.[108]

The 17th century philosopher William Derham argued that since the universe consists of such complexity and design, it could only have been conceived of and brought into being by some intelligent being equivalent to such a task; in other words, a higher power.

More modern, 20th century, philosophical thought has also been in line with and similar to the logic I used in the science-based arguments that I presented above. The "Fine-tuned Universe" argument states that because there is such order in the universe, the amazing consistency of nature's physical constants (the laws of mathematics and physics), and that achieving such perfectly consistent "rules" that have been applied so universally and perfectly since the beginning of creation, then these must have been designed. The "fine-tuning" of the Universe is far too precise to be random.

*

These views are not limited to disciples of science or even philosophy; many people with no connection to the sciences or thinkers of deep thoughts arrive at the same conclusion from a much different perspective. In the A.A. book *Experience, Strength, and Hope*, there's a story written by an early A.A. member that I find particularly powerful and thought provoking in supporting the existence of a higher power. The story is entitled "An

Artist's Concept" and is found on pages 130-134. What I found compelling about this story is that it's an argument purely from the perspective of an artist, rather than the point of view of a scientist or a philosopher. The story is beautifully written, clearly composed by the mind of an artist. I have reproduced a few lines from it, but I do recommend reading the story in full. The writer is a painter, and offers no scientific rationalization for the existence of a higher power, but bases it upon observations from the eye of an artist: "as an artist I had spent too much time communing with nature – trying to place upon canvas or paper my emotional feelings, not to know that a tremendous spiritual power was back of the universe" (p. 131-132).

Our artist struggled with addiction to alcohol, desperate for a way out. He investigated every avenue to find relief from his addiction, medicine and psychology included. All to no avail. We all know the story. In being introduced to A.A. members in recovery, he observed:

> I met over twenty men who had achieved a mental rebirth from alcoholism. Here again it was not so much what these men told me in regard to their experiences that was impressive, as it was a sense of feeling that an invisible influence was at work. What was it this man had and these other men exemplified without their knowing? They were human everyday sort of people. They certainly were not pious. They had no 'holier than thou' attitude. They were not reformers, and their concepts of religion in some cases were almost inarticulate. But they had *something*! Was it their sincerity that was magnetic? Yes, they certainly were sincere, but much more than that emanated from them. Was it their great and terrible need, now being fulfilled, that made me feel a vibratory force that was new and strange? Now, I was getting closer and suddenly, it seemed to me, I had the answer. These men were but instruments. Of themselves they were nothing.
>
> Here at last was a demonstration of spiritual law at work. Here was spiritual law working through human lives just as definitely and with the same phenomena expressed in the physical laws that govern the material world.
>
> ...These men were thinking straight – therefore their actions corresponded to their thoughts. They had given themselves, *their minds*, over to a higher power for *direction* (p. 132-133).

This man acknowledges that the concept of a higher power is personal: "the approaches of man to God are many and varied. My conception of God as Universal Mind is after all just one man's approach to and concept of the Supreme Being" (p. 134).

134

The Big Book is emphatic that the higher power concept is entirely up to each individual:

> In our personal stories you will find a wide variation in the way each teller approaches and conceives of the Power which is greater than himself. Whether we agree with a particular approach or conception seems to make little difference. Experience has taught us that these are matters about which, for our purpose, we need not be worried. They are questions for each individual to settle for himself (p. 50).

*

The 12 Step program itself may be seen as proof of a higher power in our lives, regardless of what our concept of that higher power may be. There's no way to calculate the numbers, but a reasonable estimate is that this program – which has as its cornerstone the acceptance of a higher power – has rescued tens of millions of hopeless alcoholic-addicts over the last 80+ years, after all else had failed. Given that the people in the 12 Step program have managed to take the higher power from a concept to a powerful implement of great practical use, their methods deserve our attention. One such alcoholic-addict relates:

> Here I found an ingredient that had been lacking in any other effort I had made to save myself. Here was – *power!* Here was power to live to the end of any given day, power to have the courage to face the next day, power to have friends, power to help people, power to be sane, power to stay sober. That was seven years ago – and many A.A. meetings ago – and I haven't had a drink during those seven years.... What *is* this power? With my A.A. friends, all I can say is that it's a Power greater than myself (Big Book, p. 386).

This fellow addict-alcoholic in recovery doesn't try to define this power, but describes it as a higher power, something more powerful than himself that empowered him to succeed at freeing his life from addiction-alcoholism. No matter what label we wish to put on it – call it God, or nature, or the telephone pole outside the window – it is a higher power. Many people come to the program with a pre-conceived idea of what a higher power means to them – especially those who believe in God as their higher power – but many do not. And there's no need to figure it out; the concept tends to come on its own. In the meantime, many find their need met in a simple way, such as this long-suffering alcoholic-addict: "I was able to accept the idea of a force that moved in the rooms and animated A.A.

members with a sense of unconditional love. That satisfied my spiritual needs for a long time" (Big Book, p. 367).

*

You can see from our Step Two discussion that the higher power concept can be supported from a scientific viewpoint, or from a philosophical perspective. Notice, however, that a common thread of logic runs through all arguments, regardless of the intellectual discipline making the argument; categorizations of arguments as "scientific" or "philosophical" or whatever may be an arbitrary way of describing the exact same logic. When we look around the fellowship and see the way that otherwise forlorn lives have been transformed by the higher power that was introduced into people's nettled minds through Step Two, we can definitely see the effects of a higher power even though we might not be able to see this power directly with our eyes. Like the atom, we can see the higher power not though direct visualization but through its very real and tangible effects. Perhaps then we can realize that if we want the same positive transformation in our lives that we, too, should take that leap of faith and accept what Step Two suggests of us, which is to be open to the belief that something, somewhere can help us to escape the insanity of our substance use. If we don't believe there is help for us, a way to escape the insanity of addiction-alcoholism, then there is little point in proceeding further through the Steps.

Do we really need all these arguments of science, philosophy, and logic to convince us to accept that there is something more powerful than us out there somewhere? Is there no role for simple faith? There's a beautiful passage in the Big Book that illustrates not only our capacity for faith, but also our need for it and our duty to ourselves to allow ourselves to have some faith:

> Imagine life without faith! Were nothing left but pure reason, it wouldn't be life. But we believed in life – of course we did. We could not prove life in the sense that you can prove a straight line is the shortest distance between two points, yet, there it was....
>
> Hence, we saw that reason isn't everything. Neither is reason, as most of us use it, entirely dependable, though it emanate from our best minds. What about people who proved that man could never fly? (p. 54-55).

I like this passage because it highlights an important point. In the previous pages I have put forward various evidence, arguments, and quotations from various noted scientists and philosophers showing that a higher power is not an "unscientific" or "illogical" thing to accept. However, I

136

only put forward those arguments in an effort to open the minds of people who are stuck on the "does it exist" question when it comes to a higher power. However, as the 12 Step program has amply demonstrated over the past 80+ years, and as medical research into the health benefits of connection with a higher power has shown, it doesn't matter one bit whether we can identify or believe in some great power of the universe. Rather, our recovery depends on accepting that we ourselves had no power to quit our drinking or using (Step One), but *something* outside ourselves has the power to help us do that (Step Two). We don't have to understand or even define that something, we just have to accept that there is a way out if we accept help from outside ourselves. That is the essence of Step Two.

*

We speak of "figuring out" the higher power concept. But the truest path to an understanding that fits for us turns out to be by experience, and not by direct thought. Like stumbling upon that furtive soul-mate when we are not looking for one, so it is with finding our higher power. Many grapple with the concept of a higher power because they over-think it. Consider a Chinese finger puzzle. The wretched device slides over both index fingers like a sleeve, and the challenge is to remove it. We pull our fingers away from each other so it will slide off, but instead... it tightens. Our natural instinct is to pull harder, but the harder we pull, the harder it clenches. It even starts to hurt. However, if we let go of our natural instinct to pull harder, and instead bring our fingertips back together and let go of all tension, the device just pops off of our fingers. The Chinese intended a life lesson in there somewhere, besides sharpening our swearword repertoire. Sometimes obeying our instincts to think harder to figure things out is the wrong way to solve a problem. We should not battle to define what a higher power is to us. Rather, we should stop searching and allow our answers to find us.

Nothing more than the willingness to put up our antenna and listen for an such answer is called for to get us sober: "...we of agnostic temperament have had these thoughts and experiences. Let us make haste to reassure you. We found that as soon as we were able to lay aside prejudice and express even a willingness to believe in a Power greater than ourselves, we commenced to get results, even though it was impossible for any of us to fully define or comprehend that Power..." (Big Book, p. 46). Get sober now; figure out the higher power thing later.

One alcoholic-addict who wished to remain atheist but still find sobriety in the 12 Step program did so by not allowing himself to over-think it: "many people are determined to make work out of things that require no work" (*Came to Believe*, p. 115), and "for many of us, our understanding of

God [i.e. a higher power] ends at the frustrating point of *not* understanding Him. It was a great relief to me to learn that I simply didn't have to understand. After all, you don't have to know how a tree grows to make a fence out of wood" (p. 114-115).

There's a higher power concept for all of us, even if we start by using the mind, or the group, or nature, or love, or good, or even the telephone pole outside our window as our higher power. Even better, we can just leave the higher power concept blank for now. That's enough to get sober and to start a journey of spiritual connectedness on all three levels. From there we can mature spiritually and find clearer answers as we go. Get sober now; figure out the higher power thing later.

*

One really cool research study involved a clinical analysis of A.A. members' perceptions of a higher power.[109] One of the people interviewed gave an excellent take on accessing a higher power without understanding it:

> I don't know that I have an understanding of what the HP [higher power] is. Hum, you know what it says in the literature: the important thing is that you know it's not you. And one of the things I like about AA is that you don't need to define it or understand it, you just have to believe it. It's good to not have to define it... I observed that with time, AA people seem to need less and less to understand God.[110]

I like that: the important thing is that you know it's not you! The study participants also found that their relationship with a higher power facilitated other life-affirming qualities, such as gratitude, socialization, forgiveness, tolerance, patience, and humility.[111]

The observations and experiences of the participants in the study are consistent with other research findings. For example, another (more formal) study shows that among alcoholic-addicts in recovery, higher levels of faith and spirituality (i.e. what Step Two suggests that we take on) were associated with greater life optimism, better social supports, better stress tolerance, and lower levels of anxiety.[112] Other studies show that a connection with a higher power reduces activity in a part of the brain that is responsible for managing anxiety and is important for self-regulation.[113] Reducing anxiety and improving self-regulation are certainly strengths that help us in recovery. Even more to the point, other research has shown that a close connection with a higher power is a way to providing optimal dopamine levels in the recovering alcoholic-addict's messed-up brain reward-system, thereby reducing cravings and obsessive thoughts of drinking or using.[114,115] Other studies have also demonstrated that a connection with a higher power reduces rebound depression and low mood (anhedonia) in recovering alcoholic-addicts, an important factor in relapse prevention.[116,117] Perhaps most importantly for people in recovery from substance addictions, spiritual connection with a higher power has been definitively shown to promote self-control, the development of self-regulation strength and proficiency, and the selection and pursuit of life goals.[118,119] As well, prayer – especially prayer at meetings – has been shown to increase our ability to control our impulses to relapse.[120] Prayer can help us to say no to drugs and alcohol. We'll discuss prayer in Step Eleven, but suffice it to say at this point that although most people associate prayer with religion, it's not necessarily so. Rather, it's a form of meditation where we connect with a higher power, regardless of what that higher power is.

These research findings amply demonstrate that a connection with a higher power helps us to overcome many of the psychological and mental aspects of addiction-alcoholism and acts as a buffer against relapse. It's a major factor in making recovery about healing rather than a matter of pure willpower, which would be a disaster in powerless people like us. In other words, these research findings support the basis of Step Two for long-term recovery from substance use.

*

So, we've talked about spirituality, and we've talked about a higher power, two main concepts in Step Two. These may be new to some of us, or they may be very familiar; for some they may be a new take on a familiar subject. Step Two is where we first run into these concepts, so having at least an understanding of what is meant by the terms "spirituality" and a "higher power" is important. Knowing how we feel about these things or what they mean to us is not important. Get sober now; figure that stuff out later.

In our Step Two discussion I have made it abundantly clear that we don't have to have spirituality and a higher power completely figured out, nor do we have to be entirely comfortable with these things to get sober and begin healing. Trying too hard to figure out these complex and abstract concepts and rejecting the healing process until we do can be quite costly to us, and unnecessary. As *Twelve Steps and Twelve Traditions* tells us, when it comes to Step Two, easy does it:

> Listen, if you will, to these three statements. First, Alcoholics anonymous does not demand that you believe anything. Second, to get sober and to stay sober, you don't have to swallow all of Step

139

Two right now. Looking back, I find that I took it piecemeal myself. Third, all you really need is a truly open mind. Just resign from the debating society and quit bothering yourself with such deep questions as whether it was the hen or the egg that came first. Again I say, all you need is an open mind (p. 26).

Said one individual who struggled with Step Two: "I had only to stop fighting and practice the rest of A.A.'s program as enthusiastically as I could" (*Twelve Steps and Twelve Traditions*, p. 27). As we are told in the Big Book: "we found that as soon as we were able to lay aside prejudice and express even a willingness to believe in a Power greater than ourselves, we commenced to get results, even though it was impossible for any of us to fully define or comprehend that Power..." (p. 46). After admitting our powerlessness in Step One, it's our willingness to at least consider that there is a power greater than ourselves that can restore us to sanity that empowers us: "as soon as we admitted the possible existence of a Creative Intelligence, a Spirit of the Universe underlying the totality of things, we began to be possessed of a new sense of power and direction..." (Big Book, p. 46). Easy does it: don't overwhelm yourself with figuring out who or what a higher power is: accept that there is something else besides yourself that can get you sober, and leave it at that. As the Big Book tells us: "we needed to ask ourselves but one short question. 'Do I now believe or am I even willing to believe that there is a Power greater than myself?" (p. 47). That's your Step Two.

*

The words of celebrated Austrian psychiatrist Dr. Carl Jung describe what spirituality can do for us as alcoholic-addicts: "ideas, emotions, and attitudes which were once the guiding forces of the lives of these men [alcoholic-addicts] are suddenly cast to one side, and a completely new set of conceptions and motives begin to dominate them" (Big Book, p. 27).

Step Two is where this new set of convictions and motives begin, in the form of spirituality and open-mindedness to a higher power by which we can heal and be freed from our licentious demons. Those who are atheists or agnostic have no barrier to participating, because spirituality is not religion: "we find such convictions no great obstacle to a spiritual experience" (Big Book, p. 29). Even religious people and those who believe in God may find that their concept of God doesn't fit well with what they observe and experience in the world, and may benefit from applying some open-mindedness about their God concept. People who reject this willingness to at least be open-minded about it have probably not yet reached their bottom, the point at which they are willing to do anything to end the misery of active addiction-alcoholism:

> Faced with alcoholic destruction we soon became as open minded on spiritual matters as we had tried to be on other questions. In this respect alcohol was a great persuader. It finally beat us into a state of reasonableness... we hope no one else will be prejudiced for as long as some of us were (Big Book, p. 48).

Admitting that we are powerless over alcohol or drugs in Step One leaves us very exposed: *now what?* However, Step Two suggests to us that there is a power that we can use to overcome our powerlessness. That power is our higher power.

We have completed Step Two when we accept that there is a way to end our insane behavior, through some kind of a power that is greater than the power we have within ourselves. We may not yet have any idea or understanding of what that power is to us, but we have accepted that there is something outside of ourselves that can restore us to sanity. We don't have to understand what that power is or even be able to name it; we just have to believe that there is a way out. Are you there? If so, time to move on to Step Three, if your sponsor agrees.

Step Three

Made a decision to turn our will and our lives over to the care of God as we understood him.

Step Three is the first Step where the word "God" is mentioned. For those whose spirituality includes God, that's fine, probably a comfortable fit. We must remember that the operative part of Step Three is "God *as we understood Him.*" Although the 12 Step founders chose to use the aphorism "God as we understood him," they are really referring to a higher power, whatever our concept of that higher power may be... or may not be. If our higher power is not named "God," that is no barrier to Step Three. We discussed the higher power concept in detail in our Step Two study, so we should be good to go for Step Three. Again, in our sick and precarious situation, the important thing is that we should not waste time nor should we reject our opportunity to get sober and healthy by trying to figure out what a higher power – "God as we understood Him" – is to us. Let's get healthy now, and worry about the higher power concept later.

What Step Three is asking us to do is not to accept God, or to figure out what a higher power means to us; rather, Step Three is asking us to accept that higher power as our guide for returning to health. In Step Two we acknowledged that there is some kind of a power greater than our powerless selves that can restore us to sanity, and Step Three is asking us to commit to allowing that power to do so. We will discuss in the pages that follow exactly what we mean by "turning our will and our lives over" to a power greater than ourselves.

Many people find Step Three to be the easiest and fastest Step to mount, because they are, in their desperation for an end to their misery, more than ready to give themselves over to whatever power can help them, whatever that power may be to them. They just want to get better. That's the attitude that we have when we've reached our bottom. For those who are not comfortable with the God concept, the presence of that word in Step Three may present a challenge. Others have a challenge with the idea of turning their will and life over to anything, higher power or not. My experience is that these people's reluctance is rooted in a misunderstanding of what Step Three is asking of us; we will clarify this in our Step Three study. Let's do that now.

*

For some people, the use of the word God is a bit of an elephant in the room. After all, if the 12 Step program's spirituality is all-inclusive, allowing for people to avail themselves of any concept of a higher power that works for them, then why use the word God at all? Well, we know from the A.A. publication *Pass It On* (which is a history of A.A.'s beginnings – a really interesting read that I highly recommend) that the founders of the 12 Step program intended to refer to a completely open higher power concept: "God as we understood Him." Really, this was Bill Wilson who used this terminology, and we know from *Pass It On* exactly how that came about.

We must remember that when Bill Wilson got sober, there was no 12 Step program. His story about he got sober is well documented in the first chapter of the Big Book. In those pre-A.A. days, Bill's miraculous attainment of sobriety and spiritual principles was heavily influenced by a spiritual revival organization known as the Oxford Group. Contrary to popular belief, the Oxford Group was not an alcoholism recovery group; rather, it was purely a spiritual organization. They were, they said, a system of beliefs, not a religion. The Oxford Group emphatically asserted that they were not a religion, but rather they identified themselves as an unofficial, non-sectarian gathering of people who have undertaken to live a more spiritual life by surrendering their lives to God. You can see, then, the influence of the Oxford Group in the wording of Step Three. Like the Oxford Group, the intention of the 12 Step founders was to use the word "God" in a rather generic and open way, not as part of any religion.

The tie-in between Bill Wilson's sobriety and the Oxford Group is told – indirectly – in the Big Book. Pages 26 to 28 tell the story of an unnamed alcoholic who was woefully unsuccessful in multiple exertions at getting sober, which included not a few sanitarium admissions. He ended up – the story goes – travelling to Europe to seek out the famous psychiatrist Dr. Carl Jung for help. Dr. Jung told this man that there was nothing that medicine could do for him; rather, he would require a "vital spiritual experience" (p. 27). When our alcoholic friend told Dr. Jung that he was a good church member, Dr. Jung responded by: "telling him that while his religious convictions were very good, in this case they did not spell the necessary vital spiritual experience" (p. 27). Our alcoholic friend – whose name was Rowland H., according to *Pass It On* – returned to the U.S. and sought a spiritual experience with the Oxford Group (a spiritual group), rather than through his church (a religious group). The Oxford Group taught Rowland spiritual principles that he applied to his life... and he got sober.

The link between Rowland, the Oxford Group, and Bill Wilson comes through Bill Wilson's childhood friend Ebby T., who is also mentioned in the Big Book. In 1934, when Ebby was a chronic drunk, he was visited by several men from the Oxford Group, including our friend Rowland H. Rowland became close with Ebby, and remained in contact with him after the initial visit. Ebby learned from Rowland the spiritual principles of the Oxford Group, to which he attributed his ability to finally get sober.

When Ebby visited Bill Wilson – this story appears on pages 8 to 13 in the Big Book – Bill was so impressed by Ebby's recovery and spiritual way of life that he decided that he needed to do the same. Bill was still an active alcoholic at the time of Ebby's visit (in December 1934), and wanted the sobriety Ebby had found through spirituality. So, Bill became involved with the Oxford Group, gave his life over to God according to their practice, and got sober. He realized then that spirituality was the way to sobriety for alcoholics who were otherwise beyond help.

When Bill Wilson wrote the Big Book, we must remember that he was starting from scratch; all he had was "the word-of-mouth program that [he] had been talking ever since his own experience" (*Pass It On*, p. 147). *We* are looking at the Big Book and its language and use of the word God in hindsight, but Bill had nothing to go by. Naturally, he reached out for spiritual principles from the spiritual authorities he knew and that were a factor in his getting sober, most especially the Oxford Groups. As we are told in the A.A. history, the Big Book fifth chapter "was heavy with Oxford Group principles" (*Pass it On,* p. 197), and the "first three steps were culled from his readings of James, the teachings of Sam Shoemaker [a key leader of the Oxford group], and those of the Oxford Group" (p. 199).

There was opposition among early A.A. members to the use of the word "God," especially among the fellowship members in New York. This was largely because those who were not familiar with the Oxford Group didn't understand the context of the use of the word "God" by that group, and thus the context used by Bill Wilson. Even among the fellowship members in New York, there were split opinions; some wanted the book to be fully secular, others wanted it to be full-blast Christian. The end result – a compromise, perhaps – was the phrase "God as we understood Him." Bill viewed this compromise as: "the great contribution of our atheists and agnostics. They had widened our gateway so that all who suffer might pass through, regardless of their belief..." (*Pass It On*, p. 199).

Even then, there was more pushback when the manuscript for the Big Book was submitted to the publisher for editing. The editor went at it with a heavy pen, cutting the text by about half (ouch!). A psychiatrist from Montclair, New Jersey who reviewed the manuscript – a certain Dr. Howard – felt that the book was too close to the Oxford Group, and recommended that Bill remove the word God from the entire text. Bill did not take this suggestion well: "did Bill go into a tizzy then! He almost blew his top. Here was his baby being torn apart by a screwball psychiatrist" (*Pass It On*, p. 204). The Big Book was going to have "God as we understood Him" in it. Period. And that was that. Thus, we have "God as we understood Him" rather than "higher power of our understanding." Nonetheless, the intention was the same: that **all** people could interpret the higher power – "God as we understood Him" – in their own personal way, including those people who wanted nothing to do with God.

The frame of mind of Bill Wilson in his stubborn determination can be understood by putting ourselves in his shoes for a moment. Bill was actually quite a dapper guy, and I love the classic wing-tips he used to wear, so I don't mind spending a few minutes in his shoes. Bill was a horrible alcoholic – by his own admission – and he was naturally grateful when he was finally rescued from that miserable life of insanity, after multiple hospitalizations and privations. Those of us who find transformative power in the 12 Step program and not only finally get sober but also learn a new way of handling life are understandably likewise grateful. There was no 12 Step program, no A.A. for Bill, but he found a spiritual way out of his alcoholism with the Oxford Group through Ebby and Rowland, as we discussed. His gratitude toward his higher power for his sobriety was gratitude to God, so he was understandably insistent on using the word "God" in the program as it rose from its humble beginnings.

Too, we must understand the cultural milieu of the times. The Big Book was written and reviewed by American Christians in the mid-20th century, at a time and place where the use of the word God was as linguistically, socially, and conceptually accepted as it was ubiquitous. Prayers to God were still a regular part of the school day, and reference to God was widespread in the news media, government, and society as a whole. Even now, more than 80 years on, echoes of this cultural norm still linger, as – for example – anyone can see when looking at today's U.S. currency. So much more so, then, was the term "God" an accepted part of everyday language back in the 1930s.

We should bear in mind that when the 12 Step founders used the term "God as we understood Him" they had the very best of intentions of making the program accessible for every alcoholic-addict who crawls this earth, regardless of his or her belief system or lack thereof. So, rather than take offense to how it was written, we should take it for its intended purpose: to be inclusive for all people, including the most devout atheist.

The basic text – the first 164 pages – of the Big Book contains a lot of personal anecdotes from Bill's experience and that of the first 100 or so members of A.A. Their experiences and the cultural milieu in which they lived, in a vastly different era than the one we live in now and with A.A. in its very infancy, will not necessarily be the same as our experiences and cultural milieu. So, we should try to understand rather than reject them and their language. Their stories are a snapshot from a different time and place than we now live in. Nevertheless, their experiences with alcohol or drugs were the same as ours are nowadays, even though the setting was very different. I have learned in the fellowship that we all have a remarkably similar story when it comes to the downward spiral with drugs or alcohol, but that each individual has a different thumbprint of past experiences, genetics, upbringing, belief systems, culture, and hopes and dreams. We must therefore remember that we are free to hold onto our own belief system and to express our individuality. So it is when we read the Big Book.

We must also take note that the use of the word "God" in the 12 Step program is in the abstract. It's not linked with any religious creed, nor is there any tolerance within the 12 Step fellowship for religious creed. Matters of religion and beliefs are fine – each person is encouraged to adhere to his or her own belief system – but religious pursuits are left for people to pursue outside of the fellowship. People who attend meetings know that religion and religious dogma are not discussed, nor would they be tolerated. The word "God as we understood Him," as it appears in the 12 Step program, is decidedly generic as a term intended to mean "higher power" and not connected to any religion.

So, having said all that, why is it that in more modern times the Big Book has not been changed to remove the word "God" and some of the other aspects of the Big Book that are somewhat dissonant with modern times (such as the very misogynistic language)? Well, the short answer is this: the program and the big Book work so well that it has been purposely left in its original form: "in recent years some members and friends of A.A. have asked if it would be wise to update the language, idioms, and historical references in the book to present a more contemporary image for the Fellowship. However, because the book has helped so many alcoholics find recovery, there exists strong sentiment within the Fellowship against any change to it" (*Twelve Steps and Twelve Traditions*, p. 14). And so it is. I suggest that we all be open-minded enough to take the language of the Big Book – including Step Three – for what it is intended to be: all-inclusive. Let's choose sobriety and healing over bruised sensitivities.

*

Alcoholics Anonymous co-founder Bill Wilson himself wasn't comfortable with the "God" word when he was first approached by his friend Ebby. Here's how he dealt with it:

> My friend suggested what then seemed a novel idea. He said, *'Why don't you choose your own conception of God?'*
> *It was only a matter of being willing to believe in a Power greater than myself. Nothing more was required of me to make my beginning.* I saw that growth could start from that point. Upon a foundation of complete willingness I might build what I saw in my friend. Would I have it? Of course I would! (Big Book, p. 12).

Bill had reached his bottom. He was willing to do anything to get sober at that point, and wasn't about to allow his hang-up with the word "God" stop him.

In the interviews I have conducted in my research into addictions I have heard a lot of perspectives from all varieties of people in active addiction-alcoholism and in recovery, some of whom were totally put off by the use of the word "God" in the 12 Step program. It's helpful to hear some of their answers from when I asked about how they came to terms with it and were able to participate in the program and get sober despite their reservations. Here's what some of them had to say, in their own words:

> So when I first came into A.A. I thought that all the "God" stuff might be a problem. I wasn't sure if there was a God or not and it's kind of mentioned a lot. But when I was finally willing to take the Steps my thoughts on God didn't matter anymore. I was so miserable that I would've done anything my sponsor suggested. So getting through Steps 2 & 3 was just me willing to believe. I still didn't have a higher power I truly believed in, but there was proof that the Steps work. So as dumb as I thought it was to pray every day and try to memorize the 3rd Step prayer like my sponsor suggested, I just did it. It worked for him and others, so why not just give it a shot? Maybe it'll work for me too. And I don't think I fully believed in a higher power until I got to Step 9 and started making amends. I started having amazing things happen in my life that made absolutely no sense other than a higher power working in my life. I eventually came to believe. It worked for me and I've heard similar experiences as well. For some people [Steps] 2 & 3 is just a willingness to move forward with the rest of the Steps and the God part will eventually come. IDK [I don't know] what my God/higher power looks like. And I only say God because it's quicker than higher power. I just know that there's

got to be something bigger than me working in my life. And it feels good to go from just praying because I was suggested to, to finally having a spiritual awakening and having some actual faith behind my prayers now.

This person had reached his bottom, and his desperation to heal allowed him to give the 12 Steps a chance, despite his discomfort with the word "God." As you can see, it paid off for him and he came to terms with it... on his own terms. Another alcoholic-addict in recovery explains:

It's just a word, German in origin, related to the word 'good' (Gott/gutt). I'm not religious either so I just use it as a kind of shorthand for a vague higher power which is nature/the power of good/the power of love etc. etc. It's a shame the word 'God' carries so much baggage, but don't let three little letters stand in the way of your sobriety. Keep your eye on the prize.

Another alcoholic-addict in recovery describes her experience with overcoming her reservations in order to get sober:

If you haven't read the Big Book there's a chapter called 'We Agnostics' which may help clarify AA's 'official' position.
I'll relay a bit of my own experience since it relates a bit I think. I came to A.A. as a lifelong agnostic and occasional atheist. I had a huge problem with a capital 'G' god. I still do. I have major issues with organized religion. But... after years of trying to quit drinking using my own willpower I became convinced that I could not quit on my own and needed a 'power greater than myself.'
At first it was the meetings but those are just made up of normal people and I felt I needed something more. Then it was the Steps but how could I say those were the power when they are the path to tapping into that power? Then it was nature and I felt I was getting closer. Now I use the phrase, 'The Spirit of the Universe' which I stole from the 5th Step promises, which are incredibly meaningful to me.
Once we have taken this Step, withholding nothing, we are delighted. We can look the world in the eye. We can be alone at perfect peace and ease. Our fears fall from us. We begin to feel the nearness of our Creator. We may have had certain spiritual beliefs, but now we begin to have spiritual experience. The feeling that the drink problem has disappeared will often come strongly. We feel we are on the Broad Highway, walking hand in hand with the Spirit of the Universe.

After doing my 5th Step I felt that these promises had manifested virtually overnight. I had come to believe that a power greater than myself had restored my sanity. These days I choose to call whatever that power is 'god' just because it's easier to say and quicker to be understood by others. For me it encompasses everything that we do not or cannot know. What happened before the big bang? What caused it? Why are we here? What happens after we die? What saved me from an alcoholic death? I answer god (lowercase 'g') to all those questions.

The spirit of the universe has helped me as a result of doing the 12 Steps and I haven't had a drink in over 10 years. Keep coming back. It works.

As you can see, this sister in recovery didn't figure out the "God as we understood Him" and higher power thing overnight; it was an evolving process, just as we have discussed. She got sober now, and figured out the higher power thing later. Another alcoholic-addict in recovery relates:

I was taught (and I believe) that before I came to A.A., alcohol was my 'power greater than me.' I had to rely on the program and the steps to be a power greater than me if I wanted to stay sober. I understand the mental snag that comes with the word God, as it can conjure up stuff from my past. A.A. has a lot of great sayings that work and the God one — Good Orderly Direction — is easy for me to wrap my head around. If I keep working the steps and doing what is suggested of me by my sponsor and others (with quality sobriety and whom I trust) I am taking that Good Orderly Direction that will keep me sober.

I had to let go of the capital 'G' God and just trust the process. I hope that helps and I wish you all the best.

Excellent perspective. Another fellow alcoholic-addict in recovery describes how he has left his concept of a higher power as a blank, and it works for him:

A.A. is not religious. It's spiritual. We all have our own conceptions of our own higher power. I didn't believe in any type of higher power when I joined. After going through the steps I came to believe in something. I usually just say God because I'm lazy, but I have no idea who or what my higher power looks like. I just know that I have faith in something bigger than me today. That being said, I know several people who have gone through the steps and remained atheists. The 'God' concept can be helpful for some, and unneeded for others. A.A.

can still be beneficial with or without a higher power if you give it an honest attempt, but if the word God scares you away, then IDK [I don't know] what else to say. I was miserable enough to try anything so I didn't care about all the god stuff when I got my sponsor. It works if you work it.

Another alcoholic-addict went with the higher power concept, even though he didn't know what it was, because all else had failed:

One of our mantras is that we believe that no human power could have relieved our alcoholism. We normally rely on will power or doctors to relieve us of our addiction, until we get so desperate that we are willing to try something different. I don't have a concept of a personal god but by practicing the disciplines laid out in the Steps and by working with others I have 'tapped' into something I can't explain, but I have experienced a power in the fellowship with like-minded people and my thinking, and my actions have changed as a result. I agree that god is a generic term that we use to describe something we can't fully explain. Hopefully you'll find a good meeting and hook up with a good sponsor that can walk you through the Steps that have relieved so many of us from our alcoholism.

True desperation to escape a life of insanity is a doorway to open-mindedness. One alcoholic-addict in recovery takes a more philosophical approach:

I suggest going to the A.A. meeting with an open mind. A.A. is not religious, as I have met Jews, Catholics, Christians, Muslims, Hindus, Buddhists, Atheists and Agnostics. Our 12 Steps are suggestions. Biggest thing for me was knowing I wasn't alone. 'There is a principle which is a bar against all information, which is proof against all arguments, and which cannot fail to keep a man in everlasting ignorance—that principle is contempt prior to investigation.'

Another alcoholic-addict in recovery takes a shoot-from-the-hip approach to the higher power and "God" issue:

Don't let a dumb word keep you from getting sober. All you need is to believe that you are not the biggest force in the universe.
I have heard people talk about their higher power as dogs or goodness, drag queens, or fractals. Don't worry about what you call it just focus on putting down the drink.

I agree: get sober and healthy now, and worry about the higher power thing and the "God" word later.

*

For some, the hang-up is not in believing in a higher power or God, it's in "turning their will and their life over to the care" of their higher power, as is suggested of us in Step Three. Such was the case with one alcoholic: "... I did believe there was a God of some sort, somewhere, who would help me if I really needed outside help. But I was man enough and smart enough to help myself! So I wasn't asking God, or anyone else, for help" (*Came to Believe*, p. 29). Fortunately, many people hit the bottom that breaks down their alcoholic-addict pride enough for them to accept the hand extended to them before all is lost. The man quoted above did, but not before he had lost his job, his home, his wife and children, his "impressive" car, his charge accounts: "... while playing revolving door with the Fellowship, I drank up all my excuses for not needing A.A. One evening, I sat alone in my apartment, counting my bankroll – 89 cents. There was no food in my apartment. Should I spend eighty-five cents for another bottle of wine...? Desperately, hoping He might be listening, I knelt beside my empty wine bottle and prayed very simply, 'Oh God, please help me'" (*Came to Believe*, p. 30). He found his "bottom," and his willingness to accept help, but he lost a lot before he reached his bottom. (Incidentally, hitting his bottom also rescued him from having to endure any more of that 85-cent wine, surely a high-caliber vintage!)

This same man found an interesting way to come to terms with his higher power, thanks to an electrifying analogy. Here's how he did it:

> When the Steps were read, 'God *as we understood Him*' bothered me. These people had something I was unable to grasp. I had never been able to understand God, and still didn't. Changing His name to 'Higher Power' didn't help any.
>
> One of the oldtimers used the electricity metaphor, which I later found in the Big Book [note: a previous edition]. 'A person walking into a dark room does not worry about understanding electricity,' he said. 'He just finds the switch and turns on the light.' He explained that we can turn on the switch of spirituality by simply asking God each morning for another day of sobriety and thanking Him at night for another beautiful sober day. He said, 'Do it mechanically if you really don't believe in it. But do it every day. There is probably no one who really understands the wonderful

ways of the Higher Power, and we don't need to. He understands us' (*Came to Believe*, p. 30).

We have to look at what is being asked of us in Step Three. By turning our lives and our will over to the care of our higher power we are *not* becoming limp puppets that will henceforth be controlled by someone or something else. There is no weakness or submission being asked here. We are asked to "surrender" to the program, but this is not surrender in the sense of bowing our heads in defeat. Rather, it's to let ourselves go, to stop holding back, and to do what the program suggests we need to do to stay sober from drugs and alcohol. It's more a case of "joining the winning side" than it is "surrender."

It has been widely the experience of those who are in the program that when they turned themselves over to the care of their higher power they felt immense relief. They went from trying to run their lives and the world around them, to flowing with life and living life on life's terms. It's like getting out from behind the wheel of a runaway car about to drive over a cliff; we may have been behind the steering wheel and at the controls of the car, but we really didn't have any control over it anyway and it was headed for destruction. So it is when we surrender our insane attempts at controlling our unmanageable lives and everything around us. It's very tiring to swim against the current, and a deep relief to relax and allow the strong and sure current take us along. Now we can use our energies for something else, and take the time to look around and enjoy the scenery.

The peace and serenity that comes from giving up the futile struggle against our drink and drug catches most 12 Steppers by surprise. The alcoholic-addict psychological need for control is powerfully overwhelming, and it keeps us in our disease and prevents us from seeking and accepting the help we need. Step Three is asking us to let go of that pathological disease-driven neurotic need for control. It does us no good to try to control our lives and everything around us when we are driving our life into the ground, something that drunks and addicts have a strange but consistent penchant for. It's such a relief we feel when we finally accept that we can let go and relax, that we are now involved in a program that has proven its ability to restore some normalcy and quality to our lives. Step Three is where we do just that. In the past, we gladly turned our will and our lives over to alcohol and drugs, and it quickly made us sick and our lives unmanageable. In Step Three we take our will and our lives out of the hands of alcohol and drugs and place them in the care of a power that can restore us to sanity, whatever that power may be to us.

We will come across the Serenity Prayer many times in our trip through the Steps, and it can help us right here with Step Three. The prayer asks for the serenity to accept the things we cannot change. What does this mean for Step Three? Our biggest life problem – how to stop the insanity of our substance use – is especially anxiety-inducing, but in Step One we found the serenity to accept our addiction as something we cannot change – we are powerless over it. We have tried and tried, but we have been unable to stop our addiction. In Step One we conceded and accepted that.

The next line in the prayer asks for the courage to change the things that we can. It takes courage to let go of our obsessive need for control and to place our care and the future of our lives in the hands of a higher power in the setting of the 12 Step program, something that is as yet a big unknown for us. I admire the courage that people show when they do this, because it goes against the pathological psychological drives that our disease imposes upon us. This courage comes from the wisdom to know that we can't restore our lives to normalcy and sanity by trying to fight something we are powerless over (the third line of the prayer). Thus it is that the Serenity Prayer can help us to overcome our disease-induced resistance to Step Three, and our drive to come up with any reason we can think of to avoid doing what it suggests.

This same practice of leaving something in the hands of our higher power, whatever that power is, that we first experience in Step Three becomes a big part of our ability to handle life on life's terms as we grow in our recovery. When we face adversity, it's enormously psychologically comforting to "leave it with our higher power" when the adversity is something that's beyond our control. We do our best to make the problem better, but we accept what happens because that's how life goes when something is beyond our control. This is the "peace and serenity" that the Twelve Step program rightfully promises, and it's why we sleep so well at night and enjoy life, regardless of what life sends our way. Step Three is our first introduction to this cherished life skill.

It may surprise people to find out that this "surrender" that Step Three suggests has been shown by clinical studies to increase our sense of control over our own lives.[1] It may sound like a paradox, that handing over control of our will and our lives increases our sense of control over our lives, but it really isn't. It's this process of taking the control of our will and our lives away from drugs and alcohol and handing it over to a power that can help us to heal that gives us sanity and control back in our lives. This "surrender" has also been associated with an improved sense of well-being, and a sense of purpose in life.[2] This will not surprise a Twelve Stepper, because this effect is well known among those who have done their Steps and are well-practiced in spirituality. As Bill Wilson tells us: "the more we become willing to depend upon a Higher Power, the more independent we actually are. Therefore, dependence as A.A. practices it is really a means of gaining true independence of the spirit" (*As Bill Sees It*, p.26).

Step Three suggests that we turn over our "will;" but what exactly does that mean? To fully understand what is meant by this we must look at the psychological term "willfulness," which is a cornerstone symptom of addiction-alcoholism. Willfulness is a key element of the pathological psychology of addiction-alcoholism, one that breaks our willpower and underscores our powerlessness. Our conscious decision to willingly address our substance-driven willfulness in Step Three is a key aspect of recovery: "practicing Step Three is like the opening of a door... once unlocked by willingness, the door opens almost of itself" (*Twelve Steps and Twelve Traditions,* p. 34). This door we seek to open leads to sobriety, a return to good health and function, and a new way of living life on life's terms. Surrendering our willfulness (i.e. our will) is necessary for us to take control of our own lives again, which is one of the reasons that Step Three gives us a better sense of control in our lives.

The Big Book speaks often of willfulness, but uses the term "self-will," which means exactly the same thing, so I will use the "self-will" terminology. The 12 Step literature is quite clear about what this self-will/willfulness can do to our recovery efforts: "once we have placed the key of willingness in the lock and have the door ever so slightly open, we find that we can always open it some more. Though self-will may slam it shut again, as it frequently does, it will always respond the moment we again pick up the key of willingness" (*Twelve Steps and Twelve Traditions,* p. 35). Self-will can slam shut the door to our recovery, but we can open that door again if we have a willingness to surrender our self-will, as we are suggested to do in Step Three. The Big Book tells us of Step Three: "the first requirement is that we be convinced that any life run on self-will can hardly be a success" (p. 60). So, what is this "self-will" that we are asked to relinquish in Step Three?

Self-will is a stubborn adherence to fulfilling our own desires. It's a determination to do what we want despite the consequences. To be sure, self-will is not the sole domain of the alcoholic-addict, it's a part of everyone's psyche. Self-will is that voice that tells us to satisfy ourselves by eating a box of donuts even though we are on a diet. Self-will is that thought that tells us to lie down and take a nap when we know we have work to do. Self-will is that voice that tells us to skip the workout we were planning in favor of flopping on the couch and watching TV. Self-will is that strong impulse to switch off the alarm clock and stay in bed and skip work in the morning. Every person in the world has self-will, but we can (usually) over-ride that self-will by applying a little willpower. We can use willpower to walk away from the box of donuts, skip the nap, head to the gym, and let go of the pillow and get up for work. "Normal" people can use willpower to "say no" to alcohol or drugs. However, once we cross that line into alcoholism-

154

addiction there is a psychic change that corrupts all that and renders our willpower useless. The self-will of alcoholism-addiction is a different entity, an artificial psychological force that is created by the unnatural effects of psychoactive chemicals on our brain.

Although self-will is a factor in everybody's life, the self-will of alcoholism-addiction is deadly and unique. The difference is that in active alcoholism-addiction our self-will "runs riot," as the big Books fittingly terms it. Our drive to fulfill the desire for the next drink or drug steamrolls over all other considerations and is out of control. Our self-will has no concern for others – not even our own children – but is only concerned with the self. It's the basis of our selfishness, and of our disregard for consequences, the reason alcoholic-addicts only care about the here and now. As we found out in Step One, the self-will of alcoholism-addiction renders willpower useless and thereby makes us powerless over drug and drink.

There was a time when we had the willpower to "say no" to using or drinking, but once we crossed that line into addiction-alcoholism that willpower became useless and we became powerless. I doubt if anyone anywhere would blow off their children, or risk losing their job, or their family, or spend all their savings to satisfy their self-will desire for a box of donuts. Yet, anyone who stays on the road of alcoholism-addiction long enough almost invariably gets to that point with addictive substances. People wouldn't commit crimes, or prostitute themselves, or steal from family and friends because they didn't have enough money for their next box of donuts, yet many good people are driven to do these things to obtain their next drug or drink. Nobody would risk eating a box of donuts that may contain a lethal dose of a deadly chemical, yet people will risk using drugs that may easily contain a lethal dose of fentanyl, and people with cirrhosis of the liver will continue drinking alcohol even though they know it will kill them. The self-will of alcoholism-addiction is a unique species indeed.

In alcoholism-addiction self-will – as with other psychological processes – is pushed to extremes as our disease sets in and deepens its grip on our brain's functions. We become increasingly willing to sacrifice important people, things, and responsibilities in favor of our drink or drug. When we get it in our mind to obtain and use our poison, there's nothing that will stop us; our self-will takes over our priorities. I have heard many, many loving parents – including me – tell of how they chose drink or drug over their children during their active drinking or using days. To me, that is an exemplar of self-will gone completely crazy. It's this self-will run riot that lurks behind the insanity of alcoholism-addiction; once our mind is made up to drink or use, we will do anything – *anything* – to fulfill that desire... the here and now and the self have become all that matter to us.

In order to fulfill our out of control self-will, we will attempt to manipulate, lie, cheat, steal, and do anything in order to get our drink or drug. The longer we stay on that path of alcoholism-addiction the uglier our self-will gets. Self-will run riot is why good people end up turning to crime to get their next drug or drink, or otherwise do things that they would ordinarily never even consider doing. Self-will is about needing to control everything, which is a major psychological impediment to surrendering our self-will in Step Three. Our pervasive addict-alcoholic need for control makes the thought of surrender unacceptable to us, causing resistance to Step Three. But this is a barrier that anyone who wants sobriety must overcome, whether they are involved in the 12 Step program or not. Whether someone is participating in the 12 Step program or not, there is no hope whatsoever of successful recovery unless there is the realization that the self-will has become perverted, dominant, and harmful and must be surrendered. In other words, every person – participating in the 12 Steps or not – must accomplish Step Three to get healthy and sober.

Our self-will run riot and our distorted perception and need for control make us believe that we know what is best for us. However, if we continue to follow our self-willed ideas of what is best for us it will keep us in our addiction. Look at where our self-will has already taken us. A sick mind cannot heal a sick mind.

You can see that the self-will of addiction-alcoholism is very different from the self-will of everyday life. Part of the basis of the stigma with addiction-alcoholism is that people who have not experienced our disease have difficulty understanding that the self-will for an alcoholic-addict is different from their own experience with self-will. They say: *if drinking/using drugs is making you so sick and causing you so much loss, why don't you just stop? Just don't go to the liquor store/dealer.* That's because for them, overcoming the self-will of drinking or using is not any different from overcoming the self-will of eating a box of donuts, a mere matter of old-fashioned willpower. However, once someone's brain has crossed that line into addiction-alcoholism, it's an entirely different matter, and willpower is rendered useless. It's what defines addiction. Step Three is asking us to surrender this self-will to a power outside ourselves, to commit to releasing its grip from us. And what a liberating thing it is, to finally cast aside this overpowering and destructive self-will. Even though we couldn't see it at the time, our alcoholic-addict self-will run riot was controlling every corner of our lives – and not to our benefit – and relieving ourselves of this controlling, dominating self-will is a hugely freeing thing to experience. And so our healing can begin.

*

Our alcoholic-addict self-will is exceedingly sneaky, and can bring us down in other ways than simply by trying to trigger delusions of self-satisfaction by drinking or using. This same self-will can make us pessimistic, ungrateful, and feel like victims of the world. Our pathological self-will can make us feel entitled, that everything in life should go our way. When, at some point, a problem arises and something inevitably doesn't go our way, our self-will sense of entitlement fills us with anger and resentment, which are the greatest cause of addiction-alcoholism. Life for anybody, no matter who we are, never goes our way all the time. There will be ups and there will be downs, and that's just life. However, our dysfunctional self-will won't accept that, it wants everything to go our way. When it doesn't get satisfied, that narcissistic self-will becomes a vortex of frustration, anger, resentment, self-pity, and other attributes of negative psychology. As we will learn in Steps Four and Six, these are exactly the things that make us become obsessive drinkers or users who cannot stop. The Big Book illustrates this destructive power of self-will by analogy:

> Each person is like an actor who wants to run the whole show; is forever trying to arrange the lights, the ballet, the scenery, and the rest of the players in his own way. If his arrangements would only stay put, if only people would do as he wished, the show would be great. Everybody, including himself, would be pleased....
>
> What usually happens? The show doesn't come off very well. He begins to think that life doesn't treat him right.... He becomes angry, indignant, self-pitying....
>
> Selfishness – self-centeredness! That, we think, is the root of our troubles....
>
> So our troubles, we think, are basically of our own making. They arose out of ourselves, and the alcoholic is an extreme example of self-will run riot, though he usually doesn't think so. Above everything, we alcoholics must be rid of this selfishness. We must, or it kills us! (p. 62).

That's exactly how the self-will vortex happens as we get drawn into the extreme negative psychology of addiction-alcoholism. We find it difficult to handle life's stressors; rather than see them as a normal part of the ups and downs of life, we see them as proof that God and the world are picking on us. Our self-will believes that we are entitled to a life where everything goes just right for us.

Feeling like a victim of the world – which psychologists refer to as *self-victimization* – is a terrible state of mind to be in, and the beginning of the downward vortex of self-will. We feel like the world is picking on us, isn't fair, and we feel sorry for ourselves. *Why is the world picking on me?* Self-pity is but another nail in the coffin for the addict-alcoholic. Soon, we feel like no matter what we do, bad things will happen to us, so we feel helpless and hopeless, like there is no point in trying – something psychologists refer to as *learned helplessness*. Again, another downward turn into negative psychology. Our self-will kicks in, and we want everything to go our way, for our problems to just stop. We don't do much to help things go our way, and we get angry at people, institutions, things, God, and the world because they are not behaving the way our self-will thinks they should.

The alcoholism-addiction fuse is lit when we start turning to dysfunctional ways of coping with our stress. The anger, resentments, self-pity, feeling of helplessness and hopelessness, and our frustration that other people aren't fulfilling the desires of our self-will are grievously painful feelings – the epitome of negative psychology. We soon turn to drugs or drink to numb the negative feelings, as these are the go-to coping mechanism for people like us when we are in that state of mind. Of course, the more we drink or drug, the more our life turns downwards, and the worse all those negative emotions get, which makes us drink or drug more, and so on. We all know the story.

This dysfunctional self-will – where we expect the world to fulfill our desires for how life should go for us – is an unrealistic expectation. It sets us up for failure, because life will never go anybody's way all the time. But, we don't see that at the time. Rather, we see ourselves as victims of an unfair world. Life is going to have ups and downs, no matter how rich or privileged we may be – and to expect otherwise is complete insanity.

Although everybody's story is different, this is the downward spiral of self-will and negative psychology that many people follow as they fall into active addiction-alcoholism. I just threw a lot of psychology at you, and a lot of psychological terminology, but don't fear; we'll get to know these things very well as we progress through the Steps together. In the meantime, the point is to see how surrendering this horrible self-will in Step Three is a key turning point so that we can proceed with healing and escaping the insanity as we grow and strengthen in our recovery.

*

This self-will has a powerful grip on our thoughts and behaviors, so freeing ourselves from its cruel yoke is a serious undertaking. We haven't been able to find the resources within ourselves to muscle our way out from under its dark power, otherwise we would have quit drinking and using long ago. However, the 12 Step program promises that there is a power outside ourselves that can free us from our self-will. To do so, we must wholly commit to surrendering this self-will to that power outside ourselves, because even years into successful recovery that self-will will

158

surely re-assert itself if we allow it to linger within us. Our commitment to Step Three must be absolute, and for life. Our self-will is going to try to talk us into reaching for that first drink or drug in the future, often when we least expect it. Our alcoholic-addict self-will is going to do its level best to convince us that THIS time we will be able to control our substance use. Our self-will cares only about the here and now; it wants instant gratification regardless of any consequences. However, if we give in to that first drink or drug we are surrendering our self-will right back to drugs and alcohol, and we know where that gets us. Better to hand our will over to the care of our higher power and leave it there. Our recovery will last only as long as our commitment to Step Three remains intact.

By recognizing our out of control self-will and committing to surrendering its control over us we are doing much more than simply preparing ourselves for the remainder of the Steps. We are actually neutralizing one of the major psychological causes of our addiction.

As previously mentioned, self-will is present in everybody's psychological make-up, just not usually to the degree that it's present in active alcoholism-addiction. Even in healthy recovery we will still be subjected to the regular, garden-variety self-will that everybody else deals with: we will still be tempted to sleep in when we have to get up for work, we will still be tempted to skip our workout, or to spend money that we can't afford. Those kinds of things are just normal self-will, where we can apply our willpower. If our willpower fails us and we give in to our self-will, there's really not much of a consequence. Nobody is going to lose their family or their job or their life because they hit the snooze button in the morning. That kind of self-will is just human nature, part of everybody's life. However, we must remain committed to keeping our alcoholic-addict self-will in the hands of our higher power and not in the hands of alcohol and drugs and our disease. How do we do that?

As we wind our way through the Steps and "clean house" we develop a new positive psychology, new habits, new ways of thinking and doing, and new life skills that definitively free us from alcoholic-addict self-will. When we practice the principles that we learn in all our affairs, our alcoholic-addict self-will stays where it belongs: outside of us in the hands of our higher power. In the meantime, at this stage of our trip through the Steps, when we feel our alcoholic-addict self-will trying to re-assert itself in our mind we have some tools we can use to keep it in its place. First and foremost is to call our sponsor. In the 12 Step program we must learn to shed our shyness, our tendency to close up inside of ourselves, and our predisposition to be secretive. We must shed the thought that we are bothering our sponsor by calling. If we feel our self-will trying to assert itself and talk us into using or drinking we should call our sponsor right away. The longer we leave it the harder it becomes. Sponsors can only help us if we use them, and – as we will learn in Step Twelve – when we contact our sponsors it helps them with their sobriety and their spirituality as well as it helps us. They wouldn't be sponsoring people if they didn't want to be called. If our sponsor isn't available, we should contact someone else who is in recovery.

There are other tools we can use to counter our self-will even before we have progressed any further through the Steps. We can reaffirm our Step One, because our self-will will try to convince us that we can handle a drink or drug, that we will have the power to limit ourselves to "just one." We can go to a meeting. We can pull out our Big Book, open it to any page and read. We can use the slogan "Remember When" to remind ourselves of how miserable and pathetic we had become when our alcoholic-addict self-will had its way with us. We can pray (which we will discuss further in Step Eleven). Anything is better than going backwards on our Step Three by taking our self-will back from our higher power and handing it back over to our disease.

*

Some people balk at the idea of "turning their lives over" to something greater than themselves, the other part of Step Three. They fear that doing so means that they will lose their identities and control of their lives. However, let's be honest here: when we were in active alcohol or drug use, we had turned our lives over to drugs or alcohol. We had surrendered our intellect, our health, and our happiness to our substance use. Many of us had surrendered our families, our children, our savings, our jobs, and our accomplishments to an addictive substance. Unfortunately, many have even surrendered their lives to their substance use. For those of us who stayed on the alcoholism-addiction path long enough, we were no longer living, we were just existing. And a miserable existence, at that. We had lost all ability to care for ourselves, the care of our lives was in the hands of our substance. When we are facing Step Three our life belongs to drugs and alcohol.

Step Three is asking us to be willing to take our lives back from drugs and alcohol, and hand our care over to a higher power. This doesn't mean that we will have no control over our lives and our destiny, and it doesn't mean we will become puppets of some unseen figure in the clouds. When we rely on our dentist for the care of our teeth, it doesn't mean that our teeth now become the property of our dentist. It doesn't mean that our dentist makes all the decisions about our teeth, or that the dentist will be watching our every move through hidden cameras and giving us instructions all through the day. We are still in charge of our own teeth, and we have full responsibility to brush and floss our teeth, avoid too much sugar, and make sure we do the things we need to do to keep our teeth
160

healthy. So it is when we turn our lives over to the care of God as we understand Him – i.e. a higher power. We are still responsible for our lives, we are still in control of our own actions, and we make our own decisions. Turning the care of our lives over to a higher power is a commitment to a spiritual way of living, a healthy way of living, just like turning the care of our teeth over to our dentist is a commitment to a healthy regimen for our teeth.

Twelve Steps and Twelve Traditions suggests that by coming to the 12 Step program we have already gotten a start on Step Three:

> Every man or woman who has joined A.A. and intends to stick has, without realizing it, made a beginning on Step Three. Isn't it true that in all matters touching upon alcohol, each of them has decided to turn his or her life over to the care, protection, and guidance of Alcoholics Anonymous? Already a willingness has been achieved to cast out one's own will and one's own ideas about the alcohol problem in favor of those suggested by A.A.... Now, if this is not turning one's will and life over to a newfound Providence, then what is? (p. 35).

Twelve Steps and Twelve Traditions uses a really cool analogy to allay the concerns of anyone who fears that Step Three is asking us to become non-entities, dependent on whatever we turn our will and our lives over to. The narrative (on page 36) points out that we are actually more dependent on a lot of things than our egos would allow us to realize, using the example of our dependence on electricity. We are so dependent on electricity that our society would virtually collapse if it suddenly lost all electrical power. How would your life unfold without it? No electrical lights, no Internet, our cell phones would soon be paperweights, no traffic lights to guide orderly traffic, no gas for our vehicles because the gas pumps and stations would fail, no heat for our homes and buildings because the furnace fans and circuitry would fail, no refrigerators, no grocery stores... I don't think I need to continue. When we think about it, we are completely dependent on electricity. Completely. But no one feels like a sell-out because of it, no one feels like a non-entity because of it, no one feels like their beliefs about God or a higher power are violated because of it, no one feels like they have no control over their lives because of it. Rather, we live happy, free, fulfilled lives despite being dependent upon electricity. In fact, most people don't even cast a thought to the matter. So it is when we become dependent upon a higher power for our sobriety – no matter what that higher power is to us or if we even ever figure out what that higher power means to us. Even if we forever reject the notion of God, and never figure out the higher power thing, who cares? As long as we are sober and healing, does it really matter?

Most people don't understand the complexities of electricity generation, distribution, and the physics of electricity, but they are happy to go through life dependent upon electricity. So we too, as desperate as we are to get sober, should have no qualms about being dependent upon a higher power that we don't understand or can't even define in order to go through life sober, happy, healthy, and functioning well. Step Three really doesn't ask much of us, even though our alcoholic-addict pride may make some among us recoil at the suggestion.

Most of us have tried getting sober countless times in countless ways, without success. Obviously, getting sober our way with ourselves in control and our self-will running the show was a big, fat zero. It's time to tell our self-destructive ego to back off, to open our minds to new ideas, and to try out what Step Three is suggesting that we do. After all, it has worked for millions of people who were hopelessly addicted to alcohol, drugs, gambling, over-eating, shopping, pornography, etc. It's time to air out the brain a little bit, and purge that negative psychology, as is the purpose of the Steps. With it come long-term sobriety and a return to good health and function. As it says in *Twelve Steps and Twelve Traditions*: "each of us has had his own near-fatal encounter with the juggernaut of self-will, and has suffered enough under its weight to be willing to look for something better" (p. 37-38). People who have truly reached their bottom are willing to go to any lengths to end the insanity and the misery. Step Three seems like it might not be such a barrier when we are standing at our bottom looking up.

Twelve Steps and Twelve Traditions also points out that there are some forms of dependence that are unhealthy, using the example of an adult who is still dependent upon a parent. Too, we were once dependent upon drugs or alcohol, also an unhealthy dependence. "But dependence upon an A.A. group or upon a Higher Power hasn't produced any baleful results" (p. 38). That's because dependence upon our program and a higher power is a source of strength for us, and the key to our independence. For without it we would still be slaves to our chemical dependence and our dominating alcoholic-addict self-will. Step Three is, therefore, about independence, freedom, and the ability to make our own choices in life, for we have none of those things when we are in active addiction. It's therefore a brilliant and delightful paradox of the miracle of healthy recovery in the 12 Steps that we turn the care of our lives over to a higher power in order to get back control of our lives.

*

The Big Book suggests a Third Step prayer. For anyone who's not comfortable with the idea of prayer, I suggest just saying the words and throwing them up in the air. Even if you don't know whom those words are addressed to or where they go, the simple act has a positive effect. Prayer is not necessarily an act of religion; rather, it's a communication or a meditation with a higher power outside of ourselves. We will discuss this further in Step Eleven. Think of the prayer as a call to action, an expression of willingness to consummate Step Three and move on with recovery. The prayer:

> God, I offer myself to Thee – to build with me and to do with me as Thou wilt. Relieve me of the bondage of self, that I may better do thy will. Take away my difficulties, that victory over them may bear witness to those I would help of Thy Power, Thy Love, And Thy way of Life. May I do Thy will always (p. 63).

The Big Book follows the prayer with reassurance for those who are not comfortable with the "God" part: "the wording [of the Third Step prayer] was, of course, quite optional so long as we expressed the idea, voicing it without reservation" (p. 63). The idea we are suggested to voice is the essence of Step Three: being relieved of the bondage of self; in other words, being willing to be freed of the absolute control that our self-will has had over us. We are told that committing to the Third Step will be worthwhile: "this was only a beginning, though if honestly and humbly made, an effect, sometimes a very great one, was felt at once" (Big Book, p. 63).

*

Step Three is not the time to figure out what a higher power is if we do not already have a concept that works for us. Nor is it time to balk at the program's use of the word "God," because the meaning, intent, and use of this term is widely misunderstood. Those are things that deter many from a program that would otherwise bring them health, happiness, and sobriety. Open your mind, get healthy now, and figure that stuff out later; it will come. Rather, Step Three is asking us to take a stand against that self-will run riot that has dominated our lives, forced us into insane thinking and behaviors and cost us all those things that make us healthy and happy. It's also asking us to take back our lives from drugs and alcohol and hand our care over to a power that can help us to heal, so that we can have sane control of our lives again. When you are ready for this and commit to it, you have accomplished Step Three and you are ready to move on to the "action Steps." You won't even believe what awaits you! If you are comfortable with your Step Three and your sponsor agrees, let's get to it now with Step Four.

Step Four

Made a searching and fearless moral inventory of ourselves.

Secretive drinking or using, bolstered with lies and excuses, grandiose posturing, selfish and aggressive behavior, dropped obligations and responsibilities, failed promises and resolutions, fruitless geographic escapes, alienation of family and friends, inability to initiate action – all are painful examples of the typical behavior of people in active addiction-alcoholism. Small wonder that the erosion of character brought on by addiction-alcoholism leads to a progressively worsening negative psychology characterized by guilt, shame, self-loathing and low self-esteem. The resulting state of mind is an extreme exemplar of negative psychology; so much so that it might even be called "train-wreck" psychology.

The reason that the 12 Step program works so well is that it is a remarkably effective approach to scrubbing this "train-wreck" psychology and addressing the underlying causes of addiction-alcoholism. The meat and potatoes of this process occurs in Steps Four through Nine, which are known as the "cleaning house" Steps. Steps One through Three lay the groundwork for cleaning house, and Step Four begins this wonderfully cathartic process. As a therapist I have been singularly impressed by the transformative effect of the 12 Step process, an effect whose comprehensiveness and rapidity of action few therapists could hope to emulate, even after thousands of dollars and months of therapy.

So, what do we mean by "cleaning house?" The 12 Step approach to restoring us to health and functionality is not by trying to change the world, because that's beyond our control. Rather, it focuses on guiding us through changing ourselves – a self-cleanse – by eliminating the toxic emotions, feelings, and behaviors that were both cause and effect of our obsessive substance use. That's something we can change. That's why the Serenity Prayer is so relevant to the 12 Step program; it exemplifies our approach to healing. It's also of the utmost logic: in the past we drove ourselves crazy ruminating and fuming over why the world won't change to be how we want it to be, and we blamed the world for our woes. But that didn't do us any good because we can't change the world. So, we look inside ourselves and change the things that we can do something about. And it works! We clean our own house, keep our own side of the street clean, and stop railing and driving ourselves crazy about other people's houses and their side of the street. Armed with our open-mindedness, willingness, and spiritual beginnings from Steps One through Three, we begin that process in Step Four.

Step Four is probably the single most psychologically therapeutic and transformative of the Steps, in terms of sheer potency at lifting psychological burdens from the shoulders of the troubled alcoholic-addict psyche. However, Step Four presents a major barrier to progress in the Steps for some people, a sticking point that they never get past. My own research has shown that people who get hung up on Step Four and cease their progression through the Steps are at much higher risk of relapse. This is hardly surprising, because to abnegate progress through the Steps – and Step Four in particular – is to deny oneself the healing power of the Steps, which is the key to lasting recovery within the 12 Step program. It breaks my heart to see alcoholic-addicts who end their progress before Step Four because they've missed out on a remarkably effective way of unloading the heavy burden that alcoholic-addicts carry on their shoulders every day: the guilt, regret, remorse, self-loathing, anger, resentment, and low self-esteem. In psychological terms, Step Four is a major turning point in relieving individuals of the pain of negative psychology and converting them to a positive psychology. We will discuss why Step Four presents such a barrier to some people and how to overcome that snare.

In my addictions research I have a special interest in chronic relapsers, and I have found that virtually all chronic relapsers who have participated in the 12 Step program never got past Step Four. There are many people whose 12 Step program involves the first three Steps (if even that) and meetings. I have met some people in the fellowship who have succeeded in recovery without doing the Steps, but they must not have been as sick as I was, because, personally, I needed the healing to stand a chance at recovery. Even if someone is able to maintain recovery without working through the Steps, he or she is missing a tremendous opportunity of self-improvement and spiritual and personal growth. The 12 Steps have been – for me – the most significant personal discovery and growth experience that I've ever encountered. I wish I would have been able to avail myself of the Steps when I was in my twenties, long before alcohol or drugs were a problem for me, because the life skills, spiritual well-being, and principles for living and interacting with others would have rendered me far more effective in life. So, it saddens me when I meet people who never made it through the Steps because they didn't complete their Step Four. Step Four seems to be a big sticking point for a lot of people, but let's look at the reasons why that is, so that you don't get stuck as well.

There are a variety of reasons that so many people bog down on Step Four. It's the first "action Step," where we must do some work and produce a result and then demonstrate that result to another person (i.e. to our sponsor). As well, it's a fearful and disquieting experience to reach deep down inside and confront our deepest demons, and it takes tremendous courage to do that; Step Four isn't for wusses. We are being asked to overcome our alcoholic-addict penchant for secrecy and deception. Alcoholism-addiction is essentially a form of avoidance-coping, so it goes against our very nature to stop running and directly confront and admit all those things that we had been hiding from for so long. It's like putting our hand on a hot stove and then trying to keep it there. We are being asked to confront things that we have pushed deep down inside and done our level best to ignore for many years. We drank or used partly so that we didn't have to deal with these demons, and now we are being asked to face them. For people with a profoundly painful past – such as victims of abuse – this can seem like an impossible thing to ask. The Big Book acknowledges this difficulty: "almost none of us liked the self-searching, the leveling of our pride, the confession of shortcomings which the process requires for its successful consummation" (p. 25). However, the feeling of liberation and catharsis that comes with the process is superlative. We can either continue living under the dark rule of our secrets and continue allowing them to be a reliable source of ongoing unhappiness and pain for us, or we can draw a line in the sand and screw up the courage to confront them once and for all. That's the choice we face at Step Four.

As well, many people are flat-out embarrassed by the things they must confess in their inventory in Step Four, and they make up their minds that they aren't going to do this important Step. Anticipation of this embarrassment causes fear and anxiety, because we have guarded our secrets so zealously for so long for fear of getting in trouble with friends, family, employers, and even the law. We are fearful that other people will judge us and think badly of us. We fear we will be branded as "bad." Of course, it's in the nature of the sick alcoholic-addict mind to ruminate on our fears and blow them out of proportion. So, we keep our secrets. Step Four asks us to unlock these secrets and hang them out to dry. However, once again we need to take a leap of faith. This fear is a big part of what keeps us in our addiction, and keeps our character and our behavior shameful (i.e. this fear propagates our "character defects," as we will see in Step Six). We are so accustomed to living with the fear of our past wrong-doings that we have become used to it. When we take that leap of faith and do our Step

166

Four, the sudden relief from this fear is a tremendously liberating experience. But, we must first take that leap of faith and face our fears with courage and rigorous honesty.

Another way to deal with the fear that tries to bully us as we face Step Four is to go to lots of 12 Step meetings and listen to speakers share their own dark secrets at the podium. Soon we see that we belong to a culture of rigorous honesty, and the psychological drive to belong to the group gives us a big mental boost to be honest like the rest of our brothers and sisters in recovery. We also find comfort in each other, in seeing what completing Step Four has done for others: "whenever our pencil falters, we can fortify and cheer ourselves by remembering what A.A. experience in this Step has meant to others" (*Twelve Steps and Twelve Traditions,* p. 82). People in the 12 Step fellowship who once feared taking their inventory when they first came to the program find themselves willingly sharing their inventory at the podium and with the people they sponsor. That's because by the time we complete our trip through the Steps we see that our fears were exaggerated and unfounded, and we become comfortable in our own skin. As we heal and grow our past no longer causes us fear and anxiety. We move from running and hiding from our past to accepting and owning it, thereby ceasing its power over us. We learn to accept our past as something we cannot change, and we come to terms with it by taking action to correct our actions today and for the future, which is something that we can change. As we clean house we clean out the fear and anxiety, and that begins with confronting our fears in Step Four.

*

We are told that: "Step Four is an effort to discover our liabilities" (*Twelve Steps and Twelve Traditions,* p. 6), and that: "beginning with Step Four, we commenced to search out the things in ourselves which had brought us to physical, moral, and spiritual bankruptcy" (p. 107). So, is Step Four all about self-deprecation, breaking ourselves down, making ourselves feel bad about past actions that we'd rather just forget? Do we have to throw our already low self-esteem under the bus to do our Step Four? Not at all; in fact, quite the opposite. One of the greatest effects of the Steps – especially the "cleaning house" Steps – is the development of a healthy self-esteem, an appreciation of our own self-worth that doesn't need validation from other people or putting on a false front or cutting other people down to prop it up. Step Four is absolutely essential in starting the process of self-forgiveness, so that we feel worthy of self-esteem. As we will see in Step Six, self-criticism and self-deprecation are actually character defects that we remove from our make-up as we become spiritually healthy. So, any thought that

Step Four is about beating ourselves up is dead wrong. Rather, Step Four is where we put an end to beating ourselves up over our past.

Our alcoholic-addict pride – our substance-soaked mind's pathological effort to compensate for our low self-esteem – may interfere with our ability to be willing and open-minded for Step Four: "… when A.A. suggests a fearless moral inventory, it must seem to every newcomer that more is being asked of him than he can do. Both his pride and his fear beat him back every time he tries to look within himself" (*Twelve Steps and Twelve Traditions*, p. 49). Our mind likes to make itself feel better by seeking to lay blame for our faults on others – that pesky cognitive dissonance at work again. But, we are here to heal and to establish a firm basis for recovery, so we must look beyond such mental nonsense. *Twelve Steps and Twelve Traditions* explains:

> We also clutch at another wonderful excuse for avoiding our inventory. Our present anxieties and troubles, we cry, are caused by the behavior of other people – people who *really* need a moral inventory. We firmly believe that if only they'd treat us better, we'd be all right. Therefore we think our indignation is justified and reasonable – that our resentments are the "right kind." *We* aren't the guilty ones. *They* are! (p. 45-46).

Certainly, it's seldom difficult to find other people and things that contributed to our woes. But, hanging on to this has been the basis of our resentments, which have been a constant source of mental turmoil for us; these resentments were the root cause of our obsessive substance use. We can go on hanging onto our "blame-thrower," or we can let go and find peace of mind. We can ask ourselves: *do I want to go on justifying my wrong-doings, or do I want to be happy? Twelve Steps and Twelve Traditions* explains:

> The majority of A.A. members have suffered severely from self-justification during their drinking days. For most of us, self-justification was the maker of excuses; excuses, of course, for drinking, and for all kinds of damaging conduct. We had made the invention of alibis a fine art.
>
> We thought "conditions" drove us to drink, and when we tried to correct these conditions and found that we couldn't to our entire satisfaction, our drinking went out of hand and we became alcoholics. It never occurred to us that we needed to change ourselves to meet conditions, whatever they were (p. 47).

The 12 Step publication *Living Sober* refers to this blame-game, this self-justification, this maker of excuses, this invention of alibis, as the *if trap*:

168

"each of us thought: I wouldn't be drinking this way... if it wasn't for my wife (or husband or lover)... if I just had more money and not so many debts... if it wasn't for all these family problems... if I wasn't under so much pressure..." (p. 62) and so on, you get the idea. The reason this is called the "if trap" is because it puts conditions on our sobriety: "we have begun to think sobriety is just fine – *if* everything goes well, or *if* nothing goes wrong" (p. 63). If we allow our thinking to continue in the old ways, where we believe that other people or things were responsible for our actions, the "if trap" will get us sooner or later when some mishap occurs: "somewhere, buried in a hidden convolution of our gray matter, we had a tiny reservation – a condition on our sobriety. And it was just waiting to pounce. We were going along thinking, 'Yep, sobriety is great, and I intend to keep at it.' We didn't even hear the whispered reservation: 'That is, *if* everything goes my way'" (p. 63).

We must purge this type of thinking from our mind: "those ifs we cannot afford. We have to stay sober no matter how life treats us... we have to keep our sobriety independent of everything else, not entangled with any people, and not hedged in by any possible cop-outs or conditions" (p. 63). The "if trap" gives us an out, a convenient excuse to abandon our hard-earned sobriety as soon as our disease starts knocking at the door. The way to eliminate the "if trap" is to take full responsibility for our past behaviors, including our drinking or using, to stop projecting blame for our drinking or using and related behaviors, and to accept that our recovery must not be dependent on outside issues. One of my favorite stories from the Big Book (*He Lived Only to Drink*, found on pages 446-451) makes this point beautifully:

> I realized that I had to separate my sobriety from everything else that was going on in my life. No matter what happened or didn't happen, I couldn't drink. In fact, none of these things that I was going through had anything to do with my sobriety; the tides of life flow endlessly for better or worse, both good and bad, and I cannot allow my sobriety to become dependent on these ups and downs of living. Sobriety must live a life of its own (p. 450-1).

As the alcoholic-addict who wrote that story realized, the genius of the 12 Step program is that it's not at all about not using drugs or alcohol. Rather, it's about learning to live life on life's terms, learning to stop feeling like the world's victim and getting on with life without running to the bottle or needle with every stressor. As the Serenity Prayer tells us, it's about learning to accept that life isn't always going to go our way. Not because we are cursed, not because God or the world hates us, but because that's how life is for everybody. We learn to accept life's ups and downs as they come.

We do our best to make life go our way, but when it doesn't we roll with it and accept it. The need to use drugs or alcohol to escape the overwhelming anger, resentment, self-pity, and pessimism that drive our psychology into a darkly negative domain melts away. It's such a gift to be relieved of such a painful and depressing state of mind. Step Four is a foundation stone of that new healthy and realistic mind-set. The more honest and complete we are with our Step Four, the more deeply therapeutic it is for us: "once we have a complete willingness to take inventory, and exert ourselves to do the job thoroughly, a wonderful light falls upon this foggy scene. As we persist, a brand-new kind of confidence is born, and the sense of relief at finally facing ourselves is indescribable. These are the first fruits of Step Four" (*Twelve Steps and Twelve Traditions,* p. 49-50). Let's now talk about the importance of being honest and complete.

*

It has been well established by psychological research that open and truthful disclosure reduces psychological stress and helps people come to terms with their regrets and guilt over past behaviors.[1] Most people are aware of this from personal experience; getting stuff off our chest feels good. What's more, compelling research has also demonstrated that writing out our dark secrets – as we are suggested to do in Step Four – further benefits our well-being, including our physical as well as mental health.[2]

Other studies have demonstrated that people who make partial confessions to their wrong-doings are more negatively affected psychologically than if they had made no confession at all.[3] This is probably because the partial confession draws more and renewed attention to our wrong-doings, and the act of withholding details – a lie of omission – only increases our feelings of guilt. We feel as if we are lacking credibility, and this adds to our negative feelings about ourselves. We never really get it off our chest unless we tell the *whole* story. The secrets that we keep haunt us even more when we know we should've come clean. We need to get it all out to enjoy the full benefit of Step Four, but that's a real struggle for people with alcoholism-addiction for several reasons.

As we've discussed, the psychology of active alcoholism-addiction is characterized by certain dysfunctional thought processes and behaviors that prevent truthful and honest disclosure. Ours is known as the lonely disease, because we have a tendency to shun others and self-isolate. Coming out of our shell and exposing our deepest darkest secrets does not come naturally to us. Too, alcoholism-addiction is heavily burdened with a social stigma that makes us reluctant to worsen our stigma by telling anybody without holding back, especially when our behaviors have been illegal or socially repugnant, such as drunk driving, drinking while pregnant, or resorting to

170

crime to support our addiction-alcoholism. We are already wracked with guilt, remorse, and self-loathing over these things, and we recoil from putting ourselves in a position where we will be judged by someone else by exposing our secrets. Alcoholism-addiction is also characterized by pathological lying and deception to cover up for our drinking and drug use and related behaviors; for many of us lies and deceit had become a lifestyle. We therefore come to Step Four with a predisposition to not be truthful. But that mind-set has made us sick, and we need to adopt new ways of thinking to get healthy again – our secrets keep us sick. Now is the time to let go of these addiction-related behaviors.

The human psyche is geared to make people believe that they bear no responsibility for a particular problem, or to sideswipe or minimize their responsibility, and this psychological trait is especially pronounced in alcoholic-addicts. It's that cognitive dissonance at work again. This causes us problems, especially for those of us who need some serious healing. As one psychologist puts it: "this psychological dysfunctionality [of not owning up to our mistakes] cripples a substantial portion of the human population in ways that work against the possibility of achieving worthwhile outcomes for themselves, other individuals, communities and the world as a whole."[4] We need to bust through this tendency and own our mistakes, and we need to be truthful about it. Only then can we begin healing and changing our behaviors to reflect the healthy recovery that we seek. Interestingly, psychological studies have demonstrated that people are much more likely to be truthful and accept responsibility for their actions when they believe that doing so will change their behavior.[5] Since our Step Four is part of a program designed to change our behaviors for the better, our participation in the 12 Step program itself makes us more likely to step up take on the challenge of rigorous honesty.

We are far more likely to open up and be completely honest with someone who has been through exactly what we have been through, someone who has done the same things we have done, someone we know will not be judgmental. Because of this, the 12 Step fellowship and a sponsor we trust may be the only place in the world where we can feel entirely safe in self-disclosing. They understand like no one else could.

Step Four is where the rubber meets the road for our rigorous honesty, which is necessary if we are to find healing from the Steps: "our solution which, as you know, demands rigorous honesty" (Big Book, p. 145). Step Four is where: "we subjected ourselves to a drastic self-appraisal (Big Book, p. 76). We can only deal with and overcome problems if we have the courage to confront them, and we can only do that if we are rigorously honest about them. However, our mind is geared to putting our best face forward, which makes it very difficult for us to be honest about our faults, shortcomings, and failure. That's especially true when it comes to the

171

pathetic behaviors that many among us resorted to during our active substance use. Many of our behaviors were, in hindsight, stupid, shameful, and even illegal. However, unless we confront these behaviors, we will never get them off our back and stop them from haunting our mind. Therefore, our ability to heal, and find happiness, peace of mind, and healthy recovery depends on our rigorous honesty.

The 12 Step program is tailor-made to allow us to be rigorously honest, which is one area where it's vastly superior to psychotherapy. A group of researchers who have spent years investigating whether or not people are honest with their therapists found that up to 93% of people lie to their therapist, and that among the worst offenders are people with addictions.[6] The Big Book explains why this isn't a problem in the 12 Step program:

> Highly competent psychiatrists who have dealt with us have found it sometimes impossible to persuade an alcoholic to discuss his situation without reserve. Strangely enough, wives, parents and intimate friends usually find us even more unapproachable than do the psychiatrist and the doctor. But the ex-problem drinker who has found this solution, who is properly armed with the facts about himself, can generally win the confidence of another alcoholic in a few hours. Until such an understanding is reached, little or nothing can be accomplished (p. 18).

In order to heal we must tell our story, but it must be the *whole* story. The 12 Step program offers a safe place to do that, a place where we know that no one will judge us, everybody there will understand, and there's no stigma. There's a liberating feeling that comes with getting our worst shame off our chest, and the only place where our psychology may allow us to do so freely is with receptive, non-judgmental people who are just like us.

*

Overcoming our alcoholic-addict defensive and secretive nature isn't the only barrier to a good Step Four. We must also put some effort into reflecting on the things we set down in our inventory in order to get a truthful result. It's in the nature of our mind to purposely flaw our memory of an event if that memory is painful for us, and most of us are people with a lot of painful memories. There are various mechanisms by which our mind will warp our memory and our version of past events to protect itself from discomfort.[7] This is cognitive dissonance – our disease's favorite psychological tool – once again at work, this time in distorting or shrouding our painful memories to protect us from the anguish they cause us.

172

Our memories are not like a video recording; rather, they are heavily biased by our perspective, emotions, and memory storage and recall flaws. These flaws in our memory – referred to by psychologists as *adaptive features of memory* – are an inherent defense mechanism that the mind relies on to protect itself from the discomfort of realizing that we are not as "good" as our mind wants to believe that we are – i.e. cognitive dissonance. These affect how we make memories, and our mind has specific mechanisms for distorting how we recall memories that are distasteful for us, known as *memory biases* and *recall biases*. Cognitive dissonance will induce our mind to manipulate our memories to create false or heavily distorted recollections. This is a major symptom of the psychology of addiction-alcoholism, where we blame others for our woes and carry distorted memories of events to lessen our own feelings of failure. If we recognize that our memory of events might not necessarily be the straight facts we can come up with a much more honest and complete inventory. If we allow ourselves to be open-minded and willing to face the unvarnished facts, there are ways we can improve the verity of our inventory. It hurts, but it's like ripping off a Band-Aid so that we can wash a wound and apply medicine: a quick bit of pain but worth it because of the soothing healing that follows.

Of course, forgetting is the most obvious memory flaw, but in our case the forgetting may not be necessary because we may not have formed the painful memories to begin with. Many alcoholics are blackout drinkers, which means that they are incapable of forming new memories while intoxicated. Drug use may also cause impaired memory formation during highs or withdrawal. We may have to drop our pride and listen to those who have seen our past performances to get a good picture of the extent of our wrong-doings.

Memory formation is based on perspective; we remember things that are significant to us and we are less likely to remember things that are not important to us. Addiction-alcoholism is characterized by a pathological self-centeredness – the basis of our spiritual sickness – and how our actions affect others may not matter to us much at all when we are spiritually sick. As such, we may not remember a lot of the wrong-doings we have committed because we really don't care at the time. The self-centeredness of addiction-alcoholism prevents us from even noticing how our actions affect other people. When we are in withdrawal and desperate to obtain our next drink or drug, our drive to do so may push us to wrong other people, but we are so self-focused on fulfilling the call of our self-will that the impact of our actions on others matters so little to us that we don't even register it into memory. However, as time passes in recovery the impact of our actions may start to occur to us, particularly when we seek to make amends and people begin telling us how our behaviors affected them. If we don't make efforts to remember things better our amends will fall short and we may further hurt people as we make our amends by not doing justice in our atonement. If we don't remember how we wronged them they will certainly remind us.

There are a couple of exercises that I suggest for overcoming some of the memory flaws, the effects of the drug and alcohol use on memory, and the memory formation and recall biases. The first such exercise is simply an exercise in empathy: basically putting ourselves in someone else's shoes. We can't do that for everyone we crossed paths with, but we can do it for some of the key people in our lives. This helps us to better understand our wrong-doings, so that we can get them out from their hiding places in the recesses of our mind and confront them once and for all. When we make amends in Step Nine we will fall flat on our face if we don't have a good empathetic understanding of how we have hurt or wronged the people we seek to make amends with.

Empathy – understanding and sharing the perspective and feelings of others – is a wonderful skill for spiritual health. Spirituality is about getting outside ourselves and showing more concern for others, and empathy is a great way to do that. It also helps us put together a realistic and worthwhile inventory in Step Four. A great way to generate a little empathy in order to enhance our understanding of our past actions and their effects on others is by using an exercise psychologists refer to as the *empty chair technique*. The way I suggest using this technique is to imagine yourself as a third person, sitting in a chair – sober – watching an interaction between you and another person, someone you were close with in your drinking or using days. The person you are watching from your imaginary chair is yourself, full-blast into your insane and intoxicated addict-alcoholic behavior, and the other person you are watching is sober and rational. What do you see? How does your behavior look through your eyes, sober and sitting in the chair? What would you say to yourself if you were sitting in that empty chair watching? I can give a personal example of this.

Three people who put up with A LOT when I was actively drinking and using were my sister, mother, and my girlfriend. Yet, they stuck with me, and did their best to help me, and were still there supporting me in my recovery. I was so self-focused in active addiction-alcoholism and in early recovery that I took them for granted. However, when I got to my Step Four I decided to use some "empty chair" reflection to look back at how my actions had affected them. In my imagination I sat in the empty chair – sober – and watched myself one night when I came home drunk. I sat there watching (in my imagination) as I pulled my car into the driveway – obnoxious and intoxicated – and banged my way into the house. I then imagined the horrible way I acted toward my family, and was even able to remember a lot of specifics. Looking through the eyes of a sober person I could see how insane I must have looked. And this was just one evening. I

174

put my family through this day after day, night after night, week after week, month after month. Suddenly it really began to sink in how I had caused mayhem and grief in other people's lives. I even asked myself: *would I have stood by someone else if they subjected me to such behavior?* That's a sobering question to ask ourselves, because the answer may well be *no*.

Sometimes, when I am at a social event where there is drinking, or I see some people who are drunk or high in public, I see someone who's acting like an ape, and I feel offended and angry. Then I quickly imagine how I was just the same and I subjected a lot of people to that same insane behavior. That goes a long way to helping me understand the depth of my insanity and my wrong-doings towards others. This is another example of our "empty chair" exercise in action.

The other exercise that I would suggest takes some courage. In fact, I generally recommend that people not use this technique their first time through the Steps, especially when they are in early recovery. Rather, it's more appropriate for people who have been through the Steps once and have achieved some stability and peace and self-forgiveness, and some time has passed for the rawness of their wrong-doings to settle a bit for the people in their lives. The technique is this: ask a loved one, a non-addict-alcoholic who was there during your active addiction-alcoholism, to take your Step Four inventory for you. Ask him or her to list for you what your wrong-doings were. You may find it to be a bit of an eye-opener, to say the least. Your brain may have suppressed or distorted the memories, but theirs certainly hasn't!

*

Despite our utmost efforts at remembering past events, regardless of our most devout willingness and open-mindedness, we are only human and our memories will be incomplete. Our imperfect memories, further flawed by the effects of our substance use and our inward-looking mind-set, will never perfectly reflect our past actions. That's OK; as the Big Book says: "we claim spiritual progress rather than spiritual perfection" (p. 60). However, as time goes by and our brains recover from being feasted on by chemicals of addiction, as we connect with other people and see things that jog our memory, things will come back to us. For this reason, it's important that we revisit our Step Four as things come back to us. The completeness of our Step Four is vital to our spiritual health, our wellbeing, and our recovery. Our human flaws will prevent perfection in our Step Four, but all we need is a willingness to strive for our best effort: "it is suggested that we ought to become entirely willing to aim toward perfection" (*Twelve Steps and Twelve Traditions,* p. 69), and "we shall need to raise our eye toward perfection, and be ready to walk in that direction" (p. 68). When we have completed our

Step Four and move on to Step Five we must remember that we will come back and revisit it as things come to us.

Many people in the fellowship come back to Step Four after a significant life experience, or just when they feel it necessary. For example, I recently had to go back to court for an issue around child custody with my ex, and the experience got under my skin quite a bit. I found myself becoming restless and irritable, and I knew I needed a spiritual tune-up. So, I went back and did a mini-Step Four around the event with my sponsor, which really helped me. The Steps are a process of healing and centering ourselves spiritually; they are there for us to use anytime, not just when we first come to recovery. We will see in our Step Ten discussion that taking an inventory following minor lapses in our spiritual behavior are a part of maintaining and growing our spiritual health and our recovery.

*

In order for our Step Four and subsequent Step Five to be effective there are certain conditions that need to be met for the experience to be one of healing. Psychologists have identified key aspects to admissions of wrong-doings and apologies that make them effective for what we are really looking for as we clean house: self-forgiveness and a new start on a spiritual way of living. We have already discussed the importance of rigorous honesty, and how a partial admission of wrongdoing actually does us more harm than no admission at all. As well, we must accept responsibility for our wrongdoings for Step Four to impart healing on us.[8]

It's very easy to say: *well, I was drunk/high when I did that*, thereby passing off responsibility for our action. This is especially so when we were blacked out or have no memory of the event. As well, it's in our nature to deflect blame away from ourselves by blaming others, and we must be conscious that our alcoholic-addict mind will try to get us to do that in Step Four: *I did that to her, but she did this to me.* Allowing our ailing mind to talk us into finding reasons to lessen our responsibility for our wrongdoings detracts from the healing that we stand to derive from Step Four. The two most common ways that we try to deflect our responsibility are: 1) to blame our actions on the fact that we were drunk or high, and 2) to rationalize our wrongdoing because it was in response to someone else's actions.

After high school and before I went to university I joined the army and got into officer training. I was very young and naïve when I graduated as a second lieutenant, and I learned some lessons about leadership and being an officer really quickly. One lesson that I will never forget occurred when a dude in my platoon messed up really bad, and there was a lot of trouble. One of my sergeants was punishing one of his young soldiers for a small screw-up and went a little too far with his punishment, seriously injuring the

176

soldier. Next thing I knew I was standing at attention in front of my commanding officer trying to explain what happened. I made a big mistake that day, one that I never again repeated. I tried to pass the blame for the mistake on to my subordinate – after all, it was true, it was the sergeant's fault and I had nothing to do with it; I wasn't even there when it happened. BIG mistake! My CO berated me twice as hard as he would have done if I would have straight-up accepted responsibility for the mess-up. And my CO was correct; a leader is responsible for everything that happens under his or her command, whether aware of it or not. Our Step Four is like that. We need to man/woman-up for our wrongdoings, and stop trying to hide behind blaming someone or something else. In the end, we are responsible for our actions and for how we respond to other people's actions. Step Four is therapeutically useless unless we take on the courage to do that.

Accepting responsibility for our past actions begins in our Step Four, and we must make sure that we own up to our past actions before we put any of them on paper. To allow psychological weakness to add "buts" to our list is to invite a poor result. We are not here to take other people's inventories, or to weigh out in our mind if our wrong-doings were justified, or to absolve ourselves of blame because we never would've done those things if it wasn't for the drugs or drink. If you are having problems doing that, you should discuss it with your sponsor, because you need to get past it in order to clean house, heal, and give your recovery the very best possible foundation. To be sure, there are many times that we wronged someone and they were not faultless. Nevertheless, the question we must ask is: *what was my role in the event?*

An example is in order here. The turning point for me, when I went from being take-it-or-leave-it with drugs and alcohol to an obsessive daily drinker and user was my divorce. It was a bitterly contested ordeal, and I felt that I was dealt with unfairly by the courts and by my ex-wife. The financial impact on me was crippling, and my animosity toward "the system" and the people involved grew until I burned with anger and resentment. I felt sorry for myself, convinced I was a victim. I was so filled with burning rage and resentment that the only way I could shut my mind off at night and get some sleep was by drinking alcohol. Lots of it. I went downhill fast. Soon, I was finding that the only way I could get out of bed in the morning and face the world was by drinking or using drugs to start my day, which would continue all day. When I came to the 12 Step program it was obvious to me that my anger and resentments over my divorce had to go.

When I did my Step Four it was easy for me to deflect blame for all the awful things I had said and done when it came to this watershed experience in my life. After all, my ex-wife was certainly not blameless in the matter, and the courts probably were a little hard on me. However, if I tried doing my Step Four with "buts" mixed in I was not going to heal any. If I carried the attitude that *yes, I did this, but she pushed me into it*, not only was I not going to heal but it would only have served to increase my anger and resentments. No, I had to look at **my** actions only, and take full responsibility for them.

Taking responsibility is acknowledging and accepting the choices we have made, the actions we have taken, and the results they have led to. We are here to heal and the only way to do that is to step up and own our past actions. It hurts, but it heals and it liberates the mind. It's not about who's to blame for our actions, it's about taking responsibility for our actions, claiming ownership of the circumstances of our past so that we can make them better. Taking other people's inventory and judging and criticizing their actions serves only to distance us from finding a solution to our problems. It doesn't mean that we are necessarily to blame for all the bad things that have happened in our lives, we are not lying down on the ground and accepting blame for all that went wrong. Rather, we are accepting responsibility for **our** actions and reactions – **our** part in what went wrong. It's the only way to unload ourselves of our crushing burdens. We are here to clean up **our** side of the street, not to leave it dirty while we try to clean up everyone else's side of the street.

*

In my interviews with people who got stuck on Step Four I've found that many people simply don't know how to do their Step Four, so they get stuck and never end up doing it. Many tell me that their sponsor printed out some sheets for them to fill out, but they didn't know what to do with them. They are unsure of exactly what they have to produce, what has to be on that paper and how to write it out. The Big Book gives us guidance on how to do Step Four, but the details aren't always clear. Personally, the way to do a self-inventory suggested by the Big book didn't make complete sense to me (probably because my mind was still clouded because I was still in early recovery), so I worked with my sponsor on it and came up with a way that made sense to me. I've gone back and done mini-Step Fours on a number of occasions, and I've helped others work through their Step Four, so I can pass on some suggestions. As a psychological therapist I can also offer some advice on how to do a Step Four inventory that will provide optimal release from the pain and tension from our sordid past. There's no absolute right or wrong way to do an inventory; the best thing is to find a way that makes sense for you and that allows you to free yourself of your psychological burdens. I suggest working with your sponsor to figure this out. As well, we will work through an inventory process in the pages that follow. We will dissect the Big Book and other 12 Step literature to see what it tells us about doing an awesome Step Four. Let's get to it.

*

Laying out our wrongdoings is done on paper in Step Four, and verbally in Step 5. There's special significance to this. Our brain's memory mechanisms don't work like a filing cabinet, where information about specific events is kept together in neat discrete folders. Rather, our brain stores information in a very disorganized fashion. Memories are stored as tiny little bits of information (known as *memory engrams*) that are scattered around various parts of the brain cortex (your *grey matter*).[9,10] For a specific event, we will have a small memory of a smell located in one spot in the brain, the memory of a thought over in another spot, another thought stored somewhere else, and a memory of a sound somewhere else, memory of a sight somewhere else, and so on. In order to recall the memory, we have to make a conscious effort to gather up all the scattered bits of information from all over the brain's storage system and put them together. Until we do that, these engrams are disorganized and chaotic, and the memory is nothing but scattered bits of random information. For many of us – especially after months or years of trying to avoid these memories – our Step Four is the first time we will have ever organized all these scattered engrams into a coherent memory that we can finally hold in one place and confront and deal with it.

In order to explain something to another person – either in writing or verbally – our brain must first assemble all the information and put it into a coherent package – a story – so that we can explain it to the other person. Many of us have never done that for the ugly memories of our wrongdoings and our resentments. The two ways that we can force our brain to finally assemble these scattered bits of information is by explaining the memories in writing (as we do in Step Four) and explaining them verbally to another person (as we do in Step Five). As such, Steps Four and Five allow us to finally organize our thoughts so that we can confront them and deal with them.

So, Steps Four and Five allow us to finally, after years of avoiding confronting these memories and trying to suppress them through drink or drug, put them together into a coherent package that we can hold (figuratively) in our hands in front of our eyes. We finally organize all these scattered thoughts, feelings, emotions, and sensations and can confront them head-on. That empowers us – as we hold them in our hands, so to speak – to throw them up in the air and be done with them. While this sounds simplistic, this is exactly how it works and how we finally get these awful burdens off our shoulders.

*

Step Four can be divided into three inventories: 1) our wrongdoings, 2) our resentments, and 3) our fears. Our wrongdoings and resentments are the two biggest burdens on our shoulders as alcoholics and addicts, so Step Four allows us to directly confront these adversaries to happiness and peace of mind. Our fears are also a significant burden to our mind, and a cause of anger and resentments. Our fears prevent us from taking action, and drive us to hide in the bottle or needle. We have already discussed fears and their link to addiction-alcoholism in our Step One discussion. Let's look at the wrongdoings inventory first.

The Big Book tells us how to make this inventory. Quite simply:

> We reviewed our own conduct over the years past. Where had we been selfish, dishonest, or inconsiderate? Whom had we hurt? Did we unjustifiably arouse suspicion or bitterness? Where were we at fault, what should we have done instead? We got this all down on paper and looked at it (p. 69).

For this inventory, I suggest that we list out all those things we feel guilty about, the things we've done that we regret, the things we've done where we wish we could have a do-over, and those things we have done that have hurt others. This will take some time, but it's worth it to get it right. Everything we wish to take from our conscience and make right needs to be on that list. Everything. Again, this is a good time to involve our sponsor, because a good sponsor will help draw things out of us.

The Big Book spends a lot of time discussing wrongdoings related to sex, but I personally don't see much value in doing a separate sex-related inventory unless that was a big part of your past and you wish to dedicate a separate inventory to it. (I think Bill Wilson's inordinate focus on sex-related issues was related to his past as a well-known philanderer. Sorry, Bill.) Instead, I suggest including any sex-related misdeeds on your wrongdoings inventory. If you aren't sure about it, it's best to discuss it with your sponsor.

We have discussed the impact of our disease on our memory, and our tendency to push down memories that bother us. Because of this, our inventory will not be a quick piece of work. It should be revisited and added to on a number of occasions, as things come to us. Even later on in our Step activities we may remember things that we should have had on our inventory but had forgotten. We should discuss these with our sponsor as they come up. The more complete our inventory, the more thorough our mind-cleanse, and the more thorough our healing.

When we list our wrongdoings we should decide on what's important to us. For example, for most people going all the way back to childhood to list all their wrongdoings is pointless. Listing the ones related to our drinking or using and the related behaviors is definitely appropriate. However, if there are other prior wrongdoings that bother us, that sit on our shoulders, that contribute to our self-regret and unhappiness, then these should be included in our inventory. For example, if you stole a chocolate bar from your friend when you were eight, there isn't much point in including that in your inventory unless it has really bothered you over the years. We are here to heal, not to write our life story. However, the choice is yours. Again, if you're unsure about something, discuss it with your sponsor.

I suggest taking out a piece of paper and writing down things that you have done that you regret, things that you feel guilty about, things that you wish you could go back and change, and things that have hurt others. Don't omit omissions: it's not just the actions we took but sometimes the actions we failed to take – our omissions. All those things we should have done but didn't – spending time with the kids, visiting our sick mother, and so on – can be a major source of guilt for us and should be on our list.

The more complete our list of wrongdoings the more psychological peace we will get. This psychological peace is what purges negative psychology and allows us to develop a strong positive psychology. People tend to find that the things they left out haunt them afterwards, and this can provide a locus for relapse. It's one thing to leave something important out because we didn't remember it; we can always go back and add it later. The things we leave out of our inventory because we are fearful or embarrassed or because we are still keeping secrets are like a stone in our shoe; the longer we leave it there the more it hurts us. Our secrets will kill us; we are only as sick as our secrets. As I said, Step Four is where the rubber meets the road for rigorous honesty.

Imagine a soldier in a war who was wounded by a shell-burst, and has twenty little shell fragments embedded in his body. Say the army surgeon does a fantastic job of getting out the shell fragments, but only gets 19 of the 20 little metal shards. That's great, but that single tiny missed shell fragment will cause the soldier a lot of problems. It will fester and become infected. Scar tissue will form around it, making it strongly embedded in the body tissue and very difficult to find and remove by a future surgery. That little piece of metal will disrupt the normal function of the surrounding body tissue and will become a source of chronic pain and inflammation. If only the surgeon would have gotten that one last piece of shrapnel in the beginning, so much pain and suffering could have been averted. Well, those significant secrets that we leave out of our inventory are like that tiny shard of metal left behind by the surgery.

*

The next part of Step Four is making our resentments inventory. Resentments are a manifestation of inward-looking self-involvement, powerful yet toxic emotions and beliefs that weigh heavily on our thoughts and actions in a negative way. They are one of the root causes of obsessive drug or alcohol use, and they are also caused and worsened by our substance use. As such, resentments are both a cause and an effect of addiction. As our life tumbles downwards during our chemical misadventures the dysfunctional psychology of our disease causes our resentments to become increasingly deeper and more soul-consuming. We see ourselves as victims so we deeply resent those who victimize us. Anyone who has experienced this toxic rage against other people, institutions, God, and the world knows how corrosive it can become. It often takes over our mind, so that our resentments are the first thing we think of when we wake up, the last thing we think of when we fall asleep, and cause us to erupt in rage at the smallest of stressors. For anyone who has had resentment seething from every pore, it's not hard to see why it's a major cogwheel of the spiritually sick mind and negative psychology. Many people drink or use to try to cope with these resentments. I started my drinking career by drinking at night to try to smother my resentments so that I could get some sleep, otherwise I would lay awake all night ruminating over them. The Big Book tells us of the relationship between our resentments and our sickness:

> Resentment is the 'number one' offender. It destroys more alcoholics than anything else. From it stem all forms of spiritual disease, for we have been not only mentally and physically ill, we have been spiritually sick. When the spiritual malady is overcome, we straighten out mentally and physically (p. 64).

So, how do resentments cause alcoholism and addiction? Resentments and the rumination that they bring upon us actually paralyze our problem solving skills. They cause a downward spiral of negative psychology, where we begin to develop the feelings of victimization and learned helplessness that characterize the self-pity that is so key to low self-esteem, a pessimistic life outlook, and an external locus of control. We begin to express our ruminated thoughts to others in order to get their sympathy and to have them confirm our feelings of victimization. This is exactly the negative psychology that makes people turn to substance use to cope with the toxic feelings.

Unlike the wrongdoings list, I suggest that people go back through their entire life to make sure that every resentment they hold makes it on the list. Even that teacher back in grade six who gave you detention for

182

something you didn't do: if there's still a resentment there, no matter how many cobwebs have formed around it, it needs to be on that list. There's a psychological reason for that.

Psychologists have confirmed what the A.A. founders knew back in the 1930s: that resentments are more than just unhealthy; they are a malignant emotion that causes psychological compromise.[11] Resentments lead us to ruminate, which causes growing anger over the event where we saw ourselves as being the recipient of an injustice. The result is that our anger over the event grows over time, and a single event therefore becomes a recurrent source of anger and emotional and psychological upset for us, even years after the event. One psychologist describes rumination as "a record that's stuck and keeps repeating the same lyrics."[12] Rumination is why our resentments fester as they do. It's hardly surprising that rumination has been shown to be associated with negative consequences, including depression, anxiety, post-traumatic stress, obsessive eating, and substance use.[13] The cycle of rumination that propels our resentments is a major contributor to negative psychology and, as was known to the founders of the 12 Step program back in the 1930s, a major cause of alcoholism-addiction. Letting go of our resentments in Steps Four and Five is how we stop the pernicious rumination, so any resentment we still hold needs to be included on our list, regardless of how old or trivial it may be.

The Big Book tells us exactly how to do our resentments inventory: "in dealing with resentments, we set them on paper. We listed people, institutions or principles with whom we were angry" (p. 64). The Big Book suggests that we list beside each resentment the cause behind that resentment: "we asked ourselves why we were angry" (p. 64).

This is the part that requires some self-honesty, some soul-searching, and some surrendering of our alcoholic-addict pride. As we've discussed, it's in our psychological make-up to look to others people's contributions to our failings, to assuage our cognitive dissonance by looking for blame in others when it comes to our own worst wrongdoings, failings, and mishaps. And our mind can be quite creative about it as we can become increasingly focused on what others have done to us. The alcoholic-addict "poor-me" inner focus (self-victimization) further pushes us to do this. So, when we look to the causes of our resentments we must stop this blame-game and look at **our** contributions to our resentments. As the Big book tells us: "in most cases it was found that our self-esteem, our pocketbooks, our ambitions, our personal relationships (including sex) were hurt or threatened…. Was it our self-esteem, our security, our ambitions, our personal, or sex relations, which had been interfered with?" (p. 64-65). In other words, we are resentful because someone else's actions didn't align with how we wanted them to. When we have done a proper job of it, we begin to see that our resentments are a manifestation of our selfishness;

people aren't acting the way we want them to, and life isn't treating us the way we think it should. God – or fate, or whatever – isn't making the world turn just right for us. We had unrealistic expectations that everything and everybody would go our way in life. Our resentments were based in utter selfishness, and the price was high: these resentments made us very sick indeed.

Even when our resentments are justified, as many often are, we must put them on paper. This is important for people who have truly justified resentments, such as victims of abuse. Doing this takes courage, and it always helps to have a sponsor who has had similar experiences to coach us along. One of the special things about the 12 Step fellowship is that it's filled with people from all kinds of backgrounds with all kinds of life experiences. It's never difficult to find a sponsor who shares our specific experiences. Too, this may be an opportune time to seek outside help with a counselor who specializes in trauma counseling. Asking the counselor for help in making the part of a resentments inventory that deals with the trauma is a great way to go about it. As someone who has done a lot of trauma counseling, I can say that I believe that the 12 Step process is one of the very best ways of coming to terms with things that can't be erased, such as past trauma. Medical science is very poor at helping people with past traumas – including people with full-out PTSD – because the psychological effects of traumatic experiences tend not to respond well to medications of any kind. This is part of the reason that many people with such dreadful pasts to deal with are at especially high risk for substance use, and why there are so many people in the fellowship with a history of abuse and other past traumas.[14] Smothering unbearable memories, thoughts, and emotions with drugs or alcohol is commonplace. I believe that the resentments inventory in Steps Four and Five is one of the key parts of the 12 Steps for learning to find peace in the face of such horrible memories.

*

As a psychological therapist I have always been interested in the odd relationship between the human mind and resentments. It fascinates me that even though resentments are painful, consuming, and take a lot of time and energy away from the productive use of our brain, the mind seems to revel in them. It's as if the mind somehow enjoys ruminating and burning over some real or perceived wrong that we have endured. Yet, resentments do nothing to hurt the people we resent; they actually hurt us instead: "... when we harbored grudges and planned revenge for such defeats, we were really beating ourselves with the club of anger we had intended to use on others" (*Twelve Steps and Twelve Traditions*, p. 47). Such an odd quirk of the

184

human mind, this penchant for clinging to resentments when all it yields is self-harm.

Resentments are a major cause of negative psychology in people in general, which is a shame because resentments are a useless waste of brain-power; they don't help us accomplish anything. As alcoholic-addicts, these resentments have to go: "we learned that if we were seriously disturbed, our *first* need was to quiet that disturbance, regardless of who or what we thought caused it" (*Twelve Steps and Twelve Traditions*, p. 47). We alcoholic-addicts can't afford to carry resentments because they will kill us. From the Big Book:

> It is clear that a life which includes deep resentment leads only to futility and unhappiness. To the precise extent that we permit these do we squander the hours that might have been worth while. But with the alcoholic, whose hope is the maintenance and growth of a spiritual experience, this business of resentment is infinitely grave. We found that it is fatal. For when harboring such feelings we shut ourselves off from the sunlight of the Spirit. The insanity of alcohol returns and we drink again. And with us, to drink is to die.
>
> If we were to live, we had to be free of anger. The grouch and the brainstorm were not for us. They may be the dubious luxury of normal men, but for alcoholics these things are poison (P. 66).

As I have already pointed out, in our Step Four inventories we are not listing out our greatest wrong-doings, resentments, and fears in order to beat ourselves up. Rather, we are doing this so that we can rid ourselves of being haunted by the things that we list; we are putting a stop to their crippling power over us. Step Five is where we really let go of our resentments, but in Step Four we can begin the process of changing how we look at our resentments so that we can stop their mind-crushing effect on us as we become ready to let go of them. The Big Book tells us how to rid ourselves of resentments, including justified resentments. Letting go of burning resentments goes against our human nature and its perverse penchant for hanging on to and relishing acrimony and ill feelings. This is especially true of the angry, resentful substance-soaked mind. We therefore have to go against our natural tendencies, take a leap of faith that this unnatural and painful process will help us to heal, and take on a new way of thinking about other people and events in our lives. The most potent way of letting go of resentments – especially justified resentments – is through empathy: understanding that others may be spiritually sick and plagued with selfishness, anger, resentments, and self-pity, just as we were. We are not seeking to *excuse* other people's wrongs; rather, we seek to *understand*:

> We realized that the people who wronged us were perhaps spiritually sick. Though we did not like their symptoms and the way these disturbed us, they, like ourselves, were sick too. We asked God to help us show them the same tolerance, pity, and patience that we would cheerfully grant a sick friend. When a person offended us we said to ourselves, 'This is a sick man. How can I be helpful to him?...'
>
> We avoid retaliation or argument. We wouldn't treat sick people that way (Big Book, p. 66-67).

In those cases where someone or some thing really did wrong us in an unprovoked fashion, we seek to understand the other person as a way toward letting go of the resentment. It's important to understand that it doesn't matter if our resentments are justified or not, the detrimental psychological effect is the same. Even when we were truly wronged or at the receiving end of a grievous injustice, hanging on to the resentment and allowing it to be an ongoing source of unhappiness gains nothing for us, it just keeps us sick. I don't want to be insensitive here, because some people have some highly justified resentments. In my work with people with addictions I have come to know people who have been sexually abused as children, had a child killed by a drunk driver, had a family member murdered, or other serious causes for resentment. Obviously, I am not suggesting that these events and the feelings around them can be simply shrugged off. However, even these people can loosen or even release the grip that these past events have on their lives. As we are told in *Living Sober*: "even if we actually have been treated shabbily or unjustly, resentment is a luxury that, as alcoholics, we cannot afford. For us, *all* anger is self-destructive, because it can lead us back to drinking" (p. 39).

For people who have been victims of trauma – such as crime, abuse, disease, or disaster – letting go of a resentment may seem an impossible task. However, what we are doing is letting go of the resentment's power over us. It doesn't necessarily mean that we forgive or forget, because those things may not be possible. This process may take time, may need to occur in baby-steps, and may benefit from outside help from a counselor. Even getting to the point of talking about the resentment and getting it on paper may take time. Take all the time you need. However, regardless of how long it takes, we must always hold onto the goal that we will rid ourselves of the power that our resentments hold over us. We must never allow ourselves to become comfortable with a resentment; it can kill us. Let me tell you a true story about letting go of justified resentments.

There is a story from a member of A.A. who was well known in my area, until his recent passing. I am sure he would not mind me sharing his story, as he shared it many times at the podium as a speaker, and would certainly be pleased that the legacy of his story continues to help others.

186

This man, Paul, got involved in the outlaw biker scene at a very early age. He fit the bill: big, ugly, arrogant, and ruthless. He lived the life just like you see in the movies, and ended up addicted to just about anything, and, alas, in prison for murder. While in prison he found sobriety through A.A., where he also found his higher power and a fundamental change in character. Grateful for his recovery, he sought to give back in service work to try to right some of his many wrongs. Upon release from prison he remained active in A.A. and lived a life commensurate with the principles he learned in the program. Then, unspeakable disaster struck.

Late one night Paul was awakened by a soul-shocking phone call: his twenty-something daughter had been found dead. She had been savagely raped to death. A man was in custody. To attempt to describe the blinding mix of emotions that Paul felt at that moment would be futile. Under great strain, his old biker instincts seized every fiber of his being: he had to kill this beast who had savaged his young daughter... right after picking up a bottle of Vodka. He set out to do murder, fully capable of it. However, a little mental burr caught Paul in his trance, and caused him to call his A.A. sponsor. His sponsor talked him down, and Paul collected himself. Paul was able to use his "tools" from A.A. – prayer, meditation, talking with other alcoholic-addicts, going to meetings, working his Steps – to ride through the dangerous blend of rage and anguish that turned the minutes to hours. Paul's sponsor helped him to see that the rapist was himself an alcoholic-addict, and therefore sick, and needed help. Paul found that he was able to loosen his resentment by understanding his daughter's murderer and doing his best to feel empathy, and he found his peace again.

Time passed, and the depraved rapist was sentenced to prison for his vile deeds. In prison, this man found sobriety in A.A., and, like Paul, experienced the healing power of his higher power. A fundamental change in his character paralleled that of Paul's. He worked with other alcoholics-addicts in prison. Grateful to his higher power, which was God, he studied and became an ordained minister. His behavior in prison was exemplary.

Paul was surprised one day by a call from a member of the parole board. His daughter's killer was applying for early parole. This was being seriously considered by the parole board, but they would allow a parole hearing only if Paul consented. Nobody in the world would condemn Paul for outright forbidding any consideration of early parole, but that's not what happened. Instead, Paul went and met his daughter's murderer in the flesh. He offered his forgiveness, a defining moment of courage and humility. He came away with the realization that remaining in prison wouldn't help this man or anybody else. Release from prison would allow this man to take his message of A.A. and God to others, so Paul gave his consent to the parole hearing. The man was granted early parole, and went on to do exactly the service work that he said he would do.

Paul gives us an example we can only hope to emulate. He found peace after a horrifying traumatic experience, to the point of forgiveness of someone who didn't deserve forgiveness, and showing that individual an act of mercy. Instead of allowing this dreadful tragedy to destroy his spirituality – and his sobriety – he used his spiritual principles to turn it into an opportunity to grow in spirituality. As we will discuss a little later on, we can find meaning even in suffering by how we endure our suffering – maintaining our spiritual principles and dignity despite facing adverse conditions. Although deceased, Paul lives on as an inspiring example of these principles and the healing power of the 12 Steps.

Paul's example is inspiring, but only people who have been victims of crime or abuse can understand how hard it is to loosen their resentment's grip. Again, this is not an overnight process, but everybody who has been afflicted with such a resentment should start by trying to become open-minded and willing to do their best to let go, even if gradually over time. It's about no longer allowing the object of our resentment to hold power over us. The effort is Herculean, but the rewards are great.

*

Another way to let go of resentments is to seek out our own role in the event that brought on the resentment: "putting out of our minds the wrongs others had done, we resolutely looked for our own mistakes…. Where were we to blame?" (Big Book, p. 67). We have already discussed this approach to letting go of resentments. It's about the uselessness of focusing on what other people did, but rather looking at our own role in events that have left us with resentments. Our cognitive dissonance pushes us into seeking blame for our problems and failures to get what we wanted, but the resulting resentments have been killing us; we must fight back and turn our attention to our own behaviors rather than other people's behaviors. Most situations that cause resentments are not based entirely on someone else's actions. Even when we really were innocent victims, we can apply the Serenity Prayer to how we handle our resentment. We can't change past actions, and we can't change what other people have done to us, so we need to accept those events, as unfortunate as they may be. That means stopping wasting brain power on ruminating over the past and other people's actions and doing the "what if" thing. Rather, we change the thing we do have the power to change, which is what we do with the resentment. We can either continue allowing the resentment to burn inside of us, or we can be happy and free: "it is plain that a life which includes deep resentment leads only to futility and unhappiness" (Big Book, p. 66). We apply the Serenity Prayer by accepting past happenings and other people's actions, and letting go of our need to ruminate and stew over them. The best way to do this is to become

188

focused on our role in the events that led to the resentment, and to turn it into a learning experience.

Even when someone else has wronged us, we look to what we did to bring on the event. As soon as we start taking someone else's inventory we are deviating from the healing power of Step Four:

> Putting out of our minds the wrongs others had done, we resolutely looked for our own mistakes. Where had we been selfish, dishonest, self-seeking and frightened? Though a situation had not been entirely our fault, we tried to disregard the other person involved entirely. Where were we to blame? The inventory was ours, not the other man's (Big Book, p. 67).

This is a good time to work through the resentment list with a good sponsor, because a sponsor will challenge us by asking the hard questions to draw out our contribution to our resentments.

One of the alcoholics whose story appears in the Big Book tells of a useful way to free ourselves of resentments:

> He [a clergyman in an article] said, in effect: 'If you have a resentment you want to be free of, if you will pray for the person or the thing that you resent, you will be free. If you will ask in prayer for everything you want for yourself to be given to them, you will be free. Ask for their health, their prosperity, their happiness, and you will be free. Even when you don't really want it for them, and your prayers are only words and you don't mean it, go ahead and do it anyway. Do it every day for two weeks (or more) and you will find you have come to mean it and to want it for them, and you will realize that where you used to feel bitterness and resentment and hatred, you now feel compassionate understanding and love.'
>
> It worked for me then, and it has worked for me many times since, and it will work for me every time I am willing to work it. Sometimes I have to ask first for the willingness, but it too always comes (Big Book, p. 552).

It takes a lot of grit and moxie to bring ourselves to pray for someone we resent, especially if that person did something horrible to us. This is something that some people need to take some time to work up to. However, praying for someone may be deeply therapeutic for some of us.

One of the best-loved stories from the Big Book (*Acceptance Was The Answer* written by Dr. Paul Ohliger, who died – sober – at age 83 in 2000) illustrates that the key to letting go of these resentments is acceptance;

acceptance that the world is as it is and that we can't control the world, and that people and things are not always going to go our way in life. Says Dr. O:

> And acceptance is the answer to all my problems today. When I am disturbed, it is because I find some person, place, thing or situation – some fact of my life – unacceptable to me, and I can find no serenity until I accept that person, place, thing or situation as being exactly the way it is supposed to be at this moment. Nothing, absolutely nothing happens in God's world by mistake. Until I could accept my alcoholism, I could not stay sober; unless I accept life completely on life's terms, I cannot be happy. I need to concentrate not so much on what needs to be changed in the world as on what needs to be changed in me and in my attitudes (Big Book, p. 417).

Dr. O's acceptance is the Serenity Prayer in action. The 12 Step slogan "Live and Let Live" also applies here; we concern ourselves with our own actions, and stop trying to straighten out everybody else. Says one alcoholic-addict in recovery: "I can't afford resentments against anyone because they are the build-up of another drunk. I must live and let live" (Big Book, p. 293).

In Step Four, as we make our inventory lists, we begin the process of seeing our resentments in a new light, by understanding that those who have wronged us may have been spiritually sick, by accepting the past as something we cannot change, and by endeavoring to change what we can: how we react to the past today. This forms the basis of letting go of our resentments and ending their cruel power over us. Step Five is where we take these resentments and throw them up in the air, to release ourselves from their burden.

This ability to let go of our need to hold grudges and blame our woes on others goes well beyond our Steps Four and Five. It becomes a life skill that's necessary for our ongoing spiritual growth, sobriety, and peace of mind. In the A.A. publication *Living Sober*, it tells us about applying the 12 Step slogan "Live and Let Live" to our understanding of other people's actions that don't suit us:

> In A.A. much emphasis is placed on learning how to tolerate other people's behavior. However offensive or distasteful it may seem to us, it is certainly *not* worth drinking about. Our own recovery is too important. Alcoholism can and does kill, we recall.
>
> We have learned that it pays to make a very special effort to try to understand other people, especially anyone who rubs us the wrong way. For our recovery, it is more important to understand than to be understood....

190

As time goes on, we find we are not afraid simply to walk away from people who irritate us, instead of meekly letting them get under our skin, or instead of trying to straighten them out just so they will suit us better.

None of us can remember anyone's forcing us to drink alcohol. No one ever tied us down and poured booze down our throats. Just as no one *physically* compelled us to drink, now we try to make sure no one will *mentally* 'drive us to drink,' either.

... In sobriety we have learned a new technique: We never let ourselves get so resentful toward anyone else that we allow that person to control our lives – especially to the extent of causing us to drink. We have found we have no desire to let any other person run, or ruin, our lives (p. 11-12).

The peace of mind and happiness that I have gained from the 12 Steps are precious to me. They not only enable my ongoing recovery, but they have allowed me to find a happiness and ability to get along in life that is better than I had ever previously known. This newfound peace of mind and serenity are so valuable to me that there is no way I am going to allow another person or thing to take them away from me. On a day-to-day basis, I refuse to allow another person or thing to decide whether or not I am having a good day. If I allow resentments to creep in, then I lose that battle. Step Four is where we first learn to cease allowing other people and things to get under our skin and own us. It's such a peace-giving gift, to drop the word *blame* from our vocabulary and our thoughts and to go through life without the constant mental torment of resentments. This peace of mind is the basis of our recovery and happiness, our ability to live life on life's terms, and to stop trying to constantly swim upstream against the current in the river of life.

The 12 Step program makes some further suggestions on how to head off anger and resentments if we find ourselves struggling with them. We will discuss these in detail in our Step Ten discussion.

*

Having completed our resentments inventory, we now turn our attention to taking an inventory of our fears:

We reviewed our fears thoroughly. We put them on paper, even though we had no resentment in connection with them. We asked ourselves why we had them. Wasn't it because self-reliance failed us? Self-reliance was good as far as it went, but it didn't go far enough. Some of us once had great self-confidence, but it didn't fully

191

solve the fear problem, or any other. When it made us cocky, it was worse (Big Book, p. 68).

The power of addiction to alcohol or drugs has a fear-inducing power on the brain that makes us prone to fearfulness: "we're not always sure *what* we're afraid of; sometimes it is just a vague, generalized, nameless fear" (*Living Sober*, p. 38).

Fear in general, but the fear associated with the addicted mind especially, is a dysfunctional human reaction to our environment, because it is largely a self-destructive product of our imagination. *Instinctual fear* is a natural instinct geared to self-preservation: we fear a wild bear, or walking too close to the edge of a cliff. Those are understandable, self-preserving, functional fears. However, there are few fears in our world that are functional and self-preserving. Most of the fears that dominate our thoughts and govern our actions are unhealthy, neurotic, counter-productive, and destructive. This is especially so when these fears keep us from accepting help to escape active addiction-alcoholism.

Dysfunctional, neurotic fears are seldom based in reality. Rather, they are a by-product of our past experiences, our social conditioning, and most especially the effects of psychoactive substances on our mind. This fear is based on our emotional insecurities, and the precarious fragility of our ego. These fears play on our mind like an operatic self-destruction; swirling around and provoking pessimism, dread, obsessive rumination about a future that never will be. It makes us self-focused and mistrustful of others, a major barrier to healthy, loving relationships. This fear is a major source of anger and defensiveness. When I see active alcoholic-addicts in detox desperate to get help it is their fears that make them react with anger, denial and defensiveness when we try to help them confront their demons. It's this fear that makes them indignant at the idea of admitting powerlessness. This fear is a cornerstone of the extreme negative psychology of addiction-alcoholism; it simply poisons the soul.

The most tragic thing about this dysfunctional, non-instinctual fear is that it's entirely self-manufactured, not based in reality, and unnecessary. The truth is that there are very few realistic possibilities that warrant the fears that we hold so tightly. This is what Mark Twain was referring to when he said: "I have been through some terrible things in my life, some of which actually happened." Fear is both a liar and a bully. Fears manipulate us into doing things – or, more commonly, *not* doing things.

Much of our fear is from *projecting*, which is the unfortunate human tendency to project into the future and imagine how our problems will further develop. This generates fear because we have a tendency to blow things out of proportion, to think the worst, and to be pessimistic. This is especially true when we have a negative psychology, because negative

192

psychology is heavily poisoned with pessimism. People go through life ruminating about things that will never happen, which creates fear and anxiety. We worry, dread, and fear what hasn't happened and what probably never will, thereby putting ourselves through torture for naught. Alcoholic-addicts are expert ruminators; we lay awake at night and allow ourselves to be consumed by our anxieties of the future. In the dark of night, our mind can dream up terrible, terrible things, anticipating the cruellest of evils. We suffer intense fear from our imagination, rather than anything real. The problem is that for people like us, our go-to solution to fear and anxiety is to seek refuge in the bottle or needle. So, let's stop projecting, and approach life and our problems one day at a time.

*

Our fears are self-made monsters, artificial threats. Very few of our fears are instinctual fears, the kind that protect us from danger. I have never lost a minute's sleep nor have I ever had to cower behind drugs or alcohol because I was afraid of burning my hand on the stove or being bit by a dog. Fear of bears never kept me up at night or ruined my life. Rather, the fears that kill us are fears about things that aren't even present, or don't even exist, something psychologists refer to as *anticipatory anxiety*.[15] In short, we are afraid because we imagine what *might* happen. It's this anticipatory anxiety that causes us to lose sleep and seek refuge in drug or drink.

These unfounded fears over something that *might* happen and doesn't even exist can snowball very easily. That occurs especially in alcoholism-addiction because of the negative pessimistic psychology involved and because of the depressant properties of the psychoactive substances. Anticipatory anxiety has an effect on our mind like a growing beast, through a process known as *potentiation*.[16] This is where being in a state of fearfulness about one issue amplifies our fears about other things. Things scare us more when we are already scared about something else. If we are wracked with fear and worry about our finances, then the smallest stressor will bring out disproportionate fear. These self-destructive anticipatory fears grow like a snowball rolling downhill; add alcohol or drugs to the mix, and the effect magnifies.

When we experience instinctual fears, such as happens when encountering a bear in the woods, we have a reaction that is appropriate to the danger. We either freeze until the danger passes, fight the danger (I don't recommend fighting the bear), or take flight and escape from the danger. With these proper instinctual fears based on real threats the fear resolves as soon as the danger passes. The fear and reaction are appropriate to the danger. However, with our self-invented anticipatory anxiety fears, it's a different story.

With the far more common fears based on imagined threats, we take no action. How could we; these are things that haven't happened yet, and probably never will. Our reaction is entirely psychological, and it isn't good. We quickly become overwhelmed by even a small problem because we have made it huge by projecting what might happen because of the problem. We become stuck in a state of fear, and we ruminate, complain, wallow in self-pity, blame others, grow in anger, and resign ourselves to hopelessness. Because of the potentiation effect, the more of these worries we carry, the more fear and anxiety we get about other things. For those of us who are inclined to escape uncomfortable feelings by using psychoactive substances, it's a small wonder that fear keeps us drinking and using.

This anticipatory anxiety is a truly dysfunctional state of mind. Not only does it drive us deeper into substance use and other avoidance behaviors, but it impairs our ability to deal with real problems in the here and now. It makes us feel overwhelmed, and this overwhelmed feeling causes us to avoid the problem. It robs us of reason and perspective. Doing our fears inventory is when we finally put fear in its rightful place: in the garbage bin. Time to stop allowing unfounded fears live in our mind rent-free.

*

We must recognize that we have fears that are holding us back, and that these fears are human nature, but unfounded. They are a fatal flaw of human psychology that is magnified in alcoholic-addicts. The reason we are doing our fear inventory is so that we can confront these bullies and end their power over us. Research from psychologists demonstrates that doing a Step Four fear inventory is a wise way to get fear off our back. Let's look at what psychologists tell us about managing our fears in a healthy way.

Unfortunately, people have a natural tendency to use avoidance behaviors to deal with their fears.[18] Among the most toxic and dysfunctional of avoidance behaviors is using drugs or alcohol to cope with fear, making avoidance-coping of fears a major pathway to addiction. Besides the obvious ill effects of using drugs or alcohol to avoid fears, this practice actually generalizes, as people who avoid one fear begin avoiding other fears, and eventually all fears, and then other problems, and then difficult situations, and so on.[18] When we avoid a fear we are usually left with a sense of failure and weakness, which compounds the negative feelings involved.[19] It chips away at our self-esteem and our self-confidence, which makes our fears grow as we lose confidence in our ability to face fears and handle problems. We begin to see ourselves as incapable, cowardly wimps. The effects on our negative psychology magnify, and this leads to increased drug or alcohol use as our go-to way of coping and avoiding. You can see how fears contribute to addiction-alcoholism in a progressive, snowballing way.

Psychologists advise using exposure to our fears as the best way to overcome them and gain back our confidence.[20] This takes advantage of the psychological principal of *habituation*, where our mind learns from experience that fears are usually unfounded or exaggerated, and that we can face these fears and overcome them by confronting rather than avoiding them. This is exactly the process that our fear inventory gets us to do. It's the beginning of the end for fears ruling our lives, and our need to hide behind drug or drink to cope with them. The initial process may provoke a lot of anxiety, which is why I recommend doing this inventory in close association with your sponsor and/or your support system. This may be family and friends, or other people from the 12 Step fellowship. Reading the stories in the back of the Big Book and listening to speakers at 12 Step meetings helps us to overcome fears when they arise, because we identify with other people's triumphs over fear. The 12 Step program emphasizes that recovery should not be done alone. Our alcoholic-addict minds try to get us to self-isolate, but we need to learn to engage with our sponsor, other people in recovery, and our support system. This is especially important for dealing with fear, because as soon as we discuss our fears with someone else we immediately feel better. Self-isolation and keeping our fears to ourselves leads to rumination, a dangerous pre-condition for relapse.

As we progress in our recovery, we begin to see first-hand that the fears that kept us drinking or using were unfounded. As we grow in confidence, self-esteem, connections with others, and begin to take an interest in life again we develop fewer fears about the future. When we catch our mind trying to project fears (creating anticipatory anxiety) we have the insight to halt the dysfunctional process before it takes hold of us. We apply the "One Day at a Time" slogan to stop the projecting. This is the exposure therapy the psychologists talk about; when we hold our fears up to the flame of reality, we see that they burn away.

As we complete our fear inventory and confront these fears in our Step Five, we get a sense of accomplishment and empowerment. As we apply this confrontation of our fears to life we develop a pattern of success that further boosts our self-esteem and confidence. We see from experience that our fears were exaggerated or unfounded, and that we are capable of handling scary things in life. The negative psychology that our fears brought on begins to evaporate. The need to drink or use to avoid and cope with our fear melts away. This is the value of doing a good fear inventory.

Life can be a scary place, and sometimes some of our fears will have a basis in reality. For example, if we work for a company that's down-sizing we could face the possibility of losing our job and that's frightening. However, allowing that fear to fester and grow by ruminating on it and projecting our worst fears into the future will not help us one bit, and may form a locus for relapse. We can use our tools to deal with this fear. We can get the fear out in the open by discussing it with our sponsor and hearing an objective opinion. We can practice our "One Day at a Time" slogan, by doing every day what we can to help the problem, and not wasting brain-power on "what-if's" about tomorrow. That means we can – today – start job searching, just in case, making plans for finances in case of lay-offs, and finding out more information from people in the know. We can go to a meeting, read the Big Book, engage in meditation or prayer (which we will discuss in detail in Step Eleven), and talk to someone else in recovery. And we can use our knowledge of fear and anticipatory anxiety to be mindful and challenge our dysfunctional and effort-wasting thoughts and ruminations. Perhaps the most powerful technique we have at our disposal is by engaging our higher power. Try it: take your fear, bundle it up, and leave it with your higher power. Let it go. Anything but to allow fear to rule our mind as it once did.

*

As a therapist and someone who has lived through addiction-alcoholism, I am impressed and thrilled by the power of Steps Four and Five to give us mental and spiritual release from the power of our past wrongdoings, our resentments, and our fears. The effect makes Step Four (together with Step Five) one of the most powerfully healing parts of the 12 Steps.

For those who have serious, justified resentments in their past it's important to have a proper understanding of what we can expect when we do our Step Four. I have found in my medical practice that when it comes to grief, trauma, and loss a lot of people have unreasonable expectations. People often believe that "getting over it" means that the offending experience is forgotten and no longer bothersome. That's not a realistic expectation, but many will cling to this forlorn hope for a lifetime. Realistically, "dealing with" a traumatic event means arriving at a point where we can get through our days without the event dominating our thoughts and dictating our actions. For those who have suffered serious traumatic events, the memory will always be there; what we can expect and should be striving for is that the memory be put in its proper place. We can expect that the memory no longer sits in the forefront of our mind, no longer crushes our self-esteem, no longer causes fear and anxiety, and no longer generates the constant anger and resentment that it has in the past. We no longer ruminate on these events, and no longer need to seek relief from these thoughts in drug or drink. In other words, "dealing with it" means that these events no longer "own" us.

196

Likewise, our past wrongdoings will not be forgotten; rather, they will no longer be a source of constant guilt, self-loathing, remorse, and fear. We will no longer have to lie to cover them up, hide from people because of them, or drink and use to get relief from them: we are confronting them, owning them, and putting them right, beginning in Step Four. In fact we always want to "Remember When" in our recovery, so that when our disease tries to make us remember drinking or using as "fun," we can access our memories about how miserable and painful our drinking or using had become. That's the amazing power of Step Four; it's an excellent opportunity to take control and stop our resentments, wrongdoings, and fears from owning us. Given the role of these toxic and unnecessary thoughts and feelings in creating a negative psychology and their role in our drinking and using, this is a wonderful opportunity to heal.

If you have your three inventory lists prepared, and you have spent some time reflecting on them so that they are complete and well understood, you have completed your Step Four. If your sponsor agrees, we can move on to Step Five, which is where we take action to let go of our wrong-doings, resentments, and fears and release their power over us.

The best parting words for Step Four come from the Big Book:

> If we have been through our personal inventory, we have written down a lot. We have listed and analyzed our resentments. We have begun to comprehend their futility and their fatality. We have commenced to see their terrible destructiveness. We have begun to learn tolerance, patience and good will toward all men, even our enemies, for we look on them as sick people (p.70).

197

Step Five

Admitted to God, to ourselves, and to another human being the exact nature of our wrongs.

Completing Step Four is a major accomplishment, but we're not yet done with our inventories: "at Step Five, we decided that an inventory, taken alone, wouldn't be enough. We knew we would have to quit the deadly business of living alone with our conflicts, and in honesty confide these to God and another human being" (*Twelve Steps and Twelve Traditions,* p. 108).

Step Five is a tough nut to crack; it requires courage, a commitment to rigorous honesty, and trust in the 12 Step process. However, the Big Book tells us that screwing up the courage to do an honest and uninhibited Step Five is worth it:

> We pocket our pride and go to it, illuminating every twist of character, every dark cranny of the past. Once we have taken this step, withholding nothing, we are delighted. We can look the world in the eye. We can be alone at perfect peace and ease. Our fears fall from us. We begin to feel the nearness of our Creator. We may have had certain spiritual beliefs, but now we begin to have a spiritual experience. The feeling that the drink problem has disappeared will often come strongly. We feel we are on the Broad Highway, walking hand in hand with the Spirit of the Universe (p.75).

Twelve Steps and Twelve Traditions chimes in on the value of a properly done Step Five: "the dammed-up emotions of years break out of their confinement, and miraculously vanish as soon as they are exposed. As the pain subsides, a healing tranquility takes its place" (p. 62). Sound good? Those are the rewards we can expect from a well-done Step Five. Let's talk about how we get those rewards and how we optimize them for our health, recovery, spirituality, and well-being.

*

Twelve Steps and Twelve Traditions sets the tone for Step Five: "all of A.A.'s Twelve Steps ask us to go contrary to our natural desires... they all deflate our egos. When it comes to ego deflation, few Steps are harder to take than Five. But scarcely any Step is more necessary to longtime sobriety and peace of mind than this one" (p. 55).

We have organized and put together our thoughts and memories by putting them in writing in Step Four; now Step Five deepens the unloading effect by asking us to explain these memories verbally to our higher power and another person (as well as ourselves). Certainly, it takes courage to sit in front of another person and share our inventory from Step Four. We must remember that the psychology of alcoholism-addiction is characterized by secretiveness, self-isolation, lying to cover up our wrongdoings, and an inflated false pride – all the opposite of what we need in order to do our Step Five. As such, Step Five challenges this mind-set and we must engage the willingness to prevail over our old tendencies. We must step outside our comfort zone in order to heal. It can be anxiety-provoking, but again it's like ripping off an old Band-Aid: a quick pinch at first, but necessary for healing to happen. Step Five is here for a reason; we need it for a stable recovery: "most of us would declare that without a fearless admission of our defects to another human being we could not stay sober" (*Twelve Steps and Twelve Traditions*, p. 56-57).

"Deflating our ego" – as it says in *Twelve Steps and Twelve Traditions* – is actually part of the desired effect of Step Five. We must remember that "ego" and "pride" are not the same as self-esteem, especially in the addicted mind. We have already discussed the strange pride of alcoholism-addiction as our mind's way to compensate for a low self-esteem. By challenging our ego – another word for our alcoholic-addict pride – we are breaking down its ability to make us defensive and secretive. We are ending the need to lie and present a false front to try to impress other people and hide our sickness. We are clearing the way for a proper self-esteem to take its place, accompanied by humility. We have already briefly discussed humility, and will discuss it in more detail in Step Seven. Humility carries a bad connotation in today's society, but it's a greatly misunderstood word, possibly because of its resemblance to the word "humiliation." *Twelve Steps and Twelve Traditions* explains: "another great dividend we may expect from confiding our defects to another human being is humility – a word often misunderstood. To those who have made clear progress in A.A., it amounts to a clear recognition of what and who we really are, followed by a sincere attempt to become what we could be.... More realism and therefore more honesty about ourselves are the great gains we make under the influence of Step Five" (p. 58). While it may sound paradoxical that we must deflate our ego in order to restore our self-esteem, it's not. We are replacing an inflated, artificial pride with a genuine and healthy self-esteem; no more games.

But, Step Five is not all about ego and pride, it's also about taking a huge weight off our shoulders by unburdening our crowded conscience: "if we have come to know how wrong thinking and action have hurt us and others, then the need to quit living by ourselves with those tormenting ghosts of yesterday gets more urgent than ever. We have to talk to someone about them" (*Twelve Steps and Twelve Traditions*, p. 55). It felt good to get things off our chest by writing them out in Step Four, now we unload them from our shoulders by telling them to someone else. The sense of relief that comes with a completed Step Five is huge. One of the greatest gifts that we get from the "cleaning house" Steps (Four through Nine) is self-forgiveness, and Step Five is a major piece of that process. As well, it helps release us from the resentments that have haunted our thoughts: "this vital Step was also the means by which we began to get the feeling that we could be forgiven, no matter what we had thought or done. Often it was while working on this Step with our sponsors or spiritual advisers that we first felt truly able to forgive others, no matter how deeply they had wronged us" (*Twelve Steps and Twelve Traditions*, p. 57-58).

This is the Step where we take the crushing psychological burden of our past wrong-doings, our resentments, and our fears and eject them from their dominating place in our lives. This is where we get freedom from the psychological and spiritual pain, from the reason to numb our tormented minds with substance use, which we had endured for so long. But, our disease is a powerful one, and half-measures or incomplete effort will endanger our recovery. *Twelve Steps and Twelve Traditions* warns of our tendency to want to take the easier, softer way: "but of the things which really bother and burn us, we say nothing. Certain distressing or humiliating memories, we tell ourselves, ought not to be shared with anyone. These will remain our secret. Not a soul may ever know. We hope they'll go to the grave with us" (p. 55-56). We are also warned of the dangers of an incomplete and less-than-honest Step Five: "even A.A. oldtimers, sober for years, often pay dearly for skimping this Step. They will tell how they tried to carry the load alone; how much they suffered of irritability, anxiety, remorse, and depression...." (p. 56). This is not a time for the easier softer way; rigorous honesty and a little pain are required now for much gain later on.

*

During our Step Four discussion we talked about how psychological studies have shown that doing a partial confession is actually worse for us than doing no confession at all. But, as we face Step Five, once again we are confronted with fear and anxiety and once again we must take that leap of faith that our fears are unfounded. Taking that leap of faith is required for us to avail ourselves of the wonderful effects of a completed Step Five, as we discussed at the beginning of this chapter. However, there are some things we can do to help allay our fears of doing a rigorously honest and complete Step Five.

The Big Book acknowledges that Step Five requires courage:

> *There is a solution.* Almost none of us liked the self-searching, the leveling of our pride, the confession of shortcomings which the process requires for its successful consummation. But we saw that it really worked in others, and we had come to believe in the hopelessness and futility of life as we had been living it. When, therefore, we were approached by those in whom the problem had been solved, there was nothing left for us but to pick up the simple kit of spiritual tools laid at our feet (p. 25).

If we are sick and tired of being sick and tired, if we have truly reached our bottom and we have a genuine willingness to do whatever it takes to end the insanity, then Step Five is no barrier to us:

> If you are as seriously alcoholic as we were, we believe there is no middle-of-the-road solution. We were in a position where life was becoming impossible, and if we had passed into the region from which there is no return through human aid, we had but two alternatives: one was to go on to the bitter end, blotting out the consciousness of our intolerable situation as best we could; and the other, to accept spiritual help. This we did because we honestly wanted to, and were willing to make the effort (Big Book, p. 25-26).

One thing that really helps us crush these fears is to get to know our sponsor well before we do our Step Five together. It doesn't take long before we see that our sponsor went through the same experiences we did, did the same horrible things – or worse – and is very forthcoming about discussing these things. We can also see that our sponsor is dedicated to the principle of anonymity, and will not share our dark secrets with anybody. To be honest, I have as much faith in my sponsor's respect for my personal information as I do in my doctor's legally mandated obligation for confidentiality (perhaps even more). But, the human recipient of our Step

Five doesn't necessarily have to be our sponsor. *Twelve Steps and Twelve Traditions* gives us some suggestions on choosing the person who will hear our Step Five: "we shall want to speak with someone who is experienced, who not only has stayed dry but has been able to surmount other serious difficulties. Difficulties, perhaps, like our own. This person may turn out to be one's sponsor, but not necessarily so" (p. 61). As the Big Book tells us, it may even be: "a close-mouthed, understanding friend" (p. 74). The Big Book also warns that we must take care if choosing a family member: "it may be one of our own family, but we cannot disclose anything to our wives or our parents which will hurt them and make them unhappy. We have no right to save our own skin at another person's expense. Such parts of our story we tell to someone who will understand, yet be unaffected" (p. 74).

(By the way, speaking of confidentiality and not upsetting our loved ones, I strongly suggest that you should keep your Step Four inventory lists away from prying eyes and burn them after Step Five. It does us no good to have friends or family find our inventory lists. Better to save that discussion with them for when we do our Step Nine amends.)

We may even want to break up our Step Five: "perhaps, though, your relation to [your sponsor] is such that you would care to reveal only a part of your story. If this is the situation, by all means do so, for you ought to make a beginning as soon as you can. It may turn out, however, that you'll choose someone else for the more difficult and deeper revelations. This individual may be entirely outside of A.A. – for example, your clergyman or your doctor. For some of us, a complete stranger may prove the best bet" (*Twelve Steps and Twelve Traditions*, p. 61). The important thing is not whom we choose for our Step Five; the important thing is that we are thorough, honest, and complete. It's easiest to be honest and forthcoming with someone we are comfortable with.

*

Although Step Five says that we admit the exact nature of our wrongs, I suggest that we include all three of our inventory lists in our Step Five, not just our list of wrongdoings. In other words, that we also admit the exact nature of our resentments and our fears. Although some people would argue the point, I believe that this may have been the intent of Step Five when it was written. Regardless, Step Five is so effective at helping us cast off the mental weight of our wrongdoings, it makes good sense to also use it to cast off our resentments and fears at the same time. Sharing our fears with someone outside ourselves is an excellent way to allay those fears, and to help us to see how unnecessary and unfounded they are. Likewise, sharing our resentments allows us to communicate them verbally, get them off our shoulders, and cast them aside, crushing any doubts from our Step

202

Four. The difficult part of Step Five is admitting our wrongs; admitting our resentments and fears requires little extra courage, time, or effort. Either way, this is something you may wish to discuss with your sponsor.

*

First on the list for admitting the exact nature of our wrongs is our higher power. I suggest that when people admit the exact nature of their wrongs to their higher power that they do so aloud, not just in their head. Psychologically, doing it aloud has the effect that we discussed earlier, of making the experience a chance to pull out all those scattered memory engrams and put them together. As well, it's a great dry run for doing our fifth with our sponsor.

It's really important that we not let the higher power thing in any way deter us from doing a good Step Five if we still haven't come to terms with what, exactly, a higher power is to us. As usual, we must remember that "God of our understanding" means whatever higher power makes sense to us, even if that happens to be a blank. Even for people who haven't yet figured out what a higher power is to them, there is no barrier here; going through the motions is just as therapeutic for someone who's higher power is a blank as it is for those who have a very well-defined higher power, such as those who believe in God. For those whose higher power is a blank, we can use the example of my atheist friend I told you about, who says a prayer and doesn't know who it's directed at or where exactly it goes, but just "throws it up in the air" because it makes him feel better. Likewise, there's nothing wrong with doing our Step Five with our higher power by reviewing our inventories and then "throwing them up in the air." Not having an understanding of what a higher power is to us is no impediment whatsoever to the healing power of Step Five.

The kind of weird thing about Step Five is that when we share the finished product of our Step Four with another person and with a higher power, most people seem to find it takes much more courage to admit the exact nature of their wrongs to another person than they do to their higher power. For those whose higher power is God – the supreme Judge, the All-Powerful – it would make sense that admitting wrong-doing to God would be far more difficult than it would be to do so with a mere person. However, no matter how strong the person's faith in God, it seems to almost always be the case that doing Step Five with another person is what causes the burning sweats to break out, while admitting the exact nature of our wrongs with a higher power is easy.

I believe that there are a few reasons for this. Many people see God as all-forgiving, and believe that God already knows about all our wrongdoings. Too, we don't have to look God in the eye when we do our fifth. Humans, on the other hand, are fallible and by nature judgmental, so we are very nervous when confessing our deepest, darkest, blackest secrets with a person. As such, we are more likely to be rigorously honest with our higher power, so it keeps us honest when we do it aloud with our higher power first, as we are more likely to include everything when we later do Step Five with our sponsor. So, starting our Step Five with our higher power is a great idea. We're less nervous when we do Step Five with our higher power, and it lets us get out the initial jitters that come with doing it for the first time; it's a great dress rehearsal for doing our Step Five with another human being.

*

After our higher power, the next in line to hear our Step Five is… ourselves. That might sound kind of weird; after all, we have just admitted our wrongdoings to ourselves by writing them all out in Step Four, right? Sure, but Step Five requires a little more than that, and it serves a distinct and important therapeutic psychological purpose.

When we admit our wrongdoings to ourselves in Step Five we're doing a gut-check to acknowledge our responsibility of our wrongdoings; we must take responsibility for all our wrongdoings and place the responsibility exactly where it belongs: squarely on our shoulders.

As we have discussed, the negative psychology of addiction-alcoholism is heavily characterized by our "blame-thrower." Our "poor-me" mentality, our feelings of being victims of life, and our external locus of control all propel us to place the blame for our wrongdoings outside of ourselves. And worse, our cognitive dissonance gives us an instinctual drive to look for creative and imaginative ways of placing blame for our wrongdoings on someone or something else. It's human nature, and it's especially the nature of the addicted mind. However, clinging to this defensiveness posture keeps us from cleaning house, and is therefore a barrier to spiritual health and positive psychology.

Step Five is where we own up to our wrongdoings, and stop even thinking about where the blame may lie outside of ourselves. Even if we can find a legitimate reason for something we did, now is the time to forget that and look at our own role. We aren't going to heal by admitting other people's wrongdoings or by becoming experts at blaming others. Step Five does not say "admitted other people's wrongdoings to God, to ourselves, and to another human being." Allowing ourselves to focus on other people's role in our wrongdoings takes the focus off our own blame, and just magnifies our resentments. If we're still trying to justify our wrongdoings we are doing nothing to rid ourselves of the impact of our past actions on our conscience, and we don't stand a chance of leaving our resentments and guilt behind. As well, we don't fully view an action as a wrongdoing on our

204

part if we continue believing that we were even a little bit justified in doing it. It's time to clean **our** house, and to stop the self-righteous practice of trying to clean everyone else's house for them.

An example may be in order. Let's say that I was at my son's softball league game and one of the other parents was obviously drunk (not unlike me) and being a jerk. I confronted him and it came to pushing and shoving and name-calling and we had to be separated by other parents. At the time, being half-drunk and riled up on adrenaline, all I could see was my anger and how badly I wanted to sock this guy. Afterwards, I justified it: *he started it and somebody had to confront that loser*, and I might even congratulate myself at my restraint at not hitting the guy.

When I do my Step Four, this unfortunate confrontation may (should) appear on my list, but as long as I believe that I was even partly justified in my actions I'm not going to regard it as a wrongdoing on my part. I don't think I did anything wrong, and I'll hang on to the resentment toward the other parent because I view the resentment as justified.

However, if I stop taking the other guy's inventory for a moment I can look at my own behavior. A clear, objective mind might look at the issue and ask a few questions:

- What kind of an example did I set for the children that night?
- How did I look in other parents' eyes?
- How did I look in my higher power's eyes?
- Do I think I'm the behavior police at softball games?
- How much did my drinking/using affect my behavior and choices that night?
- Was there another way this situation could have been handled?
- And so on.

Besides, even in this example, where someone else may have played a role in or triggered our wrongdoing, the entire purpose of our trip through Steps is to heal ourselves, free ourselves from the poisonous anger, resentments and other negative feelings – to clean our house. We're doing it to make ourselves spiritually well in our desperation to be well and finally escape from obsessive substance use. Looking at another person's wrongs isn't going to help us at all. And it's just plain arrogant for us to do so. Blaming others and carrying the resulting anger and resentments that derive from that blame is what kept us drinking and using when it was no longer fun. So, when we admit our wrongdoings to ourselves we must make sure that we truly accept full responsibility for our actions. Only then can we proceed with admitting our wrongs to another human being.

We should do Step Five with ourselves out loud, and as we read through our list we do a gut-check to see if we have truly accepted responsibility for our part in our wrongdoings. If we find doubts and "yeah, buts" appearing in our thoughts as we work through our list, we have some more work to do before we do Step Five with another human being. We'll never be able to relieve our crowded conscience and build a healthy self-esteem until we are looking only at our wrongdoings, not other people's faults. Alcoholic-addicts who find these doubts arising when they do Step Five with themselves should discuss the specifics with their sponsor prior to proceeding.

Doing a good Step Five with ourselves – verbally, out loud – also lowers our anxieties over doing it with another human being. When we have completed this part of Step Five, it's time to take a deep breath and call our sponsor or whomever we have chosen, and arrange to do the final part of Step Five.

*

It can be nerve-wracking even to approach and ask someone to do our Step Five with us. However, as *Twelve Steps and Twelve Traditions* explains, our anxieties once again prove to be unfounded: "when your mission is carefully explained, and it is seen by the recipient of your confidence how helpful he can really be, the conversation will start easily and will soon become eager. Before long, your listener may well tell a story or two about himself which will place you even more at ease. Provided you hold back nothing, your sense of relief will mount from minute to minute" (p. 60-61).

We may wonder why we have to share our darkest secrets with someone else. After all, we've written it out and admitted our wrongdoings to our higher power. The Big Book is very straightforward about why doing our Step Five with another person is important to our recovery:

> This is perhaps difficult – especially discussing our defects with another person. We think we have done well enough in admitting these things to ourselves. There is doubt about that. In actual practice, we usually find a solitary self-appraisal insufficient. Many of us thought it necessary to go much further. We will be more reconciled to discussing ourselves with another person when we see good reasons why we should do so. The best reason first: If we skip this vital step, we may not overcome drinking. Time after time newcomers have tried to keep to themselves certain facts about their lives. Trying to avoid this humbling experience, they have turned to easier methods. Almost invariably they got drunk. Having persevered with the rest of the program, they wondered why they fell. We think the reason is that they never completed their housecleaning. They took inventory all right, but hung on to some of

the worst items in stock. They only thought they had lost their egoism and fear; they only thought they had humbled themselves. But they had not learned enough of humility, fearlessness and honesty, in the sense we find it necessary, until they told someone else *all* their life story (p. 72-73).

Our disease is a powerful one, and that's why it can't be beaten if we're only halfway committed to the treatment. We must be all-in on our recovery, as we discussed in Step One. Now is not the time for the easier, softer way, for choosing which parts of the program suit us and which don't, for picking and choosing what parts of the Steps we do. When someone has a common cold, they don't need to see the doctor, and they don't even need to really go out of their way to take care of it; it'll pass after a few days. However, when people have cancer, they require close coordination with their doctors, and they must participate in the treatment. If they skip a part of the treatment, they risk having their disease come back. Like cancer, our disease is deadly, will not go away on its own, and can relapse very easily, so we, too, must engage ourselves fully in the treatment – our program of recovery.

Before I did my Step Five, my sponsor shared his inventory with me, essentially doing **his** Step Five with me. His honesty and the ease with which he shared his unlovely inventories REALLY put me at ease and deflated my fears and anxiety. It's reasonable to ask your sponsor to do the same if you feel that would be helpful for you.

As the 12 Step literature tells us, we are encouraged to do our Step Five with someone other than our sponsor if it will help allay our anxieties; perhaps with someone we already know and trust. I have done a complete Step Five with my sponsor and a few mini-Step Fives when I was doing the Steps again to tune up my recovery, but I did my very first Step Five with someone else. My first Step Five was with a friend who is a church minster. He happened to be in recovery in the 12 Step fellowship, and I knew that he was used to hearing people's deepest darkest secrets, so I felt comfortable with him. The point is that we do a rigorously honest and complete Step Five, and that is more likely to happen if we do it with someone we are comfortable with. We heal because we are rigorously honest and forthcoming, not because we did so with some specific person.

*

Now, having reviewed our inventories out loud with ourselves, and shared them with our higher power and another human being, it's time to end their grim effects on our conscience, our mind, and our soul. It's time to let go of our resentments, wrongdoings, and fears. Let's talk about each of these.

Letting go of resentments is one of the keys to successful long-term recovery, as well as achieving peace of mind and happiness. We have already discussed letting go of resentments in our Step Four study. There we talked about two things that help us to let go of resentments: one is understanding the object of our resentment, and the other is acceptance. Let's review these quickly and add some tools that will help us rid ourselves of resentments.

When we have a resentment toward another person, a key tool for letting go of the resentment is to understand the other person. This is not the same as forgiving them, and it certainly doesn't mean we forget what happened; that memory will always be a part of us. Rather, understanding people that we have resentments toward is about taking an empathetic look at why they may have wronged us. In most cases they have wronged us because they were spiritually sick and haunted by demons, much like we once were.

One of my long-standing resentments that had to go was my resentment toward my father. His behavior toward me and my mother and then his abandonment of us when I was young left us to suffer many hardships and affected me deeply well into adulthood. It also saddened me to see how it affected my mother. My resentments were longstanding and deep. In recovery, I needed to let go of that resentment, so I sought to understand my father. I never knew him that well, so I researched him a bit. He was an alcoholic and his behaviors were consistent with the spiritually sick behaviors of alcoholic-addicts. I, too, was spiritually sick like him in my drinking and using days. I also learned that he had been badly physically abused as a child by a step-father, and ended up living in an orphanage because his mother gave him up to appease her husband. I could easily imagine how he would've had anger, resentments, insecurities, and self-esteem issues of his own from those traumatic experiences. Understanding that my father was spiritually sick didn't excuse his behavior, and didn't necessarily mean I had to forgive him, but it helped me to understand him. When I shared this understanding of my father with my sponsor it really helped me let go of my resentment.

Using acceptance to help us let go of resentments is about invoking the Serenity Prayer. We ask for the serenity to accept the things we cannot change. We cannot change the things that people have done to us in the past, and we require serenity to accept that. The serenity to accept the past comes from stopping the ruminating, the anger, and the "what ifs" so that our mind can cool down and think. That's the serenity our mind requires to accept the past. We have two choices: 1) we can keep ruminating and obsessing about the past so that it continues to be a daily source of unhappiness for us, or 2) we can accept the past as a done-deal and move on with life. As alcoholic-addicts we must choose option #2 if we want to find health and sobriety.

Besides acceptance, and understanding the object of our resentment, there are some techniques from psychology that help us to let go of resentments. Let's go through those now.

Commit to doing no harm to the offender. This does not amount to forgiveness or excusing the behavior. Rather, it's a decision on our part to completely drop thoughts of revenge or retribution from our mind. We stop harboring fantasies of the person we resent coming to harm. Rather, we wish the person well and even pray for him or her. We must become willing to abolish from our mind any thoughts of vengeance or malicious wishes, and then commit to it... forever. Those kinds of thought are no longer allowed to be a part of us. The guy whose daughter was raped and murdered found this technique to be a powerful tool for letting go of his resentment, which he had to do to stay sober and spiritually healthy.

Consider forgiveness. This may be something that takes time, but that's OK. When it comes to very deep traumatic resentments, outside help in the form of trauma counseling may be advisable. I suggest that every person, no matter how bad the event that caused the resentment, should aim for forgiveness, even if it takes a long time. And that forgiveness must be unconditional. It must not require that the other person show remorse, or ask for our forgiveness. If we wait for that to happen we are handing power back to our offender. And forgiveness doesn't need to be offered to the other person. In many cases having contact with the other person would not be helpful.

If the thought of forgiving someone who did you wrong is repulsive to you, and you feel that they don't deserve it, then think again. Forgiveness is not for the benefit of the other person; rather, it's for **our** benefit. It's the ultimate release from the power that past traumas have held over us.[1] Anger and resentments are physically and mentally toxic to our bodies, so it's not surprising that forgiveness has been shown by research to improve our physical and mental health.[2] And it's certainly good for our spiritual health and recovery.[3] Keep an open mind about this if you have deep-seated or justified resentments; you will almost certainly find it worthwhile.

Take on a new healthy, spiritual identity. As part of a life-changing conversion from a negative psychology to a positive psychology, spiritual health, and recovery we take on a new identity. This happens during the transformative process of the 12 Step process. Human psychology has a quirk where we seek identities: things, personas, idiosyncrasies, and even eccentricities that we identify with.[4] When we have such things that we identify with, we naturally strive to fulfill those identities, and it can really change who we are. As part of our Step Five, as we seek to let go of our resentments, we should be open to taking on a new, healthy, spiritual identity as someone who empathizes with others, someone who forgives, someone who can ask a resentment to leave and it does. We reap huge benefits from that. It's key to sobriety, and it relieves us of being ongoing daily victims of past events, over and over again.

*

Let's explore the issue of ridding ourselves of really difficult resentments a little more, because many people who develop addictions are survivors of some serious past traumas and carry justified resentments. Even those who aren't in that category may carry some resentments that they are finding difficult to shed. The amount of pain and dysfunction that result from being a victim of sexual or physical abuse, serious illness, crime, or disaster can leave people with profound legitimate resentments. However, I have seen many people in the program find relief from these resentments, and this has clearly greatly relieved the pain and dysfunction that they suffer from their past traumas. Many probably wouldn't be sober without this release from resentment. As a therapist I believe that the 12 Step process is one of the most potent approaches to healing for people who suffer ongoing deep pain and related issues from traumatic experiences. That includes but is not just limited to people with post-traumatic stress disorder (PTSD). Many people do not have full-out PTSD but are still deeply troubled and suffer physical and psychological symptoms from horrible past experiences. I believe that the Steps Four and Five are especially therapeutic in this regard. This is an important observation, because medical science is woefully poor at treating post-traumatic symptoms.

However, I don't kid myself. I have been involved in the care of many such people as a physician and as a therapist, and I know very well that it doesn't just all go away, especially for people with deep psychological scars. Again, we must have realistic expectations. "Getting over it" doesn't mean that all is forgotten and forgiven; rather, it means that these experiences no longer dominate our thoughts and behaviors, and no longer propel us to seek refuge in the bottle or needle.

Some kinds of pain never fully heal, especially those caused by deep trauma. I have a suggestion to people who live with that kind of pain, over and above the suggestions that we have already used to lessen the grip of resentments on our psyche: the suggestion is to find meaning in their pain and suffering. That may sound strange, "finding meaning" in pain, but let's talk about what that means.

One of my favorite books is Viktor Frankl's 1959 book *Man's Search for Meaning*.[5] Many people have never heard of this book, but it has sold more than 12 million copies, and is still in print. The New York Times has called Frankl's book one of the most important books of the 20th century. Among psychologists it's an important work that has had a profound impact on trauma counseling, but the beauty of the book is that you don't have to be a psychologist to read it and find personal enrichment from it. It's a very short book, but a beautiful read for people who are seeking to grow in spirituality.

Viktor Frankl was an Austrian psychiatrist of the Jewish faith. As an Austrian Jew during the Nazi era he and his wife and kids were dragged from their home, completely dispossessed, and sent to the Auschwitz death camp in Poland. All that was left of their worldly possessions was a suitcase of items they were permitted to bring with them, and even that was stripped from them at the camp. Upon arrival, Frankl's wife and two children were immediately murdered: gassed and cremated. The only thing Frankl had left in the world – the clothes he was wearing – were taken from him and he was given the ragged striped camp uniform so that he looked just like everyone else. Even his identity was taken: his head was shaved to make him look nondescript, and he was no longer permitted to use his name. He was now officially known only by the number tattooed on his left arm. In a matter of a few days, Frankl went from being a respected physician with a thriving practice, with a beautiful home and family and all the trimmings, to having nothing. He didn't even have the ashes of his wife and children or a grave to visit. There was nothing left of his life but a shell. Frankl could easily be forgiven for feeling like a victim, and holding deep seething resentments for his situation.

It must be remembered that concentration camps like Auschwitz were not simply a prison for Jewish people. The Jews who were not sent to the gas chambers on arrival were sent to work, but the purpose was to work them to death. Historical studies have produced ample evidence that productivity of the Jews' work was secondary to their demise; in fact they were often given heavy work with no purpose whatsoever except to wear them down, such as carrying sacks of cement across a field and piling them up and then moving them right back again.[6] The Nazis thought it to be some kind of ironic justice to work these people to death. As a consequence, only 1 in 28 Jewish people who went to concentration camps survived.[7]

Many among us would view Frankl's life in the concentration camp as life not worth living. He and his fellow prisoners were given about 400 Calorie a day diet of poor quality food – usually watery nettle soup once a day (I don't know what nettle soup is, but the sound of it doesn't exactly make my mouth water) – well below a starvation diet, and were worked mercilessly 18 hours a day. They were very poorly clothed with wooden clogs and only one set of clothes. They endured sub-zero temperatures in the winter without warm clothing. They suffered random clubbings and killings. Worse, they knew that the intention was for them to die, and that there was no hope of release.

As such, Frankl could have been forgiven for losing all hope in life, and wanting to die. Many of his fellows did; it was commonplace that they would throw themselves on the high voltage electrified fence or just not get out of their bunk in the morning and perish at the hands of the enraged camp guards. Frankl also noticed that most prisoners who did not give up and die became degraded to behaving like animals, acting only out of pure instinctual self-interest to survive the day. They abandoned all human civil principles and became willing to steal and even kill just to survive. Frankl was determined not to become like that.

Despite having literally nothing left to live for Frankl found hope within himself and spread that hope to others, saving a number of lives by doing so. He found hope by finding purpose – meaning – in his suffering. This is not to be confused with philosophical search for the meaning *of* life, the reason life exists. To a psychologist, that search for the meaning *of* life is irrelevant to our happiness and health. To me, the search for the meaning *of* life is futile, unanswerable, and a waste of time; finding meaning *in* life, however, is what makes life worth living, even in difficult times. The need for meaning in life is a fundamental need for humans, and lacking meaning in life leads to hopelessness and a negative outlook. Loss of meaning in life is one of the underlying causes of the extreme negative psychology of addiction-alcoholism.

Frankl could have become like the others. He could have felt sorry for himself, he could have filled his soul with anger and resentment, he could have raged with blame for others, he could have ruminated on what *should* have been. But, no; Frankl decided that he wasn't going to be a victim of circumstances beyond his control. He wasn't going to be consumed by pessimism, hate, anger, resentment, selfishness, and self-pity. Rather, he was going to endure the suffering, maintain his principles, and not allow his circumstances to "own" him, no matter how grave they were. He was going to find meaning in his suffering. But how did he do that?

*

Frankl frequently cites German philosopher Friedrich Nietzsche: "he who has a *why* to live can bear almost any *how*." That "why" is meaning in life; (s)he who has meaning in life can endure anything. Frankl's experience in the concentration camp proved that Nietzsche was absolutely correct. Frankl found meaning in life and that carried him through the experience and enabled him to help others to likewise endure the experience and find a reason to survive. Amazingly, even though Frankl didn't resort to his fellow prisoners' tactics of stealing food and clothing from each other (he even gave his own meager food to others on occasions), he ended up being one of the 3% of Jewish people who survived the camp. Frankl found meaning in life – even his bare, naked existence – in three ways: loving and caring for someone, leaving a legacy, and work that is meaningful.

Frankl's wife and children had been murdered at the camp, and he didn't know what had become of any of his extended family. There was no one he knew in the camp. So, instead of finding meaning in loving and caring for family and friends, he decided he would reach out and help as many of his fellow inmates as he could. While most other inmates were doing anything they could to survive, even if it meant doing harm to others, Frankl helped others survive by helping them find food, evade murderous work, and stay mentally strong without giving up and dying.

Frankl found meaning in his work, even while at the concentration camp. Prior to being rounded up by the Gestapo he had been working on a book about psychiatry. When he left for the concentration camp one of the few belongings that he took with him was his precious manuscript, which was promptly ripped up by one of the German guards at the camp when he arrived. To Frankl, finishing his manuscript was deeply important to him, so he began to collect scraps of paper and jot down notes for re-writing his manuscript. The idea of one day finishing his manuscript and publishing his book gave Frankl meaning, a reason to endure and survive this adversity. (By the by, after the war, when Frankl was liberated from the concentration camp, he had managed to keep those scraps of paper and ended up finishing and publishing his book.)

The other way that Frankl found meaning in what was left of his life was by finding meaning in his suffering. That may sound strange, but to him, his suffering became meaningful by exercising his freedom to choose how he endured that suffering. Many people understandably degenerated to near-animals, displaying extreme selfishness, theft, and even violence in their drive to survive. Rather, Frankl found meaning in maintaining his principles and dignity in the face of his suffering. Not only did he not give in to his instincts to survive at any cost, but he even reached out to help others, putting concern for others above his own welfare.

*

What can we learn from Dr. Frankl? He was subjected to the most extreme form of trauma: murder of his entire family, loss of everything he owned, wrongful imprisonment, repeated vicious physical and mental abuse, and the trauma was ongoing with no end in sight. Yet, he found that focusing on meaningful activities kept him from obsessing and ruminating on his deplorable traumatic past and present. He was able to free himself of the mental torment of the anger, resentments, self-pity, and "what-ifs" that

213

would have come with focusing on the injustice of his situation. Unlike most of his fellow prisoners, he was able to maintain his principles and dignity, maintain his hope and outlook, and survive the camp.

So, too, can those who are haunted by memories and thoughts of past traumas free themselves from mental torment by focusing on activities that give meaning to life. This doesn't mean that terrible past experiences will be forgotten or even forgiven; rather, like Dr. Frankl, it's about preventing ourselves from becoming a product of our past traumas, dominated by their presence in our mind. It's about not allowing ourselves to be defined by our past experiences. Let's apply Frankl's wisdom to our situation.

Frankl found meaning in loving and helping others. We, too, can find life-affirming meaning in loving and helping others, and they don't necessarily have to be family or friends. Mental health research has shown that survivors of trauma find significant relief in altruism (helping others and expecting nothing in return) directed toward people who have suffered similar trauma.[8,9,10,11,12] For example, sexual assault survivors were able to find significant relief from the lingering mental effects of the assault by doing volunteer work to help other sexual assault victims. This same principle is used in the 12 Step program, and in fact forms the basis of Step Twelve. As we will see in Step Twelve, the way in which alcoholic-addicts are best able to maintain peace of mind, happiness, positive psychology, and sobriety is by helping others, especially other alcoholic-addicts. In the meantime, this same principle can be applied to those who have trouble letting go of resentments, especially justified resentments. Placing our attention and care on others turns our mind away from a dangerous inward-focus.

As well, Frankl found that meaningful work is a powerful way to prevent a self-pitying inward-focus. This isn't necessarily work in the sense of our job. If we find meaning in our job, that's great, but work that is most meaningful to us usually involves something outside of our employment. Frankl found meaning in the book he was writing, and a determination to survive the camp and finish his book was a strong motivator for him to never give up; he attributes this to being a major factor in his beating the odds and surviving the camp. Meaningful work tends to be something that helps others, makes a difference, and leaves our mark on the world. My mother has endured a lot of hardship in her life, and she finds great joy in her work as a volunteer. She knits mittens and warm hats for underprivileged children, she visits lonely elderly people in nursing homes, and has taken – on her own initiative – responsibility for keeping a stretch of a nearby street clean of garbage. For her, these activities are meaningful work that helps others, makes a difference, and leaves her mark on the world. This work gets her outside herself and stops her from feeling sorry for herself or focusing on her woes. Step Twelve helps us to find meaningful

214

work that helps us to heal, grow in spirituality, maintain sobriety, and find meaning in life. Stay tuned for that, but in the meantime seeking out meaningful work is a great therapeutic measure for those who suffer lingering effects from past traumas.

Dr. Frankl also sought to find meaning in his suffering, and we can do the same when we are suffering from painful memories. Frankl decided that he would maintain his spiritual principles and dignity despite his suffering and the strong natural tendency to abandon those principles in order to survive. Likewise, we, too, can maintain our principles in our suffering, by not hating people who have done hateful things to us, striving to forgive the unforgiveable, being happy in unhappy circumstances, being positive in the face of our negative situation, and taking the high road when we have been wronged in the lowest of manners. This may take a major change in attitude and thinking – a paradigm shift – for some of us, and this won't happen overnight. I suggest starting by making a commitment to spiritual principles and dignity in the face of suffering from someone else's past wrongdoings. Then, we should pursue that commitment. The 12 Step process is – in my opinion – by far the every best approach to achieving this healthy and healing mind-set. Talking with a counselor who specializes in trauma may be helpful for some as well.

*

One of the most important lessons in Dr. Frankl's remarkable experience is also one of the most important lessons in the 12 Step program: acceptance. We cannot expect nor should we seek a life devoid of pain and suffering. Our situation is what it is, we can't go back in time and change it. Rather, we should find some meaning in how we bear that pain and exercise our freedom to choose how we let it affect our attitude and behavior.

Frankl could have railed and obsessed over his unjust situation, and no one would blame him for it. But he would have driven himself crazy and accomplished nothing but his own mental torment. Rather, he accepted what he couldn't change – his situation – and instead changed what he could – how he behaved in the face of his situation. It's the Serenity Prayer applied to life. Says Frankl:

> We must never forget that we may also find meaning in life even when confronted with a hopeless situation, when facing a fate that cannot be changed. For what then matters is to bear witness to the uniquely human potential at its best, which is to transform a personal tragedy into a triumph, to turn one's predicament into a human achievement. When we are no longer able to change a situation... we are challenged to change ourselves.[13]

215

Acceptance is a key component of letting go of our resentments. Things that have happened to us in the past have happened; we can't change that fact. So, we have no choice but to accept them, or do we? Unfortunately, we do have a choice, and many people refuse to accept the past and let it go. Resentments involve an inability or unwillingness to let go of things that we can't change. Acceptance doesn't mean we concede that what has happened to us in the past was OK. Acceptance doesn't mean that those things will go away and stop being painful for us; many people have had some really terrible things happen to them. Rather, acceptance is about making a decision about whether or not we allow these things to "own" us, to dominate our thoughts, to make us angry, to rob us of any chance of having peace and tranquility of mind, and to continue being a reliable source of daily unhappiness. Most people will go through their whole life with their resentments, but you and I don't have a choice, we are not like most people. We are addicted to alcohol or drugs and our resentments were keeping us in our cups. We don't have the luxury of harboring our resentments and anger, for us it's a life and death matter. If we can't let go of our resentments and anger then we will die. We must let go of our resentments. THAT is the purpose of Steps Four and Five.

It might sound like I am being idealistic, but let me tell you about some people who know something about acceptance. In my medical practice I have always been amazed by people who have lived with disabilities for a long time. These people schooled me on what acceptance means. I'm talking about people who have been blind since birth or childhood, or confined to a wheelchair, or afflicted with birth defects, such as being born with stumps for arms without working hands. What amazes me is that even when we are specifically discussing their disability, I never hear them express anger or resentment about it. And these are people who have every right to shout out: *why me???* and be resentful. They have every right to ruminate about what they cannot do. But that's not what I see from them. These are people who have long ago realized that the price of carrying resentments over something you cannot change is very high, and they have gotten on with life through acceptance.

Likewise, I have met many people in the fellowship who have a history of deep personal trauma – such as sexual abuse as a child – but who have learned to accept their past and stop allowing it to own them. I suspect that this is a large part of the reason that they have succeeded in their recovery. It's certainly why they are able to lead happy, healthy lives, free from resentments. It's not that they have forgotten, or that the memory isn't painful, and it doesn't necessarily mean they have forgiven their assailant, it just means that they have stopped allowing the memory and the resentment to dominate their minds.

I would suggest that anyone who is having difficulty shedding resentments about deeply hurtful things from their past seek out someone in the fellowship who has a similar history, and get to know that person a little. They don't necessarily have to be your sponsor, just someone you can talk to a bit. You don't even have to share your story, necessarily, just hear theirs. One of the rich benefits of the fellowship is that no matter what your past, what you've done, or what you've experienced, there are always other people there who have lived the same experience.

*

I have suggested including our fear inventory in Step Five. In our Step One discussion we talked about the huge role that fear plays in our addiction-alcoholism and how it keeps us from sobriety. We have also discussed fear in Step Four. We talked about how the vast majority of our fears are unfounded, the by-product of an over-active, troubled mind. Our negative psychology makes us fearful, and our tendency to ruminate and blow things out of proportion causes us to fear things that *might* happen – and probably never will. We have discussed in Steps One and Four the various ways that we can overcome our fears, including learning to take life one day (chunk) at a time (the psychological principle of chunking), listening to other people tell of how their fears proved to be unfounded (by listening at meetings and reading the stories in the Big Book), learning to accept that not everything in life will always go our way, and the psychological principle of habituation (where we gain confidence as we challenge our fears and expose them as unfounded). As we pass through the Steps and develop a positive psychology, our mind will become increasingly less prone to pessimism, projecting disaster in the future, and generating fear. I believe that sharing our fear inventory in Step Five helps that process along, because we get our fears off our chest, using our sponsor as our sounding board. This usually results in a discussion about how fears prove to be unfounded, non-productive, and a waste of brain-power. It reassures us to share our fears. Psychologists tell us that this practice of sharing our fears is an important way to engage the fear-crushing principle of habituation.

Similarly, when we share our wrongdoings inventory in Step Five, we are completing an important part of the process of cleaning house. The end result is that by the time we have completed Step Nine we find self-forgiveness, and a release from the guilt, shame, self-loathing, and regret that have been plaguing our minds and killing our self-esteem for so long. A complete and sincere wrongdoings inventory in Steps Four and Five is necessary for a proper completion of the remaining "cleaning house" Steps.

Even though a complete purging of our fears and the effects of our wrongdoings comes with completion of the upcoming Steps, sharing our inventories in Step Five provides us with considerable psychological and spiritual relief. We have finally come out of hiding and stopped the lies, deceit, and secretiveness. We have committed ourselves to a path toward a spiritual way of life and a positive psychology. Completing Step Five – for all the fear we carried going into it – feels good! I always welcome the opportunity to do another fourth and fifth Step, because every time I do I find the experience to be spiritually and psychologically refreshing. I feel really good for the rest of the day.

*

The Big Book tells us how to wrap up our Step Five:

> Returning home we find a place where we can be quiet for an hour, carefully reviewing what we have done. We thank God from the bottom of our heart that we know Him better. Taking this book down from our shelf we turn to the page which contains the twelve Steps [i.e. pages 59-60 in the Big Book]. Carefully reading the first five proposals we ask if we have omitted anything, for we are building an arch through which we shall walk a free man at last. Is our work solid so far? Are the stones properly in place? Have we skimped on the cement put into the foundation? Have we tried to make mortar without sand?
>
> If we can answer to our satisfaction, we then look at STEP SIX (p. 75-76).

We are ready to move on from Step Five when we are able to take responsibility for and admit to all of our wrongdoings, we are ready to let go of our resentments, and we have confronted our fears. For resentments that are too deeply seared into our consciousness, such as those caused by deep trauma, we must be willing to commit to working toward lessening and purging these resentments, as this may take some time and work.

If your sponsor agrees, let's move on to Step Six.

Step Six

Were entirely ready to have God remove all these defects of character.

I have a weird hobby: I collect character defects. When I did my Step Six I found that the list of character defects that I made was deficient, because I kept thinking of other ones weeks and months later. We can only address the character defects we set our mind to correcting; the ones that aren't on our list won't receive our attention and consideration. So, I began keeping a list of character defects. Every time I would think of another descriptive that identified a character defect I would jot it down on my list.

I've found Step Six to be a really good one to revisit from time to time, and every time I do I pull out my list so that I have a pretty complete accounting to mull over and meditate on. My list also helps me a lot with my Step Ten, as we will discuss later. If you're interested, I've included my running list of character defects as appendix 2 at the back of the book. If you can think of any that I can add, please email me and let me know.

Step Six is an especially salutary one from the point of view of a therapist. It represents a major leap forward in cleaning house and developing a healthy and strong spirituality and positive psychology. The way we interact with other people and handle life's situations changes after we have accepted this sixth suggestion from the program. By now you may have noticed that a major theme in correcting dysfunctional thoughts and behaviors in ourselves involves awareness of those thoughts and behaviors, which is the basis of mindfulness. This self-awareness is a powerful technique for correcting unwanted behaviors, and it's known to psychologists as metacognition. Step Six provides us with the basis for an awareness of our character defects, many of which have been with us for so long that we may not even notice them anymore; they're just a part of us, as comfortable as an old shoe.

Step Six is similar to Steps Four and Five in that it allows us to properly relieve our conscience and begin liking ourselves again. We are much more likely to be able to forgive ourselves when we have taken measures to eliminate the ugly character traits and behaviors that filled us with remorse, guilt, self-loathing, and low self-esteem in the first place. We will never be able to forgive ourselves for past behaviors unless we first stop the behaviors. These very same character defects made us behave in a very un-spiritual and unhealthy way. They also gave rise to our anger, resentments, and blame for others. These character defects are not only a manifestation of negative psychology – they are also a cause. Character defects and negative psychology feed off each other in a downward spiral of painful and negative feelings and emotions that drive us further into our drinking or using. Step Six is where we commit to stopping the vicious cycle.

You may notice, too, that these character defects are responsible for all the stuff that made it onto our inventory lists in Step Four. As such, we can refer back to our inventories to help us identify the character defects that we need to consider in Step Six (using my cheat-sheet at the back of the book might help, too).

*

In order to become entirely ready to have our higher power remove our defects of character, we must first identify what those defects of character are. Naturally, we can only deal with the character defects that we are aware of. That's why we should prepare a list of our character defects for our Step Six.

A character defect is a behavioral tendency that results in wrongdoings, harm to ourselves or others, and moral failings. Most of them are rooted in selfishness and self-will run riot. Character defects detract from our spirituality because they harm our connections with other people, the world in general, and a higher power. They make us toxic and socially undesirable. Character defects are the result of acting on some of the primitive instincts that still lurk within the primordial areas of our brain, left over from our ancient ancestors' struggles for survival long ago. These character defects are both cause and effect of an obsessive need to drink or use. They are our tools for protecting our drug or alcohol use and concealing it from others. They have to go if we are to escape the quicksand of addiction-alcoholism.

There are certain character defects that I refer to as *cluster character defects*. These are character defects that are particularly important to deal with because they cause a whole cluster of other character defects by their effects. The 12 Step program acknowledges the importance of these special character defects, because they repeatedly appear in the pages of the Big Book and other 12 Step literature (although the term "cluster" character defect is my own contrivance, not one you will see in the Big Book or other 12 Step literature).

220

The cluster character defects are: selfishness, self-criticism, hubristic pride, and self-pity. Because of the importance of these toxic core character defects I will go through each one and offer some insight on the nature of these afflictions and how best to send them packing. The more insight we have into these vile beasts the better equipped we will be to absolve ourselves of their deleterious effects on our spirituality and recovery.

*

Steps Six and Seven are about reining in our character defects, those anti-spiritual aspects of our thoughts and behaviors that have made so much work for us in Step Four. Unfortunately, controlling our sordid tendencies is a bit of an uphill battle, because most of our character defects are, in fact, in our nature as humans, embedded in our very DNA.

Our ancient ancestors lived in a world of constant danger and struggle for survival. They had to scratch out a living in an environment of scarce resources, in the setting of vicious competition for those resources. Saber-toothed tigers, cave-bears, woolly mammoths, and other humans were worthy adversaries. The mind became shaped by pressure to survive and reproduce. The evolutionary principle of "the survival of the fittest" in an environment of limited resources predisposed individuals to selfishness.[1] Similarly, people who were aggressive, dishonest, and unscrupulous also had a survival advantage. Likewise, competition for mates for reproducing favored those who were aggressive, jealous, selfish, and ruthless. As such, over time these traits became ingrained in human nature.

As grim as that sounds, our instincts aren't *all* bad. Pro-social behavior – behavior that favors cooperating with and caring for others, and doing things for the group rather than for the self – was also an evolutionary advantage. Thus it is that we humans have a psychological dichotomy embedded in our DNA and in the workings of our brainstem, the most primitive part of our brain. We have these anti-social survival instincts that make us aggressive, selfish, greedy, and envious; and then we have these pro-social instincts that make us want to love and care for others, share, and cooperate.

It's striking, though, how readily the anti-social aspects of our human nature come out in our behavior. I take my Step Six very seriously, and I make a tremendous effort to keep my character defects in check. Yet, sometimes it's a constant battle. We are especially likely to show our anti-social side when we react unthinkingly, such as when someone does something wrong toward us and we lash out. It seems to be our brain's go-to response.

Likewise, it's amazing how much alcoholism-addiction brings our character defects to the forefront. Drinking and drug use starts the downward nose-dive of negative thoughts and behaviors that lead to the crushing guilt, remorse, shame, blaming others, anger and resentments – in other words, the negative psychology and spiritual sickness – that keep us drinking or using in order to smother those negative feelings, if only for a while. Our drive to satisfy our willful cravings for our next drug or drink pushes us to increasingly uglier behaviors, and character defects become our tools for making sure our willful desires are fulfilled. Small wonder that active alcoholic-addicts usually don't like themselves, and other people don't like them either.

*

However, just because these ugly character traits are in our nature doesn't mean that we have to allow them to dictate our behavior. Just as these unlovely mannerisms are in our nature, so are love, kindness, empathy, and selflessness. Step Six is about making a decision about which of our natural aspects we will allow to win out and determine how we behave toward ourselves and others. You may have heard the story about the two wolves inside us.

An old parable of uncertain origin – although it probably originated with the Cherokee Indians – illustrates what Step Six suggests that we do. A young Cherokee boy came home one day angry and determined to get revenge against another boy who had just wronged him. He expressed his anger to his grandfather:

> The old Cherokee chief said to his grandson, 'I too, at times, have felt a great hatred for those who have taken so much with no sorrow for what they do.
>
> 'Hatred wears you down, and hatred does not hurt your enemy. Hatred is like taking poison and wishing your enemy would die. I have struggled with these emotions many times.
>
> 'It's as though a fight is continuously going on inside me. It is a terrible fight and it is between two wolves.
>
> 'One wolf is good and does no harm. He is filled with joy, humility, and kindness. He lives in harmony with everyone around and does not take offense when no offense was intended. He will only fight when it is right to do so and in the right way.
>
> 'The other wolf is full of anger, envy, regret, greed, and self-pity. The littlest thing will set him into a fit of temper. He fights everyone all the time and for no reason. When blinded by his anger and hatred, he does not have a sound mind. It is helpless anger, because his anger will change nothing.

'It is hard to live with these two wolves inside me. These two wolves are constantly fighting to control my spirit.

'Young man, the same fight is going on inside you and inside every other person on this earth.'

The grandson thought about it for a moment and then asked his grandfather, 'Which wolf will win inside you, grandpa?'

The old Cherokee chief smiled and replied, 'The one I feed.'

Dear readers, which wolf inside are you feeding?[2]

So, think of Step Six as separating the two wolves within us and making a decision to commit to feeding the good wolf. Our peace of mind, happiness, serenity, spiritual health, and sobriety depend upon it.

*

What does the Big Book say about Step Six? The Big Book emphasizes "willingness as being indispensable" (p. 76): "are we now ready to let God remove from us all the things which we have admitted are objectionable? Can He now take them all – every one? If we still cling to something we will not let go, we ask God to help us" (p.76). This is actually a bigger task than some may initially realize. Now that we have listed our character defects, we must search within ourselves and really see if we are truly willing to give them up. We really need to think about this and dig deep: "at Step Six, many of us balked – for the practical reason that we did not wish to have all our defects of character removed, because we still loved some of them too much" (*Twelve Steps and Twelve Traditions*, p. 108). This is one of those times for rigorous honesty with the person we have the most difficulty being honest with – ourselves. We can list all the character defects we want and profess to the world that we intend to clear them from our character, but if we aren't truly ready – deep down inside – to give them up then it's nothing but bluster. Let's look at an example.

Let's say this guy named Pat is doing his Step Six, and he has identified lust as one of his character defects. When he was drinking and using he allowed his weakness for seeking carnal fulfillment to run amok. His numerous affairs were hurtful to his wife and family and caused a lot of conflict and mayhem with the women he got involved with; he always promised a lot more than what he was willing to give. His lust brought on a number of other character defects: he had to lie and put on airs to get women to take an interest in him, he had to lie to cover up his debauchery, he had to lie to cover up his lies. His guilt, shame, and regret kept piling up higher and higher as his behavior continued and he saw the effects. His cognitive dissonance was driven deeper and deeper into the dark nether-zones, causing him to drink and use more. After a while, he was seeking to

223

"score" with women just to boost his injured self-esteem, a sort of one-night stand co-dependency. In other words, that one character defect – lust – really played havoc with him, deepened his negative psychology, and contributed greatly to his drinking and using.

Step Six is about being truly willing to surrender our character defects to our higher power. To have that willingness, Pat needs to look deep down inside and realize what that commitment means. He can't just stop his mind from being lustful or noticing an attractive woman, those kinds of thoughts are things that he can't control. As we are told in the 12 Step literature: "it is nowhere evident, at least in this life, that our Creator expects us to fully eliminate our instinctual drives. So far as we know, it is nowhere on the record that God has completely removed from any human being all his natural drives" (*Twelve Steps and Twelve Traditions*, p. 65). If Pat thinks that to succeed in Step Six he must no longer have a lustful thought or feel a physical attraction to a woman then he is setting himself up for failure. Pat will sometimes be attracted to members of the opposite sex, and lustful thoughts will enter his head from time to time. That's human nature, which will never change. What Pat must do for Step Six is to commit to a willingness to stop acting on those thoughts when they occur. This is the Serenity Prayer again, accepting what we can't change while changing the things we can. We can't stop such thoughts from entering our mind, but we can change how we act on those instinctual lusts.

Twelve Steps and Twelve Traditions has something to say about Pat's character defect:

> What we must recognize now is that we exult in some of our defects. We really love them…. To think of *liking* lust seems impossible. But how many men and women speak love with their lips and believe what they say, so that they can hide lust in a dark corner of their minds? And even while staying within conventional bounds, many people have to admit that their imaginary sex excursions are apt to be all dressed up as dreams of romance (p. 66-67).

Psychologically, this character defect of being lustful has a yo-yo effect on Pat's alcoholic-addict pride and self-esteem. He gets a prideful boost out of propping up his ego when he "scores" with a woman – after all, for someone to give themselves to us in body is the ultimate affirmation – yet it later further drags down his self-esteem as he feels guilt and regret and swears to himself that he won't do it again. Then, his lowered self-esteem soon drives him to repeat the cycle in order to prop up his pride. As Pat works his way through the Steps and true self-esteem blossoms within him, he will probably find that his drive to seek affirmation of his worth as a person by seeking sexual encounters falls away. In the meantime, though, he needs to become entirely ready and willing to surrender this character defect.

With this character defect, Pat may be fighting another addiction. Sexual intercourse stimulates our brain's reward system – the same one that drugs and alcohol target – and can therefore be addictive.[3] In fact, the feel-good brain chemicals (neurotransmitters) produced by sexual gratification are about one-tenth to one-half the level of that produced by addictive substances.[4] People like us can easily replace one addiction with another. So, Pat must decide in his Step Six if he is willing to surrender his lust, even though it makes him feel good and boosts his ego. It may take some soul-searching for him to arrive at that willingness. The willingness that the Big Book tells us we need for Step Six does not always come easily.

Allowing our sexual lust to run away with our thoughts disrupts our spirituality in that we see other people as physical objects rather than looking for the inside connections that make up our spiritual connections. By indulging our fantasies in our mind or acting on them we are allowing our character defect of lust to flourish. This is that same willfulness that we discussed in Step Three.

The Big Book has a lot to say about sexual impropriety and its effects on us. It suggests that to give it up we should place our efforts into getting outside ourselves:

> To sum up about sex: We earnestly pray for the right ideal, for guidance in each questionable situation, for sanity, and for the strength to do the right thing. If sex is very troublesome, we throw ourselves the harder into helping others. We think of their needs and work for them. This takes us out of ourselves. It quiets the urge, when to yield would mean heartache (p. 70).

Pat may find his lustful thoughts and urges quiet down after a while of living spiritually, and with practice he will find it easier to stop such thoughts from turning into fantasies and actions when they occur. Before he goes and chats up a woman he needs to be mindful and ask himself: *am I going to talk to her because I really want to talk to her, or is it because I'm acting out of lust?* or *would I be going to talk to her if she was a guy?* Perhaps a good litmus test of his motivations would be: "am I being in any way selfish, dishonest or inconsiderate by doing this? Will I unjustifiably arouse jealousy, suspicion or bitterness?" (Big Book, p. 69, paraphrased). The earlier on in a given situation that he does this, the better he will fare: "sex-related problems complicate the lives of many alcoholics. The first consideration in handling them is to stop the trouble at its source. Honesty is a prime factor in the lives of all members and leaves no room for adultery."[5]

225

In *Twelve Steps and Twelve Traditions* we are told that: "... any person capable of enough willingness and honesty to try repeatedly Step Six on all his faults – without any reservations – has indeed come a long way spiritually, and is... sincerely trying to grow" (p.63). If Pat reaches down deep and finds he is not fully ready to give up on acting on his lustful instincts, then he should talk this over with his sponsor. He can be proud of his honesty with himself and with his sponsor, as this shows a sincere desire to find a way to beat this injurious character defect. He should also take it up with his higher power, and we will discuss in detail how he can do that to maximum effect when we get to Step Eleven. Meanwhile, he can continue his progress through the Steps, working on this character defect every time it presents itself.

The example of Pat's character defect illustrates that we sometimes must really look deep inside to see if we are truly willing to surrender a character defect, especially if it's one that has been a long-standing part of our behavior and if it's one that we derive some kind of reward or pleasure from. While we used lust as an example, it could be any other character defect, such as being an angry driver, or being greedy. If the character defect keeps re-appearing in our behavior even after we have been through the Steps, we may have to return to Step Six and reconsider that specific character defect. Talking out such issues with our sponsor or another person in the fellowship often helps us with this.

*

When it comes to our character defects we must find a balance between our spiritual ideals and realistic expectations. As we have discussed, the behavioral tendencies that constitute character defects are an innate part of our make-up. Like the example of Pat's lustful drives and instincts, we must be very careful not to set ourselves up for failure by setting false expectations in our Step Six. As for Pat, he must not beat himself up about his lustful thoughts. As the Big Book tells us: "we all have sex problems. We'd hardly be human if we didn't" (p. 69), but then asks: "what can we do about them?" (p. 69). We must remember that we are human, that we cannot simply eliminate our natural instincts, and they will sometimes get the better of us. Pobody's nerfect (that's right, I said "pobody's nerfect"). A passage from Chapter 5 of the Big Book explains:

> Do not be discouraged. No one among us has been able to maintain anything like perfect adherence to these principles. We are not saints. The point is, that we are willing to grow along spiritual lines. The principles we have set down are guides to progress. We claim spiritual progress rather than spiritual perfection (p. 60).

Whenever one of our character defects gets the better of us and we act in a way that is not consistent with our spiritual ideals, we should remind ourselves of this passage rather than beat ourselves up over the matter. Spiritual progress is about admitting that we faltered, learning from it, and committing to doing better. As we will discuss shortly, the alcoholic-addict tendency for self-criticism – beating ourselves up over our mistakes – is itself a character defect, and a dangerous one.

While Pat struggles with his willingness to give up flirting and all the physical manifestations of his professed character defect of lustfulness, it's important that he not halt his progress through the Steps. If he has found the willingness and the honesty, then that gives him the tools he needs for spiritual progress, and that's what Step Six asks of us. As we are told in *Twelve Steps and Twelve Traditions*: "[Step Six] states perfect ideals. They are goals toward which we look, and the measuring sticks by which we estimate our progress…. The only urgent thing is that we make a beginning and keep trying" (p. 68). However, we must be honest with ourselves, so that we are not simply using our imperfection as an excuse to continue living with our vice. That will leave a stone in our shoe that will grind away at our spirituality and our sobriety. Rather, we must be honest with ourselves and with our higher power about whether or not we are truly willing to remove this defect of character. If we're not, then we must say so and talk to someone about it.

Keeping our character defects in check is like playing whack-a-mole; every time we knock down one character defect another pops up… then you whack that one and two more pop up. When we play whack-a-mole it would be unrealistic to expect that no moles would pop up or that they would whack themselves. The above Big Book passage tells us to expect our character defects to pop up, and that our job is to keep whacking. As we have discussed, character defects are hard-wired into our brain. Expecting that they will disappear is unrealistic.

It's true that expectations are premeditated resentments. When we place expectations on ourselves to be character defect-free and then we act out on a character defect – as we inevitably will – we become angry and resentful at ourselves for it, and our alcoholic-addict mind will start looking to blame others for our failed expectations. You get the picture. We have worked too hard on purging our resentments to start making new ones by placing impossible demands upon ourselves. Psychological research has found that placing unreasonable expectations on ourselves is a natural human tendency, a *self-enhancement bias*, and that it operates outside of our awareness.[6,7] So, this tendency to place unreasonable expectations on ourselves is itself a character defect that we should endeavor to correct. Let's shoot for progress rather than expect perfection.

Setting reasonable expectations on ourselves becomes more and more natural as we progress in our spirituality because as we learn humility we learn to recognize and accept our limitations as human beings. As well, as our self-esteem becomes more and more rooted in who we are rather than outwards shows of wealth and success, we lose the expectation to succeed at everything we do in order to prop up our feelings of self-worth. Easy does it, it gets easier and better.

*

Earlier I spoke of what I refer to as "cluster" character defects, which are character defects that are especially important because they trigger a number of other character defects that all occur together in a cluster. The first cluster character defect we will discuss is crucial to recovery, and absolutely critical for establishing a healthy, positive psychology, but many people overlook it in their Step Six. That character defect is self-criticism.

People often overlook self-criticism as a character defect because it's one that harms ourselves, and we tend to focus on the character defects that cause harm to other people. However, we must remember that our character defects are not simply behaviors that cause harm to others; they also include the ones that cause harm to ourselves because these self-directed character defects make us sick. Just as we endeavor to stop being angry, resentful, judgmental, impatient, and intolerant toward others, so we must endeavor to stop the same behavior toward ourselves. We grow in spirituality by being loving, kind, generous, supportive, and tolerant toward others; likewise we must also be loving, kind, generous, supportive, and tolerant toward ourselves. We have beat ourselves up during our morally corrupt days of drinking and using, and we have a rock bottom self-esteem and inflated pride to show for it. In Step Six it's time to become ready to stop the self-flagellation. That comes a lot easier to us after Step Nine and we are finding self-forgiveness, but we must recognize this self-defeating behavior as a character defect now and commit to stopping it.

Self-criticism is firmly embedded in human nature, and – to a certain extent – it may help some people to regulate their actions and improve on their mistakes. However, there's a fine line between constructive self-criticism and self-abuse, and very few people are able to walk that line (we will discuss shortly exactly how we can find the right balance). Self-criticism is super-harmful to people with a negative psychology, particularly the extreme negative psychology that characterizes spiritually sick people in active drug or alcohol use.[8,9,10] The internal dialogue of self-criticism quickly veers away from being a productive way to admit to and learn from our mistakes and gets to the point where we beat ourselves up mercilessly. We criticize not just our actions, but also our appearance, our thoughts, our intellect, everything. Our self-esteem doesn't stand a chance.

Self-criticism is, for most of us, deeply ingrained in our psyche because it became a learned behavior from very early on in life.[11,12] Children and adolescents are highly self-aware through most of the stages of childhood development and are therefore exquisitely sensitive to criticism from anyone. If they have a parent with high expectations or a teacher who is especially harsh or critical they internalize the criticism they receive, and that inner critic can last a lifetime. Children even internalize stuff that – to any outside observer – had nothing to do with them. For example, if their parents fight a lot they often internalize the conflict in an egocentric way, by looking for shortcomings within themselves that they feel explain why their parents don't get along. As well, if children have a sibling or a friend who excels in some area then they are likely to compare themselves to that other person, again internalizing the difference in accomplishments as a self-failing. This is especially a problem for children who grow up in the shadow of an older sibling.

Social rejection in children is especially harmful to their sense of self-worth. Rejection by a group or a romantic interest, or ostracization, or bullying all have a powerful impact on propelling the dysfunctional, excessively self-criticizing inner voice. Our experiences in adulthood can worsen this inner critical voice, as we become sensitive to social rejection, criticism at work, and our inability to keep up our appearances, income, and status to the "norms" that we see on social media and advertising. That self-critical inner voice often becomes the go-to inner explanation whenever anything goes wrong in life. The inner critic does more than criticize; it belittles, condemns, and nags.

As our life tumbles downward with the progression of our drinking and using we can become very contemptible in our own eyes, and this is magnified by other people's disgust with our "choices" and behaviors, and by the social stigma that surrounds addiction-alcoholism in general. Our pessimistic, negative psychology deepens our inner critic, and we can become mercilessly critical of ourselves. That same anger, resentment, impatience, intolerance, and blame that we pour onto other people is also directed inwards at ourselves. By the time we come to recovery and get to our Step Six we have been our own punching bag for quite a while, and we must recognize this self-criticism as a character defect.

Does this mean that we stop negatively evaluating our negative behaviors? No, not at all. In fact, stopping the inner critic helps us to better evaluate and learn from our mistakes and shortcomings.[13] Self-criticism impairs our ability to learn from our mistakes. Rather than analyze what went wrong and take a lesson from it our inner narrative demeans and devalues our own ability or worthiness as the cause of the failure. It's like the teacher who screams at children who got their math question wrong versus the teacher who explains things. Self-criticism can generate a variety of feelings including shame, guilt, sadness, anger, frustration, disappointment, helplessness, and hopelessness. It contributes to our anger; anger at ourselves and our own perceived shortcomings. It leads to frustration, because if we see our very nature as a person as the cause of our failure. If we feel we are a failure because of our very nature, then there is no point in trying, and we tend to give up on things. This can fuel rumination and contribute to the overall negative feelings that we tried to numb and escape from with our drinking or using.

Self-criticism, for most people, is not an objective tool for self-improvement. Rather, it's based on an unfounded core belief that we are not good enough, and that our failures are based on our shortcomings. Most people have lived with this belief since early childhood so for them it's entrenched in their nature. Many people mistakenly believe that self-criticism is a good motivator and a sign of humility, but it isn't. On the contrary, it contributes greatly to the low self-esteem, cognitive dissonance, and negative psychology that keep us drinking or using. As we will see in Step Seven, humility is based on a realistic understanding of our capabilities and limitations, not on a merciless negative critical inner voice.

People with addictions tend to be extra hard on themselves because they share society's stigma for substance addiction, and they apply this unfair stigma to themselves. This negative view of the self is a major cause of the negative feelings that keep us continuing in our drug or alcohol use. This was especially the case for me. My experience in medical school and in medical practice left me with a firm conviction that addicts and alcoholics are bad people who wake up every day and choose to make bad decisions. When I myself was caught in the downward spiral of addiction I applied this same stigma to myself. Many others among us do the same thing, turning society's stigma about addiction-alcoholism inwards on themselves.

As a therapist I believe that one of the greatest healing effects of the Steps (especially the first nine Steps) is self-forgiveness. Being around other people in the fellowship shows us that what has happened to us is common and happens to many people. As such, we develop an understanding that ADDICTION IS A MATTER OF BIOLOGY, NOT A MATTER OF MORALITY, AND IT CERTAINLY ISN'T A MATTER OF CHOICE. When we come to understand that, we can let up on ourselves and free ourselves from the self-imposed stigma.

Too, many people are predisposed to self-criticism because of a self-imposed neurotic perfectionism. It seems that alcoholics and addicts are especially likely to suffer from setting impossible standards for themselves:

It is often said that problem drinkers are perfectionists, impatient about any shortcomings, especially our own. Setting impossible goals for ourselves, we nevertheless struggle fiercely to reach those unattainable goals.... We angrily punish ourselves for being less than super-perfect (*Living Sober*, p. 41).

This effect goes well beyond our last drink. In my research into recovering addicts-alcoholics I have noticed that impatience with themselves seems to be a common and rather prominent character defect, especially among those in early recovery. They call addiction the disease of more, and so it is. People like us tend to want everything now. Three weeks from our last drink but we want our twenty-year recovery medallion. When we apply this impatience to ourselves we become hypercritical of ourselves. Easy does it!

*

We alcoholic-addicts can't allow this character defect of self-criticism go unchecked; it's too destructive to our spirituality, our positive psychology, and our recovery. Step Six is our time to recognize our inner critic for what it is, and to commit to an ongoing effort to rid ourselves of its persistent and long-standing bullying. For most of us, this inner critic has been nagging at us since childhood, so it'll take some time and practice to overcome – like most of our other character defects. In Step Six our job is to recognize it as a toxic defect of character and to become willing to do our utmost to purge ourselves of its power over us.

And toxic it is. Self-criticism has been proven by research to adversely affect our mental and physical health.[14] Specifically, it has been shown to be associated with depression, anxiety, eating disorders, substance addiction, behavioral disorders, suicidality, and a long list of physical disorders.[15] In other words, everybody would benefit by freeing themselves from the inner bully, not just those of us who are in recovery.

Psychologists have identified the value of cutting ourselves some slack – something they call *self-compassion* – for our emotional and psychological well-being.[16] So much so, that replacing dysfunctional self-criticism with self-compassion is a major focus of psychotherapy for many of their patients. It's about giving ourselves a break. Research has shown that self-compassion is associated with an improved sense of inner strength, resilience to stress, physical health, motivation, interpersonal relationships, and overall psychological function.[17] Sound good? Good, let's talk about how to curb the inner critic and get some self-compassion.

While psychotherapists spend a lot of time helping their patients to learn self-compassion – in other words, to give themselves a break and stop beating themselves up – I believe that the most effective therapy for self-criticism and all the negative psychology that it brings is a good trip through the 12 Steps. If the 12 Steps teach us anything it's humility, and a big part of humility is learning to respect ourselves. As the program reminds us: "now is the time, the only time there is. And if we are not kind to ourselves right now, we certainly cannot rightfully expect respect or consideration from others" (*Living Sober*, p. 42). Finding self-forgiveness, becoming spiritually healthy, and learning healthy humility by doing the 12 Steps is the best path to self-compassion. However, there are also a few tricks we can use to help us along.

Perhaps the most effective way to put nonproductive self-criticism in its place is to be mindful of this inner critic when it appears. We must recognize it when we beat ourselves up, and then challenge the skewed opinion and bad advice that this inner enemy gives us. When we start beating ourselves up, *Living Sober* makes a suggestion about how to center ourselves:

> Take stock. Have we refrained from taking a drink this 24 hours? That deserves honest self-commendation. Have we made ourselves eat properly today? Have we tried to fulfill our obligations today? Have we, in short, done about the best we could, and all we could today? If so, that's all it is fair to expect.
>
> Maybe we can't answer yes to all those questions. Maybe we have fallen short somehow.... So what? We are not perfect creatures. We should settle for small progress, rather than bemoan any lack of perfection (p. 41-42).

It took me a long time to recognize that self-criticism was a character defect when I was in early recovery and working the Steps; it wasn't on my list the first time I did Step Six. I was so focused on character defects that affected other people that I completely overlooked character defects that affected me, even though these self-directed character defects played a huge role in my addiction-alcoholism. I had a particularly bad case of self-criticism; for most of my life I was always beating myself up over everything. I would ruminate on the past and all the things I should have said or should have done. I would even lay awake at night, replaying all my mistakes in my mind and doing the "what-if" thing. It was not compatible with peace of mind, serenity and positive psychology. What saved me is the "One Day at a Time" slogan, which I made my mantra. Letting go of the past became a great source of peace for me. After all, what do we gain from ruminating and beating ourselves up over things that we cannot change? Wasted brain-power. Better to expend that energy on doing our best today, which is something we can control. Once again, the Serenity prayer holds a valuable lesson for us.

When we mindfully notice that our inner critic is trying to bully us we need to change the channel right away. Refuse to listen to that crap. If we must, we should occupy ourselves, keep the mind and body busy rather than giving any more attention to this useless waste of brain-power. One thing I like to do is to imagine if a friend came to me and told me about a mistake she made. I would be encouraging and helpful, and tell her not to worry about it and move on. No point in beating herself up over past mistakes. So, we should apply that same advice to ourselves. Would we call our friend an idiot? No, probably not, so why should we call ourselves an idiot? As one psychologist puts it, it's about: "turning the inner critic into an inner ally who will refuse to disparage [us] in ways [we] would never disparage those [we] care about."[18]

Psychologists teach their patients a technique known as *dis-identifying*.[19] This is where we separate that inner critical voice from being a part of us and look at it as a foreign, unwelcome entity. Sometimes it even helps to give it a name. Then, when we hear that inner critic starting in with its self-defeating browbeating we can dis-identify – detach – ourselves from it. We look at the inner critical voice as an individual separate from ourselves and tell it to bugger off. Studies have shown that it works![20]

As well, we can examine the evidence. If we look at the situation objectively, we can see that our inner critic focuses only on the bad, and usually makes it look worse than it was. So, we examine the evidence and challenge the inner critic. This is usually easiest to do once our emotions have cooled. If we're upset over something that we just did and our inner critic calls us an idiot, it's best to wait until our initial emotional outburst has cooled and then take a realistic look at what just happened. What were the positives? Was our action really that stupid, or that bad? What would it have looked like through another person's eyes? And, even when there are negatives, we accept that no situation will ever be 100% pure positives. There will always be some negatives, so why get hung up on them when they occur? Our inner voice seems to think that any negatives are unacceptable, but we know better, so we can challenge that notion. Pobody's nerfect, right?

Likewise, when our inner critic tells us we are deficient or inferior, we should review evidence to the contrary. We should think about all the things we're good at, the things we've done well, our talents and strengths. This becomes second nature to us as we grow in humility, something we will look at more closely in Step Seven.

Using self-talk to challenge the inner critic is another technique that psychologists teach their patients to help them overcome the self-sabotage. Many people have an inner "voice" – although it's really thoughts, not an actual voice that they hear – that provides a running dialogue as they go about their day. Self-talk includes not only our conscious thoughts but also our unconscious beliefs and assumptions. When our inner voice is self-critical and pessimistic, that's our inner critic speaking to us. Much of the time, this pessimistic inner voice is distorted and self-defeating, especially for those with damaged self-images.[21] We can practice self-talk when we challenge that inner critic. Repeating to ourselves: *my mistakes do not define me!* is a good self-talk technique.

Another thing we can do is to look at our perceived shortcomings or mistakes with an objective scientific viewpoint. *What can I learn from it?* Analyze it once, take a lesson from it, use it to improve ourselves, and then move on and let it go. Although we can often learn from our past mistakes, beating ourselves up over them serves no purpose whatsoever, and only makes us feel bad. In other words, we replace self-criticism with self-correction... and then let it go. We make a statement of action, such as: *in the future, I commit to _____* ... and then we drop the matter. Any further discussion with our inner critic will only do us harm.

As we pass through the Steps and begin living according to spiritual principles it becomes more difficult for our inner critic to bully us. We find self-forgiveness, we clean house, and we strive to live by spiritual principles. We help others (Step Twelve) as part of our spirituality. Our inner critic naturally melts away. However, when that voice does start its self-defeating work, we must recognize it as a dangerous character defect and treat it as such. It was a part of our downfall in the past, so we crush it when it tries to make a comeback.

*

Another cluster character defect that results in a cascade of anger, resentment, and selfishness and that drives us to drink or use is self-pity. Self-pity is a psychological disaster; it's a major contributor to negative psychology also an effect of negative psychology. Self-pity is based in deeply pessimistic feelings of hopelessness and helplessness, and is thereby a major reason for us to seek escape in our drink or drug. When we are in active addiction-alcoholism, self-pity becomes our excuse to keep on with the substance use: *you'd drink/use too if you had my spouse/problems/job/life, etc.* Addressing self-pity is a major step toward achieving positive psychology and long-term sobriety.

Like most people in the 12 Step fellowship, I give out my phone number to a lot of people in the program, especially newcomers. I'll take calls pretty much any time of the day. Ideally, if people call me when they're in trouble or not doing well, they'll call before resorting to taking a drink or drug, but that's often not the case. I've noticed that when people call me when they are drunk or high, the call is virtually always a burst of self-pity coming from the other end. It's striking how much self-pity is tied into drinking or using, including in relapse. I always think that if only the individual on the other end of the phone line would have dealt with this self-pity by doing the Steps, he or she would not be drunk or high right now.

In Step One we talked about learned helplessness and an external locus of control. That's where we become so negative-minded that we focus on all the bad in our lives, and we even magnify it to make it sound worse than it is. After a while we begin to develop an external locus of control, where we believe that our destiny is determined by factors completely outside our control and we are nothing but passive puppets of the outside world. As it progresses we become so convinced that our efforts don't matter that we even stop trying to succeed at things: *nothing I do matters, so why even try?* Self-pity brings about this mind-set of hopelessness, which in turn worsens the self-pity. This is a crippling outlook on life and one of the horrible emotions and feelings that we try to numb by using alcohol and drugs.

Living Sober nails the psychology of self-pity:

> This emotion [self-pity] is so ugly that no one in his or her right mind wants to admit feeling it. Even when sober, many of us remain clever at hiding from ourselves the fact that we are in a mess of self-pity. We do not like at all being told that it shows, and we are quick to argue that we are experiencing some other emotion – not that of loathsome poor-me-ism. Or we can, in a second, find a baker's dozen of perfectly legitimate reasons for feeling somewhat sorry for ourselves.
>
> Hanging over us long after detoxification is the comfortably familiar feeling for suffering. Self-pity is an enticing swamp. Sinking into it takes so much less effort than hope, faith, or just plain moving. (p. 55-56).

That passage highlights an aspect of human psychology that has always amazed me: in some sort of perverse way we enjoy feeling the victim. We deny it when we are indulging our mind in its strange love for self-pity and we even become defensive about it. We must overcome this and not allow pride to dissuade us from recognizing and admitting our self-pity when we do Step Six. As *Living Sober* tells us: "once we recognize self-pity for what it is, we can start to do something about it other than drink" (p. 57).

There's no point in holding onto self-pity, because – despite our mind's perverse pleasure in playing "poor-me" – it does us no good: "such thinking is a great ticket to the barroom, but that's about all" (*Living Sober*,

235

p. 56), and "sitting in our own pool of tears is not a very effective action" (p. 56). Besides, as we shall see shortly, self-pity costs us our positive psychology and wrecks our spirituality. Psychologists refer to self-pity as *self-victimization* because our mind turns us into victims of the world. I like that terminology, because we become victims when we allow self-pity to flourish in our mind, and our mind loves to do it. We need to recognize this weird human affinity for self-pity and resolve to rid ourselves of its horrible dominion over us.

Self-pity and its best friend learned helplessness force us into inaction. We believe that nothing we can do will matter, so we do nothing. It robs us of the wisdom to know the difference between the things we cannot change and the things we can. The Serenity Prayer tells us to drop the self-pity by accepting the things we cannot change, and finding the courage and resolve to get off our butts and change the things that we can. Sounds like a much better plan than wallowing in self-pity.

Think for a moment of all the other character defects that this poor-me, "I'm a victim" self-pity and negative-focused mentality brings out. We become angry that we are victims of the world and that life is treating us so unfairly. We begin to resent other people, institutions, life, and even God for our lamentable situation. We are jealous of others because in our eyes they have life so much better than us; we may even hate them for it. Our self-esteem takes a swan dive, so our artificial alcoholic-addict's pride needs to be coddled, and we begin lying about ourselves, and cutting others down around us to prop up our own pride. Some people may become sexually promiscuous and manipulative to prop up their pride. We don't care about other people; in fact we delight in their mishaps because it makes us feel better about our situation (this is known as *schadenfreude*). We may even try to sabotage others. It starts getting pretty dark inside our head. Our spirituality is deadened and our psychology is negative. This mind-set is a breeding ground for substance use.

Just yesterday I received a call from someone who's been in and out of the fellowship for some time (who, by the by, has never got past Step One despite being in the program for several years) and she was drunk. Not really a rare occurrence because she's a chronic relapser. And she was ANGRY. She was complaining about her "stupid sponsor," and her stupid sponsor – she says – is why she has been drinking and using. She was complaining about her life situation and how it's not fair. She was even complaining about the stupid weather and how many problems it causes for her. She was blaming everybody for her relapse... except herself. It was clear to me that her raging self-pity was keeping her from sobriety. By this point, as you are working on Step Six, I'm sure you can recognize all the symptoms of alcoholism-addiction in her, including self-victimization/self-pity. Until she takes ownership of her life and stops with the blame and resentments

236

and self-pity she has no hope of lasting sobriety. To do this, she needs to do the Steps. It saddens me to see people suffer so, when the solution is right under their noses.

Psychological studies in self-pity have shown that people who feel sorry for themselves are high in neuroticism (an older term that essentially refers to obsessive-compulsive behaviors), sadness and depression, a heightened sense of injustice, envy of others, dysfunctional anger reactions, and beliefs that they are controlled by external factors, including powerful others and chance.[22] They also found that people high in self-pity are ambivalent toward life and goals, yet they worry excessively about the future. As well, they tend to feel lonely. That aligns quite well with our experiences with self-pity as alcoholic-addicts; those symptoms are deeply entwined with the downward spiral of obsessive substance use.

Psychologists have found that self-pity is a natural human response to stress, failure, loss, or illness.[23] Some people respond with self-pity and a feeling of victimization to the smallest of stressors, while others seldom, if ever, feel self-pity. Those who respond to stress with self-pity are described as "psychoneurotic," or "thin-skinned," and are over-sensitive to stress and experience great insecurity when confronted with difficulties.[24] They may just lie down and let things happen to them. They are likely to be depressed or have depression just under the surface. Almost anyone can develop the pessimistic frame of mind that leads to self-pity, either because they are overwhelmed by stressors, experiencing depression or other mental health symptoms, or because they are naturally predisposed to that frame of mind. As well, substance use can itself induce or worsen the negative frame of mind that leads to self-pity because of the depression-inducing after-effects of any kind of substance use. As such, self-pity and substance use become locked in a downward spiral of negative psychology and substance dependence. Bill Wilson describes his experience with self-pity: "no words can tell of the loneliness and despair I found in that bitter morass of self-pity. Quicksand stretched around me in all directions. I had met my match. I had been overwhelmed. Alcohol was my master" (Big Book, p. 8).

Active alcoholic-addicts usually become "psychoneurotic," thin-skinned, over-sensitive to stress, and insecure – in other words, they become weapons-grade self-pity-ers. Studies have shown that self-pity-ers are likely to "over-indulge" in obsessing on their failures, hardships and setbacks.[25] They ruminate on their perceived failures, shortcomings, and problems and ignore all the positives in life. This negative frame of mind is what turns many among us to respond to these horribly negative feelings by trying to numb them with drink or drug. By engaging our substance use we give ourselves a brief high – the opposite of the sadness and helpless feelings of self-pity – and escape for a little while. It's an extreme form of stress avoidance, known as *escapism*. And, it's not just people who use substances who do this. Compulsive gambling, sex addiction, co-dependency, compulsive shopping, and other behavioral addictions (sometimes called *process addictions*) are also dysfunctional forms of escapism that can ruin people's lives.

As well, it has been shown that people use self-pity to seek empathy, sympathy, attention, and help from others.[26] However, this strategy may work in the short-term, but invariably fails and leads to rejection. Social psychologists have found that the people we tell our sob stories to may respond to a display of self-pity initially and may be quite generous in their response, but the length of time that this persists is very short.[27] People don't like whiners. It's in our nature to expect people to stop complaining, accept their situation, and do something about it or move on. After all, people all have their own problems, and they hold in contempt those who think that everyone should pity them for their problems. This social rejection just leads to more self-pity, anger, resentment, lowered self-esteem, and – in people like us – drinking or using. We just add the people who don't respond to our appeals for pity to our long list of resentments. Small wonder that self-pity has been associated with social and emotional isolation and loneliness.[28]

Self-pity is a matter of perspective; anybody, even the most fortunate individual alive, could easily come up with reasons to rationalize self-pity. People who have a negative mind-set – such as the extreme negative psychology of addiction-alcoholism – are especially prone to the pessimistic perspective that creates self-pity. As we progress through the Steps and develop a positive psychology and begin to see that life is valuable and worthwhile, our self-pity will naturally fall away. However, self-pity comes so naturally to us that we must be vigilant for when it tries to creep back into our psyche. If allowed to fester, self-pity can become a locus for relapse.

So we can see how destructive self-pity is to our spirituality. We are selfishly focused on ourselves, and we resent others. Our spiritual need to get outside ourselves is impaired by this inward-focus on our perception of our own victimization. We drink or use to shut everyone and everything out. We can also see how this one character defect – self-pity – can lead to a cluster of other character defects. And it gets us nowhere! It's gotta go. That's what Steps Six and Seven are for, so make sure this character defect finds its way onto your list. Let's now talk about some ways we can challenge self-pity and send it where it belongs: somewhere other than between our ears.

*

The human mind's weird love affair with self-pity is a true oddity of the human psyche, because it gets us nowhere and it's psychologically disastrous. I always wondered why people seem to love feeling sorry for themselves, when they gain nothing from it; it's just a weird aspect of human psychology. Worse, it's a major factor in addiction-alcoholism. So let's look at a few really great ways to rid ourselves of self-pity. The 12 Step program is designed to get us outside ourselves and stop the self-pity cycle, so we will look to the 12 Step literature. Ordinarily, I would add some suggestions from counseling psychology, but the 12 Step program has unmatched expertise at teaching people to overcome self-pity because it's such a powerful part of our disease, and psychology has very little to add to the 12 Step process. The key tools for ending self-pity are: 1) awareness, 2) getting outside ourselves by helping others, 3) making a gratitude list, 4) using humor, 5) going to a meeting, 6) doing some "book-keeping," and 7) reading the Big Book. Let's go through these now.

Technique 1: awareness. Just plain awareness of self-pity is one of the gifts that we get from Step Six, and it gives us great power to free ourselves from this mind-sucking mind-set. Self-pity is, as we know, a natural human response to adversity, and a natural effect of feeling down. As such, people usually aren't even aware of its presence and its effects. In fact, people even deny self-pity when confronted about it. However, we alcoholic-addicts now have an awareness of it, so that we can recognize it when it happens, recognize its negative effects, and engage our tools to deal with it.

This awareness should be coupled with a determination to face life on life's terms and an acceptance that nobody's life will ever be without adversity. We make a conscious decision to accept the things we cannot change and change the things that we can, rather than questioning whether our problems are "fair" and cowering behind the resulting self-pity.

Our awareness of our tendency toward self-pity also empowers us to question our perceptions: *am I really so unfortunate? Is my luck really always bad? Am I really so hard-done-by in life?* Leaving our perceptions of victimization unchallenged can cause them to become self-fulfilling prophecies. We never have to look far to see people who are much worse off than we are, if we open our eyes to it. Suddenly, our situation doesn't seem so bad when we put our own situation in perspective.

Technique 2: getting outside ourselves by helping others. Bill Wilson tells of how getting outside himself saved him from self-pity:

> I was not too well at the time, and was plagued by waves of self-pity and resentment. This sometimes nearly drove me back to drink, but I soon found that when all other measures failed, work with another alcoholic would save the day. Many times I have gone to my old hospital in despair. On talking to a man there, I would be amazingly

lifted up and set on my feet. It is a design for living that works in rough going (Big Book, p. 15).

My own experience has mirrored that of Bill's. When I am sponsoring a newcomer and I see that he is stuck in self-pity, I interrupt his "poor-me" inward-focus by helping him get outside himself. In our area there is a program called "out from the cold," where local churches rotate on a schedule to provide homeless persons an evening meal and a chance to come in from the weather and sleep in a warm and safe place. When I take people who are stuck in self-pity to volunteer at out from the cold for an evening, it's amazing how quickly their self-pity dries up. I mentioned earlier that a colleague of mine (who is not an alcoholic-addict) was caught in a depressive mind-set of the "poor-me's" and I suggested she go volunteer at the local soup kitchen for an afternoon. She did, and it worked; she now goes back once a week. She likes how it makes her feel. I signed up as a volunteer at a local retirement home and started going to sit and visit with people who had no friends or family. I also like going to help put on 12 Step meetings at the local detox center. Such activities take us outside ourselves and even make us feel foolish for any thoughts of self-pity that we might be harboring. As a doc I often see people who are very sick or badly disabled, and I find that helps keep me grounded. There are many ways to keep our perspective fresh and healthy, and we will discuss these further in our Step Twelve study.

It's amazing to experience the healing power of getting outside ourselves; a testament to the power of spirituality. Our most serious character defects – selfishness, self-pity, hubristic pride, and self-criticism – occur when we are caught up in looking inward with all our concern placed squarely on ourselves. These character defects give us negative feelings, so getting outside ourselves is a salubrious exercise indeed. Feeling down? Feel like your spirituality and your recovery need a boost? Engage your spirituality and do something to get outside yourself.

Technique 3: making a gratitude list. I always say that it's impossible to be unhappy while you're holding a bunch of balloons. Likewise, it's impossible to feel gratitude and self-pity at the same time. So, if you find yourself wallowing in self-pity, replace it with gratitude; it'll push that feeling of being life's victim right out of your head. The most effective way to do that is to write a gratitude list.

This involves simply sitting down with a pad and paper and writing out everything that you are grateful for. This may sound easy, but you'd be surprised at how many important things we take for granted and don't even think of when we make our list. That's why I suggest getting some help from your sponsor until you get the hang of it. I have found that when I work with newcomers in the detox center even people who have been living under a bridge can find a lot of things to put on a gratitude list if properly coached. Your sponsor can coach you if you want to improve your ability to make such list.

A lot of people don't do well with their list until they've had a chance to be exposed to people less fortunate than themselves. That's one way that giving of our time to help others helps our recovery: it makes gratitude come a lot easier when we need to call upon it to chase away the self-pity monster.

I find doing a gratitude list to be so uplifting that I do them all the time, often a few times a week. Sometimes I just do one in my head while I'm driving or out for a walk. It keeps me grateful, chases away depression and self-pity, and keeps me grounded in humility. Try it!

Technique 4: using humor. This awesome technique for addressing self-pity comes to us from *Living Sober*:

> Another excellent weapon is humor. Some of the biggest belly laughs at A.A. meetings erupt when a member describes his or her own latest orgy of self-pity, and we listeners find ourselves looking into a fun-house mirror. There we are – grown men and women tangled up in the emotional diaper of an infant. It may be a shock, but the shared laughter takes a lot of the pain out of it, and the final effect is salutary (p. 57).

As a psychologist and someone who is in recovery, I am always fascinated by the capacity of the men in the U.S. Navy SEALs for mental resilience in the face of arduous situations. These guys are psychological rock-stars, and we can learn from them. I have noticed from my readings and from watching video recordings of their training program that their sense of humor comes to the surface whenever times get really tough. We don't have to be Navy SEALs to realize that when we look at the light side of things with another person it helps release tension, fear, anxiety, and self-pity. An overwhelming body of research evidence has shown that humor and laughter improve our mood, help us see the world as a better, kinder place, and reduce stress.[29,30,31,32] However, it's necessary to stick to uplifting humor, not jokes that demean or disparage others – including ourselves.[33]

Technique 5: going to a meeting. There's something about the fellowship that has a tremendous centering power. I can really see why some people use the fellowship as their higher power. There are many ways to engage the fellowship to help us to stay sober and to fend off the negative feelings and character defects that make us drink or use, especially self-pity.

One recovery tool that I strongly recommend is to make contact with someone in recovery every day. That can be as simple as a text. It doesn't have to be anything more than a: *Hey! How's it going?* message. Some people text or call their sponsor every day. I like scrolling through my contacts and picking out someone I haven't been in contact with for a while and shooting him a text. It reminds us of who we are, and it gets us outside ourselves. These are people who understand us, who get us, and who speak our language. If we send them a text that says: *I've been feeling some self-pity lately* they will know exactly what we are talking about and what the significance of that is for people like us. They can help us with it. Chances are they might suggest that we go to a meeting.

However, there's a major difference between routine contact with "regular" people (i.e. people who are not recovering alcoholic-addicts) and routine contact with people in the fellowship. When regular people ask us how we are doing, they usually expect us to say: *fine, thanks!* Many would be annoyed or feel awkward if we poured out our feelings to them. However, when we text other people in recovery, we should engage our rigorous honesty and tell them how we feel if they ask. If we feel fine, then we should say so. If we don't, then we should say so. Keeping things to ourselves when we are not well is a red flag for relapse. Our secrets make us sick.

I love showing up for meetings early to connect with people from the fellowship. In early recovery I used to show up early and leave late, because I knew that I needed to break my well-used spiritually sick habit of self-isolating. That still applies, but now that I'm pretty stable in working my recovery I see other benefits, including getting outside myself and centering myself in my spirituality. Somehow, when I interact with other people at meetings it makes me feel better, and reminds me that I am not alone in my pursuit of spiritual principles. It definitely helps if I'm suffering from a case of the "poor-me's."

When I find myself doing the self-victimization thing, there's one guy in the fellowship that I really look for at meetings. I was fortunate in that before my drinking and using career got going I was able to put together a life: get myself educated, surround myself with wonderful family and friends, and put together a good work history. My friend was not. His drug and alcohol use started while he was a teen, so he never finished high school, never got an education or a trade, never built up any kind of positive work history, and never developed any meaningful relationships. When he finally got sober when he was almost 60, he had the same employability as a teenager who hasn't finished high school. As a result he does minimum wage manual labor jobs, barely survives paycheck to paycheck, and lives a very simple life. He does without a lot of things that some of us take for granted. However, he is by far one of the most grateful people I've ever met. He's so wonderfully grateful for life, his sobriety, and the few material things he does have that I find him to be an inspiration, especially when my human nature gets the better of me and self-pity creeps in.

Anytime we become aware of self-pity welling up inside us, we should engage the fellowship by contacting others in recovery, meeting our sponsor for a coffee, and/or going to a meeting. It works for just about anything that ails us before it degenerates into a desire to drink or use.

Technique 6: doing some "book-keeping." Another suggestion for crushing self-pity when it sneaks up on us is by doing some "book-keeping." This is similar to doing a gratitude list, but it's much quicker and we can do it in our mind no matter where we are or what we're doing. The suggestion comes to us from *Living Sober*:

> When we catch self-pity starting, we also can take action against it with instant bookkeeping. For every entry of misery on the debit side, we find a blessing we can mark on the credit side. What health we have, what illnesses we don't have, what friends we have loved, the sunny weather, a good meal a-coming, limbs intact, kindnesses shown and received, a sober 24 hours, a good hour's work, a good book to read, and many other items can be totaled up to outbalance the debit entries that cause self-pity (p. 57).

Technique 7: reading the Big Book. This is one of my go-to recovery tools. I love reading the big Book; I find it interesting, informative, insightful, and it has deep meaning for me. It's the only book on my shelf that has saved my life. I have read it through a number of times. I go through it from start to finish – a little at a time – and when I get to the end I go back to the beginning and start again. No matter where I am in recovery or what's going on in my life, when I read the Big Book new things pop out at me that I hadn't noticed before. It's like the Big Book is growing with me as I grow in recovery and spirituality.

I suggest that everyone in the program make reading the Big Book one of their regular recovery activities. Even for people who are not into books it's an easy read, because we are learning all about our favorite subject – ourselves!

Whenever I'm feeling down, or my alcoholic-addict mind starts going where it shouldn't, I pull out my Big Book and take 10 minutes to read. Sometimes I just pick a story from the back and read it, or I pick up reading where I last left off. Some people say to just open it to any page and start reading. This incredible book has the power to calm me down and center me when I need it, and it definitely helps me keep self-pity in check.

*

The next cluster character defect that we'll discuss is hubristic pride and its good buddy, low self-esteem. We have already encountered the paradoxical pride of addiction-alcoholism and its destructive effects on our psychology and recovery in our study of the earlier Steps. Pride is so central to addiction-alcoholism that it must necessarily be discussed in virtually every Step. Pride is one of the Seven Deadly Sins, and is often referred to as the sin from which all others arise. While it's OK to be proud of our accomplishments, the dysfunctional pride we are speaking of goes well beyond that. This pride needs to go if we are to be healthy and spiritually well. Let's talk about this major character defect, why it exists, and how we can deal with it.

The pride involved in the minds of alcoholics is distinct and unusual. For most people, pride is a reflection of their accomplishments, abilities, and feelings of self-worth. In other words, they have something to at least partly back up their pride, over-inflated as it may be. In the practicing alcoholic, pride is over-inflated and defensive in nature, with nothing to back it up. Yet, it is powerful enough to prevent us from accepting our powerlessness over alcohol, and keeps us from accepting help.

The irony is that the pride that feeds our disease is driven by low self-esteem. This sickness-induced pride is an instinctive mechanism of denial of our situation to help reduce the psychological pain that comes from knowing how low we have become. In order to compensate for our own sorry behavior and our pathetic situation, we will project a fabricated positive view of ourselves on others by inflated demonstrations of pride, and conversely by criticizing and nit-picking others in efforts to cut them down beneath us.

Oddly, the person we try the hardest to convince with our fake displays of pride is ourselves. The whole purpose of this false pride is to reduce our mind's discomfort with how low we've become, and how far removed our behaviors and situation are from what we believe is "good" – in other words, it's how our mind tries to relieve our cognitive dissonance. We seek affirmation from others to validate our pride, and when we don't get it we become angry and resentful at those who aren't giving us the praise and respect that we feel we deserve: *don't you know how awesome I am?* We become consumed by being "right" and can't admit when we are wrong, and we can't acknowledge our defects. It's dysfunctional to the extreme, and it makes us intolerable to be around.

*

Psychologists identify two types of pride: authentic (good) pride versus hubristic (bad) pride.[34] Hubristic pride is the kind that's arrogant, boastful, self-absorbed, conceited, and narcissistic. Authentic pride is when we are proud of a legitimate accomplishment, but we aren't shoving it in everybody's face. The dysfunctional pride that rules the hour in the addicted mind is hubristic; it's an attempt to cover up for a rock bottom self-esteem. Our cognitive dissonance doesn't like how pathetic we've become in our drinking or drug use, so the mind compensates by trying to project a false image of how awesome we are, through this fake pride. Our mind needs to convince itself that we are awesome, despite how our life is crashing down. That's the paradox of the pride that's characteristic of our disease: it's inflated pride as a result of a deflated self-esteem.

Good pride (authentic pride) is not a bad thing; we are right to be proud of our accomplishments. In fact, authentic pride is part of healthy humility. That's right, humility includes well-placed, justified authentic pride. As we will discuss in Step Seven, humility includes acknowledgment of our strengths and accomplishments. Authentic pride can be a great motivator and a healthy part of our positive psychology. However, there can be a fine line between authentic and hubristic pride, so we should be mindful. Let's look at an example.

I'm proud of my sobriety. Rightfully so, because it's hard-earned, and one of the most miraculous achievements of my life. That pride can be healthy, authentic pride as long as I approach it with humility. I use my pride for my recovery to motivate me to continue doing the work that I need to do to stay sober, and I use it as a reward every time I reach a milestone in my recovery. I use my recovery to help others to find the same. I include my recovery in my humility by recognizing my sobriety as one of my personal strengths. That's healthy and natural. However, that pride can also become hubristic. If I start boasting about my sobriety time, using it to project superiority over people with less recovery time, or to be judgmental and intolerant of people who are still sick and suffering, then it has become hubristic and unhealthy. So we must be vigilant for when we cross that thin line into hubristic pride in recovery.

Twelve Steps and Twelve Traditions shows us how our pride (the hubristic, dysfunctional pride of alcoholism-addiction) can explode into a number of other toxic character defects:

> Self-righteous anger can be very enjoyable. In a perverse way we can actually take satisfaction from the fact that many people annoy us, for it brings a comfortable feeling of superiority. Gossip barbed with our anger, a polite form of murder by character assassination, has its satisfactions for us, too. Here we are not trying to help those we criticize; we are trying to proclaim our own righteousness (p. 67).

These character defects – self-righteous anger, and gossip – are especially toxic for our recovery because they are anti-spiritual. They interfere with our ability to connect with others. Gossip is pure poison for spirituality, "murder by character assassination." Gossip has driven many people away from the 12 Step fellowship, and it has hurt many others. People gossip because they still have some hubristic pride that wants to be propped up by bringing down other people. It's a nasty, venomous tendency we have when our self-esteem needs some work. A recent study published in the *Journal of Social Psychology and Personality Science* found that people spend an average of 52 minutes a day gossiping – talking about people who aren't present.[35] Gossip is a form of *schadenfreude*, which is when we derive pleasure from another person's misfortune.

Another recently published study shed some light on schadenfreude that is relevant to our Step Six efforts.[36] The researchers reviewed three decades of psychological research to put together a coherent picture of this psychological phenomenon. Unsurprisingly, the researchers found it to be an ugly aspect of human nature; they referred to it as "the darker side of humanity." The study authors found that schadenfreude was motivated by feelings of aggression, rivalry, and justice; seeing someone else knocked down a peg somehow makes us feel better about all the times we felt victimized after being knocked down a peg. The researchers believe that schadenfreude involves a dehumanization of the person whose downfall amuses us, and that it's related to sadism, narcissism, and even psychopathy. Suffice it to say that schadenfreude, which includes gossip, involves a complete lack of empathy, and represents a vain effort to prop up an unhealthy pride.

It takes a lot of work to maintain an unhealthy, hubristic pride. We are always scheming, looking for other people's weaknesses and failings, and expending considerable effort to figure out what other people think of us, and then we fret about it non-stop. We are always trying to project and maintain appearances, many of them false or exaggerated. It's so much easier to let go of all that and just be ourselves when we are comfortable in our own skin with a healthy self-esteem and humility. Ironically, research has shown that people like us and respect us more when we stop trying to project an inflated image.[37]

When our self-esteem is low and we try to compensate with an elevated hubristic pride, we trigger a cluster of other character defects. We become angry and resentful when other people don't validate our pride to our satisfaction, we engage in gossip and schadenfreude and other efforts to bust people down in order to boost our own image, we become judgmental and critical of others, our focus becomes inward-looking so that we lack empathy for others, and we become selfish and willing to wrong others to boost our own situation. Hubristic pride is toxic to our spiritual health and our sobriety.

So, the strange pride of alcoholism-addiction can lead to a whole cluster of character defects. Fortunately, as we progress through the Steps we find self-forgiveness, self-acceptance, and humility, and our old pride melts away, replaced by a healthy self-esteem. Thus, if we come to be willing to abandon our hubristic pride in Step Six, the endowment of a healthy self-esteem that we get from our trip through the 12 Steps is the very best way to rid ourselves of this horrible character defect.

*

The final core "cluster" character defect is selfishness. Like the other cluster character defects, selfishness is given a lot of attention in the Big Book and other 12 Step literature because of its central importance to negative psychology, spiritual sickness, and addiction-alcoholism.

Selfishness is one of the most noxious of character defects, and is the root of many problems in society in general, including among people who are not alcoholic-addicts. In its most benign form it involves being concerned for one's own well-being, profit, and pleasure with no regard for others. In its more toxic forms it involves seeking to gain at the expense of others, not caring if one's own actions may harm others. In its most pernicious form it involves seeking one's own interests by using and manipulating others; this is the basis of narcissism (the pursuit of gratification of ego, inflated self-image, and pleasure above all other pursuits), anti-social personality disorder (the view of others as only having value in as much as they can be manipulated and used to satisfy one's own selfish desires, also known as sociopathy), and psychopathy (an extreme sociopathy where one is willing to commit crimes and even kill to satisfy one's selfish needs and desires).

In alcoholism-addiction selfishness takes on a rather unique face. This disease-specific form of selfishness is rooted in the self-will of addiction, where we get to the point where we will do anything for our next drink or drug, no matter whom we have to crush under our heel to get it. We discussed this toxic self-will of alcoholism-addiction in our Step Three study, and how it stands out from all other forms of self-will. Our self-will when we crave a donut when we are on a diet won't propel us to spend our life savings, blow off our children, push away family and friends, lose our job, turn to criminal activities, or risk our lives by taking toxic substances. However, once we have crossed the line into addiction-alcoholism, our self-will around getting our next drink or drug will propel us to do all of those things and more. This self-will propels us to a level of selfishness beyond normal human limits.

Recently, a couple of guys in my town stole a big delivery truck, then drove it in the middle of the night to a closed convenience store and drove the truck through the wall. They had to back up the truck and drive it into the wall seven times to smash through. Then, they ran into the dark store and pulled out the ATM and made off with it. A few miles away they transferred everything to their own vehicle and drove off after setting the delivery truck on fire.

It didn't take long for the police to find these guys and arrest them. They had made about $2,000 in their little enterprise that night, and it was all gone within two days. It turned out that they were alcoholic-addicts who were so desperate for their next hit that they undertook this insane venture to get the money that they needed. Their selfishness was such that they caused $150,000 worth of damage to the convenience store, over $100,000 by burning the truck, and put the convenience store – a "mom-and-pop" family operation – out of business for weeks. They cost over a quarter of a million dollars in damage and a lot of heartache to other people to get $2,000 for themselves, and then blew it all in a couple of days. The level of selfishness involved is incomprehensible to people who don't understand addiction-alcoholism.

People who are addicted to alcohol might look at these two guys and say: *I would never do that to get a drink!* However, these two guys were addicted to cocaine, which can easily swallow up $1,000 a day if you have the money. If alcohol was that expensive and that difficult to obtain, I'm sure more than a few alcoholics would be driven to the same lengths. As the Big Book tells us:

> Here is the fellow who has been puzzling you, especially in his lack of control. He does absurd, incredible, tragic things while drinking. He is a real Dr. Jekyll and Mr. Hyde.... His disposition while drinking resembles his normal nature but little. He may be one of the finest fellows in the world. Yet let him drink for a day, and he frequently becomes disgustingly, and even dangerously anti-social. He has a positive genius for getting tight at exactly the wrong moment, particularly when some important decision must be made or engagement kept. He is often perfectly sensible and well balanced concerning everything except liquor, but in that respect he is incredibly dishonest and selfish (p. 21).

By all accounts, our two would-be robbers were – before their lives became completely taken over by their drug use – normal, nice guys. One even has a wife and three kids. It doesn't matter, though. Once we go far enough down that road to addiction-alcoholism the selfishness trumps all other considerations, and anyone can end up there, no matter how high their starting point and how normal and nice they are. Our disease has sharp teeth.

However, we don't have to commit such a selfish act as these two guys did to have selfishness take sway over our lives and fill us with other character defects. Selfishness is a bad enough defect of character in many

248

people who don't have our disease, but when addiction to alcohol or drugs is added to the mix, the selfishness becomes malignant. Driven by our self-will to get to our next drink or drug, we will lie, cheat, steal, evade responsibility, blow off our job or family, and spend our last dollar. That's a lot of character defects, but it gets worse. If anyone gets in our way or tries to stop us, our selfishness propels us to become defensive, aggressive, judgmental, impatient, angry, and resentful. As our life deteriorates and our self-esteem drops our selfish need for pride drives us to lie, and cut down others. Jealousy, schadenfreude, gossip, and down-talking others become part of our behavior. Our selfish pride renders us willing to harm others to satisfy our own need for validation. The selfishness of alcoholism-addiction truly is a "cluster" defect of character.

As with so many other aspects of the psychology of alcoholism-addiction, I'm amazed by the oddness of the selfishness that accompanies our disease; it's truly a paradox. Here we have a sickness that we would do anything to stop, yet we are willing to engage in the most extreme selfish acts to keep it going. I'm willing to bet that both of those guys who robbed the convenience store wished that they could just snap their fingers and be free of their addiction, yet they were willing to commit the most extreme selfish act to feed their addiction. As the Big Book says: "many of us felt that we had plenty of character. There was a tremendous urge to cease forever. Yet we found it impossible. This is the baffling feature of alcoholism as we know it – this utter inability to leave it alone, no matter how great the necessity or the wish" (p. 34). Bizarre, but such is the weird pathological psychology of our disease.

Selfishness is the opposite of empathy, the opposite of altruism, and the opposite of spirituality. So, it makes sense that the best way to rid ourselves of selfishness is to become rich in spirituality, empathy, and altruism. And that's exactly how selfishness is dealt with in the 12 Step program. As we progress through the Steps and grow in spiritual health and wealth our selfishness shrinks and recedes. When we practice empathy and altruism as part of our ongoing program of recovery (as we will discuss in Step Twelve) we keep selfishness at bay. Ironically, our past extreme selfishness and selfish acts help us to help others when we are in recovery. Says one alcoholic-addict in recovery: "those events that once made me feel ashamed and disgraced now allow me to share with others how to become a useful member of the human race" (Big Book, p. 492). Another paradox, that our past selfishness makes us better at doing the things we need to do to keep selfishness at bay. However, we must be realistic and keep our guard up, because selfishness is a natural human tendency, and in the past we had become very comfortable with it indeed. If we allow it to snake its way back into our psyche we risk much. In the meantime, Step Six asks us to recognize and acknowledge this ruinous character defect and to become willing to surrender it to our higher power.

*

The Big Book pulls no punches about the role of selfishness in making us drink and use: "selfishness – self-centeredness! That, we think, is the root of all our troubles. Driven by a hundred forms of fear, self-delusion, self-seeking, and self-pity, we step on the toes of our fellows…" (p. 62). This is a character defect that must go if we hope to beat our addiction: "… the alcoholic is an extreme example of self-will run riot, though he usually doesn't think so. Above everything, we alcoholics must be rid of this selfishness. We must, or it kills us!" (Big Book, p. 62).

The Steps are a potent way to purge us of our selfishness, but we must first become willing to surrender that poisonous aspect of human nature. Among the ninth Step promises: "we will lose interest in selfish things and gain interest in our fellows. Self-seeking will slip away" (Big Book, p. 84). In our pursuit for spiritual progress we not only remove this selfishness, but we seek to push it out through acts of selflessness, as we will see in Step Twelve. Psychologists involved in research about positive psychology have acknowledged the role that selflessness plays in positive psychology, as embodied by the Chinese proverb "if you want happiness for a lifetime, help someone else."[38]

Research into social motivation has shown that selfishness comes at a price that greatly outweighs any benefits that we gain from selfish acts.[39] This is especially so for people like us, whose selfishness can result in a downward cascade of character defects, guilt, negative psychology, and relapse. After all, it's happened to us before. If we see selfish thoughts and behaviors rearing their ugly head in our lives, we should take heed. Our recovery, happiness, peace of mind, and positive psychology are all dependent upon our spiritual health, and selfishness is a symptom of spiritual decline. Spirituality is about getting outside ourselves, while selfishness is about staying locked inside the self. Likewise, our humility – a key virtue that helps keep us in sobriety – is failing if we find ourselves becoming selfish. We spoke earlier about the importance of finding meaning and a sense of purpose in life, and selfishness has been shown to rob us of these important aspects of happiness and wellbeing.[40] It's human nature to deny selfishness if we are confronted on the issue, but we must overcome this natural tendency to become defensive and deny, for the sake of our recovery and well-being. In fact, we should recognize selfishness when it finds its way into our thoughts and actions, and talk to our sponsor about it. Selfishness is poisonous to our spirituality and our sobriety, so we should see it for the red flag that it is.

250

*

While we're on the subject of selfishness, we should take the opportunity to clear up something that a lot of newcomers to the program find confusing; I know I did. We are told that we must overcome selfishness, as it is one of the main drivers of the spiritual sickness of our disease, yet we are also told when we come to recovery that we must seek recovery for ourselves, not for someone else. *Wait, what? I need to stop being selfish, yet I must be here for myself and not for anybody else? How does that work?*

While this may sound selfish, it really isn't. Experience has taught us that people who try to recover from substance use and are doing it for their wife or their kids, or to save their job have much less chance of succeeding. We must, by necessity, be there for ourselves, otherwise our commitment will be less than complete. As we learned in Step One, if we aren't all-in in our recovery efforts, success is unlikely. While getting clean and sober will really be a good thing for our kids, and our kids are definitely part of our motivation, and it might save our job, we must be there in recovery for ourselves. This seeming negative selfishness is actually positive, because we must do this little bit of selfishness in order to have our best chance at giving the very best gift we could give to our kids: our sobriety and a full return into their lives as a properly functioning parent. *Living Sober* explains:

> Does this mean you rank sobriety ahead of family, job, and the opinion of friends?
>
> When we view alcoholism as the life-or-death matter it is, the answer is plain. If we do not save our health – our lives – then certainly we will have no family, no job, and no friends. If we value family, job, and friends, we must *first* save our own lives in order to cherish all three (p. 32).

This is the basis of the A.A. slogan "First Things First!" Our recovery **must** come first, or all the other things will be lost. In order to succeed in recovery – as decades of experience has taught us – we must be there for ourselves.

Psychologists distinguish between good, bad and neutral selfishness, and so should we.[41,42,43] Neutral and bad selfishness are pretty easy to figure out. Bad selfishness is when we satisfy our desire for greed, pleasure, or laziness at the expense of others. We know when we are doing it, because it sets off a tingling sensation inside our head. We know we are being selfish. Neutral selfishness is when we do some self-care – like getting ourselves ready for our day in the morning, going to the gym, and that sort of thing.

We benefit from those efforts, but they aren't really done at the expense of others. Those are things that we need to do to be in good health and function.

Then there's good selfishness, where we benefit and so do others, such as when we spend money to take our family on a holiday together. There are some really important things that we must do in recovery that may outwardly seem like bad selfishness, but we must come to recognize them as good. That includes doing our detox and recovery for ourselves, going to meetings, taking our alone time away from the family to do our recovery work (such as prayer/meditation, reading the Big Book, and doing our Step Ten work). We are taking time for ourselves, but it benefits those around us because they benefit richly from our spiritual health and our recovery. There are times when we know that we need to take some "me-time" to do our recovery work, and we must not feel selfish or guilty because of it. We must get this concept into our heads and help our loved ones to understand it as well. First Things First; without recovery we have nothing.

*

So, we have discussed the "cluster" character defects in detail, because they are the ones that are especially dangerous for our spiritual health and our recovery. We have made a list of our character defects, working closely with our inventory lists from Step Four. We have discussed what it means to truly be ready to give up these character defects by surrendering them to our higher power. Some of these character defects are going to take time, as many behavioral changes take time and practice and coaching. However, this starts with a willingness to give it our all to remove them from our thoughts and actions, which is the point of Step Six.

A parting word about becoming willing to surrender our character defects in Step Six comes to us from the Big Book: "when I am willing to do the right thing I am rewarded with an inner peace no amount of liquor could ever provide. When I am unwilling to do the right thing, I become restless, irritable, and discontent. It is always my choice" (p. 317).

When we feel confident that we have identified our defects of character and we are ready and willing to surrender these defects of character to our higher power, we are ready for Step Seven. If your sponsor agrees, let's move on to the next Step.

Step Seven

Humbly asked Him to remove our shortcomings.

I was saddened, recently, to read an opinion on someone's 12 Steps blog that Step Seven is a "filler" Step, a "do-nothing" Step that was only stuck in there to bring the Steps to an even twelve. On the contrary, a properly done Step Seven is the basis of the most important character virtue for our spirituality and sobriety, and a turning point for the development of our recovery-enhancing life skills. So, let's make sure we do an awesome Step Seven!

Twelve Steps and Twelve Traditions tells us in no uncertain terms what Step Seven is about: "the whole emphasis of Step Seven is on humility" (p. 76). It also tells us how to start out on our Step Seven: "since this Step so specifically concerns itself with humility, we should pause here to consider what humility is and what the practice means to us" (p. 70). So, we'll do just that: we'll talk first about what, exactly, humility is, why it's so valuable to our spiritual well-being and recovery, and why so many people think it's a bad thing. Then we'll look at why humility is so important to Step Seven and how we can optimize this virtue for our spiritual well-being and recovery.

If we have done a thorough and honest job in Step Six, then Step Seven should be a seemingly easy one. But, there's something that must be accomplished in Step Seven that takes some conscious effort: nailing down humility. After all, Step Seven is about asking our higher power to remove our shortcomings, but this isn't done by sitting back and waiting for our higher power to magically remove our ugliest tendencies. Far from being a "do-nothing" Step, Step Seven requires us to lay the foundation for the replacement of our character defects with the healthy character virtues that we seek by establishing a deep understanding of humility and how to apply it to our lives. We'll discuss why that is and how to go about doing exactly that.

Personally, I have found that the development of a measure of enduring humility has become one of my most valuable assets in life, particularly for its power for allowing me to handle life's adversities. Initially, I wondered what was meant when humility was described as "a healer of pain" (*Twelve Steps and Twelve traditions*, p. 75). However, I faced some catastrophic life circumstances in early recovery and I attribute my newfound humility to my ability to survive the times. It protected me from pain that in other times would have driven me to drink or use. Indeed, *Twelve Steps and Twelve Traditions* tells us that humility will be an asset for dealing with any problems we may have: "if that degree of humility could enable us to find the grace by which such a deadly obsession [our addiction] could be banished, then there must be hope of the same result respecting any other problem we could possibly have" (p. 76). I have found that to be utterly true.

However, people tend to recoil at the sound of the word humility. It sounds just like the word "humiliation" and that's the association that most people make when they hear "humility:"

> Humility, as a word and as an ideal has a very bad time of it in our world. Not only is the idea misunderstood; the word itself is often intensely disliked. Many people haven't even a nodding acquaintance with humility as a way of life (*Twelve Steps and Twelve Traditions*, p. 70).

For most people, the word humility evokes connotations of having a low opinion of oneself, being meek and lowly, and being insignificant or unworthy. Population studies have confirmed that humility is widely misunderstood as being related to low self-esteem or self-criticism.[1] However, that concept of humility doesn't conform with reality, because many rich, famous, powerful, and accomplished people are known for their humility. Billionaire Warren Buffett – the third richest man in the world – is well-known for his humility, yet he engages in no self-abasement, definitely doesn't belittle himself or diminish his accomplishments, and he is definitely not lowly, insignificant, or unworthy. Nor does he come across as meek, and he definitely doesn't have a low opinion of himself. He commands the admiration and respect of every friend to human nature. So how can people who believe that humility is a negative attribute involving self-abasement explain someone like Warren Buffett?

We can look to psychology to understand the inconsistencies between people's understanding and the true meaning of the word "humility." With the advent of positive psychology as a field of study, interest in the considerable benefits of humility as a character strength that promotes human flourishing has spurred much research into the subject.[2]

254

Researchers who pooled data from a number of studies concluded that there are two types of humility that are, oddly enough, nearly polar opposites. These are: 1) *appreciative humility*, which involves celebrating the positives in ourselves and others, and 2) *self-abasing humility*, which involves self-demeaning and a low opinion of oneself.[3]

Obviously, when we refer to humility in our 12 Step program we are referring to appreciative humility. This type of humility has been associated with authentic pride (this is the "good" pride that we discussed in Step Six), spirituality, quality interpersonal relations (due to likability and forgiveness), pro-social behavior (including helping others), and psychological and physical well-being.[4] Besides these spiritually uplifting benefits of humility, humility has been proven to improve self-control, which is of great practical importance to relapse prevention.[5]

Humility is a complex personality trait, so rather than trying to define humility in a few sentences, let's instead look at the characteristics of humility in order to solidify our understanding of the concept. A review of the psychology literature shows some key traits of healthy (appreciative) humility:[6,7,8,9,10]

- an accurate (not overinflated or underestimated) sense of our abilities and achievements,
- a willingness to share due credit for accomplishments,
- the ability to acknowledge and accept responsibility for our mistakes, imperfections, gaps in knowledge, and limitations,
- openness to new ideas, contradictory information, and advice,
- keeping our abilities and accomplishments in perspective,
- relatively low focus on the self, and a lack of self-preoccupation,
- empathy, gentleness, respect, and appreciation for the equality, autonomy, and value of others,
- lack of a desire to distort information to "self-enhance" or make ourselves look and feel better,
- a non-judgmental and open-minded disposition to considering new and divergent ideas and seek new information,
- a general desire and openness to learn,
- gratitude,
- appreciation of the value of all things, as well as the many different ways that people and things can contribute to our world,
- an awareness of our place in, and connection to, the world and cosmos, and
- a willingness to consider or connect with God or some higher power.

By looking at these characteristics, we can see that humility involves overcoming our natural tendency to see ourselves as a priority or privileged above all others. Since much of this selfish tendency is rooted in the hubristic (bad) pride that tries to compensate for low self-esteem, the process of developing a healthy, intact self-esteem – as we do in the Steps – does much to boost our humility. As well, humility is about seeing ourselves more objectively, as one among many other worthy people, and that means that we don't self-criticize and treat ourselves more harshly than anyone else. As super-pastor and best-selling author Rick Warren famously said: "humility is not thinking less of yourself, it's thinking of yourself less."[11] The late C.S. Lewis accurately described humility:

> Do not imagine that if you meet a really humble man he will be what most people call 'humble' nowadays: he will not be a sort of greasy, smarmy person, who is always telling you that, of course, he is nobody. Probably all you will think about him is that he seemed a cheerful, intelligent chap who took a real interest in what you said to him. If you do dislike him it will be because you feel a little envious of anyone who seems to enjoy life so easily. He will not be thinking about humility: he will not be thinking about himself at all.[12]

The 12 Step literature offers a simple but spot-on definition of humility: "… humility – a word often misunderstood. To those who have made clear progress in A.A., it amounts to a clear recognition of what and who we really are, followed by a sincere attempt to become what we could be" (*Twelve Steps and Twelve Traditions*, p. 58).

There's another definition of humility that I like because it's not formal or scientific. Although it comes to us from the psychology scholarly literature, it's heartfelt and consistent with our spiritual outlook:

> Humility does not consist in handsome people trying to believe they are ugly, and clever people trying to believe they are fools.… True humility is more like self-forgetfulness.… It leaves people free to esteem their special talents and, with the same honesty, to esteem their neighbor's. Both the neighbor's talents and one's own are recognized as gifts and, like one's height, are not fit subjects for either inordinate pride or self-deprecation.[13]

Feeling good about the self can yield benefits, such as positive emotions and the confidence to pursue goals. But society's eagerness to facilitate positive views of the self at all costs has created this pervasive view of humility as being an undesirable quality. However, as we shall see shortly, research in psychology and the social sciences has shown that this

256

"positive self-view at all costs" and low humility mentality is very harmful indeed. And, as the 12 Step program has been telling us since the 1930s, this mentality can be a major contributor to the development of addiction-alcoholism.

Humility is about perspective. A broken-down addict-alcoholic who has lost everybody and everything can have a huge chip on his or her shoulders and be completely lacking in humility, while someone like Warren Buffett (for example) who is in control of his faculties and has tremendous power and resources can be rich in humility. This shows that humility has nothing to do with our material wealth, or station in life, or the power or influence that we carry; rather, humility is all about perspective, how we see ourselves and others. *Twelve Steps and Twelve Traditions* speaks of how prideful alcoholic-addicts have lost their perspective: "here, of course, we have lost all perspective, and therefore all genuine humility" (p. 45). Therefore, finding and growing in humility is not about gaining material wealth, influence, and power. Rather, it's about a healthy change in our perspective: "for we had started to get perspective on ourselves, which is another way of saying that we were gaining in humility" (*Twelve Steps and Twelve Traditions*, p. 48).

*

Humility was a part of the 12 Step program that caught me by surprise. Because of my background in counseling psychology I knew that humility was not the opposite of self-esteem, but I didn't have a true appreciation of its value for positive psychology, well-being, and spirituality until I came to experience those benefits for myself. This underscores the central importance of humility to recovery, spirituality, and happiness:

> Indeed, the attainment of greater humility is the foundation principle of each of A.A.'s Twelve Steps. For without some degree of humility, no alcoholic can stay sober at all. Nearly all A.A.'s have found, too, that unless they develop much more of this precious quality than may be required just for sobriety, they still haven't much of a chance of becoming truly happy (*Twelve Steps and Twelve Traditions*, p. 70).

I just want to emphasize a sentence from that passage: "the attainment of greater humility is the foundation principle of each of A.A.'s Twelve Steps." We can demonstrate that we are guided to a state of healthy humility by each one of the Steps, in four basic phases:[14]

Phase 1: Steps One through Three are about admitting that we are powerless over alcohol, that we cannot get better on our own, and that we need help from some kind of a higher power. This is referred to as the "humility of honestly admitted powerlessness,"[15] and marks the beginning of our transformation from prideful, selfish, self-pitying beings to individuals rich in humility.

Phase 2: Steps Four through Seven are about the humility of admitting our deepest darkest secrets, and bringing them out from the dark corners of our psyche into the bright light of redemption. This part of the humility process may be referred to as "humility of truthful inner accuracy and transparency."[16]

Phase 3: Steps Eight through Ten can be referred to as "humility of contrition, making apologies and amends."[17] Heartfelt apology and amends require a level of humility that lifts us to new level of this quality, and wins us the admiration or respect of those we seek to make amends with.

Phase 4: Steps Eleven and Twelve are about expending less concern on ourselves and more concern about others. This gets us outside ourselves and away from the inner-focused character defects such as selfishness, greed, and pride. This may be regarded as the "humility of living a rightly ordered and transformed new life."[18]

*

The odd thing is that despite all the repeated humiliations that we endure as active drunks or addicts we never learn humility from the experience: "while this was a humiliating experience, it didn't necessarily mean we had yet acquired much humility" (*Twelve Steps and Twelve Traditions*, p. 58). Quite the contrary, our substance-soaked mind stubbornly makes us cling even more to our dysfunctional pride with every new humiliation. We seek artificial self-esteem with our inflated pride, rather than a healthy self-esteem based in humility:

> In all of these strivings [our search for security, prestige, success, and romance], so many of them well-intentioned, our crippling handicap had been our lack of humility. We had lacked the perspective to see that character-building and spiritual values had to come first, and that material satisfactions were not the purpose of living (*Twelve Steps and Twelve Traditions*, p. 71).

There's a major distinction between the humility that comes with repeated humiliations during our drinking days, and the humility that we seek in recovery. The humility we find while in our cups may be better described as "eating humble pie," so it amounts to self-abasing humility forced upon us against our will, and it stirs up the hornets nest of our anger and resentments. We do not want humility, and our reaction is a need to compensate by blaming others for our humiliations, and further pushing up our alcoholic-addict pride. And, of course, we drink or use more to cope with the negative feelings.

The humility we find in recovery is based on a desire for healthy humility, rather than based on eating humble pie. As we are told in *Twelve Steps and Twelve Traditions*:

> We saw we needn't always be bludgeoned and beaten into humility. It could come quite as much from our voluntary reaching for it as it could come from unremitting suffering. A great turning point in our lives came when we sought for humility as something we really wanted, rather than as something we *must* have. It marked the time when we could see the full implication of Step Seven: 'Humbly asked Him to remove our shortcomings' (p. 75).

Alcoholics Anonymous co-founder Bill Wilson understood humility. Throughout his life he alternated between extremes of financial and professional success, and rock bottom privation. Then, as A.A. grew, so did his fame, reaching international levels. Yet he spurned the fame because he knew that humility was the basis of the 12 Steps and his sobriety, and because he knew that sacrificing his anonymity would cost A.A. and set a counter-example of humility for others in the fellowship. As we can see from reading about the history of A.A. (such as in *Pass It On*), Bill turned down lucrative job appointments, the fame of being named in national media publications, and even honorary degrees because of his commitment to humility, which included his anonymity. His alcoholic-addict pride would have hungrily grabbed at those opportunities, but his humility based in healthy self-esteem respectfully declined. He didn't need those things to pump up his ego or to prove himself to the world, but he did need his humility and anonymity to remain sober.

So, humility is a core virtue for successful recovery, spirituality, and happiness in life. But true humility doesn't come easily to us, as we must fight our natural tendencies and overcome habits left over from our drinking or using days. Although Step Seven requires us to adopt humility as the basis of our spiritual recovery, we must remember that the most important thing in Step Seven is to establish our willingness, for humility is not a virtue we can master overnight:

So it is that we first see humility as a necessity. But this is the barest beginning. To get completely away from our aversion to the idea of being humble, to gain a vision of humility as the avenue to true freedom of the human spirit, to be willing to work for humility as something to be desired for itself, takes most of us a long, long time. A whole lifetime geared to self-centeredness cannot be set in reverse all at once. Rebellion dogs our every step at first (*Twelve Steps and Twelve Traditions*, p. 73).

Easy does it, one day at a time.

*

The character defects that have prevented our humility (resentments, blame for others, selfishness, greed, pride, etc., etc.): "must be dealt with to prevent a retreat into alcoholism once again" (*Twelve Steps and Twelve Traditions*, p. 73). But these character defects come naturally to us and we have practiced them unrestrained for quite some time, at least as long as we were drinking and using, and sometimes even before. So, how to overcome them? Well, the main thing to remember is that this is a process. We alcoholics and addicts are not patient people, we want everything now. But finding the humility that comes with surrendering our character defects takes time and effort. Easy does it. Step Seven doesn't require a mastery of humility and our character defects; rather, it requires a willingness to commit to the process of spiritual growth. Remember the fifth chapter of the Big Book: "we claim spiritual progress rather than spiritual perfection" (p. 60). But our willingness must be sincere: "but again we are driven on by the inescapable conclusion which we draw from the A.A. experience, that we surely must try with a will or fall by the wayside" (*Twelve Steps and Twelve Traditions*, p. 73-74).

The process requires daily commitment and a steep learning curve, but take heart: once we get a taste of the peace of mind that comes with surrender, the spiritual boost that comes with the commitment we make in Step Seven and we begin to experience true, healthy humility, can be quite intoxicating. We begin to see that humility isn't something best left for the meek and mild after all: "where humility had formerly stood for a forced feeding on humble pie, it now begins to mean the nourishing ingredient which can give us serenity" (*Twelve Steps and Twelve Traditions*, p. 74). You may notice that as you begin to live life with a commitment to purging your character defects you begin to feel really good about yourself, perhaps in a way that is new to you. That good feeling is brought about by the surge of healthy self-esteem in your psyche, and the humility that comes with it.

260

Psychological studies have supported and confirmed the 12 Step program's emphasis on humility as a therapeutic tool and key to happiness, health, and sobriety.[19,20,21,22] Many studies show a close association between humility and numerous positive attributes and character strengths, suggesting that humility is a powerfully pro-social virtue with psychological, physical, and social benefits.[23] More specifically, research by psychologists has identified many salutary benefits to humility: improved prosocial behaviors (such as forgiving, cooperation, honesty, friendship), better academic and job performance, excellence in leadership, improved interpersonal relationships, and generosity, to name but a few.[24] As well, humility as been confirmed by independent research to boost markers of psychological well-being, such as openness to experience, optimism, hope, positive life-regard, secure attachment, positive growth, personal relationships, decisiveness, comfort with ambiguity, and openness to experience.[25]

Humility is a key tool for preventing anger and resentments from cropping up and threatening our spiritual well-being and sobriety. Humility is the antidote for that horrible human habit of believing that it's up to us to straighten out other peoples' affairs. This is the basis of the 12 Step slogan "Live and Let Live." Think of all the times we raged because other people weren't driving the way we'd like them to, for example. Some of us even believed that it's up to us to become self-righteous traffic police and straighten out other drivers, or teach them a lesson. It's all just wasted brain-power, and a terrible way to allow our disease to sneak anger and resentment back into our vulnerable mind. There are so many among us who have done things they later regret while acting on such impulses, when humility would have saved everybody the trouble. It's so much easier to live and let live, and humility allows us to do that.

In fact, the 12 Step slogan "Live and Let Live" is a good way to give our humility a spot-check. If we find that if we find we are becoming upset because of other people's behaviors, or we find that we are responding to that urge to set everyone straight, or other people's behaviors are getting under our skin, it may be a good idea to ask ourselves some questions:

- Am I being self-righteous?
- Is it my place to straighten people out?
- Is it possible that my way isn't the "right" way?
- It is possible that there is more than one "right" way to do something?
- Am I acting out of emotion (anger, impatience, intolerance, fault-finding, self-righteousness, and a belief that my way is the right way) or am I acting out of spiritual principles (love,

tolerance, empathy, patience, understanding, humility, and open-mindedness)?

- Am I acting out of a need to be in control?
- Am I trying to project my will on someone else?
- How would I feel if I was on the receiving end of my behavior?

In the end, the best overall question to ask ourselves is: *would I rather be "right," or would I rather be happy?* If there's any doubt, our best bet is to take a few breaths, detach ourselves from the situation, and examine our thoughts (awareness is, once again, a powerful tool for living according to healthy spiritual principles). When our emotions settle down, we can center ourselves, ask ourselves these questions, and re-evaluate our actions. Better to act on thought-out humility rather than the emotional reactions and base instincts that possess us in the moment.

*

So, we seek humility, but what about pride? Being humble certainly doesn't mean that we self-deprecate or ignore our accomplishments. Rather, it involves a shift in our pride from the dysfunctional and strange pride of alcoholism-addiction (i.e. hubristic pride) to a healthy authentic pride. We should take pride in who we are and what we do, and not in how big our house is, how expensive our car is, or how many toys we have. Healthy pride in our accomplishments in life is fine as long as it's coupled with humility and gratitude.

But does living with humility mean that we have to allow people to walk all over us? Does expressing humility and charity and tolerance and patience and giving and putting others before ourselves mean that we can't have self-esteem and self-worth? Does it mean that we can't be ambitious and competitive? What if we have a job that requires us to be aggressive and uncompromising? Do we have to quit our jobs to stay sober? Does it mean we can't stand up for ourselves in a dispute? Does it mean that we can't negotiate with someone for a better deal? These are questions we must answer before we walk out the door and face the world endowed with our newfound humility.

Warren Buffett – if you'll forgive me for once again using his example, but he is a great exemplar – definitely doesn't allow anybody to walk all over him, nor does he back down in a scrap. Humility is no bar to doing the things we need to do in life, including being tough and assertive when we must. The difference is that when we do behave in that way, we do so with humility and according to the spiritual principles that spring forth from humility. We still treat others with the respect they deserve, and we don't allow our actions to be governed by anger, resentments, jealousy, greed, or a need to boost our ego. Being tough, assertive, and confident is consistent with humility.

The Big Book is careful to tell us that humility does not mean that we become the world's doormat: "we should be sensible, tactful, considerate and humble without being servile or scraping. As God's people we stand on our feet; we don't crawl before anyone" (p. 83).

*

As if to contradict the popular conception of humility as a negative quality, humility provides us with numerous advantages in life, whether in dealing with other people and situations, working toward goals, or maintaining a positive outlook consistent with being content and happy in life. Most especially, it is advantageous for our spiritual well-being and recovery from alcoholism-addiction.

One of the reasons that people believe that humility is a negative trait is because of the belief that humility lowers our self-esteem and negatively affects other people's evaluation of us. However, psychologists have determined that the opposite is true.[26] For example, well-designed studies have shown that people who are high in humility are better liked by peers, co-workers, family, and friends.[27] This is due to the positive personality qualities of humility, but also because people find boasting and grandiose attitudes about the self to be annoying.[28] Spiritual people who endeavor to cultivate their humility are more focused on people and things outside themselves, and care more about other people's interests rather than being focused entirely on their own. They are not seeking to boost themselves, and other people recognize and appreciate their sincerity and regard for others. This leads to better quality interpersonal relationships and higher levels of respect and liking from others.[29]

Humility is the basis of a healthy self-esteem, because it enables us to let go of the need for outward shows of vainglory and a need for other people's validation in order to feel good about ourselves. We find our self-esteem in the awareness of our own strengths and abilities, not in what we are pretending to be. Our self-esteem doesn't depend on stamps of approval from others. Healthy self-esteem can exist in a vacuum, but pride-based ego can only exist when surrounded by other people whom we can try to impress. People with healthy self-esteem are comfortable in their own skin, whereas those who depend upon hubristic pride wear their displays of success as armor that protects their fragile ego. Possessing healthy self-esteem a great way to be, and humility is the key.

Psychologists know that in the absence of humility our drive to prop up and validate our pride is psychologically distressing for us.[30] The constant need for validation and the never-ending efforts to maintain our inflated image of ourselves to compensate for our lack of self-esteem creates a psychological burden that promotes a desire to escape through dysfunctional ways, including by using substances. Humility, especially if accompanied by self-transcendence (i.e. spirituality) relieves us of this burden.[31]

A number of studies have shown that people who lack humility lash out at others who threaten or challenge their self-views, or who don't fulfill their need for acknowledgement to overcome low self-esteem.[32] People low in humility are known to be unhealthily competitive (they are competitive for need of validation, which can turn ugly if they don't win), dominant over others (which does little to earn respect or friendship), hostile, aggressive, and angry.[33] People with an unwarranted high view of themselves tend to react to failure – which can be anything that contradicts their view of themselves – by lashing out, sometimes with violence. They are hyper-sensitive and respond defensively to advice or teaching and react by rejecting opportunities for growth and learning. If people are not preoccupied with maintaining highly positive self-views, they are freed from this burden that propels and perpetuates negative psychology. Such is the gift of humility.

When we lack humility, our sense of hubristic pride and our ego imbue us with a sense of entitlement, and we are infuriated when we aren't given what we feel is due to us. I am reminded of the parable of the wedding feast, from the Christian New Testament:

> He [Jesus] spoke a parable to those who were invited, when he noticed how they chose the best seats, and said to them, "When you are invited by anyone to a marriage feast, don't sit in the best seat, since perhaps someone more honorable than you might be invited by him, and he who invited both of you would come and tell you, 'Make room for this person.' Then you would begin, with shame, to take the lowest place. But when you are invited, go and sit in the lowest place, so that when he who invited you comes, he may tell you, 'Friend, move up higher.' Then you will be honored in the presence of all who sit at the table with you. For everyone who exalts himself will be humbled, and whoever humbles himself will be exalted" (Luke 14:7-14).

We, with our hubristic pride and ego intact, would not only be ashamed when we got sent to the lowliest seat, but we would also be infuriated. And, we'd likely get drunk at the feast because of it. Nobody likes people with a sense of entitlement.

One of the most common reasons that people seek out a psychological therapist is because they want help for their low self-esteem. It would probably amaze people to know how many people who display an outward mask of ego to the point of arrogance are actually troubled by low self-esteem. This is due to the perception among most people that humility means low self-esteem while ego and pride mean high self-esteem or self-confidence. It has always amazed me how much time, energy, and money that people expel on building up material and other signs of material success in misguided efforts to build self-esteem. And they spend a tremendous amount of brain-power worrying and fretting over what other people think of them and how their own display of well-being stacks up against everyone else's ("keeping up with the Jones"). Many people spend their entire life striving for more ego, in the belief it may fix their insecurities and lack of self-confidence. Ironically, the key to self-esteem and escaping from the rat race of ego lies precisely in the thing they have always sought to avoid: humility. What they are missing is the realization that we are not in this world to live up to others' expectations, and others are not in this world to live up to ours.

Think of how many bad decisions we have made in life because we were trying to prop up our ego, how many times we have spent money on a house or car we couldn't afford, how many times we have bought over-priced clothes so that we could impress others with the brand label, and so on. Our quest for ego-validation may even lead to us to pursuits that are counter-productive and even harmful, such as taking steroids or spending money we don't have. In hindsight, I often wonder if my decision to go to medical school was the best decision for me, or if it was based in ego. Ten years of university and $200,000 later, it might not have been what I really wanted from life. Two guys I went to medical school with went on to become neurosurgeons, which involves a grueling, punishing 12 years of training after medical school. My impression of both of these guys was of an utter lack of self-esteem. I'm convinced that the biggest reason they chose neurosurgery was to prop up their hubristic pride, as they felt that this was the most prestigious specialty. *Everybody respects and is in awe of a brain surgeon, right?* While it might not be fair of me to say that, I think I make my point: a lack of self-esteem can lead us unhappily through life by the nose, even to the point of controlling our major life decisions. And it can make us drink or do drugs. When our ego isn't giving us the self-esteem we seek, or other people aren't validating our ego to our satisfaction, the anger, resentment, and negative feelings can drive us to drink or use.

The odds are stacked heavily against us in the ego-humility wrestling match. Unless we come to the 12 Step program or some other program of deep introspection and guided self-awareness we may never put any thought into humility. We've probably always seen humility as something to beat, and ego as something to build. We've probably looked at people with a great deal of material success and saw their inflated egos as the reason that they are so "successful" while in reality it's the other way around. With a little insight, the realization that this is all a sham comes to us.

Our culture really does much to stack the odds against seeing humility as a virtue. Have you ever noticed that the people most admired in our society show very little, if any, humility? Rock stars, movie stars, sports stars, political leaders, corporate CEOs, and so on. Even the fictional characters in TV and film are seldom icons of humility. Quite the opposite, they are often self-important, glamorized, arrogant, self-absorbed, and aggressive.

Humility is key to our efforts to rid ourselves of our character defects and replace them with character strengths, which is what we endeavor to do by invoking the help of our higher power in Step Seven. It leads to many other qualities that we need to keep sober, and it helps us lead a life of integrity and respect for ourselves and others.

We have spoken about open-mindedness as a key ingredient to our trip through the Steps, starting right back in Step One. Open-mindedness comes from humility, because being fixated on our pre-existing ideas and beliefs to the exclusion of all others is a form of intellectual pride, if not intellectual arrogance.

Importantly, humility leads us to leave behind our sense of inadequacy and our sense of unworthiness. This, in turn, is how we stop exaggerating our accomplishments, being envious of others, and generally making fools of ourselves. As such, humility does much more than win us the respect of those around us – it allows us to gain our own unconditional self-respect. What a wonderful way to be, especially in contrast to the mangled heap of ugly emotions and motives that led us around by the nose for so long. As one alcoholic explains: "one of the primary differences between alcoholics and non-alcoholics is that non-alcoholics change their behavior to meet their goals and alcoholics change their goals to meet their behavior" (Big Book, p. 423).

*

Now let's look at the question: *how is Step Seven all about humility?* After all, it seems to be about casting off character defects and little else. Well, a clue lies in the wording of the Step: "humbly asked...." In Step Seven we ask our higher power to remove our defects of character, and we fill the void left by removal of our character defects with spiritual virtues, the character strengths that put an end to our negative psychology and spiritual sickness. Psychologists have described humility as a "foundational virtue," in that it's a personality virtue that needs to be in place in order for other positive personality virtues to develop.[34] Likewise, more than 2,500 years ago, Chinese philosopher Confucius recognized the same: "humility is the

266

solid foundation of all virtues." In other words, to replace our character defects with character virtues we must first have humility in place as the basis from which all other character strengths grow. The 12 Step program recognized this truth long before psychologists worked it out: "everywhere we saw failure and misery transformed by humility into priceless assets" (*Twelve Steps and Twelve Traditions*, p. 75).

Simply asking for our shortcomings to be removed does not automatically make them go away. We can't just sit back and watch them float out of our head. Higher powers help those who help themselves. We are not going to beat this disease and get healthy by inaction. As we have discussed, these character defects are imprinted in our brainstem and encoded in our DNA – they are part of us. So, we must take action to remove these toxic aspects of our personality. That's why I'm saddened when I hear people refer to Step Seven as a "do nothing" Step.

Since the foundation of the character virtues we seek in order to live by spiritual principles is humility, we must learn about humility in Step Seven. We should take the time to understand what humility is and how it will fit into our lives.

Taking action to remove our defects of character requires humility so that we recognize when we are not being "right-sized." If we feel special or entitled above other people then we won't recognize our selfish behaviors for what they are, and we won't be willing to give them up because we feel entitled to special treatment. Humility gives us the perspective we need to carry out Step Seven, and we can't do our Step Seven and proceed on our journey through the rest of the Steps without this humility. When we ask our higher power to remove our shortcomings we must do so humbly, recognizing that we are neither too big nor too small. Grandiose self-entitlement is the target of our Step Seven.

Addiction-alcoholism is a bizarre affliction, filled with paradoxes. As we grow in our recovery the learning curve is steep, but we must learn about our disease in order to help ourselves and others. Humility is the only way we can do this: "only by discussing ourselves, holding back nothing, only by being willing to take advice and accept direction could we set foot on the road to straight thinking, solid honesty, and genuine humility" (*Twelve Steps and Twelve Traditions*, p. 59). Anyone who has sponsored others in recovery knows that an alcoholic-addict coming to recovery needs to be "teachable" to succeed. We require humility to make this transition to open-mindedness and willingness to take on new ways of thinking and behaving, and proper completion of Step Seven requires focus on this humility.

*

Humility and gratitude are closely tied together, so gratitude is an excellent portal to improving our humility and self-esteem. Psychological research has confirmed in recent years what the 12 Step program has been telling us for the past 80+ years: humility is found through gratitude. When it comes to growing in humility, psychological studies have found a reciprocal correlation between humility and gratitude.[35] That tells us that working on our gratitude, as we discussed in Step Six, improves our humility. Likewise, as we grow spiritually in humility our ability to feel gratitude will improve. For example, one study found that people who wrote a letter expressing their gratitude showed higher humility than those who performed a neutral activity, and people's baseline humility predicted the degree of gratitude they felt after writing the letter.[36] Also, a person's level of humility can be predicted by the amount of gratitude that he or she shows.[37]

Some of the most content people I know are people in recovery who have glaringly little in terms of material treasures. This is because they appreciate the sobriety, peace, and serenity that they have found in the 12 Step program, and because they have humility-based perspectives about their situation and place in the world. Their peace comes from acceptance, and gratitude fills them with appreciation. Their program of recovery has taught them that we are a success today if we don't drink or use today. So, they feel like a success every day, regardless if their material worth advanced that day. They have chosen to rid themselves of the unhappy yoke of unsatisfiable envy.

As we read in *Living Sober*: "feeling gratitude is far more wholesome, makes staying sober much easier. It will come as a pleasant surprise to discover that it is not difficult to develop the habit of gratitude if we just make some effort... but it soon becomes easier, and can become a strong and comfortable force in our recovery. Life was meant to be enjoyed, and we mean to enjoy it" (p. 48).

Changing our perspective can, in fact, have a robust effect on our happiness in life. One man in recovery from substance use puts it this way: "when I focus on what's good today, I have a good day, and when I focus on what's bad, I have a bad day. If I focus on a problem, the problem increases; if I focus on the answer, the answer increases" (Big Book, p. 419). We're lucky here – changing our perspective is easy to do. It's a free way to have better days!

It's unfortunate that humility doesn't come naturally to the human mind, because it's such a peace-giving virtue. Humility helps us to find gratitude by allowing us to recognize that everything we have came to us because of what we were capable of working for, and for which we put in the required effort. Maybe some of it came by chance, or maybe we sometimes came up short for our efforts, but humility is about acceptance of who and what we are. Humility also allows us to gauge our own abilities so that we can set our sights on wants that are realistically achievable for us, so that we can make the plans necessary to realize those goals, rather than wasting our time and energy burning with envy over things that are out of reach for us. Humility keeps us from allowing our unrealistic wants to "own" us, to occupy our minds, to cloud our thoughts with jealousy and envy and resentment. Humility keeps us grounded in reality. Some people were born into wealth and had many opportunities in life that I have never had. For me to focus my thoughts and energy on wishing I could live their lifestyle is a waste of brain-power that distracts me from realistic pursuits. I can chase my dreams but doing so with a measure of humility focuses my efforts in a way that I can achieve success. As long as we are focused with envy on other people's possessions and situations we can't feel gratitude for our own possessions and situations, and the way to humility will be barred from us. We must foster gratitude in order to grow in humility.

*

So, what else can we do to develop humility? Well, the field of psychology has determined that humility is something that is learned, and not something we are born with. That bodes well for those of us who are endeavoring to grow in healthy humility and are (mostly) starting at zero. However, psychotherapy is lacking in formal interventions designed to directly improve humility. In fact, I am quite leery about psychotherapy for people who seek help for low self-esteem. You and I know from our knowledge about pride, humility, and alcoholism-addiction that the most appropriate way to healthy self-esteem is through humility; however, that concept is lost on some therapists. They risk helping their patients develop hubristic pride by teaching them to push their own self-worth through accomplishments. This hubristic pride can easily be mistaken for self-esteem by the uninitiated, and these people may be learning some harmful habits from their therapist.

My experience – both personal and professional – is that the 12 Steps are by far the most effective and direct way to help people develop a healthy self-esteem, humility, and positive psychology. As I explain in my book *The Alcoholic/Addict Within*, the 12 Steps are actually a very powerful program of psychotherapy that is highly successful in moving individuals from the most negative possible psychology, to a positive psychology. Therefore, my greatest recommendation for striving for humility is to do the Steps with rigorous honesty and an open mind, to go to meetings, get a sponsor, read the Big Book, watch the long-timers, and interact with other people from the program.

However, there are a few techniques that we can glean from the psychology literature that may help us to improve on our humility as well. One is to develop a mindfulness of what psychologists call our *competitive reflex*.[38] This competitive reflex is pretty much just like it sounds: a natural, subconscious instinct to react in social situations by trying to establish our dominance over others, and being ultra-sensitive and offended by perceived challenges to our superiority. It involves an excessively strong tendency to react aggressively when we feel we are being pushed around or treated with less respect than what we think we deserve. It pushes us to distort information in order to defend, repair, or boost our own image.

A large body of research in social cognition suggests the existence of a pervasive, reflexive drive to look and feel better than average, and to resort to inflating our accomplishments to do so.[39] This is our competitive reflex. When that doesn't work out, our knee-jerk reaction – in the past – has been to drink or use to cope with the deeply felt frustration. Meanwhile, our anger and resentments grow as other people fail to validate our ego as we feel they should. As with other unhelpful natural reflexes, our best defense is to mindfully recognize the existence of this natural behavioral tendency, and put it in its place when it tries to manipulate us.

Psychologists have also recognized that we can't just will ourselves into a healthy humility; we must live it by changing our words and our behavior to reflect our desired level of humility.[40] Again, this fits perfectly with the 12 Step program, which is based on a new "design for living" (Big Book, p. 8). Humility is "worn" by people who do the Steps, not talked about or bragged about. When living with humility, there should be no indulging our natural drive toward self-importance and no burning need to see or present ourselves as being better than we actually are.

The "action" involved in living the 12 Step program involves more than the action required for completing the Steps. It also requires that our day-to-day actions reflect our new way of living – we live the program's principles (as we will discuss further in Step Twelve). We are challenged to consider: *if I couldn't speak, would people know by my actions what I stand for?* We gain much more than we give by living principled lives. As the Big Book tells us: "the spiritual life is not a theory. *We have to live it*" (p. 83).

*

Just as our character defects feed off each other and snowball out of control during our drinking or using days, so do our positive virtues grow together as our healing takes place as we progress through the Steps. As we find self-forgiveness in the first nine Steps, our self-esteem leaps forward. We begin to see our own inestimable worth and that our behaviors during our active addiction-alcoholism do not define us. This healthy self-esteem pushes our humility forward, as our need to find a feeling of self-worth from outside sources falls away. Our intact self-esteem removes our competitive reflex and we no longer need to deflate others in order to elevate ourselves. We can now appreciate the worth of others and be supportive and encouraging for them. We no longer thrive from their failings. Our ability to connect with other people increases, something social psychologists refer to as *social intelligence*.[41] Our spiritual connections improve.

So it is that our humility, self-esteem, and spirituality are tied together and as we grow in each of these qualities we grow in them all. Meanwhile, these three virtues – spirituality, self-esteem, and humility – crush our character defects. We are no longer seeking faults in others, being judgmental, intolerant of their shortcomings, or impatient with them. Our perverse love of schadenfreude deflates because we no longer relish in others' failings in order to feel better about ourselves. When other people don't validate our ego like we want them to we don't become angry or vengeful. We no longer need to blame our shortcomings and life's problems on others and become resentful. We are finding peace of mind, calm, and serenity. The negative feelings and emotions that we used to hide from with alcohol or drugs are no longer there.

Such is the value of the Seventh Step.

*

Twelve Steps and Twelve Traditions gives us a focus for doing our Step Seven:

> As we approach the actual taking of Step Seven, it might be well if we A.A.'s inquire once more just what our deeper objectives are. Each of us would like to live at peace with himself and with his fellow. We would like to be assured that the grace of God can do for us what we cannot do for ourselves. We have seen that character defects based upon shortsighted or unworthy desires are the obstacles that block our path toward these objectives. We now clearly see that we have been making unreasonable demands upon ourselves, upon others, and upon God (p. 76).

The Big Book explains quite simply how to do our Step Seven:

> Are we now ready to let God remove from us all the things which we have admitted are objectionable? Can He now take them all – every one? If we still cling to something we will not let go, we ask God to help us be willing.

When ready, we say something like this: 'My Creator, I am now willing that you should have all of me, good and bad. I pray that you now remove from me every single defect of character which stands in the way of my usefulness to you and my fellows. Grant me strength, as I go out from here, to do your bidding. Amen.' We have then completed *Step Seven* (p. 76).

Simply put, our Step Seven is completed when we have – with humility – asked our higher power to remove these defects of character that have plagued our conscience and driven our behaviors to the point of insanity. We have a list of these defects of character that we can hold in our hands, and we simply leave those defects of character in the hands of our higher power.

Now that we have completed Step Seven, we have clean hearts and we proceed to live our lives with humility, and without our defects of character to the utmost of our ability. It is essential to our spirituality, to our mental and physical health, to our happiness and peace of mind, to our well-being, and to our sobriety. If your sponsor agrees, we are ready to make amends.

Step Eight

Made a list of all persons we had harmed and became willing to make amends to them all.

Steps Eight and Nine are the capstone for our cleaning house and progression to self-forgiveness. They also provide a big leap forward in our attainment of humility by imbuing us with what may be called "humility of contrition."[1] Steps Eight and Nine – the amends Steps – can seem kind of scary when we are facing them, but the healing effect of making amends is tremendous. We heal our own long-suffering psyche and we heal our relationships with others. We've spoken about fear and how it can be an impediment to recovery, and we've discussed how to put fear in its place; we should be mindful of this as we begin Step Eight. A great way to dispel fear over the amends Steps is to have a coffee with our sponsor or someone else from the fellowship and listen to his or her experiences with making amends. As usual, our fears prove to be unfounded and manufactured by our fickle minds. Hearing another person's experiences with making amends helps us to see that.

Twelve Steps and Twelve Traditions explains clearly the value of Step Eight for our recovery: "every A.A. has found that he can make little headway in this new adventure of living until he first backtracks and really makes an accurate and unsparing survey of the human wreckage he has left in his wake" (p. 77).

Besides our own psychological well-being, the amends-making Steps are concerned with interpersonal relations and therefore represent a major step forward in our spiritual connections with people outside ourselves. These Steps are a great chance to put into action our newfound life skills where we mindfully allow our actions to be guided by humility and spirituality, rather than by our character defects. Most of the people we make amends with will be warmly surprised by this change in our demeanor. People respect people who have the fortitude and integrity to own up and make contrition.

Our Step Four is a useful source for identifying the people we list for our Step Eight, but we need to dig a little deeper. We must remember that we have been living a long time in a mind-set where our blame-thrower was turned on high, and we saw ourselves as victims. In order to do our Step Eight we must re-evaluate old impressions and take a good look at our role in things that we had previously blamed others for. My personal experience has been that when I took an honest backward look through the eyes of my newfound humility, I found that I saw a lot of people whom I previously resented and disliked in a whole new light. In many cases they had wronged me with good reason because of how I was behaving or what I had done to them. Sometimes they simply came between me and my drink or drugs. In many cases they hadn't wronged me at all. My un-brotherly and unlovely behaviors toward them had failed them in matters of fellowship, and I became the rightful recipient of what – to me at the time, through my alcoholic-addict eyes – was unjustified wrath.

Even for those who have indeed wronged us, we are not here to open a ledger of wrongs and rights to weigh out who wronged whom. Rather, we are only interested in how we have wronged others, regardless of the accounting. We are not making amends only to those we like or who have only done good things for us, we are making amends to those we have wronged.

Step Eight is a sort of a gut-check to make sure that we have made headway in the previous Steps. In order to add any name to our list, we must have first let go of our anger and resentments, and we must have taken seriously our commitment to rid ourselves of our character defects. Step Eight won't work if we are still being selfish, resentful, or defensive. *Twelve Steps and Twelve Traditions* explains:

> The moment we ponder a twisted or broken relationship with another person, our emotions go on the defensive. To escape looking at the wrongs we have done another, we resentfully focus on the wrongs he has done us. This is especially true if he has, in fact behaved badly at all. Triumphantly we seize upon his misbehavior as the perfect excuse for minimizing or forgetting our own (p. 78).

We learned back in Step Four that one way to let go of our resentments towards others is to try to understand the others. We can see that they are sick people who have issues that bring out character defects, just as we were sick and clouded with character defects back in our drinking or using days. We should apply the same understanding in our Step Eight:

> Let's remember that alcoholics are not the only ones bedeviled by sick emotions. Moreover, it is usually a fact that our behavior when

drinking has aggravated the defects of others. We've repeatedly strained the patience of our best friends to a snapping point, and have brought out the very worst in those who didn't think much of us to begin with.... If we are about to ask for forgiveness for ourselves, why shouldn't we start out by forgiving them, one and all? (*Twelve Steps and Twelve Traditions*, p. 78).

Step Eight also requires an open mind. There may be a lot of people who should be on our list but don't make it because we once lacked the empathy to realize the harm we were doing them. Even now, at first glance we may not see how our behaviors hurt them or cost them. We should remember that there were times that our intoxication prevented us from remembering or being aware of the impact of our actions. This is especially true for people who are blackout drinkers. Even when we do remember our past deeds, we often lacked the perspective to realize at the time how our actions may have harmed others. Blinded by our selfishness and our laser-focus on protecting our access to the next drink or drug, our mind may not have registered it when we stepped on others' toes. We thought only of ourselves, and our brain didn't register our impact on others because it didn't matter to us; all that mattered was that next drink or drug. So, we need to take another look at past events as we prepare our list.

We have previously discussed cognitive bias, a major tool that our disease uses to propagate our substance use. If you recall, a cognitive bias is a defect in how our mind works that causes us to make errors. There are some psychological cognitive biases that can interfere with our Step Eight. One of these is known as the *empathy gap*.[2] The empathy gap is the limitation of our ability to put ourselves in other people's shoes and see things from their perspective. This would greatly impair our ability to understand the effects of our past actions on other people and could therefore impair our ability to do a thorough job with our Step Eight.

As we just discussed, the empathy gap is a particular problem with alcoholic-addicts, because of the inward-looking mind-set and obsession for obtaining the next drink or drug that accompany addiction. The solution is accomplished by improving our empathy, but it's only possible to feel empathy for someone else when we get outside ourselves and put ourselves in the other person's shoes. Luckily for us, our spirituality is about exactly that: getting outside ourselves and connecting with others in a meaningful way. So, by the time we reach Step Eight we should be capable of the necessary empathy to make a complete list of the people we had wronged. But, it takes some deep thought and introspection, reviewing our past actions through the lens of our newfound spirituality.

As we continue to grow in spirituality, so we also grow in empathy, and our empathy gap will get smaller and smaller. Therefore, as time passes we should keep our mind open for other people who should have been on our list from our Step Eight, and we may have to revisit our amends Steps from time to time to address missed amends as they come to light. As with our Step Four inventories, the more complete our Step Eight list, the more complete the healing. As we are told in *Twelve Steps and Twelve Traditions*, making our list: "is a task which we may perform with increasing skill, but never really finish" (p. 77). We never close that list.

I recently got schooled on my empathy gap, and in the process learned something relevant to my Step Eight, despite being years since I first went through the Steps. I was at a relative's house for dinner, and a guy who was drinking heavily began acting out. As the evening wore on he was being increasingly obnoxious and an outright jerk. His wife was embarrassed and in tears, his children were wailing and the otherwise pleasant evening ended on a crappy note when the police arrived due to a noise complaint.

Thoughts of that evening stuck with me for a while, as I had just learned first-hand what it's like to be a sober person watching someone like me drink and behave like I used to. I was a blackout drinker and I seldom remembered any details about my drinking bouts, but I was handed a "remember when" on the matter that night to fill in the blanks from my own patchy memories. It shocked me to see first-hand what I must have looked like. It really hit me how awful it must have been for my family and friends – and any other unfortunate soul who happened to be there – to live through my intoxicated behavior day in day out. All of a sudden my perspective on why I must make amends became clearer than ever before, and on that day my empathy gap narrowed considerably.

Another cognitive bias that can affect our ability to make a complete list in Step Eight is the *social desirability bias*.[3] This is the natural human tendency to over-emphasize our socially desirable behaviors and underestimate our negative behaviors. This, too, is usually much worse in people with the pathological psychology of substance addiction. Cognitive dissonance and our alcoholic-addict pride both tend to make us view ourselves and our behaviors in a positive light, or to blame others for our misdeeds so as to excuse our own behaviors.

The social desirability bias is a big problem for psychologists and researchers when they collect self-report data – such as when the research subjects fill out a questionnaire or answer questions about their own past behaviors. The study subjects believe they are acting truthfully, but their social desirability bias is causing the information they provide to be heavily skewed in their own favor. Likewise, this bias can affect our accuracy and completeness as we make out our list in Step Eight.

There are a couple of ways that I suggest overcoming such biases so that we can achieve an accurate and complete Step Eight. The first and most obvious is to make sure that we do Step Eight in close conjunction with our sponsor. Sponsors challenge us and guide us, as they have experience with the process themselves, as well as with helping others through the process. They are there to keep us on track, keep us rigorously honest, and to call us on our BS. An experienced 12 Step sponsor can smell BS from a mile away.

Another way to reduce error and bias is to be aware that these cognitive biases are part of human psychology, so that we expect them and recognize that we may need to challenge our own impressions and memories. I suggest taking some time to reflect on your Step Eight list prior to moving on to Step Nine so that some proper introspection can be done. We can be mindful of these biases and ask ourselves if we are perhaps sugar-coating our list in order to spare our own feelings.

Our spirituality is itself a good tool for overcoming these biases. As we grow in humility, our mind has less of a need to warp our memories to try to make us look better than we are. With a healthy self-esteem we no longer have any need to maintain a false pride, and we are much more receptive to recognizing our shortcomings. Too, as we grow in spirituality and get better at getting outside ourselves and seeing things from other people's viewpoints – being empathetic, in other words – our biases will fall away.

The final suggestion to overcome these biases is only for the brave. This involves picking someone close to us and asking him or her how our drinking or using has affected them, and compare what they say to our own impression of how we had harmed them. Usually, we will be surprised. We should be careful, though, because sometimes the pain and resentment is still too raw for this exercise to be done without causing further upset to our loved one. It may be best to save such an exercise for a later time, when amends have been made and some time to heal has passed. We must not hurt others in our recovery efforts, no matter how well-intentioned we are. Many people we have harmed may still have raw feelings about it, and they need to see us walking the walk before they are ready to talk. Easy does it.

*

As we'll see in our Step Nine discussion, it's also necessary for us to take into account the people that we can't name in Step Eight. Sometimes we can't identify a particular person or group of people, but we wronged them and potentially harmed them very much by our actions. Many times this weighs heavily on our conscience, and we need to put things right in order to heal and move forward. Allow me to illustrate with an example.

In my drinking and using days, I drove drunk and/or high many times. Many times. I never got caught, but it was a regular thing for me. Every single individual whom I passed on the highway or who drove by me, or who was walking on the sidewalk as I drove by was wronged by me. I put their lives at risk because of my insane behavior. I can't possibly name those people on a list, because there are thousands of them and I couldn't possibly know who they are. However, this horrible wrong weighed heavily on my mind, and I needed to make some kind of amends in order to find self-forgiveness and to feel right spiritually. Leaving something like that undone can be like a stone in our shoe that can become a locus for relapse. As such, I had to put those people on my list as a group, so that I can make amends in Step Nine. We'll discuss how we can make amends to people or groups that we can't name in our Step Nine discussion. Meanwhile, we need to make sure they aren't left out of our list. There are many other examples of how we need to include "nameless" people on our list. Let's look at one more example.

All those times I did my very best to appear sober while buying alcohol at the liquor store I could have gotten the store clerk who checked me out in big trouble. They're required to recognize people who are intoxicated and refuse the sale of more alcohol. When I succeeded in buying more booze I could have gotten the store clerk fired, especially if I would have gotten into a drunk driving accident after leaving the store. I knew that what I was doing could harm these innocent people, but I cared only about myself and my next drink. These people had to be on my Step Eight list, even though I couldn't name them or find out who they were.

While it seems odd to include people or groups of people whom we can't specifically name on the Step Eight list, it's important to do so. The first nine steps are very much about self-forgiveness, and the quality of our self-forgiveness will depend on the thoroughness of the job that we do in Steps Eight and Nine. Let's get all those rocks out of our shoes.

*

So, how, exactly, do we do Step Eight? The Big Book is sparse on the details, saying only: "we have a list of all persons we had harmed and to whom we are willing to make amends. We made it when we took inventory. We subjected ourselves to a drastic self-appraisal" (p. 76). This says that we simply take our list directly from our Step Four inventory. I suggest taking a sheet of paper and making two columns. In the column on the left, write down the name of the person harmed. In the right-hand column, beside the name, write down a brief annotation of the harm done to that person. Just a point-form note or a phrase that jogs your memory, no need to write out the whole story.

Bill Wilson, in the Big Book chapter *Bill's Story* tells of how he did what was later to become our Step Eight:

> We [Bill and an "old school friend"] made a list of people I had hurt
> or toward whom I felt resentment. I expressed my entire willingness

to approach these individuals, admitting my wrong. Never was I to be critical of them. I was to right all such matters to the utmost of my ability (p. 13).

It can be said that doing our amends Steps takes courage, but what it really takes is humility. We should remember, too, who the true beneficiary of these amends is:

In many instances we shall find that though the harm done others has not been great, the emotional harm we have done ourselves has. Very deep, sometimes quite forgotten, damaging emotional conflicts persist below the level of consciousness. At the time of these occurrences, they may actually have given our emotions violent twists which have since discolored our personalities and altered our lives for the worse (*Twelve Steps and Twelve Traditions*, p. 79-80).

Of the willingness required for our amends Steps, the Big Book tells us: "if we haven't the will to do this, we ask until it comes. Remember it was agreed at the beginning we would go to any lengths for victory over alcohol" (p. 76). Some among us might find it helpful, when we work on our list, to invoke the Step Eight prayer:

Heavenly Father, I ask Your help in making my list of all those I have harmed. I will take responsibility for my actions, and begin to clear my past mistakes. Grant me the willingness to begin my restitution. Amen.

If you're not comfortable with prayer try just saying the words to your higher power. If your higher power is a blank, just say the words and throw them up in the air.

As with anything, it's important to find balance when we do Step Eight. Addiction-alcoholism has many of the same characteristics as obsessive-compulsive disorder, and we can be an obsessive lot. We don't want to over-do our Step Eight list. We should avoid cluttering the list with petty wrongs and matters that don't affect our conscience. This is just our neurotic perfectionism trying to assert itself again. We should be making our list based on our wrongdoings that were related to our substance use, or anything from the past that really bothers us, and we let go of the rest. Otherwise, the exercise would detract from the value of our amends-making. No point in making amends over that chocolate bar we stole in grade eight, unless that incident still bothers us or there was some kind of lasting harm to the other person. If you're not sure about some of the stuff that you want to put on your list, it's best to run it by your sponsor.

Our amends Steps represent one of those instances of "positive selfishness" that we previously discussed, where doing something that's for our own benefit also benefits others. Although our amends are for us and our mental and emotional well-being, they are necessary for us to heal and keep from resorting to drug or drink again. If we are to be of use to anyone we must be healthy and sober. So, for our sake and the sake of those we would harm by going back to drinking and using, we should dive into our amends with the same vigor with which we would want a cancer removed from our body: "thoroughness, we have found, will pay – and pay handsomely" (*Twelve Steps and Twelve Traditions*, p. 79).

Our Step Eight is one place where we should be careful that our self-critical voice doesn't go unchallenged. We must not beat ourselves up when we reflect on the harms we have done. The amends Steps are not an exercise in self-flagellation, nor are they a form of punishment. *Twelve Steps and Twelve Traditions* reminds us of this: "we should avoid extreme judgments, both of ourselves and of others involved. We must not exaggerate our defects or theirs. A quiet, objective view will be our steadfast aim" (p. 82).

Allowing that errant inner self-critic to have its say as we undertake amends is counter-productive. Self-criticism is a cluster defect, so if left unchecked it will cause a cascade of those ugly and unnecessary negative emotions that used to drive us to drink or use. Self-criticism isn't at all productive; instead, it begets shame, remorse, anger at ourselves, blame, anger and resentment at those we blame, lowered self-esteem, and so on. You get the picture. We learned back in Step Six that we must replace self-criticism with self-correction – in other words, learning from our mistakes and then dropping the issue – and the amends Steps are about self-correction, putting things right. So let's not allow the character defect of self-criticism to ruin that for us.

When we discussed self-criticism as a character flaw in Step Six we discussed different ways to beat this self-defeating nonsense before it has a chance to get under our skin. One way to do that is to recognize that inner voice and challenge it, and another is by replacing self-criticism with self-correction. Rather than beat ourselves up over our past wrongdoings, let's look at the lessons we can learn from the experience and resolve to apply those lessons to our lives as we move forward. We can't change our past behaviors, but we certainly can change our future behaviors. As you look to how you can self-correct for past wrongdoings so that the same behaviors aren't repeated, you will notice that the answer lies in living by spiritual principles. Since that's exactly what we are doing here by working through the Steps, we can satisfy ourselves that we are self-correcting. It's much easier to forgive ourselves for sins of the past when we are taking action to correct our faults – as we are doing here – rather than just saying the words. Our amends Steps, Eight and Nine, constitute affirmative action to self-correct for our past wrongs to others.

There may be times that our amends can cross the line from being a form of positive selfishness to being negative selfishness. When making overt amends hurt ourselves or someone else, then we must put them on our list, but make amends in a quiet way, between ourselves and our higher power. We can involve our sponsor as well. When we make our list in Step Eight we should take note of which things on our list – if any – require this kind of discretion to prevent doing further harm to anyone. We will discuss this further in Step Nine.

*

When we leave our Step Eight we must remember that this is a list that we should never consider closed; making our list: "is a task which we may perform with increasing skill, but never really finish" (*Twelve Steps and Twelve Traditions*, p. 77). Over time memories will come back, we will run into old acquaintances, and we will think of things that we overlooked when we first did our Step Eight. Too, as we will see in Step Ten, we make amends as needed as we go forward, in order to stay on top of our wrongs to others lest they fester and cause that same downward spiral of character defects that has caused us so much harm in the past.

Remembering that our Step Eight is never done is a great tool to help boost our humility. If we remember that there is no possible way for us to list everyone who was harmed by our drinking and using, it really helps us in those times when we get angry or impatient with someone else. For example, when I get that feeling of road rage welling up inside me, I think back to all those times that I drove drunk and endangered the lives of countless people. Suddenly, my humility comes back and I calm down. How could I ever put all of those people on my Step Eight list and make amends? I can't. So, instead, I will make amends by calming myself and being a respectful and courteous driver no matter how much I don't like other people's driving.

If my wife or my kids are getting on my nerves, I calm myself by remembering that – even though they are on my Step Eight list – they endured countless days and nights of my horrible drunken behavior, I spent money on my drink and drugs that was rightfully theirs, and they lived without a functional husband and father. How could I ever really make a complete list accounting for everything I put them through? I can't. So I look upon situations like that as an opportunity to contribute towards my amends by being patient, tolerant, understanding, and loving.

Keeping it in the back of our mind that our amends are never really finished helps to calm us and keep our character defects in check. Ironically, this provides us with a great way to make amends to specific people and the world in general on an ongoing basis.

*

I've heard some people say that maintaining their sobriety is amends enough. While it's true that keeping ourselves sober and healthy is a part of our amends, it's not fair to ourselves and others that we take the easier softer way out:

> The alcoholic is like a tornado roaring his way through the lives of others. Hearts are broken. Sweet relationships are dead. Affections have been uprooted. Selfish and inconsiderate habits have kept the home in turmoil. We feel a man is unthinking when he says that sobriety is enough" (Big Book, p. 82).

This attitude robs us of the tremendous healing power that proper amends hold for our own peace of mind and serenity, and it also robs us of the tremendous impact that amends-making has on our interpersonal relationships: "Steps Eight and Nine are concerned with personal relations.... Having thus cleaned away the debris of the past, we consider how, with our newfound knowledge of ourselves, we may develop the best possible relations with every human being we know" (*Twelve Steps and Twelve Traditions*, p. 77). Our making amends is how we let others know that we mean business, and that things will be different from now on. People in our lives have heard our heartfelt promises many times in the past: *THIS time I'm done with the drink and drugs!* and they've seen us fail time and again. Our words are rightfully meaningless to them; we are the boy who cried wolf, on steroids. However, although our words have lost all verity, our actions mean something. Our amends-making is meaningful action, and it's our chance to show people that we are taking action to end our drinking or drug use. Making amends gives us a fresh start after the damage done to our spiritual relationships during our active drinking or using days. It also shows ourselves that we mean business, thereby deepening our commitment to recovery, because our resolve is always strengthened when we back it up with action.

By making amends we display to others that we acknowledge our harm to them, which is meaningful. It opens their hearts (usually, anyway) to renewed relationships. Some will take time, for some we have deeply hurt. However, by showing them that we mean business by continuing in the program and living by our spiritual principles we seldom fail to win hearts. The key is that we are *showing* them, rather than *telling* them. We have the tools we need to do this. All we have to do is to keep our freshly cleaned house from becoming dirty again. Try to live each day without building up a new inventory like the one we made in Step Four. Truly, Step Eight: "is the beginning of the end of isolation from our fellows and from God" (*Twelve Steps and Twelve Traditions*, p. 82).

*

If Step Eight is never truly finished, how do we know when we are ready to move on to Step Nine? Well, I suggest that you not be in a huge rush, and take some time to really ponder your past and who was affected; especially the people whom you didn't really encounter that much, such as someone you picked a fight with at a wedding, or other "relatively minor" events. Any wrongdoing or action that has left a burr in our crowded conscience – no matter how small – must be met with an amend. The more complete the list, the more complete the healing. I also suggest you run your list by your sponsor for feedback and advice. Once you have given it some truly reflective thought and you are satisfied with the list – and if your sponsor agrees – it's time to move on.

Step Nine

Made direct amends to such people wherever possible, except when to do so would injure them or others.

Step Nine can be a source of fear for some of us, while others are gung-ho to get out there and start making amends and repairing broken relationships. Step Nine is a wonderful chance for us to showcase the amazing transformation we are undergoing. To outsiders, this spiritual transformation from zero to hero seldom fails to impress. Nonetheless, amends are made to set our spirit free, lift tremendous burdens from our shoulders, and find serenity and real peace of mind – regardless of how an amend is received. As with our other Steps, the better and more complete the effort, the better the healing.

Once again, willingness and humility are at the forefront of our ability to perform this soul-invigorating Step. By this point in our progress through the Steps we should be pretty comfortable with finding the willingness to do what each Step suggests, as we are seeing the benefits of a willing and earnest effort in our previous Steps. However, to proceed with Step Nine we must understand what is asked of us and be sure of our readiness to do what it takes:

> We attempt to sweep away the debris which has accumulated out of our effort to live on self-will and run the show ourselves. If we haven't the will to do this, we ask until it comes. Remember it was agreed at the beginning *we would go to any lengths for victory over alcohol* (Big Book, p. 76).

Step Nine has several purposes. First, it's a superb tool for growing and maturing in humility. Second of all, it's the final piece of the process of finding self-forgiveness. Third, it's meant to improve our inter-personal relationships, thereby advancing our spirituality immeasurably. Finally, Step Nine is just plain the right thing to do. As Bill Wilson said in one of his

General Service Conference talks: "we must enlarge upon the joys and gifts we had received... we found we were doing these things because they were right, because we ought to do them" (*Our Great Responsibility*, p. 48). Step Nine certainly enlarges upon our spirituality and allows us to project our positivity onto people who deserve some atonement. After all the harm we have caused, we owe amends to those we have harmed. It's what good people like us do.

Many of the people we make amends with may not be, until now, aware that we were in recovery, let alone that we are so healthy and high functioning as to be out doing amazing things like taking responsibility for our past and putting things right. Many are impressed and are left with a brand new impression of us. Some are indifferent, and may not even recall the wrongdoings for which we are making amends. Others are angry and not yet ready to let go of past transgressions. Some weren't even aware of our addiction-alcoholism, although most will admit that they knew something wasn't right. Regardless of their reaction, being approached by someone earnestly seeking to make amends seldom fails to impress. People respect honesty, they respect integrity, and they respect people who own up to their wrongdoings.

*

If you're putting a check mark beside each Step as you progress through them and fulfill their requirements before moving on to the next one, then Step Nine might disappoint you. This one should be left open-ended for the rest of our life. One of our tools for keeping our character defects in check is that we always remain mindful that we owe amends that can never be fully completed. It helps us maintain humility.

We don't complete Step Nine and move on because we've made all amends and there is nothing more to do. Rather, we are ready to move on when we've made initial amends to everyone on our Step Eight list, as long as it doesn't harm anyone to do so, and we've laid the groundwork for ongoing amends for those that can't be addressed with a single gesture. Let's look at a couple of examples.

I put on an awful drunken performance at a pool party at a guy's house back in the day, and I broke some stuff in his backyard. Planters and a chair, as I recall. When I did my Step Nine, I went over to his house to make amends. I gave him and his wife a heartfelt apology, offered them money to pay for the damages that I made (which they declined), and I stayed and helped the guy out for the afternoon because he was building a shed and needed a hand. It's a guy I don't really know that well and I probably won't ever see again, but I told him to give me a call if there was ever anything I could do for him. When I left that day, I was satisfied that my amends were made.

Unlike the nice, tidy amends I made at that guy's house, my amends with my mother were a different story. During my drinking and using days I put my dear mother through hell. How do you make simple amends when your wrongdoings were prolonged and profound? So, I approached her and made my apologies in detail, which she accepted. However, I'll be making amends to her for life. I am always ready to support her, help her out, and look for any opportunity to do something helpful and nice for her. Those are my ongoing amends. To satisfy the requirements of my Step Nine, I made my apologies to her, and laid the groundwork for my ongoing amends.

*

Step Nine is one of those suggestions where we need some finesse to find the right balance: "good judgment, a careful sense of timing, courage, and prudence – these are the qualities we shall need when we take Step Nine" (*Twelve Steps and Twelve Traditions*, p. 83). It's easy to lose objectivity when planning our amends, so it's a good idea to do this Step in close conjunction with a sponsor. Too, approaching some long-timers in the fellowship for advice is useful, because they have seen many different Step Nine situations themselves and they will have many fresh suggestions for us. Many times, when I was stumped about how to make amends, I was given great suggestions by long-timers in the fellowship. They really helped me feel my way through Step Nine without stubbing my toe. Long-timers are there to help us, but we have to ask; they are only a great resource for us if we access them. Finesse and balance are key, because acting in haste or in the spur of the moment may result in approaching someone too soon or too bluntly in our efforts to check that box. In our enthusiasm for our amends we can lose sight of people's sensitivities and go in commando-style with an indelicate timing and approach.

We can easily offend someone or mess up an amend because we rushed into it too quickly, so easy does it. This is a great time to be in close contact with our sponsor so that we can use him or her as a sounding board. After all, when we make amends we are doing something that goes against human nature. When we are responsible for harming someone, our natural instinct is to look for someone to blame it on (especially the person we did harm to), to try to rationalize or excuse our behavior rather than taking responsibility for it, to lie to cover our transgression, or to avoid the person we harmed.[1] This is especially true of people like us, because alcohol and drug use are usually part of an avoidance behavior, where we run from problems and responsibilities. So, our instinct is to avoid the person and dodge confronting the situation head-on. As such, we are usually somewhat

286

out of sorts when we approach people to make amends, and some objective advice will help keep us from stubbing our toe.

Step Nine is not for wusses. It takes courage, integrity, humility, and a commitment to heal and do what's right. However, the rewards are great. This is the final of the cleaning house Steps, and the feeling of self-forgiveness and even liking ourselves again becomes even more complete as we make our way through our amends. Some people may find it takes time even after Step Nine to really forgive themselves and like themselves again, but the ingredients are all there by the time we are ready to move on to Step Ten.

*

Twelve Steps and Twelve Traditions (p. 83) tells us of two conditions that should be met prior to setting out to make our amends: 1) we have made our list of those we have harmed and reflected carefully upon each one on the list, and 2) we have the right attitude in which to proceed. In doing our Step Eight we have taken care of requirement number one. In terms of item number two, we should make sure that we prepare ourselves mentally prior to setting out to do our amends. Let's discuss that now.

First of all, we need to do a gut-check about our anger and resentments involving the people we will be making amends with. If we are harboring some residual negative feelings toward them we should discuss that with our sponsor and do a mini-Step Four to let go of those. If we get a negative reaction from some people we are making amends with and we still hold some resentment or blame toward them, it may easily turn ugly. Nothing's worse than a negative Step Nine call! Even if someone we are making amends with has wronged us, even if he or she is to blame for some hardship or humiliation in our life, we are not there to take their inventory.

Second of all, we must make sure that our expectations are correct. Our Step Nine is about self-forgiveness, righting wrongs as best we can, and getting a new start for meaningful relationships with people outside ourselves. If we are expecting people to react positively, or we are expecting them to forgive us, or we are expecting them to reciprocate with an apology for their past wrong-doings we are setting ourselves up for disappointment and we are there for the wrong reasons. As spiritual people we do not place expectations on other people; expectations breed resentments. Failed expectations lead to anger, resentment, and negative interpersonal connections. Now is the time to live and let live.

I wish to emphasize here that the success of our Step Nine does **not** depend upon whether or not we receive forgiveness from people. We are motivated by selfishness if we are approaching people to make amends with the self-serving expectation to have them say *I forgive you* and then we walk away feeling all warm and fuzzy. The amends are about them, not about us, but the psychological release we get from the process more than makes up for it. We should set out to make our amends and expect nothing in return, including forgiveness. We should not try to take credit or seek kudos for our amends, but we should be gracious about it when we do receive praise. We're not there for an ego boost.

If some people tell us that they forgive us, then that's well and good. But it's arrogant for us to believe that our decision to seek them out and make amends should automatically provoke forgiveness in return. Step Nine does not say: "sought forgiveness from people." Besides, we are just setting ourselves up for failure if we approach our amends with the expectation of a reciprocal gesture of forgiveness, because that may not be forthcoming. Some people may find the wrongs that we did unforgiveable, or they may need time to process the significant changes that we have made in ourselves, or they might be very suspicious of our motives and our ability to stay sober, or they may themselves be spiritually sick and clinging to anger, resentments, and blame. As we shall see shortly, psychologists have determined that most people who forgive someone after an apology do so within several weeks, so just because we did not get an affirmation of forgiveness at the time of our amends doesn't necessarily mean that it's not forthcoming.

When we're fortunate enough to gain forgiveness from those we have harmed it's a very positive thing. It helps our own self-forgiveness, it shows that we did a good job with our amends, and it gives our relationships with the people we have harmed a huge boost. In fact, many members of the fellowship have found that after making amends with people, they have developed new friendships where only mutual dislike previously existed. Making amends makes us very likeable, and our spirituality makes us worthwhile friends.

*

Although we shouldn't go into our amends with expectations of forgiveness, forgiveness is a desirable outcome and a source of healing for both parties, so let's look at how we can improve the odds of forgiveness. Research by psychologists into what makes apologies effective gives us some useful information that we can use when we make our amends, and increase the likelihood of receiving forgiveness. There are three elements to an apology that make it more likely to be effective, repair relationships, and lead to healing.[2] These are: 1) apologizing: by saying: *I'm sorry!* We are openly acknowledging responsibility and regret for our actions, 2) offering compensation: this shows genuine remorse and an interest in repairing the damage done, and 3) taking responsibility: some people make "non-

288

apologies" by making excuses or "hollow apologies" by apologizing for hurt feelings or any inconvenience caused, rather than apologizing for their actions. Dodging responsibility for our actions obliterates the usefulness of our amends. All three of these qualities should be part of all of our amends.

Again, we can turn to research in psychology to get an idea of how our amends may lead to forgiveness. We have just discussed the three key aspects of an apology that maximize the chances of interpersonal healing and forgiveness. Studies have shown that forgiveness doesn't always come straight up.[3] Understandably, some people need some time to process our apology – after all, that kind of contrition isn't exactly a common event in today's society. As well, some people won't believe us, and may need to see us continuing to walk the walk and getting sobriety time under our belt before they let their guard down, which is understandable. After all, they've been burned by us in the past.

Studies have shown that following a (proper) apology the level of forgiveness rises for several weeks after, and the level of anger toward the offender decreases during the same time period.[4,5] Two factors are most influential in increasing forgiveness and decreasing anger: 1) if the offender (the person doing Step Nine) makes a proper apology that includes the three elements previously discussed, and 2) the transgressor is seen as less likely to engage in hurtful behaviors in the future and is genuinely seeking to do better. When those two elements are in place, the offender (us) is perceived as more valuable, stable, and reliable as a friend and more worthwhile of forgiveness and friendship, since the offender places enough importance on the relationship to make the amends. This is why we should briefly explain our program of recovery as we make amends, so that people will see that we have changed our old behaviors and have committed to a newfound spiritual way of living – a way of living that will prevent a repeat of past harms.

*

Twelve Steps and Twelve Traditions (p. 83) divides the people we approach to make amends into four categories:

1) Those we ought to approach as soon as we become reasonably confident we can maintain our sobriety,
2) Those to whom we can make only partial restitution because complete disclosure to them would cause more harm than good,
3) Those where action should be deferred, and
4) Those whom we will never be able to approach at all due to the nature of the situation.

There are two kinds of amends that we can make to others, both of which provide us with healing: 1) our verbal acknowledgement of the harms we have done, given directly to the affected individual (i.e. *verbal amends*), and 2) our action-based amends. We can use either of these types of amends or both in combination to make sure that we cover all four types of people on our amends list. Let's talk about each of these in turn, starting with verbal amends.

Verbal amends are where we approach the people on our list and make a verbal acknowledgement of the harm we have done to them and an affirmation that we are undergoing a program of recovery to free ourselves from the sickness that led to such behavior. These verbal amends are sometimes referred to as *direct amends*.

Our verbal amends could be described as an apology, but somehow that word just doesn't seem to fit. An apology is something like: *I'm sorry I walked through your kitchen with my muddy shoes.* Our verbal amends are more involved than that, because the deeds being apologized for are personal, hurtful, and more profound in depth and duration. The term "amends" is more appropriate to our situation because it implies taking action to put things right, and offering an apology may be only one of those actions.

People want to know what makes us tick in times of pain, and if we don't provide the back-story they will make their own conclusions.[6] People who don't know about or understand our drinking or drugging problem may assume that we just don't like them, or they may internalize it and blame themselves. One of the things that our verbal amends does is to free them from that burden. Many people, too, are unfamiliar with alcoholism-addiction and the behaviors that typify the disease. Hearing the back-story actually provides them with relief, and puts into context our explanation of how we are committed to a process of healing and recovery. So we shouldn't use our disease as an *excuse* for our behaviors to absolve ourselves of responsibility, but we should use our disease as a *context* for our behaviors, because it helps people to understand us, and to see that we are taking steps (twelve of them!) to correct the problem.

We should not sound like we are blaming all of our misdeeds on drugs or alcohol, but we should point out that our lives and behaviors spiraled downwards during our addiction. People get that our behavior was influenced by our addiction, but they may be offended by our efforts to excuse things because of it. If we find that we are being defensive or not accepting full responsibility for what happened, then we are not yet ready for Step Nine, and we should have a conversation with our sponsor.

We should be direct and to the point when we approach people to make our verbal amends:

These conversations can begin in a casual or natural way. But if no such opportunity presents itself, at some point we will want to summon all our courage, head straight for the person concerned, and lay our cards on the table. We needn't wallow in excessive remorse before those we have harmed, but amends at this level should always be forthright and generous (*Twelve Steps and Twelve Traditions*, p. 85-86).

This really needs to be done face-to-face. Using a text message to apologize for a small incident may work for our Step Ten amends, but when we are making amends for the momentous harm we have done during our active substance use, a text message is not appropriate at all. Text messages carry none of the feeling, emotion, eye contact, body language, or interpersonal contact that are part of our verbal amends. Besides, the last thing we want to do is trivialize our amends, which may, rightfully, insult or anger the other person. A text message does not convey sincerity. *Sorry dude, LOL* just doesn't cut it.

How about an email for those we cannot meet in person? Emails are a bit better than text messages because they are more formal and can include more of a back-story. However, I suggest not using email unless it's absolutely not possible to meet in person. Personally, the only emails that I sent for my verbal amends involved letting people know that I wished to speak to them about my past behaviors so that I could put things right. Then, I would arrange in the email to meet in person. Better to wait to make the amend when we can do it face-to-face than to do it by email now. Email is fine, though, if we are unlikely to be able to see the other person in the near future, but a phone call is much better than email.

When we meet with someone to make verbal amends we are emotionally and spiritually charged and ready to go. We have an agenda, we're on a mission, and we've probably rehearsed what we are going to say a dozen times. However, easy does it: a key part of our verbal amends involves **not** dominating the conversation. We can start out with a soliloquy that expresses our verbal amends, but we must allow the other person to speak. To feel heard and understood is really important for those we have harmed. It shows genuine concern on our part, and allows us to get outside ourselves and hear the other individual's point of view. It's a good opportunity to compare our own impression of past events with how it was perceived by someone else. We show empathy, caring, and concern by listening.

Going back to the previously discussed research on what makes apologies effective, we can draw on some tips for our verbal amends.[7] First, the verbal amends should involve saying: *I'm sorry*. This is an open statement of regret and responsibility. The second key aspect involves offering a way to help the healing process. This shows that we really do care about the individual, that we truly are sorry and want them to heal from the harm we have done them, and that we are committed to our amends. The third aspect of the most effective verbal amends is to take responsibility. A "non-apology," where we evade responsibility for the harm we have done, is insulting and ineffective. It's tempting to blame everything on the drugs or alcohol, but it really takes the wind out of our apology. We should allow the other person to understand that we were behaving like an addict-alcoholic, but be sure to avoid any appearance of using that to excuse our behavior. Again, we use our addiction-alcoholism to put our past behaviors in context, not to excuse them.

We must be careful, too, not to use the words "if" or "but" as these are sneaky ways that we try to dodge full responsibility for our actions. "I'm sorry *if* I hurt you..." or "I'm sorry I hurt you, *but*..." amount to non-apologies. We should also avoid the tendency to make apologies sound like they imply that the other person is the one with the problem: "I'm sorry you felt hurt...." This sounds passive-aggressive, and it sounds like we are apologizing for how the other individual felt, not for our own actions. Our amends must be rigorously honest and responsibility-laden, so we must be aware of the human tendency to try to sugar-coat our behavior when making an apology.

Another study showed that the effectiveness of an apology is further boosted if it includes an expression of empathy, particularly if that empathy is specific to that individual.[8] That means expressing our impression of how our actions affected the other person, and then listening and allowing the other person to speak to express his or her feelings about the matter.[9] This makes the verbal amends personalized and heartfelt.

The second type of amends is our *action amends*, sometimes referred to as *indirect amends*. These tend to be hugely fulfilling, because they make us feel good and warm inside, and they also fit nicely with our Step Twelve work, as we shall see. Importantly, any time we find our character defects welling up, or if we find ourselves getting selfish or self-pitying, action amends are remarkably effective for getting outside ourselves to chase away the selfish negativity. Going out of our way to do something random and thoughtful for someone on our amends list is wonderfully therapeutic for both parties.

Our action amends may be direct, such as doing some gardening and lawn care for the lady next door whose lawn we ripped up in a drunken driving performance late one night. Or, it may be indirect things, such as remaining dedicated to our 12 Step program for life to make amends to our family, who are benefitting from our sobriety and spiritual health. These indirect action amends are very good for making amends to people whom we can't possibly list or track down when we do our Step Eight. For example, when I do volunteer work at the detox center, it's part of my amends for all those people I harmed but can't possibly name or find – I'm doing something to reduce the impact of addiction-alcoholism in our community, which benefits everyone.

Action amends are kind and thoughtful selfless acts done while expecting nothing in return. They are especially psychologically and spiritually uplifting when we do indirect action amends anonymously. Doing them anonymously goes against human nature, because our ego screams for acknowledgement and praise when we do something good. Old fragile egos die hard, and always try to re-establish themselves, regardless of how solid our self-esteem may be. With practice, it becomes much easier to do good deeds anonymously and avoid the willful desire to seek credit. For people who believe in karma, there's no better investment than anonymous good deeds.

One type of action amend that we make is simply by maintaining our new way of living. We make immense amends to others by remaining committed to our spiritual program and remaining in recovery. This is sometimes referred to as *living amends*. Living amends are a way of making amends to specific people in our lives and to the world in general. It's one way that we can feel that we are making amends to all those people we cannot possibly list or know, the world at large.

While living amends are useful and make good sense, we must be careful not to rely on them too much. It's tempting to take the easier softer way and avoid our action amends by rationalizing that the act of staying sober and living by spiritual principles alone is enough. This is especially true of the people closest to us, whom we have usually harmed the most. Sure, they benefit every day from our sobriety, but our amends need to reflect the harm that's been done.

Our action amends don't necessarily have to be directed specifically at someone we injured with our behavior. When we help the old lady next door carry in her groceries, stop to help someone in distress, or even hold the door for someone at the bank we are making action amends to the world in general. We brighten someone's day, spread some positivity and spirituality around, and make the world just a little bit better. Given the amount of harm we have caused society and the world in general, these kinds of non-specific action amends are an appropriate way to apply Step Nine and get outside ourselves. If we're ever feeling down, or irritable, or otherwise off, doing such non-specific good deeds have an amazing ability to give us a boost.

It's amazing how often in life we somehow cross paths with people we owe amends to and are given an opportunity to do a really good and rewarding amends long after the fact, when doing amends with them would have been impossible or injurious back when we were first in recovery. Life, fate, a higher power, luck, or whatever else seems to allow us to cross paths with such people when the time is right. We often hear such stories at the podium or in print. Here's an example. Remember the guy whose pool party I ruined? After I made my amends and waved goodbye I didn't think I'd ever see or hear from him again. However, a couple of years later he called me out of the blue and asked me if I was still in A.A. When I said yes, he told me his cousin was staying at his house after the guy hit rock bottom with an alcohol and crystal meth addiction. He asked if I could help. So, I went over and did a Step Twelve call, took the guy to the detox center, and helped him get into a rehab program. When he got back I picked him up and drove him to meetings. He did well. My friend from the pool party was so grateful, we became good friends, and I knew I had more than made good on my past wrongdoings. Life has a way of giving our Step Nine a boost, often years after our initial trip through the Steps.

We can think of our Step Nine as an "emotional bank account." Every time we do someone wrong, we make a withdrawal, and every time we do something good and kind we make a deposit. So, Step Nine is our way of making sure that we keep our emotional bank account in the black, where our good deeds outweigh the bad.

*

Part of Step Nine is the admonition that our amends should not injure the other person or others. Sometimes our desire to clean house and get that load of guilt and remorse off our shoulders can make us a little over-zealous with our verbal amends. However, we must always think through the consequences of every verbal amend that we make. If there is the risk of upsetting or harming someone else in our efforts to make ourselves feel better, then our amends-making moves from positive selfishness – where our actions help ourselves and others – to negative selfishness – where we look after our own interests at the expense of others.

The 12 Step literature gives a few examples of dilemmas where making amends may be harmful, such as revealing or discussing details of an extramarital affair, or revealing financial indiscretions in the workplace. These can be found on page 84 of *Twelve Steps and Twelve Traditions*, and pages 76-84 of the Big Book. Our real purpose is not to make ourselves feel better about ourselves at any cost; rather: "our real purpose is to fit ourselves to be of maximum service to God and the people about us" (Big Book, p. 77).

I suggest carefully thinking through each verbal amends to anticipate how it may play out and affect others and ourselves. I also suggest close contact with your sponsor while doing this planning. The Big Book tells us: "in meditation we ask God what we should do about each specific matter.

294

The right answer will come if we want it.... Counsel with other persons is often desirable, but we let God be the final judge" (p. 69). We will discuss in Step Eleven the powerful tool of meditation and prayer, and how it can be just as powerful for those whose higher power is not named "God." In the meantime, quiet reflection on each of our amends before we act is certainly a wise precaution against folly.

In the end, there may be situations where we aren't quite sure how to proceed, as there may not be a black-and-white right-or-wrong answer: "of course, there is no pat answer which can fit all such dilemmas. But all of them do require a complete willingness to make amends as fast and as far as may be possible in a given set of conditions" (*Twelve Steps and Twelve Traditions*, p. 87). I suggest that the bottom line is that if there is any doubt, we should err on the side of not offending or harming someone else with our amends. Remember, too, from the list of four different situations that we listed above that there are times when deferring verbal amends until the dust has settled and old wounds are not as fresh may be wise in some situations. Easy does it, Step Nine is, after all, a lifelong pursuit. We don't have to check every box before we move on with the rest of the Steps.

*

In order to put our past behaviors behind us, the amends should fit the wrongdoings. This requires us to apply some empathy elbow grease as we reflect on the list we made in Step Eight. We reflect back on the people we affected and do our very best to imagine what it was like to be on the receiving end of our crapulence during our drinking and using days. As I mentioned, this becomes much easier when we observe someone else who is drunk or high or fully engaged in his or her drug- or alcohol-seeking selfishness.

There are others who had to put up with our behavior, fix the physical damage we caused, explain or make excuses for us to our kids, cover for our shirked responsibilities, and otherwise baby-sit a selfish, insane cur. For many of the people we had wronged a simple apology won't do. It would demean their experience and make it look to her like we feel that the hurt and harm that we brought upon them was so trivial as to be worthy of nothing more than a verbal apology or living amends. Our behaviors made those closest to us feel unvalued, unwanted, unworthy, and unloved. So, we should be focusing our efforts at amends that make these special people feel loved, special, valued, and needed. In many cases, verbal amends alone won't accomplish that, so we must make some meaningful action amends to show people how much we care. The amends should fit the wrongdoings.

We should take the attitude that our amends are never done when it comes to these people who were so deeply affected by our insanity. It makes us better friends, family members, spouses, co-workers, sons or daughters, and so on. It's also a powerful tool for our spiritual principles, because it helps our humility, gratitude, interpersonal relationships, and selflessness. Making action amends gets us outside ourselves. When we lose our cool or feel like someone is annoying us remembering that we still owe amends to that person (and the world in general) helps bring us back down to earth. All this comes from taking the attitude that our amends are never fully done.

*

Some particularly tough amends situations may arise when we owe amends to someone we don't like, someone we feel doesn't deserve it, or when we must make restitution with someone we owe something material.

Our amends are not just directed at people we like, or people who have been kind to us, or even people who are important to us. We are cleaning *our* house, and leaving things undone because they are distasteful for us will leave behind nasty cobwebs in our otherwise clean house. These become the rocks in our shoes that can become a locus for relapse. So, we need to be thorough, regardless of our feelings for the other person:

> The question of how to approach the man we hated will arise. It may be he has done us more harm than we have done him and, though we may have acquired a better attitude toward him, we are still not too keen about admitting our faults. Nevertheless, with a person we dislike, we take the bit in our teeth. It is harder to go to an enemy than to a friend, but we find it much more beneficial to us. We go to him in a helpful and forgiving spirit, confessing our former ill feeling and expressing our regret.
>
> Under no condition do we criticize such a person or argue. Simply we tell him that we will never get over drinking until we have done our utmost to straighten the past. We are there to sweep off our side of the street, realizing that nothing worthwhile can be accomplished until we do so, never trying to tell him what he should do. His faults are not discussed. We stick to our own. If our manner is calm, frank, and open, we will be gratified with the result (Big Book, p. 77-78).

When someone we don't like makes it onto our Step Eight list, we can be tempted to skip that one or put it on the back burner. However – paradoxically – these can be the most rewarding amends to make. My own experience has been that people are so impressed with our humble approach, our initiative, and the fact that we care enough to make contrition – rare qualities in today's world – that antipathy and hostility melt away on

296

both sides. There's no guarantee that this will happen; we still risk rejection and indignation, but we get an immense boost in our growth in humility regardless of the outcome, and the feeling of having the guilt and remorse lifted from our shoulders is that much sweeter. After all, it takes great strength of character and humility to even approach someone we don't like to make amends.

We are here to deal with our own inventory, not to take other people's inventory for them. We clean up our side of the street, and leave others to clean up their side of the street. If they don't do that, then we must let go and live and let live. So, when we make amends with an unsavory acquaintance it's very important that we have no expectations for a warm reception or reciprocation.

In the uncommon occasion that someone rejects our attempts at verbal amends, we simply walk away and leave it with our higher power. We check ourselves that we do not become angry or resentful over the matter; we have no cause to feel entitled, because these people owe us nothing. Perhaps when time has provided some measure of healing and we have proved ourselves through some sobriety, life will cause us to cross paths with this individual under more favorable circumstances. We can still make action and living amends in the meantime. Step Nine is not a rush job; we remain open to opportunities for furthering this Step the rest of our lives. Easy does it. Step Nine is not a rush-job.

Similarly, we must check ourselves when we are tempted to dodge making amends with people we owe money:

> Most alcoholics owe money. We do not dodge our creditors. Telling them what we are trying to do, we make no bones about our drinking; they usually know it anyway, whether we think so or not. Nor are we afraid of disclosing our alcoholism on the theory it may cause financial harm. Approached this way, the most ruthless creditor will sometimes surprise us.... We must lose our fear of creditors no matter how far we have to go, for we are liable to drink if we are afraid to face them (Big Book, p. 78).

I must say that my own experience has mirrored these words from the big Book exactly. Creditors are so accustomed to errant people dodging them and using whatever means possible to avoid paying, that they are pleasantly surprised and well disposed to make satisfactory arrangements when a debtor seeks them out to make contrition. My experience when dealing with individuals and even with institutions has been that when they hear my story and I explain that it may be some time before I have income again to make payments they are most understanding and willing to work with me. People respect recovery, and they respect honesty. The feeling of integrity and courage that replaces the guilt and fear is immensely uplifting.

As we stumble in our resolve when we face making verbal amends in situations that are distasteful or fearful for us, we should remember:

> Above all, we should try to be absolutely sure that we are not delaying because we are afraid. For the readiness to take the full consequences of our past acts, and to take responsibility for the well-being of others at the same time, is the very spirit of Step Nine (*Twelve Steps and Twelve Traditions*, p. 87).

If fear begins to interfere with our amends, our knee-jerk reaction should be to discuss our fears with our sponsor, and to spend some time in meditation or prayer contemplating and visualizing moving forward and facing our fears. If we allow these fears to fester in our thoughts they will become a burr in our ability to move forward.

One of the most oft-quoted and beloved passages in the Big Book is the Ninth Step promises:

> If we are painstaking about this phase of our development, we will be amazed before we are half way through. We are going to know a new freedom and a new happiness. We will not regret the past nor wish to shut the door on it. We will comprehend the word serenity and we will know peace. No matter how far down the scale we have gone, we will see how our experience can benefit others. That feeling of uselessness and self-pity will disappear. We will lose interest in selfish things and gain interest in our fellows. Self-seeking will slip away. Our whole attitude and outlook upon life will change. Fear of people and of economic insecurity will leave us. We will intuitively know how to handle situations which used to baffle us. We will suddenly realize that God is doing for us what we could not do for ourselves. Are these extravagant promises? We think not. They are being fulfilled among us—sometimes quickly, sometimes slowly. They will always materialize if we work for them (p. 83-84).

I have been impressed by how universally the Ninth Step promises come true for people who embrace the 12 Steps, regardless of how low their bottom and how far they were gone in their addiction-alcoholism when they came into the program. It's a perfect example of what people are missing out on when they participate in the 12 Step fellowship without doing the Steps.

*

There's one name that people don't usually put on their list in Step Eight, but is nonetheless the person we wronged the most by our drinking or using: ourselves. While Step Nine is not about making amends to ourselves, I would like to point out that remembering to make amends to ourselves is a spiritually useful tool. The humility that we learn from making amends to others is priceless, but there's a deeper lesson buried in there. That lesson is that humility is never just about empathy for others; it's also about empathy for ourselves.

In our Step Six discussion we talked about some cluster character defects, so-named because they cause a number of other character defects to occur in clusters. One of those cluster defects was self-criticism. When we do Step Nine, which is a very humbling Step that is focused on our wrongdoings and the harm we have done to others, it's very easy for that inner critic voice to start up again, without us even noticing. Step Nine is not about giving ourselves an emotional horsewhipping. Rather, it's the final of the house cleaning Steps, and is therefore designed to help us to finally feel comfortable in our own skin. Allowing the inner critic to start bullying us will derail that necessary quality.

Now is a great time to use those tools we discussed in Step Six for putting that inner critic in its place. One of those tools is to turn self-criticism into self-correction. The very best way to do this is to make some amends to ourselves. Just like when we make amends to others, our action amends to ourselves should fit the damage they are intended to repair.

We ripped ourselves apart mentally, physically, socially, financially, vocationally, and spiritually by our addiction. It's OK to look ourselves in the mirror and apologize for that, making verbal amends to ourselves. We can also take the opportunity in Step Nine to make living amends to ourselves, by renewing our commitment to our powerlessness and our commitment to complete our Steps and to continue doing the things we need to do to stay sober (such as going to meetings, reading the Big Book, connecting with our sponsor and others in recovery, living by our spiritual principles, and so on). We should commit to remaining with the program and fellowship for life. This is our best way to never have to go through that devastating experience again, and it's also the best way to repair the psychological and mental damage done by our substance use.

As well, we can make action amends to ourselves by doing some self-care. Step Nine is a great chance to take a look at self-care, because for most of us it has been a very long time since we have done anything like that, and good habits can be difficult to initiate. Turning our attention to proper diet, starting an exercise program of some sort, taking leisure time rather than allowing our obsessive tendencies keep us too work-focused, and getting some regular and adequate sleep are a good start. I also suggest that all people in recovery get a family doctor and become involved in their own health. One particularly nice amends we can do for ourselves for the mental and spiritual aspects is meditation. In our Step Eleven discussion we will explore exactly what meditation is, the powerful things it can do for us, and how to do it. Embracing meditation and making it a regular habit is a really nice self-care amends to ourselves.

Too, self-care should involve giving ourselves some well-deserved treats on a regular basis. Little things, like going for a mani/pedi, planning a trip, going for a nice night out, buying ourselves something nice that we totally don't need, and so on.

While Step Nine is not about self-focus, it's an important aspect of our ongoing health and well-being that we learn to take care of ourselves after the years of self-abuse and self-neglect. We are no good to anyone if we are not in good physical, mental, and spiritual health. Sick bodies do not house healthy minds.

*

Meditation and prayer prior to each verbal amend is an excellent tool for keeping our focus on what our amend is really about, and giving us a gut-check to make sure that our motives for making the amend are correct and that our plans are sound. It also provides a way to involve our higher power in the process. The Big Book does not give us a ninth Step prayer, but I have heard a few suggested ones passed around the fellowship. Here are four of them:

> Higher power, I pray for the right attitude to make my amends, being ever mindful not to harm others in the process. I ask for your guidance in making amends. Most important, I will continue to make amends by staying abstinent, helping others & growing in spiritual progress.

> Higher power, give me the strength and direction to do the right thing no matter what the consequences may be. Help me to consider others and not harm them in any way. Help me to consult with others before I take any actions that would cause me to be sorry. Help me to not repeat such behaviors. Show me the way of patience, tolerance, kindliness, and love and help me live the spiritual life.

> Higher power, with regard to this amend, give me the strength, courage and direction to do the right thing, no matter what the personal consequences may be. Help me not to shrink from anything. Help me not to delay if it can be avoided. Help me to be

sensible, tactful, considerate and humble without being servile or scraping.

Where I have done wrong, help me do right.
I have done enough harm, and I ask your help, so that I may do no more.
I'll need more courage than I've got, help me be strong.
I've been selfish, help me be selfless.
Come what may, help me bear it.
As I have in the past harmed completely, help me to finish this, completely.
I have been willful and hurtful; please grant me humility and humanity.
Help me be better for you and for others.

If you aren't comfortable with the idea of prayer, it's appropriate to think of prayer as a brief, focused meditation directed at a higher power, whatever that may be to you. More on that in Step Eleven.

*

Be ready for lots of surprises as you progress through Step Nine. The greatest surprise that I had when doing my amends was with my kids. They were 11 and 12 years old when I got sober, old enough to comprehend that I had been an absolute zero as a father during my drinking and using days. They could remember from beforehand that I had always been an active and involved father, so they could see how far downhill I went when my drinking and using took over my life. Then, I constantly chose alcohol and drugs over them.

For example, I remember one Friday when they came to my house for the weekend. There was a new Star Wars movie out that we all wanted to see, so we planned to go to the movies that night. I steeled myself that I wouldn't drink until after the movie, so as not to let down my kids... again. However – predictably – by the time movie time came around I was drunk and passed out on the couch. When the kids woke me to go to the movies I told them I was feeling sick and we couldn't go. Great.

Next morning, when I came to, I was wracked with guilt about ruining our plans to go out to the movies, so I told the kids we'd make up for it by going to the beach that afternoon. Again, I steeled myself to stay sober and follow through with my promise. Once again, the kids woke me – passed out drunk on the couch – and once again the plans were a bust. We ended up spending the entire weekend without leaving the house, with the kids fending for themselves by helping themselves to whatever they could find in the fridge for their meals. Another wasted, irretrievable weekend of being a zero as a father.

When it came time to make my verbal amends with my kids I was terrified. I knew they were going to be very hard on me and I knew I deserved it. I put it off until the last of my planned verbal amends. I talked it over with my sponsor many times, I consulted a friend who is a church minister, and I talked to a number of other parents in the fellowship. When I finally screwed up the courage I approached each of my kids and explained everything to them, acknowledged the harm I had done them, and told them that I was healing and getting better so that this wouldn't happen anymore.

So, what happened? Well, in both cases they said exactly the same thing: *OK dad!* That was it. They let me off the hook. I thought that maybe in six months everything I had said would sink in and they would unload on me with both barrels. However, here it is years later and they haven't said a word about it. I think they were just glad that the experience was over and they had a dad again.

Speaking of kids, I've noticed that a lot of parents in the fellowship carry guilt because they believe that they have passed the "alcoholism-addiction" gene on to their kids. While a review of the specifics is beyond the scope of our discussion here, suffice it to say that this guilt is misplaced. The genetics of alcoholism-addiction don't operate in a straightforward way, and have a variable effect on our kids. Genetics are only half the cause, the other half being life circumstances. Besides, our knowledge of our disease and its causes and our ability to smell addiction behavior from a mile away make us incredibly adept parents in terms of talking to our kids about addiction and helping them when they are in trouble. We can talk to our kids about drinking and drugs like no other parent can. In the end, we remember the advice of the Serenity Prayer, which tells us to accept the things we cannot change – like our genetics – and the courage to change the things we can – such as how we talk to our kids about drugs and alcohol. Anyone who wants to know more about the heritability of addiction-alcoholism and the effects of our disease on our children is invited to check out my book *The Alcoholic/Addict Within: Our Brain, Genetics, Psychology, and the Twelve Steps as Psychotherapy.* The specifics of genetics and our disease and whether or not our kids will be affected is explained in detail in that informative book. I'm told it's an excellent read!

*

Holding on to any guilt or remorse for amends that we cannot make is an exercise in self-harm; it's just our inner critic and our neurotic need for perfection trying to bully us. Easy does it, many of our amends come with

302

time, sometimes years into recovery. After all, we can never undo the past, we can only do our best to make amends as the opportunities arise.

Step Nine is one that we never really finish, so how do we know when it's time to move on to Step Ten? When we have made our verbal amends with everyone on our Step Eight list whom we can reach, and for whom immediate verbal amends are appropriate, when we have a plan for our action amends, living amends, and deferred amends in place, and when we have initiated the habit of doing action amends on an ongoing basis, we are ready to move on. If you're there and your sponsor agrees, let's now move on to Step Ten.

Step Ten

Continued to take personal inventory and when we were wrong promptly admitted it.

Step Ten is where: "we commence to put our A.A. way of living to practical use, day by day, in fair weather or foul" (*Twelve Steps and Twelve Traditions*, p. 88). We have completed the "action Steps" and cleaned house, and Step Ten is how we keep the house clean. While Steps Ten through Twelve are sometimes referred to as the "maintenance Steps," I prefer to call them the growth Steps. It's true that these are the Steps that enable us to maintain recovery for a lifetime, but they are also the Steps that enable ongoing spiritual growth, thereby strengthening our health, happiness, and well-being. We can't be satisfied with maintenance, or we will stagnate; we must seek growth.

We have just completed a thorough and salutary house cleaning. However, our character defects will always be locked in battle with our spirituality for control of our thoughts and behaviors. We have just experienced a miraculous psychological and spiritual transformation by our trip through the first nine Steps. We're starting to feel better physically. Things are coming back to us. We may even be on a pink cloud. We're feeling pretty good about ourselves, and it's a natural reaction to congratulate ourselves and then lay back and be happy with what we've achieved. But, as the Big Book reminds us: "it is easy to let up on the spiritual program of action and rest on our laurels. We are headed for trouble if we do, for alcohol is a subtle foe. We can flat out become cocky in our recovery and lose contact with our higher power and let go of our program of recovery. We are not cured of alcoholism. What we actually have is a daily reprieve contingent on the maintenance of our spiritual condition" (p. 85). The purpose of Step Ten is to make sure that we don't make the mistake of resting on our laurels and becoming complacent. We've worked hard to clean house, and Step Ten provides us with the tools to keep it clean. Step Ten is there to safeguard and strengthen the amazing progress we have made. We get better at spiritual living and learn from our day-to-day experiences, which strengthens our recovery and makes us better able to help others.

Simply maintaining our spiritualty requires ongoing attention, but we want more than that; we want to *grow* in spirituality. To do this, we must take care of our spirituality just as we take care of our bodies: "for the wise have always known that no one can make much of his life until self-searching becomes a regular habit, until he is able to admit and accept what he finds, and until he patiently and persistently tries to correct what is wrong" (*Twelve Steps and Twelve Traditions*, p. 88). We use exercise, healthy food, and our daily self-care rituals (such as taking a shower, brushing our teeth, etc.) to take care of our body, and we use Step Ten to take care of our spirituality. Step Ten is the toothbrush for our mental and spiritual well-being.

Recent discoveries into the anatomical and physiological changes to the brain that occur with addiction lend authority to what the Big Book has been telling us since the 1930s: we are never cured of addiction.[1,2,3,4,5] These addiction-related brain changes endure for the rest of our life, and can be reactivated at any time, even decades into recovery. As such, the science confirms that recovery is, in fact, a daily reprieve from the effects of these brain changes, and even a single drink or drug can put us back to where we were before, or worse. This has been the vast experience of the fellowship over the past near-century, and it has been validated by these recent discoveries from neuroscience. We need our growth Steps to maintain our recovery, good health, and function, and we need them to grow in our spirituality and recovery. This all starts with the conscientious practice of our Step Ten.

*

Step Ten involves doing a mini-version of Steps Four through Nine every day: "we continue to take personal inventory and continue to set right any new mistakes as we go along... to grow in understanding and effectiveness" (Big Book, p. 84). The value of this exercise in living is that it keeps us from accumulating the same anger, resentments, and other mental chaos that once led up to our obsessive substance use. Step Ten allows us to correct and learn from our mistakes on a daily basis, rather than allowing them to accumulate and snowball. As we've discussed in our earlier Steps, the character defects and unlovely tendencies that once ruled our lives are ingrained in human nature, and old tendencies can easily creep back in as we face life in sobriety. Step Ten provides us with the tools to keep us vigilant against the ever-present character defects that are embedded in human nature. We already have the skills from the previous nine Steps; Step Ten is where we blend them with our daily lives to make them our blueprint for healthy living.

Step ten involves taking inventory of our actions on a daily basis ("continued to take personal inventory"). There are two ways that we do this: 1) a review of our day at the end of the day, and 2) spot-checks as significant events occur through the day. *Twelve Steps and Twelve Traditions* explains:

> There's the spot-check inventory, taken at any time of the day, whenever we find ourselves getting tangled up. There's the one we take at day's end, when we review the happenings of the hours just past. Here we cast up a balance sheet, crediting ourselves with things well done, and chalking up debits where due (p. 89).

This is where we grow and learn in spirituality. Despite our house cleaning, we remain human, subject to human nature and weaknesses of mind and spirit. But, we can get better. Rather than allow our spiritual failings to accumulate as guilt, or allow our inner-critic to beat ourselves up over it, Step Ten is the process whereby we turn to self-correction and reject self-criticism. The Big Book reminds us that spirituality is a virtue that must be worked on:

> Do not be discouraged. No one among us has been able to maintain anything like perfect adherence to these principles. We are not saints. The point is, that we are willing to grow along spiritual lines. The principles we have set down are guides to progress. We claim spiritual progress rather than spiritual perfection (p. 60).

Step Ten is our tool for ensuring spiritual progress. Some people do a big Step Ten overhaul every once in a while to complement their daily reflections:

> Then there are those occasions when alone, or in the company of our sponsor or spiritual adviser, we make a careful review of our progress since the last time. Many A.A.'s go in for annual or semiannual housecleanings. Many of us also like the experience of an occasional retreat from the outside world where we can quiet down for an undisturbed day or so of self-overhaul and meditation (*Twelve Steps and Twelve Traditions*, p. 89).

To illustrate the value of Step Ten to sobriety as well as peace of mind and happiness we can step back for a moment and look at what it does from a psychological perspective. Obsessive substance use, regardless of how it started, becomes a coping mechanism for life's difficulties. Compulsive substance use is, at its core, a dysfunctional coping mechanism. There comes a point where the substance use is no longer fun or enjoyable, but it becomes a necessary ongoing activity to avoid withdrawal and to escape from an increasingly intolerable life and a malignant negative psychology.

Up to this point our Step activities have been about converting ourselves from a deeply negative psychology to a positive psychology. This allows us to begin accepting life on life's terms, accepting the things in life that we cannot change as life's reality, and finding the courage to face the life problems that we can do something about. The key to preventing the same conditions that was both cause and effect of substance use – the downward spiral of feeling overwhelmed and victimized by life, and the negative feelings and emotions – we must use our tools to prevent life from getting under our skin. Step Ten is our daily check and balance that we are not surrendering our peace and serenity to other people or things.

At the end of each day, as we turn our attention to our Step Ten, we can look back and review how we reacted to the significant events of the day. Rather than allow things to accumulate and begin their inevitable downward spiral, we can catch things and learn from them. We practice self-correction rather than self-criticism: "we must be careful not to drift into worry, remorse or morbid reflection, for that would diminish our usefulness to others. After making our review we ask God's forgiveness and inquire what corrective measures should be taken" (Big Book, p. 86). This not only keeps our house clean, but is also how we fortify our recovery and spirituality: "we grow by our willingness to face and rectify errors and convert them into assets" (Big Book, p. 124).

Wait, what? We have to do Step Ten every day? What a pain in the butt! Actually, not so much. As we get used to taking the few minutes we need to reflect back on our day, it becomes a daily practice that allows us to go to bed at night at peace with the day, and in good spiritual standing. Good habits take some time to establish, but over time the Step Ten reflection at the end of the day becomes automatic, and often quick: "... at length our inventories become a regular part of everyday living, rather than something unusual or set apart" (*Twelve Steps and Twelve Traditions*, p. 90). Some days, there's not much to think over. As we become more practiced in our daily Step Ten reflection the process becomes efficient and streamlined. Soon, we find that if we skip our daily Step Ten reflection we feel out of sorts. That out of sorts feeling can be the beginning of a downward slide, possibly to relapse. Brushing our teeth takes a little time and effort, but we make it part of our daily routine in order to maintain our teeth. How much more sense does it make to take the little time and effort to maintain our peace of mind and recovery?

*

As you may recall from our discussion of Step Six, I have this little hobby where I collect character defects on a list, and my list appears at the end of the book in Appendix 2. A little routine that I use in my daily Step Ten practice is that I pick three character defects off the list and reflect back on how I have been doing with them lately. I go through the list from start to finish, picking three character defects every day to ponder. This gives me a way to make sure that I don't have any character defects that are flying under the radar undetected. For each character defect I reflect on how and when it has been coming up, and what lessons I can take from the experiences so as to better myself. It works for me, as a little Step Ten trick to help me do a better job of playing whack-a-mole with my character defects.

Most people go through life carrying some degree of anger, resentments, and many are governed by their character defects, blissfully unaware of the negative psychology and detriment to their happiness and peace of mind that comes from it. There are a lot of very angry and resentful people out there, some a little bit, some a lot. You only have to drive on a busy roadway to see that for yourself. That's fine for them, they can afford to be like that. For us, however, it's a matter of life and death, because in the past such anger and resentment drove us to drink or drug, and old habits can easily find us again as our disease tries to snake its way back into our psyche. As *Living Sober* tells us: "hostility, resentment, anger – whatever word you use to describe this feeling – seems to have a close tie-up with intoxication and maybe even a deeper one with alcoholism" (p. 37). If we allow those things to well up in us again, we may well relapse right back to where we were. Step Ten is our defense from that happening.

*

From a medical and psychological point of view, Step Ten fulfills two functions: 1) to maintain, strengthen, and improve upon the high level of positive psychology achieved from doing the first nine Steps, and 2) to prevent relapse to drug or alcohol use. Step Ten is about maintaining and growing in spirituality, but the reason we are here is to seek a daily reprieve from our obsession with drug and alcohol, for: "we are not cured of alcoholism. What we really have is a daily reprieve contingent on the maintenance of our spiritual condition" (Big Book, p. 85). So, our newfound spirituality is a wonderful thing for allowing us to live life with newfound
308

life skills, but the bottom line is maintaining our daily reprieve; i.e. relapse prevention. We are using our spirituality to avoid that downward spiral of negative psychology that leads people like us to seek solace in drugs or alcohol. Our spirituality is what stands between us and our next drink or drug, so we need to take care. In my work I have seen time and again where people who have let go of maintaining their spirituality fall into relapse, much like my friend Liam, who relapsed just before the ten year anniversary of his sobriety. I'll tell you about Liam shortly.

When you look at the relapse prevention techniques that are used by professional addiction counselors in accredited addiction treatment programs, they are all derived from the 12 Step program. So, let's have a quick look at these and tie them in to our own recovery.

Surveys of people who have relapsed show a few common factors: stress intolerance, depressed mood, anxiety, drug-related cues, temptations and boredom, and lack of positive supports (e.g., job, family, relationships, responsibilities).[6] These are generalities, and some factors may be more of a danger than others for specific people. As well, there are other factors, such as feeling lonely, but these were the most prevalent factors identified in published studies. As alcoholic-addicts in recovery, it's good for us to be aware of the kinds of things that lead to relapse so that we can be mindful and take action if these things are occurring with us.

Each person in recovery should reflect on what his or her own triggers are. A tool for recognizing common relapse triggers is the HALT acronym. HALT stands for **H**ungry, **A**ngry, **L**onely, or **T**ired. The purpose of HALT is to allow us to recognize these factors when they occur, so that we can act on them lest they become a trigger for relapse. These are all self-care issues that mean that we need to take a moment to look after ourselves. Race car drivers know that they can't win a race unless they pull over for a pit-stop once in a while, and so it is with us. We can ask friends and family members to alert us if they notice we are edgy, or self-isolating, or not eating properly, or not getting enough rest. And we must listen to them, because denial is in our nature. Our Step Ten reflection should include some mindful reflection to see if we have been experiencing any of these factors. We should have an action plan if any HALT symptoms or other relapse-related cues become a factor for us. First and foremost, if we see relapse factors in ourselves we should get it out. We can talk to family or friends about it, but it's always best to speak with someone who understands our disease and has some experience in recovery; talking to our sponsor about it, going to a meeting and sharing, or talking to someone else in the fellowship are all great ways to head off the beginnings of a relapse.

Research into relapse has shown that relapse is a process, not an event.[7] One study found that people admitted that their relapse had been developing over a period of at least three weeks, often longer. So, recognizing and arresting the process of relapse before it plays out is key. We will discuss exactly how to do that. We will also discuss how these actions to head off relapse can be planned out and practiced in advance as part of an effective relapse prevention strategy. Step Ten plays heavily into that process, because it involves a daily examination of how our recovery and spiritual health are doing, as well as a commitment to taking action if all is not well.

Another important principle for relapse prevention is realizing that recovery requires much more than just quitting drinking or using. If we don't address all the mental stuff that put us there in the first place and worsened during our active drinking and using, then we will be at very high risk of relapse. That's the genius of the 12 Step program: it's directed specifically at cleaning up the mental carnage that was both cause and effect of our substance use. I noted when I came to the 12 Step program that nobody in the fellowship ever said to me: *dude, you need to stop drinking and using drugs, you're going to lose everything and kill yourself.* Nobody ever said that to me. The focus of our program is not on "saying no" to drinking or using drugs. Rather the focus is on mental and spiritual health, a state of healthy positive psychology whereby the need for drink and drug as an escape from life and negative emotions falls away. When we are addicts or alcoholics we cope with stress by drinking or using drugs. It's what we do. So, in order to stay in recovery we need to develop new, healthy coping mechanisms. Our spiritual principles allow us to handle life on life's terms, without allowing life to get under our skin. We become master copers. Of course, once we achieve the healthy mind-set and way of living that rescued us from our addiction-alcoholism, we must maintain that same positive psychology to remain in recovery. Our Step Ten is our daily check-up on this process, the key to our ongoing recovery.

The U.S. National Institute of Drug Abuse (NIDA) developed the acronym TIPS to remind alcoholics and addicts in recovery of how to cope with difficult life situations. TIPS stands for: **T**ruth, **I**nformation, **P**riorities, and **S**upport. These principles are taken straight from the 12 Step program. Let's take a look at them, because they reinforce some important aspects of our program in general, and Step Ten's role in relapse prevention in particular:

> **Truth** means that we need to be rigorously honest about any struggles we are experiencing. The human tendency to keep our struggles to ourselves is magnified in alcoholic-addicts, because we tend to isolate, avoid, and run when we are in trouble. The fellowship provides us with ample safe, understanding, and trustworthy people to talk to at any time of day when we need to.

Information means we learn about our disease and what things we need to do to stay healthy, spiritually well, and in recovery. Reading the Big Book and other 12 Step literature, absorbing information from meetings and interacting with other members of the fellowship, and reading about the science of addiction and relapse prevention help us build a knowledge base that we can use for mindful practice of our Step Ten, as well as for helping others.

Priorities means that we see the number one priority as staying sober. If we put our recovery first, all the other good stuff will follow. If we put other stuff ahead of our recovery and we relapse, we will lose everything again. So, recovery must come first. This is the basis of the slogan "First Things First."

Support reminds us to turn to others for support when we're in a difficult situation, before it's too late. Again, our fellowship and our sponsor fulfill this role in a way that someone who is not in recovery wouldn't be able to. Many people who relapse are lacking in a healthy support system. The fellowship provides a rich source of experience, support, and understanding, and our spiritual way of living promotes the healthy interactions needed to also establish a support system outside of the fellowship.

Addiction counselors teach their clients to use the "big three" relapse prevention tools, all of which are – again – borrowed from the 12 Step program. Again, let's have a quick look at these so that we can relate them to our program and be sure that they form a part of our relapse prevention tool-kit:

Remember when: when our addict-alcoholic mind starts telling us that drinking or using is or was fun, we defeat the deceit by thinking back to all the pain, misery, sickness, loss, and regret that our substance use caused us, how badly we wanted to be able to stop, and how hard it was to stop. Remembering specific situations that were especially painful during our drinking or using days is helpful. "Remember When" is one of the 12 Step slogans. In our Step Eleven study we will discuss how to combine this slogan with some simple meditation techniques to crush psychological cravings for drug or drink.

Follow the tape through to the end: when our disease tries to talk us into drinking or using, it just thinks about "the party." However, by playing the tape through to the end, we follow through in our mind what happens after the party, the next day, and so on. We imagine the guilt, self-disappointment, shame, sickness, and renewed obsession to drink or use that will follow "the party." This is sometimes described as "following the drink or drug through to its inevitable outcome." This challenges our disease's powerful ability to rationalize just about anything, and provides an effective counter to the "insanity of alcoholism-addiction" – which is our belief that THIS time we will be able to control our drinking or using.

Actively avoid high-risk situations: it's much easier to say no at the beginning than it is at the end. We should cut off a high-risk situation as soon as we recognize it developing, rather than allow it to progress to where getting ourselves out of it will be very difficult. Many of the people who relapse do so after allowing themselves to get into a situation that they knew very well was high-risk. This is the basis of the 12 Step slogan "New People, Places, and Things." Hanging around with people who are still drinking or using, in the places where we used to drink or use, and doing the same things we used to do when we were in active addiction are going to get us in trouble. We need new people, places, and things.

*

There's one aspect related to relapse that we should especially watch out for in our Step Ten reflection: complacency. If we lose touch with our Step One – our appreciation of our powerlessness over addictive substances – and if we take our recovery for granted, or we stop doing our recovery activities we court disaster. Whether we have been in recovery for 10 days or 10,000 days, our next drink or drug is only an arm's length away. We must always remain grateful for our last 24 hours of recovery, and do what we need to do to make sure the next 24 hours will be safe and sober. It has widely been the experience within 12 Step program that as people drift away from the fellowship they become increasingly susceptible to relapse. When we have had some success with our recovery, and the drug or alcohol obsession, thoughts and cravings have long ago faded, we can easily become complacent and even cocky.

I have a special interest in studying relapse in my research activities, and what I have found from hundreds of interviews that I have conducted is that as people drift away from the program, they lose touch with their Step One. Their belief in their powerlessness fades and they get into trouble. It's as if our disease really is out in the parking lot doing push-ups waiting for us to falter.

As I mentioned in our Step One study, when it comes to recovery, I consider myself to be privileged to be able to live and walk among "normal" humans, and to live a normal, happy and productive life despite my horrible substance addiction. Although I am privileged to live among "normal" people, I can only do so as long as I remember ONE thing: I am not like them. They can go out for beer after work, but I can't. As long as I remember that, I will be fine. When I remain in the program I have constant reminders of my powerlessness – meetings, reading my Big Book, working with newcomers, doing my Step Ten every day – and it keeps my head in the game. But if I drift away from the program eventually my alcoholic-addict brain begins to think that because I live among normal people, I must be like them. That's when we relapse. It really does work that way.

I have a friend in the program whose experience is a good illustration of what I'm talking about. My friend Liam – I mentioned him a few pages ago – was a low-bottom cocaine and alcohol addict who found healthy recovery in the 12 Step program. He ran a good program, did all the stuff suggested of him, and benefited with a full return to good health and function without the obsession to drink or use drugs. And then he let go of his recovery program.

Just after he celebrated nine years of recovery Liam drifted away from the 12 Step fellowship. He lost contact with most of the people he knew in the fellowship, including his sponsor, he no longer sponsored or reached out to newcomers, he stopped reading his Big Book, he no longer went to meetings, he stopped his Step Ten reflection at the end of the day, and he stopped praying/meditating regularly. In other words, he stopped doing those things he needed to do to be in recovery. His rationale: he was too busy for that stuff now, and he was good anyway; after all it had been nearly a decade since his last drink or drug, *right?*

When he was only a few weeks from what would have been his tenth anniversary in recovery Liam was travelling through Italy with his girlfriend. They had stopped for the night in a little Italian town and were having dinner at the *locanda* (inn) where they were staying. In that town there was a specific traditional liqueur that had been made locally since the 19th century, and the innkeeper came to Liam's table and offered Liam and his girlfriend a shot of this special liqueur on the house. Liam declined, of course, but the innkeeper appeared nettled by the refusal to partake, so Liam's girlfriend pressed him to take it. *It's just one shot, Liam!* She knew he was an alcoholic-addict, but she didn't understand the nature of our disease. She also hadn't known him when he was in active addiction-alcoholism. So, Liam acquiesced and took the innocuous-looking little one-ounce shot. After all, *what harm could it do? It had been ten years, right?*

For the next three days, as Liam and his girlfriend toured Italy, Liam was completely rocked by an obsession with that one innocent little shot of alcohol that he had taken; he could think of nothing else. No matter what they did or saw, Liam could only think of that shot of liqueur. When they got on the plane to go home he got so drunk that he had to be helped off the plane in a wheelchair when they landed. So started an eight-month bender of alcohol and $1,000 a day cocaine use that again took him to his bottom. I'm pleased to say that Liam is once again with us in recovery in the 12 Step fellowship, this time with us to stay, I'm sure.

As Liam discovered, we need to keep our head in the game, and staying the course in the program is the best way for us to do that. The cost is too high when we wander away. Based on Liam's experience, which is far from unique, I suggest that we recognize a red flag if, during our Step Ten reflection, we note any of the troubling signs of losing contact with the program, such as: becoming cocky or over-confident in our recovery, entertaining the belief that we could drink or use again and control it because we've been in recovery long enough, or stopping doing the things we need to do to stay in recovery (our Step-related practices from Steps Ten, Eleven, and Twelve, going to meetings, contact with our sponsor and other people in recovery, reading the Big Book, learning about our disease, etc.).

I suggest a few measures if we feel we are slipping away from our program. Getting together with our sponsor to discuss it, contacting other people in recovery to maintain that spiritual contact, meditating/praying on the subject, reading the Big Book, or going to a meeting.

If you find yourself getting bored with your recovery program I suggest making it interesting again. Go to some different groups for meetings, reach out to newcomers, get involved in putting on meetings at the local jail or detox center or hospital, get involved in (or even start) a Big Book study group, pick up a book from the 12 Step literature that you haven't read before, get involved in service work, and so on. Write a book, if that's your thing.

There's no prescribed number of meetings that we should go to, and some people have limited access to meetings due to geographical, health, or financial reasons. There are excellent on-line meetings for those who have a problem with getting out. How many we need depends a lot on where we are in our recovery and what's going on in our lives. When I was in the detox center the counselors suggested that I should attend 90 meetings in the first 90 days of my recovery, and I thought they were crazy. However, I must have been the one who was crazy, because I ended up doing 172 meetings in 90 days. I really liked the meetings and they helped me. Nowadays, I go to two or three meetings a week, but there are times when I only get to one for some reason or other, but I don't allow it to become a habit. Sometimes I need more. People can tell when they're not getting to enough meetings. If they're feeling restless, irritable, like life is getting under their skin, or their addiction is trying to assert itself again, they probably need more meetings, more contact with others in recovery, more time with their sponsor, more time to read the Big Book, and more time for prayer/meditation. When facing a particularly stressful time in our lives – which is bound to happen from time to time – going to more meetings is likely a good idea, especially if we find that the stress is getting to us. Our Step Ten reflection is a good time to identify if we need to hit more meetings.

*

When we do our Step Ten reflection we should remember that we are there to take our inventory for the day, and we should resist the urge to take inventory for the other people we encountered that day. That applies especially to situations where we have allowed people or things to get under our skin, to make us angry or resentful. We want to address our anger and resentments, not the perceived wrongdoings of the people we allowed to get under our skin. As we are told in *Twelve Steps and Twelve Traditions*: "it is a spiritual axiom that every time we are disturbed, there is something wrong *with us*. If someone hurts us and we are sore, we are in the wrong also" (p. 90). It doesn't matter if our anger toward the other individual is justified or not, what matters is that anger and resentments kill people like us:

> Few people have been more victimized by resentments than have we alcoholics. It mattered little whether our resentments were justified or not. A burst of temper could spoil a day, and a well-nursed grudge could make us miserably ineffective. Nor were we ever skillful in separating justified from unjustified anger. As we saw it, our wrath was always justified. Anger, that occasional luxury of more balanced people, could keep us on an emotional jag indefinitely. These emotional 'dry benders' often led straight to the bottle. Other kinds of disturbances – jealousy, envy, self-pity, or hurt pride – did the same thing (*Twelve Steps and Twelve Traditions*, p.90).

This is important. If we find ourselves ruminating on someone else's wrongs during our Step Ten reflection, then we are feeding a new resentment. It benefits our spirituality and our recovery not one bit to reflect on other people's perceived wrongs. We apply the Serenity Prayer and accept the things we cannot change – someone else's actions – but we change the things we can – our reactions. Besides, other people wronging us is a normal part of life; anybody who really expects to go through life without anybody ever hurting or wronging them are not living life on life's terms, and they are setting themselves up for frustration, anger, and resentment. Expectations lead to resentments, and when we expect that everyone in the world is going to behave just the way we want them to and in a way that is pleasing to us we are asking for frustration and resentment.

So, even if we were done wrong we reflect on what we did with it, how we handled it, why we allowed it to get under our skin. And then we let it go; we leave it with our higher power. If it's still bothering us we should discuss it with our sponsor. In Step Eleven we will discuss how to use simple meditation to calm the spirit and let go of ugly emotions. Those negative emotions are like a tiny stone in our shoe; if left there long enough they can cause festering wounds. In the meantime, we have our tools from Steps Four and Five for unburdening ourselves of anger and resentment. If our Step Ten reflection doesn't do it, we should consider doing a mini-Step Four with our sponsor to crush the resentment and learn from the experience.

*

As we become more accustomed to our Step Ten routine, we find ourselves doing a quick mental Step Ten reflection during the day's events, as significant events happen. This is when we catch ourselves when some person or thing gets under our skin and we feel those unlovely character defects surging up inside of us: "a spot-check inventory taken in the midst of such disturbances can be of very great help in quieting stormy emotions... especially those where people or new events throw us off balance and tempt us to make mistakes" (*Twelve Steps and Twelve Traditions*, p. 90-91).

All the better for us if we catch ourselves before, caught up in the initial anger, we lash out or do something we'll regret. With time, we get accustomed to this "spot-check" inventory, and we are able to catch ourselves before we react out of emotion in the heat of the moment. Better to catch ourselves and use our higher brain functions to get through the situation with thought and consideration and with our spiritual principles intact, rather than react out of emotion and primitive reflexes. This situational Step Ten "spot-check" is a great tool for enabling us to live according to our spiritual principles in bad times as well as in good: "in all these situations we need self-restraint, honest analysis of what is involved, a willingness to admit when the fault is ours, and an equal willingness to forgive when the fault is elsewhere" (*Twelve Steps and Twelve Traditions*, p. 91).

We are not perfect spiritual beings; sometimes we fail to catch ourselves, and our natural tendencies to lash out get the better of us. That's fine. We can't undo the past and rather than beat ourselves up about it we use our tools to turn off the self-criticism and turn it into self-correction. We do this by reflecting on the incident in our Step Ten reflection at the end of the day: "we need not be discouraged when we fall into the error of our old ways, for these disciplines are not easy. We shall look for progress, not

316

perfection" (*Twelve Steps and Twelve Traditions*, p. 91). We give ourselves a break, easy does it.

Just as we let go of anger and resentments in Steps Four and Five, so can we use our tools to let go of anger and resentments when we fulfill our Step Ten. Understanding people who have wronged us, or whom we don't like helps us to change our attitude:

> Finally, we begin to see that all people, including ourselves, are to some extent emotionally ill as well as frequently wrong, and then we approach true tolerance and see what real love for our fellows actually is. It will become more evident as we go forward that it is pointless to become angry, or to get hurt by people who, like us, are suffering from the pains of growing up (*Twelve Steps and Twelve Traditions*, p. 92).

When we realize that other people who behave in an unkind or selfish way are sick, albeit probably less so than we once were, we can at least understand them. Our behavior before we undertook a program of spiritual wellness was deplorable, after all. Let he or she who is without sin cast the first stone. We are fortunate in that we have a program that helped us to become well and to rid ourselves of those dark character defects that haunted our lives and drove our actions. If anything, we should feel compassion and empathy for those angry people who don't have a program like ours and are still ruled by anger, resentment, and defects of character.

When someone wrongs us or there's interpersonal animosity, there's little that offers the ability to repair negative feelings like a kind word or a good deed to that person. When we catch ourselves with our "spot-check" inventory as an unsavory life situation unfolds, nothing defuses the anger and conflict like applied spirituality: "courtesy, kindness, justice, and love are the keynotes by which we may come into harmony with practically anyone" (*Twelve Steps and Twelve Traditions*, p. 93). A kind word, or even a smile will help defuse an otherwise difficult or tense situation, and usually surprises us with the outcome that it produces. That's spirituality applied to life: using a healthy connection with another person in order to head off using a defect of character, with positive results.

Despite our newfound spiritual health, to expect to go through life without feelings of anger welling up from time to time is entirely unrealistic. Rather, our spiritual health depends on what we do with those angry feelings when they well up and seep out of our pores. The undisciplined mind will react and lash out, but we are learning to end anger's power to determine our actions for us. *Wait, what?* How do we get a "disciplined" mind? We'll talk about that in our Step Eleven discussion. In the meantime, we can use our spiritual tools to help us stop anger's power over us in our

Step Ten "spot-checks." Our sobriety and spiritual health depend on it. Being angry sucks. Something as small as stopping up our mouth and taking a few deep breaths may be all it takes, especially as we become practiced at living by our spiritual principles.

Spirituality is our greatest asset to admitting our mistakes, being open-minded to other people's opinions and ideas, and defusing unnecessary conflict. Pride and ego that require validation and propping up do not allow people to admit they are wrong or to take the high road when they are right. Our spirituality promotes a healthy self-esteem, humility, and patience, tolerance and empathy. This mind-set allows us to be the bigger person to defuse difficult situations. We no longer need to be "right" like we did when we were ruled by ego. Spirituality allows us to get outside ourselves and to see things from others' perspective, and to understand them when they are wrong. Besides our spirituality, the program lays at our feet other tools for those times that our spirituality falters.

The 12 Step literature offers some suggestions about some tools we may use to deal with feelings of anger when they arise (these suggestions are found on pages 39 to 40 of *Living Sober*). The focus is on coping with anger (and other negative feelings) when they arise, whether or not we feel they are justified. These tools include: 1) taking something to eat or drink, 2) picking up the phone and talking to our sponsor or another alcoholic-addict in recovery, 3) pausing to think about whether or not we are over-tired (or over-stressed), 4) pondering the 12 Step slogan "Live and Let Live," 5) switching to an activity that has nothing to do with the source of our anger, 6) losing ourselves in exercise or listening to music, 7) contemplating the ideas of the Serenity Prayer – often what we are angry about is something that we cannot possibly change, so the sensible thing to do is just accept it rather than boil inside or turn to alcohol or drugs, 8) changing the thing we are angry about if we can, rather than raging about it, 9) using the "as if" idea – we think about how a mature, well-balanced person would handle the situation and we act "as if" we were that person, and 10) seeking outside help (such as a counselor or a person of the clergy). The overall idea is that: "simply repressing, glossing over, or damming up anger rarely helps. Instead, we try to learn not to act *on* it, but to do something about it. If we don't, we increase enormously our chances of drinking" (*Living Sober*, p. 40).

*

Our spiritual spot-checks are great for helping us defeat our primitive urges to answer the call of our character defects, but the meat of Step Ten is: "when evening comes, perhaps just before going to sleep, many of us draw up a balance sheet for the day" (*Twelve Steps and Twelve Traditions*, p. 93). This is our daily inventory, the real substance of our Step Ten, and it's a life-

318

long commitment: "this is not an overnight matter. It should continue for our lifetime. Continue to watch for selfishness, dishonesty, resentment, and fear. When these crop up, we ask God at once to remove them. We discuss them with someone immediately and make amends quickly if we have harmed anyone. Then we resolutely turn our thoughts to someone we can help. Love and tolerance is our code" (Big Book, p. 84).

It may seem like a lot to ask, to add yet another thing to our already hectic day. However, before too long the Step Ten reflection becomes a welcome end to the day, a healthy habit that helps us wind down and gives us a nice feeling, as any good habit does. And we get better at it. It often amounts to a matter of a few minutes, especially if nothing particularly bothersome happened that day. After everything we've been through and how far we've come in our progress through the Steps, it's a small price to pay for ongoing peace of mind, serenity, spiritual growth, and sobriety.

Twelve Steps and Twelve Traditions tells us how to do our Step Ten reflection at day's end. We search for our motives when our thoughts or actions appear to be wrong: "here we need only recognize that we did act or think badly, try to visualize how we might have done better, and resolve with God's help to carry these lessons over into tomorrow, making, of course, any amends still neglected" (p. 94). In other words, we run through a quick version of Steps Four through Nine. Our amends are usually simple, even as simple as sending a text the next day to someone we owe a word of contrition to. Unlike Step Nine, here we are making amends for small incidents of wrongdoing, righting our wrongs as we go.

We are also advised to watch out for cases where: "our old enemy, rationalization, has stepped in and has justified conduct which was really wrong. The temptation is to imagine that we had good motives and reasons when really we didn't" (*Twelve Steps and Twelve Traditions,* p. 94). This is scientifically valid because, as we have discussed, the bizarre psychology of addiction-alcoholism includes an uncanny ability to rationalize just about any behavior, no matter how illogical or far-fetched the chosen justification may be. We are in recovery from addiction now, but old habits and tendencies may still prevail and, as we are told on page 94 of *Twelve Steps and Twelve Traditions*, we must keep watch lest our old enemy, rationalization, tries to disguise our character defects in a psychological smoke screen.

We are given a few examples of this in *Twelve Steps and Twelve Traditions*, but there is one that I would like to focus on because of its psychological significance and its powerfully negative effect on our spirituality, positive psychology, and recovery. That example: "we 'constructively criticized' someone who needed it, when our real motive was to win a useless argument" (p. 94). I have long been fascinated and perplexed by the human need to be "right." Many, many arguments and other interpersonal conflicts are driven by this neurotic need to be right, even in cases where the topic being argued doesn't have a right or wrong answer, such as when choosing a political party to vote for.

Whether it be a marriage, a friendship, a co-worker, or even the boss at work, this neurotic need to be right can spark impassioned conflict and some very negative feelings on both sides, even when the topic of the argument is trivial or frankly stupid. And the worse the argument gets, the more people dig in their heels and become more doggedly committed to pressing their point. This even occurs once the argument has degenerated well past the point where either side stands any chance whatsoever of persuading the other person to switch opinions. Yet the arguments continue.

Behavioral science studies have established that arguing and other interpersonal conflicts are a significant threat to our psychological well-being, and that an argument can leave us feeling unhappy and overwhelmed for days.[8] Further, arguing has been shown to be counter-productive: when we argue we are less likely to arrive at a good decision and more likely to lose focus on the matter that we were arguing about.[9] This begs the question: *so why do we argue, then?* Psychologists have identified the reasons that propel us to fight and argue with others. Their findings show that if we are arguing with others we likely have some deficits in our spiritual health, and our Step Ten work offers a perfect opportunity to work on these emerging character defects. Let's look at what the psychologists tell us.

If other people are not offering us the respect we feel we deserve, we are likely to argue with them in order to establish our superiority or assert our worthiness.[10] In other words, our arguing and neurotic need to be "right" is ego-driven. We do this subconsciously when other people are not validating our pride as we feel they should. An awareness that our bruised ego may be a reason that we got sucked into an argument gives us cause to reflect on the health of our humility, the very basis of our spirituality.

Other studies have shown that inadequate sleep predisposes us to argue with others.[11] If we find in our daily reflection that we have been irritable and argumentative, then perhaps we are failing in our self-care by not getting enough sleep, rest, and relaxation time. Our amends to ourselves involve good self-care, and we are failing in our amends to others if they are bearing the brunt of our tired psyche. We owe it to them and to ourselves to take good care of ourselves, and being argumentative and irritable probably indicates that we haven't been doing so. Our Step Ten reflection is the perfect time to recognize this and resolve to take steps to address the issue.

A wide range of psychological studies have shown that when we argue we are not seeking the truth but instead we are after arguments supporting our views; in fact we may resist obvious truths or persuasive reasoning if

320

they don't support our side of the argument.[12] You may recall that we discussed cognitive biases, which are irregularities in our thought processes that lead to irrational thinking and skewed decision-making. Well, this tendency to ignore facts and sound reasoning that don't support our viewpoint and to cling to less logical reasoning or flawed facts that do support our argument is a cognitive bias known as the confirmation bias. Of course, the confirmation bias is pushed to extremes by our character defects: the need to be "right," anger, impatience, and intolerance, for example. So, arguing is counter-productive in terms of arriving at the truth, and allows our character defects to assert themselves into our behavior. Arguing is just bad for our spirituality, our psychological health, and our recovery.

I do quite a bit of marriage counseling and it always amazes me how a couple will get sucked into useless, futile, unwinnable arguments about the same tired subjects time and time again. They end up enraged, hurt, and indignant, and it chips away at their relationship. However, in the end, it's pretty much always the case that whatever subject they were arguing over wasn't even the point of the argument; rather, they were re-fighting a thousand previous arguments, and in the heat of the moment unleashed the worst of their character defects on each other, which eliminates all reason, compassion, love, and common sense. They will argue all night over something pointless, because neither has even the slimmest of chances of persuading the other, and they know it. It's as if their ego needs the other person to concede, kneel before them, and beg forgiveness for not having the wisdom to see it their way. But that will never happen. Yet, the argument escalates and goes on and on, often for days or longer. Arguing brings out the worst in us. Arguing is absolutely futile, and absolutely psychologically and spiritually destructive.

So, the next time we feel that need to argue welling up inside ourselves, we should ask ourselves: *am I trying to prop up my ego here? Am I tired and irritable? Is there likely to be any kind of useful outcome to this argument?* And, of course, the big question: *would I rather be right or would I rather be happy?*

At the end of the day, when we do our Step Ten reflection, we should look back at any argument that we allowed ourselves to become involved in and recognize the futility of it, and note the number of character defects that we pulled out during the argument. We should let go of any hard feelings or bruised ego that we were left with. And we should decide to learn from the experience by avoiding futile arguments in the future.

Great advice about this matter can be found in *Living Sober*:

> The change begins with a tentative willingness to wait and see, to accept for a moment the hypothesis that the other person just

possibly might be right. Before rushing to judgment, we suspend our own argument, listen carefully, and watch for the outcome.

It may, or may not prove us to be in the wrong. That is not the important issue here. Whichever way the chips fall, we have at least temporarily freed ourselves from our driving need to always be right, or one-up. We have found that a sincere 'I don't know' can be rejuvenating. Saying, 'I'm wrong, you're right' is invigorating when we are sufficiently at ease with ourselves not to be bothered about actually being in the wrong. We are left feeling relaxed and thankful that we can be open to new ideas (p. 48-49).

It really goes against human nature to be "big" enough to behave this way when we get drawn into an argument. We may feel we are eating crow when we do it, but it feels really good afterwards, and people rightfully respect us for it. After we've done it a few times, it gets a lot easier. As we grow in healthy self-esteem, our need to be "right" for the sake of our ego and pride begins to melt away, along with our ego and hubristic pride. In the meantime, I once again ask people to remember this question to ask themselves when they find themselves arguing: *do I want to be right, or do I want to be happy?*

*

Let's take a more detailed look at how to do our daily Step Ten reflection. Although Step Ten is about taking a personal inventory at the end of the day and then admitting our wrongdoings, it's a little different from the inventory and admission of wrongdoings that we did in Steps Four and Five. It differs in two ways: 1) we also do the same things we did in Steps Six through Nine in our Step Ten inventory, and 2) we look at the positives as well as the negatives. In Step Ten we look back at our day and give ourselves a spiritual check-up. Where did we have conflict, or experience anger or impatience today? Do we have anger or resentment left over from the day? Did we fail anybody in matters of fellowship or spirituality today? Did any of our character defects appear in our behavior today? Was our behavior consistent with our spiritual principles today? Do we owe anybody amends for any of our behaviors or failings today? Did our disease try to talk us into drinking or using today? Did we do the things we need to do to stay sober today? Were we useful to our higher power and other people today?

Too, we should give ourselves credit for what we did well today. We should give ourselves kudos for the miracle of another day of sobriety. What else did we do well today?

Overall, what lessons did we learn today? What things did we do well today? What things did we do today that worked well for us? What can we learn from our mistakes today? What character defects need some extra attention? Then, we renew our admission of our powerlessness over drugs and alcohol.

It's important that we not allow our Step Ten reflections to turn into a tool for our inner critic to beat us up. Our Step Ten reflection is not just about what didn't go well and how we failed in our spiritual principles. We must also reflect on things we did well; spiritual successes we achieved. We should recognize how awesome we are. In matters where we didn't do well, we practice self-correction, not self-criticism. That's important, because Step Ten reflections are a very positive practice.

Over time we become quite good at Step Ten. Most of us end up keeping a running list in our mind, mentally noting things down as they happen through the day. This helps regulate our behavior during the day and gives us a pre-made inventory for our Step Ten reflection. Usually, Step Ten only takes a few minutes, but when times are tough or we are struggling we may find ourselves spending more time in our quiet reflection. This is not only therapeutic for us, but it helps us mull things over and put things in perspective. It's a useful practice for helping us figure out our problems.

Despite the suggestions I have made, there is no set format for our Step Ten practice. We will discuss meditation and prayer in Step Eleven, and our daily reflection time is a perfect opportunity to do some of that. It's also a great time to do some recovery reading, such as reading the Big Book or other 12 Step literature.

Throughout our Step Ten discussion, our daily reflection has been discussed as an "end of the day" activity. However, lots of people do this at another time of day that works for them. I have a friend in the fellowship who does his Step Ten reflection in the mornings. His wife and kids know that he needs his "recovery time" in the mornings, so they leave him undisturbed when he takes his 15 minutes of quiet time on his own every morning. It's just part of the routine in their house. They're so pleased to have him in recovery, I'm sure it doesn't bother them in the least that he takes the time to maintain his recovery.

Step One – our admission of powerlessness over drug and drink – is so overwhelmingly crucial to maintaining sobriety that it deserves special mention in our Step Ten study. During our reflection we should reflect back to see if the "insanity of alcoholism-addiction" spoke to us. Did we think about drinking or using in a positive way? Did we entertain the idea that it might be OK to drink or use again, that THIS time we could control it? Certainly, we need to identify it when this disease-specific distorted thinking emerges, and recognize it for what it is. And we must not keep it a secret. We should discuss it with our sponsor, go to a discussion meeting and share it – get it out in the open to someone who understands this kind of thinking.

And what if we're having relapse dreams? Relapse dreams are a source of confusion and guilt for many people in recovery. They're a unique type of dream, often so vivid that people wake from them honestly believing that they really did relapse. Sometimes they even taste alcohol or drugs in their mouth or feel like they are drunk or high, or hung over or in withdrawal. People tend to believe that a relapse dream indicates that they subconsciously want to relapse, or that it represents a prediction that they will relapse, and they consequently feel guilt and fear from the dreams. While I won't get into a detailed discussion about relapse dreams here, suffice it to say that these dreams are **not** an indication of a subconscious desire to drink or use. Rather, they are a normal part of recovery for many people, related to the brain changes from substance use. They occur in many people in recovery, sometimes even many years after the last drink or drug. I have noticed that people tend to keep it to themselves when they have relapse dreams because they feel guilty about them, but I recommend getting them out in the open when they occur. Phone your sponsor and talk about it as soon as you wake up; go to a meeting that day and discuss it. Confront the dream. Anyone who wants to know more about these fascinating aspects of addiction psychology and the research into why relapse dreams happen and what they mean can learn more in my book *The Alcoholic/Addict Within: Our Brain, Genetics, Psychology, and the Twelve Steps as Psychotherapy.*

*

It deserves mention in our Step Ten study that we should also give our mental health symptoms a quick check-up during our daily reflection, if those are a factor for us. As we discussed in the introduction to this book, more than half of people who become addict-alcoholics got there because they were "self-treating" mental health symptoms with drugs or alcohol. The most common mental health disorders we see in people with our disease are depression and anxiety, but others occur as well, especially PTSD and bipolar disorder. Sometimes we don't fully notice if mental health symptoms are breaking through unless we put some conscious thought into the matter. As such, I suggest that people with a history of a mental health disorder learn about symptoms specific to their own situation and watch for them as part of their Step Ten reflection.

Because of the huge amount of overlap between mental health disorders and addiction-alcoholism, certain symptoms may be a red flag for both. These include, for example, such symptoms as depressed mood, anxiety, social isolation, loss of interest in life's activities including ones that are enjoyable (anhedonia), or thoughts of suicide. Such symptoms may indicate that it's time to seek medical attention; suicidal thoughts are a medical emergency and require immediate attention. As with other disease-related causes, our ability to recognize and address such red flags is crucial to our happiness, well-being, and sobriety.

*

On our way through the Steps we've covered a lot of principles and tools that contribute to making us happy, at peace, fulfilled, and possessed of a positive outlook – in other words, the basis of positive psychology. By far the greatest way to a positive psychology is through spiritual well-being, and we've discussed why that is and the overwhelming amount of research evidence that backs that up. It has a lot to do with gratitude and humility, and being at peace with our place in the world. The Serenity Prayer helps us to remain focused on letting go of the stuff we can't do anything about, and getting off our butts to fix the things we can. We are no longer the world's victims. We no longer allow outside events or people to decide whether or not we are having a good day and whether or not we are happy; we no longer assign anyone or anything else that much power over our life. Happiness is about perspective; we can either rail about the things we don't have or learn gratitude for the things we have. We have learned that happiness is an inside job. This whole positive mind-set – based on our spiritual health – is the basis of our sobriety and our quality of life. We must guard it and protect it and never give it away, lest we fall again. Step Ten is our bastion against slipping back to the miserable mind-set that was previously the basis of our downfall. It's our daily check-up for our spiritual well-being.

From a psychological point of view, Step Ten is a tremendously effective self-care practice that supports spirituality, recovery, and a positive psychology. Step Ten deploys our recently learned principles into a brief daily mindful practice that endows us with an exceptional tool for resilience, even in the face of hardships. Psychological therapists can't prescribe Step Ten to their clients because it doesn't work unless the individual has acquired the mind-set, positive psychology, support system, and skill set that are imbued by the previous nine Steps. We truly have something special here that can't be obtained even with tens of thousands of dollars of professional therapy.

Step Ten plays a huge role in our recovery from the need for using psychoactive substances for escaping negative thoughts, life's stressors, negative feelings, or whatever else we were trying to smother. As we continue to grow in spirituality, and our new way of living becomes more comfortable for us, the obsession and cravings for mind-altering substances fall away. That's the genius of the 12 Step program: nobody ever nags us to stop drinking or using. Rather it's about learning to handle life on life's terms:

> And we have ceased fighting anything or anyone – even alcohol. For by this time sanity will have returned. We will seldom be interested in liquor. If tempted, we recoil from it as from a hot flame. We react sanely and normally, and we will find that this has happened automatically. We will see that our new attitude toward liquor has been given us without any thought or effort on our part. It just comes! We are not fighting it, neither are we avoiding temptation... as long as we keep in fit spiritual condition (Big Book, p. 85).

From a psychological standpoint, the part "we are not fighting it, neither are we avoiding temptation" is particularly significant. As we found in our discussion about the scientific basis for powerlessness in our Step One study, willpower is not only of little use in overcoming addiction, but it's actually harmful. Fighting and avoiding temptation are not part of 12 Step recovery, which is perfectly aligned with what the science of addiction tells us.

Our Step Ten reflections give us better skills at living our life spiritually and avoiding conflict and strife. We don't self-criticize at the end of the day, we self-correct. That means that we seek lessons from things that didn't go as we would have liked them to. Life is made up of many types of events – good, bad, and ugly – that tend to repeat themselves over time. So, when we take a lesson from our Step Ten from a given situation, we have a tool for doing better the next time that same situation arises. Because we run into similar situations over and over again in life, Step Ten ensures that we get better and better at it.

At the end of the day, the essence of our Step Ten is summed up by *Twelve Steps and Twelve Traditions*:

> Learning daily to spot, admit, and correct these flaws is the essence of character-building and good living. An honest regret for harms done, a genuine gratitude for blessings received, and a willingness to try for better things tomorrow will be the permanent assets we shall seek.
>
> Having so considered our day, not omitting to take due note of things well done, and having searched our hearts with neither fear nor favor, we can truly thank God for the blessings we have received and sleep in good conscience (p. 95).

After years of tortured sleep and unlovely dreams, to sleep in good conscience is a blessing indeed!

*

Step Ten is a "maintenance and growth" Step, meaning that we practice it on an ongoing basis for life. So, how do we know when we are ready to move on to Step Eleven? When we have established a routine for our daily Step Ten practice and it's working for us, we're ready to move on, as long as our sponsor agrees. If you're there, let's head into one of my favorites: Step Eleven.

Step Eleven

Sought through prayer and meditation to improve our conscious contact with God as we understood Him, praying only for knowledge of His will for us and the power to carry that out.

Brain hygiene.

That's what Step Eleven does for us. It sounds good, doesn't it? Clean out the old dysfunctional self-destructive thoughts and mind-set and replace them with positive psychology, and replace self-will run riot with an invigorating connection with a higher power. But, there's more to it than that.

Brain hygiene is a pretty cool concept. It's where we use the brain's "plasticity" (or *neuroplasticity*) to enhance its performance for improved physical, mental, emotional, social, and spiritual well-being. Just like our muscles benefit from exercise, so too does our brain. I mentioned neuroplasticity way back in the introduction to the book, but we'll review the concept quickly here. Sitting around with an inactive brain watching TV doesn't do much for the brain. Getting drunk or high does even less! Regular physical exercise, yoga, deep breathing, sound sleep, relaxation, socialization, positive thinking, hobbies, a healthy diet, sports, listening to music, meditation, reading, and mindfulness are very enhancing activities for the brain and mind. Good brain hygiene helps us to better tolerate stress, and think our way through adversity, as well as relapse urges.

Although it may feel like our brains were made out of plastic when we look back at our past behaviors, that's not what's meant by "brain plasticity." Rather, brain plasticity refers to the brain's ability to adapt and change according to what we're using it for. Just about any tissue in the body has plasticity built into it. For example, our muscles will adapt according to what we use them for; when we are lazy and sedate, they lose size and tone, and when we are active and we exercise, they grow and strengthen. Our brain is one of the most plastic of all body tissues. When we

328

exercise our brain and challenge it to do new things, it strengthens and increases its capabilities. When we use it to do positive things, it strengthens in positivity. As we all know from our drinking days, when we abuse our brain and do nothing to improve it, it becomes a couch potato. Of course, substance use worsens this deleterious effect; as we have previously discussed, addictive substances cause inflammatory changes in the brain that disrupt and re-arrange our brain cell connections and pathways. These changes result in the creation of permanent "addiction pathways" that can be re-activated at any time in the future with exposure to drugs or alcohol. This is negative plasticity – our brain adapting to our negative behaviors. Now, in recovery, we are working on positive brain plasticity, which is precisely what we accomplish with our trip through the Steps.

So, "brain hygiene" involves taking advantage of the brain's natural plasticity to make positive, healthy, and functionally advantageous changes in our brain's structure and function. The skills we learn and make a part of our daily life in a properly done Step Eleven impart the most important mechanism that we have available to us for brain hygiene and positive neuroplasticity. So, let's get to it and do an awesome Step Eleven!

*

Step Eleven is one of my favorites, because I have been practicing meditation for a long time – more than twenty-five years – and I was delighted to find out that it could be an important part of my recovery. Of course, like most other good habits, meditation went completely out the window during my drinking and using days. Step Eleven was a perfect occasion to make it a part of my life again, as well as part of my recovery. If you aren't a meditator, Step Eleven gives you a great opportunity to explore this powerful and gratifying brain hygiene technique; if you're already an experienced meditator Step Eleven gives you a chance to tune up your skills and apply them to your recovery and healing. If you're spooked by the idea of meditation, fear not. I'll take you through how to meditate and make it an enjoyable part of your day.

First, let's clear up a couple of misconceptions that are sometimes attached to Step Eleven. First of all, meditation is not a wonky, new-age, voodoo thing. Meditation has been extensively studied in proper medical and psychological research studies and has many proven benefits, as we shall see. When I tell you how I came to be a meditator you'll see for yourself that it's a very real and practical thing. The 12 Step program, too, is clear that meditation is in fact a serious tool for recovery, not some frivolous pastime: "let's always remember that meditation is in reality intensely practical" (*Twelve Steps and Twelve Traditions,* p. 101). The other misconception that we need to clear up is the belief that prayer is a religious ritual reserved for those who practice religion. Sure, religious people pray, but so do non-religious people. I will explain why this is, and how prayer can help all of us in our recovery, including hard-core atheists and people who haven't yet figured out the higher power thing. Like meditation, the benefits of prayer have been well documented with proper research studies. For those who get their hackles up when they hear the word "prayer," I once again ask that you keep an open mind and open yourself up to taking a leap of faith.

I suggest that skeptics of meditation or prayer give it a heartfelt try: "it has been well said that 'almost the only scoffers at prayer are those who never tried it enough'" (*Twelve Steps and Twelve Traditions*, p. 97). (Note the word "enough" in that passage.) Once again the 12 Step program is asking us to be open-minded, to give something new an honest try, and to put aside that ubiquitous character defect of close-mindedness. As we are reminded in *Twelve Steps and Twelve Traditions*: "when we turn away from meditation and prayer, we… deprive our minds, our emotions, and our intuitions of vitally needed support" (p. 97).

So far in our journey through the Steps keeping an open mind and trying new things has paid off, so Step Eleven shouldn't be much of an obstacle for any of us, regardless of our belief system or lack thereof. We've got nothing to lose, but stand to gain much. But first, let's talk about meditation. We'll go through what exactly meditation is, how it works, its effects on our mental and physical health, and how to properly meditate. We'll also discuss how to use meditation to strengthen and optimize our spirituality and recovery.

*

When I was in the detox center and met the people from A.A. who came in to put on meetings I admired them for their recovery, but I didn't think *I* could do it. No way. My concern was that I knew that I lacked the strength to beat my cravings; they talked about one day at a time, but for me it was one minute at a time. However, I soon learned that my old meditation skills could help me. The guys from A.A. told me that meditation was part of the Steps, and they also told me that the slogan "Remember When" would help me when my disease tried to talk me into drinking or using. So, I put the two together and did some "remember when" meditation. This absolutely crushed my cravings and pushed my recovery ahead. As I grew in recovery and progressed through the Steps I learned many other ways that my meditation skills could help me heal, stay healthy, grow in spirituality and positive psychology, and stay the course in my recovery. As *Twelve Steps and Twelve Traditions* explains, the idea is: "to point our imagination toward the right objectives. There's nothing the matter with *constructive*

330

imagination; all sound achievement rests upon it. After all, no man can build a house until he first envisions a plan for it. Well, meditation is like that, too; it helps us to envision our spiritual objective before we try to move toward it" (p. 100).

The beautiful thing about meditation is that it can be used to help us with much more than killing off our cravings for drink or drug. With a little practice, it helps center the mind, calm the body, and rein in our primitive character defect-driven reactions when life tries to get under our skin. Allowing life to get under our skin once made us seek shelter in drugs and alcohol, so meditation is a powerful life-saving skill for us that we can add to our recovery toolbox, allowing us to approach life in a wiser, controlled, and more thought-out way. It allows us to balance our emotions, rather than allowing volatile emotions carry us through life and dictate our actions to us.

Another beautiful thing about meditation is that it takes surprisingly little time and effort to become really good at it and see it making a huge difference in life. Good thing for me, because I definitely have attention deficit disorder, so no way am I going to sit there meditating for hours on end like some cloistered monk.

Another really cool thing about meditation is that the sky's the limit; you can use it in its very basic form to help your sobriety and spirituality, or you can take it as far as you want to go with it. Meditation is a tool with much depth, and you can keep learning about it and improving your skills and doing new things with it, making it a fulfilling activity in its own right. There are many people in the program who have become expert meditators and really enjoy it as a relaxing and enjoyable pursuit, a hobby. Once we learn some basic concepts and skills, we can totally personalize meditation, and meditate in a way that makes sense to us and works for us. As *Twelve Steps and Twelve Traditions* tells us: "meditation is something which can always be further developed. It has no boundaries, either of width or height. Aided by such instruction and example as we can find, it is essentially an individual adventure..." (p. 101).

So what about prayer? Prayer is simply a form of meditation that gives us that connection on the third level of spirituality. Remember, we defined spirituality as connections outside ourselves, and these connections can occur on three levels: 1) connections with other people, 2) connections with the world around us, and 3) connections with a power greater than ourselves. Prayer is how we make that connection with a power greater than ourselves. For people who find their higher power in God, prayer is their connection to God. For those who have another higher power, prayer is their connection to that higher power. For those who do know yet have a higher power, prayer is a form of meditation that allows for exploring and projecting these thoughts. It's like a dialogue of focused thought with all distractions removed. In other words, prayer is simply a specific type of meditation. We'll talk about how to pray, no matter what your belief system, and how to use it to tune up your spirituality and your recovery.

*

The way I first came to know meditation was definitely not because of some new-age pursuit. Believe it or not, I was first introduced to it as a young man as part of my training in martial arts. I had no desire to learn meditation; I was just doing it because it was a requirement for getting my belt promotions. Its benefits were never really explained to me, we just went through the motions of learning how to do it and we practiced it. I discovered the remarkable benefits of meditation by accident on my own as meditation increasingly became a part of my life. Soon I was doing meditation because I enjoyed it and liked what it was doing for me, not because I had to do it to get my martial arts belts.

The basic premise of meditation is that the human mind is inherently weak, and it wanders off on its own wherever it wants to go. That's why we tend to get distracted so easily. I refer to the "wandering" mind as an "undisciplined" mind, and I compare it to a child sitting in class staring out the window at the soccer game going on outside rather than listening to the lesson. The teacher keeps rebuking the child, drawing his attention back to the blackboard, but the child is soon focused on the soccer game outside again. Our "undisciplined," wandering mind is yet another weakness of our psychology that our disease takes advantage of to keep us from recovery. For alcoholic-addicts in recovery, our disease uses this weakness to provoke the mind to wander off into areas where it shouldn't, such as thoughts of drinking or using, or ruminating on our problems and blowing them out of proportion. Too, our character defects work their way into our mind when our mind wanders off on its own. Rather than think our way through a stressful situation, our undisciplined mind will instead – on its own initiative – focus on anger, fear, or other primal emotions that distract us from thinking through the situation and responding logically.

In fact, the undisciplined mind will react to distractions really quickly, reflexively, without first consulting our brain's higher thought processes and decision-making functions. These instantaneous reactions remove our higher mind functions – such as reasoning, planning, and thinking – from determining our actions, and our primitive instincts – such as lashing out in anger – take over. That works well when we touch a hot stove and reflexively jerk our hand away, but it doesn't work so well when someone offends us in our day-to-day lives. The hot stove is a stimulus where our knee-jerk reaction saves us from harm, but a knee-jerk reaction to a stimulus involving a daily stressor, such as someone bumping into us, can

332

land us in trouble. Better we think about it a second and smile and say "excuse me" than to lash out and insult and push the person who bumped us. For we alcoholic-addicts, indulging our tendency to anger can be the beginning of a fatal downslide into the pit of anger and resentment that once kept us drinking or using.

Meditation is about learning to keep our mind from darting off on its own. It's about stopping the undisciplined mind from making its own snap decisions without consulting our higher reasoning faculties as we face various situations in our day-to-day life. Through meditation we can teach our mind to be disciplined, more under the control of our higher, intelligent brain functions and less under the control of our primitive, instinctual reactions. Then, when we run into stressful events through the day we are able to give measured, thought-out responses rather than lashing out unthinkingly. Think back to all those times in life when you wish you could take back something you said or did out of haste, and you will see the value of having better control over the undisciplined mind's tendency to react unthinkingly.

*

It may sound strange that the peaceful practice of meditation is a required learning for martial arts, but the reason for it illustrates perfectly what meditation can do for people like us in recovery. Meditation, as I learned it, was intended to help a fighter who takes an injury to focus on finishing the fight rather than focusing only on the pain of his injury. Let's use an example to illustrate. A person is assaulted, punched on the nose. Getting punched on the nose produces a blinding, debilitating pain that only someone who has experienced it can truly understand. The undisciplined mind will immediately focus only on that pain and forget everything else, and the person will therefore double over, turn away from the assailant, and cover his nose. This will result in a defenseless posture against a further, more thorough, beating. However, the mind that is well trained in meditation can maintain focus on the assailant, ignoring the pain for the moment, and deal with the attack by fighting back, or escaping, or whatever it takes to prevent further injury. Once the danger is over, then the focused mind can deal with finding help for the pain. The person with meditation skills maintains his or her mind on proper thought and decision-making, rather than allowing the mind to run off wherever it wants to go, in this case on the distracting stimulus, the pain from being hit on the nose.

However, as I came to learn, the true value of meditation for martial arts lies in its power to help us to avoid a fight, rather than winning a fight. Therein lies its usefulness for us in recovery. As we alcoholic-addicts are well aware, the undisciplined human mind has impulse control problems, as our self-will tries to assert itself. When we feel slighted we usually respond with a burst of angry emotion that, if we act on it, could make us do something we ordinarily wouldn't do or that we might later regret. The undisciplined mind acts out of impulse, rather than first letting the thought filter through our higher brain processes and consider our options and the ramifications. Thus, the disciplined mind can avoid lashing out in situations that might lead to conflict or a fight.

The experienced meditator can head off ill-advised impulses by not letting the naturally weak mind go where it wants to in an uncontrolled fashion. During my sickness of active addiction-alcoholism the benefits of a disciplined mind became lost to me as my disease took over and my weak mind led me around by the nose, day in and day out, in total service to my obsession with drugs and alcohol. My self-will was in control, not my higher brain functions. This is typical of our disease, and those of us who stay in active substance use long enough will invariably get to that point. However, in recovery, we need to stop our disease's control over our mind by asserting some mental discipline for when our disease tries to assert itself – because it will. For those who don't have any experience with meditation, Step Eleven is the perfect time to learn.

Step Eleven also suggests that we use prayer. We'll discuss exactly how to use meditation to enhance the meaningfulness of prayer and to deepen our connection with our higher power. For those who are not religious, we'll discuss how to use prayer as a non-religious meditation, an important part of everybody's spirituality and recovery.

*

As you have probably noticed by this point in our trip through the Steps, the most up-to-date science agrees completely with and supports the utility of the 12 Steps for restoring us to good health and function. Step Eleven is certainly no exception. The medical and scientific community has long recognized the positive effects of meditation, and there has been much empirical study into the effects of meditation on our health and well-being in recent years. Let's have a quick look at some of the research findings about meditation, so we can use the science to our advantage.

One interesting study found that a short program of meditation improved immune function (as measured by response to flu vaccine), as well as baseline brain activity.[1] Meditation has also been shown to be an effective approach to reducing physical pain. One clinical trial published in *The Journal of Neuroscience* looked at how meditation affects our perception of pain.[2] The researchers used a special type of functional magnetic resonance imaging (fMRI) to assess the neural mechanisms by which meditation influences perception of pain. After four days of meditation

334

training, the test subjects were exposed to pain-inducing stimuli (I don't know how they suckered people into participating in this study!). Meditation reduced pain perception by 57% and pain-intensity ratings by 40% when compared to rest. The brain scans showed that meditation worked on multiple brain sites involved in pain perception processing. Meditation helps reduce how much pain we feel. Other research has shown that meditation works in a manner different from any existing pain medications, which means that it can be used to enhance pain reduction in people who are already using medications.[3]

We know that mental stress is a major cause of disease exacerbation for virtually any kind of not only mental, but also physical illness, especially inflammatory diseases like arthritis (joint inflammation), gastritis (stomach upset and pain), and Crohn's Disease (bowel inflammation). Given that meditation is focused on relaxation and stress-reduction, the natural question to ask is if this stress reduction affects the severity of physical diseases. Indeed it does. For example, in one study, meditation was used for stress-reduction, and then post-stress inflammatory responses were compared to participants who underwent a non-meditation stress-reduction program. The results showed that stress-reduction in general reduced inflammation, but meditation was significantly better.[4]

A number of studies have suggested that meditation is an effective way to reduce high blood pressure – the "silent killer" – which is hardly surprising given the well-known association between stress and high blood pressure.[5] Speaking of killers, meditation has also proven effective in smoking-cessation trials.[6]

It has been well established by numerous studies that meditation reduces depression, anxiety, stress, and feelings of loneliness.[7,8] Meditation increases social connection, emotional stability, self-control (including over relapse in addiction recovery), and compassion.[9,10] Physically, it increases brain size and density in areas involving concentration, higher brain functions, attention span, multi-tasking, and creativity.[11]

Meditation also has innumerable positive effects on our body's physical function, such as improvements in hormone levels (especially via reduction of the stress hormone *cortisol*), improved regulation of digestive functions, as well as blood pressure, heart rate, immunological, respiratory, and neuroplastic function.[12] I'm not going to dwell on the effects of meditation on physical and mental health, because there are innumerable research studies that have been done to support meditation. Rather, my purpose here is to make a point: meditation can have far-reaching positive effects for our physical and mental health. It is indeed a powerful tool for health and well-being.

So, meditation clearly has impressive mental and physical health benefits. But, let's get down to brass tacks; what does meditation do for recovery from addiction-alcoholism? After all, that's why we're here. First of all, it makes sense that meditation would help us in our recovery because successful recovery comes from developing healthy coping skills which replace our previous go-to dysfunctional and self-destructive coping mechanisms. There's a strong body of research evidence which clearly upholds meditation as a powerful healthy coping mechanism to replace destructive coping mechanisms, such as substance use or other escape behaviors.[13,14] Further, meditation is known to give the ability to maintain self-insight and an awareness of one's vulnerabilities and destructive thought processes, and to challenge these processes before they take over our behaviors.[15] As we have seen in previous Steps, this self-awareness is a key tool for changing our behaviors for the better.

Addiction counseling professionals and addiction treatment centers have recognized the overwhelming scientific evidence supporting the use of meditation in addiction treatment and recovery, and most have adopted meditation as an integral part of their treatment and relapse prevention programs.[16,17,18,19] Studies of meditation in people with addiction-alcoholism have demonstrated that it eases detoxification, boosts recovery motivation and commitment, reduces the effects of stress, increases relaxation while reducing tension, improves self-confidence, improves anger management, improves interpersonal and social function, and improves our overall sense of well-being.[20,21] Now that you are at Step Eleven and you have a deeper knowledge of the causes and effects of addiction-alcoholism, you can see the benefits of these effects of meditation on recovery. What's more, meditation is a low-cost and enjoyable approach to recovery – so enjoyable that it has been referred to as a "positive addiction."[22]

Significant research has looked at very specific effects of meditation on the addicted brain, such as its effects at increasing the function of the brain circuitry responsible for self-control (in the anterior cingulate cortex of the brain, for you science-nerds).[23,24,25,26] Similarly, separate studies have confirmed the positive effects of meditation on promoting healthier function of the brain's mechanisms for emotional regulation and stress reduction.[27] Moreover, these effects on the brain have been shown to reduce substance use in people with addictions.[28,29,30]

Meditation has been shown to be an effective intervention for the treatment of addiction, as well as for long-term relapse prevention.[31,32,33] A large body of research into the neuroscience of the effects of meditation on addiction recovery has shown that it does so through multiple mechanisms in the brain, modulating cognitive, affective (i.e. emotional), psychological, and physiological processes that positively support recovery and relapse prevention by modifying negative behaviors, promoting healthy self-regulation, and normalizing reward processing, all of which are severely disrupted by addiction-alcoholism.[34,35] Again, I don't want to turn our discussion into a scientific review, but I simply want to make the point that the meditation aspect of Step Eleven is heavily supported by research evidence as an effective tool for health and recovery.

Now, let's get to it and go through the basics of how to meditate.

*

Meditation isn't some kind of arcane ancient ritual, and it's not mystical. You don't have to belong to a secret society to learn how to do it. It's not some kind of otherworldly hypnosis. It's a very practical thing, and it's easy to get started at doing it. You don't even have to be good at it to start feeling its benefits, especially when it comes to recovery.

A few things that meditation is not: time consuming, sitting in weird positions, chanting, religious, or otherworldly. In fact, it's about being comfortable, takes only a few minutes or can be done momentarily on the fly through the day, involves an active mind, and it's very real and practical: I did it to get my black belt in martial arts, and the United States Marine Corps teaches it to their soldiers. U.S. Navy SEALs rely heavily on meditation for their mental strength and resilience. And we alcoholic-addicts in recovery use it in our Step Eleven to fortify our recovery.

To start out, we should find a comfortable position that suits us. Sitting on the couch or floor, cross-legged or not, with your posture as you like to sit. Some people like to meditate lying down, but I don't. You'll be surprised by how incredibly relaxed your mind becomes as you meditate, and I have a tendency to drift off to sleep when I meditate lying down. In fact, on nights that I find myself unable to sleep I will start meditating on something pleasant and it always helps me get to sleep.

I recommend closing your eyes, as it's much easier to concentrate and focus the mind with the eyes closed. Meditating with eyes open can be a part of more advanced meditation, but to start out it's usually best to have eyes closed, shutting out the outside world. Even though eyes open can be an advanced meditation technique, I have been meditating a long time and I still prefer keeping my eyes closed.

Breathing is very important for starting out, because we want to send a burst of fresh oxygen to our brain to kick-start the lazy thing into action. Even though our brain makes up only 2% of our body, it uses 25% of our entire oxygen intake. Our brain needs to breathe, especially during a brain hygiene workout like meditation. While we meditate, we breathe in through the nose and out through the mouth. If we keep our back straight and erect it gives our diaphragm – the big breathing muscle between our chest and abdomen – more room to do its job as it contracts to draw fresh air into our lungs.

We start with three deep breaths in through the nose and out through the mouth, but no more than three big ones. We don't want to make ourselves dizzy. Some call these three initial deep breaths "cleansing breaths." As we meditate we will continue breathing in through the nose and out through the mouth, but we'll just breathe normally as we do. As people get good at meditation, their breathing rate, pulse, and blood pressure lower, indicating deep physical and mental relaxation. Sometimes our breathing is barely perceptible when we're in a good meditation.

After our cleansing breaths, we focus our mind and all our thoughts, with eyes closed, on dark, empty space. Blackness. Nothing. Every time our mind starts thinking about something, including what we are doing, we guide it back to focusing solely on the nothingness. This can be done for increasingly longer periods of time. It's important to keep your mind focused, not allowing it to wander. You will notice your mind wandering, to some problem you've been dealing with, something someone said to you, something you forgot to do, what to have for supper, some big task coming up, and so on. That's your challenge: to not allow your mind to go wherever it wants to. Quite often, you will find yourself thinking about something during meditation and you don't even realize it initially, until after you've been thinking on it for a while. If you feel your mind wandering, snap it back in focus. Try doing this exercise for a few minutes at a time initially, and as you get better at it begin increasing the time. With practice, we get better and better at keeping our mind on task: keeping focused on the black nothingness and nothing else.

Once you've done this initial meditation a few times, and you've gotten a bit used to guiding your mind away from distraction and back onto the darkness, let's try a little meditation mind relaxation exercise. Now, when you breathe imagine breathing in cool, blue air, always through the nose. Imagine the cool air actually being blue in color, cool, very fresh, and clean. The blue air we are inhaling is cool and calm. When we exhale, imagine hot, red, bad, toxic air going out through the mouth. It's actually red in color, very warm, dirty, angry air. This red air is turbulent and poisonous. Our lungs are filled with it. Continue breathing in this cool blue air, in through the nose, and exhaling this hot red air, out through the mouth. Visualize the cool blue air going deep down inside you and swirling around your lungs, and pushing out the hot red air, which rushes out through your mouth and dissipates into the sky.

As you continue breathing in and out, visualize the cool blue air starting to gradually replace the hot red air down deep in your lungs. Visualize how, with each breath, there becomes progressively more blue air deep down in your lungs, and less and less red air as it gets pushed out by the cool, fresh, blue air. Gradually, there is less and less red air, and more and more blue air, until finally there is just blue air, blue air coming in when you breathe in – your lungs full of cool blue air – and cool blue air coming out through your mouth when you exhale. There's nothing but cool, blue, calm, clean, smooth air in and out. At this point, your mind is relaxed. You will probably be unaware of your body at this point, and without any thoughts beyond your breathing. If your mind tries wandering off, snap it right back to the cool, blue air going in and out.

The cool blue air represents peace, serenity, confidence, love, goodwill, cleanliness, health, and positivity. The red air represents anger, hatred, conflict, fear, and resentment. Now, imagine the cool blue air filtering through your entire body, as it leaves your lungs and circulates in your blood, diffusing throughout your body. Feel the cool, peaceful, serene, confident, loving, positive effects of the cool blue air throughout your body, and feel it tingling as it reaches the tips of your fingers and toes. Keep visualizing this and let it affect your mood. For the rest of your meditation just keep your mind focused on the clean, cool blue air coming in and out, reaching every part of your body.

This exercise is an excellent way to practice relaxing and focusing your mind. Once you have practiced this visualization a few times, you can use it to focus your mind and center your mood at the start of a meditation, or you can use it as the entire meditation for its calming, centering effects.

After a while, when you feel you are good at doing this and it's effortless to keep focused on the breathing for your entire meditation session, you can try moving from visualizing your breathing to visualizing an object. I suggest a plain white candle burning in a dark, black space. Start with your comfortable position, eyes closed, cleansing breath, and your cool blue air relaxation exercise. Then, visualize the candle, the texture of the wax, the streaks of melted wax trailing down its sides. Notice every detail, even the barely perceptible sound of the flame burning and melting the wax. Visualize the flame, sometimes still, sometimes flickering. See the soft orange flame surrounding the black wick, with a halo of blue flame around the orange, tapering up to the hot white tip of the flame, with a thin wisp of black smoke rising straight up from the tip. Continue breathing in through your nose and out through your mouth while you are doing this. If your mind wanders away from the candle flame, bring it right back into focus. Some people enjoy enhancing the candle flame meditation by using an actual candle in a dark room; feel free to try that as well. The point is to focus your mind on every small detail of the candle and flame (without hurting your eyes) and snapping your mind back on task every time it attempts to wander off.

Practice this mind-focusing until it becomes easier and easier, with less and less interruption by the weak mind trying to go where it wants to go. Meditation is like any other skill or form of exercise: the more you practice the better and stronger you get at it and the easier it becomes.

Remember: because of neuroplasticity your brain will rise to the challenges that you set for it, kind of like lifting weights for the brain. You don't need to meditate for long periods of time. Even just 3-5 minutes initially is fine. Meditation is not a skill that requires a lot of time commitment. As you get better and better at it, and as you have more and more things you wish to meditate on, you may start spending more time at it. It becomes something to look forward to, a reward at the end of a long day. The relaxation helps center us and purge our minds of all the turmoil of the day.

When you are finished meditating, simply open your eyes, slowly allow your mind to come back to reality, get up, and you are done your session. Congrats: you now have some basic meditation skills!

*

Thus far, we've done some basic meditation that helps us – with practice – to accomplish two things: 1) to relax our mind and body, and 2) to discipline our mind by keeping it focused and not allowing it to wander off on its own. The more we practice these basic skills, the better we get at those two important goals. When you feel ready, we can take the next step and introduce some focused meditation.

We've already gone through two different ways of focusing our meditation: the blue and red breathing and the candle flame visualization. Focusing our meditation can do two things for us. First, it gives us something to center our mind and thoughts on so that we can practice keeping our mind focused. Second, we can choose a specific meditation focus to help us address specific concerns or problems we are facing, including eliminating our cravings or thoughts of drinking or using.

We can choose any meditation focus we wish, based on our current needs, goals, or interests. So far we've used either darkness, our breathing, or a candle flame as the center of our meditation. A good example of focused meditation is the practice of Step Ten, where we are suggested to review our actions each day to see if any character defects reared their ugly heads and took over our actions that day. We can do this by meditating on our day, keeping our mind focused on putting together our inventory for the day.

In fact, the best way to do an effective Step Ten is with the mental concentration that we get by meditation. At the end of the day we get into position, do our breathing, and focus our mind. Then we review our day, centering on incidents that stand out, and analyze our thoughts and actions in each situation. We review each incident by asking ourselves these questions: did I react spontaneously, or was my reaction well thought-out and measured? How would my actions look from someone else's perspective? Were there any character defects that showed through in my actions? Would someone be able to know what I stand for by my words and

340

actions? While we are doing this, our weak mind will try to run over to how the other people in our ugly encounters were at fault, how they have character defects. Feelings of anger or anxiety might well up and ruin our concentration, but we must bring our thoughts back on task. Meditating on other people's faults is a waste of time and effort, so we use our newfound mind discipline to focus on our own role in what happened. Then, we meditate on how we could do better next time if we were faced by an identical situation. I don't want to re-invent Step Ten now in our Step Eleven study, I just want to point out that using our meditative concentration and disciplined mind helps us to do a really good Step Ten review. So, we can apply our Step Eleven skills to our daily practice of Step Ten.

Before too long, we will find ourselves automatically doing a mini-Step Ten spot-check meditation in our mind immediately after or even during significant incidents during our day. When this begins happening our spirituality is taking on a whole new level, because our meditation skills are allowing us to regulate our behaviors at the time they play out. That's a pretty big deal for us low-bottom alcoholic-addicts. We've come a long way!

Our improved behavior as we are confronted by stressors in our daily routine doesn't go unnoticed. People react to our response much better when our reaction is measured and appropriate. If we lash out at them they are likely to do the same in kind. When we respond to anger with patience, understanding, and restraint it has a calming effect on the other person and the situation. Difficult situations diffuse away rather than escalate. We become known as rational, measured people who handle stressors well. People start respecting us, maybe even wanting to be like us. Life becomes easier, and we come home at the end of the day with much less frustration and anger than we once did. Not only do other people like us better, but we like ourselves better. We are handling life in a better way. The practice of spirituality has many benefits besides just keeping us sober.

*

By choosing a focus of meditation and keeping our mind on topic, we are further honing our mind-discipline skills. Our focus of meditation can be anything we want, it doesn't have to be all about self-evaluation as it is in Step Ten. If we've had a rough day and just want to wind down, or if we are dealing with anger we want to purge, or if our mind is too active for us to sleep, we may want to simply meditate on something pleasant and soothing. Again, we get set up, do our breathing, get our mind cleared and centered, and then allow our mind to fill with a beautiful scene, or a fun event, or some other thing that's really nice for us. Every time our mind tries to slip off our beautiful scene and back onto our anger, or our finances, or when is garbage day this week, or otherwise become overactive and jump around, we bring it back to our pleasant scene. Once it has stopped trying to get off topic, and surrenders to enjoying our pleasant meditation it's a safe bet that we will be more relaxed and better able to sleep when we finish our meditation. And our mind is that much more disciplined.

The more we meditate, the better we become at it, and the more disciplined our mind becomes. The goal is an awareness of what the mind is doing, and an ability to pull it back when it tries to go off on its own. After a while, this ability begins to show itself all day long, not just when we're actively meditating. So, when someone does something that would anger us and our mind darts to thoughts of retaliation or harsh words or worse, we immediately recognize that our mind is operating on its own, and we pull it back and use our higher brain functions to assess the situation and our response to it. Eventually, with practice in meditation, this occurs spontaneously, as our mind becomes accustomed to staying centered, including in times of stress. Rather than having anger carry us away, our higher brain functions determine our actions. Our mind is disciplined. A disciplined mind is a huge life asset that many people will never possess unless they learn to meditate. Psychologists recognize this mental discipline as a valuable life skill that allows people to function optimally in all life situations; they refer to it as *trait mindfulness*. If everybody had strong trait mindfulness, psychologists would go broke, because they'd have very few patients. Given our history of self-will run riot, meditation is a crucial skill for success for our recovery. But this skill also serves us well in other aspects of life, such as work, relationships, parenting, and problem-solving.

*

There are many ways we can focus our meditation, and the 12 Steps give us a huge – nearly endless – variety of excellent and deeply useful areas of focus for meditation. Many of these have already come up in our discussions of the previous Steps. For example, we have already talked about meditating on our readiness to give up our character defects in Step Six, our daily meditation as part of our Step Ten, and we will discuss shortly using "remember when" meditation to put an end to cravings or thoughts of relapse.

The Big Book provides suggestions for a focus for morning and evening meditations. These are found on pages 86 and 87. The suggested focus for meditation at night is a review of our day and our actions, and how we could have done better; basically a Step Ten review. The morning focus is on visualizing the upcoming day and asking our higher power for guidance in being the kind of person who lives by spiritual principles. We want to start our day focused on the day ahead and being at our best as we head into it. I suggest throwing in a brief affirmation of our powerlessness over addictive substances every morning as well.

Sometimes we may wish to choose a problem-and-solution-based meditation focus. Here we meditate on a specific problem we are facing, and work through the problem and come at it from different perspectives and angles. We keep our mind from going to the emotions that surround the problem, and we instead focus on a detached view of the problem and potential solutions. This may be the only time we will consider all possible approaches to the problem and we may even realize some aspects of the problem or repercussions from it that we hadn't previously considered. You may be surprised at how much clarity and perspective that you get from meditating on a problem: "meditation… helps to envision our spiritual objective before we try to move toward it (*Twelve Steps and Twelve Traditions,* p. 100). However, when focusing on a problem we must be mindful to keep our mind on task, rather than allowing it to wander off and generate anger, resentment, or self-pity because of the problem we are considering. That kind of negative psychology must not be allowed to invade our meditation.

If we become mindful of feeling down, or we are indulging in self-pity, or feeling short-changed in life, it's therapeutic to meditate on gratefulness. This centers us, and moves our psychology away from the negative. We focus our meditation on all the things in life that we are – or should be – grateful for and what life would be like without these things. I find myself smiling when I come out of my gratefulness meditations. I do these gratefulness meditations a couple of times a week and whenever I need a boost. They really help me a lot. Sometimes it really helps defeat our human tendency to do the self-pity thing when we include in our gratefulness meditation an appreciation for some of the terrible things that we *don't* have in our lives, and which we take for granted. For example, I think of people who are incarcerated, or who live in a dangerous country, or in a war zone, or who are dying, or who have lost a child, and so on, and then I think of how grateful that I am that I am not facing those kinds of challenges. Always, I meditate on how fortunate I am that I'm not still out there sick and suffering from addiction-alcoholism, as many people are.

Meditation is a powerful way to "psyche ourselves up" for something that's creating fear or worry for us. I'll use a boxing match as an example. Prior to getting in the ring with another fighter, a boxer will have trained for years as a boxer, and for months specifically for that particular fight. The constant fear is of failure: losing the fight, performing poorly, getting knocked out on the canvas. Imagine any of those things happening in front of a large crowd of people and maybe even on TV. Just imagine the fear of getting knocked out in front of all those people. So how does a boxer even work up the nerve to get in the ring? How does a boxer heading to the ring

343

in front of a huge crowd not become suddenly overcome with anxiety over the possibility of being beat and humiliated in front of all those people? It's about being psyched up. For that, boxers and other athletes use visualization by meditation.

Using visualization as a focus of meditation helps us to "psyche ourselves up" for a difficult task, including working up the courage to face the task, but it also helps us to prepare and plan for the task. If you don't have a boxing match coming up, you can use the same technique to overcome performance anxiety for a job interview, public speaking, or any other task that's causing you anxiety. Our focus of meditation here is the visualization of ourselves doing the task, and playing it through to the end. As we do so, we are able to foresee potential problems we will face so that we are mentally prepared for them, and this enables us to develop our plan of action. We should not abandon this line of meditation until we have worked through a viable, workable approach to our task and a plan of action for any problems that we may foresee cropping up. The undisciplined mind will – on its own initiative – visualize failure, and that's what creates fear. This fear is exaggerated, because the undisciplined mind has a penchant for blowing things out of proportion, and the fear is dysfunctional because it doesn't protect us from failure, but can actually make us more likely to stumble. This fear can cripple us, and become a self-fulfilling prophecy. Some people freeze up or shut down from this fear, the so-called "performance anxiety." Meditating on success, or gracious acceptance if things don't go the way we would want them to helps alleviate that fear, and gives us a much better chance of success. Preventing the mind from wandering off and creating dysfunctional and exaggerated fear is a goal of meditating prior to a stressful task. That same mental discipline allows us to keep our mind from scaring us and paralyzing us with fear by visualizing failure at the time we do our task.

It really is an odd thing that the nature of the mind is to visualize and anticipate failure, because this in itself can be a cause of failure, becoming a self-fulfilling prophecy. For some reason, our mind loves to stew on something, to dream up worst-case scenarios, and then to blow those out of proportion. It gets worse at night, when all is quiet and our undisciplined imaginations outrun us, and even outrun reality. Before you know it, we can't sleep and we are so shaken that we can't even face what's bothering us. "Getting psyched up" is about defeating that process, which can only be done by reining in our weak mind when it tries to do this self-destructive exercise in futility. Meditation is exactly how we do this. A practiced meditator has a disciplined mind, which is not allowed to wander off and visualize failure and create anxiety. Rather, through meditation we can guide it into projecting a more realistic outcome, and then a pathway to success and an outcome that's very positive for us. Not false hope, but a

344

realistic positive outcome that's within reach of our abilities. We can back up our meditation by taking action to support that positive outcome, filled with our confidence that we have the ability to complete our task.

This technique of stopping the mind from its useless, self-destructive tendency to envision the worst possible failed outcome is the basis of sports psychology. Elite athletes can lose at their sport if this terrible mental process isn't halted. Imagine the NHL goaltender who allows his mind to envision failure before a playoff game; the anxiety will stunt his performance and could actually bring on failure. Likewise with the boxer before an important bout or the major league batter stepping up to the plate in the World Series. However, regular people like us can also be defeated by an undisciplined mind, especially prior to stressful tasks, such as public speaking or a job interview. Our mind can leave us "freaked out," frozen by fear, completely unfocussed on our game plan for the task. When our mind does this to us our poor performance will be certain; our undisciplined mind will have talked us into failing. In such cases, our Step Eleven meditation techniques can become a powerful ally to success. Even people who don't get performance anxiety can benefit from "psyching up" meditation, to prepare for possible barriers to success and to improve self-confidence.

Properly psyching ourselves up usually doesn't happen with just one meditation session. We may have to revisit the meditation to keep our mind focused and on task, especially if the task we are psyching ourselves up for is a big one. Each time we can consider things that hadn't previously occurred to us, and strengthen our mind's purchase of reality. The more we have meditated in our preparation for the stressful event, the less likely it is that our mind will be able to run away with us and smother us with fear at the time of the challenge. It's about handling life on life's terms.

*

It's a really nice thing to spotlight our meditation on a specific person sometimes, and this can be part of our gratitude meditation. On Mothers' Day – for example – it's a great gift and tribute to mom to meditate on how much we love her, how much she does for us, and to reflect back on all the things she has done for us from earliest childhood. Also, it helps our gratitude to meditate on how it would affect us if she suddenly disappeared from our lives. If mother is deceased, this same meditation will fill us with warm feelings and provide a worthy tribute to her life on Mother's Day, the anniversary of her death, or her birthday. Any particular day where we miss our mother the most and are most reminded of and saddened by her death is a good day to do such a meditation. Perhaps your experiences with your mother weren't good. If you still harbor anger or resentment, meditation around Mothers' Day may be a good time to use our tools to unburden

345

ourselves of these negative feelings, using the same tools that we discussed in Step Four. Meditating on mom's past experiences to understand that she was sick – like we once were – may help us to let go. We can also meditate on how useless and harmful it is for us to allow these negative emotions to live in our head rent-free. This, too, may help us to let go. When we are in a relaxed and positive state of mind during meditation, we are more likely to let go of the negative.

If we have been fighting with our spouse or partner lately, the relationship is strained, or there are hard feelings, it will almost certainly help us to find peace in our home if we meditate on our partner. We do this in a similar way to our "meditation for mom" example. We can meditate on what our partner means to us, the good times we've had, and how we would feel if he/she suddenly passed away (hopefully this would be sad). This helps our relationship and us. Gratitude for another person in our lives makes us much more likely to have positive interactions with that person.

One type of meditation that's particularly uplifting is a focus on togetherness. The power of "we" is potent and salubrious, if we allow it to be. After all, "we" is how we came to sobriety. After failing to do it our way, on our own, we found recovery when we let other people in. Ours is an uncommon fellowship, and the 12 Steps is definitely a "we" program. The first word of Step One is "we." Meditating on togetherness, on our connections with people outside ourselves, fills us with strength, warmth, and hope. It helps us to realize that we are not alone, to value people in our lives, and to reciprocate to others in our life. Finishing the meditation with prayer for those we care about completes the process and adds to our amends to them.

*

It can be very relaxing and calming to allow our senses to be the focus of a meditation. Meditating in a beautiful place, whether in nature – such as overlooking a lake set in the trees – or something man-made – such as overlooking the majestic architecture of a bustling city, is how we do this. Meditating on something specifically made for contemplation – such as a painting or a sculpture or while listening to an inspiring piece of music – is a natural way to relax. Here we focus our mind on our senses and examine these senses. We use our sight to contemplate every minute detail – especially the ones we ordinarily wouldn't notice as we go about our daily lives. We focus on the smells and the freshness of the air if we are in nature, we allow our mind to lose itself in the sounds – this is especially nice if we are meditating with music. Listen to rain falling. Pick out every sound, especially the ones we usually don't notice or divert our attention to. Our touch is a fantastic focus as part of our meditation. Pick up a leaf and hold it

346

with eyes closed, feeling its texture, its details, its softness. Run rich soil through your hand. Feel the fresh air as it touches your whole body. Taste the air, taste the smells, or put something of flavor in your mouth and focus on breaking it down. Think of how you would put that flavor into words or emotions.

Now let's carry that memory of these sensual meditations with us, so that we can revisit them mentally when we need some spiritual and mental relaxation. During the day when the stress is adding up we can lean back and close our eyes and revisit the place we meditated, or the music, or whichever sensation-focused meditation appeals to us at the time. At the end of a stressful day we can do a proper meditation where we again focus on this meditation. We can visualize the place we meditated without even being there, by focusing our mind on the memory. A particularly useful application of revisiting our sensation-based meditation is when we are laying in bed at night unable to sleep, when our thoughts are keeping us up, or our problems and challenges are cycling through our mind. In times of stress many of us project our problems into the future, making issues worse in our mind, and we face a long night of sleeplessness. Instead, as we lie there, we can close our eyes and meditate on one of our relaxation sensual meditations. Next thing we know we're asleep. It works.

*

A really important recovery-based focus of meditation is our "remember when" meditation. There are a lot of flaws in our memory processes that are used by our disease against us in our recovery. These include a tendency to remember the good times and forget the bad as time passes, and the tendency for our mind to make itself feel better about our past drinking or using by trying to convince us that there was good reason for it, or that it was fun. This is known as a *recall bias*, one of the cognitive biases that we have previously discussed. The human mind has an in-born capacity for self-deception – largely from these cognitive biases – and these are magnified in the addicted mind. These biases are driven by our cognitive dissonance, which motivates us to change how we remember things because the truth hurts. Our motivations strongly influence our memories and interpretations, and our disease tries to use this fact to push us back into drinking or using by recalling biased pleasant memories of our past life, while forgetting the bad memories. And it succeeds in tripping up many good people in recovery who aren't vigilant and doing the things they need to do to remain in recovery, such as our Step Eleven activities. This recall bias that distorts our memories can cause us to have thoughts and cravings of drinking or using, even decades into recovery. This is especially likely to happen if we are facing really rough times, or really good times.

By far the most effective way of defeating the obsession, thoughts, distorted memories, and cravings of substance use is to combine the 12 Step slogan "Remember When" with our meditation techniques. I have mentioned this technique for overcoming cravings a few times already, but let's now take a closer look at it. This potent neuroplasticity technique is especially useful in early recovery, but revisiting "remember when" meditation is important further on in recovery if we find thoughts of drinking or using creeping back in. This is a remarkably effective technique for putting such thoughts in their place. This isn't just based on experience; studies in the cognitive science of memory function and addiction has shown that these meditation practices help us to form new, healthy brain pathways to overcome the brain changes that came from our substance use.[36] This represents a significant boost for relapse prevention in the short- and long-term.

The 12 Step slogan "Remember When" suggests that we make a conscious effort to remember all the misery and mishap and loss that our substance use caused us, in order to counter the recall bias. However, we can use our Step Eleven meditation to give this slogan a huge boost. By focusing our meditation on remembering the specifics of how sick, miserable, and hopeless we were when we were in active substance use provides a much greater impact than merely "remembering." When we meditate on all this misery and loss – as painful as it is to do so – we build new memory pathways that overlay the fake pleasant memories that our disease tries to boost to leverage us back into drinking or using. This defeats the natural self-destructive tendency of our mind to remember our drinking or using days as good times. Our disease tries to convince us that it was great to be drunk or high, partying, and having life's problems lifted off our shoulders by drug or drink. Our disease's ability to play with our memories like that is powerful, and many people fall to relapse from little else. However, "remember when" meditation over-rides this self-destructive trick of the mind, and conditions our mind to associate our drug or alcohol use with what it really became: the worst experience of our life. Thoughts of relapse and cravings melt away when we achieve that.

We know that our "remember when" meditation is working when thoughts of drinking or using make us shudder, feel physically sick, and make the hair on the back of our neck stand up. This powerful mental conditioning makes us associate drinking or using with misery, loss of all the things in life that are important to us, and sickness. That's our "remember when" meditation at work. If you don't feel that association, perhaps some more remember when meditation is in order. I did this kind of meditation every day in early recovery, and I was amazed by how quickly it removed my cravings and obsessive thoughts of drinking or using. Remarkably, I was able to accomplish this with only three or four minutes of remember when meditation a day. I can honestly say that my first year in recovery was a lot easier than I thought it would be, and I attribute a lot of this to my remember when meditation.

You may hear 12 Step members talking about "playing the tape through to the end," a technique that we have already discussed. Playing the tape through to the end means that if we are having thoughts of drinking or using we must think beyond the "party," and think through to where it will lead – right back to that same misery that beat us down in the past. It takes some mental discipline to do this, because the addicted mind will focus on the here and now of that first drink or drug, and ignore what happens after. Addiction is, after all, a disease of the "here and now." It's easy to fall victim to this shallow, dysfunctional thinking, but the disciplined mind will recognize this self-destructive thinking and play the tape through to the inevitable end. We can do this with a brief bout of "walking meditation" at the very time that we find ourselves faced with an urge to pick up that first drink or drug. This, too, is a powerful tool for preventing relapse.

*

Wait a minute... I just used the term "walking meditation." What, exactly, is walking meditation? That's a term I use for brief mini-meditations where we center our mind and pull it in when it's doing something it shouldn't be doing as we go about our day. When we become practiced at meditation and used to snapping our mind back on track when it wanders off during meditation, that skill begins to appear in our day-to-day life. This is that "trait mindfulness" that psychologists so revere. When our mind wanders off we take notice and snap it back in place when we need to. This is important because it helps keep us from reacting out of emotion and letting our character defects take over when something stressful happens. If someone bumps into us or does something we don't like and our mind goes instinctually to an anger reaction and tells us to lash out we recognize our errant mind and snap it back into place, often without even thinking about it. Similarly, if our alcoholic-addict mind begins thinking about how nice a drug or drink would be, we are able to snap our mind back from the grip of our disease and engage our remember when tool.

When our mind gets really angry an experienced meditator can pause and consciously bring it back on track. A lot of people who struggle with "road rage" find this very helpful because they otherwise find it difficult to curb their anger and stop themselves from lashing out at other drivers during their commute. That's an important benefit to meditation and a disciplined mind, because road rage is a very un-spiritual thing and can get us in trouble. It really puts on a bad show for other people, especially anyone who's unfortunate enough to be in the car with us. Besides, it's a terrible thing to show up at work every day already edgy and in a bad mood from the commute. I have done therapy for a number of my patients who are really nice people but suffer terribly from road rage and uncontrollable anger when they drive. Always, I teach them some basic meditation skills, and it always works.

Sometimes (when we are not driving) we can even sit back for a moment as we go about our day and do a very brief mini-meditation where we close our eyes, detach ourselves from a stressful situation, and center our mind. For the experienced meditator, this takes but a moment. We can do this, too, while driving, but with our eyes open. When we center our mind and snap it back from an emotional, character defect-driven response to a stressor we are allowing our higher brain functions take over rather than allowing instinct and emotion to drive our actions. I'm sure we've all had times in our lives when we wished we could have a do-over for some unfortunate and not thought-out reaction to a stressor. When we recognize that our mind is going somewhere we don't want it to go and consciously snap it back into place as we go about our day, I refer to this as "walking meditation." This is a great tool for our spirituality and our ability to maintain our peace of mind and serenity, and a great life skill. It's one of the advantages of practicing meditation.

Twelve Steps and Twelve Traditions makes a suggestion relevant to walking meditation: "if at these points our emotional disturbance happens to be great, we will more surely keep our balance, provided we remember, and repeat to ourselves, a particular prayer or phrase that has appealed to us in our reading or meditation" (p. 103). In meditation lingo, this prayer or phrase that we repeat in stressful times is known as a *mantra*. Personally, I find the third Step prayer and the slogans "Easy Does It," and "One Day at a Time" to be meaningful mantras. Each of us should have a few of these in our back pocket for use in stressful times. For example, when I become angry, impatient, or intolerant of some person or situation, repeating "Easy Does It" to myself really helps me center myself, and gives me something to focus my mind on other than my anger. The simple slogans that our fellowship embraces are truly powerful tools, *if* we use them.

*

We must remember that many of us got caught in addiction-alcoholism because life became overwhelming, or we had poor coping skills, or we were trying to cope with mental health symptoms, or a combination of those factors. The 12 Step program is designed to help us learn to handle life without becoming overwhelmed, to find healthy coping mechanisms, and to seek the outside help we need to treat our mental health symptoms if that's a problem for us. The reason that meditation found its way into the 12

Step program – via Step Eleven – is because it's an extremely potent way to give us precisely those life skills that the program seeks to impart. Meditation is a robust coping mechanism for whatever life has to dish out at us, and it helps us to find the self-awareness to recognize when things aren't right with us.

When we use meditation to help us get our head around life and its problems, we take away the chance for our disease to take advantage of a stressed-out mind to worm its way back into our lives. Life is so much more manageable when we face our problems and challenges realistically, rather than with undue fear caused by allowing our weak mind to run away on us and blow everything out of proportion. This is where we get the fear, self-pity, pessimism, and anger that once caused us to feel overwhelmed and try to escape life in drink or drug. We are using a positive coping mechanism – our meditation – to crush the need for a dysfunctional coping mechanism – our drinking or using. Again, I use the example of the mental techniques used by the U.S. Navy SEALs, because their techniques are derived directly from meditation principles, and the SEALs are experts at applying these principles to the most stressful of situations. The SEALs employ the same meditation techniques that we use in recovery, and they put in the time and practice necessary to get good at it, because they need the mental strength to endure any kind of hardship that life may throw at them – or, as they put it, to "embrace the suck." The whole SEALs selection and training process is designed to select the individuals who are capable of believing in their ability to get through any challenge, and who don't allow their mind to talk them out of success by its natural tendency to cast doubt, project failure, and cause fear and pessimism. They are looking for people who don't give up and surrender to fear, no matter what. We, too, must never again give up and surrender to our disease. That's exactly the approach that our Step Eleven meditation brings to us. We learn to discipline our mind, and to have the awareness to refocus when our mind is creating negative, unfounded, and self-defeating thoughts and made-up fears.

We can add other positive coping mechanisms to our meditation: exercise, family time, going to meetings and our other recovery activities, eating properly, etc. However, we are addict-alcoholics, so we must be mindful of other dysfunctional coping mechanism that can seep into our lives, such as: unhealthy sex practices, pornography, gambling, impulsive shopping, compulsive eating, co-dependent relationships, or self-harm. These are known as behavioral addictions (sometime referred to as *process addictions*) that actually involve very similar brain processes as substance addiction. It's very easy to replace one addiction with another, so we must be mindful and vigilant of this tendency. Better to develop meditation and prayer skills as a way to cope with stress and life than to inadvertently resort to old habits by slipping into a new addiction.

*

There are various techniques or disciplines or styles of meditation, such as Vipassana meditation, Zen meditation, mantra meditation, transcendental meditation, Buddhism, and mindfulness meditation. I don't get hung up on different dogmatic meditation styles, but some people may enjoy exploring some of these for themselves. What's important is just finding what makes sense for you and works for you. What's nice is that nowadays you no longer have to climb the Himalayas to consult a guru to sample different meditation styles; rather, you can check them out by using YouTube videos, making it really easy to do. The various types of meditation and advanced meditation techniques are beyond the scope of our discussion here, but I encourage anyone who enjoys meditation and wishes to explore it further to do so. Joining a meditation class, attending a retreat, or even watching YouTube videos on meditation are great ways to learn more and try new things. Some of the guided meditations available on YouTube are quite nice.

I would, however, like to mention mindfulness, because I have used the term "being mindful" a number of times in our trip through the Steps, and "mindfulness" is an important aspect of challenging dysfunctional thoughts and behaviors. As we have discussed, self-awareness is a core technique for overcoming virtually any dysfunctional or harmful thoughts and behaviors. I find that so-called "mindfulness meditation" – as a specific meditation discipline – is inappropriate for our purposes for one major reason: it involves being non-judgmental of our thoughts and feelings; acting as an accepting observer of our thoughts rather than challenging dysfunctional thoughts.[37] It suggests that our thoughts or feelings are neither right nor wrong, so we should observe them and learn to live with them as they are. This concept would be harmful for our purposes, because as alcoholic-addicts we have been plagued by thoughts that are definitely harmful and wrong, and have led to our spectacular demise, and could potentially kill us if they go unchallenged. We must confront our dysfunctional thoughts and feelings and root out the ones that propagate our disease.

So, rather than practice "mindfulness meditation," we can benefit from being mindful, meaning that we learn to have an awareness of our thoughts, emotions, and behaviors and challenge them when we recognize them as harmful or dysfunctional. So, when I speak of being mindful I am not referring to the doctrine of "mindfulness meditation;" rather, I am referring to the practice of being aware of our thoughts and feelings and using our knowledge of our disease to root out those which would put us back to where we were: overcome by negative psychology, and spiritually, mentally, and physically sick.

Now, let's look at a specific type of meditation: prayer.

*

We'll begin our discussion of prayer by noting that prayer is a powerful tool for everyone, not just the religious or those whose higher power is called God. The word prayer has come to be saddled with an inescapable religious connotation, but we need to look at it differently within the 12 Step program, because it's used by many people who are not religious, and it's an important type of meditation. You may note as you read through the Big Book that although the prayers are often directed to God, none of them are incantations of worship, such as you may see in a religious service. Rather, they are communications in which we ask our higher power for help, which is the true purpose of prayer in the 12 Step program: "prayer, as it is commonly understood, is a petition to God. Having opened our channel as best we can, we ask for those things of which we and others are in the greatest need. And we think that the whole range of our needs is well defined by that part of Step Eleven which says: '... knowledge of His will for us and the power to carry that out'" (*Twelve Steps and Twelve Traditions*, p. 102). We've already discussed in our Step Three study why the 12 Step program founders decided to use the word "God" in the Big Book, and how they intended it as an open concept encompassing anyone's beliefs or non-beliefs, referring to a higher power of our understanding (or *not* understanding).

Scientific research has – as we will discuss – upheld prayer as a therapeutic type of meditation. So, let's start out by changing our way of thinking of prayer: sure, it's something used by religions, but it's also something that can be used by those who are not religious. The Big Book equates meditation and prayer on a number of occasions (on pages 83, 87, and 164), as does *Twelve Steps and Twelve Traditions* (on pages 96, and 101-102). For our purposes in the 12 Step program, regardless of anybody's definition of prayer, we use prayer as a form of meditation to help us grow in spirituality, maintain a positive psychology, and fortify our recovery. Let's think of prayer as a way of connecting with a higher power through meditation.

We'll discuss how prayer can be a good and meaningful fit for atheists, and for those who haven't yet figured out exactly what a higher power is to them. We'll also discuss how those among us who are religious or whose higher power is known as God may be able to tune up their prayer to make it more supportive of their recovery, and more directed to healing from the physical, mental, and spiritual sickness of addiction-alcoholism. Best of all,

353

we'll discuss how to use the type of meditation we refer to as prayer as a powerful spiritual tool. We'll look to the 12 Step literature and research from the behavioral sciences to help us learn how to do that.

*

There's peace of mind that comes with learning to pray: "peace, love, and joy can be sought through quiet thinking and honest prayer. The wholeness, the new awareness, that is produced affects one's relationship with God and man.... There is a joining of inner forces with outer forces. The Power greater than ourselves puts us in tune with the world.... I believe completeness is waiting for anyone who will take the time to make the effort, through quiet thinking, honest prayer, chosen reading, and exercise. These are the ingredients. It is an adventure so worthwhile that all else fades in comparison, yet it makes all else worthwhile" (*Came to Believe*, p. 65-66). This is why those among us who are leery about the word "prayer" should be open-minded about it and give it a chance. By this point in our trip through the Steps, we've taken an open-minded approach to many new ideas, and we've taken more than a few leaps of faith, so this should be almost second nature to us by this point.

There's a tremendous body of research evidence supporting prayer as an immensely effective way of coping with life's problems, which – as you well know at this point in the Steps – is central to the success of our recovery. We discussed in Step Three the scientific evidence that shows that "surrender" of our will to a higher power gives us a greater sense of personal control, and prayer has been shown to augment that effect.[38] Other research has consistently shown prayer to increase our sense of well-being, our sense of purpose in life, self-esteem, and satisfaction with life.[39,40,41] As well, prayer has been shown to reduce alcohol cravings and consumption.[42, 43,44]

There's a great body of evidence from well-designed medical clinical trials that shows that prayer has many benefits to our physical health.[45] As one researcher puts it: "prayer, like meditation, influences our state of mind, which, in turn, influences our state of body."[46] Perhaps most notable for us is that prayer has been shown to reduce cortisol levels in our blood, with a significant impact on our health, and how we feel.[47,48] Cortisol is known as the "stress hormone," and it causes a lot of detrimental effects to our physical and mental health; cortisol is the reason that stress is so harmful to our health. As such, by reducing cortisol levels, prayer exerts a very real contribution to our resilience to life's stressors, both physically and mentally. Prayer reduces the experience of anxiety, elevates a depressed mood, lowers blood pressure, stabilizes sleep patterns, and impacts autonomic functions like digestion and breathing.[49] Further, in influencing

354

our state of body-mind, prayer and meditation also influence our thinking. This prompts a shift in the habits of the mind, and, subsequently, patterns of behavior. These changes, in turn and over time, induce changes in the brain, further influencing our subjective and objective experience of the world and how we participate in it.[50] Speaking strictly in medical terms, prayer, spirituality, and connection with a higher power are potent catalysts for positive neuroplasticity, a necessary process for the brain to recover from substance use and addiction-alcoholism.

So, prayer, by any name – whatever label you wish to put on it – can do a lot for us.

*

Who prays? Lots of us do. More than half (55%) of Americans say they pray every day, according to a Pew Research Center study, while 21% say they pray weekly or monthly.[51,52] Even 20% of those who don't belong to any religion pray daily. About 12% of atheists say they pray.[53,54] Prayer seems to hold an appeal for a lot of people, and a lot of well designed medical and scientific research studies over the last forty years tell us why. The benefits go well beyond the spiritual, and there are many known measurable physical and mental benefits.

Prayer, like spirituality, means something different to everyone. Keeping our prayer personal and informal, as a meaningful conversation with our higher power, is important because we know that prayer can lose its force if it becomes fixed, formulaic, and impersonal or if it is performed simply as a custom.[55] Even prayer that involves simple listening, reflection of gratitude, quietly thinking about our higher power, or experiencing a sense of presence is related to higher feelings of well-being.[56] In fact, psychological studies have shown that meditative prayer was correlated with spiritual well-being and satisfaction, as well as feelings of closeness to a higher power and a sense of purpose in life.[57] Prayer carried out in the form of *informal* and familiar speech was correlated with happiness. On the other hand, petitionary and ritual prayer had no demonstrated positive effects. As well, those who pray frequently and use meditative forms of prayer are more likely to have positive experiences from the prayer.[58]

Based on these research findings – and on the long-standing suggestions from the 12 Step literature – I suggest that we think of prayer as a form of meditation. The deeper level of concentration without the mind wandering off makes our prayer much more meaningful and productive. The 12 Step program agrees with this suggestion: "there is a direct linkage among self-examination, meditation, and prayer. Taken separately, these practices can bring much relief and benefit. But when they are logically related and interwoven, the result is an unshakeable foundation for life (*Twelve Steps and Twelve Traditions*, p. 98).

A well-designed clinical analysis of A.A. members' perceptions of the higher power (we discussed this study in our Step Two discussion) included a look at A.A. members' perceptions of prayer.[59] This research is particularly interesting for our purposes because it identifies what prayer means to 12 Steppers. This study amply demonstrates that the 12 Step program has succeeded in making prayer personal, meaningful, and practical – regardless of participants' belief system. Let's look at some of the notable points brought out by this interesting research.

A recurrent theme among the study participants was that atheism or agnosticism were no barrier to praying. One A.A. member said: "I know a lot of atheists that pray." Some participants identified themselves as atheists who pray despite personal struggles with the concept of a higher power. One such atheistic person regularly prayed by citing the Eleventh and Third Step prayers, finding that mouthing these prayers helps his sobriety. That individual even found those prayers to be meaningful, despite his atheistic views. Another atheist observed: "you can almost gauge people's level of contentment – their external level of contentment anyway – from their degree of contact with their HP [higher power]. Those people who maintain a constant dialogue with their HP – whatever that is – seem to be happier than the people who struggle with it. The problem that causes me is that intellectually I struggle with it... I try not to let it worry me too much!" Some of the study participants found prayer valuable to their sobriety and life despite not knowing who or what they were praying to. These people are making spirituality and prayer work for them even though they don't know where it fits with their belief system. Their open-mindedness and desire to go to any lengths to stay sober has resulted in them finding a powerful tool for recovery in prayer.

Among the study participants, the simplest form of prayer consisted of asking for another day of recovery in the morning and expressing thanks for the past day of recovery in the evening. Some also relied on set prayers such as the Serenity Prayer or Francis of Assisi's prayer, carried out in meetings or in solitude. One member commented: "without failure I do say the Lord's prayer because... it calms me down."

Morning prayers were important to the interviewees, setting the tone for the day. One said: "if I don't pray in the morning or meditate, my day will not go right. If I do, even if there are problems, it will be ok." Another observed: "people have gone out [i.e. relapsed] after 25 years, 40 years... probably they stopped praying."

The issue of praying for ourselves was addressed by the study participants. Though the focus is on praying for others, asking for help was not taboo: "sometimes I suffer from nightmares, violent, really nasty...:

'Please take this away! I can't handle this!' – gone!" One sister in recovery prays, but not to ask for things for a specific reason: "I'm careful not to pray for stuff because that's taking back my self-will. And my self-will doesn't get me anywhere basically... I don't pray for things to get better but I pray for me to get through something... I pray... 'O let me do the best I can... just be with me, give me guidance'... I have 10 little marbles and in the morning I put them out, one for each thing I'm worried about, I hand that over, and then the same marbles at the end of the day are for the things that I'm grateful for. So I'm starting my day by handing over things to God that I am scared of, and I'm finishing it by the things that I'm thankful for." That's an interesting point: she prays to get through things, not for those things to be magically solved for her. As we will discuss shortly, her point about not praying for everything to go exactly her way is consistent with the suggestions in the Big Book, and is a very valid psychological point.

The issue of contrast between prayer at religious gatherings and the prayers in A.A. came up. One woman reflected on her experiences from her Catholic background: "sometimes, I struggle with the prayers because again of my upbringing. There's a lot of saying of prayers and not really thinking about what they mean, and that's still a habit." Participants like to apply the slogan "Keep it Simple" to prayer. They felt that it's OK to pray with others, but we should have our private moments of meditation in prayer that is aligned with our spiritual goals: growth, positive psychology, and stable recovery.

Among the study participants, prayer was widely seen as a way to benefit from connecting with a higher power: "I couldn't have enjoyed my present peace without improvement in contact with my HP." This emphasizes the role of prayer in our growth in our connection with our higher power, which is the third level of spirituality. This is something that we must incorporate into our daily routine to become practiced and to continue to experience the positive effects: "contact with the HP has to be constantly worked at." Participants found that prayer made them feel more connected with their higher power and with the universe – a connection that some hadn't been able to find elsewhere: "I didn't feel a connection... not just with the church but with anything I was turning to: it didn't seem authentic." Things seemed to have more purpose than ever before. A higher power was described as "a force we can access" and prayer and altruism were suggested as the way to exercise that access. Expressing gratitude held a prominent place in prayer: "remembering the past gives me overwhelming gratitude to the HP for the present... I am grateful for the HP's protection from negative thinking, which is part of the addictive disease."

Interestingly, not one of the randomly selected people involved in the study disparaged prayer, including the atheists and agnostics.

Convincing research has shown that prayer increases our ability to resist temptation by improving self-control.[60] What's especially interesting and relevant to our Step Eleven discussion in this particular research study is that this effect was shown to exist even among atheists when they pray. Further, the improved self-control effect was found to exist even when the prayer was not about resisting temptation – the prayer could be on any subject. So prayer, any kind of prayer, improves our ability to resist temptation.

Another very cool study used a state-of-the-art neuro-imaging technique known as fMRI to examine the functional effects of prayer on the brains of A.A. members.[61] The researchers compared the A.A. members who were praying to members who were not praying, and found that the group who were praying had significant changes in the parts of the brain associated with suppressing cravings (for you science nerds, those parts of the brain were the left-anterior middle frontal gyrus, left superior parietal lobule, bilateral precuneus, and bilateral posterior middle temporal gyrus). The prayer group also had a significantly reduced emotional reaction to an alcohol-related stimulus, and had the parts of their brain related to reduced cravings and improved self-control light up on the scans, showing measurably increased activity. Here we have a research study looking into serious, measurable effects of prayer on our disease, with results that clearly show the benefits of prayer. Overall, the study concluded that prayer among A.A. members is associated with the engagement of brain mechanisms that control attention, emotion, self-control, and cravings.

Numerous other studies have shown that prayer increases our ability to abstain from alcohol, which reflects this improved self-control.[62,63] Interestingly, four different studies demonstrated that even among non-alcoholics prayer lowered their alcohol consumption by about one-half and prevented their progression to problem drinking.[64] Given that other addictive substances affect the same brain mechanisms as does alcohol, it is reasonable to interpolate and apply these results to alcoholism-addiction in general.

Although the effects of prayer on alcohol addiction have been studied more that the effects of prayer on drug addiction, the same effects have been upheld by studies of prayer and drug use.[65] Medically, alcohol and drugs are not separate entities; rather they are all addictive substances that have the same neural pathways leading to addiction. In other words, science does not distinguish alcoholism from drug addiction. As such, it is entirely reasonable and physiologically viable to expect the same advantages from prayer regardless of our choice of drug.

In the end, we have ample studies from behavioral science as well as neuroscience that confirm the benefits of prayer for overall well-being as well as for recovery from our disease. As one review of studies concluded: "whether or not a divine power truly does exist might be a matter of opinion, but the neurophysiological effects of religious/spiritual belief are scientific facts that can be accurately measured."[66] Bill Wilson was right on the money when he made prayer and meditation a part of the 12 Step program in Step Eleven.

*

Prayer is a really great way to make action amends to people on our list from Step Eight. Praying for someone is a really nice thing to do for them, allowing us to further our ongoing amends, and allowing us to make amends to the people we haven't been able to reach in Step Nine.

Prayer is also great way to make amends for the hell we put our partner and family through. Besides staying sober, the next best thing we can do is to be the best spouse we can be. Research has shown that prayer helps us do that. It has been shown that if we pray for our spouse we are happier with them, more willing to compromise, and more likely to be satisfied with not being "right."[67] The research compared people who prayed for their spouse against people who just engaged in positive thought about their spouse, and it was prayer that made the difference. This research also demonstrated that we are more likely to forgive our spouse when we pray for him or her, and that we are also less likely to react with anger when our spouse offends us. That's a great way to make amends – and to keep our home happy and healthy.

Further studies have demonstrated that prayer enhances trust between couples and makes them more likely to stay together.[68] Given that by the time we find our way into recovery we have completely destroyed any trust that our partner had in us, this makes prayer an important tool for regaining that important relationship virtue.

These positive effects of prayer on our relationships are a great amends for our partner, but it also helps our own recovery and happiness. Stable relationships provide, after all, an important support structure for our recovery, and make for a better life for our entire family, including the kids. Several research studies have shown that when a couple prays together, even just twice a week for four weeks, they have an increased level of trust and feelings of unity. The same effect was not seen in couples that just talked about positive things for the same period of time.[69]

The 12 Step literature even suggests that we may consider involving our spouse or family in our meditation and prayer (see the Big Book page 87, and *Twelve Steps and Twelve Tradition,* page 134).

So, just to quickly summarize, prayer makes us nicer, more forgiving, less needful of being "right," and improves our bond with our spouse. It also helps us gain back the trust of our spouse, and brings us closer together. Further, it helps our physical and mental health in numerous ways, most especially by reducing the circulating levels of cortisol (the stress hormone) in our hot blood. It provides a powerful boost to our resilience to stress and adversity. It's also a potent "brain hygiene" technique that deploys our neuroplasticity to overcome the devastating effects of substance use on our brain, thereby strengthening our mental health, brain function, and resistance to relapse. Sound good? Let's now look at how to pray.

*

Step Eleven holds the key for effective prayer in its simple wording: *praying only for knowledge of His will for us and the power to carry that out.* What that phrase is telling us is that we must avoid the temptation to make prayer into a "wish-list." Many people's prayers are focused on everything going their way, like a wish list for life. They pray that they will get that job they applied for, that their health will be good, maybe even that they will win the lottery. However, this selfish way of praying is disastrously dysfunctional for our spirituality and for our recovery. Turning prayer into a petition for willfulness destroys what we accomplished in Step Three.

The 12 Step program has a much different take on prayer than the selfish wish-list style of prayer that many people adhere to. When Bill Wilson shares about the moment he found sobriety, it was about letting go to his higher power: "I humbly offered myself to God, as I then understood Him, to do with me as He would. I placed myself unreservedly under His care and direction. I admitted for the first time that of myself I was nothing; that without Him I was lost" (Big Book, p. 13). He did this while – once again – hospitalized for his drinking, deathly sick. That was the moment from which he counts his sobriety, as he never had a drink again. His prayers from then on reflected his focus on selflessness and a desire to be "useful:" "... asking only for direction and strength to meet my problems as He would have me. Never was I to pray for myself, except as my requests bore on my usefulness to others. Then only might I expect to receive. But that would be in great measure" (Big Book, p. 13).

It's tempting to turn our prayers into our wish list for life, asking for good things to happen to us. However, such a selfish and inward-looking mind-set harks back to the negative psychology of our drinking and using days. Besides, we're setting ourselves up for spiritual and psychological disaster, because when something in life doesn't go our way – as is bound to happen from time to time – after we have prayed and prayed for it to go just right for us, we become disappointed, angry, and resentful. Remember:

360

expectations are the prelude to resentments, and putting expectations upon our prayer and higher power is no exception. Rather than ask for everything to go our way as we face a stressful event, we ask for the strength to do our best and to get through the stressful event and still uphold our spiritual principles, dignity, and sobriety, regardless of how it turns out. An alcoholic-addict in recovery explains:

> If I am facing a life crisis, I no longer pray for my Higher Power to make that crisis go away. Instead, I ask for the strength and courage to accept His will, and to guide me through the experience: Thy will, not mine, be done. No more asking my Higher Power to do things my way. It's about living 'life on life's terms,' which is the same as saying 'life on my Higher Power's terms.'
>
> It's merciful that our Higher Power doesn't just make everything in life go our way. How could life go everybody's way? There have to be winners and losers, not everyone can win. It doesn't even make sense for us to ask for life to go our way. To ask for another 24 hours of sobriety, though, is what we do. Many people pray as though to overcome the will of a reluctant God, instead of taking hold of the willingness of a loving God (*Came to Believe*, p. 26).

The 12 Step literature explains further: "our immediate temptation will be to ask for specific solutions to specific problems, and for the ability to help other people as we have already thought they should be helped. In that case, we are asking God to do it *our* way. Therefore, we ought to consider each request carefully to see what its real merit is. Even so, when making specific requests, it will be well to add to each one of them this qualification: '...if it be Thy will'" (*Twelve Steps and Twelve Traditions*, p. 102). We can end up trying to force our self-will on ourselves and others through prayer if we aren't careful about how we pray. As such, prayer can easily become a tool for our self-will, arrogance, selfishness, and need for control to re-assert themselves:

> Of course, it is reasonable and understandable that the question is often asked: '*Why* can't we take a specific and troubling dilemma straight to God, and in prayer secure from Him sure and definite answers to our requests?' This can be done, but it has hazards. We have seen A.A.'s ask with much earnestness and faith for God's explicit guidance on matters ranging all the way from a shattering domestic or financial crisis to correcting a minor personal fault, like tardiness. Quite often, however, the thoughts that *seem* to come from God are not answers at all. They prove to be well-intentioned unconscious rationalizations. The A.A., or indeed any man, who tries

361

to run his life rigidly by this kind of prayer, by this self-serving demand of God for replies, is a particularly disconcerting individual. To any questioning or criticism of his actions he instantly proffers his reliance upon prayer for guidance in all matters great or small. He may have forgotten the possibility that his own wishful thinking and the human tendency to rationalize have distorted his so-called guidance. With the best of intentions, he tends to force his own will into all sorts of situations and problems with the comfortable assurance that he is acting under God's specific direction. Under such an illusion, he can of course create great havoc without in the least intending it (*Twelve Steps and Twelve Traditions*, p. 103-104).

As we discussed in Step Three, recovery from alcoholism-addiction requires a willingness to surrender our self-will, that trademark of our disease where our drive to fulfill our desires rule our life despite negative consequences to ourselves or others. When we pray for our self-will to be fulfilled – even if it is with good intentions – we are simply trying to manipulate our higher power into enabling our self-will.

*

So, what should we pray for? The Big Book doesn't suggest an eleventh Step prayer, but the third Step prayer echoes what Step Eleven suggests to pray for:

> God, I offer myself to Thee – to build with me
> And to do with me as Thou wilt.
> Relieve me of the bondage of self,
> That I may better do Thy will.
> Take away my difficulties, that victory over them
> May bear witness to those I would help of
> Thy Power, Thy Love, and Thy Way of Life.
> May I do Thy will always! (Big Book, p. 63).

The Big Book suggests that our prayer should reflect our new selflessness: "how can I best serve Thee – Thy will (not mine) be done" (Big Book, p. 85). As we progressed through the Steps we worked hard to rid ourselves of the selfishness and self-will run riot of our past miserable ways. This kind of prayer is a manifestation of who we now aspire to be, as selfless people living by spiritual principles. Our prayer reflects our desire to focus on others' needs in keeping with this new way of thinking outside ourselves. As we pray, we should pray for those in need. We can name specific people who are in need of specific help, or we can be more general: we can pray generically for those who are hungry or thirsty, those who are tired, those who are in trouble or despair, those who are sick or suffering, those who are lost, those who are afraid, those who are in the throes of alcoholism-addiction, those who are alone or lonely, those who are poor or destitute, those who are in danger, and those who do not have the comfort of a higher power.

When we pray, there are three things we should ask for when it comes to ourselves: 1) we should give thanks for having another 24 hours of sobriety, and ask for another 24 hours of sobriety, 2) we should ask that we be useful to our higher power and to others, and 3) we should ask for guidance on what our higher power would have us do. That's not to say that we expect that our higher power is there to direct us through life and control our every move. Rather, that's saying that we ask to choose to do what our higher power would have us do; we are saying that we want to do the right thing. It's a rare thing that we don't know the right thing to do when it comes to our recovery: whether to seek revenge or lash out at that person we think has wronged us, or to rid ourselves of anger and resentment and to pray for the person instead; whether or not to go to that party where the drugs and alcohol will be flowing; whether go to a much-needed meeting or to stay home and watch TV. In other words, we are asking for help to do what we should do, not what our self-will wants us to do.

Properly done, this conscious contact with our higher power through prayer provides rich benefits. We have already discussed the science research into the benefits of prayer, but we also have the experience of the millions of people who have found spiritual wellness in the 12 Step program before us:

> We discover that we do receive guidance for our lives to just about the extent that we stop making demands upon God to give it to us on order and in our terms. Almost any A.A. will tell how his affairs have taken remarkable and unexpected turns for the better as he tried to improve his conscious contact with God. He will also report that out of every season of grief or suffering, when the hand of God seemed heavy or even unjust, new lessons for living were learned, new resources of courage were uncovered, and that finally, inescapably, the conviction came that God *does* 'move in a mysterious way...' (*Twelve Steps and Twelve Traditions*, p. 104-105).

So, when we pray, we don't pray for ourselves in support of our willfulness. Likewise, when we pray, we must take care not to project our will on others:

We form ideas as to what we think God's will is for other people. We say to ourselves, 'This one ought to be cured of his fatal malady,' or 'That one ought to be relieved of his emotional pain,' and we pray for these specific things. Such prayers, of course, are fundamentally good acts, but often they are based upon a supposition that we know God's will for the person for whom we pray. This means that side by side with an earnest prayer there can be a certain amount of presumption and conceit in us. It is A.A.'s experience that particularly in these cases we ought to pray that God's will, whatever it is, be done for others as well as for ourselves (*Twelve Steps and Twelve Traditions*, p. 104).

The Big Book even suggests including a prayer when we do our walking meditation: "as we go through the day we pause, when agitated or doubtful, and ask for the right thought or action.... We are then in much less danger of excitement, fear, anger, worry, self-pity, or foolish decisions" (p. 87-88).

The Big Book also suggests concluding our meditations with a prayer: "we usually conclude the period of meditation with a prayer that we be shown all through the day what our next step is to be, that we be given whatever we need to take care of such problems. We ask especially for freedom from self-will, and are careful to make no request for ourselves only. We may ask for ourselves, however, if others will be helped. We are careful never to pray for our own selfish ends" (Big Book, p. 87). This is a great way to connect our higher power with our meditation.

Although prayer is a personal thing, the Big Book offers some suggestions about what to pray about and when on pages 86 to 88. (We have covered these suggestions in our discussion here.) This is a good starting point for those who are not sure about prayer, but they are just suggestions and we should explore prayer on our own and allow it to blossom for us in our own way as we find our connection with our higher power.

For those whose higher power is not named God, all this talk about "God's will" may be unsettling. However, the essence of the message is that we must not try to project our will for how things should go in life for us or anybody else through prayer. Life will go as life goes (this is what's meant by "God's will") and we are setting ourselves up for disappointment and resentment by trying to project our will into future events that are beyond our control.

*

I don't participate in organized religion, but I was intrigued to see what the clergy would think about the 12 Step approach to prayer. I spoke to a number of members of the clergy from several religions, and found that they agree very much with the concept of selfless prayer. The reason behind it is that – according to these clergy members – God has a plan for all of us, our "destiny," as it were. Because we pray to God every night that we want this to happen or that to happen is not going to change God's plan for us. In fact, it just makes us come across as selfish and a little greedy. By praying for help in correcting our defects of character, and praying for knowledge of God's will and the power to carry that out we are showing a willingness to accept God's plan.

Science, too, has something to say about praying for others. It has been well established by research that praying for others reduces anger and aggression, even directly after a provocation.[70] The research demonstrated that praying for a stranger who just angered us reduces our anger and aggression more than simply thinking about them in a positive way. We are past victims of our own anger and resentments, and selfless prayer is a helpful way to defeat these terrible demons. Prayer that isn't focused on ourselves has also been shown to improve our sense of well-being, including: self-esteem, optimism, meaning in life, and satisfaction with life.[71]

So, praying for others is good for us. It's easy to pray for the people we love and care about; however, a difficult aspect of praying for others involves praying for those we don't like. Believe it or not, this helps us too. Let's look at that now.

*

We spoke in our Step Four study about praying for people we don't like as a way of letting go of anger and resentments, and we can continue this practice as we advance in our recovery. In Step Four, I quoted the story from pages 544-552 of the Big Book, which suggests that we should pray for someone we don't like for two weeks. The name of that story – *Freedom From Bondage* – gives us an indication of what we can expect from such an exercise. The suggestion to pray for someone we don't like may seem like a big ask, but it's a very therapeutic exercise. Taking the high road is always calming to the soul, even if not at the time. It may go against every fiber of our being in the moment, but it always feels good later on, and we are better for it. When someone wrongs us, it's our primitive instincts that make us brew up in anger, vengeful thoughts, and aggression. The dark corner of our heart wants a piano to fall on the person in question and the thought of praying for him or her may be repulsive to us. These are exactly the primitive thoughts that we are overcoming with our meditation-disciplined mind, so that we use our higher thought processes to guide our actions and behaviors, rather than allowing our primitive reflexes to control us. What better way to keep our character defects in check? Our willfulness wants to indulge those thoughts of lashing out and getting revenge on those who have wronged us, or secretly wishing for their demise, but it's our willfulness that nearly killed us in our addiction-alcoholism, and we committed to surrendering that willfulness in Step Three. We have our hard-earned peace and serenity and we don't want to lose it – or go back to old habits – because of new or on-going anger and resentments. Praying for those we don't like helps us to do that. Besides, anybody can pray for someone they like, but it's a true test of a strong and virtuous character to pray for someone we don't like. And we want our character to be good; we need spiritual health to stay sober.

It's key to our serenity and peace of mind that we re-frame how we think of those we don't like. We need a new paradigm here, and meditating on it is our best way to work that into our mind. We must remember that when someone is being mean or selfish toward us, they have their own anger and resentments and character defects that are propelling them to their unsavory behavior. They have a similar sickness to what we had, although their sickness may or may not have propelled them into addiction-alcoholism like it did to us. Or, perhaps they are active alcoholic-addicts and they are just as sick as we once were. Either way, we should see them as sick people, and treat them as such: "we asked God to help us show them the same tolerance, pity, and patience that we would cheerfully grant a sick friend. When a person offended we said to ourselves, 'This is a sick man. How can I be helpful to him? God save me from being angry. Thy will be done'" (Big Book, p. 67). As we did in Step Four when we let go of our resentments by understanding those we resented, so we do now:

> We avoid retaliation or argument. We wouldn't treat sick people that way. If we do, we destroy our chance of being helpful. We cannot be helpful to all people, but at least God will show us how to take a kindly and tolerant view of each and every one…. Putting out of our minds the wrongs others had done, we resolutely looked for our own mistakes. Where we had been selfish, dishonest, self-seeking, and frightened? Though a situation had not been entirely our fault, we tried to disregard the other person involved entirely. Where were we to blame? … We admitted our wrongs honestly and were willing to set these matters straight (Big Book, p. 67).

Then, we take it a step further by applying the Serenity Prayer. We cannot control how other people behave toward us. However, we can control how we react and behave toward them. Therefore, we need to stop criticizing how the other person is behaving and instead examine our own role in the conflict and reflect on how we can set these things straight. Often our anger and instinctual need to blame others makes us completely lose sight that maybe we played a role in the conflict, and makes us completely unable to see things from the other person's perspective. When we use our newfound skills to calm ourselves and think through our dislike for the other person we can prevail in our spiritual principles.

If we pray for this person who wronged us or whom we don't like, then we are taking action to show our commitment to spiritual growth. Psychologically, when we do an action our mind will get behind that action and adopt the reasoning behind it, because the mind likes our actions and our beliefs to be congruent. That's where we get the expression "it's easier to act yourself into thinking than it is to think yourself into acting."

To help us prepare to swallow what might seem a bitter pill of praying for someone who probably doesn't deserve it, some meditation may be in order. We can try focusing our meditation on our new role as a pray-er for others, including people we don't like or care for, and on our new paradigm where we view other people's unsavory behavior as being simply symptoms of a sickness.

*

Psychological research supports the use of prayer as an effective healthy coping mechanism, and has demonstrated that the use of prayer during difficult times is not at all a passive response to problems.[72,73,74,75] In particular, turning things over to a higher power – the form of prayer most advocated in the 12 Step program – is an active surrender of the outcome and a move to differentiate what cannot be changed. This enhances our healthy humility, our ability to let go of our alcoholic-addict's need to try to control everything, and our ability to accept that we can do our best in every life situation, but we can't necessarily control the outcome. Prayer and leaving the outcome with our higher power is a key to spirituality that leads to freedom by letting go of our inherent need for perceived control, accepting that much of our life is beyond our control, and accepting with gratitude what life has to offer. When we do this it provides a great release from worry and anxiety over things that are beyond our control: "'Thy will be done.' We are then in much less danger of excitement, fear, anger , worry, self-pity, or foolish decisions. We become much more efficient. We do not tire so easily, for we are not burning up energy foolishly as we did when we were trying to arrange life to suit ourselves. It works – it really does" (Big Book, p. 88). We must remember that an obsessive need for a sense of control over our out-of-control life was a large part of what kept us addicted to our substance use. When that obsessive need for control tries to re-assert itself, we must be mindful of it: "our immediate temptation will be to ask for specific solutions to specific problems... in that case, we are asking God to do it *our* way" (*Twelve Steps and Twelve Traditions*, p. 102). Of course, citing the Serenity Prayer helps remind us of this.

By this point in working the Steps, you have (hopefully) learned that keeping an open mind is an important part of overcoming addiction-alcoholism. For those who still see prayer as religious and are reluctant to accept it, now would be a good time to keep an open mind and give it an honest try. As the Big Book points out: "it [prayer] works, if we have the proper attitude and work at it" (p. 86).

When we have a problem that's really weighing us down, disrupting our serenity, keeping us up at night, it's of great comfort to leave it with our higher power. Try it next time you're wracked with worry over something. Do your very best to make the problem work out the way you would like it to, but leave the outcome with your higher power. If you don't yet have a higher power, just throw it up in the sky or leave it with fate, or with whatever works for you. It's a simple yet effective way to enact the Serenity Prayer: having the wisdom to accept what we cannot control (the outcome of the problem), but having the courage to do what we can to make the problem work out the way we would like it to. We do our best (what we can control), then leave the outcome (what we can't control) with our higher power.

We should ask for guidance and strength in doing what we need to do to handle our problems. That's what we do when we say the Serenity Prayer. We *don't* ask our higher power to solve all our problems or make them go away from us; that would be cowardly and unrealistic. We have to live life on life's terms, and facing our problems and rolling with the outcome is part of that. Nonetheless, it's of great comfort when we leave our anxieties and worries about such things with our higher power, rightfully throwing it off our own shoulders.

*

The 12 Step literature is very clear about the benefits to be derived from the proper practice of Step Eleven:

> In A.A. we have found that the actual good results of prayer are beyond question. They are matters of knowledge and experience. All those who have persisted have found strength not ordinarily their own. They have found wisdom beyond their usual capability. And they have increasingly found a peace of mind which can stand firm in the face of difficult circumstances (*Twelve Steps and Twelve Traditions*, p. 104).

I can certainly vouch for that personally. The quality of our sobriety and our health and happiness will depend on the amount of effort we put into our healing and our recovery. Step Eleven is one part of the program where putting in the time and effort will pay large dividends, and will make a big difference in our well-being. I hope you plan to make Step Eleven a part of your daily routine.

*

So, we have discussed how to meditate and pray, and how to improve our connection with our higher power, the two main suggestions of Step Eleven. How do we know when it's time to move on to Step Twelve? Well, like Step Ten, Step Eleven is a maintenance and growth Step, meaning that we are never finished with it. Rather, our practice of Step Eleven is meant to become a part of our daily routine toward our daily reprieve from our alcoholism-addiction. As we grow in our skills and ease with meditation and prayer, so we grow in spirituality, health, serenity, and sobriety. The 12 Step literature warns us of the dangers of letting go of this important tool for our spiritual health and recovery: "when we turn away from meditation and prayer, we likewise deprive our minds, our emotions, and our intuitions of vitally needed support" (*Twelve Steps and Twelve Traditions,* p. 97).

Once you have gotten yourself into the regular practice of meditation and prayer and committed to it as a lifelong pursuit, and if your sponsor agrees, you are ready for Step Twelve.

Step Twelve

Having had a spiritual awakening as a result of these steps, we tried to carry this message to alcoholics, and to practice these principles in all our affairs.

"The joy of living is the theme of A.A.'s Twelfth Step, and action is its keyword" (*Twelve Steps and Twelve Traditions,* p. 106). Step Twelve is our roadmap for ongoing spiritual health, which is the absolute requirement for our ongoing recovery and well-being. We've put considerable time and effort into cleaning house and doing brain hygiene, and Step Twelve is how we go about keeping everything clean and hygienic.

You may have noticed that throughout our discussion of the Steps, I seldom use the terms "Step-work" or "working the Steps." This is because I really don't like conveying the impression that this remarkably life-affirming and healing process constitutes work. As with the earlier nine Steps, the maintenance/growth Steps – Ten through Twelve – should be viewed as a valuable opportunity to incorporate incredibly healthy and beneficial new practices and daily habits into our lives, rather than looking at them as some kind of chore that we must tend to in order to stay sober. If these new life skills are not enjoyable for you, you should talk to your sponsor about it, and look to adjust how you are going about it. When you find the right way to incorporate these practices in your life, the result is new daily habits that are a relaxing refuge from the chaos of life, not a chore. Those of us who have found our "spiritual groove" – successful incorporation of these recovery activities into our daily routine – miss these calming, centering practices if they go undone, and we feel "off" if we let go of our spiritual maintenance and growth practices.

Bill Wilson explained why our ongoing spiritual growth is so important:

Is sobriety all that we are to expect of a spiritual awakening? No, sobriety is only a bare beginning; it is only the first gift of the first awakening. If more gifts are to be received, our awakening has to go on. As it does go on, we find that bit by bit we can discard the old life – the one that did not work – for a new life that can and does work under any conditions whatever (*Came to Believe*, p. 39).

This illustrates perfectly why we need a design for living, why simply attaining sobriety isn't enough. Lest we go back to what we know, the way of doing things that previously led to our demise, we must continue on in our spiritual growth. It really is a happier, healthier, and more effective way to live. And it's how we stay sober.

*

To the newcomer, Step Twelve may raise some questions: 1) what is a spiritual awakening, and how do I know if I've had one?, 2) what are "these principles" that we are to practice in all our affairs?, and 3) why do I have to carry the 12 Step message to other alcoholic-addicts in order to maintain **my** sobriety? We'll answer all these questions in our Step Twelve discussion.

Step Twelve is our third maintenance and growth Step, our lifetime guide to renewing our daily reprieve from our disease. The importance of Step Twelve for our long-term recovery is emphasized in the Big Book, and at the risk of sounding repetitive I wish to repeat a previously used quote: "it is easy to let up on the spiritual program of action and rest on our laurels. We are headed for trouble if we do, for alcohol is a subtle foe. We are not cured of alcoholism. What we really have is a daily reprieve contingent on the maintenance of our spiritual condition" (p. 85).

When the co-founders of A.A. first met, they collectively realized that the solution to their unending sickness was spiritual. Bill Wilson related: "the man [Dr. Bob] agreed that no amount of will power he might muster could stop his drinking for long. A spiritual experience, he conceded, was absolutely necessary..." (Big Book, p. 155). This spiritual experience can be otherwise referred to as a spiritual awakening, and is usually the "light bulb switching on moment" for the alcoholic-addict. It seems to be the moment the spiritual cure is found. We'll discuss what, exactly, this spiritual experience is shortly. We need to have this discussion, because – according to research – most people experience a spiritual awakening as a gradual process, and may not even realize that it has happened to them.

*

Dr. Silkworth, a well-known alcoholism specialist from the time of A.A.'s foundation, is quoted in the Big Book (all from p. xxvii-iii): "men and women drink essentially because they like the effect produced by alcohol. The sensation is so elusive that, while they admit that it is injurious, they cannot after a time differentiate the true from the false. To them, their alcoholic life seems the only normal one." Further: "unless this person can experience an entire psychic change there is very little hope of his recovery." The 12 Steps are designed to produce exactly the psychic change that Dr. Silkworth was speaking of. In the language used in the Big Book, this psychic change is referred to as a "spiritual awakening." Dr. Silkworth continues: "once a psychic change has occurred, the very same person who seemed doomed, who had so many problems he despaired of ever solving them, suddenly finds himself easily able to control his desire for alcohol. One feels that something more than human power is needed to produce the essential psychic change."

So, what exactly is this spiritual awakening that is talked about so much in the 12 Step program? Is it unique to the 12 Step program? How do I know if I've had one? It's OK to be unfamiliar with the concept; it's not something that many people know about or talk about. Dr. Carl Jung – whom we will discuss shortly – describes a spiritual awakening as a "phenomenon." A phenomenon is something that is unique in the universe, not like anything else in existence. As such, a spiritual awakening is a unique experience, unlike anything else that we know, and many people go through life without even hearing this term. As we will discuss, most people don't become aware of the concept until they need a psychic change to survive a life crisis.

The term "spiritual awakening" is not specifically defined in the Big Book, but the experience of a spiritual awakening is described a number of times, in the basic text and in the stories in the back of the book. Perhaps it's not defined because it's a very personal and individualized experience: "maybe there are as many definitions of spiritual awakening as there are people who have had them" (*Twelve Steps and Twelve Traditions*, p. 106). However, despite the elusive definition and the wide variety of individual experiences, these vital spiritual events share some common features:

> Certainly each genuine one has something in common with all the others.... When a man or a woman has a spiritual awakening, the most important meaning of it is that he has now become able to do, feel, and believe that which he could not do before on his unaided strength and resources alone. He has been granted a gift which amounts to a new state of consciousness and being. He has been set on a path which tells him he is really going somewhere, that life is not a dead end, not something to be endured or mastered. In a very

real sense he has been transformed, because he has laid hold of a source of strength which, in one way or another, he had hitherto denied himself (*Twelve Steps and Twelve Traditions,* p. 106-107).

The Big Book, too, regards a spiritual awakening as a very individualized experience that's necessary for lasting healthy recovery from our disease: "the terms 'spiritual experience' and 'spiritual awakening' are used many times in this book which, upon careful reading, shows that the personality change sufficient to bring about recovery from alcoholism has manifested itself among us in many different forms" (p. 567).

A spiritual awakening is not necessarily a bright burst of white light that immediately changes your whole world. In some of us, it's a "sudden and spectacular upheaval," but in others, it's not. It can be a very subtle, gradual event that may even go unnoticed, as gradual changes often do. In fact, a clinical research study into the spiritual awakening phenomenon in 12 Step members found that 60% of the study participants had experienced their spiritual awakening gradually over time.[1] The Big Book, too, warns us that our spiritual awakening may not be sudden and spectacular: "our first printing gave many readers the impression that these personality changes... must be in the nature of sudden and spectacular upheavals. Happily for everyone, this conclusion is erroneous" (p. 567).

In the Big Book, the story is told from the early days of A.A. of an alcoholic named Fred. Fred, a chronic relapser, was once again in hospital, deathly ill from his latest chemical forays. Desperately seeking sobriety, Fred agreed to a visit from two members of AA. Says Fred:

> Then they outlined the spiritual answer and program of action which a hundred of them had followed successfully. Though I had been only a nominal churchman, their proposals were not, intellectually, hard to swallow. But the program of action, though entirely sensible, was pretty drastic. It meant I would have to throw several lifelong conceptions out of the window. That was not easy. But the moment I made up my mind to go through with the process, I had the curious feeling that my alcoholic condition was relieved, as in fact it proved to be (p. 42).

Fred had a spiritual awakening during that visit. Some may argue: *how was **that** a spiritual awakening*? However, that's exactly what happened to him. Two members of A.A. had just explained the spiritual solution to his alcohol addiction and he accepted surrender of his willfulness to his higher power, experiencing a psychic change that changed his life. He somehow knew that his life was about to change. Fred had experienced a spiritual awakening, and his sobriety followed from that. This was no religious experience, no angels descended from Heaven, there were no bright flashes of light, and no voice thundered from the clouds. It was as subtle as can be, but it was a definable turning point for Fred, one that changed his life. For some, their spiritual awakening is more dramatic, but Fred's story is typical. My own spiritual awakening was very similar to Fred's.

There's a story in the Big Book that highlights the fact that there's no call for a preconceived idea of a higher power to experience a spiritual awakening. The alcoholic in this story had been brought to an A.A. meeting by a friend. She didn't think A.A. was for her, but she reluctantly went along. She tells her story:

> It was the second meeting that clinched my sobriety... the chairperson called upon me to share.... As I spoke, I looked around the room. More importantly, I looked at the faces of the people in the room and I saw it. I saw the understanding, the empathy, the love. Today I believe I saw my Higher Power for the first time in those faces. While still up at the podium, it hit me – this is what I had been looking for all of my life. This was the answer, right here in front of me. Indescribable relief came over me; I knew the fight was over (Big Book, p. 326).

This woman experienced a spiritual awakening on her first A.A. meeting, right there at the podium.

Another sister in recovery describes her spiritual awakening, which led to her finally finding a lasting sobriety:

> Then the miracle happened – to *me*! It isn't always so sudden with everyone, but I ran into a personal crisis that filled me with a raging and righteous anger. And as I fumed helplessly and planned to get good and drunk and *show them*, my eye caught a sentence in the book lying open on my bed [the Big Book of AA]: 'We cannot live with anger.' The walls crumpled – and the light streamed in. I wasn't trapped. I wasn't helpless. I was *free*, and I didn't have to drink to 'show them.' This wasn't 'religion' – this was freedom! Freedom from anger and fear, freedom to know happiness, and freedom to know love.... That was the beginning of a new life, a fuller life, a happier life than I had ever known or believed possible (Big Book, p. 206).

Another person in recovery had a more gradual "vital spiritual experience," but which had the same end result as a sudden awakening:

Step Three, I now believe, was the key that opened some door within my being and allowed spirituality to enter, not in a sudden flow, but as a trickle, on occasions just a drop at a time. As I progressed through the Steps, I began to see some change in my thinking and my attitudes toward people. At the completion of Step Nine, I now believe, I did have a spiritual awakening. I came to the point where, not only could I give love and compassion to my fellow man, but, more important, I could receive love and compassion. Now spiritual experiences, as I understand them, began to happen (*Came to Believe*, p. 69).

Non-dramatic spiritual awakenings are common, and perhaps even the norm. One God-phobic alcoholic who wanted nothing to do with the spiritual bit, not seeing what it had to do with not drinking, was advised: "pray with disbelief; but pray with sincerity; and the belief will come." This didn't sit well with him, but he was desperate: "pray? How could I pray? I didn't know how to pray. Still, I was ready to go to any lengths to get my sobriety and some semblance of a normal life. I guess I just gave up. I stopped fighting. I accepted that which I did not really believe, much less understand" (*Came to Believe*, p. 47). This brother in recovery thinks that this surrender led to a spiritual awakening, as non-dramatic as it was: "in my view, some of the evidences of a spiritual awakening are: maturity; an end to habitual hatred; the ability to love and to be loved in return; the ability to believe, even without understanding, that Something lets the sun rise in the morning and set at night, makes the leaves come out in the spring and drop off in the fall, and gives the birds song (p. 48).

For many, a spiritual awakening is but an impactful realization, a change in attitude: "I knew I had to have a new beginning, and this beginning had to be here. I could not start anywhere else. I had to let go of the past and forget the future. As long as I held on to the past with one hand and grabbed at the future with the other hand, I had nothing to hold on to today with. So I had to begin here, now" (*Came to Believe*, p. 46).

Have you had a spiritual awakening? Have you found sobriety and now think differently than you did when drinking and using? Do you have a new outlook on life that keeps you sober? Do people around you see a difference in your behavior? Have you admitted your powerlessness and accepted that you need help from something or someone more powerful than your willpower? Then you almost certainly have had a spiritual awakening. You may not be able to identify a clear moment when and where this occurred, because it may have occurred gradually as you progressed through the Steps. However, think back, think hard, back to that point where you finally *got it* – when you finally surrendered to your powerlessness and committed to the program of recovery, when you finally knew you could do this. If you can remember that moment, then you are probably remembering your spiritual awakening.

The stories in A.A. reveal that many people have a spiritual awakening so gradually that they don't even realize it until it's pointed out to them. They undergo a psychic change, and develop a new outlook on life, a new approach to life, to live by a new set of values, and their sobriety becomes a reality. Often it's their families or other people close to them who point this out because they didn't recognize the gradual change in themselves. As one sister in recovery noted: "in common with many A.A.'s I never enjoyed the luxury of a large and conscious spiritual experience, and I felt a little deprived" (*Came to Believe,* p.41). But, she did experience a spiritual awakening "… by way of [the] program, though I have recognized the process only in retrospect" (p. 41).

Like this alcoholic, many of us will only recognize our spiritual awakening in retrospect. If you have embraced the suggestions of all these Steps that we have gone through, like it or not, you have changed. Big time. You are a different person with different ways of doing things, a different perspective about life and other people, a different outlook, and perhaps even a different set of values and beliefs. Your way of thinking, your thought processes, your daily habits, and your behaviors have all changed – you have undergone a psychic change, a spiritual awakening, even if you are only really realizing that as you read this paragraph. One alcoholic-addict in recovery explains his awareness of his psychic change unfolding every day:

> Gradually, I began to see another part of me emerging – a grateful me, expecting nothing, but sure that another power was beginning to guide me, counsel me, and direct my ways. And I was not afraid.
>
> Then, as this power began to unfold new selves within me, a greater understanding of my fellowmen began. With a new awakening each day – new strengths, new truths, new acceptance of A.A. people and people not in A.A. – a new world opened up. And every day it still does (*Came to Believe,* p. 45).

The Big Book gives us some insight into this gradual type of spiritual awakening:

> Quite often friends of the newcomer are aware of the difference long before he is himself. He finally realizes that he has undergone a profound alteration in his reaction to life; that such a change could hardly have been brought about by himself alone…. With few exceptions our members find that they have tapped an unsuspected inner resource which they presently identify with their own conception of a power greater than themselves (p. 567-568).

I never tire of hearing people in recovery speak of their own experiences with spiritual awakenings, because it's always touching to hear, and because the stories are as varied and interesting as the people who tell them. One thing that you commonly hear is that people experience more than one spiritual awakening. One example that I have heard is that of a parent who had a child come along while he was in recovery, and he has been experiencing the joy of watching this child grow and experience the world, while his two older children, who grew up while he was in the throes of alcoholism-addiction, are – tragically – absent from his memories. When he realized this he was moved to tears by the privilege he felt by being a sober, involved parent, and felt reaffirmed in his recovery. He describes this moment as his second spiritual awakening.

No matter how the awakening is experienced, Step Twelve tells us that the "psychic change" that occurs with a spiritual awakening is necessary for long-term recovery. Early in the development of the A.A. program, "a certain American business man" (this man's name was Rowland H., and we briefly met him way back in our Step Three discussion) consulted the world-renowned Psychiatrist Carl Jung in Europe. When medical treatment of Rowland's addiction failed, Dr. Jung pronounced him "utterly hopeless," and doomed. Dr. Jung did, however, upon further pressing, admit that exceptions do exist to the prognosis: "here and there, once in a while, alcoholics have had what are called vital spiritual experiences. To me these occurrences are phenomena. They appear to be in the nature of huge emotional displacements and rearrangements. Ideas, emotions, and attitudes which were once the guiding forces of the lives of these men are suddenly cast to one side, and a completely new set of conceptions and motives begin to dominate them" (Big Book, p. 27). Further, the eminent doctor explained: "that while his [Rowland's] religious convictions were very good, they did not spell the necessary vital spiritual experience" (p. 27).

This highlights two points: 1) a "vital spiritual experience" (what we call a spiritual awakening) is the path to sobriety, and 2) this is not necessarily a religious experience. The Big Book quotes a doctor (Dr. William Silkworth, director of the Charles B. Towns hospital for alcoholism in New York): "...the general hopelessness of the average alcoholic's plight is, in my opinion, correct.... Though not a religious person, I have profound respect for the spiritual approach in such cases as yours. For most cases, there is virtually no other solution" (Big Book, p. 43). The spiritual awakening is well placed in our program for people who are powerless over alcohol or drugs.

*

To put a fine point on the matter, it's important that we not fail to recognize our own spiritual awakening as we contemplate the issue in Step Twelve, because many among us may hold the mistaken belief that spiritual awakenings occur only as a sudden and spectacular event. To the contrary, in most people the spiritual awakening develops: "slowly over a period of time. Quite often friends of the newcomer are aware of the difference long before he is himself. He finally realizes that he has undergone a profound alteration in his reaction to life; that such a change could hardly have been brought about by himself alone" (Big Book, p. 567). Once this experience has been realized, A.A. members: "find that they have tapped an unsuspected inner resource which they presently identify with their own conception of a Power greater than themselves" (Big Book, p. 567-8). It's true: our sobriety comes from an "unsuspected inner resource" that we weren't able to access prior the psychic change that we experienced as a result of these Steps.

As with the pursuit of spirituality in general, the experience of a spiritual awakening is not limited to religions. There's a large population of people who are heavily into spirituality but do not belong to any religion. They have their own robust body of literature that gives us insight into the phenomenon of the spiritual awakening, from a perspective outside of that of the 12 Step program. I have spent considerable time researching this body of literature, and I find that it's completely consistent with the spiritual practices of the 12 Step program. Although there are some really out-there spiritual practices that I wouldn't touch with a ten-foot butterfly net, the non-addict-alcoholics out there who have made spirituality a part of their lives are doing basically the same things as we are. However, we alcoholic-addicts have a significant advantage over the average people who seek to incorporate spirituality into their lives. *How is that?*

Well, as we shall see shortly, clinical research into the phenomenon of a spiritual awakening has shown that people coming out of the traumatic experience of active addiction-alcoholism are especially primed for spirituality and a spiritual awakening. As well, we have the 12 Step program, which is (literally) a step-by-step guide to rapidly adopting a spiritual way of living and experiencing a psychic change; most people don't have access to such a program or any impetus to seek one out. Indeed, the 12 Step program has a spiritual awakening as an endpoint – a goal – in Step Twelve. Too, with the 12 Step program we have someone to guide us through this spiritual process (our sponsor), as well as a fellowship and a rich body of literature to keep us growing and thriving in spirituality. Most people pass through life completely unaware of the incredible positive effects of spirituality on health, relationships, happiness, and life function. Unless they have some sort of life crisis – such as hitting their bottom as alcoholic-addicts – they may never need, seek, or find spirituality and a spiritual awakening. We, through the 12 Step program, are introduced to this

378

enriching practice, which was heretofore unknown to most of us. That's why many among us describe ourselves as "grateful" alcoholics or addicts.

*

So, how does a spiritual awakening relate to our recovery and getting our life back? As usual, we'll take a look outside of the 12 Step literature for research studies to see if the 12 Step program and principles have any science to back them up.

One robust clinical study of the experience of the spiritual awakening made some interesting findings that are relevant to our healing and recovery.[2] In this study, the investigators identified four main triggers for spiritual awakenings: 1) psychological turmoil, 2) contact with nature, 3) spiritual practice, and 4) engagement with spiritual literature. That demonstrates that those of us who find sobriety through the 12 Step program are naturally primed for a spiritual awakening. We have certainly been through psychological turmoil, we are introduced to spiritual practices through the Steps (for many of us, for the very first time in our lives), and we are engaged with spiritual literature as we read through the Big Book and other 12 Step literature. Many of us are also primed by contact with nature, as we seek a spiritual connection with the world around us. Therefore, the 12 Step program provides the ideal setting to nurture and foster the psychological and spiritual requirements for a spiritual awakening.

Another clinical study of addict-alcoholics found that when they were psychologically ready to accept help for recovery they were not only primed but even mentally hungry for a psychic change.[3] This study, which was not based solely on people in a 12 Step program, described addiction-alcoholism as a "spiritual vacuum," and found that spirituality provided an energizing function to fill that psychologically painful void. The study authors found that addiction-alcoholism was typically associated with a great sense of loss – either from painful loss or trauma earlier in life or from pain and loss during the active substance use – and that this sense of loss was a source of pain that kept the drug or alcohol use going. They found that spirituality – especially following a spiritual awakening – provided a sense of filling the emptiness from loss and a source for understanding and accepting the loss, as well as optimism for life moving forward. Rather than filling this void with alcohol or drugs, living by spiritual principles following a spiritual awakening fulfills our deepest needs. The researchers also found that spirituality provided "containment" for people who were looking for reasonable boundaries for healthy living after living a life without boundaries or limits. Within this group, the higher power concept provided a source of comfort and strength, and supported their belief that life's challenges could be met face-on without substance use. Study participants also found that the higher power concept and spirituality in general provided a sense of a life with meaning. These highly supportive qualities were part of what contributed to a sense of spiritual awakening in these individuals, who were suddenly filled with the knowledge that there was a way out of addiction-alcoholism and that life would be different. In other words, they underwent a psychic change. The results of this study confirm the entire premise of the 12 Step program as a spiritual treatment for our socially, mentally, physically, psychologically, and spiritually devastating disease.

The study also identified the characteristics of after-effects of the experience of a spiritual awakening. These effects included: a shift in perspectives and values, an intensified awareness (mindfulness), a transformation of our vision of the world and our place in the world, a sense of clarity, and a sense of well-being. Of course, a sense of connection was also a prominent after-effect, which is the essence of spirituality. This demonstrates the value of a spiritual experience in finding a spiritual way of life, positive psychology, long-term stable recovery, and the healing needed for a return to health, happiness, and good function. What an awesome change from the train-wreck state of mind that many among us suffered during our active addiction-alcoholism!

Another research study looked at the effects of a spiritual awakening specifically in A.A. members.[4] This study found highly significant changes in the study subjects that followed their spiritual awakening experience in a number of measures: reduced cravings, reduced depression, improved interpersonal relationships, increased service to others, higher likelihood of abstinence from substance use, improved awareness of sensory experiences, better understanding of meaning in life, and a more positive mood. This further demonstrates that those who participate in the 12 Step fellowship but don't complete their Steps are robbing themselves of the magnificent healing and life-boosting effects of the program.

When you look at the list of benefits described by these and other clinical studies, it's not surprising that spirituality and a spiritual awakening are known to be a source of strength in other ailments besides alcoholism-addiction. We have discussed in our Step Two study some of the research evidence that supports the remarkable effects of spirituality on health and disease, and it's therefore not surprising that similar findings have been established for the effects of a spiritual awakening experience in overcoming physical and mental illness.[5]

Spirituality, connection with a higher power, and a spiritual awakening have been touted by one researcher as being: "the most robust protective factor against depression known to medical and social sciences."[6] Given that more than half of alcoholic-addicts have underlying mental health disorders – of which depression is the most common – this makes spirituality and the spiritual awakening a particularly important part of our recovery.[7] It also makes it an important adjunct to treatment for depression and other mental health disorders, and therefore is an important contributor to our function, mental health, and ongoing sobriety.

*

A review of the research and lay literature shows other "symptoms" of having had a spiritual awakening that are commonly experienced by 12 Step members.[8,9,10] The experience begins by a desire to slow down, change, and simplify our complicated life, and re-examine who we are and what our life means to us. There's a desire to break free from restrictive patterns, our substance-dominated life-draining consumptive lifestyle, and escape from toxic people and situations. There's a sudden feeling that we are somehow different from our old self, and perhaps from those around us. We sense that everything in our life is new and altered, that we have left our old self behind. We are filled with a knowledge that we are getting it, that we are on the right track. We are filled with a desire for personal integrity; after years of addictive behavior we are tired of the lies and trying to remember our lies, and we want the freedom and peace of mind that comes with being honest and truthful. Integrity has become attractive and interesting to us, and has become a cherished part of our self-identity.

We find an inner peace that becomes so valuable to us that we avoid any type of conflict that will threaten our newfound peace and serenity. We lose interest in drama and shed the need to be "right" at all costs; it just isn't worth it to us anymore. We choose our battles. For the same reason, we learn to let go of rumination and worrying, freeing our mind for other things. Our actions become based on reality and not on fear. Experience soon teaches us that our fears were unfounded anyway.

Feelings of gratitude accompany our newfound peace and serenity. The gratitude is especially strongly felt for how well we feel, and how much different we feel than we did in active addiction-alcoholism prior to our spiritual awakening. We learn the crucial key to happiness of being thankful for what we have, rather than resenting and ruminating on what we don't have.

These studies confirm what people in the fellowship report in their stories and experiences, as we hear at meetings and read in A.A. Grapevine and in the Big Book and other 12 Step literature. By the time we reach Step Twelve – having had a spiritual awakening as a result of these Steps – we should identify with these experiences. Sometimes we must take a moment to reflect back on how we were before the Steps and how we are now to really recognize that we have indeed undergone a psychic change.

*

A spiritual awakening has been a well-known quantity since the very beginnings of the study of human psychology. Abraham Maslow was a ground-breaking psychologist whose theories of human motivation and needs from the 1950s still hold up to scrutiny even today. You may recall his name, because his famous *hierarchy of needs* theory is taught in high school biology and psychology courses. Maslow's theory identifies the things that humans need to survive (such as food, shelter, water), thrive (such as love, belonging, and connection), and to be fulfilled. A spiritual awakening, the vitalizing psychic change that we experience when we progress through the 12 Steps, is precisely what Maslow referred to as a "peak experience."[11] A peak experience is at the very apex of our needs, and is required for humans to achieve their peak fulfillment. Unfortunately, many people – probably most – never enjoy a "peak experience" in their lifetime, and pass on without ever having had that final piece of psychological fulfillment. This is especially true nowadays, when social media, streamed TV, and myriad other distractions divert most people's attention from such matters as spirituality and peak experiences. We are fortunate, indeed, that we have the 12 Step program in our lives, even if it took hitting our bottom to find it.

Maslow's own research linked a peak experience with a positive attitude, and reduced anxiety, fear, and doubt. Those who had a peak experience underwent a change of perspective, and felt fortunate and reaffirmed in the worthiness of life. Maslow believed that every person is capable of a peak experience. He also found in his research that people who are emotionally healthy are much more likely to experience a peak experience, which explains why people who are doing the Steps and move from an extreme negative psychology to a robust positive psychology almost invariably experience a spiritual awakening during the process.

*

Even when it occurs gradually, a spiritual awakening is a life-changing event, and the contrast as we transition from an extreme negative psychology to a strong positive psychology becomes especially obvious after a spiritual awakening. However, this – like our sobriety – is something that must be maintained once it has been achieved, and this is how we maintain our sobriety. We must strive to improve and maintain our improved self. We have inventoried, admitted, and made amends for our wrongs. We have identified and asked for help in removing our defects of character which led to these wrongs and which played a part in our addiction-alcoholism. Now we must continue to inventory our day-to-day actions and strive to correct

382

our defects as they do their best to invade our daily lives, which is the basis of Step Ten. To do this, we must learn to meditate and, if you choose, connect with a higher power through prayer, which is the basis of Step Eleven. Applying all that we have learned to everyday living – outside of the rooms of 12 Step meetings – is the basis of the other aspect of Step Twelve, which is "to practice these principles in all our affairs."

Finding spirituality and experiencing a spiritual awakening is not something that happens and then we just drop it. Our recovery depends on our ongoing maintenance and growth of our spiritual wellness. Besides, the benefits of this new way of living are so gratifying that we owe it to ourselves to grow in it and practice its principles in all our affairs. As the Big Book tells us: "the spiritual life is not a theory. *We have to live it*" (p. 83). As we have discussed throughout our study of the 12 Steps, the experiences of millions of people who have lived a life based on spiritual principles, as well as an overwhelming body of research evidence, have shown that the effects of spirituality on our physical and mental health, our relationships with others, our ability to cope with life, our happiness and peace of mind, and – of course – our recovery are profound indeed. To let go of this new spiritual way of life rather than to grow in it and realize its benefits would be to squander an incredible gift. However, for people with our disease, it's more than a matter of taking advantage of an incredible gift – for us it's also a matter of life and death, for our recovery depends on it.

Although practicing these spiritual principles in all our affairs requires adding some new aspects to our daily routine – such as meditation/prayer, reading the Big Book and other relevant literature, keeping in touch with other people in recovery, getting to meetings, practicing our Step Ten daily – these quickly become a part of our routine when we stick with them. You will often hear people in the fellowship say they feel "off" when they aren't doing these things. These practices are how we maintain our hard-won sanity.

Like it or not, we are alcoholic-addicts, and we will be for life. For those of us who hit a low bottom before we came to recovery, it seemed like life was over. We had burned all our bridges, lost people and things, were in the cruelest possible frame of mind (i.e. negative psychology), and we were physically, mentally, and spiritually bankrupt. Life seemed over, no longer worth living, and hopeless. Many among us pondered or even tried suicide. Many of us woke up every day regretting that we hadn't died in our sleep. We had wronged so many people, and done so many other things that weighed heavily on our crowded conscience that it hurt to even think. Yet, here we are. We've had a spiritual awakening, we've progressed through the Steps, and we've had that huge load removed from our shoulders. We are sober and enjoying recovery, we are getting healthy, and life worth living is coming back to us. To go back to where we were is unthinkable.

We have been gifted a second shot at life, despite our past actions and misdeeds. Now, we are privileged to walk among "normal" people and live a normal life. However, even though we live among "normal" people and lead a full and productive life, we are not like other people. We are alcoholic-addicts, and our recovery depends upon a daily reprieve from our disease. In order to continue on with our new shot at life we must take care of doing the things we need to do to maintain our recovery. Step Twelve requires us to accept that fact, and to renew our ongoing commitment to "practice these principle in all our affairs." We'll discuss shortly what, exactly, these principles are that we must practice.

There may be times when it feels like a burden to get to a meeting when we know we need one, or to get together with our sponsor, or to otherwise do the things we need to do to remain in recovery and grow spiritually. As a full life comes back to us we may feel the press of other responsibilities and priorities. However, we must maintain our perspective; if we relapse all those other things in life that compete for our time and attention will be lost. That's the basis of the slogan "First Things First." We must take care of our recovery first, or everything else will go up in smoke. We know this from past experience and from the stories of others. Fortunately, as time goes on and our spiritual activities become more embedded in our life we may become more efficient at them, and some of them may not require as much time as when we were in early recovery. For example, people who have completed the Steps and live the spiritual principles may not need to attend as many meetings as they did in early recovery. However, there will be times when we know that our recovery needs some attention, and that's when we must put it first. Many people begin to feel restless, irritable, and discontent when their recovery activities are insufficient. Sometimes my wife will say to me: *you've been really edgy lately, you need to get to a meeting* (although she usually doesn't say it quite so politely), and she's right. She knows. She's seen me sick and she's seen me healthy. Too, when our disease begins speaking to us again, trying to convince us that a drink or drug would be good right now, or that we have been in recovery long enough that we can handle drinking or using, that THIS time we will be able to control it, those are sure signs that we need to take better care of our recovery.

*

So, what, exactly, are these principles that Step Twelve suggests that we practice in all our affairs? Certainly, in our trip through the Steps we've committed to adopting a lot of spiritual principles, all aimed at improving our connections with other people, the world in general, and a higher power. These same principles are the basis of cleaning house and keeping it

384

clean, and now in Step Twelve we are to apply them to our life – practicing these principles in all our affairs. But, can we name these principles that we are supposed to live?

The Big Book doesn't explicitly list what "these principles" are, but coming as it does on the heels of the previous twelve Steps on page 59 of the Big Book, the implication of Step Twelve is that "these principles" are found in the previous eleven Steps that have just been named. These are the principles that allowed us to take on humility with every Step, to admit to our powerlessness in Step One, to take on willingness and open-mindedness in Steps Two and Three, and so on.

Although it's not taken from the Big Book, there's a list of the "12 Principles" that's discussed within the 12 Step fellowship. These 12 Principles are based on the spiritual principle considered to be central to each of the 12 Steps. There are a number of different versions of the "12 Principles," with some of the principles differing between versions. Let's take a look at them (the numbers correspond to the Step related to each principle):

1) Honesty,
2) Hope,
3) Faith (some versions say Commitment),
4) Courage,
5) Integrity (Truth),
6) Willingness,
7) Humility,
8) Love (Reflection),
9) Discipline (Responsibility),
10) Patience and Perseverance (Discipline, Vigilance),
11) Awareness (Spirituality), and
12) Service.

However, nothing in the primary 12 Step literature – the Big Book and *Twelve Steps and Twelve Traditions* – says anything about "12 Principles," nor is any list given. The same applies to the other 12 Step literature that I have reviewed, including such books as *As Bill Sees It*, and *Pass it On*. Nor have I seen such a list produced in any of Bill Wilson's many talks and essays published in A.A. Grapevine. (If I am wrong and there is such a list appearing in the 12 Step literature, I would appreciate an email to enlighten me.) It would seem a bit frivolous and a little bit limiting, therefore, to arbitrarily boil down the spiritual principles to twelve, as good and spiritual as those principles may be. There are many other principles that come out in our study and practice of the Steps that must be practiced in all our affairs. For example, the principles of anonymity, open-mindedness,

385

tolerance, striving for growth, doing the right thing, and giving are not mentioned in the "12 Principles" but are important principles that emerge as we study our Steps. There are many other principles that make up our new way of living, much more than twelve. I would suggest that we can summarize the principles as "doing the right thing, consistent with spiritual values." We know when we aren't doing the right thing, and we know when we are; kind of like the cartoon figure who's pondering a decision with a little devil sitting on one shoulder and a little angel sitting on the other.

Twelve Steps and Twelve Traditions is quite clear about the importance of applying these principles to our recovery: "the A.A. member has to conform to the principles of recovery. His life actually depends upon obedience to spiritual principles. If he deviates too far, the penalty is swift; he sickens and dies" (p. 130). That sounds a little drastic, maybe even a little alarmist, doesn't it? But, let's just take a look for a moment at what happens if we don't practice these principles in ALL our affairs. Let's look at just one example: the principle of honesty.

If we don't practice honesty in all our affairs, it means we have given ourselves permission to lie. Even something seemingly unrelated to recovery like lying on our taxes is not practicing honesty in all our affairs. When we give ourselves permission to lie about one thing, we have violated our principles and it becomes much easier to give ourselves permission to lie about other things, because we have already crossed that line. When we lie it's usually to indulge our self-will. Lying on our tax return is done in order to indulge our self-will's call to gain ourselves some money, even if it's done dishonestly and we must lie to do it. We alcoholic-addicts are people who nearly destroyed ourselves by lying and deceiving to satisfy our self-will run riot in past times, and we are in the 12 Step program to put an end to our old ways and never go back. The program tells us that we must practice honesty in all our affairs, yet here we are listening to our self-will again, rather than our program of recovery, by lying on our taxes. And there's more.

That lie can become like a rock in our shoe. We can stew and ruminate on it, guilt and self-loathing can set in. Our old alcoholic-addict mind-set can assert itself again by rationalizing our lie – *after all, what does the government care if I lied a little on my taxes? It doesn't hurt anybody, right?* Then our inner self-critic starts up on us, after all that work that we've done to put it in its place. We may have to lie to cover for our lie. We may feel guilt when we get our money from our tax lie. This rock in our shoe can cause a wound that can grow and grow.

Maybe the guy next door, or the girl at work lie on their taxes and get away with it, and even get money out of it. That's fine for them. But we must remember that we are not like other people – we are alcoholic-addicts, and our happiness, well-being, and even our life depends on our spirituality and recovery. To maintain those things we must practice the principles that have saved our lives... in ALL our affairs.

Once we have violated our spiritual principle of honesty, it becomes easier to violate other principles as well. We have crossed a line, and it takes less rationalization to cross it in other ways. Soon, we discover that our spiritual principles were there for a reason: they keep our character defects in check. Keeping our character defects in check is key to our spirituality, which is key to our positive psychology. Our character defects breed negative interactions with other people, the world in general, and our higher power. They breed guilt, self-loathing, self-doubt, and regret. They take a chunk out of our humility and our healthy self-esteem, so our ego and hubristic pride become necessary to compensate. Self-will and selfishness begin asserting themselves again. I'm not saying that telling one lie will cause our world to come crashing down on us, but by letting go of our commitment to practicing our spiritual principles in all our affairs we risk a downward slide which, over time, will represent a decline in our well-being and recovery. I used just one example of not practicing our principles in all our affairs; imagine the effect if we are engaging in multiple "slip-ups" (I hate that word!) of multiple spiritual principles. This is the same downward spiral that once nearly killed us. This is what's meant when *Twelve Steps and Twelve Traditions* warns us that when we deviate from our spiritual principles we sicken and die.

This is likely a large part of the reason that drifting away from our program and fellowship carries such a risk of relapse. When we are part of the fellowship we belong to a "culture of recovery" that reminds us of who we are and what we must do to remain sober. Living by our spiritual principles is at the forefront of our attention when we are interacting with other people who do the same, listening to speakers, and reading our recovery literature that remind us of our spiritual way of living. Belonging to our program and fellowship keeps our head "in the game."

In the end, we don't need to memorize a list of the principles that we must practice in all our affairs. We know it when we are violating our principles. A little alarm goes off in our brain, and we know that we are doing something wrong. When that little alarm goes off, we are well advised to repeat a little mantra to ourselves: *practice these principles in ALL our affairs... practice these principles in ALL our affairs... practice these principles in ALL our affairs!*

*

We're covering a lot of ground, here, but, as our blueprint for life-long recovery, Step Twelve is a big one. So far we've discussed two of the parts of Step Twelve – having a spiritual awakening, and practicing these principles in all our affairs – and now we turn to the third part: "we tried to carry this message to alcoholics." Let's take a look at that now.

"This is our twelfth suggestion: Carry this message to alcoholics! You can help when no one else can. You can secure their confidence when others fail. Remember they are very ill" (Big Book, p. 89). The "service" part of Step Twelve, where we carry the message to alcoholic-addicts who still suffer, was part of 12 Step program from the very beginning of Bill Wilson's sobriety, before the 12 Steps had even been invented. From the chapter *The Doctor's Opinion* in the Big Book:

> In the course of his [Bill Wilson's] third treatment [the third time he was admitted to hospital for his alcoholism] he acquired certain ideas concerning a possible means of recovery. As part of his rehabilitation he commenced to present his conceptions to other alcoholics, impressing upon them that they must do likewise with still others. This has become the basis of a rapidly growing fellowship of these men and their families (p. xxv).

Alcoholism-addiction is not like other diseases, where a diagnosis is made, treatment is given, and all is well. Rather, someone must be ready to seek and accept help, and even then a level of trust and understanding are required. There's no one better qualified to gain that trust and understanding and take the message to an alcoholic-addict than another one in recovery:

> Highly competent psychiatrists who have dealt with us have found it sometimes impossible to persuade an alcoholic to discuss his situation without reserve. Strangely enough, wives, parents and intimate friends usually find us even more unapproachable than do the psychiatrist and the doctor. But the ex-problem drinker who has found this solution, who is properly armed with the facts about himself, can generally win the confidence of another alcoholic in a few hours. Until such an understanding is reached, little or nothing can be accomplished (Big Book, p. 18).

Service work – taking the message to those who still suffer, helping others, acts of kindness, giving of ourselves with no expectations of reciprocity – is one of the strongest actions we can do for our spiritual maturity. A large part of spirituality is connectedness with other human beings, and the connectedness that occurs when helping others in need is nearly without parallel:

To watch the eyes of men and women open with wonder as they move from darkness into light, to see their lives quickly fill with new purpose and meaning, to see whole families reassembled, to see the alcoholic outcast received back into his community in full citizenship, and above all to watch these people awaken to the presence of a loving God in their lives – these things are the essence of what we receive… (*Twelve Steps and Twelve Traditions*, p. 110).

To see these things happen – a real life saved and restored – is no small spiritual experience.

The experience of carrying the message can be a double-edged sword, and we need to meditate in preparation for doing this kind of work, in order to protect ourselves. We may end up seeing some tough situations – people, including children, in a bad state of affairs, disastrous living conditions, the worst examples of people practicing character defects in all their affairs, ugly fallout from years of an ugly addiction. We will almost certainly see people doing well who fall again. We must be prepared for the devastation we feel when people we are emotionally and spiritually attached and committed to end up failing horribly and seeming to become someone different, rejecting us and all we have done for them. We require insulation from this lest we fall ourselves from the emotional and spiritual trauma. Meditative mental preparation for this eventuality, and meditation-prayer after are how we can best accomplish this. Discussing this with someone experienced in Step Twelve work – such as our sponsor – is also a key resource to help us prepare for what may come, especially if we are new at it.

The 12 Step literature warns us of the emotional entanglements that can ensue from our Step Twelve work:

We may set our hearts on getting a particular person sobered up, and after doing all we can for months, we see him relapse. Perhaps this will happen in a succession of cases, and we may be deeply discouraged as to our ability to carry A.A.'s message. Or, we may encounter the reverse situation, in which we are highly elated because we seem to have been successful. Here the temptation is to become rather possessive of these newcomers. Perhaps we try to give them advice about our affairs which we aren't really competent to give or ought not to give at all. Then we are hurt and confused when the advice is rejected, or when it is accepted and brings still greater confusion…. We are presented with the temptation to overmanage things, and sometimes this results in rebuffs and other consequences which are hard to take (*Twelve Steps and Twelve Traditions*, p. 111).

Taking the message to a newcomer is a highly emotionally-charged activity. The whole situation hits close to home for us, because we have been there and back ourselves, which makes carrying the message a deeply meaningful experience. We pour our hearts out because we want with all our might for the person we are helping to succeed as we did. We are heartbroken if they don't succeed, and we can be frustrated and angry as well. After all, our message is so plain and obvious to us, so we wonder why the other person doesn't get it. Even though we are in recovery and getting healthy, we are, after all, alcoholic-addicts and we are somewhat emotionally fragile. So, we must proceed with some care and some self-protection. This means not getting too emotionally engaged in our Step Twelve work (which is easier said than done), and not taking the process too personally (also easier said than done). We must find balance in our approach. Knowledge and experience is key, so newcomers should consider doing their Twelfth Step work with or in close conjunction with their sponsor for a while.

As a doctor, perhaps I can provide some insight into this aspect of carrying the message. After all, doctors also try to help people with complex medical conditions and can easily become deeply emotionally involved in the outcome and suffer great pain when their patients' disease relapses or they die. That's no different from how we can feel when we watch as someone we've been helping falls into relapse and perhaps even dies. So how do we protect ourselves?

Doctors are trained to maintain a level of emotional detachment with their patients, but that doesn't mean what it sounds like. Doctors are humans, not robots, so of course they become mentally and emotionally engaged when they try to help someone with a disease, especially over time as they get to know the patient and the family. However, the trick is to not allow our emotional health and well-being become tied into the outcome of how the person makes out with his or her disease. We anticipate that things might go terribly wrong, and we accept that these things are largely beyond our control, so that we don't turn it into a futile exercise of *where did I go wrong?* when things don't work out. We can learn from the experience, but we mustn't allow our inner critic to start bullying us every time there's an adverse outcome. Doctors who don't get this don't last long, and neither will we.

We, too, as alcoholic-addicts practicing our Step Twelve must likewise be ready to see people we help end up stumbling and falling, despite our best efforts. We want with all our heart to see them succeed like we did, and it's easy to feel defeated when that doesn't happen. However, there's one thing we must accept before we reach out to help anyone: we will not always succeed, and it's not our fault. People who sponsor or help others in recovery can easily blame themselves when their sponsees don't make it, and this can be an absolute disaster. There are other tools we can engage when we carry the message and it's rejected, or the person relapses, or dies. You are already familiar with these tools, and they should already be in place in your life: get it out by talking about it with your sponsor or at a meeting, read the Big Book or other 12 Step literature, pray and meditate, recognize that self-destructive inner critic and put it in its place, and apply your knowledge of alcoholism-addiction to the situation to realize that ours is a cunning and powerful disease that kills, despite everyone's best efforts to help.

Too, as the passage from *Twelve Steps and Twelve Traditions* points out, it can be frustrating for us when the targets of our Step Twelve efforts don't follow our suggestions or buy into what we say. We must avoid forcing the message on anyone or pressing too hard, regardless of our urges to do so. The message is plain to us, but it's in the nature of our disease that people will only seek or accept help when they are ready to, when they have hit their bottom. Before that, the obsessive need for control and the alcoholic-addict pride keeps them from surrendering, and they will pick and choose which of our suggestions they take. When the addict-alcoholic mind is not yet ready to let go of drug or drink, open-mindedness and willingness are impossible to impart. That's why we mustn't shout our message from the rooftops and be aggressive in our efforts to carry the message. Rather, it's best to let those who need help know that we are there for them with a solution when they are ready. That message will be ever-present in their brain and gnaw at them. When they are ready, hopefully they will seek us out. In the meantime, we must back off.

Discussion about Step Twelve brings up the topic of sponsorship. Sponsoring other alcoholic-addicts in the program can be a part of our responsibility to carry the message. There are entire books written about sponsorship in the 12 Step program and the 12 Step literature includes an excellent booklet on sponsorship, so a discussion about how to be a sponsor is beyond my scope here. That's something that people who are well into their recovery should consider doing. I do suggest that people consider waiting until they have some significant sobriety and have a good familiarity with the 12 Step literature prior to offering themselves as sponsors.

Carrying the message to someone who is still sick and suffering or a newcomer packs benefits that will surprise people even before they come to Step Twelve: "even the newest of newcomers finds undreamed rewards as he tries to help his brother alcoholic" (*Twelve Steps and Twelve Traditions*, p. 109). Even newcomers can reach out to others at their own level, by inviting them to meetings, introducing them to people in the fellowship, or telling them about what they have found in the program. Most of us are surprised at how good we feel when we take the message to another alcoholic-addict:

"practically every A.A. member declares that no satisfaction has been deeper and no joy greater than in a Twelfth Step job well done" (*Twelve Steps and Twelve Traditions,* p. 110). The Big Book gushes over the effects of carrying the message:

> Carry this message to other alcoholics! You can help when no one else can. You can secure their confidence when others fail.... Life will take on new meaning. To watch people recover, to see them help others, to watch loneliness vanish, to see a fellowship grow up about you, to have a host of friends – this is an experience you must not miss.... Frequent contact with newcomers and with each other is the bright spot of our lives (p. 89).

Some of our greatest contributions to carrying the message to others are based in our indirect actions. Praying for those who still suffer, even when not by name, and living principled lives are a significant part of carrying our help to those who still suffer. People will notice and admire our character and deportment, as it is uncommon in today's world. When they see that we were once low-bottom drunks or addicts, they will marvel at how well we are doing now when we set an example of living by our spiritual principles. When people want what we have we speak volumes in favor of our program, including to those who still suffer. Wanting what people in the program had was a major draw to the 12 Step program for me.

*

Chapter 7 of the Big Book – *Working With Others* – is the definitive guide to taking the message to others. As those who have read my book *The Alcoholic/Addict Within* will be aware, the 12 Steps are actually a type of psychotherapy. As a therapist, I find the 12 Step program to be brilliant, and part of its genius is that it's delivered by people with no formal training or degrees, but who are unquestionably qualified due to their past experiences, and the wisdom they have obtained from doing the Steps themselves. Chapter 7 of the Big Book is like a textbook on how to approach a fellow alcoholic-addict, how to earn rapport, and how to establish a therapeutic relationship. These are all things that professional psychotherapists do with great difficulty, but our past experiences and our own spiritual growth make it come naturally to us. I suggest that reviewing Chapter 7 of the Big Book is a necessary part of preparing to take on service work.

*

Altruism – giving to others and expecting nothing in return – is an aspect of the 12 Step program that, at first glance, defies logic. How could that possibly be the key to maintaining long-term sobriety? Yet the role of altruism – service work – in long-term sobriety is given great reverence within the 12 Step program and even holds pride of place as part of the final of the Steps. Yet it seems like a paradox: how does helping others help **us** to stay sober?

One person in recovery sheds light on who really benefits from service work: "we no longer ask only what everyone can do for us; we also ask what we can do for them. We no longer only seek out situations that comfort only us; we also discover ways to comfort. We find that we feel better about ourselves when we help others. We learn from our Program that what we may have been searching for our whole lives is wrapped up in service to others."[12]

Dr. Bob Smith, co-founder of A.A., was well known for the amount of time, effort, and selfless sacrifice that he and his wife Anne put into helping other alcoholic-addicts and their families. He explained why he did service work:

> I spend a great deal of time passing on what I have learned to others who want it and need it badly. I do it for four reasons:
> 1. Sense of duty.
> 2. It is a pleasure.
> 3. Because in so doing I am paying my debt to the man who took time to pass it on to me.
> 4. Because every time I do it I take out a little more insurance for myself against a possible slip (Big Book, p. 180-1).

Once we are at a point in our recovery where we are ready for service work, the level of commitment suggested by Step Twelve is deep:

> Never avoid these responsibilities, but be sure you are doing the right thing if you assume them. Helping others is the foundation stone of your recovery. A kindly act once in a while isn't enough. You have to act the Good Samaritan every day, if need be. It may mean the loss of many nights' sleep, great interference with your pleasures, interruptions to your business. It may mean sharing your money and your home, counseling frantic wives and relatives, innumerable trips to police courts, sanitariums, hospitals, jails, and asylums. Your telephone may jangle at any time of the day or night. Your wife may sometimes say she is neglected. A drunk may smash your furniture or burn your mattress. You may have to fight with him if he is violent. Sometimes you will have to call a doctor and

administer sedatives under his direction. Another time you may have to send for the police or an ambulance. Occasionally you will have to meet such conditions (Big Book, p. 97).

Fortunately, it's seldom (or never) that we'll be called to this level of service, but that level of commitment radiates through the fellowship. I have seen many instances of such commitment to service among members of the fellowship, and even experienced it myself when I was at my bottom coming into the program (although I never burned anyone's mattress). At the time, I was overwhelmed by the kindness of these munificent strangers, but I couldn't understand why they were so willing to put themselves out to help me – a drunken, addicted wretch who looked like he'd been dragged behind a car.

The Big Book is clear about the importance of service work: "practical experience shows us that nothing will so much ensure immunity from drinking as intensive work with alcoholics. It works when other activities fail" (p. 89).

It's counter-intuitive, but somehow this giving to strangers and asking nothing in return in fact benefits the giver abundantly. Another A.A. member describes his experience with service work: "in telling newcomers how to change their lives and attitudes, all of a sudden I found I was doing a little changing myself.... I discovered in pointing out to the new man his wrong attitudes and actions that I was really taking my own inventory, and that if I expected him to change, I would have to work on myself too... [and] the dividends have been tremendous" (Big Book, p. 230). Although we ask for nothing in return, we receive much.

Service work as part of our Step Twelve growth isn't just about taking the message to others:

> Nor is this the only kind of Twelfth Step work. We sit in A.A. meetings and listen, not only to receive something ourselves, but to give the reassurance and support which our presence can bring. If our turn comes to speak at a meeting, we again try to carry A.A.'s message. Whether our audience is one or many, it is still Twelfth Step work. We can be the ones who take on the unspectacular but important tasks that make good Twelfth Step work possible, perhaps arranging for the coffee and cake after the meetings.... 'Freely ye have received; freely give...' is the core of this part of Step Twelve (*Twelve Steps and Twelve Traditions*, p. 110).

That shows that our mere presence within the fellowship, participation in meetings, and even setting up chairs or making coffee constitutes Step Twelve service work. Still, that constitutes Step Twelve work with other alcoholic-addicts, and our service work must look beyond the fellowship.

It's important to remember that our Step Twelve service work is not just limited to deeds dedicated to helping fellow alcoholic-addicts. Part of practicing our spiritual principles in all our affairs includes acts of kindness directed at people who have nothing to do with our disease: "you are expected, at some point, to do more than carry the message of A.A. to other alcoholics. In A.A. we aim not only for sobriety – we try again to become citizens of the world that we rejected, and of the world that once rejected us. This is the ultimate demonstration toward which Twelfth Step work is the first but not the final step" (*As Bill Sees It*, p. 21). In other words, we direct our service work at the world in general, in order to become exemplary "citizens of the world" again. This does much for our spirituality and therefore our recovery. It adds depth and emotion to our connections outside ourselves, it improves our connections with the world in general, and it helps us to make amends to the world after all we took from it during our drinking and using days. Acts of kindness directed at others outside the fellowship also allows us to carry the message through our example of spirituality, and helps to keep us from becoming "12 Steps hermits," whose good deeds and positive interactions are focused only on the fellowship. It's also a great way to keep our character defects in check.

The connections that we form when we do a good deed for someone and expect nothing in return are deep, indeed. No matter how small these acts may be, they the carry powerful benefits of altruism. Allowing someone to pull in front of us in heavy traffic, shoveling our sick neighbor's driveway after a snow storm, or even offering a kind word, a smile, or a hug to someone who needs it are small but deeply spiritual acts.

*

Service work is how we grow in spirituality and our sobriety – if we stagnate we fall. Spirituality is about getting outside ourselves and making connections, and there is no better way to get outside ourselves and crush our selfish tendencies than to reach out to help others. Other less obvious dividends abound. We are never fully able to make amends to those we have harmed: someone can't be located... someone would be harmed by our amends... someone is offended by our efforts... a certain amend would land us in jail to no one's benefit... or there is nothing we could do that would equal the harm we have brought on someone. Some alcoholic-addicts working the Steps are deeply bothered by these unattainable amends. Service work provides us a way of making amends indirectly, by doing good now to counter past misdeeds, to our immense psychological relief. Further, as we help others, so others will help us in our times of need. It makes the

12 Step community much more than the fellowship it claims to be... it makes it a kinship, a brotherhood/sisterhood. And there's more. No matter how well we hide our good deeds, they become known to others, inside and outside of the program. We earn respect and trust from people without even being aware of it. We reap benefits from this that far outweigh the efforts we put forth. Trust and respect of others is a deep psychological need whose satisfaction can't be bought.

We discussed in earlier Steps the psychological dysfunctions that fuel our alcoholism-addiction. You will recall that it has much to do with cognitive dissonance, the psychological discomfort we feel when how we act doesn't line up with how we believe a good person should act. The psychic changes we enjoy from progressing through the 12 Steps alleviate this dissonance, this pain, by bringing our actions back in line with our set beliefs and values. However, service work nails it for us, because by putting others before ourselves and by giving with no expectations of anything in return we make our actions even better than our set beliefs about how we should behave. Service work is a stake through the heart of cognitive dissonance. Instead of pain, our actions now bring us joy. No wonder they help us maintain our sobriety. We no longer need drugs or alcohol to feel joy in our lives.

*

The medical, psychological, and behavioral sciences support the Step Twelve suggestion of altruism. An overwhelming body of research evidence has provided proof of far-reaching benefits of altruism for our mental, social, and even physical health.[13,14,15]

Research has demonstrated that being too self-focused is harmful to our emotional and physical health.[16] In psychological terms, this is referred to as *self-focused attention*, the same selfishness and self-focus that we seek to eliminate with our efforts at spiritual health. As we become more self-focused, personality and behavioral pathologies (sicknesses) begin to emerge. Most notably, these pathologies that are brought on by excessive self-focus can include depression, anxiety, substance use, suicide, and social isolation.[17] Researchers have also demonstrated that by reducing self-focus, these pathological conditions can be reduced and overall well-being improved.[18] That's the basis of why the spiritual approach to recovery of the 12 Steps works so well. Of course, altruism is a potent way to shift the focus away from the self, which explains why helping others is such a potent way to maintain recovery.

Studies have also demonstrated that voluntarily helping others results in improved life satisfaction, sense of well-being, happiness, self-esteem, and hopefulness.[19,20,21] In other words, our Step Twelve work contributes significantly to our positive psychology. Further, altruism reduces symptoms of depression, anxiety, and the physical symptoms of mental health disorders. In fact, giving help was found to be significantly more beneficial for mental health symptoms than was receiving help.[22] Given the prevalence of mental health disorders – especially depression and anxiety – among alcoholic-addicts, this makes Step Twelve a great protective factor against relapse.

The social benefits of altruism are obvious, but have been confirmed by studies in the social sciences. Helping others is associated with enhanced social integration, better connectedness with others (i.e. spirituality), enhanced meaningfulness in life, and an improved perception of one's own self-efficacy and competence.[23,24]

Surprisingly, helping others also impacts our physical health. One large study that followed people over 30 years to study what factors determined their health found that those who voluntarily helped others were significantly less likely to develop serious illness.[25] Other studies have demonstrated that volunteering and helping others is also associated with longer life.[26,27] Helping others has also been found to be linked to other important physical parameters, such as energy levels, reduced fatigue, and self-reported good health.[28]

Interestingly, studies into the effects of altruism have shown that helping others reduces negative emotions, many of which are the same negative emotions that cause addiction-alcoholism: fear, anxiety, depression/sadness, anger, and hostility.[29] Says one researcher: "it is difficult to be angry, resentful, or fearful when one is showing unselfish love toward another person."[30] Researchers theorize that the positive effects of altruism stem from enabling people to emerge from preoccupation with the self, which is precisely our goal in our quest for spirituality.[31]

The research has, however, identified one landmine that can turn helping others into a negative: becoming too involved, or allowing ourselves to become too emotionally engaged in our efforts at altruism can be harmful to us.[32] We alcoholic-addicts sometimes lack an off-switch when we do things; our disease has been described as "the disease of more." As with all things, we must strive to find a balance. So where does that balance lay?

Altruistic behavior is linked to health and well-being benefits when it's not experienced as overwhelming.[33] When we become overwhelmed by helping tasks that are chronic and unchanging, like being a caretaker for a family member with Alzheimer's disease, we may be at greater risk for depression.[34] Altruism does us harm if our emotional and physical health diminish as a result of our altruistic behavior. However, when helping is voluntary, not experienced as a burden, not enduring and repetitive, there are numerous mental and physical benefits.[35,36] The key to keeping a balance – especially for chronic tasks such as caring for a sick family member – is to ensure that we take time and space for self-care. This is something we must be mindful of as we carry out service work.

*

There's another important aspect of altruism that has deeply therapeutic effects for those of us who are recovering from addiction-alcoholism, and that's its effects for helping us to recover from trauma or, as it's known in psychology, its capacity to help us to experience *post-traumatic growth*.[37] Past trauma is a leading contributor to addiction-alcoholism, as people who have difficulty coping with the after-effects of trauma are at high risk for substance use. Trauma does not necessarily have to be a crisis as awful as having been sexually or physically abused, or having witnessed a death. It can also be the result of having lived through difficult circumstances, or a prolonged period of adverse conditions, such as years of bullying at school or work, or a childhood scarred by uncaring parents.

Too, we must recognize that living through addiction-alcoholism is, in itself, a deeply traumatic experience. It destroys self-esteem, self-confidence, and disrupts normal brain function. It's associated with great loss: material wealth, employment, family and friends, health, and happiness. It's a miserable and prolonged experience, a struggle of a lifetime. The longer the active addiction, the more severe the dysfunction, the lower the bottom, the greater the trauma.

The condition known as post-traumatic stress disorder (PTSD) has become a household name because of its life-disrupting symptoms. Given the severity of the psychological symptoms of PTSD, it's not surprising that there is a very high association between PTSD and substance addiction. There is very little medical science can do to heal PTSD, so affected people are prone to seeking refuge in drugs or alcohol. In my opinion, however, the 12 Step process – including the altruism suggested in Step Twelve – is among the very best of therapies for people with PTSD, mainly because of its focus on acceptance, confronting and then letting go of the past, and because of the coping tools, such as meditation, group support, and spirituality. However, true PTSD isn't nearly as common as people would believe by the amount that the term is bandied about; in fact, only about 20% of people who experience severe trauma will go on to develop PTSD.[38] However, people don't need to develop full-out PTSD or even experience severe trauma to develop significant disruptive and painful symptoms related to past experiences that contribute to addiction-alcoholism.

Many survivors of trauma – especially deliberate trauma at the hands of others – live life with a deep sense of insecurity and mistrust because of their past experiences. They don't view the world as a safe place, and they

398

put up walls that prevent closeness with other people. Getting close to anyone – including people in the 12 Step fellowship – is unthinkable to some of these people. Easing into service work, especially service work directed at people who have been through similar experiences, can be a therapeutic way to begin to allow the outside world back in again. These unfortunates should work closely with a qualified therapist to get to a point where they can ease their way into trusting relationships. This is a slow process and a sponsor in the 12 Step program with a similar background is helpful.

Investigations have been done to identify the brain changes that occur following trauma. This research has identified specific neural pathways that result from traumatic experiences and cause the dysfunctional thought processes, behaviors, and emotions. Similarly, further research has shown that selflessness, altruism, and social support all help to reroute those disrupted brain connection networks back to their normal state.[39,40] As you know, these are all important parts of the 12 Step program.

Altruism and past trauma have a kind of a reciprocal relationship. Psychological research has demonstrated that people who have been through traumatic experiences are more likely to empathize for others and also more likely to wish to reach out to help those they empathize with.[41,42] They can understand what others are going through, and are better equipped to reach out to them. Some survivors of trauma internalize it, but others are driven to try to address their trauma by reducing the adversities that they themselves have experienced. In psychology, this is known as a *survivor mission*, where the individual derives healing benefits from giving meaning to their personal trauma by transforming it into positive social action.[43] This phenomenon, where people who are themselves survivors of trauma are driven to find healing by helping others is known as *altruism born of suffering.*[44,45] This is the type of altruism that Step Twelve positions us to perform. Altruism born of suffering is deeply therapeutic, and Step Twelve makes sure that we avail ourselves of this rich source of healing. This can apply to alcoholic-addicts helping other alcoholic-addicts, or sexual assault victims helping other sexual assault victims, and so on. We are best equipped to help those we can identify with, and this trauma-specific altruism helps us to heal.

Altruism born of suffering is important for more than simply its healing properties. Therapists try to facilitate it with their trauma patients because the healing prevents a repeating cycle of trauma, where the anger, rage, resentments, and negative psychology can lead to a cycle of perpetual unhappiness, negative psychology, substance use, and even violence.[46,47,48] Like trauma therapists, the 12 Step program facilitates altruism born of suffering in Step Twelve. Further, studies have shown that altruism is most effective for healing from trauma when it is mentored, done within the context of a support system, and with some healing already accomplished.[49,50] This is exactly why altruism appears in Step Twelve, after we've had the benefit of the healing powers of the first eleven Steps, and it's exactly what happens when we do service work within the context of the 12 Step fellowship and with the guidance of a sponsor.

*

The healing power of Step Twelve for past trauma is not the only positive effect that service work does for us in strengthening and maintaining our recovery and spirituality. It's true that our mind will follow wherever our actions go: actions have a weightier impact on our minds than do words. By carrying out the action of service work our minds become much more committed to our program of recovery. Our minds strive to justify our efforts, especially if we are not receiving material compensation in return for our acts of kindness and self-giving, and it does so by increasing our belief in the value of what we are doing. In other words, our mind becomes much more psychologically committed to our own recovery by helping others with theirs. Likewise, when we help people with non-recovery related altruism, our mind becomes much more committed to our spiritual way of living.

Helping others provides a new healthy coping mechanism to replace our old dysfunctional coping mechanisms, including escapism and avoidance (such as drinking or using drugs) to run away from our problems in life. Helping others is known to release endorphins, those feel-good chemicals that improve our mood, motivate us, and give us energy.[51] We get a feeling of satisfaction that distracts us from our own problems and helps us to feel grateful for what we have, rather than indulging in self-pity for our problems.[52] They are spiritual acts that take us outside ourselves, which is known to improve our self-confidence and outlook on life.[53] As such, kind acts can give us the ease and relief that we used to get with that first drink or drug, and that becomes our go-to feel-good coping mechanism as we practice it more and more.

Earlier, I told you about a physician friend of mine – who is not an alcoholic-addict – who was struggling with feeling down about life and wallowing in self-pity. I suggested that she try volunteering at a soup kitchen in order to get outside herself, develop a sense of gratitude, give her some deeper meaning in life, and to boost her humility. She found the exercise to be so therapeutic that she now does it weekly to keep her mind in the positive. So it is with us, whether we are helping out other alcoholic-addicts or people in general; if life is getting to us, a good dose of altruism is exactly what we need.

Service work roots out other old tendencies. Alcoholism and addiction drag us into deep selfishness, and altruistic service work is the authoritative

400

antidote for selfishness. Our minds follow our actions, and by acting selfless our minds accept ourselves as selfless, and this stamps out the last flames of selfishness and keeps it from smoldering back to life. Service work also helps us in our humility, a virtue that is central to our purging of character defects. Both of these virtuous character strengths are key to our recovery and are strengthened by our service work.

The dividends are tremendous, as it's through this service work that 12 Step members stay sober for life. A commonly held sentiment is: "I could not expect to keep what I had unless I gave it away" (Big Book, p. 253). Step Twelve teaches us to make giving it away a part of our psychological makeup and our lives. Besides, service work is how we stay in recovery for the long term: "never avoid these responsibilities... helping others is the foundation stone of our recovery" (Big Book, p. 97).

Another aspect of service work that's very important to our and other people's recovery is service work within the 12 Step program. The 12 Step program doesn't have a formal infrastructure with paid employees. Rather, it's a member-driven recovery organization that only exists because of members who give of their time and effort to make the program available for those in need, including you and me. The program couldn't operate without people who make service work to the program a part of their Step Twelve. I encourage all to give back to the program at some point in their recovery. This may include showing up early at meetings to help set up, staying after to help clean up, attending business meetings at the home group, and taking on organizational responsibilities, such as group treasurer, or literature rep. It can also mean stepping up to be a general service rep or other inter-group responsibilities. Many people find such service work to be an important part of their recovery and a great way to give back for all they have received. I encourage all to learn about the 12 Traditions, which provide excellent insight into how and why the 12 Step program functions, and how it has survived so successfully for nearly a century.

*

There are two aspects of service work that can give us an extra-special boost in our fight against character defects and our efforts to foster humility. These are doing service work anonymously, and expecting nothing in return. Our old ego – the one we are trying to stamp out through healthy self-esteem and humility – screams for recognition when we do a good deed. However, even though we deserve a pat on the back for our efforts, foregoing recognition or a reward gives us a much bigger bonus: a major boost in self-esteem and humility. The first time we do a good deed anonymously our ego will make us dizzy by pushing us hard to seek kudos.

However, with each successive unacknowledged or anonymous act our ego's push becomes less and less – our ego loses its power over us. Soon, with practice, we really don't want the recognition that usually comes with good deeds; we are satisfied with the spiritual rewards.

Anonymity is a founding principle of the 12 Step program, and a character virtue that can keep us out of trouble. I suggest that anyone who wants to know more about the importance of anonymity in our works read the excellent historical record of the 12 Step program in the book *Pass It On*. This engaging 12 Step publication gives insight into our program straight from the mouths of its founders. Bill Wilson discusses at length how he declined some huge opportunities for international recognition and personal rewards (including an honorary degree and a lucrative job) because of the importance of anonymity to his recovery. His humility won out over his ego, to the benefit of his spirituality and his sobriety.

*

There are other things we must do to continue to grow in spirituality and in our recovery. Everyone should – on his or her own level – continue learning about addiction-alcoholism, about the 12 Step program, and about spirituality. Drugs and alcohol will always be but an arm's length away from us, and we don't want to stagnate in our recovery or in our spirituality, the two things that stand between us and relapse.

Part of the genius of the 12 Step program is that we don't have to understand addiction-alcoholism in order to get better. Good thing, too, because it's a disease of paradoxes and odd behaviors that don't make sense to the outside observer. However, many people want to understand more about what happened to them and to understand the effects it has had on their mind. We learn much about addiction and alcoholism just by working with newcomers and listening at meetings. Much of the data that I collected for my research on addictions came from people's stories in the program. For those wish to learn more, I recommend my book *The Alcoholic/Addict Within*. The book is a guided tour through the genetics, psychology, behavioral science, and brain changes that are involved in addiction-alcoholism and recovery. The information is presented in a way that is accessible for anyone. Although knowledge doesn't keep us sober, it certainly helps us understand ourselves to the benefit of our sobriety. As we have discussed throughout our study of the Steps, self-awareness is a key tool for correcting our dysfunctional thoughts and behaviors.

Part of taking the message to newcomers means making 12 Step meetings a safe place for all people. We know that nearly half of all alcoholic-addicts are women, yet my experience has been that women almost never represent half of the people present at 12 Step meetings. I

402

know from interviews in my research that many women have been driven away from the wonderful 12 Step program by offensive behavior that made them uncomfortable or afraid. Part of our Step Twelve work must include keeping vigilance for such behavior and doing our very best to root it out and address it appropriately. We need to do our best to make our meetings safe and comfortable for our sisters in recovery. That's a Step Twelve obligation for each and every one of us to uphold.

*

Step Twelve is about continuing to do those things we need to do to maintain sobriety. The activities in Steps Ten, Eleven, and Twelve give us the tools we need to continue to maintain our sobriety and spirituality, and to grow as the kind of people we aspire to be. Earlier, I compared our disease to someone with diabetes, in that both diseases can be put in remission with proper daily care, but can never be cured. Like people with diabetes, we must continue to give attention to our alcoholism-addiction, regardless of how long we've been sober. We do this by practicing the principles we have learned in our trip through the Steps in all our affairs.

Time and time again I have seen the same pattern emerge, both in my experiences within the fellowship and in my experiences as an addictions researcher: people who end up drifting away from their program of recovery and way of living and who subsequently end up relapsing, even after many years in recovery. The progression to relapse may occur gradually, but as our practice of our recovery activities decline, so too does that thin line between us and our return to old tendencies. The reasons for our need to stay with the 12 Step fellowship for the long-term – for life – are many. Primarily, it's to prevent the things that caused us to become obsessive and compulsive drug or alcohol users from re-asserting themselves. However, the most important thing that our ongoing commitment to the program does is to "keep our head in the game," as I like to put it. When we're living a normal life around normal (i.e. non-alcoholic-addict people), it becomes easy to forget that we're different, in that we're people who can never drink or use again, lest we fall as we did before. When we maintain our place in the program and fellowship, we are constantly reminded of our powerlessness. When we slip away, our alcoholic-addict mind begins to forget and to talk us into believing that it's OK for us to drink or use again, that THIS time we'll be able to handle it. While that sounds like an over-simplification, the psychology of addiction-alcoholism works precisely that way. Keep coming back. Life is too precious to go backwards by giving up what we have.

Early in my recovery I was given a yellow wallet-sized card that was printed by A.A. World Services. It lists various slogans, prayers, and contact numbers. Also, it lists the "Big Six" things we need to do to maintain our recovery:

1. Get a sponsor and keep in touch with him or her,
2. Get a Big Book and read it,
3. Get a home group and get active,
4. Work the Steps and finish them,
5. Get involved in prayer and meditation, and
6. Get involved in service work.

This provides a good checklist for making sure that we're engaging in our program. The overall point is to not let go of our program and the practice of our spiritual principles. Now that you've been through the Steps, the tools are right there at your feet, and you have only to pick them up. We see far too many people who stray from the program and end up getting in trouble with substance use again, and we see many deaths occur as a result. At the risk of being repetitive, I once again point out what the Big Book has to say on the matter: "it is easy to let up on the spiritual program of action and rest on our laurels. We are headed for trouble if we do, for alcohol is a subtle foe. We can flat out become cocky in our recovery and lose contact with our higher power and let go of our program of recovery. We are not cured of alcoholism. What we actually have is a daily reprieve contingent on the maintenance of our spiritual condition" (Big Book, p. 85).

*

So it is that we arrive at the end of our trip through the Steps. Whether it's your first time through, or one of many, or you're just deepening your knowledge of the program, may it not be your last. It seems appropriate to end our study of the Steps with a quote from the 12 Step literature:

These little studies of A.A.'s Twelve Steps now come to a close. We have been considering so many problems that it may now appear that A.A. consists mainly of racking dilemmas and troubleshooting. To a certain extent, that is true. We have been talking about problems because we are problem people who have found a way up and out, and who wish to share our knowledge of that way with all who can use it. For it is only by accepting and solving our problems that we can begin to get right with ourselves and the world about us, and with Him who presides over us all. Understanding is the key to right principles and attitudes, and right action is the key to good living; therefore the joy of good living is the theme of A.A.'s Twelfth Step.

With each passing day of our lives, may every one of us sense more deeply the inner meaning of A.A.'s simple prayer:

God grant us the serenity to accept the things we cannot change,
Courage to change the things we can,
And wisdom to know the difference.

(*Twelve Steps and Twelve Traditions,* p. 125).

Appendix 1

<u>Why Addiction-Alcoholism is a Disease.</u>

The disease model of addiction-alcoholism (presently referred to by the medical community as "substance use disorders") still stirs up debate, and many people unfortunately continue to view addiction to drugs or alcohol as a choice, a failing of morality. The view of substance addiction as anything but a disease presents a barrier to recovery for those suffering from addiction-alcoholism, and perpetuates harmful stigma.

Much of the opposition to the acceptance of addiction as a disease is economically and politically motivated. Insurance companies generally oppose the disease concept because of the billions of dollars in costs they incur if they cover addiction treatment if it is labeled as a disease. Likewise, government policy-makers – for various motivations, including the powerful lobby of the health insurance industry – may also oppose the medicalization of addiction. Social stigma of addiction as a choice and a failing of morality is based on a widespread lack of understanding of addiction and is the driving force behind the opposition to the disease model. Political officials who weigh in on the debate on the side of addiction as a disease may risk alienating large portions of their electorate; people in active addiction generally don't vote or make campaign contributions.

A disease may be defined as a disorder of structure or function that produces specific signs or symptoms that affect a specific system, organ, or organs of the body. Disease is caused by various agents, such as infection, inflammation, environmental factors, genetic defect, or toxins, but usually does not include injury (e.g. a broken leg is not a disease). For example, let's look at a virus, such as the HIV virus. A virus causes disease by entering the body, and inserting itself into the body's cellular DNA and using the cells' innate protein synthesis apparatus to reproduce itself and make baby viruses, thereby using the body's own natural processes to propagate itself. The result is specific signs and symptoms that are caused by the virus's effects on a body organ or system (in the case of the HIV virus, that system is the immune system).

Like viruses, addictive substances enter the body and target and alter the brain's natural physiological, functional, and psychological processes to propagate their continued use to the detriment of the host's body. The result is specific signs and symptoms that affect certain organs (mostly the brain, but other organs, such as the liver, kidneys, and digestive systems are affected as well). As well, like many diseases, addiction has a strong genetic component, with about 40-60% of the basis of addiction being genetic in nature, depending on the individual.

As with other diseases, addiction causes physiological and structural changes to the body as it exerts its effects. We know that addictive substances cause a low-level inflammation of the brain, and that this inflammation causes a breakdown of existing attachments of brain cells (neurons) and a subsequent rearrangement of these attachments into new pathways that support and propagate continued substance use. This inflammation is not because the addictive substances are foreign bodies; rather, it occurs because these substances change DNA expression in brain cells at the molecular level, causing a disruption of the neuroimmune system that creates the inflammation. As such, addiction-alcoholism is very much a physical disease that causes physical changes in the body to propagate itself.

As substance use crosses the line to addiction-alcoholism, it creates dysfunctional, pathological patterns of thoughts and behaviors that favor continued substance use, prevent seeking help, and favor relapse in people who attempt to stop. Addictive substances do so by leveraging the weaknesses and flaws in human brain function, as we discuss in our trip through the Steps. These patterns of symptoms are remarkably uniform between different people and different addictive substances, making alcoholism-addiction a syndrome disease (one that is characterized by a cluster of symptoms).

One might say: alcohol and other addictive drugs don't have a brain, so how can you say that they purposely do these things? Well, viruses don't have a brain or an ability to think, neither do bacteria, cancers, or diabetes, or almost any other disease (the only exception would be infections by parasites, such as lice or worms). Nonetheless, even without a brain all of these diseases use the body's quirks and weaknesses to propagate themselves as diseases.

The fact that alcoholism-addiction is a disease can be further illustrated by the fact that affected individuals lose control as the disease asserts itself. "Normal" people – i.e. non-alcoholic-addicts – will stop drinking or using drugs when they see that it's causing them problems in life. However, once someone is afflicted with our disease, that control is no longer possible. Even when the drinking or using is no longer fun and their lives are being ruined, alcoholic-addicts have lost the ability to stop despite the absolute earnest desire to do so. They are now under the power of a disease, and they are no more able to make it go away than cancer victims can close their eyes, bear down, and make the cancer go away. When we cross the line to where alcohol or drug overtakes the power of our higher brain functions, it becomes a disease.

The disease model of alcoholism-addiction is important for many reasons. First of all, when it's classified as a disease people have a much easier time of getting their medical insurance to cover treatment, and they have an easier time of getting sick leave to take care of their treatment and recovery. As well, the disease model is crucial for reducing the social stigma around addiction-alcoholism. Employers are much more likely to hire someone in recovery when they realize that the person was afflicted with a disease and not possessed of weakness, or a flawed personality. The disease model helps alcoholic-addicts to understand that there is treatment available, and that remission is possible. It also helps those in recovery to forgive themselves. The disease model is a major factor in ending the destructive "War on Drugs" that focused on users, jailing them for simple possession. It helps us to see that addiction-alcoholism is a matter for the medical system rather than the criminal justice system.

In other words, the disease model helps people at all levels of society and government to realize that: ADDICTION-ALCOHOLISM IS A MATTER OF BIOLOGY, NOT A FAILING OF MORALITY!

Appendix 2

<u>Defects of character</u>

Resentful
Angry (also quick-tempered, bad-tempered)
Fearful
Cowardice
Willfulness (also self-indulgence)
Self-pity
Self-justification (also rationalization)
Selfishness (also self-centeredness, self-absorbed)
Egotism (also false pride, prideful, grandiosity, arrogance, hubristic)
Opinionated (also know-it-all)
Haughtiness (also pretension, boastfulness, presumptuousness, self-importance, fake)
Self-condemnation (also self-criticism, over-apologetic, insecure, self-deprecating, self-hatred, self-loathing, self-punishing)
Guilt
Lying (also dishonesty, deceitfulness)
Dishonesty by omission
Evasiveness
Impatience
Phoniness
Denial
Jealousy (also envy, covetousness)
Laziness
Procrastination
Insincerity
Negative thinking
Immoral thinking
Perfectionism
Intolerance
Gossip (also loose talk)
Greed (also avarice)
Contempt (also criticizing, cynicism, sarcasm)
Hatred
Snobbishness

Close-mindedness (also rigidity, inflexibility, dogmatic, stubborn)
Discontent
Tension
Distrust
Anxiety
Suspicious
Belligerency
Vindictiveness
Unreliable (also false promising, exaggerating, not following through,
          undependable, untrustworthy)
Self-satisfaction
Vanity
Impertinence (also disdain)
Conceit
Imprudence (also rashness, recklessness, foolishness, injudiciousness,
          disregard, irrationality, impulsiveness)
Neglectful (of self, others, responsibilities)
Irresponsibility
Thoughtlessness
Squandering (also wastefulness, excessive)
Sloppiness (also carelessness)
Corruption
Unfairness (also unjust, favoritism)
Immorality (also sinfulness)
Depravity (also degeneracy, brutality, cruel)
Crookedness
Secretive (also secret-keeping)
Dishonorable
Hypocrisy
Self-seeking (also narcissism)
Lust (also filthy-mindedness)
Sloth
Gluttony
Disrespect
Miserliness (also stinginess)
Meanness (also rudeness, cold-heartedness, lacking compassion, harsh,
          insensitive, insulting, coarse)
Impolite (also gruff, inconsiderate, unkind, ill-mannered)
Foul-mouthed (also base, crassness, dirty, offensive, loutish, obscene,
          vulgar, swearing)
Negativity
Antagonistic (also hostile, oppositional, combative, leering)
Unloving (also inhospitable, unfriendly, unneighborly, cold, uncivil)

410

Unhelpful
Alienating (also rejecting, judgmental)
Needing to be "right" (also argumentative, preachy, proselytizing)
Inaction
Abusiveness
Uncaring (also aloofness, indifference)
Obsessiveness (also neurotic, compulsive)
Bigotry (also sexism, racism, discrimination)
Nosy (also busybody)
Meddling (also playing God)
Blamefulness
Lacking boundaries
Codependence
Cheating
Over-competitive (also unsportsmanlike)
Complaining
Controlling
Dependent
Destructive
Devious (also scheming, calculating)
Disorganized
Unfaithful
Fanatical
Frustrated
Ignoring self-care
Refusing help when needed
Schadenfreude (also wishing ill on others, malice)
Immodesty (also showing off)
Impulsiveness
Indecisiveness
Self-righteousness (also taking others' inventories)
Isolating (self or others)
Excuse-making
Manipulative
Messy (also unclean, slovenly)
Negative body image (also negative self-image)
Pre-occupation with self-image (also vain, narcissistic)
Overcompensating
Vengeful
Remorseful
Remorseless
Attention-seeking (also melo-dramatic)
Setting expectations

Stealing (also theft)
Ungrateful (also lack of stewardship of possessions, unappreciative)
Uncharitable
Thrill-seeking
Undisciplined
Worrying
Aggressive
Domineering (also bossy, controlling, possessive)
Uncooperative (also disruptive, difficult, obstinate)
Disloyal
Frightening
Moody (also grouchy)
Shallow
Unforgiving
Desperate
Extravagant (also materialistic)
Facetious (also patronizing)
Flippant
Fussy
Withdrawn
Shameless

Chapter References

Note: full bibliographic information appears in the "Works Cited and Consulted" section.

Introduction

1. Ackerman, 2019; 2. Voss, Thomas, Cisneros-Franco, & de Villers-Sidani, 2017; 3. Perlovsky, 2013; 4. NIH, 2008.

Step One

1. Garavan & Stout, 2005; 2. American Psychiatric Association, 2013; 3. Sack, 2012; 4. Bechara, 2005; 5. American Psychological Association, 2012; 6. Garavan & Stout, 2005; 7. Garavan & Stout, 2005; 8. Batho, 2017, p. 12; 9. Batho, 2017; 10. Batho, 2017, p. 12; 11. Pearson, Janz, & Ali, 2015; 12. NIDA, 2003; 13. American Psychological Association, 2012; 14. Hardy, 2018; 15. Snoek, Levy, & Kennett, 2016; 16. Hardy, 2018; 17. Dash, 2018; 18. Noël, Bechara, Brevers, Verbanck, & Campanella, 2010; 19. American Psychological Association, 2012; 20. American Psychological Association, 2012; 21. Carl Jung, 1968, p. 99; 22. Albrecht, 2015; 23. Aten, 2019; 24. Austin, 2012; 25. Nielsen & Marrone, 2018; 26. Post, Johnson, Lee, & Pagano, 2015; 27. Post, Pagano, Lee, & Johnson, 2016; 28. Wright, Nadelhoffer, Perini, Langville, Echols, & Venezia, 2017; 29. Austin, 2012; 30. Post, Pagano, Lee, & Johnson, 2016; 31. Aten, 2019; 32. Post, Johnson, Lee, & Pagano, 2015, p. 464; 33. Post, Johnson, Lee, & Pagano, 2015; 34. G., Kate, 2017; 35. Rufus, 2016; 36. NIDA, 2010; 37. Shakespeare, Henry VI, Act V, Scene II; 38. Korteling, Brouwer, & Toet, 2018; 39. Groome, 2014; 40. Croskerry, Singhal, & Mamede, 2013a; 41. Croskerry, Singhal, & Mamede, 2013b; 42. Maier & Seligman, 2016; 43. Feldman & Dinardo, 2009; 44. Psychology Today, 2020; 45. Stoeber, 2003; 46. Stoeber, 2003; 47. Feldman & Dinardo, 2009; 48. Donovan, Ingalsbe, Benbow, & Daley, 2013; 49. Moos & Timko, 2008; 50. Crews & Vetreno, 2014; 51. Cui, Shurtleff, & Harris, 2014 ;

52. Nennig & Schank, 2017; 53. NIDA, 2018; 54. NIDA, 2018; 55. Dong, Taylor, Wolf, & Shaham, 2017; 56. Morse, 2017; 57. Egevari, Ciccocioppo, Jentsch, & Hurd, 2018.

Step Two

1. Wade & Halligan, 2004; 2. Skinner, 2016; 3. Yuill, Crinson, & Duncan, 2010; 4. Skinner, 2016, p. 2-3; 5. Tanyi, 2002; 6. Tanyi, 2002; 7. van Niekerk, 2018; 8. Omelicheva & Ahmed, 2018; 9. van Niekerk, 2018; 10. Hanfstingl, 2013; 11. Diamond, 2008; 12. Puchalski, 2001; 13. Fischer, 2011; 14. Krentzman, 2012; 15. Krentzman, 2012; 16. Krentzman, 2012; 17. Barton & Miller, 2015; 18. Krentzman, 2012; 19. Barton & Miller, 2015; 20. Barton & Miller, 2015, p.839; 21. Krentzman, 2012; 22. Krentzman, 2012; 23. Krentzman, 2012; 24. Galanter, 2007; 25. Irani, 2018; 26. Irani, 2018; 27. Irani, 2018; 28. Barton & Miller, 2015; 29. Smith, 2004; 30. Heine, Proulx, & Vohs, 2006; 31. Walach & Reich, 2005, p. 423; 32. Sagan, 1995; 33. Tyson, 2014; 34. Albert Einstein; 35. Albert Einstein; 36. Albert Einstein; 37. Hawking, 1998; 38. Walach & Reich, 2005, p.425; 39. Lightman, 2018, para. 2; 40. Lightman, 2018, para. 1; 41. Lightman, 2018, para. 3; 42. Lightman, 2018, para. 8; 43. Lightman, 2018, para. 16; 44. Sagan, 1995; 45. Tanyi, 2002; 46. Tanyi, 2002; 47. du Maurier, *Rebecca*, ch. 2; 48. Smith, 2004; 49. Smith, 2004; 50. Pesut et al., 2008; 51. Heine, Proulx, & Vohs, 2006; 52. Mark, 2018; 53. Tanyi, 2002; 54. Mark, 2018; 55. no citation available, this has been attributed to de Chardin, but is not in his writings; 56. Johnson, 2001; 57. Johnson, 2001; 58. Hynes, 2019; 59. Hynes, 2019; 60. Hynes, 2019; 61. Hynes, 2019; 62. Hynes, 2019; 63. Hynes, 2019; 64. Hynes, 2019; 65. Hynes, 2019; 66. Hynes, 2019; 67. Hynes, 2019; 68. Umberson & Montez, 2010; 69. Cacioppo et al., 2011; 70. Cacioppo et al., 2011; 71. Cacioppo et al., 2011; 72. Wong, Stanton, & Sands, 2014; 73. Saavedra, Perez, Crawford, & Arias, 2018; 74. Le Boutillier & Croucher, 2010; 75. Cacioppo et al., 2011; 76. Cacioppo et al., 2011; 77. Cacioppo et al., 2011; 78. Cacioppo et al., 2011; 79. Wong, Stanton, & Sands, 2014; 80. Saavedra, Perez, Crawford, & Arias, 2018; 81. Perkins & Repper, 2018; 82. Le Boutillier & Croucher, 2010; 83. dos Santos, Barros, & Huxley, 2018; 84. LaNae & Feinauer, 1993; 85. Shuler, Gelberg, & Brown, 1994; 86. Kennedy, Davis, & Taylor, 1998; 87. Brome, Owens, Allen, & Vevaina, 2000; 88. Galanter, 2007; 89. Heinz, Disney, Epstein, Glezen, Clark, & Preston, 2010; 90. Koenig, 2012; 91. Pardini, Plante, Sherman, & Stump, 2000; 92. Pesut, Fowler, Taylor, Reimer-Kirkham, & Sawatzky, 2008; 93. Nelson, 2009; 94. Arnaud, Kanyeredzi, & Lawrence, 2015; 95. Pardini, Plante, Sherman, & Stump, 2000; 96. Pardini, Plante, Sherman, & Stump, 2000; 97. Fischer, 2011; 98. Pardini, Plante, Sherman, & Stump, 2000; 99. McConnell & Dixon, 2012; 100. Hall & Fincham, 2008; 101. Hall & Fincham, 2005; 102. Krause & Ellison, 2003; 103. Sagan, 1995; 104.

Achenbach, 2014; 105. John D. Morris; 106. Voltaire; 107. St. Thomas Aquinas; 108. Hume, 1779; 109. Arnaud, Kanyeredzi, & Lawrence, 2015; 110. Arnaud, Kanyeredzi, & Lawrence, 2015, p. 14-15; 111. Arnaud, Kanyeredzi, & Lawrence, 2015; 112. Pardini, Plante, Sherman, & Stump, 2000; 113. Inzlicht, McGregor, Hirsh, & Nash, 2009; 114. Markou, Kosten, & Koob, 1998; 115. Leventhal, et al., 2008; 116. Leventhal, et al., 2008; 117. Pardini, Plante, Sherman, & Stump, 2000; 118. McCullough & Willoughby, 2009; 119. Barton & Miller, 2015; 120. Shariff & Norenzayan, 2007.

Step Three

1. Pardini, Plante, Sherman, & Stump, 2000; 2. Pardini, Plante, Sherman, & Stump, 2000.

Step Four

1. Penneback, 2016; 2. Penneback, 2016; 3. Peer, Acquisti, & Shalvi, 2014; 4. Burrowes, 2018, para. 2; 5. Schumann & Dweck, 2014; 6. Blanchard & Farber, 2015; 7. Schacter, 1999; 8. Hammond, 2017; 9. Tonegawa, Liu, Ramirez, & Redondo, 2015; 10. Poo et al., 2016; 11. Enright, 2017; 12. Tartakovsky, 2018, para. 1; 13. Tartakovsky, 2018; 14. NIDA, 2010; 15. Grupe & Nitschke, 2013; 16. Tsaousides, 2015; 17. Shpancer, 2015; 18. Shpancer, 2015; 19. Shpancer, 2015; 20. Shpancer, 2015;

Step Five

1. McCullough, Pedersen, Tabak, & Carter, 2014; 2. Weir, 2017; 3. Ross & Dolan, 2017; 4. Cinoğlu & Arıkan, 2012; 5. Frankl, 2006; 6. Goldhagen, 1996; 7. Frankl, 2006; 8. Staub, 2011; 9. Staub & Vollhardt, 2008; 10. Steakley, 2013; 11. Irani, 2018; 12. Post, 2005; 13. Frankl, 2006.

Step Six

1. Heylighen, 1992; 2. Belludi, 2014; 3. Georgiou, et al., 2018; 4. Dowling, 2011; 5. Little Red Book, p.86; 6. Becker-Phelps, 2010; 7. Johnson, J.A., 2018; 8. Golden, 2019; 9. Morin, 2018; 10. Shahar, 2017; 11. Golden, 2019; 12. Bernhard, 2016; 13. Shahar, 2017; 14. Shahar, 2017; 15. Shahar, 2017; 16. Bluth & Neff, 2018; 17. Bluth & Neff, 2018; 18. Bernhard, 2016, para. 1; 19. Bernhard, 2016; 20. Bernhard, 2016; 21. Culpepper, 2016; 22. Stober, 2003; 23. Stober, 2003; 24. Stober, 2003; 25. Stober, 2003; 26. Stober, 2003; 27. Stober, 2003; 28. Stober, 2003; 29. Wild, Rodden, Grodd, & Ruch, 2003; 30. Savage, Lujan, Thipparthi, & DiCarlo, 2017; 31. Martin, & Kuiper, 2016; 32. Louie, Brook, & Frates, 2016; 33. Markman, 2017; 34.

Winch, 2014; 35. Robbins & Karan, 2019; 36. Wang, Lilienfield, & Rochat, 2019; 37. Winch, 2014; 38. Crocker, Canevello, & Brown, 2016; 39. Crocker, Canevello, & Brown, 2016; 40. Crocker, Canevello, & Brown, 2016; 41. Heylighen, 1992; 42. Crocker, Canevello, & Brown, 2016; 43. Johnson, 2015.

Step Seven

1. Wright et al., 2017; 2. Weidman, Cheng, & Tracy, 2018; 3. Weidman, Cheng, & Tracy, 2018; 4. Weidman, Cheng, & Tracy, 2018; 5. Weidman, Cheng, & Tracy, 2018; 6. Peterson & Seligman, 2004; 7. Weidman, Cheng, & Tracy, 2018; 8. Buri, 1988; 9. Post, Johnson, Lee, & Pagano, 2015; 10. Wright et al.; 2017; 11. Warren, 2012; 12. Lewis, 2015; 13. Buri, 1988; 14. Post, Johnson, Lee, & Pagano, 2015; 15. Post, Johnson, Lee, & Pagano, 2015, p.19; 16. Post, Johnson, Lee, & Pagano, 2015, p.19; 17. Post, Johnson, Lee, & Pagano, 2015, p.19; 18. Post, Johnson, Lee, & Pagano, 2015, p.19; 19. Austin, 2012; 20. Albrecht, 2015; 21. Nielsen & Marrone, 2018; 22. Wright, et al., 2017; 23. Wright et al., 2017; 24. Austin, 2012; 25. Wright et al.; 2017; 26. Wright, et al.; 2017; 27. Wright, et al.; 2017; 28. Wright, et al.; 2017; 29. Wright, et al.; 2017; 30. Amodeo, 2015; 31. Peterson & Seligman, 2004; 32. Peterson & Seligman, 2004; 33. Peterson & Seligman, 2004; 34. Wright, et al.; 2017; 35. Wright, et al.; 2017; 36. Wright, et al., 2017; 37. Wright et al., 2017; 38. Albrecht, 2015; 39. Post, Pagano, Lee, & Johnson, 2016; 40. Post, Pagano, Lee, & Johnson, 2016; 41. Riggio, 2014.

Step Eight

1. Post, Pagano, Lee, & Johnson, 2016; 2. Newman, 2016; 3. Grimm, 2010.

Step Nine

1. Dowden, 2014; 2. Dowden, 2014; 3. McCullough, Pedersen, Tabak, & Carter, 2014; 4. McCullough, Pedersen, Tabak, & Carter, 2014; 5. Dowden, 2014; 6. Taibbi, 2018; 7. McCullough, Pedersen, Tabak, & Carter, 2014; 8. Fehr & Gelfand, 2010; 9. Winch, 2010.

Step Ten

1. Crews & Vetreno, 2014; 2. Cui, Shurtleff, & Harris, 2014; 3. Dong, Taylor, Wolf, & Shaham, 2017; 4. Egevari, Ciccocioppo, Jentsch, & Hurd, 2018; 5. Noël, Bechara, Brevers, Verbanck, & Campanella, 2010; 6. Ramo & Brown, 2008; 7. Melemis, 2015; 8. Wickham, Williamson, Beard, Kobayashi,

& Hirst, 2016; 9. Almost, 2013; 10. Anicich, Fast, Halevy, & Galinsky, 2016; 11. Gordon & Chen, 2014; 12. Mercier & Sperber, 2011.

Step Eleven

1. Davidson et al., 2003; 2. Zeidan et al., 2011; 3. Zeidan et al., 2011; 4. Rosencrantz et al., 2013; 5. Shi, 2017; 6. Tang, Tang, & Posner, 2013; 7. McGee, 2008; 8. Keng, Smoski, & Robins, 2011; 9. McGee, 2008; 10. Keng, Smoski, & Robins, 2011; 11. Seppälä, 2013; 12. Telles, Gerbarg, & Kozasa, 2015; 13. Pruett, Nishimura, & Priest, 2007; 14. Carlson & Larkin, 2009; 15. Pruett, Nishimura, & Priest, 2007; 16. Young, DeLorenzi, & Cunningham, 2011; 17. Kus, 1995; 18. Carlson & Larkin, 2009; 19. Priester et al, 2009; 20. Young, DeLorenzi, & Cunningham, 2011; 21. Kus, 1995; 22. Young, DeLorenzi, & Cunningham, 2011; 23. Tang, Posner, Rothbart, & Volkow, 2015; 24. Tang, Tang, & Posner, 2016; 25. Tang & Leve, 2016; 26. Shonin & Van Gordon, 2016; 27. Tang, Tang, & Posner, 2016; 28. Tang, Tang, & Posner, 2016; 29. Carlson & Larkin, 2009; 30. Tang & Leve, 2016; 31. Zgierska et al., 2008; 32. Marlatt & Chawla, 2007; 33. Hsu, Grow, & Marlatt, 2008; 34. Garland & Howard, 2018; 35. Priddy et al., 2018; 36. Priddy et al., 2018; 37. Wegela, 2010; 38. Jeppsen, Pössel, Winkeljohn, Bjerg, & Wooldridge, 2015; 39. Whittington & Scher, 2010; 40. Simão, Caldeira, & de Carvalho, 2016; 41. Krause & Hayward, 2013; 42. Kus, 1995; 43. Lambert, Fincham, Marks, & Stillman, 2010; 44. Neighbors, Brown, Dibello, Rodriguez, & Foster, 2013; 45. Simão, Caldeira, & de Carvalho, 2016; 46. Koenig, 2012; 47. Simão, Caldeira, & de Carvalho, 2016; 48. Koenig, 2012; 49. Koenig, 2012; 50. Koenig, 2012; 51. Pew Research Center, 2015; 52. Pew Research Center, 2014; 53. Lipka, 2016; 54. Pew Research Center, 2014; 55. Whittington & Scher, 2010; 56. Nelson, 2009; 57. Whittington & Scher, 2010; 58. Nelson, 2009; 59. Arnaud, Kanyeredzi, & Lawrence, 2015; 60. Friese & Wänke, 2014; 61. Galanter, Josipovic, Dermatis, Weber, & Millard, 2017; 62. Lambert, Fincham, Marks, & Stillman, 2010; 63. Neighbors, Brown, Dibello, Rodriguez, & Foster, 2013; 64. Lambert, Fincham, Marks, & Stillman, 2010; 65. Heinz, Disney, Epstein, Glezen, Clark, & Preston, 2010; 66. Sandoiu, 2018, para. 1; 67. Lambert, Fincham, & Stanley, 2012; 68. Lambert, Fincham, LaVallee, & Brantley, 2012; 69. Lambert, Fincham, LaVallee, & Brantley, 2012; 70. Bremner, Koole, & Bushman, 2011; 71. Whittington & Scher, 2010; 72. Krause & Hayward, 2013; 73. Kus, 1995; 74. Formica, 2010; 75. Whittington & Scher, 2010;

Step Twelve

1. Galanter, Dermatis, & Sampson, 2014; 2. Taylor, 2017; 3. Green, Fullilove, & Fullilove, 1998; 4. Galanter, Dermatis, & Sampson, 2014; 5. Cerfolio, 2016; 6. Miller, 2013, para. 1; 7. NIDA, 2010; 8. Taylor, 2018; 9. Davis, 2014; 10. Mager, 2014; 11. Hoffman, 2011; 12. Drop the Rock, p. 42; 13. Post, 2005; 14. Filkowski, Cochran, & Haas, 2016; 15. Irani, 2018; 16. Irani, 2018; 17. Irani, 2018; 18. Irani, 2018; 19. Post, 2005; 20. Filkowski, Cochran, & Haas, 2016; 21. Irani, 2018; 22. Post, 2005; 23. Post, 2005; 24. Irani, 2018; 25. Post, 2005; 26. Post, 2005; 27. Filkowski, Cochran, & Haas, 2016; 28. Post, 2005; 29. Post, 2005; 30. Post, 2005, p. 72; 31. Post, 2005; 32. Post, 2005; 33. Post, 2005; 34. Irani, 2018; 35. Irani, 2018; 36. Post, 2005; 37. Collier, 2016; 38. Steakley, 2013; 39. Steakley, 2013; 40. Filkowski, Cochran, & Haas, 2016; 41. Irani, 2018; 42. Staub & Vollhardt, 2008; 43. Irani, 2018; 44. Staub & Vollhardt, 2008; 45. Staub, 2011; 46. Irani, 2018; 47. Staub & Vollhardt, 2008; 48. Staub, 2011; 49. Staub & Vollhardt, 2008; 50. Staub, 2011; 51. Bourg-Carter, 2014; 52. Bourg-Carter, 2014; 53. Post, 2005;

Works Cited and Consulted

Achenbach, J. (2014, July 10). Carl Sagan denied being an atheist. So what did he believe? *The Washington Post*. Retrieved from https://www.washingtonpost.com/news/achenblog/wp/2014/07/10/carl-sagan-denied-being-an-atheist-so-what-did-he-believe-part-1/

Adler, N., Glymour, M., & Fielding, J. (2016). Addressing social determinants of health and health inequalities. *JAMA, 316(16),* 1641-1642. Retrieved from https://cdn.ymaws.com/hpaapta.site-ym.com/resource/resmgr/Resource/social_Determinants_Adler_20.pdf

Albrecht, Karl. (2015). The paradoxical power of humility [Web log post]. *Psychology Today.* Retrieved from www.psychologytoday.com/blog/brainsnacks/201501/the-paradoxical-power-humility

Alcoholics Anonymous. (2001). *Alcoholics Anonymous* (4th ed.). New York, NY: Alcoholics Anonymous World Services.

Alcoholics Anonymous. (2019). *Our great responsibility.* New York, NY: Alcoholics Anonymous World Services.

Alcoholics Anonymous. (1989). *Twelve steps and twelve traditions.* New York, NY: Alcoholics Anonymous World Services.

Almost, J. (2013). Review: Conflict on the treatment floor: An investigation of interpersonal conflict experienced by nurses. *Journal of Research in Nursing. 19,* 38-39. doi: 10.1177/1744987113485841.

419

American Psychiatric Association. (2013). *Diagnostic and statistical manual of mental disorders* (5th ed.). Washington, DC: Author.

American Psychological Association. (2012). *What you need to know about willpower: The psychological science of self-control*. Retrieved from http://www.apa.org/helpcenter/willpower

Amodeo, J. (2015). Why pride is nothing to be proud of [Web log post]. *Psychology Today.* Retrieved from https://www.psychologytoday.com/ca/blog/intimacy-path-toward-spirituality/201506/why-pride-is-nothing-be-proud

Anicich, E., Fast, N., Halevy, N., & Galinsky, A. (2016). When the bases of social hierarchy collide: Power without status drives interpersonal conflict. *Organization Science, 27(1),* 123-140. https://doi.org/10.1287/orsc.2015.1019

Anonymous. (1987). *The little red book.* Hawthorne, CA: BN Publishing.

Arnaud, Y., Kanyeredzi, A., & Lawrence, J. (2015). AA members understandings of the higher power (HP): A qualitative study. *Journal of Addiction Research & Therapy, 6,* 233. doi:10.4172/2155-6105.1000233

Ashim, K., & Tridip, C. (2017). Stress and its vulnerability to addiction. *Glob J Intellect Dev Disabil, 3(5).* DOI: 10.19080/ GJIDD.2017.03.555623

Aten, J. (2019). Humility and resilience [Web log post]. *Psychology Today.* Retrieved from https://www.psychologytoday.com/intl/blog/heal-and-carry/201901/resilience-and-humility

Austin, Michael W. (2012). Humility [Web log post]. *Psychology Today.* Retrieved from www.psychologytoday.com/blog/ethics-everyone/201206/humility

B., Cheryl. (2011). The third time is the charm. *A.A. Grapevine.* Retrieved from http://www.aagrapevine.org/feature/1055 (Permission to reprint The AA Grapevine, Inc., copyrighted material in this publication, organization, does not in any way imply affiliation with or endorsement by either Alcoholics Anonymous or The AA Grapevine, Inc.)

Barton, Y., & Miller, L. (2015). Spirituality and positive psychology go hand in hand: An investigation of multiple empirically derived profiles and related protective benefits. *Journal of Religion & Health, 54*, 829–843. DOI 10.1007/s10943-015-0045-2

Bartone, P., Hystad, S., Eid, J., & Brevik, J. (2012). Psychological hardiness and coping style as risk/resilience factors for alcohol abuse. *Military Medicine, 177(5)*, 517-524. Retrieved from https://watermark.silverchair.com/milmed-d-11-00200.pdf

Batho, D. (2017). Addiction as powerlessness? Choice, compulsion, and 12-Step programmes green paper (November 2017). *University of Essex.* 10.13140/RG.2.2.20695.16809.

Bechara, A. (2005). Decision making, impulse control and loss of willpower to resist drugs: A neurocognitive perspective. *Nature Neuroscience, 8,* 1458-1463. https://doi.org/10.1038/nn1584

Becker-Phelps, L. (2010). The secret of success: Lower your expectations [Web log post]. *Psychology Today.* Retrieved from https://www.psychologytoday.com/ca/blog/making-change/201007/the-secret-success-lower-your-expectations

Belludi, N. (2014). *Feed the right wolf: An American-Indian parable on cultivating the right attitudes* [Web log post]. Retrieved from https://www.rightattitudes.com/2014/01/15/the-two-wolves/

Bernhard, J. (2016). A sure-fire way to silence your inner critic [Web log post]. *Psychology Today.* Retrieved from https://www.psychologytoday.com/ca/blog/turning-straw-gold/201604/sure-fire-way-silence-your-inner-critic

Blanchard, M., & Farber, B. (2015). Lying in psychotherapy: Why and what clients don't tell their therapist about therapy and their relationship. *Counselling Psychology Quarterly, 29(1)*, 90-112. https://doi.org/10.1080/09515070.2015.1085365

Bluth, K., & Neff, K. (2018). New frontiers in understanding the benefits of self-compassion. *Self and Identity, 17(6),* 605-608. https://doi.org/10.1080/15298868.2018.1508494

Bourg-Carter, S. (2014). Helper's high: The benefits (and risks) of altruism [Web log Post]. *Psychology Today.* Retrieved from www.psychologytoday.com/blog/high-octane-women/201409/helpers-high-the-benefits-and-risks-altruism

Bremner, R., Koole, S., & Bushman, B. (2011). Pray for those who mistreat you: Effects of prayer on anger and aggression. *Personality and Social Psychology Bulletin, 37(6)*, 830–837. doi: 10.1177/0146167211402215

Brome, D., Owens, M., Allen, K., & Vevaina, T. (2000). An examination of spirituality among African American women in recovery from substance abuse. *Journal of Black Psychology, 26(4)*, 470-486. Retrieved from http://citeseerx.ist.psu.edu/viewdoc/download?doi=10.1.1.854.8715&rep=rep1&type=pdf

Buri, J. R. (1988). The nature of humankind, authoritarianism, and self-esteem. *Journal of Psychology and Christianity, 7*, 32–38. (Obtained from academic library sources).

Burrowes, R. (2018). Human psychology: The delusion 'I am not responsible.' *Global Research.* Retrieved from https://www.globalresearch.ca/human-psychology-the-delusion-i-am-not-responsible/5535678

Cacioppo, J., Reis, H., & Zautra, A. (2011). Social resilience: The value of social fitness with an application to the military. *American Psychologist, 66(1)*, 43-51. http://dx.doi.org/10.1037/a0021419

Carlson, B., & Larkin, H. (2009). Meditation as a coping intervention for treatment of addiction. *Journal of Religion & Spirituality in Social Work: Social Thought, 28(4)*, 379-392, DOI: 10.1080/15426430903263260

Cerfolio, N. (2016). Loss, surrender and spiritual awakening. *Palliative and Supportive Care, 14*, 725–726. doi:10.1017/S1478951516000304

Cinoğlu, H., & Arıkan, Y. (2012). Self, identity and identity formation: From the perspectives of three major theories. *Journal of Human Sciences, 9(2)*, 1114-1131. Retrieved from https://www.j-humansciences.com/ojs/index.php/IJHS/article/view/2429/972

Collier, L. (2016). Growth after trauma. *American Psychological Association Monitor on Psychology, 47(10)*, 48. Retrieved from https://www.apa.org/monitor/2016/11/growth-trauma

Crews, F., & Vetreno, R. (2014). Neuroimmune basis of alcoholic brain damage. *International Review of Neurobiology, 118*, 315-57. doi: 10.1016/B978-0-12-801284-0.00010-5

Crocker, J., Canevello, A., & Brown, A. (2016). Social motivation: Costs and benefits of selfishness and otherishness. *Annual Review of Psychology, 68*, 299-325. https://doi.org/10.1146/annurev-psych-010416-044145

Croskerry, P., Singhal, G., & Mamede, S. (2013a). Cognitive debiasing 1: Origins of bias and theory of debiasing. *BMJ Quality & Safety, 22*, 58-64. http://dx.doi.org/10.1136/bmjqs-2012-001712

Croskerry, P., Singhal, G., & Mamede, S. (2013b). Cognitive debiasing 2: impediments to and strategies for change. *BMJ Quality & Safety, 22*, 65-72. http://dx.doi.org/10.1136/bmjqs-2012-001713

Cui, C., Shurtleff, D., & Harris, R. (2014). Neuroimmune mechanisms of alcohol and drug addiction. *International Review of Neurobiology, 118*, 1-12. doi: 10.1016/B978-0-12-801284-0.00001-4

Culpepper, L. (2016). Positive psychology and spirituality. *Journal of Psychology and Clinical Psychiatry, 6(7)*, 00407. DOI: 10.15406/jpcpy.2016.06.00407

Dash, M. (2018). F.A.T.E. from addict to entrepreneur, with Joe Polish of The Genius Network. *Thrive Global.* Retrieved from https://thriveglobal.com/stories/f-a-t-e-from-addict-to-entrepreneur-with-joe-polish-of-the-genius-network/

Davidson, R., Kabat-Zinn, J., Schumacher, J., Rosenkranz, M., Muller, D., Santorelli, S., et al. (2003). Alterations in brain and immune function produced by mindfulness meditation. *Psychosomatic Medicine, 65 (4)*, 564–570. doi: 10.1097/01.PSY.0000077505.67574.E3).

Davis, B. (2014, Oct. 10). Life after a spiritual awakening. *The Huffington Post.* Retrieved from https://www.huffpost.com/entry/life-after-a-spiritual-aw_b_5962252?guccounter=1&guce_referrer=aHR0cHM6Ly93d3cu

Z29vZ2xlLmNvbS8&guce_referrer_sig=AQAAAFBRJtnnSO5wsrWfxS
25y_0qUzUX9HIWK2gc62wvSv7Snaarz-
dJgVXtVkyc9pxy2FpHnoQV08J20sSNMuf1PEtJH3b-
QHPKibwxi7pEmzwDRQtP7jaUDwc89Xh7ljjoJdwvqpepQwq4feOWa
iovX8NYxN_mGkxjEnlPCsq6Pi-x

deGrasse Tyson, N. (2014). *Death by black hole: And other cosmic quandaries.* New york, NY: W.W. Norton & Company.

Diamond, S. (2008). The psychology of spirituality [Web log post]. *Psychology Today.* Retrieved from https://www.psychologytoday.com/blog/evil-deeds/200812/the-psychology-spirituality

Dickens, C. (1998). *The mystery of Edwin Drood & other stories* (Wordsworth ed.). Hertfordshire, UK: Wordsworth Classics.

Dong, Y., Taylor, J., Wolf, M., & Shaham, Y. (2017). Circuit and synaptic plasticity mechanisms of drug relapse. *Journal of Neuroscience, 37(45),* 10867-10876; DOI: 10.1523/JNEUROSCI.1821-17.2017

Donovan, D., Ingalsbe, M., Benbow, J., & Daley, D. (2013). 12-step interventions and mutual support programs for substance use disorders: An overview. *Social Work in Public Health, 28(3-4),* 313–332. doi:10.1080/19371918.2013.774663

dos Santos, J.C., Barros, S., & Huxley, P.J. (2018). Social inclusion of the people with mental health issues: Compare international results. *International Journal of Social Psychiatry 2018, 64(4),* 344–350. DOI: 10.1177/0020764018763941

Dowden, C. (2014). The 3 keys to a real apology [Web log entry]. *Psychology Today.* Retrieved from https://www.psychologytoday.com/ca/blog/the-leaders-code/201408/the-3-keys-real-apology

Dowling, G. (2011). *Advances in drug abuse and addiction research from NIDA: Implications for treatment* [Power point presentation]. Retrieved from https://www.bumc.bu.edu/care/files/2011/08/02-Keynote-CRIT-2011.pdf

Du Maurier, R. (1938). *Rebecca.* New York, NY: HarperCollins.

Egevari, G., Ciccocioppo, R., Jentsch, J., & Hurd, Y. (2018). Shaping vulnerability to addiction – the contribution of behavior, neural circuits and molecular mechanisms. *Neuroscience & Behavioral Reviews, 85,* 117-125. https://doi.org/10.1016/j.neubiorev.2017.05.019

Enright, R. (2017). Why resentment lasts – And how to defeat it [Web log post]. *Psychology Today.* Retrieved from https://www.psychologytoday.com/ca/blog/the-forgiving-life/201703/why-resentment-lasts-and-how-defeat-it

Fehr, R., & Gelfand, M. (2010). When apologies work: How matching apology components to victims' self-construals facilitates forgiveness. *Organizational Behavior and Human Decision Processes, 113(1),* 37-50. https://doi.org/10.1016/j.obhdp.2010.04.002

Feldman, R., & Dinardo, A. (2009). *Essentials of understanding psychology* (3rd Canadian ed.). Toronto, ON: McGraw-Hill.

Filkowski, M., Cochran, R., & Haas, B. (2016). Altruistic behavior: Mapping responses in the brain. *Neuroscience and Neuroeconomics, 5,* 65-75. https://doi.org/10.2147/NAN.S87718

Fischer, J. (2011). The Four Domains Model: Connecting spirituality, health and well-being. *Religions, 2,* 17-28; doi:10.3390/rel2010017

Frankl, V. (2006). *Man's search for meaning.* Boston, MA: Beacon Press.

Friese, M., & Wänke, M. (2014). Personal prayer buffers self-control depletion. *Journal of Experimental Social Psychology, 51,* 56–59. https://doi.org/10.1016/j.jesp.2013.11.006

G., Kate. (2017). Fear and acceptance [Web log post]. *BRC Recovery.* Retrieved from https://www.brcrecovery.com/fear-and-acceptance/

Galanter, M. (2007). Spirituality and recovery in 12-step programs: An empirical model. *Journal of Substance Abuse & Treatment, 33(3),* 265–272. doi: 10.1016/j.jsat.2007.04.016. S0740-5472(07)00186-9

Galanter, M., Dermatis, H., & Sampson, C. (2014). Spiritual awakening in Alcoholics Anonymous: Empirical findings. *Alcoholism Treatment Quarterly, 32(2-3),* 319-334. DOI: 10.1080/07347324.2014.907058

425

Galanter, M., Josipovic, Z., Dermatis, H., Weber, J., & Millard, M. (2017). An initial fMRI study on neural correlates of prayer in members of Alcoholics Anonymous. *The American Journal of Drug and Alcohol Abuse, 43(1)*, 44-54. DOI: 10.3109/00952990.2016.1141912

Garavan, H., & Stout, J. (2005). Neurocognitive insights into substance abuse. *Trends in Cognitive Sciences, 9(4)*, 194-201. doi:10.1016/j.tics.2005.02.008

Garland, E., & Howard, M. (2018). Mindfulness-based treatment of addiction: Current state of the field and envisioning the next wave of research. *Addiction Science & Clinical Practice, 13(1)*, 14. doi:10.1186/s13722-018-0115-3

Georgiou, P., Zanos, P., Bhat, S., Tracy, K, Merchentaler, I., McCarthy, M., et al. (2018). Dopamine and stress system modulation of sex differences in decision making. *Neuropsychopharmacology. 43*, 313–324. https://doi.org/10.1038/npp.2017.161

Golden, B. (2019). How self-criticism threatens you in mind and body [Web log post]. *Psychology Today.* Retrieved from https://www.psychologytoday.com/intl/blog/overcoming-destructive-anger/201901/how-self-criticism-threatens-you-in-mind-and-body

Goldhagen, D. (1996). *Hitler's willing executioners: Ordinary Germans and the Holocaust.* New York, NY: Random House.

Gordon, A., & Chen, S. (2014). The role of sleep in interpersonal conflict: Do sleepless nights mean worse fights? *Social Psychological and Personality Science, 5(2)*, 168–175. https://doi.org/10.1177/1948550613488952

Green, L., Fullilove, M., & Fullilove, R. (1998). Stories of spiritual awakening: The nature of spirituality in recovery. *Journal of Substance Abuse Treatment, 15(4)*, 325–331. (Obtained from academic library sources).

Grimm, P. (2011). Social desirability bias. In: J. Sheth & N. Malhotra (eds.). *Wiley International Encyclopedia of Marketing.* West Sussex, UK: John Wiley & Sons. doi:10.1002/9781444316568.wiem02057

Groome, D. (2014). *An introduction to cognitive psychology* (3rd ed.). New York, NY: Routledge.

Grupe, D., & Nitschke, J. (2013). Uncertainty and anticipation in anxiety: An integrated neurobiological and psychological perspective. *Nature Reviews Neuroscience, 14(7)*, 488–501. doi:10.1038/nrn3524

Hall, J., & Fincham, F. (2005). Self-forgiveness: The stepchild of forgiveness. *Journal of Social and Clinical Psychology, 24(5)*, 621-637. Retrieved from http://citeseerx.ist.psu.edu/viewdoc/download?doi=10.1.1.452.7231&rep=rep1&type=pdf

Hall, J., & Fincham, F. (2008). The temporal course of self-forgiveness. *Journal of Social and Clinical Psychology, 27(2)*, 174–202. Retrieved from http://fincham.info/papers/jscp-The%20temporal%20course%20of%20self-forgiveness.pdf

Hammond, C. (2017). The 7 steps of accepting responsibility [Web log post]. *Psych Central.* Retrieved from https://pro.psychcentral.com/exhausted-woman/2016/05/the-7-steps-of-accepting-responsibility-for-wrongdoing/

Hanfstingl, B. (2013). Ego and spiritual transcendence: Relevance to psychological resilience and the role of age. *Evidence-based Complementary and Alternative Medicine.* 949838. doi:10.1155/2013/949838

Hardy, B. (2018). Why willpower makes things worse, not better [Web log post]. *Psychology Today.* Retrieved from https://www.psychologytoday.com/us/blog/quantum-leaps/201803/why-willpower-makes-things-worse-not-better

Hawking, S. (1998). *A brief history of time.* New York, NY: Bantam Books.

Heine, S.J., Proulx, T., & Vohs, K.D. (2006). The Meaning Maintenance Model: On the coherence of social motivations. *Personality and Social Psychology Review, 10(2)*, 88-110. DOI: 10.1207/s15327957pspr1002_1

Heinz, A., Disney, E., Epstein, D., Glezen, L., Clark, P., & Preston, K. (2010). A focus-group study on spirituality and substance-user treatment. *Substance Use & Misuse, 45(1-2),* 134–153. doi:10.3109/10826080903035130

Heylighen, F. (1992). Evolution, selfishness and cooperation. *Journal of Ideas, 2(4),* 70-76. Retrieved from https://pdfs.semanticscholar.org/fc6d/93966c24f1ac8b6ded84d53 de5d04cdc746f.pdf

Hoffman, E. (2011). What was Maslow's view of peak-experiences? [Web log post]. *Psychology Today.* Retrieved from https://www.psychologytoday.com/ca/blog/the-peak-experience/201109/what-was-maslows-view-peak-experiences

Hsu S., Grow J., & Marlatt A. (2008). Mindfulness and addiction. In: L. Kaskutas & M. Galanter (eds.). *Recent developments in alcoholism.* New York, NY Springer. https://doi.org/10.1007/978-0-387-77725-2_13

Hume, D. (1779). *Dialogues concerning natural religion* [Reprint edition, 1990]. London, UK: Penguin Classics Reprints.

Hynes, M. (Host). (2019, Sept 20). *Headlines and rejection: Interview with Dr. Steven Stosny* [Radio broadcast interview]. In Meyer, M., & Mahoney, S. (Producers), Tapestry. Toronto, ON: CBC Radio.

Inzlicht, M., McGregor, I., Hirsh, J., & Nash, K. (2009). Neural markers of religious conviction. *Psychological Science, 20(3),* 385-92. doi: 10.1111/j.1467-9280.2009.02305.x.

Irani, A. (2018). Positive altruism: Helping that benefits both the recipient and giver [Master's thesis]. *University of Pennsylvania.* https://repository.upenn.edu/mapp_capstone/152

Jeppsen, B., Pössel, P., Winkeljohn, S., Bjerg, A. & Wooldridge, D. (2015). Closeness and control: Exploring the relationship between prayer and mental health. *University of Louisville Counseling Psychology Commons.* Retrieved from https://ir.library.louisville.edu/cgi/viewcontent.cgi?article=1174&c ontext=faculty

Johnson, J. (2015). Good, neutral, and bad selfishness [Web log post]. *Psychology Today.* Retrieved from https://www.psychologytoday.com/ca/blog/cui-bono/201501/good-neutral-and-bad-selfishness

Johnson, J. (2018). The psychology of expectations [Web log post]. *Psychology Today*. Retrieved from https://www.psychologytoday.com/ca/blog/cui-bono/201802/the-psychology-expectations

Johnson, M.H. (2001). Functional brain development in humans. *Neuroscience, 2,* 475-483. Retrieved from http://www-inst.eecs.berkeley.edu/~cs182/sp06/readings/Johnson%20-%202001.pdf

Jung, C. (1968). *Psychology and alchemy.* Princeton, N.J.: Princeton University Press.

Kennedy, J., Davis, R., & Taylor, B. (1998). Changes in spirituality and well-being among victims of sexual assault. *Journal for the Scientific Study of Religion, 37,* 322-328. Retrieved from http://www.jeksite.org/research/assault.pdf

Keng, S., Smoski, M., & Robins, C. (2011). Effects of mindfulness on psychological health: A review of empirical studies. *Clinical Psychology Review, 31(6),* 1041–1056. doi:10.1016/j.cpr.2011.04.006

Kobasa, S. C. (1979). Stressful life events, personality, and health: An inquiry into hardiness. *Journal of Personality and Social Psychology, 37(1),* 1-11. http://dx.doi.org/10.1037/0022-3514.37.1.1

Koenig, H. (2012). Religion, spirituality, and health: The research and clinical implications. *ISRN Psychiatry*, 278730. https://doi.org/10.5402/2012/278730.

Korteling, J., Brouwer, A., & Toet, A. (2018). A neural network framework for cognitive bias. *Frontiers in Psychology: Cognitive Science.* https://doi.org/10.3389/fpsyg.2018.01561

Krause, N., & Ellison, C. (2003). Forgiveness by god, forgiveness of others, and psychological well-being in late life. *Journal for the Scientific Study of Religion, 42(1),* 77–94. doi:10.1111/1468-5906.00162

Krause, N., & Hayward, R. (2013). Prayer beliefs and change in life satisfaction over time. *Journal of Religion and Health, 52(2),* 674–694. doi:10.1007/s10943-012-9638-1

Krentzman, A.R. (2013). Review of the application of positive psychology to substance use, addiction, and recovery research. *Psychology of Addiction Behavior, 27(1),* 151-65. doi: 10.1037/a0029897

Kus, R. (1995). Prayer and meditation in addiction recovery. *Journal of Chemical Dependency Treatment, 5(2),* 101-115, DOI: 10.1300/J034v05n02_08

Lambert, N., Fincham, F., LaVallee, D., & Brantley, C. (2012). Praying together and staying together: Couple prayer and trust. *Psychology of Religion and Spirituality, 4(1),* 1-9. DOI: 10.1037/a0023060

Lambert, N., Fincham, F., & Stanley, S. (2012). Prayer and satisfaction with sacrifice in close relationships. *Journal of Social and Personal Relationships , 29(8),* 1058 -1070. https://doi.org/10.1177/0265407512449316

Lambert, N., Fincham, F., Marks, L., & Stillman, T. (2010). Invocations and intoxication: Does prayer decrease alcohol consumption? *Psychology of Addictive Behaviors, 24(2),* 209-219. DOI: 10.1037/a0018746

Lanae, V., & Feinauer, L. (1993). Resilience factors associated with female survivors of childhood sexual abuse. *American Journal of Family Therapy, 2193, 216-24.* (Obtained from academic library sources).

Le Boutillier, C. & Croucher, A. (2010). Social Inclusion and Mental Health. *The British Journal of Occupational Therapy. 73(3),* 136-139. 10.4276/030802210X12682330090578.

Leipold, B., & Greve, W. (2009). Resilience: A conceptual bridge between coping and development. *European Psychologist, 14(1),* 40-50. doi:10.1027/1016-9040.14.1.40

Leventhal, A., Kahler, C., Ray, L., Stone, K., Young, D., Chelminski, I., et al. (2008). Anhedonia and amotivation in psychiatric outpatients with fully remitted stimulant use disorder. *The American Journal on Addictions / American Academy of Psychiatrists in Alcoholism and Addictions, 17*(3), 218–223. http://doi.org/10.1080/10550490802019774

Lewis, C. (2015). *Mere Christianity*. New York, NY: HarperCollins.

Lightman, A. (2018). Fact and faith: Why science and spirituality are not incompatible. *Science Focus.* Retrieved from https://www.sciencefocus.com/the-human-body/fact-and-faith-why-science-and-spirituality-are-not-incompatible/

Lipka, M. (2016). 5 facts about prayer. *Pew Research Center*. Retrieved from http://www.pewresearch.org/fact-tank/2016/05/04/5-facts-about-prayer/

Louie, D., Brook, K., & Frates, E. (2016). The laughter prescription: A tool for lifestyle medicine. *American Journal of Lifestyle Medicine, 10(4),* 262–267. doi:10.1177/1559827614550279

Mager, D. (2014). What constitutes a spiritual awakening? [Web log post]. *Psychology Today.* Retrieved from https://www.psychologytoday.com/ca/blog/some-assembly-required/201404/what-constitutes-spiritual-awakening

Maier, S., & Seligman, M. (2016). Learned helplessness at fifty: Insights from neuroscience. *Psychological review, 123(4),* 349–367. doi:10.1037/rev0000033

Mark, J. (2018). Religion in the ancient world. *Ancient History Encyclopedia.* Retrieved from https://www.ancient.eu/religion/

Markman, A. (2017). Humor sometimes makes stressful situations better [Web log post]. *Psychology Today.* Retrieved from https://www.psychologytoday.com/ca/blog/ulterior-motives/201706/humor-sometimes-makes-stressful-situations-better

Markou, A., Kosten, T., & Koob, G. (1998). Neurobiological similarities in depression and drug dependence: A self-medication hypothesis. *Neuropsycho-pharmacology, 18,* 135–174. Retrieved from https://www.ncbi.nlm.nih.gov/pubmed/9471114

Marlatt, G., & Chawla, N. (2007). Meditation and alcohol use. *Southern Medical Journal, 100(4),* 451. (Obtained from academic library sources).

Martin, R., & Kuiper, N. (2016). Three decades investigating humor and laughter: An interview with Professor Rod Martin. *Europe's Journal of Psychology, 12(3)*, 498–512. doi:10.5964/ejop.v12i3.1119

McConnell, J., & Dixon, D. (2012). Perceived forgiveness from God and self-forgiveness. *Journal of Psychology & Christianity, 31(1)*, 31-39. (Obtained from academic library sources).

McCullough, M., Pedersen, E., Tabak, B., & Carter, E. (2014). Conciliatory gestures promote forgiveness and reduce anger in humans. *Proceedings of the National Academy of Sciences, 111(30)*, 11211-11216. doi:10.1073/pnas.1405072111

McCullough, M., & Willoughby, B. (2009). Religion, self-regulation, and self-control: Associations, Explanations, and Implications. *Psychological Bulletin, 135(1)*, 69-93. DOI: 10.1037/a0014213

McGee, M. (2008). Meditation and psychiatry. *Psychiatry, 5(1)*, 28–41. (Obtained from academic library sources).

Melemis S. M. (2015). Relapse prevention and the five rules of recovery. *The Yale Journal of Biology and Medicine, 88(3), 325*–332. Retrieved from https://www.ncbi.nlm.nih.gov/pmc/articles/PMC4553654/

Mercier, H., & Sperber, D. (2011). Why do humans reason? Arguments for an argumentative theory. *Behavioral and Brain Sciences, 34(2)*, 57-74. https://ssrn.com/abstract=1698090

Miller, L. (2013). Spiritual awakening and depression in adolescents: A unified pathway or "two sides of the same coin." *Bulletin of the Menninger Clinic, 77(4)*, 332-48. doi: 10.1521/bumc.2013.77.4.332.

Moos, R., & Timko, C. (2008). Outcome research on twelve-step and other self-help programs. In M. Galanter, & H. Kleber (Eds.), *Textbook of substance abuse treatment* (4th ed. pp. 511-521). Washington, DC: American Psychiatric Press. Retrieved from https://www.mentalhealth.va.gov/providers/sud/selfhelp/docs/4_moos_timko_chapter.pdf

Morin, A. (2018). 7 ways to overcome toxic self-criticism [Web log post]. *Psychology Today*. Retrieved from https://www.psychologytoday.com/intl/blog/what-mentally-strong-people-dont-do/201801/7-ways-overcome-toxic-self-criticism

Morse, E. (2017). Addiction is a chronic medical illness. *North Carolina Medical Journal, 79(3),* 163-165. doi: 10.18043/ncm.79.3.163

National Institute on Drug Abuse (NIDA). (2003). *Epidemiology.* Retrieved from https://archives.drugabuse.gov/publications/diagnosis-treatment-drug-abuse-in-family-practice-american-family-physician-monograph/epidemiology

National Institute on Drug Abuse (NIDA). (2010). Comorbidity: Addiction and other mental illnesses. *Research Report Series.* Retrieved from https://www.drugabuse.gov/sites/default/files/rrcomorbidity.pdf

National Institute on Drug Abuse (NIDA). (2015). *National survey of drug use and health* [Data file]. Retrieved from https://www.drugabuse.gov/national-survey-drug-use-health

National Institute on Drug Abuse (NIDA). (2018). *Principles of drug addiction treatment: A research-based guide* (3rd ed.). Retrieved from https://www.drugabuse.gov/publications/principles-drug-addiction-treatment-research-based-guide-third-edition

Neighbors, C., Brown, G., Dibello, A., Rodriguez, L., & Foster, D. (2013). Reliance on God, prayer, and religion reduces influence of perceived norms on drinking. *Journal of studies on alcohol and drugs, 74(3),* 361–368. doi:10.15288/jsad.2013.74.361

Nelson, J. (2009). *Psychology, religion, and spirituality.* New York, NY: Springer-Verlag.

Newman, S. (2016). Understanding and closing the empathy gap [Web log post]. *Psychology Today.* Retrieved from https://www.psychologytoday.com/ca/blog/singletons/201602/understanding-and-mastering-the-empathy-gap

Nielsen, R. & Marrone, J. (2018). Humility: Our current understanding of the construct and its role in organizations. *International Journal of Management Reviews, 20,* 805-824. doi:10.1111/ijmr.12160

Nennig, S., & Schank, J. (2017). The Role of NFkB in Drug Addiction: Beyond Inflammation. *Alcohol and Alcoholism, 52(2),* 172–179. doi: 10.1093/alcalc/agw098

Noël, X., Bechara, A., Brevers, D., Verbanck, P., & Campanella, S. (2010). Alcoholism and the Loss of Willpower: A Neurocognitive Perspective. *Journal of Psychophysiology, 24(4),* 240–248. doi:10.1027/0269-8803/a000037

Omelicheva, M., & Ahmed, R. (2018). Religion and politics: Examining the impact of faith on political participation. *Religion, State and Society, 46(1),* 4-25, DOI: 10.1080/09637494.2017.1363345

P., A. (2017). *The alcoholic/addict within: Our brain, genetics, psychology, and the twelve steps as psychotherapy.* St. Catharines, ON: Recovery Folio.

P., B., W., T., & S., S. (2005). *Drop the rock* (2nd ed.). Seattle, Wash.: Hazelden Publishing.

Pardini, D., Plante, T., Sherman, A., & Stump, J. (2000). Religious faith and spirituality in substance abuse recovery: Determining the mental health benefits. *Journal of Substance Abuse Treatment, 19,* 347-354. DOI: 10.1016/s0740-5472(00)00125-2

Pearson, C., Janz, T., & Ali, J. (2015). Mental and substance use disorders in Canada. *Statistics Canada.* Retrieved from https://www150.statcan.gc.ca/n1/pub/82-624-x/2013001/article/11855-eng.htm

Peer, E., Acquisti, A., & Shalvi, S. (2014). "I cheated, but only a little": Partial confessions to unethical behavior. *Journal of Personality and Social Psychology, 106(2),* 202–217. https://doi.org/10.1037/a0035392

Penneback, J. (2016). Does confessing our secrets improve our mental health? *Scientific American Mind, 27(2),* 71. doi:10.1038/scientificamericanmind0316-71a

Perkins, R. & Repper, J. (2018). Thinking about recovery and well-being in a social context. *Mental Health and Social Inclusion, 22(4),* 161-166. https://doi.org/10.1108/MHSI-08-2018-058

Perlovsky, L. (2013). A challenge to human evolution-cognitive dissonance. *Frontiers in Psychology, 4,* 179. https://doi.org/10.3389/fpsyg.2013.00179

Pesut, B., Fowler, M., Taylor, E.J., Reimer-Kirkham, S. & Sawatzky, R. (2008). Conceptualising spirituality and religion for healthcare. *Journal of Clinical Nursing, 17,* 2803–2810. doi: 10.1111/j.1365-2702.2008.02344.x

Peterson, C., & Seligman, M. (2014). *Character strengths and virtues: A handbook and classification.* New York, NY: Oxford University Press. Retrieved from http://ldysinger.stjohnsem.edu/@books1/Peterson_Character_Strengths/character-strengths-and-virtues.pdf

Pew Research Center. (2014). Frequency of prayer. *Religious Landscape Study.* Retrieved from https://www.pewforum.org/religious-landscape-study/frequency-of-prayer/

Pew Research Center. (2015). *Religious practices and experiences.* Retrieved from https://www.pewforum.org/2015/11/03/chapter-2-religious-practices-and-experiences/#private-devotions

Poo, M., Pignatelli, M., Ryan, T., Tonegawa, S., Bonhoeffer, T., Martin, K., et al. (2016). What is memory? The present state of the engram. *BMC Biology, 14(40).* Retrieved from https://bmcbiol.biomedcentral.com/articles/10.1186/s12915-016-0261-6

Post, S. (2005). Altruism, happiness, and health: It's good to be good. *International Journal of Behavioral Medicine, 12(2),* 66-77. (Obtained from academic library sources).

Post, S., Johnson, B., Lee, M., & Pagano, M. (2015). Positive psychology in Alcoholics Anonymous and the 12 Steps: Adolescent recovery in relation to humility. *The American Psychological Association Addictions Newsletter,* 18-20. Retrieved from http://www.helpingotherslivesober.org/documents/publications/Positive_Psychology_in_Alcoholics_Anonymous_and_the_12_steps_Adolescent_Recovery_in_Relation_to_Humility.pdf

Post, S., Pagano, M., Lee, M., & Johnson, B. (2016). Humility and 12-Step recovery: A prolegomenon for the empirical investigation of a cardinal virtue in alcoholics anonymous. *Alcoholism Treatment Quarterly, 34(3),* 262–273. doi:10.1080/07347324.2016.1182817

Priddy, S., Howard, M., Hanley, A., Riquino, M., Friberg-Felsted, K., & Garland, E. (2018). Mindfulness meditation in the treatment of substance use disorders and preventing future relapse: Neurocognitive mechanisms and clinical implications. *Substance Abuse and Rehabilitation, 9,* 103–114. doi:10.2147/SAR.S145201

Priester, P., Scherer, J., Steinfeldt, J., Jana-Masri, A., Jashinsky, T., Jones, J., et al. (2009). The frequency of prayer, meditation and holistic interventions in addictions treatment: A national survey. *Pastoral Psychology, 58,* 315. https://doi.org/10.1007/s11089-009-0196-8

Pruett, J., Nishimura, N. & Priest, R. (2007). The role of meditation in addiction recovery. *Counseling and Values, 52,* 71-84. doi:10.1002/j.2161-007X.2007.tb00088.x

Psychology Today. (2020). *Learned helplessness.* Retrieved from https://www.psychologytoday.com/ca/basics/learned-helplessness

Psychology Today. (2019). *Spirituality.* Retrieved from https://www.psychologytoday.com/ca/basics/spirituality

Puchalski, C. M. (2001). The role of spirituality in health care. *Proceedings (Baylor University. Medical Center), 14(4),* 352–357. Retrieved from https://www.ncbi.nlm.nih.gov/pmc/articles/PMC1305900/

Ramo, D., & Brown, S. (2008). Classes of substance abuse relapse situations: A comparison of adolescents and adults. *Psychology of Addictive Behaviors : Journal of the Society of Psychologists in Addictive Behaviors, 22(3),* 372–379. doi:10.1037/0893-164X.22.3.372

Riggio. (2014). What is social intelligence? Why does it matter? [Web log post]. *Psychology Today.* Retrieved from https://www.psychologytoday.com/ca/blog/cutting-edge-leadership/201407/what-is-social-intelligence-why-does-it-matter

Robins, M.; & Karan, A. (2019). Who gossips and how in everyday life. *Journal of Social Psychology and Personality Science.* https://doi.org/10.1177/1948550619837000

Rosenkranz, M., Davidson, R., MacCoon, D., Sheridan, J., Kalin, N., & Lutz, A. (2013). A comparison of mindfulness-based stress reduction and an active control in modulation of neurogenic inflammation. *Brain, Behavior, and Immunity, 27*, 174–184. https://doi.org/10.1016/j.bbi.2012.10.013

Ross, H., & Dolan, S. (2017). Forgiveness and its importance in substance use disorders. *Journal of Psychology and Christianity, 36(3),* 250-266. Retrieved from https://www.researchgate.net/publication/322339237_Forgivenes s_and_Its_Importance_In_Substance_Use_Disorders

Rufus, S. (2016). The other higher powers. *Spirituality & Health.* Retrieved from https://spiritualityhealth.com/blogs/worthy-a-self-esteem-blog/2016/07/29/anneli-rufus-other-higher-powers

Saavedra, J., Perez, E., Crawford, P., & Arias, S. (2018). Recovery and creative practices in people with severe mental illness: Evaluating well-being and social inclusion. *Disability And Rehabilitation, 40(8),* 905-911. http://dx.doi.org/10.1080/09638288.2017.1278797

Sack, D. (2012). Does willpower play a role in addiction recovery? [Web log post]. *Psychology Today.* Retrieved from https://www.psychologytoday.com/ca/blog/where-science-meets-the-steps/201211/does-willpower-play-role-in-addiction-recovery

Sagan, C. (1995). *The demon-haunted world: Science as a candle in the dark.* New York, NY: Random House.

Sandoiu, A. (2018). What religion does to your brain. *Medical News Today.* Retrieved from https://www.medicalnewstoday.com/articles/322539.php#1

Savage, B., Lujan, H., Thipparthi, R., & DiCarlo, S. (2017). Humor, laughter, learning, and health! A brief review. *Adv Physiol Educ, 41,* 341-7. https://doi.org/10.1152/advan.00030.2017

Schacter, D. (1999). The seven sins of memory: Insights from psychology and cognitive neuroscience. *American Psychologist, 54(3),* 182-203. Retrieved from https://www.researchgate.net/profile/Daniel_Schacter/publication /13099436_The_seven_sins_of_memory_-

_Insights_from_psychology_and_cognitive_neuroscience/links/0c96
052f3f81c5ece0000000.pdf

Schumann, K., & Dweck, C. (2014). Who accepts responsibility for their
transgressions? *Personality and Social Psychology Bulletin, 40(12)*,
1598-1610. https://doi.org/10.1177/0146167214552789

Seppälä, E. (2013). 20 Scientific reasons to start meditating today [Web
log post]. *Psychology Today* Retrieved from
https://www.psychologytoday.com/blog/feeling-it/201309/20-
scientific-reasons-start-meditating-today

Shahar, G. (2017). The hazards of self-criticism [Web log post].
Psychology Today. Retrieved from
https://www.psychologytoday.com/ca/blog/stress-self-and-
health/201708/the-hazards-self-criticism

Shariff, A., & Norenzayan, A. (2007). God is watching you: Priming God
concepts increases prosocial behavior in an anonymous economic
game. *Psychological Science, 18*, 803–809. doi: 10.1111/j.1467-
9280.2007.01983.x

Shi, L., Zhang, D., Wang, L., Zhuang, J., Cook, R., & Chen, L. (2017).
Meditation and blood pressure: A meta-analysis of randomized
clinical trials. *Journal of Hypertension, 35(4)*, 696-706. doi:
10.1097/HJH.0000000000001217

Shonin, E. & Van Gordon, W. (2016). The mechanisms of mindfulness in
the treatment of mental illness and addiction. *International Journal
of Mental Health & Addiction, 14*, 844.
https://doi.org/10.1007/s11469-016-9653-7

Shpancer, N. (2015). How to stop worrying and get on with your life
[Web log post]. *Psychology Today*. Retrieved from
https://www.psychologytoday.com/ca/blog/insight-
therapy/201501/how-stop-worrying-and-get-your-
life?collection=168048

Shuler, P., Gelberg, L., & Brown, M. (1994). The effects of
spiritual/religious practices on psychological well-being among
inner city homeless women. *Nurse Practitioner Forum, 5(2)*, 106-
113. (Obtained from academic library sources).

438

Simão, T., Caldeira, S., & de Carvalho, E. (2016). The effect of prayer on patients' health: Systematic literature review. *Religions, 7(11)*. doi:10.3390/rel7010011

Skinner, w. (2016). A bio-psycho-social plus approach to addiction and recovery. *York University*. (Obtained from academic library sources).

Smith, S. (2004). Exploring the interaction of trauma and spirituality. *Traumatology, 10(4)*, 231-243. https://doi.org/10.1177/153476560401000403

Snoek, A., Levy, N., & Kennett, J. (2016). Strong-willed but not successful: The importance of strategies in recovery from addiction. *Addictive Behaviors Review, 4*, 102-17. https://doi.org/10.1016/j.abrep.2016.09.002

Soleimani, M., Sharif, S., Zadeh, A., & Ong, F. (2016). Relationship between hardiness and addiction potential in medical students. *I J Psych Behav Sci, e6225*. DOI: 10.17795/ijpbs-6225

Staub, E. (2011). Altruism born of suffering: The value of kindness [Web log post]. *Psychology Today*. Retrieved from https://www.psychologytoday.com/blog/in-the-garden-good-and-evil/201112/altruism-born-suffering

Staub, E., & Vollhardt, J. (2008). Altruism born of suffering: The roots of caring and helping after victimization and other trauma. *American Journal of Orthopsychiatry, 78(3)*, 267-80. doi: 10.1037/a0014223.

Steakley, L. (2013). How the brain processes trauma and why support, altruism can ease fear. *Stanford Medicine Scope*. Retrieved from https://scopeblog.stanford.edu/2013/04/16/how-the-brain-processes-trauma-and-why-support-altruism-can-ease-fear/

Stoeber, J. (2003). Self-pity: Exploring the links to personality, control beliefs, and anger. *Journal of Personality, 71(2)*, 183-220. https://doi.org/10.1111/1467-6494.7102004

Tang, Y., & Leve, L. (2016). A translational neuroscience perspective on mindfulness meditation as a prevention strategy. *Translational Behavioral Medicine, 6(1)*, 63–72. https://doi.org/10.1007/s13142-015-0360-x

Tang, Y., Posner, M., Rothbart, M., & Volkow, N. (2015). Circuitry of self-control and its role in reducing addiction. *Trends in Cognitive Sciences, 19(8),* 439-444. https://doi.org/10.1016/j.tics.2015.06.007

Tang, Y., Tang, R., & Posner, M. (2013). Brief meditation induces smoking reduction. *Proceedings of the National Academy of Sciences, 110(34),* 13971-13975. DOI: 10.1073/pnas.1311887110

Tang, Y., Tang, R., & Posner, M. (2016). Mindfulness meditation improves emotion regulation and reduces drug abuse. *Drug and Alcohol Dependence, 163(Supp 1),* S13-S18. https://doi.org/10.1016/j.drugalcdep.2015.11.041

Tanyi, R.A. (2002). Towards clarification of the meaning of spirituality. *Journal of Advanced Nursing, 39(5),* 500-509. https://doi.org/10.1046/j.1365-2648.2002.02315.x

Taylor, S. (2018). The after-effects of awakening [Web log post]. *Psychology Today.* Retrieved from https://www.psychologytoday.com/ca/blog/out-the-darkness/201802/the-after-effects-awakening

Taibbi, R. (2018). The art of the apology [Web log post]. *Psychology Today.* Retrieved from https://www.psychologytoday.com/ca/blog/fixing-families/201811/the-art-the-apology

Tartakovsky, M. (2018). Why ruminating is unhealthy and how to stop it [Web log post]. *PsychCentral.* Retrieved from https://psychcentral.com/blog/why-ruminating-is-unhealthy-and-how-to-stop/

Taylor, S. (2017). Exploring awakening experiences: A study of awakening experiences in terms of their triggers, characteristics, duration and after-effects. *International Journal of Transpersonal Studies, 49(1),* 45-65. (Obtained from academic library sources).

Telles, S., Gerbarg, P., & Kozasa, E. (2015). Physiological effects of mind and body practices. *Biomedical Research International.* http://dx.doi.org/10.1155/2015/983086

Tonegawa, S., Liu, X., Ramirez, S., & Redondo, R. (2015). Memory engram cells have come of age. *Neuron, 87(5),* 918-931. https://doi.org/10.1016/j.neuron.2015.08.002

Tsaousides, T. (2015). 7 things you need to know about fear [Web log post]. *Psychology Today.* Retrieved from https://www.psychologytoday.com/ca/blog/smashing-the-brainblocks/201511/7-things-you-need-know-about-fear

Umberson, D., & Montez, J. K. (2010). Social relationships and health: A flashpoint for health policy. *Journal of Health and Social Behavior, 51(Suppl),* S54–S66. doi:10.1177/0022146510383501

van Niekerk, B. (2018). Religion and spirituality: What are the fundamental differences?. *HTS Theological Studies, 74(3),* 1-11. https://dx.doi.org/10.4102/hts.v74i3.4933

Voss, P., Thomas, M., Cisneros-Franco, J., & de Villers-Sidani, É. (2017). Dynamic brains and the changing rules of neuroplasticity: Implications for learning and recovery. *Frontiers in Psychology, 8,* 1657. https://doi.org/10.3389/fpsyg.2017.01657

Wade, D., & Halligan, P. (2004). Do biomedical models of illness make for good healthcare systems? *BMJ, 329(7479),* 1398-1401. doi: 10.1136/bmj.329.7479.1398

Walach, H., & Reich, K.H. (2005). Reconnecting science and spirituality: Toward overcoming a taboo. *Zygon, 40(2),* 423-441. (Obtained from academic library sources).

Wang, S., Lilienfield, S., & Rochat, P. (2019). Schadenfreude deconstructed and reconstructed: A tripartite motivational model. *New Ideas in Psychology, 52,* 1-11. DOI: 10.1016/j.newideapsych.2018.09.002

Warren, R. (2012). *The purpose driven life.* Grand Rapids, MI: Zondervan.

Wegela, K. (2010). How to practice mindfulness meditation. *Psychology Today.* Retrieved from https://www.psychologytoday.com/ca/blog/the-courage-be-present/201001/how-practice-mindfulness-meditation

Weidman, A., Cheng, J., & Tracy, J. (2018). The psychological structure of humility. *Journal of Personality and Social Psychology, 114(1),* 153-178. http://dx.doi.org/10.1037/pspp0000112

Weir, K. (2017). Forgiveness can improve mental and physical health. *American Psychological Association Continuing Education, 48(1),* 30. Retrieved from https://www.apa.org/monitor/2017/01/ce-corner

Wickham, R., Williamson, R., Beard, C., Kobayashi, C., & Hirst, T. (2016). Authenticity attenuates the negative effects of interpersonal conflict on daily well-being. *Journal of Research in Personality, 60,* 56-62. https://doi.org/10.1016/j.jrp.2015.11.006

Winch, G. (2014). The key difference between pride and arrogance [Web log post]. *Psychology Today.* Retrieved from https://www.psychologytoday.com/ca/blog/the-squeaky-wheel/201407/the-key-difference-between-pride-and-arrogance

Winch, G. (2010). The science of effective apologies [Web log post]. *Psychology Today.* Retrieved from https://www.psychologytoday.com/ca/blog/the-squeaky-wheel/201012/the-science-effective-apologies

Whittington, B., & Scher, S. (2010). Prayer and subjective well-being: An examination of six different types of prayer. *The International Journal for the Psychology of Religion, 20,* 59-68. https://doi.org/10.1080/10508610903146316

Wild, B., Rodden, F., Grodd, W., & Ruch, W. (2003). Neural correlates of laughter and humour. *Brain, 126(10),* 2121-38. 2003. (Obtained from academic library sources).

Wong, Y.I., Stanton, M.C., & Sands, R.D. (2014). Rethinking social inclusion: Experiences of persons in recovery from mental illness. *American Journal of Orthopsychiatry, 84(6),* 685–695. http://dx.doi.org/10.1037/ort0000034

Wright, J.C., Nadelhoffer, T., Perini, T., Langville, T., Echols, M., & Venezia, K. (2017). The psychological significance of humility. *The Journal of Positive Psychology, 12(1),* 3-12. doi: 10.1080/17439760.2016.1167940

Young, M., DeLorenzi, L. & Cunningham, L. (2011). Using meditation in addiction counseling. *Journal of Addictions & Offender Counseling, 32,* 58-71. doi:10.1002/j.2161-1874.2011.tb00207.x

Yuill, C., Crinson, I., & Duncan, K. (2010). *Key concepts in health studies.* Los Angeles, CA: Sage.

Zeidan, F., Martucci, K., Kraft, R., Gordon, N., McHaffie, J., & Coghill, R. (2011). Brain mechanisms supporting modulation of pain by mindfulness meditation. *The Journal of Neuroscience, 31(14),* 5540–5548. http://doi.org/10.1523/JNEUROSCI.5791-10.2011

Zeidan, F., Adler-Neal, A., Wells, R., Stagnaro, E., May, L., Eisenach, J., et al. (2016). Mindfulness-meditation-based pain relief is not mediated by endogenous opioids. *Journal of Neuroscience, 36(11),* 3391-3397. doi: 10.1523/JNEUROSCI.4328-15.2016

Zemore, S. (2007). A role for spiritual change in the benefits of 12-step involvement. *Alcoholism: Clinical & Experimental Research, 31(S3),* 76S–79S. DOI: 10.1111/j.1530-0277.2007.00499.x

Zgierska, A., Rabago, D., Zuelsdorff, M., Coe, C., Miller, M., & Fleming, M. (2008). Mindfulness meditation for alcohol relapse prevention: a feasibility pilot study. *Journal of Addiction Medicine, 2(3),* 165–173. doi: 10.1097/ADM.0b013e31816f8546.

<u>Notes</u>

Notes

Printed in Great Britain
by Amazon

45522995R00270